Garfield

FAT CAT 3-PACK

VOLUME 22

Garfield
FAT CAT 3-PACK
VOLUME 22

BY
JIM DAVIS

BALLANTINE BOOKS · NEW YORK

Published in the United States by Ballantine Books, an imprint of Random House,
a division of Penguin Random House LLC, New York.

BALLANTINE and the HOUSE colophon are registered trademarks of Penguin Random House LLC.

NICKELODEON is a Trademark of Viacom International, Inc.

GARFIELD FEEDS HIS FACE was published separately by Ballantine Books, an imprint of
Random House, a division of Penguin Random House LLC, in 2017. GARFIELD EATS AND RUNS and
GARFIELD NUTTY AS A FRUITCAKE were each published separately by Ballantine Books, an imprint of
Random House, a division of Penguin Random House LLC, New York, in 2018.

ISBN 978-0-593-15638-4

Printed in China on acid-free paper

randomhousebooks.com

9 8 7 6 5 4

Garfield
FEEDS HIS FACE

BY JIM DAVIS

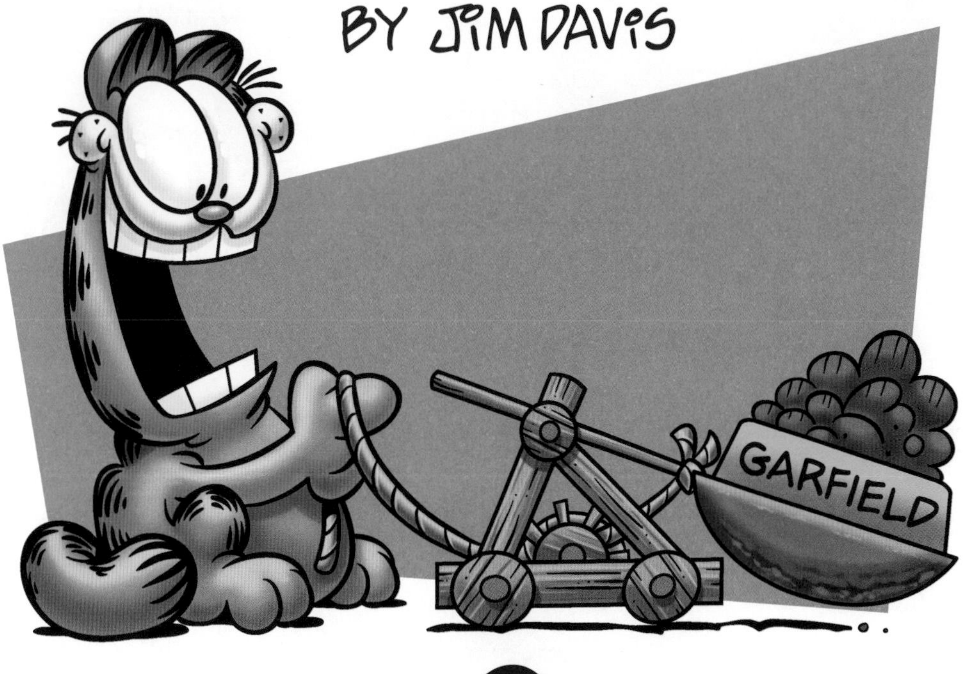
GARFIELD

Ballantine Books • New York

GARFIELD'S PET FORCE

ORDINARY PETS GARFIELD, ODIE, ARLENE, AND NERMAL HAVE THEIR LIVES CHANGED FOREVER WHEN THEY'RE SUCKED INTO A PARALLEL UNIVERSE AND TRANSFORMED INTO FOUR FURRY SUPERPOWERED DEFENDERS OF JUSTICE: GARZOOKA, ODIOUS, STARLENA, AND ABNERMAL.

TOGETHER, THIS TITANIC TEAM PROTECTS THE COSMOS FROM EVIL VETERINARIAN VETVIX AND HER MANIACAL MUTANT MINIONS.

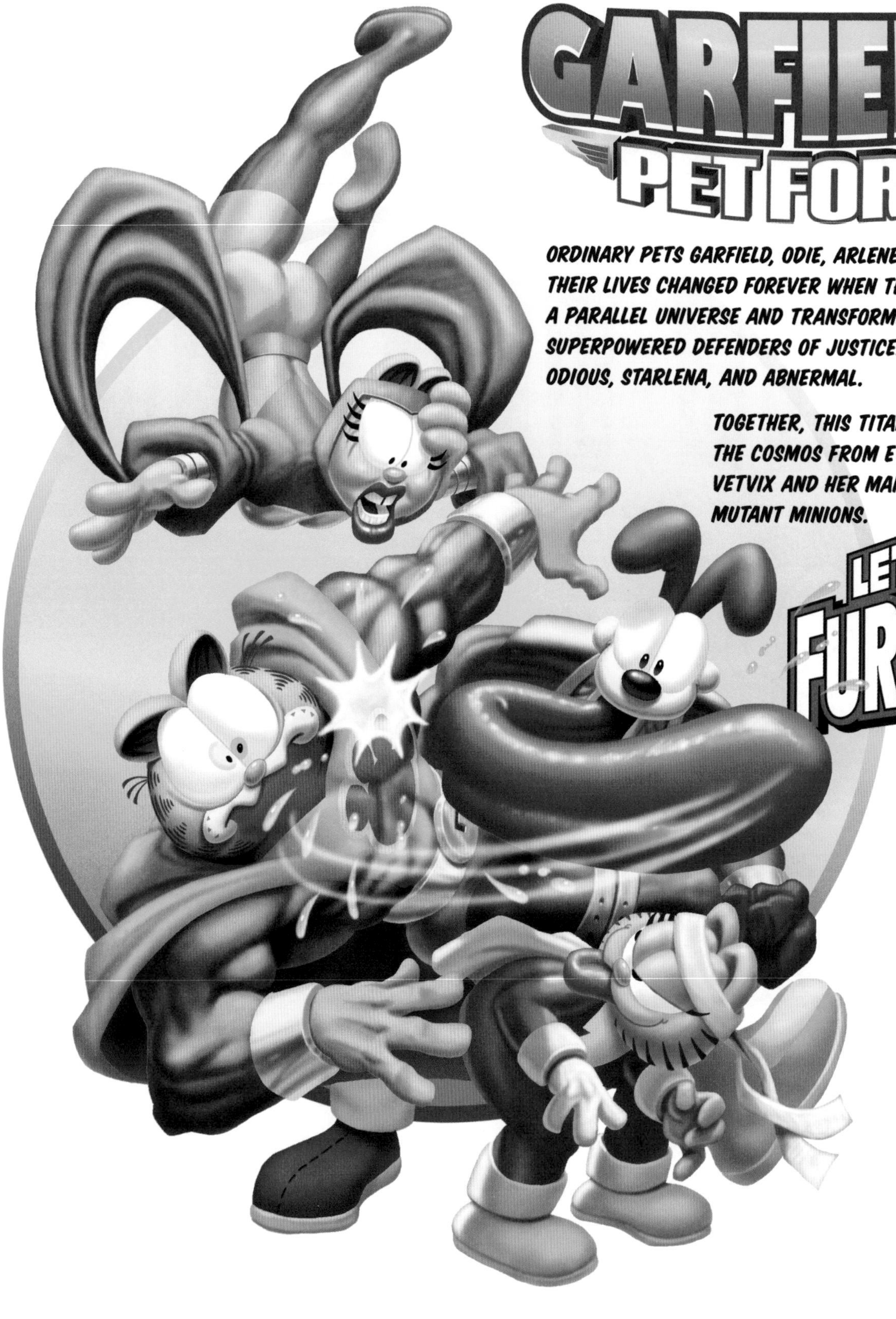

LET THE FUR FLY!

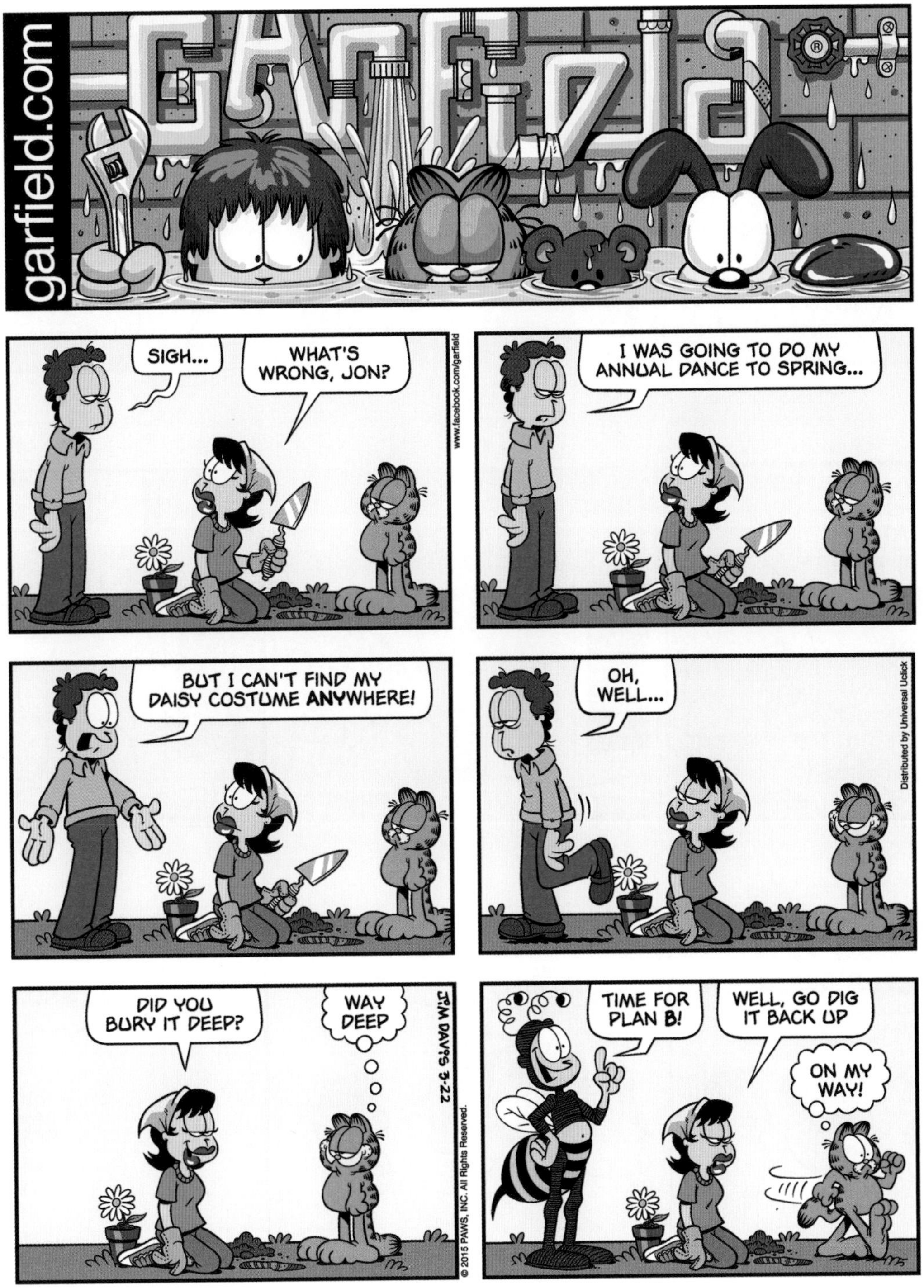
garfield.com
SIGH...
WHAT'S WRONG, JON?
www.facebook.com/garfield
I WAS GOING TO DO MY ANNUAL DANCE TO SPRING...
BUT I CAN'T FIND MY DAISY COSTUME ANYWHERE!
OH, WELL...
Distributed by Universal Uclick
DID YOU BURY IT DEEP?
WAY DEEP
JIM DAVIS 3-22
© 2015 PAWS, INC. All Rights Reserved.
TIME FOR PLAN B!
WELL, GO DIG IT BACK UP
ON MY WAY!

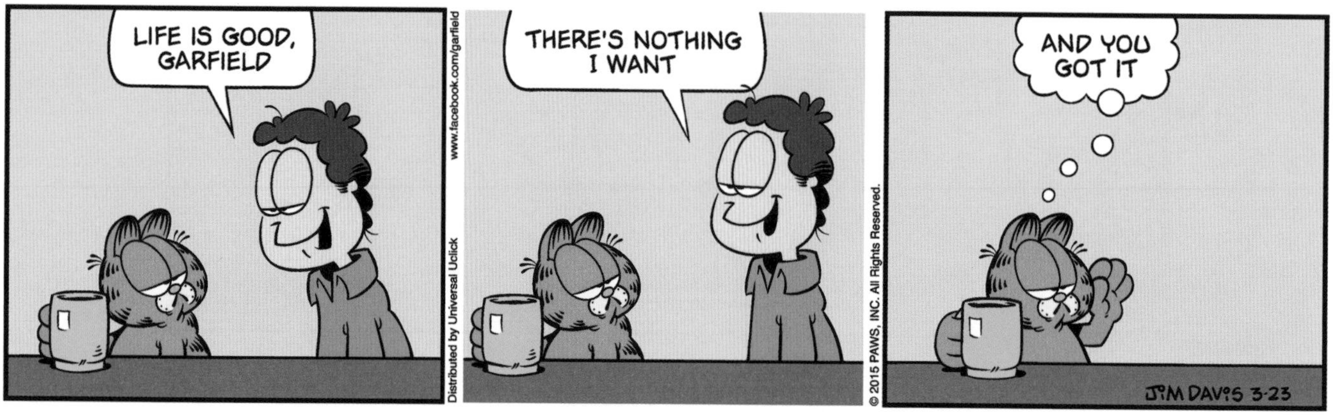
LIFE IS GOOD, GARFIELD
Distributed by Universal Uclick www.facebook.com/garfield
THERE'S NOTHING I WANT
© 2015 PAWS, INC. All Rights Reserved.
AND YOU GOT IT
JIM DAVIS 3-23

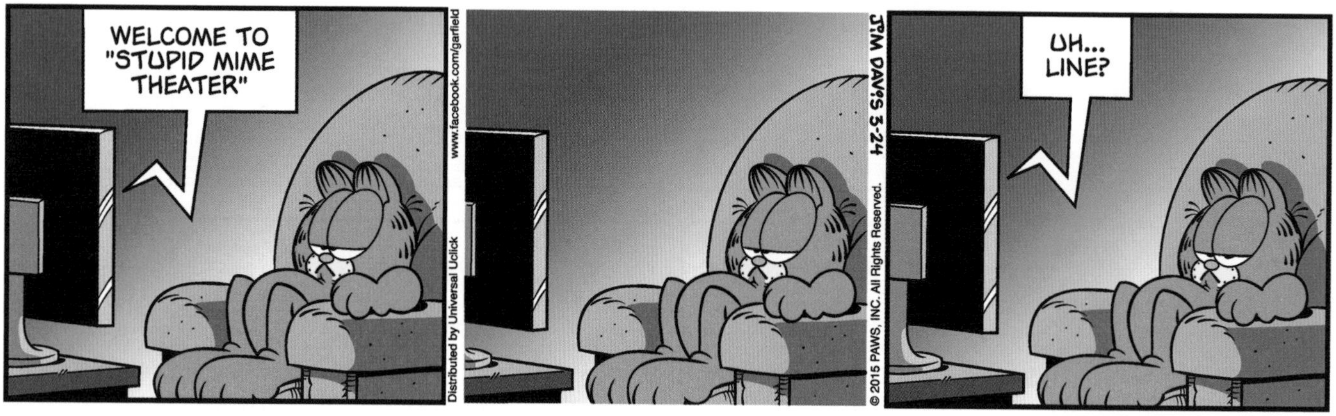
WELCOME TO "STUPID MIME THEATER"
Distributed by Universal Uclick www.facebook.com/garfield
JIM DAVIS 3-24
© 2015 PAWS, INC. All Rights Reserved.
UH... LINE?

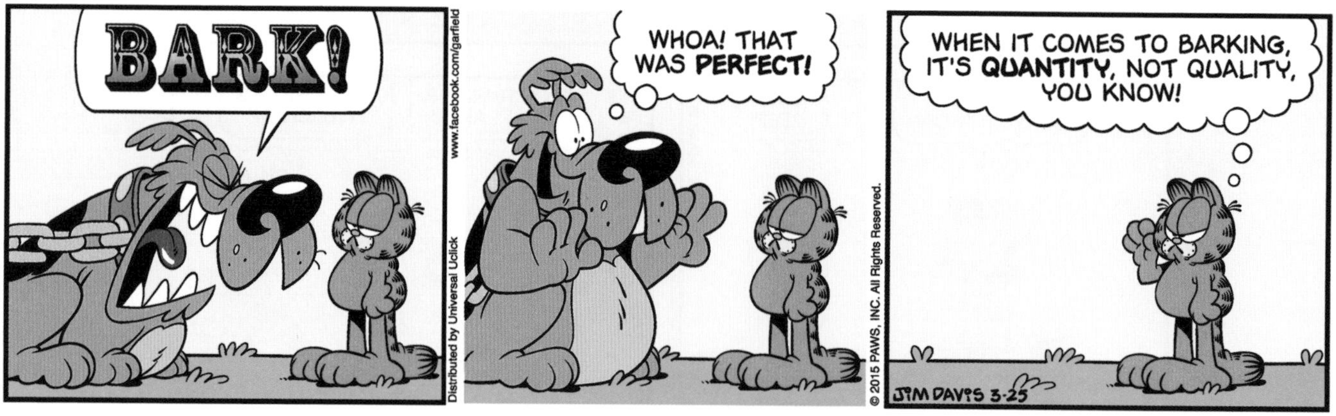
BARK!
Distributed by Universal Uclick www.facebook.com/garfield
WHOA! THAT WAS PERFECT!
© 2015 PAWS, INC. All Rights Reserved.
WHEN IT COMES TO BARKING, IT'S QUANTITY, NOT QUALITY, YOU KNOW!
JIM DAVIS 3-25

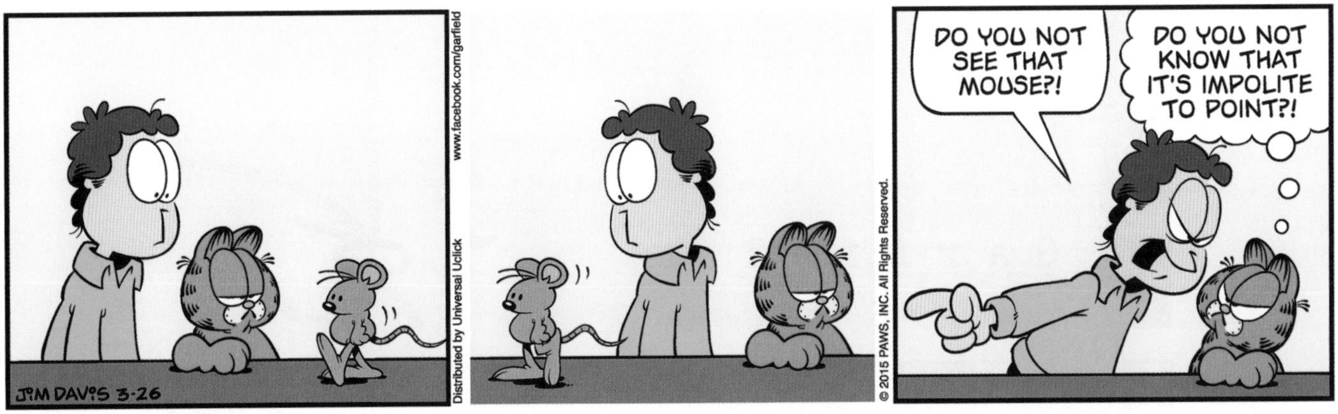
JIM DAVIS 3-26
www.facebook.com/garfield
Distributed by Universal Uclick
DO YOU NOT SEE THAT MOUSE?!
DO YOU NOT KNOW THAT IT'S IMPOLITE TO POINT?!
© 2015 PAWS, INC. All Rights Reserved.

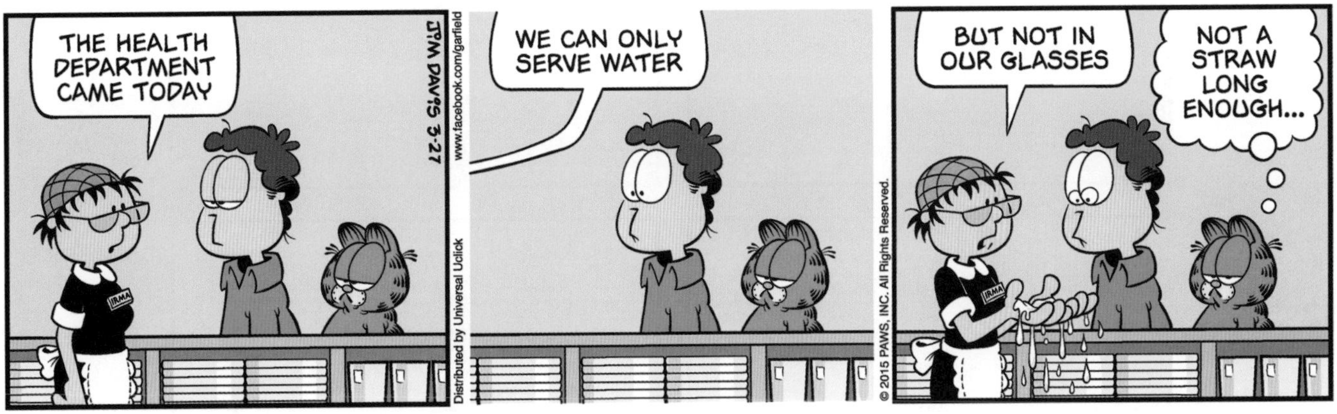
THE HEALTH DEPARTMENT CAME TODAY
JIM DAVIS 3-27
IRMA
www.facebook.com/garfield
Distributed by Universal Uclick
WE CAN ONLY SERVE WATER
BUT NOT IN OUR GLASSES
NOT A STRAW LONG ENOUGH...
© 2015 PAWS, INC. All Rights Reserved.

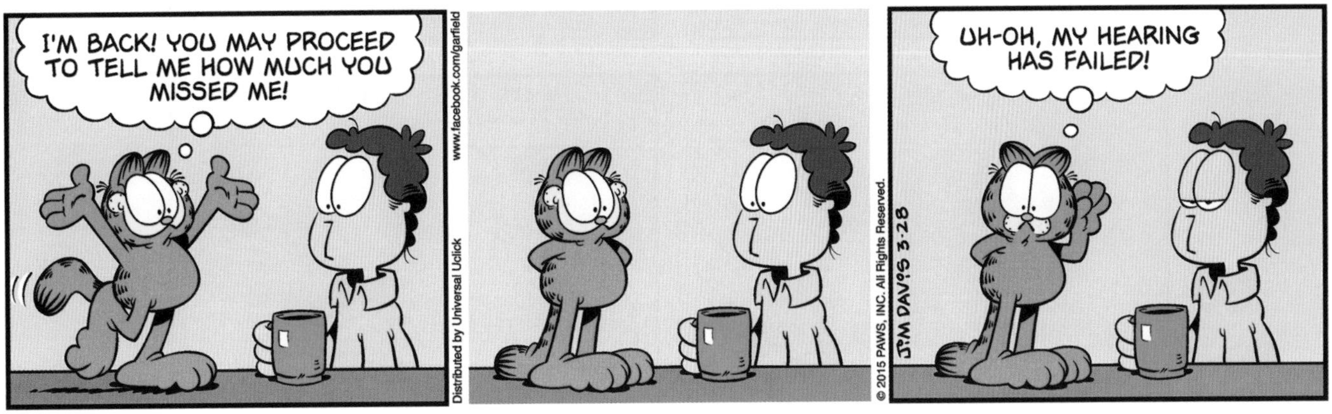
I'M BACK! YOU MAY PROCEED TO TELL ME HOW MUCH YOU MISSED ME!
www.facebook.com/garfield
Distributed by Universal Uclick
UH-OH, MY HEARING HAS FAILED!
JIM DAVIS 3-28
© 2015 PAWS, INC. All Rights Reserved.

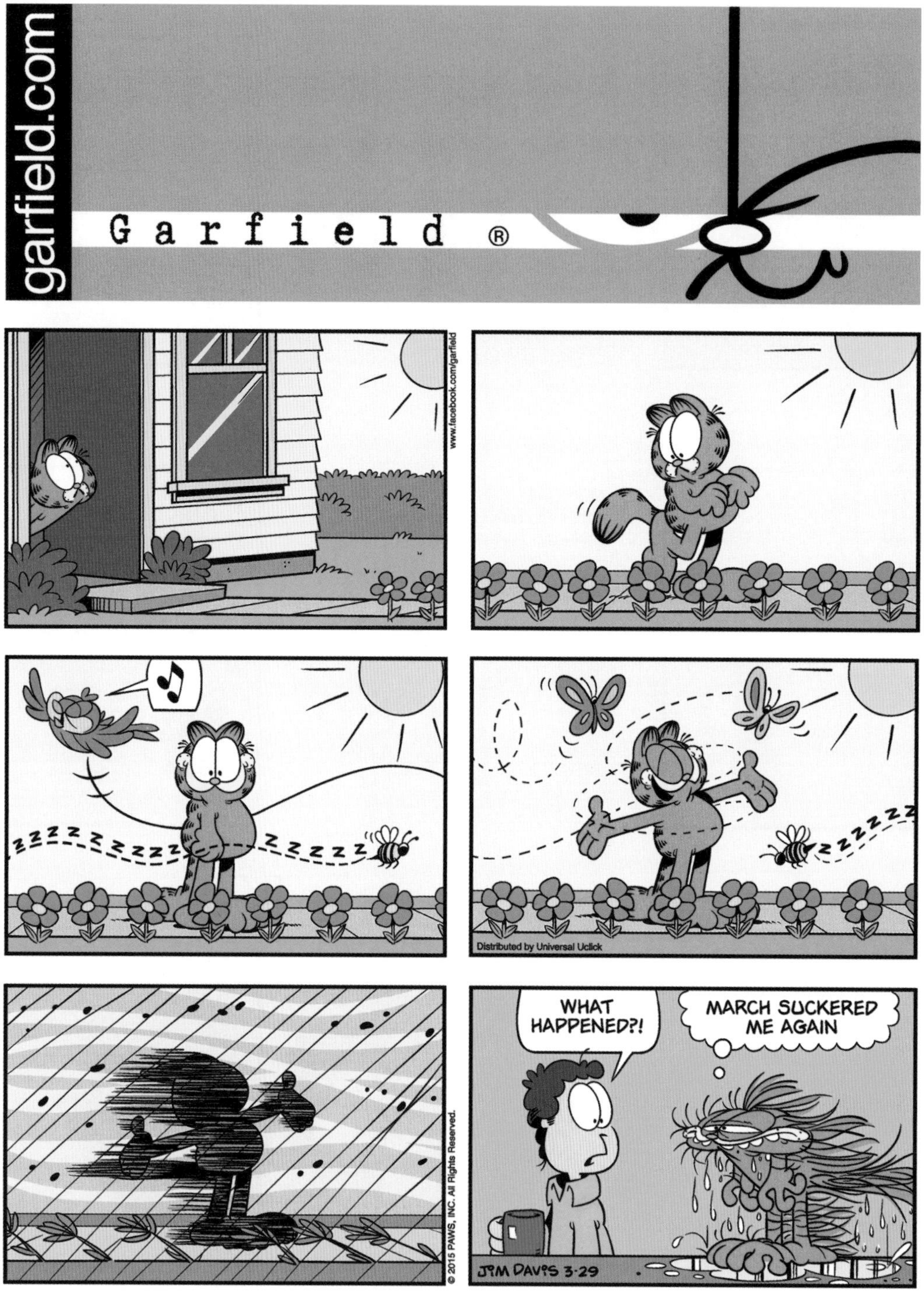
garfield.com
Garfield ®
www.facebook.com/garfield
Distributed by Universal Uclick
© 2015 PAWS, INC. All Rights Reserved.
WHAT HAPPENED?!
MARCH SUCKERED ME AGAIN
JIM DAVIS 3-29

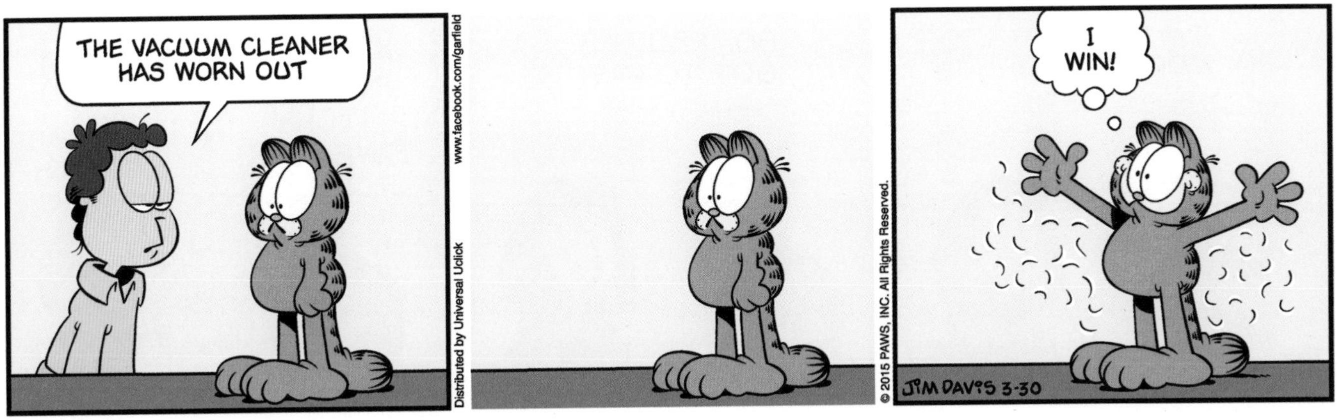
THE VACUUM CLEANER HAS WORN OUT
I WIN!
www.facebook.com/garfield
Distributed by Universal Uclick
© 2015 PAWS, INC. All Rights Reserved.
JIM DAVIS 3-30

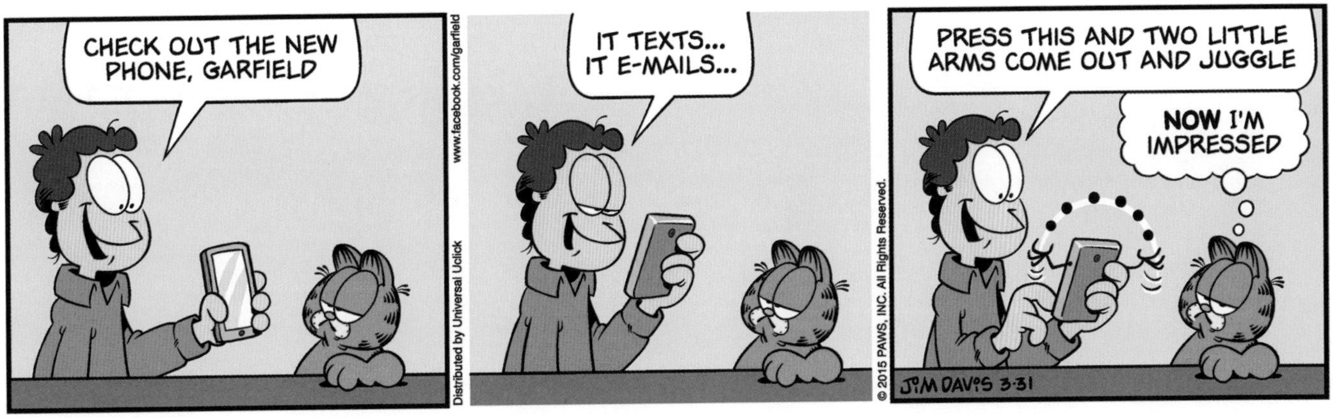
CHECK OUT THE NEW PHONE, GARFIELD
IT TEXTS... IT E-MAILS...
PRESS THIS AND TWO LITTLE ARMS COME OUT AND JUGGLE
NOW I'M IMPRESSED
www.facebook.com/garfield
Distributed by Universal Uclick
© 2015 PAWS, INC. All Rights Reserved.
JIM DAVIS 3-31

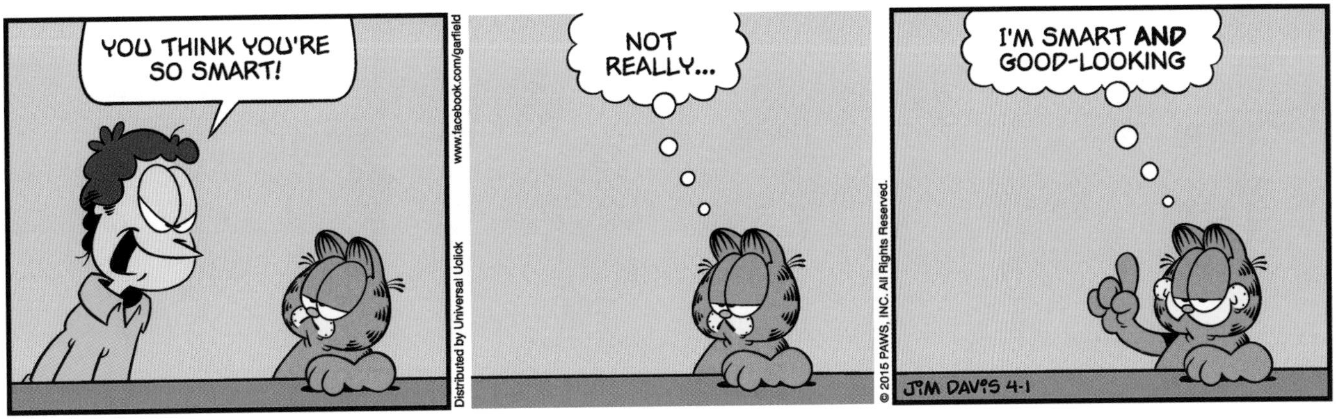
YOU THINK YOU'RE SO SMART!
NOT REALLY...
I'M SMART AND GOOD-LOOKING
www.facebook.com/garfield
Distributed by Universal Uclick
© 2015 PAWS, INC. All Rights Reserved.
JIM DAVIS 4-1

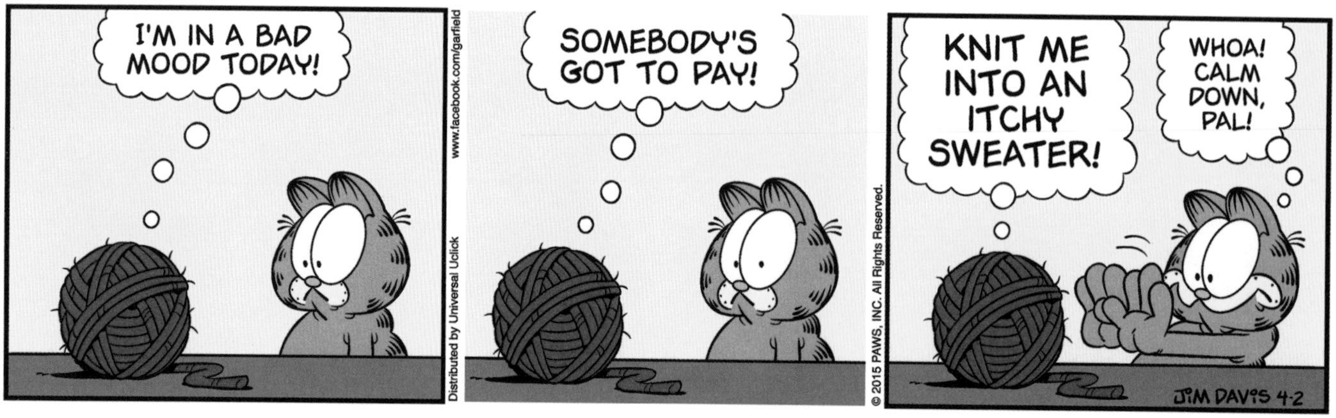
I'M IN A BAD MOOD TODAY!
www.facebook.com/garfield
Distributed by Universal Uclick
SOMEBODY'S GOT TO PAY!
© 2015 PAWS, INC. All Rights Reserved.
KNIT ME INTO AN ITCHY SWEATER!
WHOA! CALM DOWN, PAL!
JIM DAVIS 4-2

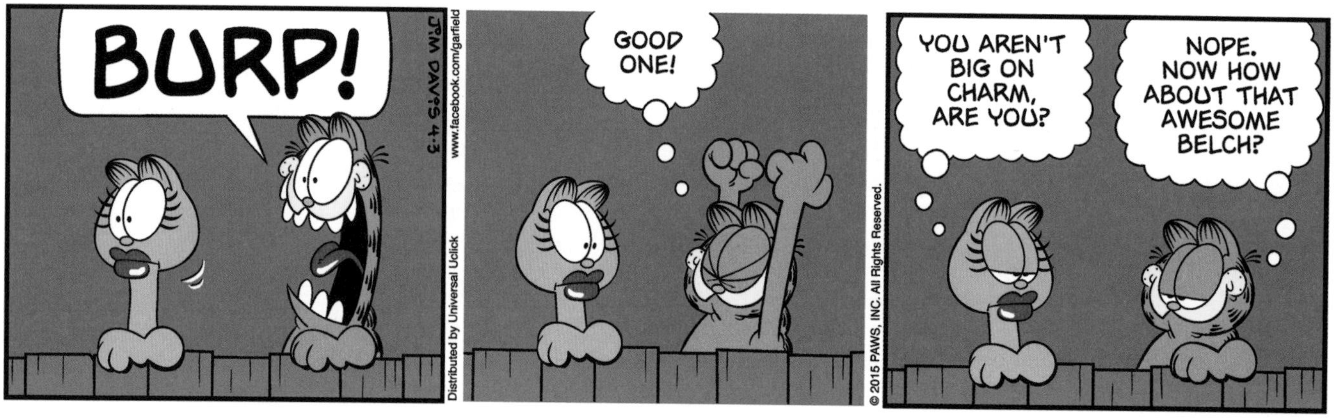
BURP!
JIM DAVIS 4-3
www.facebook.com/garfield
Distributed by Universal Uclick
GOOD ONE!
© 2015 PAWS, INC. All Rights Reserved.
YOU AREN'T BIG ON CHARM, ARE YOU?
NOPE. NOW HOW ABOUT THAT AWESOME BELCH?

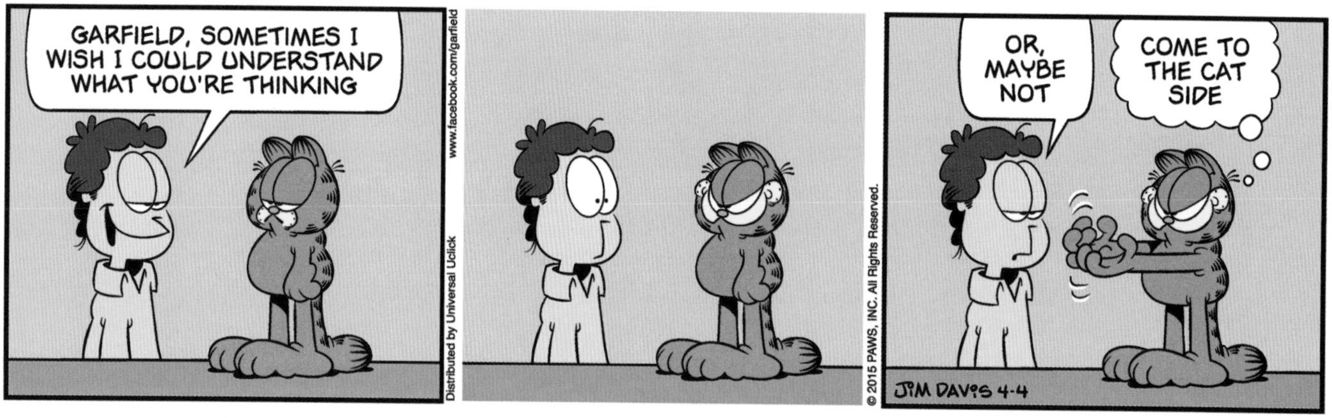
GARFIELD, SOMETIMES I WISH I COULD UNDERSTAND WHAT YOU'RE THINKING
www.facebook.com/garfield
Distributed by Universal Uclick
© 2015 PAWS, INC. All Rights Reserved.
OR, MAYBE NOT
COME TO THE CAT SIDE
JIM DAVIS 4-4

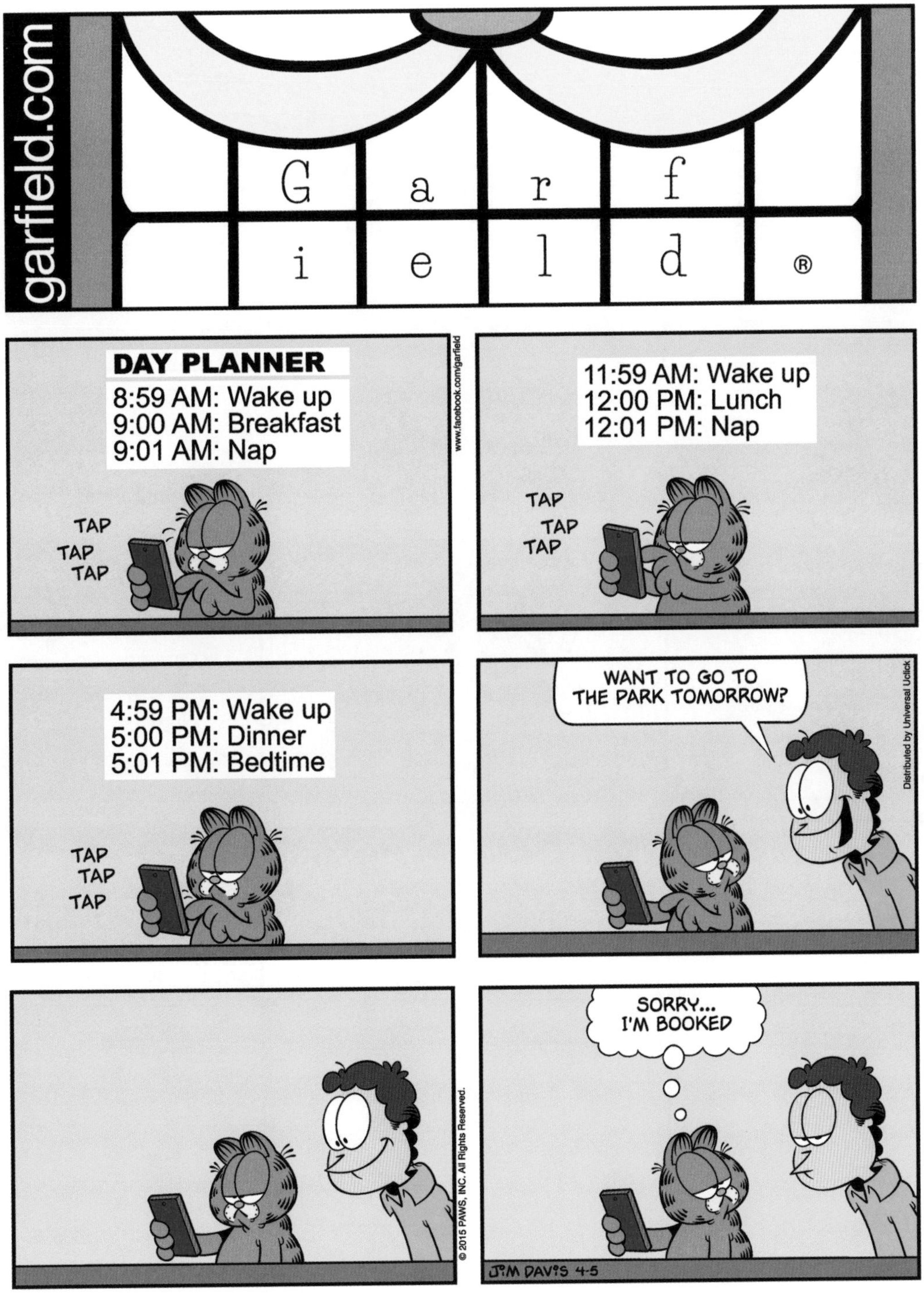

garfield.com
Garfield®
DAY PLANNER
8:59 AM: Wake up
9:00 AM: Breakfast
9:01 AM: Nap
TAP TAP TAP
www.facebook.com/garfield
11:59 AM: Wake up
12:00 PM: Lunch
12:01 PM: Nap
TAP TAP TAP
4:59 PM: Wake up
5:00 PM: Dinner
5:01 PM: Bedtime
TAP TAP TAP
WANT TO GO TO THE PARK TOMORROW?
Distributed by Universal Uclick
© 2015 PAWS, INC. All Rights Reserved.
SORRY... I'M BOOKED
JIM DAVIS 4-5

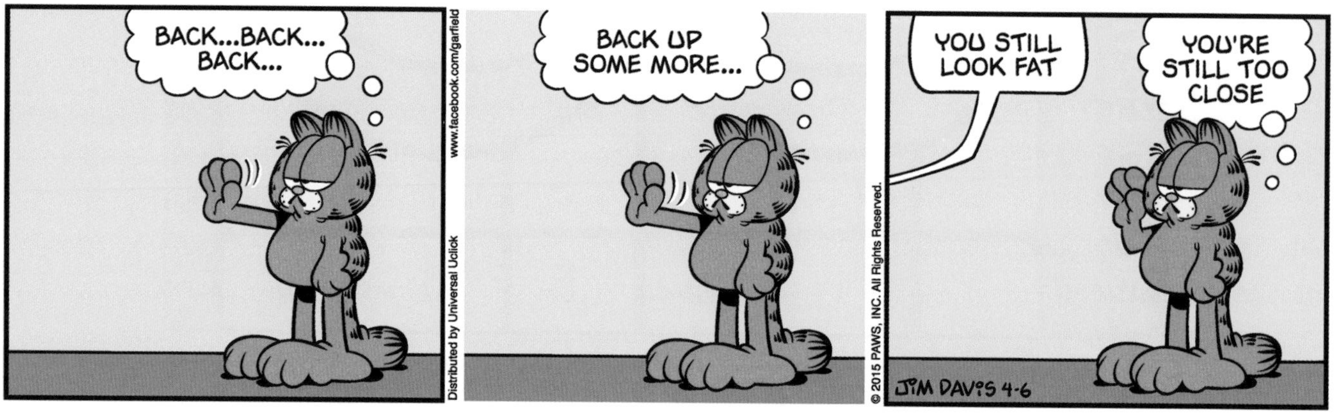
BACK...BACK... BACK...
BACK UP SOME MORE...
YOU STILL LOOK FAT
YOU'RE STILL TOO CLOSE
JIM DAVIS 4-6
Distributed by Universal Uclick www.facebook.com/garfield
© 2015 PAWS, INC. All Rights Reserved.

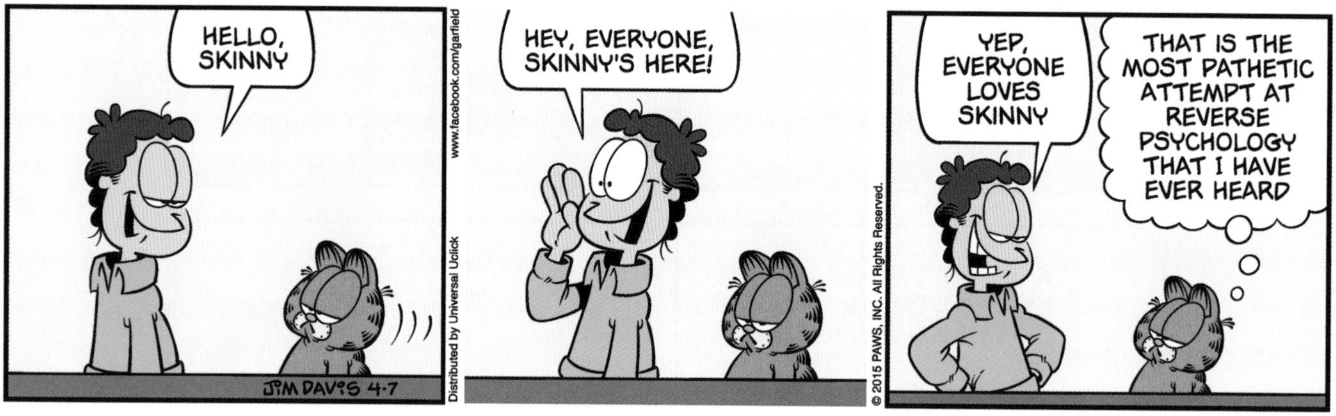
HELLO, SKINNY
HEY, EVERYONE, SKINNY'S HERE!
YEP, EVERYONE LOVES SKINNY
THAT IS THE MOST PATHETIC ATTEMPT AT REVERSE PSYCHOLOGY THAT I HAVE EVER HEARD
JIM DAVIS 4-7
Distributed by Universal Uclick www.facebook.com/garfield
© 2015 PAWS, INC. All Rights Reserved.

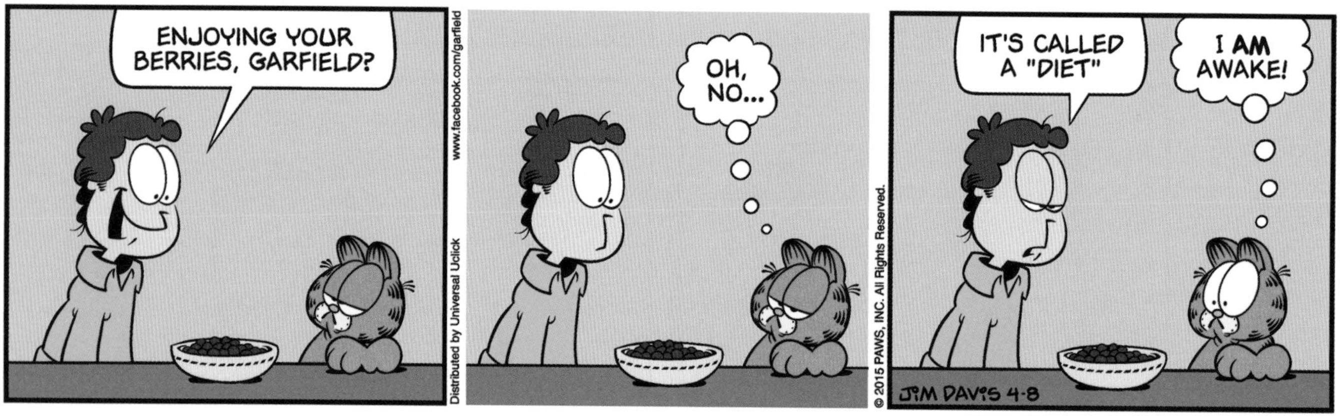
ENJOYING YOUR BERRIES, GARFIELD?
OH, NO...
IT'S CALLED A "DIET"
I **AM** AWAKE!
JIM DAVIS 4-8
Distributed by Universal Uclick www.facebook.com/garfield
© 2015 PAWS, INC. All Rights Reserved.

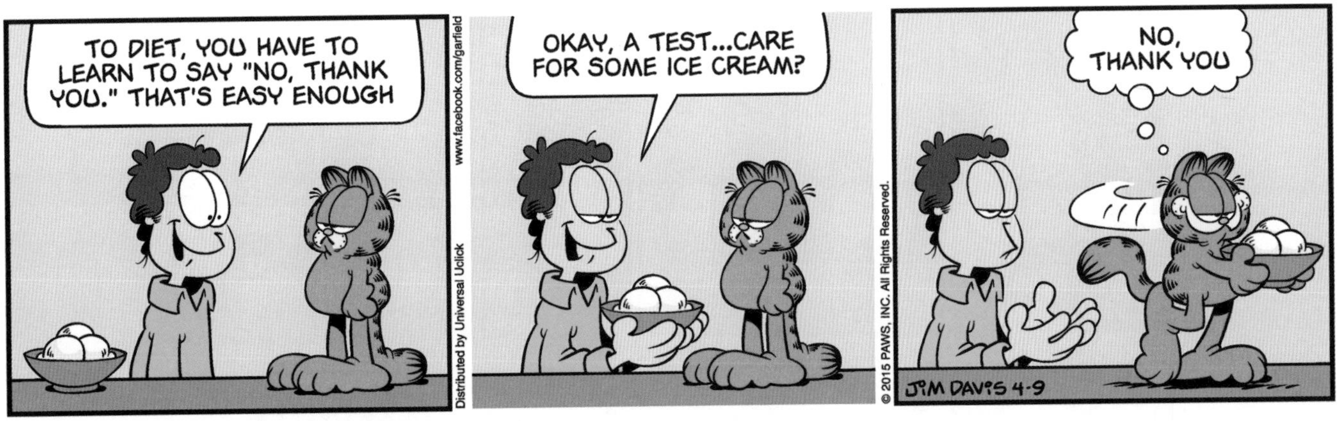
TO DIET, YOU HAVE TO LEARN TO SAY "NO, THANK YOU." THAT'S EASY ENOUGH
OKAY, A TEST...CARE FOR SOME ICE CREAM?
NO, THANK YOU
JIM DAVIS 4-9
Distributed by Universal Uclick www.facebook.com/garfield
© 2015 PAWS, INC. All Rights Reserved.

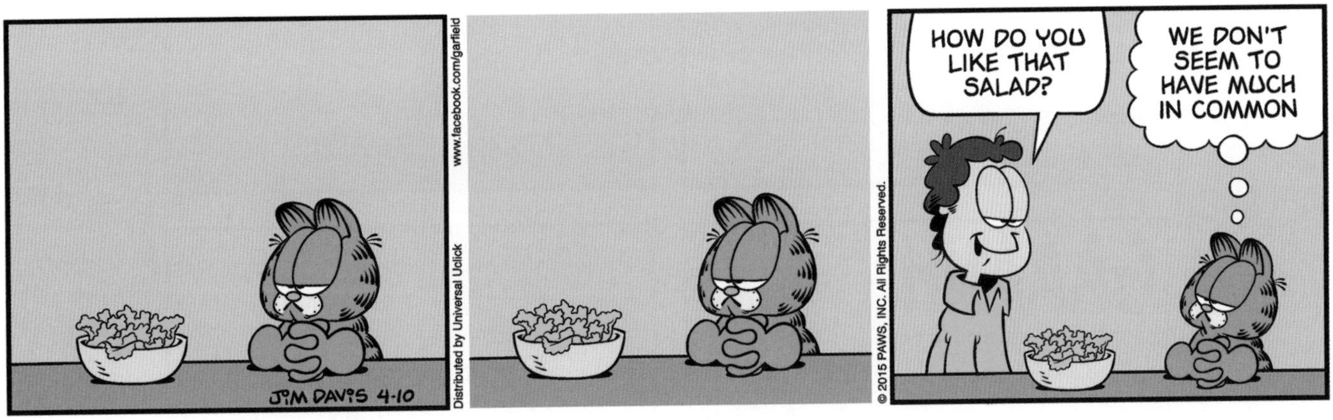
JIM DAVIS 4-10
HOW DO YOU LIKE THAT SALAD?
WE DON'T SEEM TO HAVE MUCH IN COMMON
Distributed by Universal Uclick www.facebook.com/garfield
© 2015 PAWS, INC. All Rights Reserved.

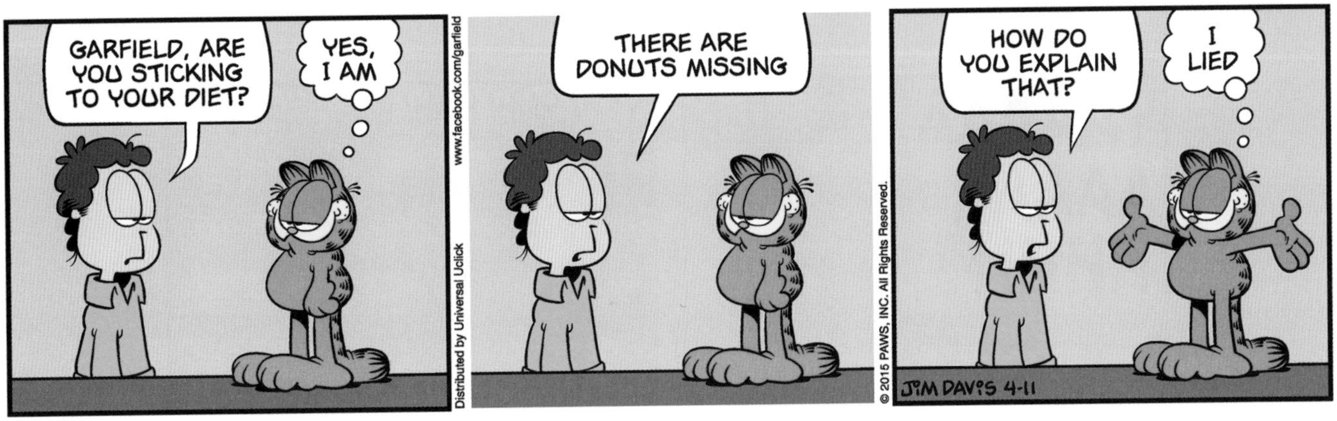
GARFIELD, ARE YOU STICKING TO YOUR DIET?
YES, I AM
THERE ARE DONUTS MISSING
HOW DO YOU EXPLAIN THAT?
I LIED
JIM DAVIS 4-11
Distributed by Universal Uclick www.facebook.com/garfield
© 2015 PAWS, INC. All Rights Reserved.

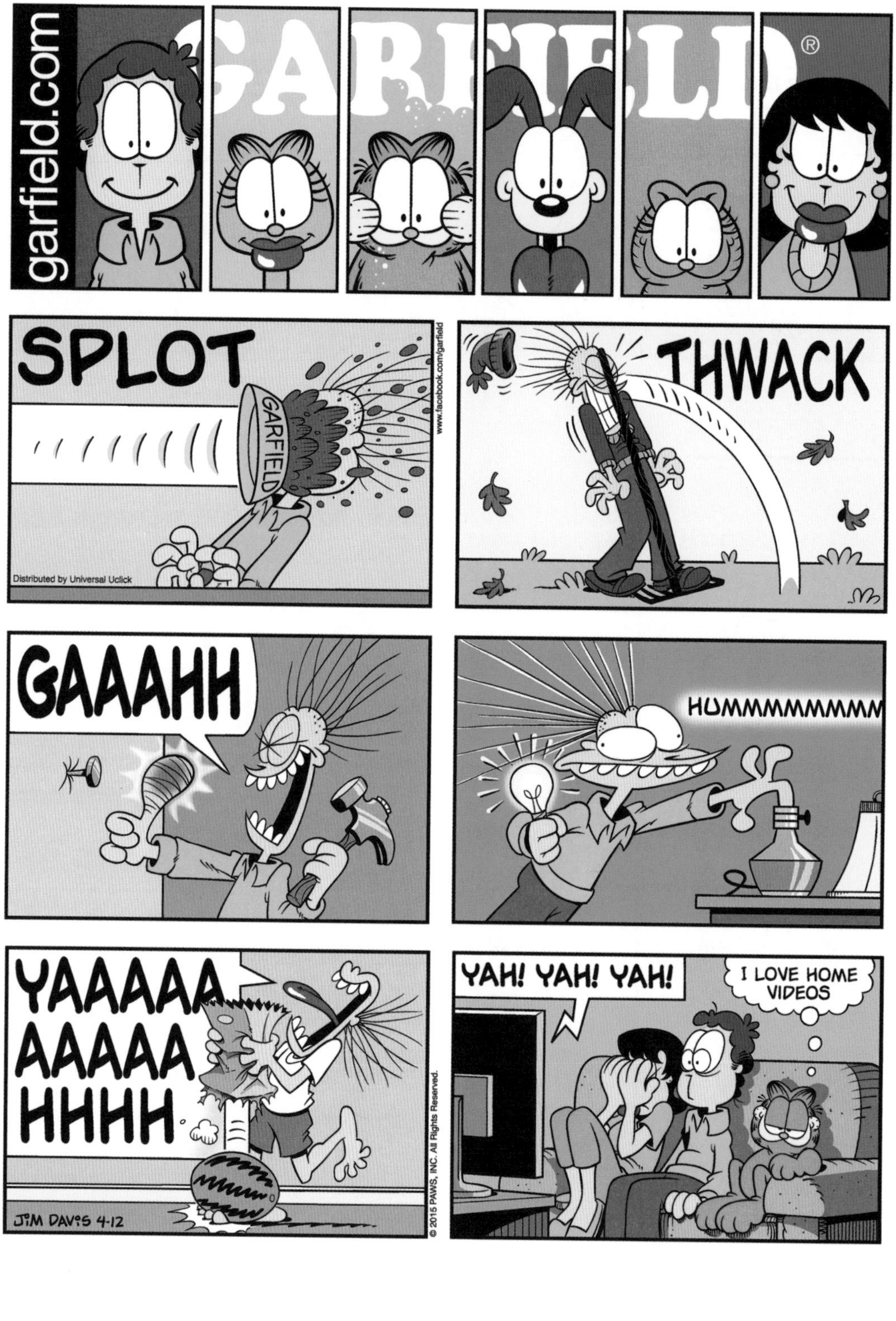
garfield.com
GARFIELD®
SPLOT
GARFIELD
www.facebook.com/garfield
Distributed by Universal Uclick
THWACK
GAAAHH
HUMMMMMMMM
YAAAAA AAAAA HHHH
JIM DAVIS 4-12
© 2015 PAWS, INC. All Rights Reserved.
YAH! YAH! YAH!
I LOVE HOME VIDEOS

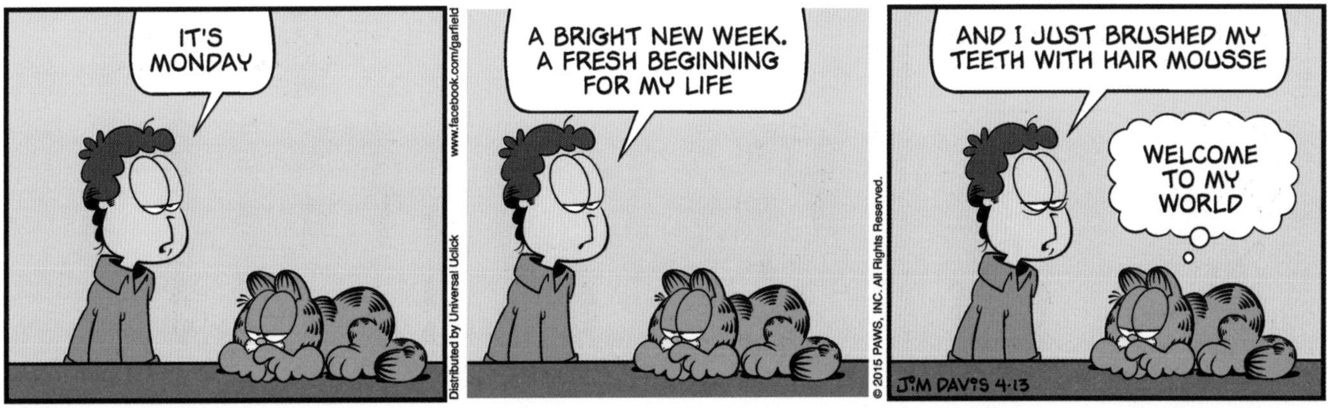
IT'S MONDAY
A BRIGHT NEW WEEK. A FRESH BEGINNING FOR MY LIFE
AND I JUST BRUSHED MY TEETH WITH HAIR MOUSSE
WELCOME TO MY WORLD
JIM DAVIS 4-13
Distributed by Universal Uclick www.facebook.com/garfield
© 2015 PAWS, INC. All Rights Reserved.

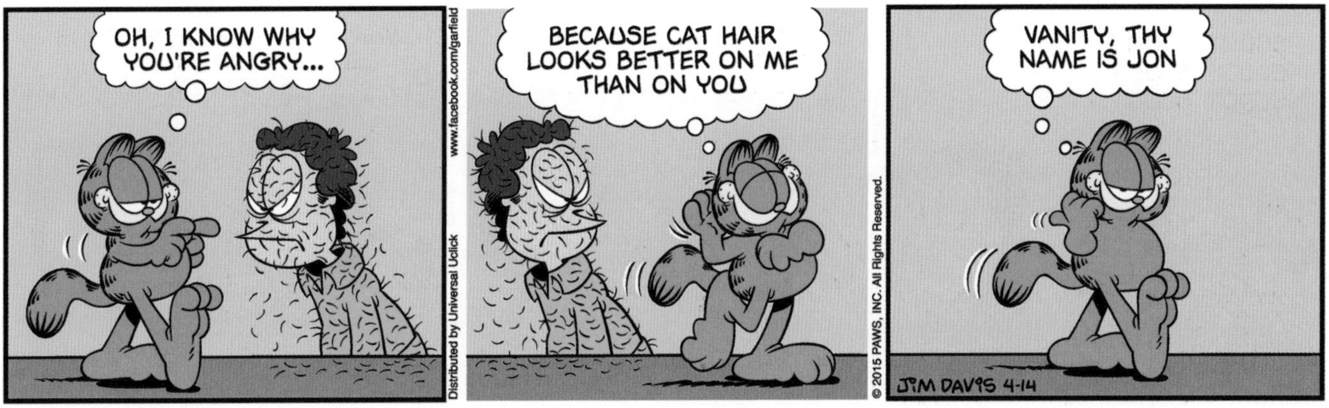
OH, I KNOW WHY YOU'RE ANGRY...
BECAUSE CAT HAIR LOOKS BETTER ON ME THAN ON YOU
VANITY, THY NAME IS JON
JIM DAVIS 4-14
Distributed by Universal Uclick www.facebook.com/garfield
© 2015 PAWS, INC. All Rights Reserved.

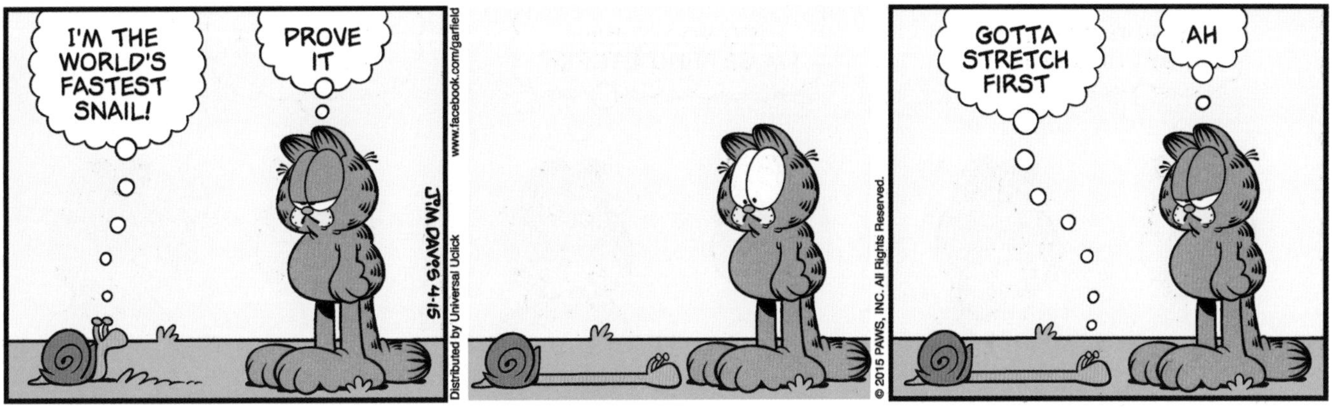
I'M THE WORLD'S FASTEST SNAIL!
PROVE IT
GOTTA STRETCH FIRST
AH
JIM DAVIS 4-15
Distributed by Universal Uclick www.facebook.com/garfield
© 2015 PAWS, INC. All Rights Reserved.

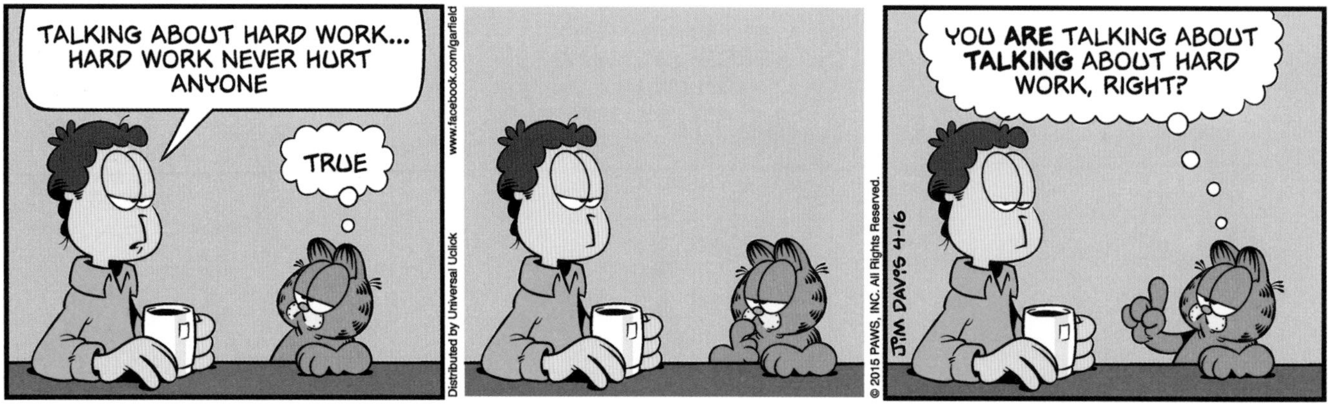
TALKING ABOUT HARD WORK... HARD WORK NEVER HURT ANYONE
TRUE
Distributed by Universal Uclick www.facebook.com/garfield
YOU **ARE** TALKING ABOUT **TALKING** ABOUT HARD WORK, RIGHT?
© 2015 PAWS, INC. All Rights Reserved.
JIM DAVIS 4-16

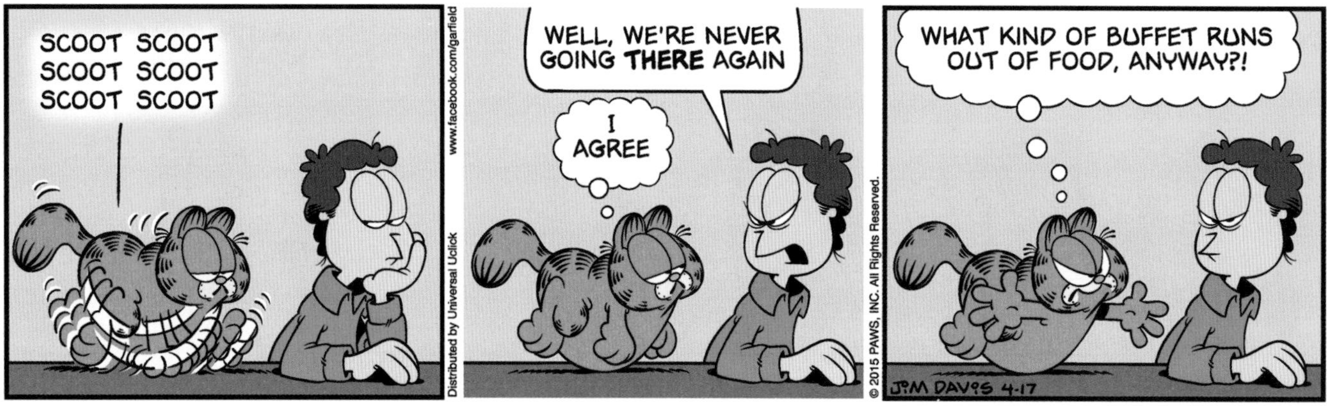
SCOOT SCOOT SCOOT SCOOT SCOOT SCOOT
Distributed by Universal Uclick www.facebook.com/garfield
I AGREE
WELL, WE'RE NEVER GOING **THERE** AGAIN
WHAT KIND OF BUFFET RUNS OUT OF FOOD, ANYWAY?!
© 2015 PAWS, INC. All Rights Reserved.
JIM DAVIS 4-17

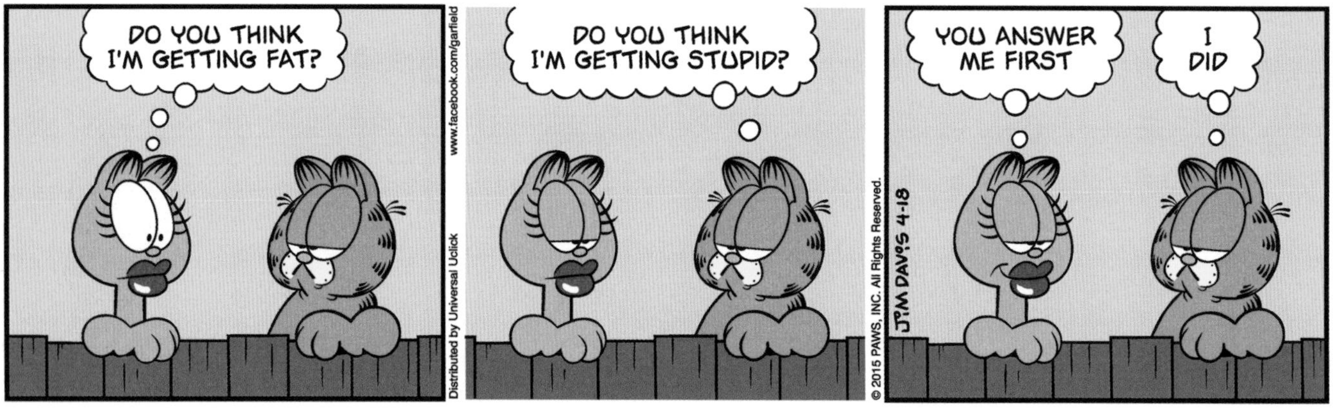
DO YOU THINK I'M GETTING FAT?
Distributed by Universal Uclick www.facebook.com/garfield
DO YOU THINK I'M GETTING STUPID?
YOU ANSWER ME FIRST
I DID
© 2015 PAWS, INC. All Rights Reserved.
JIM DAVIS 4-18

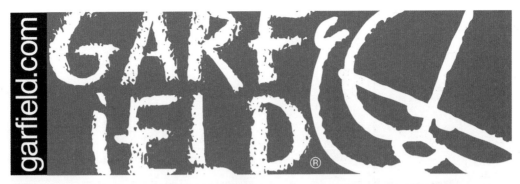

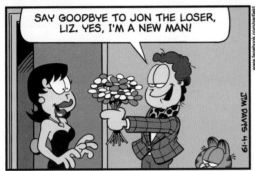

garfield.com
GARFIELD®
SAY GOODBYE TO JON THE LOSER, LIZ. YES, I'M A NEW MAN!
JIM DAVIS 4-19
www.facebook.com/garfield
I'VE GIVEN UP MY LOSING WAYS, AND I'M...HEY, LOOK! A STREET FAIR!
LOOK DEEEP INTO MY EYEEEES...
OH, PLEASE
ONLY $
WHAT SIZE HAT DO YOU
I'M GOOD!
Distributed by Universal Uclick
SO, IS EVERYONE READY TO EAT?!
SURE, WHY NOT
CHEZ GRUB
© 2015 PAWS, INC. All Rights Reserved.
THIS "NEW MAN" STUFF IS EASY!
I'LL CREATE A DIVERSION, AND YOU RUN LIKE THE WIND
Menu

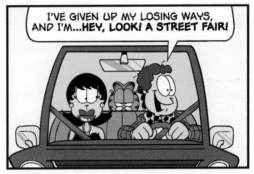

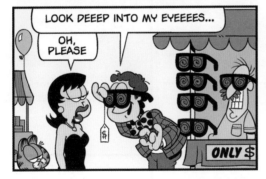

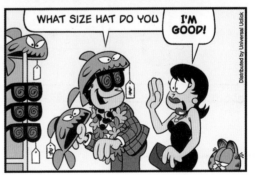

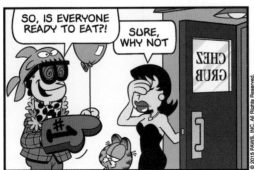

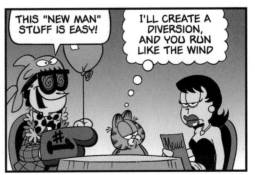

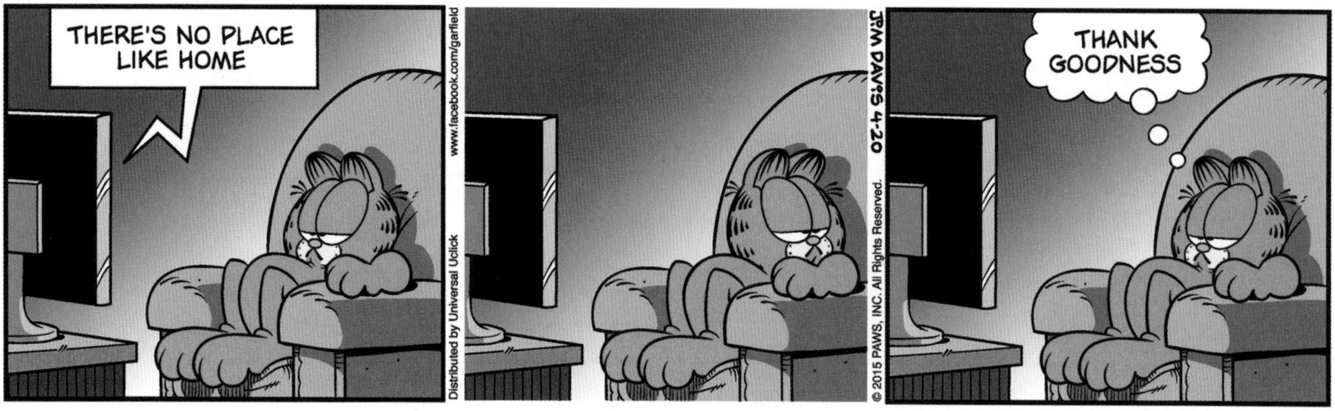
THERE'S NO PLACE LIKE HOME
THANK GOODNESS
JIM DAVIS 4-20
Distributed by Universal Uclick
www.facebook.com/garfield
© 2015 PAWS, INC. All Rights Reserved.

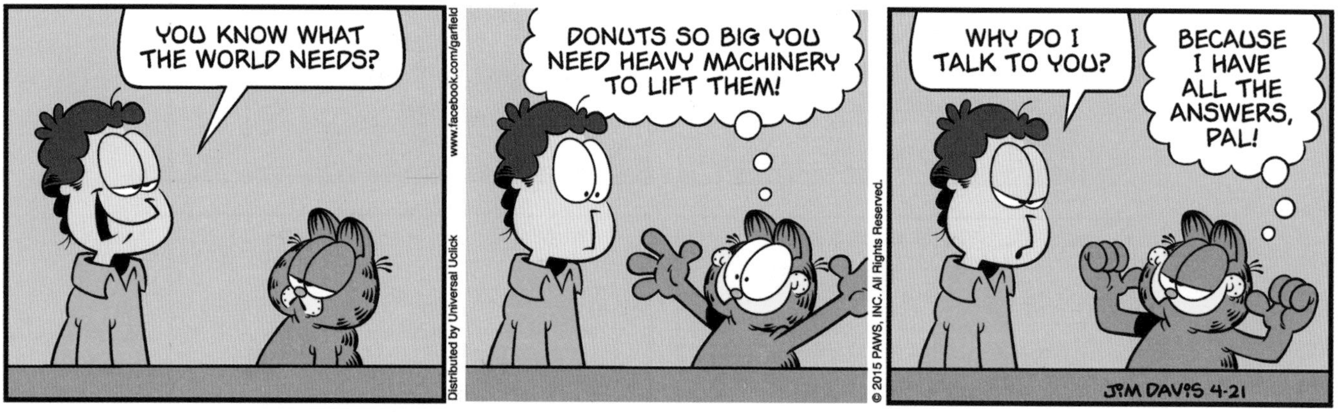
YOU KNOW WHAT THE WORLD NEEDS?
DONUTS SO BIG YOU NEED HEAVY MACHINERY TO LIFT THEM!
WHY DO I TALK TO YOU?
BECAUSE I HAVE ALL THE ANSWERS, PAL!
JIM DAVIS 4-21
Distributed by Universal Uclick
www.facebook.com/garfield
© 2015 PAWS, INC. All Rights Reserved.

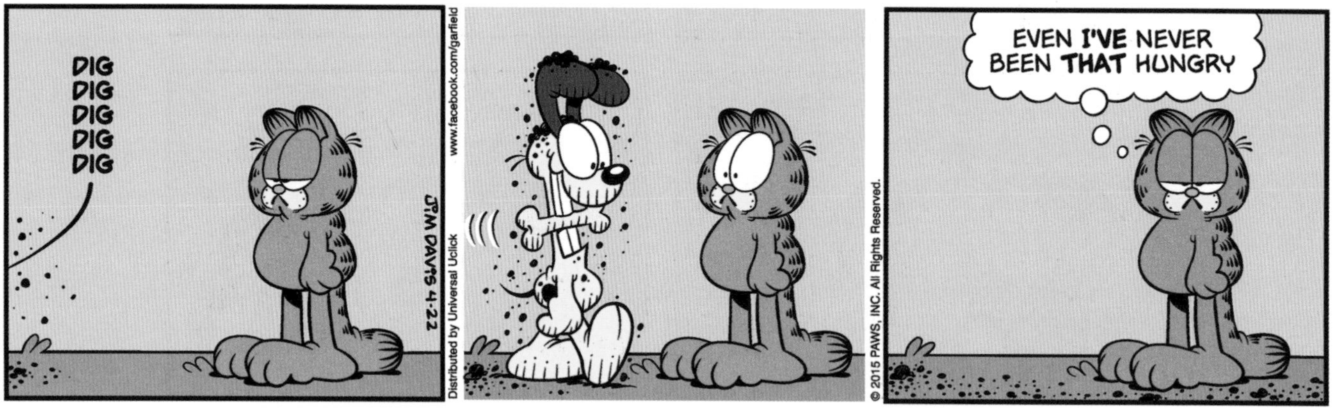
DIG DIG DIG DIG DIG
EVEN I'VE NEVER BEEN THAT HUNGRY
JIM DAVIS 4-22
Distributed by Universal Uclick
www.facebook.com/garfield
© 2015 PAWS, INC. All Rights Reserved.

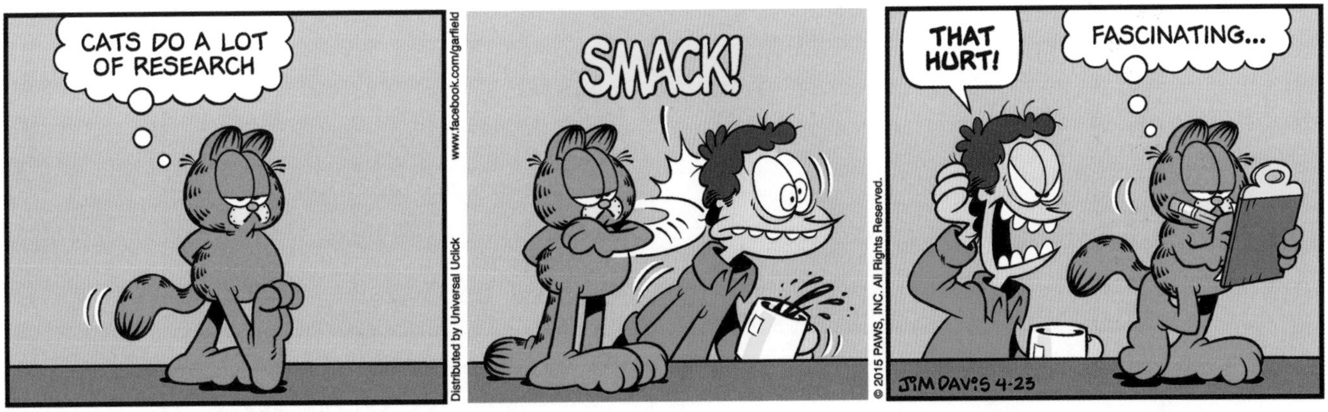
CATS DO A LOT OF RESEARCH
www.facebook.com/garfield
Distributed by Universal Uclick
SMACK!
THAT HURT!
FASCINATING...
© 2015 PAWS, INC. All Rights Reserved.
JIM DAVIS 4-23

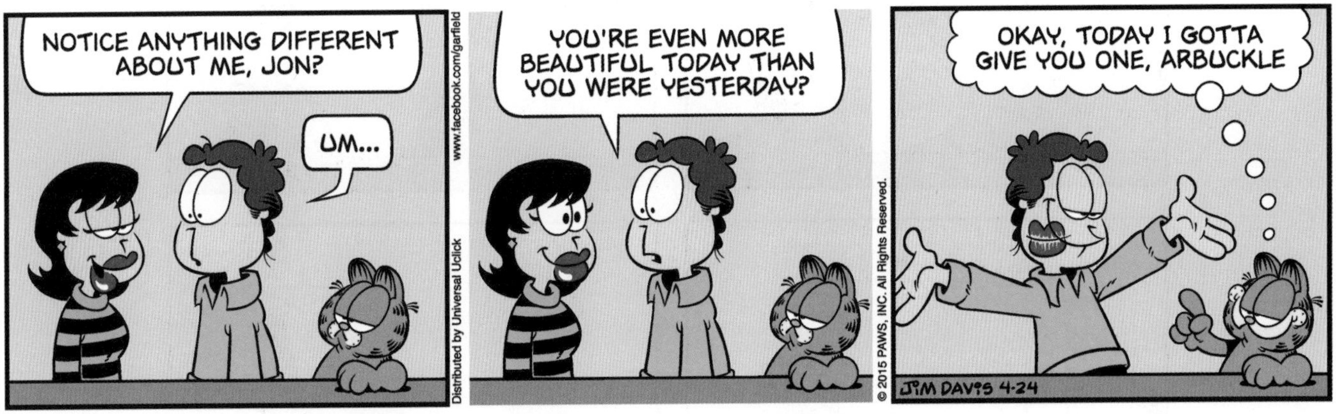
NOTICE ANYTHING DIFFERENT ABOUT ME, JON?
UM...
www.facebook.com/garfield
Distributed by Universal Uclick
YOU'RE EVEN MORE BEAUTIFUL TODAY THAN YOU WERE YESTERDAY?
© 2015 PAWS, INC. All Rights Reserved.
OKAY, TODAY I GOTTA GIVE YOU ONE, ARBUCKLE
JIM DAVIS 4-24

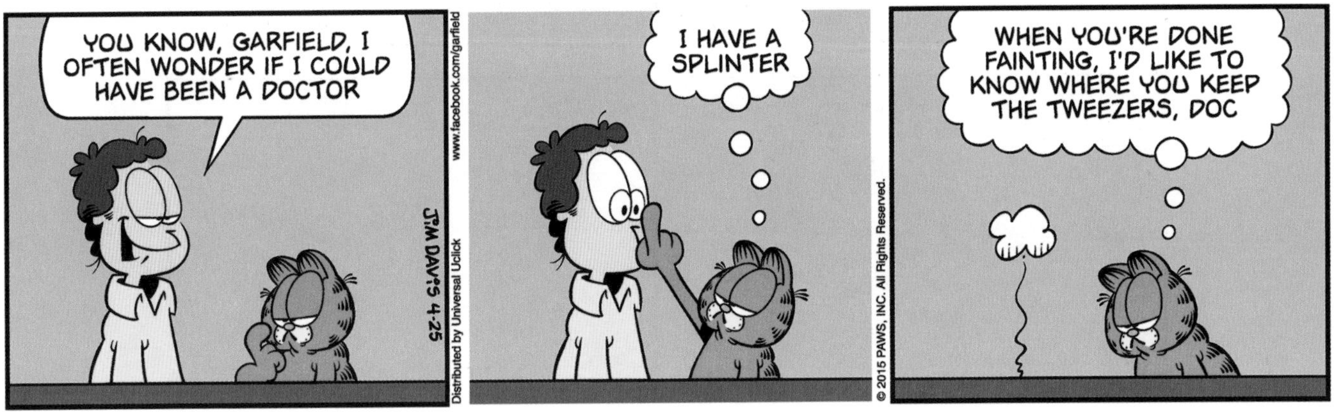
YOU KNOW, GARFIELD, I OFTEN WONDER IF I COULD HAVE BEEN A DOCTOR
JIM DAVIS 4-25
www.facebook.com/garfield
Distributed by Universal Uclick
I HAVE A SPLINTER
© 2015 PAWS, INC. All Rights Reserved.
WHEN YOU'RE DONE FAINTING, I'D LIKE TO KNOW WHERE YOU KEEP THE TWEEZERS, DOC

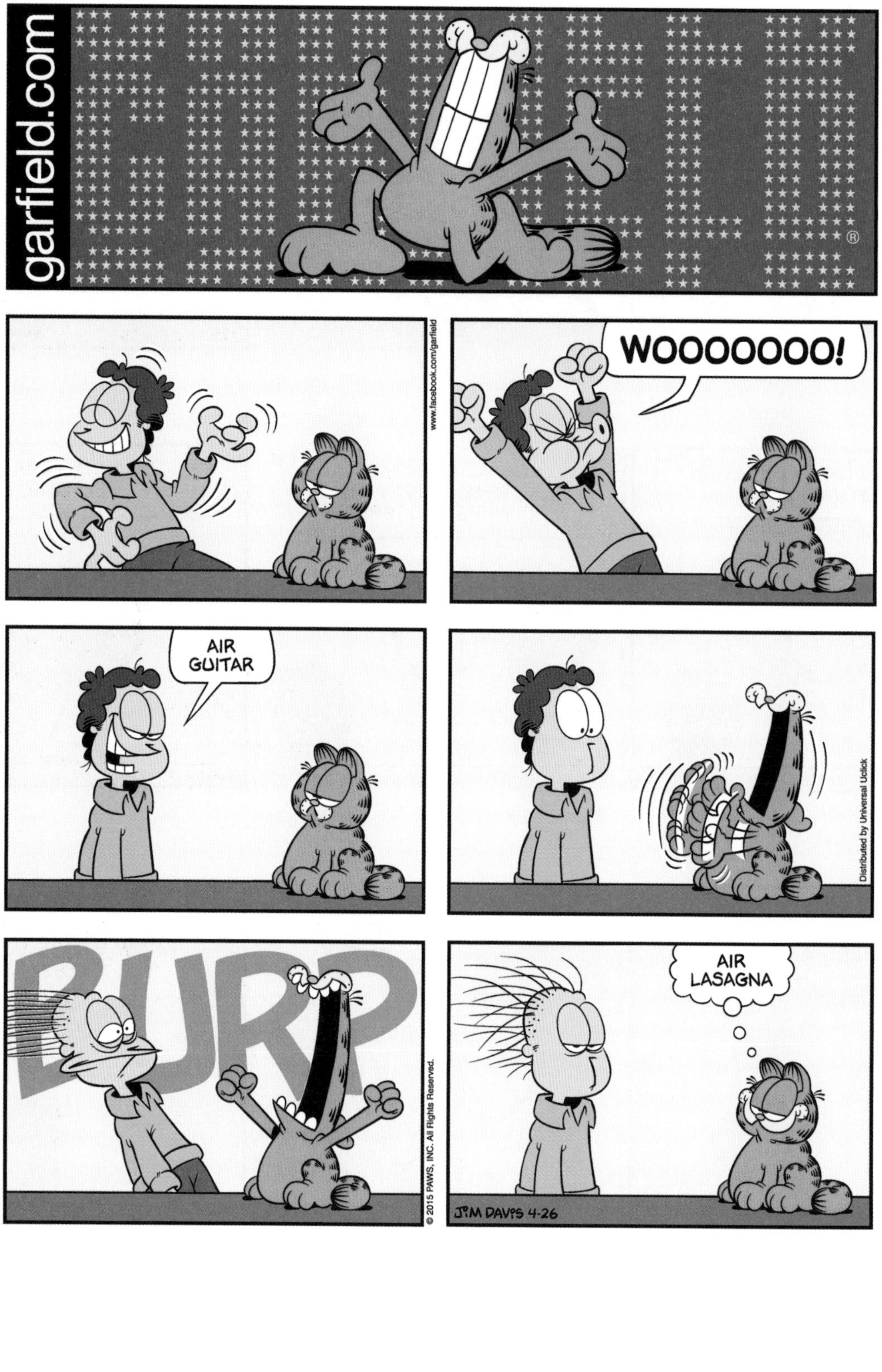
garfield.com
www.facebook.com/garfield
WOOOOOOO!
AIR GUITAR
Distributed by Universal Uclick
BURP
© 2015 PAWS, INC. All Rights Reserved.
AIR LASAGNA
JIM DAVIS 4-26

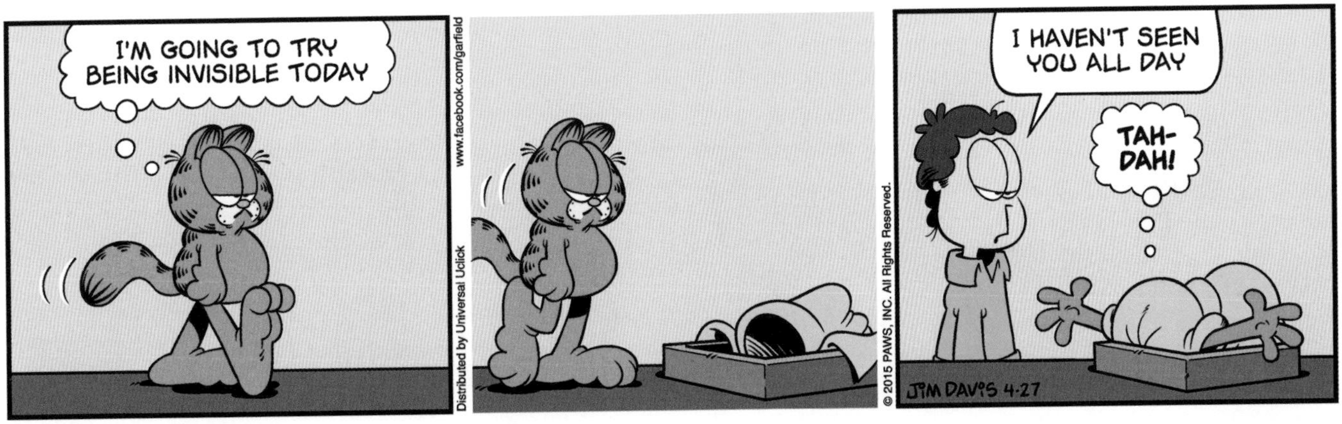
I'M GOING TO TRY BEING INVISIBLE TODAY
www.facebook.com/garfield
Distributed by Universal Uclick
© 2015 PAWS, INC. All Rights Reserved.
I HAVEN'T SEEN YOU ALL DAY
TAH-DAH!
JIM DAVIS 4-27

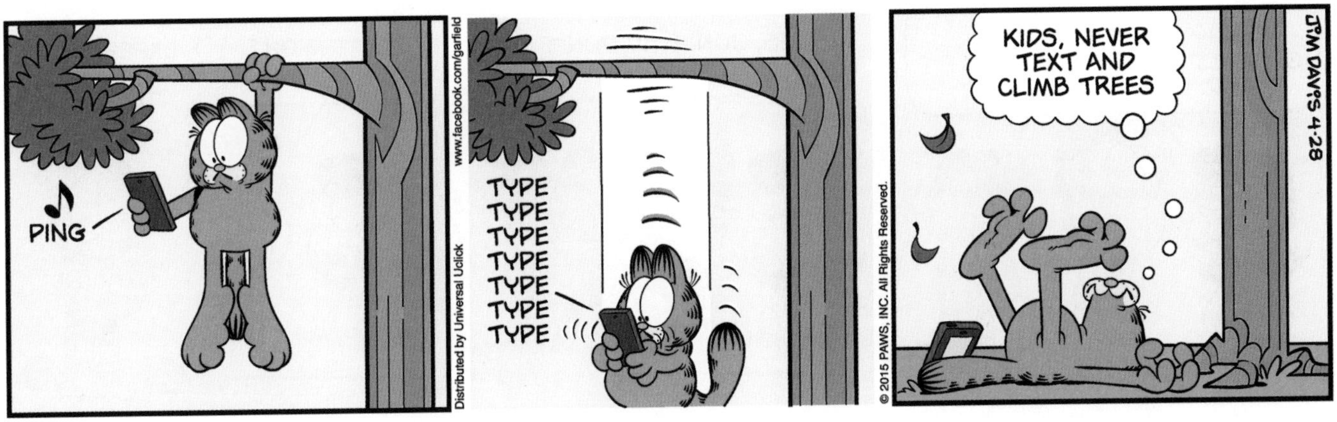
PING
www.facebook.com/garfield
Distributed by Universal Uclick
TYPE TYPE TYPE TYPE TYPE TYPE TYPE
© 2015 PAWS, INC. All Rights Reserved.
KIDS, NEVER TEXT AND CLIMB TREES
JIM DAVIS 4-28

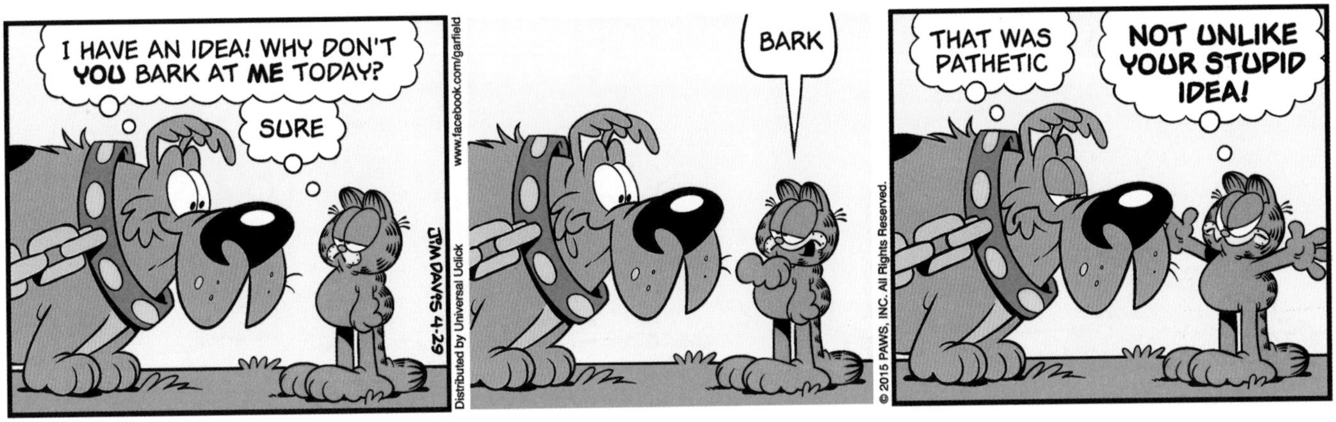
I HAVE AN IDEA! WHY DON'T YOU BARK AT ME TODAY?
SURE
JIM DAVIS 4-29
www.facebook.com/garfield
Distributed by Universal Uclick
BARK
© 2015 PAWS, INC. All Rights Reserved.
THAT WAS PATHETIC
NOT UNLIKE YOUR STUPID IDEA!

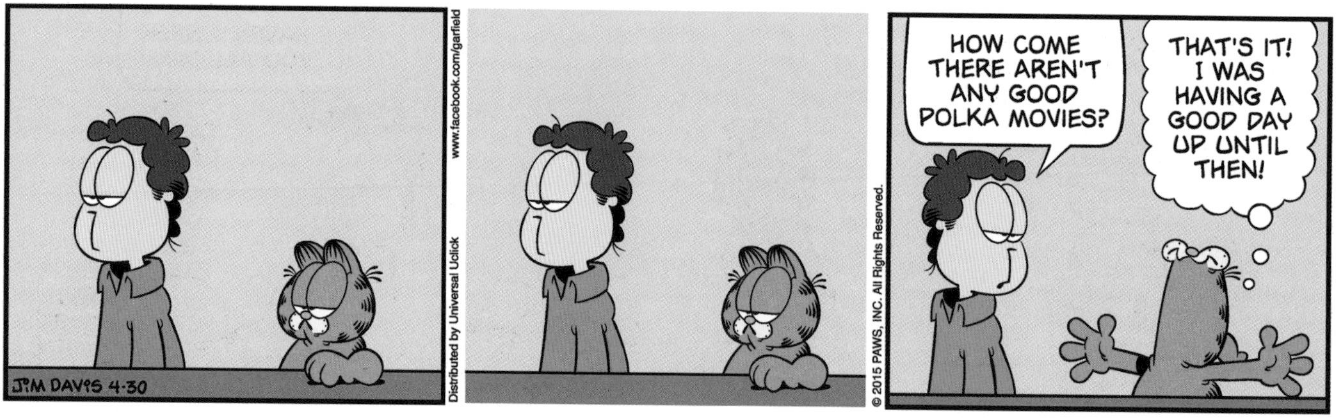
JIM DAVIS 4-30
Distributed by Universal Uclick www.facebook.com/garfield
HOW COME THERE AREN'T ANY GOOD POLKA MOVIES?
THAT'S IT! I WAS HAVING A GOOD DAY UP UNTIL THEN!
© 2015 PAWS, INC. All Rights Reserved.

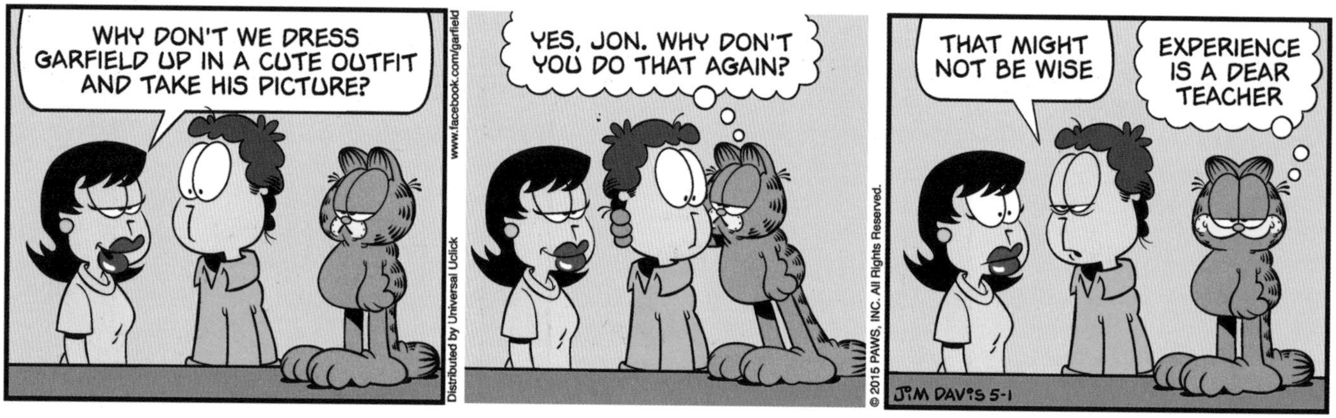
WHY DON'T WE DRESS GARFIELD UP IN A CUTE OUTFIT AND TAKE HIS PICTURE?
Distributed by Universal Uclick www.facebook.com/garfield
YES, JON. WHY DON'T YOU DO THAT AGAIN?
THAT MIGHT NOT BE WISE
EXPERIENCE IS A DEAR TEACHER
JIM DAVIS 5-1
© 2015 PAWS, INC. All Rights Reserved.

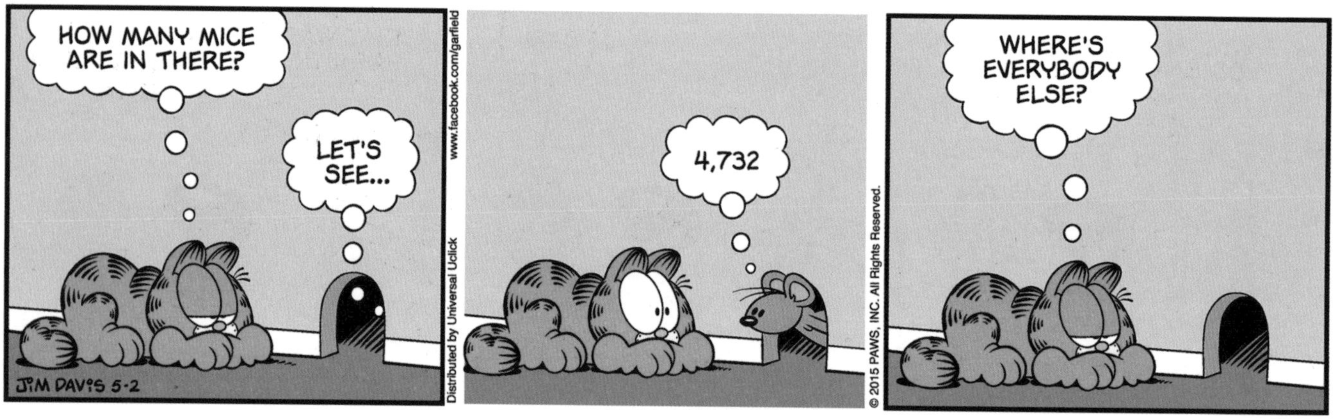
HOW MANY MICE ARE IN THERE?
LET'S SEE...
JIM DAVIS 5-2
Distributed by Universal Uclick www.facebook.com/garfield
4,732
WHERE'S EVERYBODY ELSE?
© 2015 PAWS, INC. All Rights Reserved.

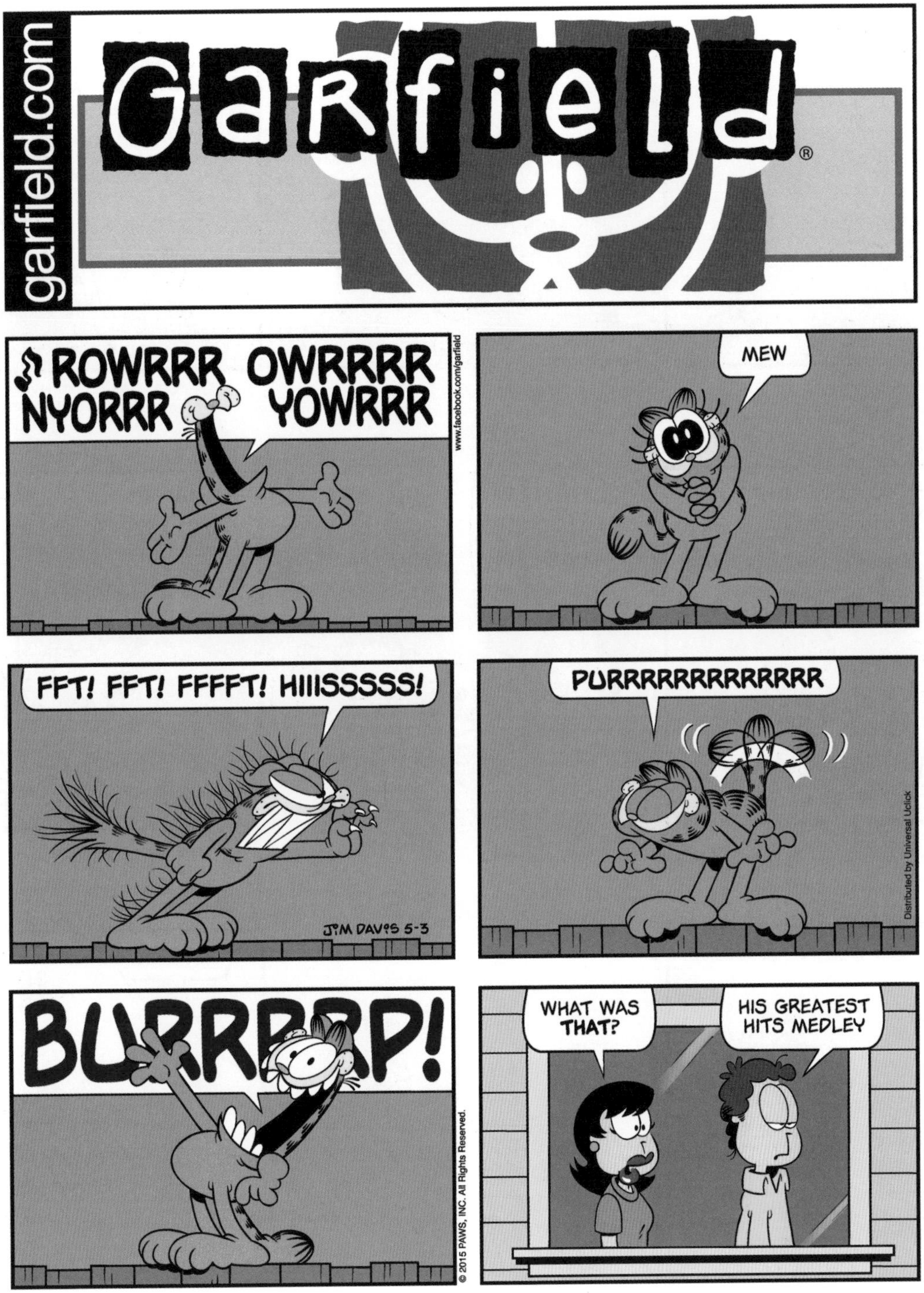
garfield.com
Garfield
ROWRRR OWRRRR NYORRR YOWRRR
MEW
FFT! FFT! FFFFT! HIIISSSSS!
PURRRRRRRRRRRRR
BURRRRP!
WHAT WAS THAT?
HIS GREATEST HITS MEDLEY
JIM DAVIS 5-3
www.facebook.com/garfield
© 2015 PAWS, INC. All Rights Reserved.
Distributed by Universal Uclick

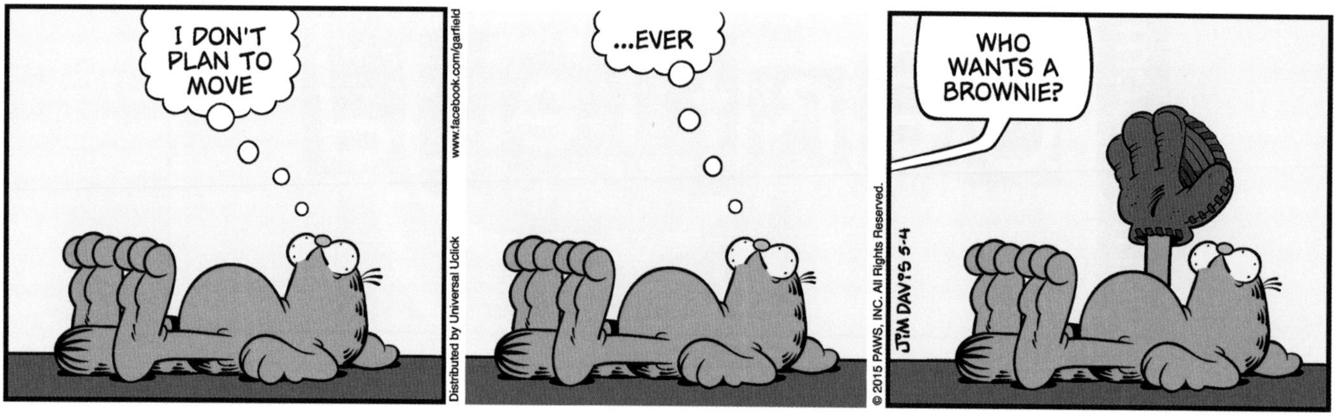
I DON'T PLAN TO MOVE
...EVER
WHO WANTS A BROWNIE?
JIM DAVIS 5-4
Distributed by Universal Uclick www.facebook.com/garfield
© 2015 PAWS, INC. All Rights Reserved.

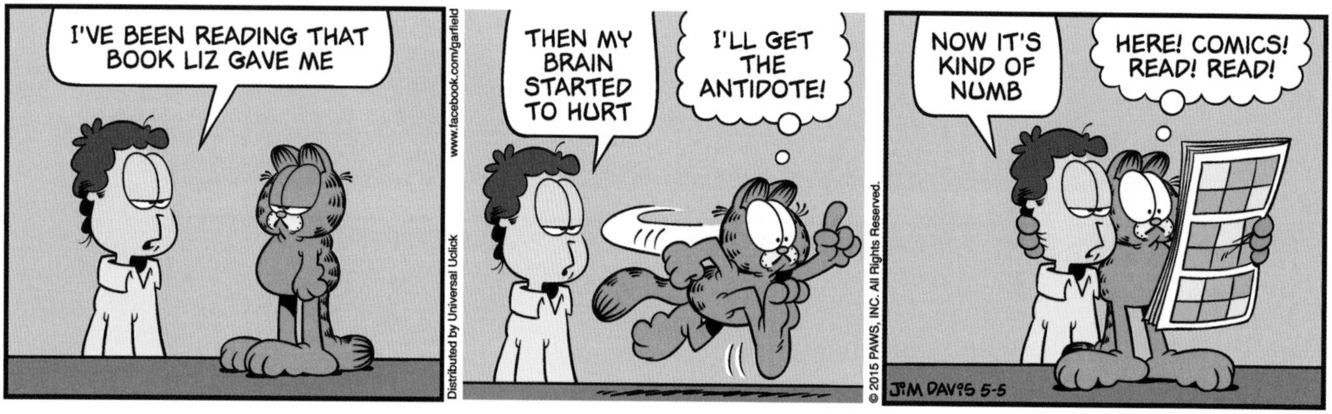
I'VE BEEN READING THAT BOOK LIZ GAVE ME
THEN MY BRAIN STARTED TO HURT
I'LL GET THE ANTIDOTE!
NOW IT'S KIND OF NUMB
HERE! COMICS! READ! READ!
JIM DAVIS 5-5
Distributed by Universal Uclick www.facebook.com/garfield
© 2015 PAWS, INC. All Rights Reserved.

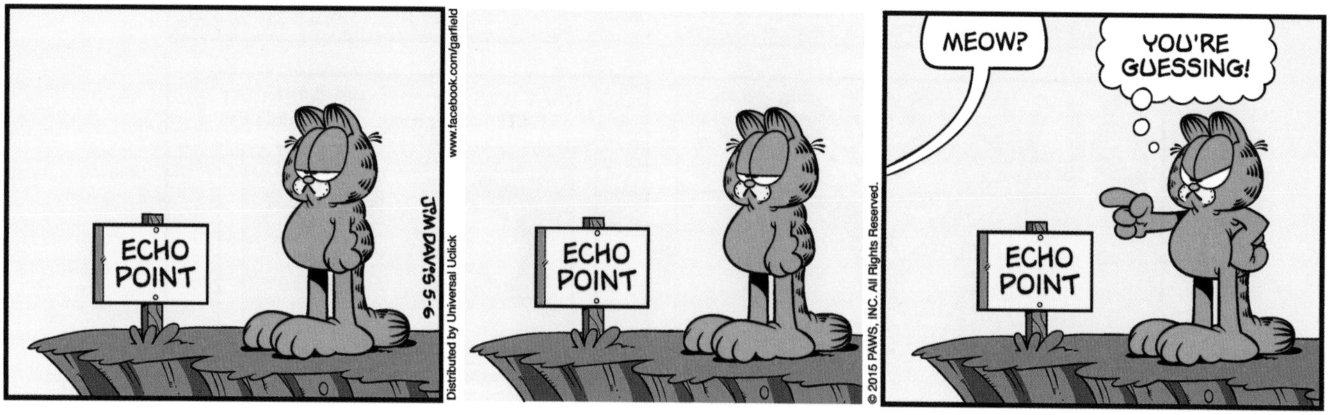
ECHO POINT
ECHO POINT
MEOW?
YOU'RE GUESSING!
ECHO POINT
JIM DAVIS 5-6
Distributed by Universal Uclick www.facebook.com/garfield
© 2015 PAWS, INC. All Rights Reserved.

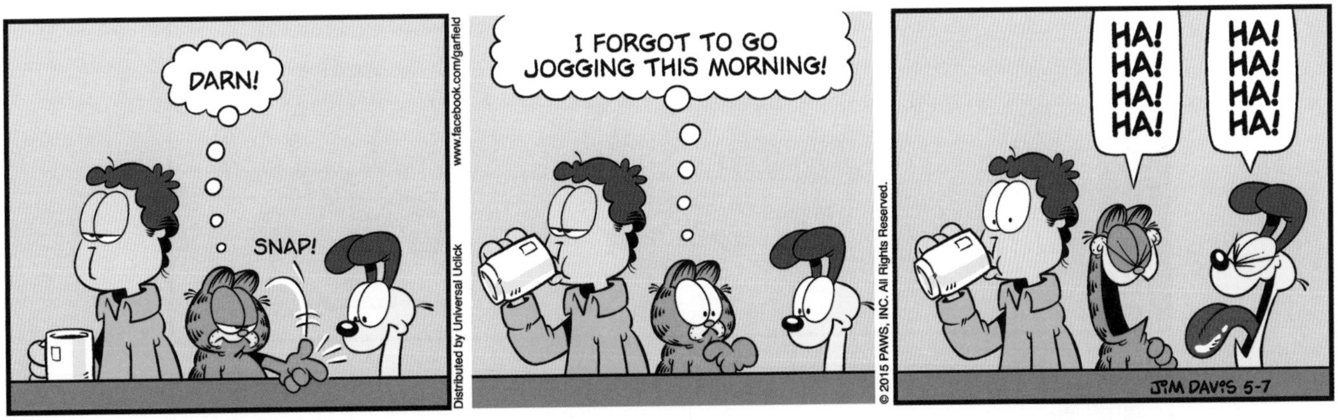
DARN!
SNAP!
www.facebook.com/garfield
Distributed by Universal Uclick
I FORGOT TO GO JOGGING THIS MORNING!
© 2015 PAWS, INC. All Rights Reserved.
HA! HA! HA! HA!
HA! HA! HA! HA!
JIM DAVIS 5-7

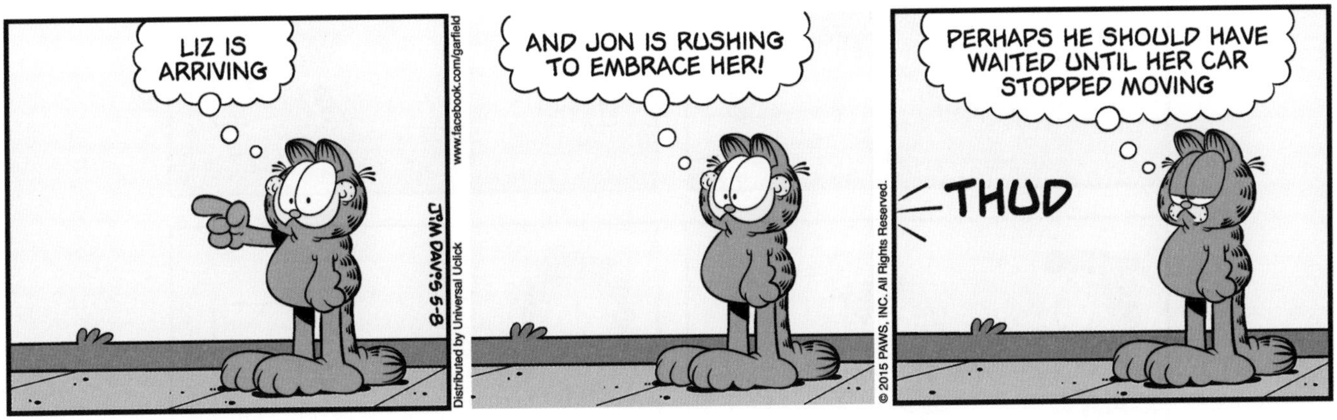
LIZ IS ARRIVING
JIM DAVIS 5-8
www.facebook.com/garfield
Distributed by Universal Uclick
AND JON IS RUSHING TO EMBRACE HER!
© 2015 PAWS, INC. All Rights Reserved.
THUD
PERHAPS HE SHOULD HAVE WAITED UNTIL HER CAR STOPPED MOVING

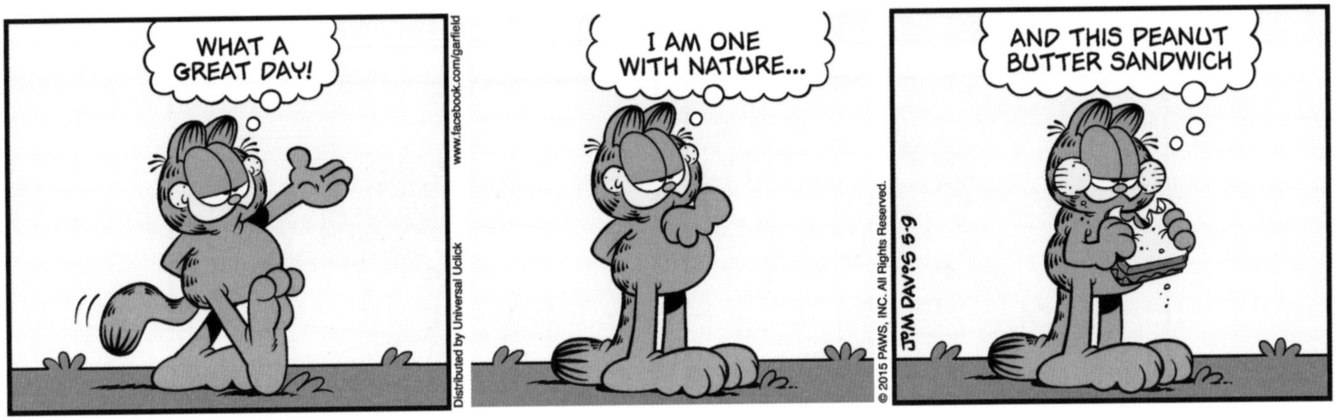
WHAT A GREAT DAY!
www.facebook.com/garfield
Distributed by Universal Uclick
I AM ONE WITH NATURE...
© 2015 PAWS, INC. All Rights Reserved.
JIM DAVIS 5-9
AND THIS PEANUT BUTTER SANDWICH

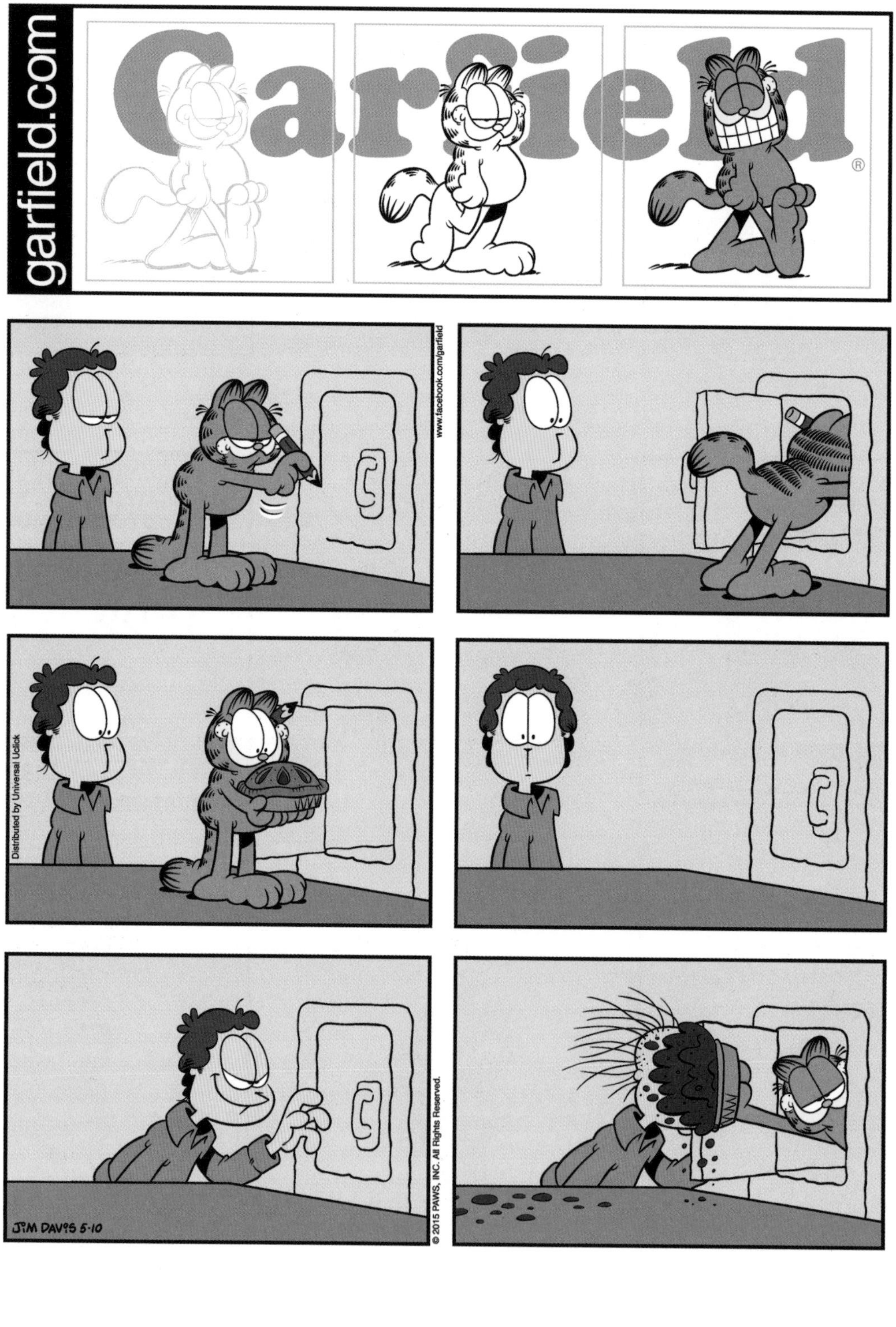
garfield.com
Garfield
www.facebook.com/garfield
Distributed by Universal Uclick
© 2015 PAWS, INC. All Rights Reserved.
JIM DAVIS 5-10

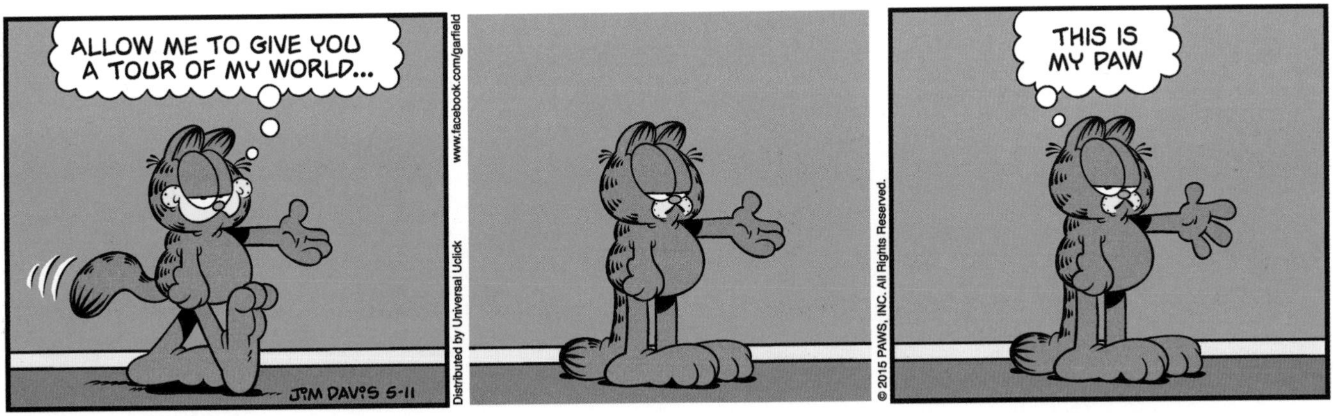
ALLOW ME TO GIVE YOU A TOUR OF MY WORLD...
JIM DAVIS 5-11
Distributed by Universal Uclick www.facebook.com/garfield
THIS IS MY PAW
© 2015 PAWS, INC. All Rights Reserved.

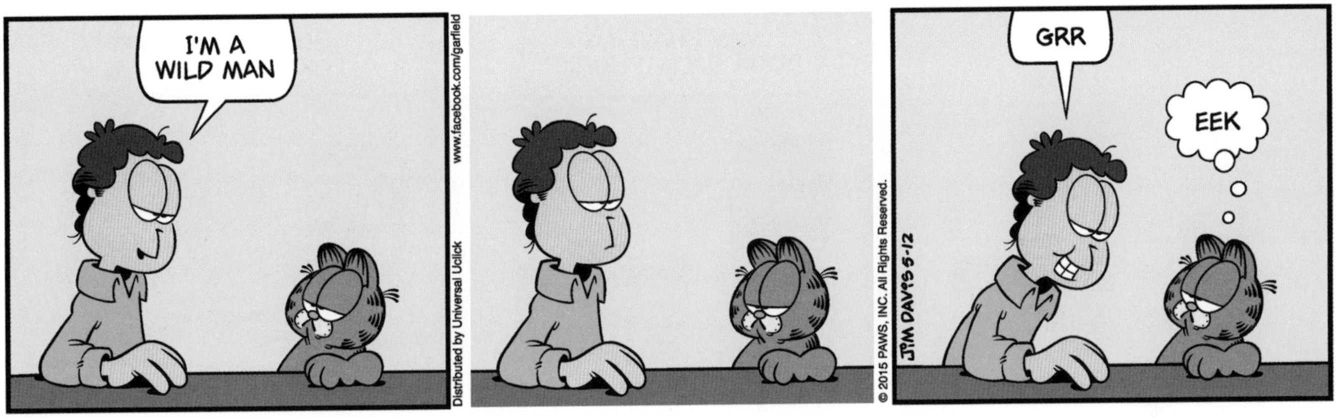
I'M A WILD MAN
Distributed by Universal Uclick www.facebook.com/garfield
© 2015 PAWS, INC. All Rights Reserved.
JIM DAVIS 5-12
GRR
EEK

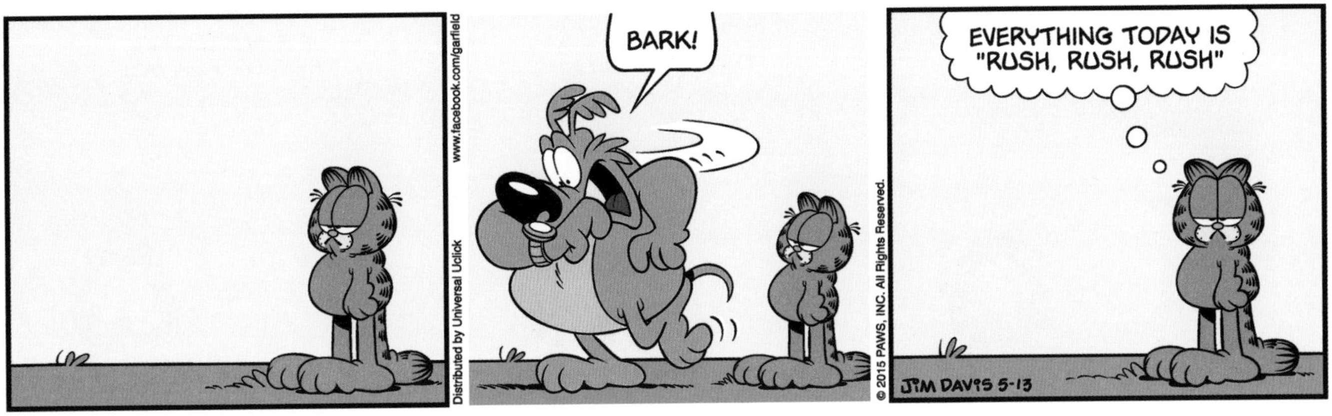
Distributed by Universal Uclick www.facebook.com/garfield
BARK!
© 2015 PAWS, INC. All Rights Reserved.
JIM DAVIS 5-13
EVERYTHING TODAY IS "RUSH, RUSH, RUSH"

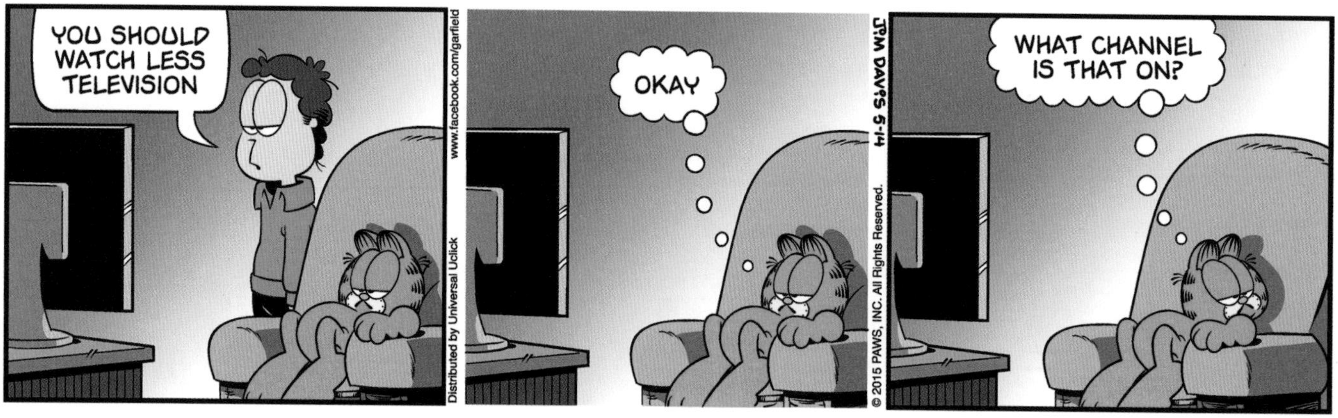
YOU SHOULD WATCH LESS TELEVISION
OKAY
WHAT CHANNEL IS THAT ON?
JIM DAVIS 5-14
Distributed by Universal Uclick www.facebook.com/garfield
© 2015 PAWS, INC. All Rights Reserved.

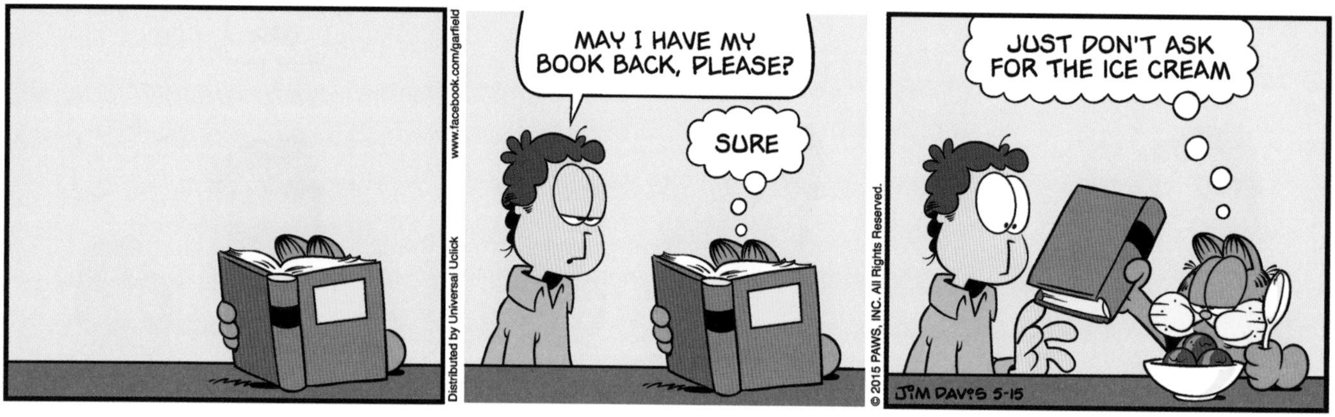
MAY I HAVE MY BOOK BACK, PLEASE?
SURE
JUST DON'T ASK FOR THE ICE CREAM
JIM DAVIS 5-15
Distributed by Universal Uclick www.facebook.com/garfield
© 2015 PAWS, INC. All Rights Reserved.

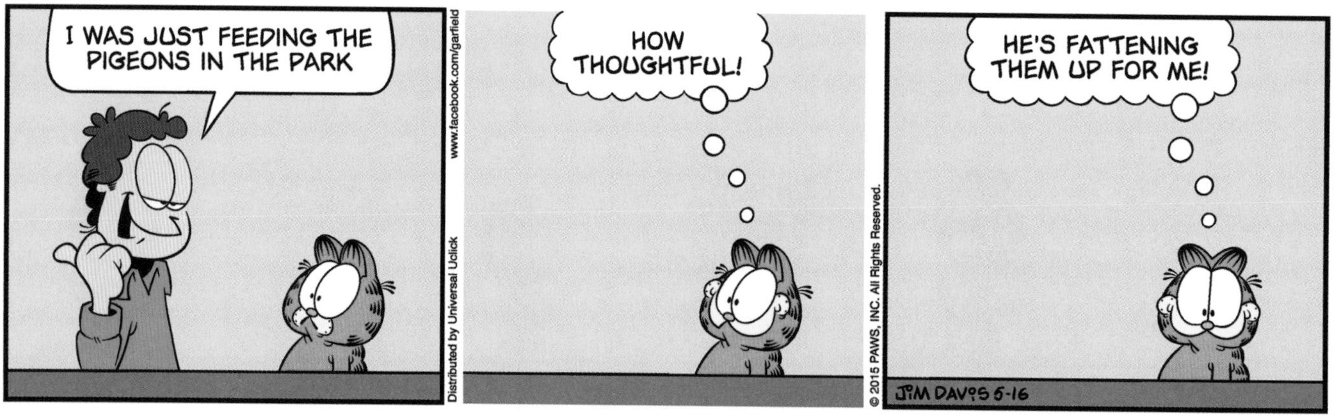
I WAS JUST FEEDING THE PIGEONS IN THE PARK
HOW THOUGHTFUL!
HE'S FATTENING THEM UP FOR ME!
JIM DAVIS 5-16
Distributed by Universal Uclick www.facebook.com/garfield
© 2015 PAWS, INC. All Rights Reserved.

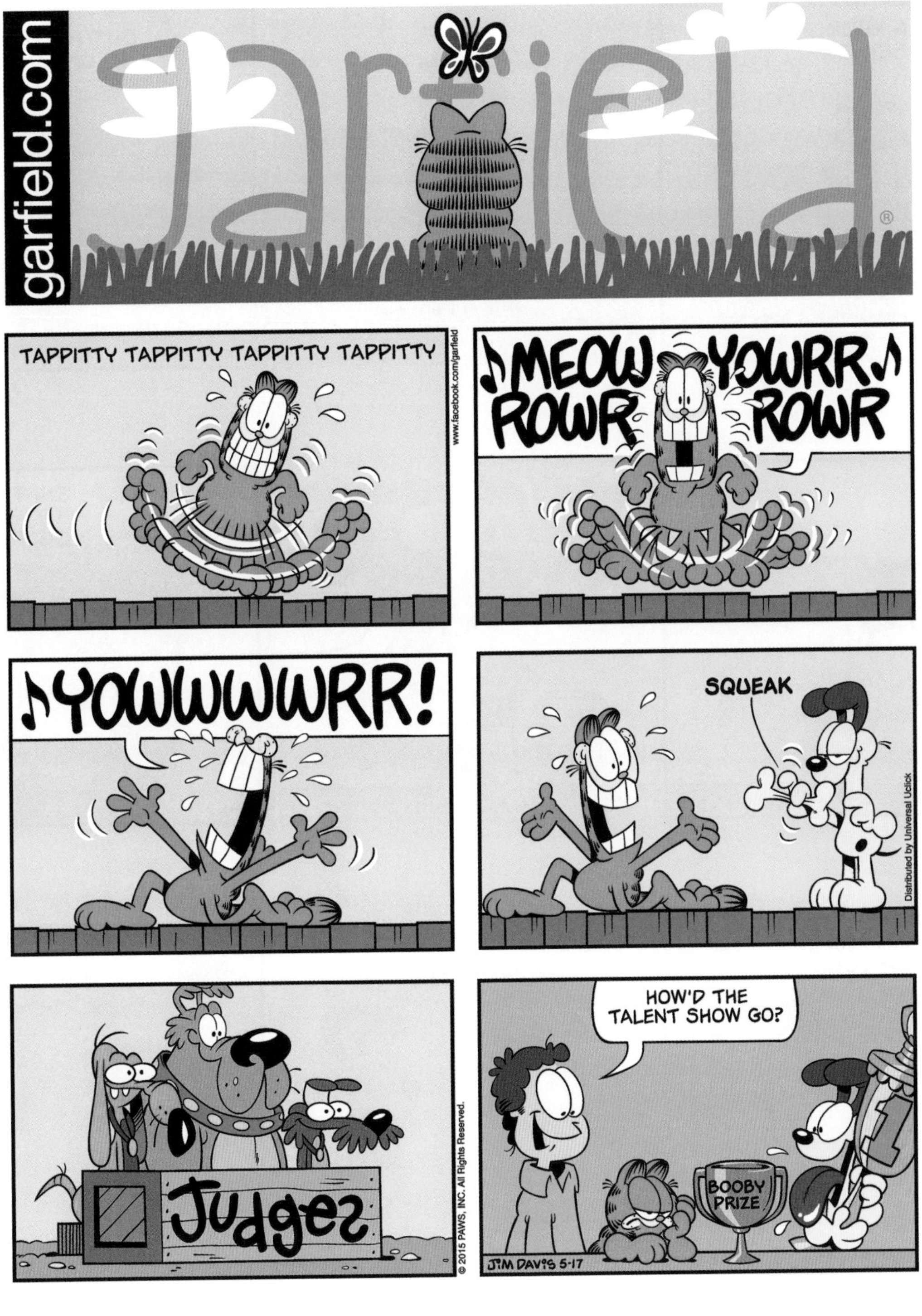
garfield.com
garfield
TAPPITTY TAPPITTY TAPPITTY TAPPITTY
www.facebook.com/garfield
♪MEOW YOWRR♪ ROWR ROWR
♪YOWWWWRR!
SQUEAK
Distributed by Universal Uclick
Judges
© 2015 PAWS, INC. All Rights Reserved.
HOW'D THE TALENT SHOW GO?
BOOBY PRIZE
JIM DAVIS 5-17

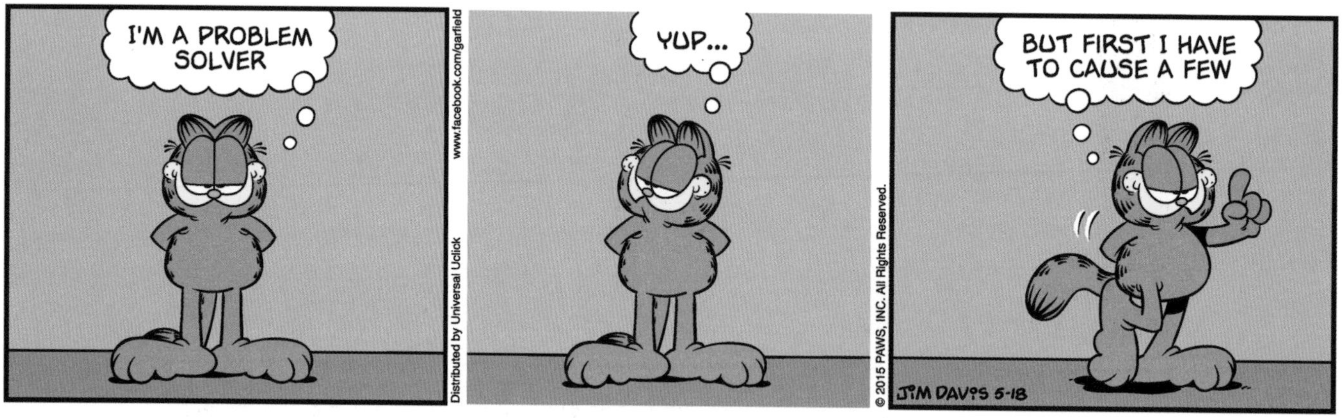
I'M A PROBLEM SOLVER
Distributed by Universal Uclick www.facebook.com/garfield
YUP...
© 2015 PAWS, INC. All Rights Reserved.
BUT FIRST I HAVE TO CAUSE A FEW
JIM DAVIS 5-18

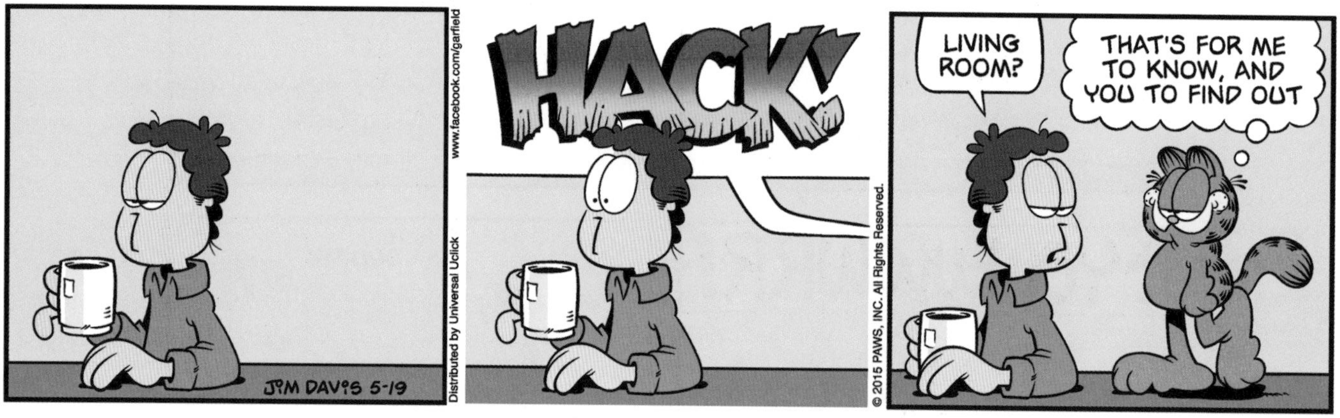
JIM DAVIS 5-19
Distributed by Universal Uclick www.facebook.com/garfield
HACK!
© 2015 PAWS, INC. All Rights Reserved.
LIVING ROOM?
THAT'S FOR ME TO KNOW, AND YOU TO FIND OUT

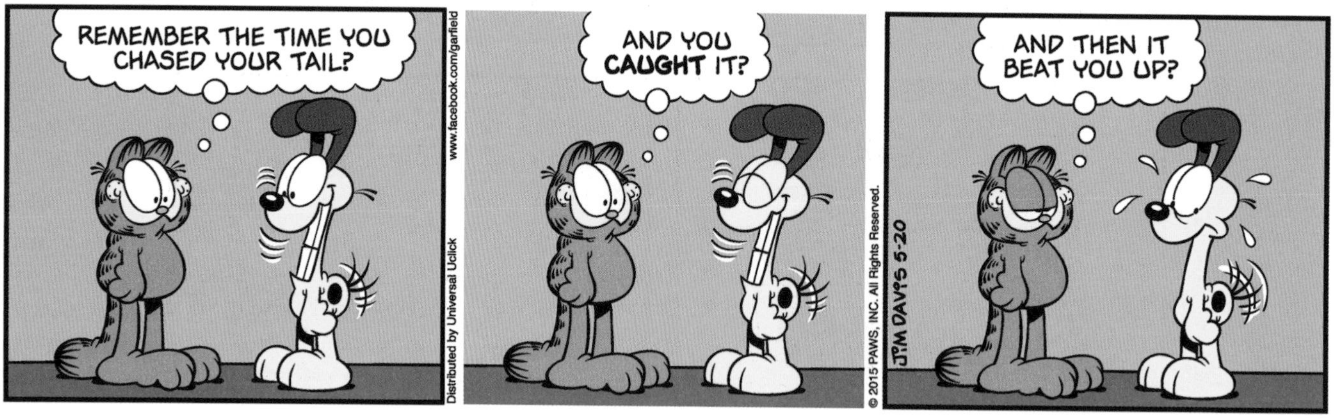
REMEMBER THE TIME YOU CHASED YOUR TAIL?
Distributed by Universal Uclick www.facebook.com/garfield
AND YOU CAUGHT IT?
© 2015 PAWS, INC. All Rights Reserved.
JIM DAVIS 5-20
AND THEN IT BEAT YOU UP?

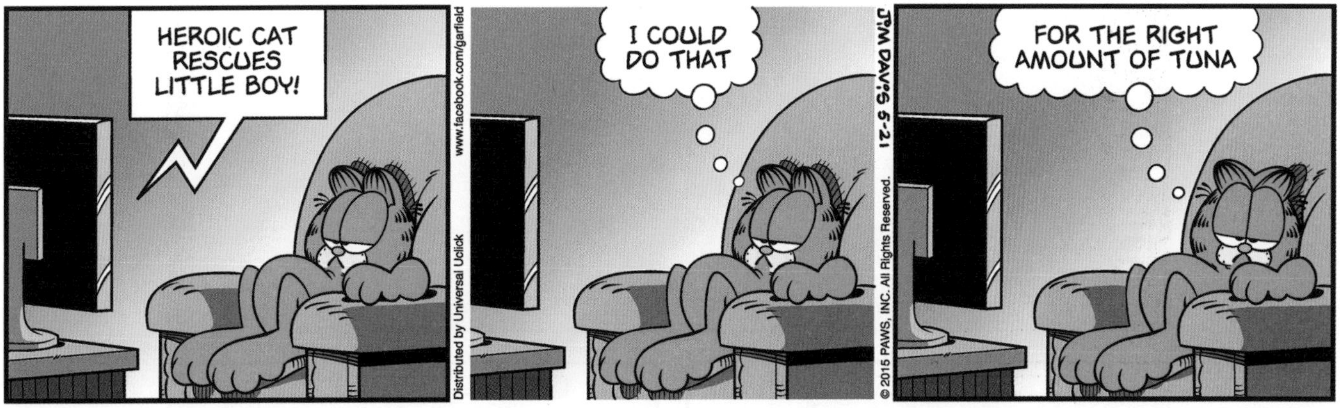
HEROIC CAT RESCUES LITTLE BOY!
I COULD DO THAT
FOR THE RIGHT AMOUNT OF TUNA
JIM DAVIS 5-21
Distributed by Universal Uclick www.facebook.com/garfield
© 2015 PAWS, INC. All Rights Reserved.

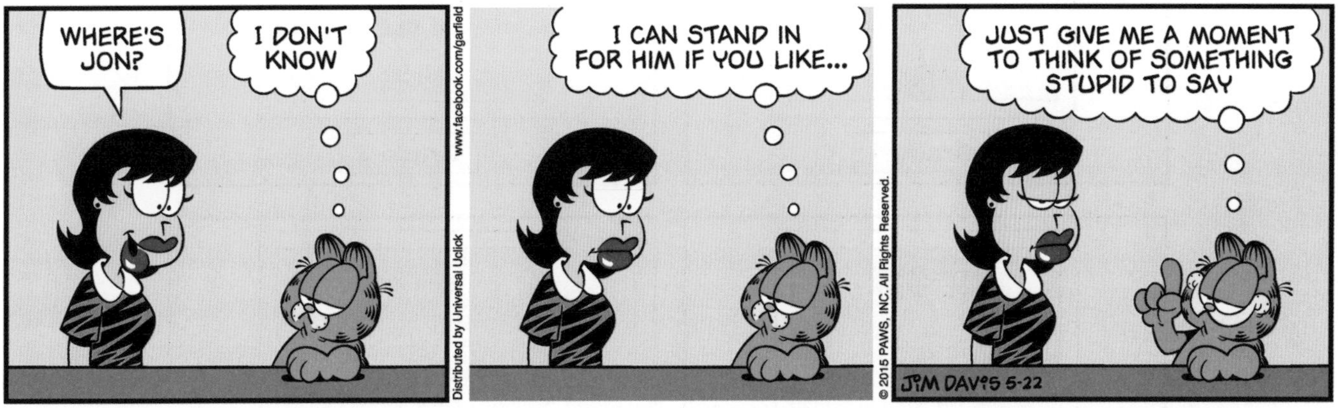
WHERE'S JON?
I DON'T KNOW
I CAN STAND IN FOR HIM IF YOU LIKE...
JUST GIVE ME A MOMENT TO THINK OF SOMETHING STUPID TO SAY
JIM DAVIS 5-22
Distributed by Universal Uclick www.facebook.com/garfield
© 2015 PAWS, INC. All Rights Reserved.

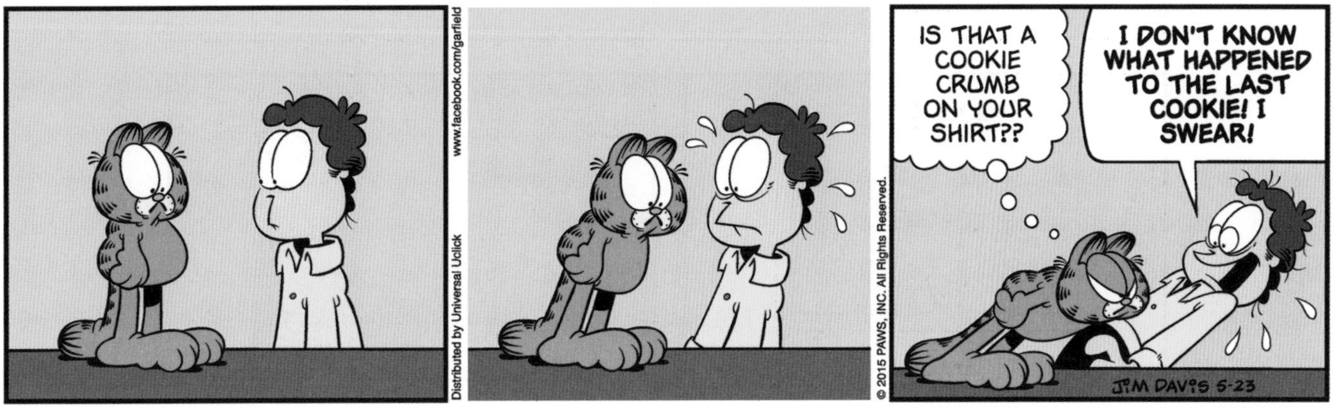
IS THAT A COOKIE CRUMB ON YOUR SHIRT??
I DON'T KNOW WHAT HAPPENED TO THE LAST COOKIE! I SWEAR!
JIM DAVIS 5-23
Distributed by Universal Uclick www.facebook.com/garfield
© 2015 PAWS, INC. All Rights Reserved.

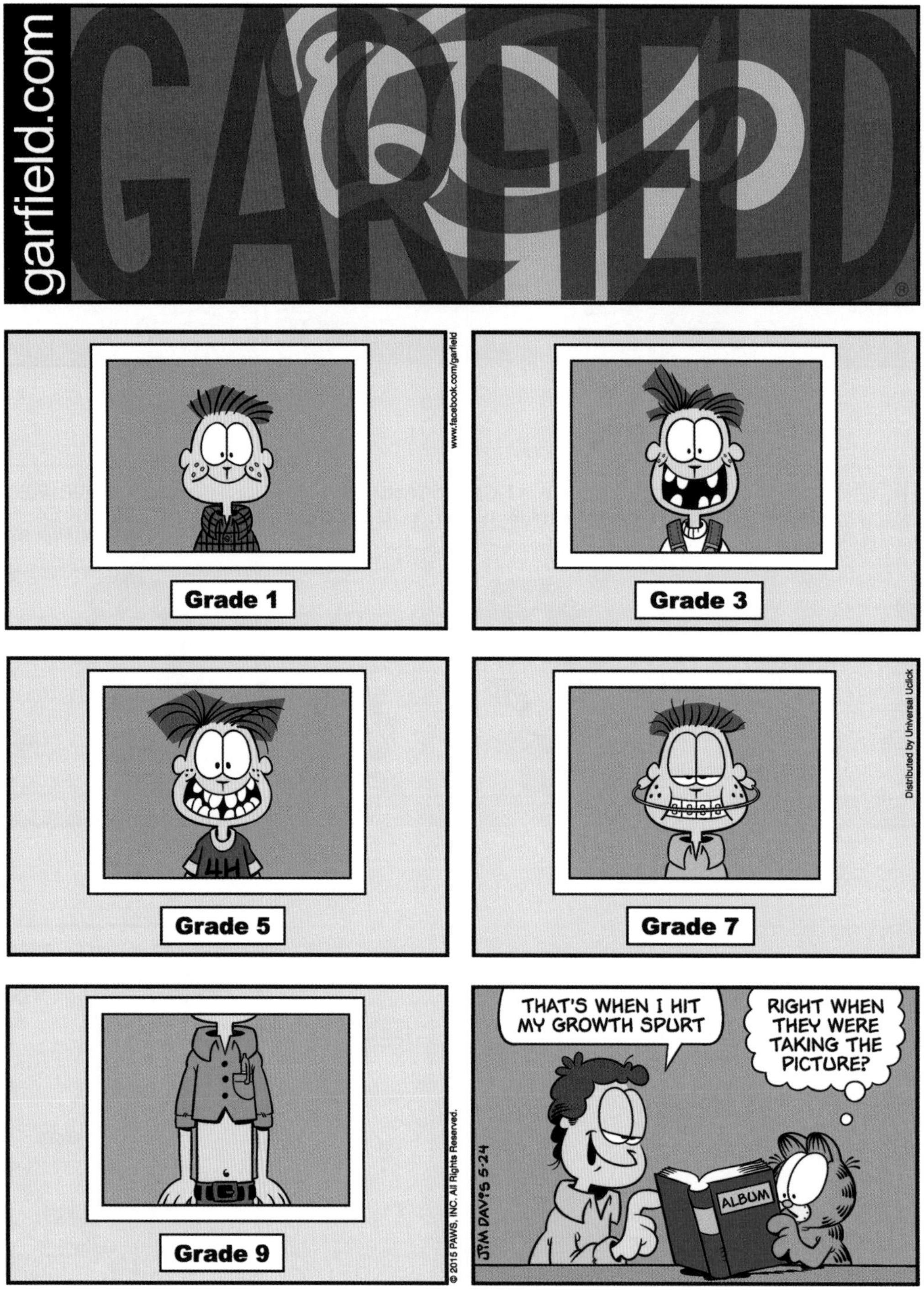
garfield.com
GARFIELD
www.facebook.com/garfield
Grade 1
Grade 3
Grade 5
Grade 7
Distributed by Universal Uclick
Grade 9
© 2015 PAWS, INC. All Rights Reserved.
JIM DAVIS 5-24
THAT'S WHEN I HIT MY GROWTH SPURT
RIGHT WHEN THEY WERE TAKING THE PICTURE?
ALBUM

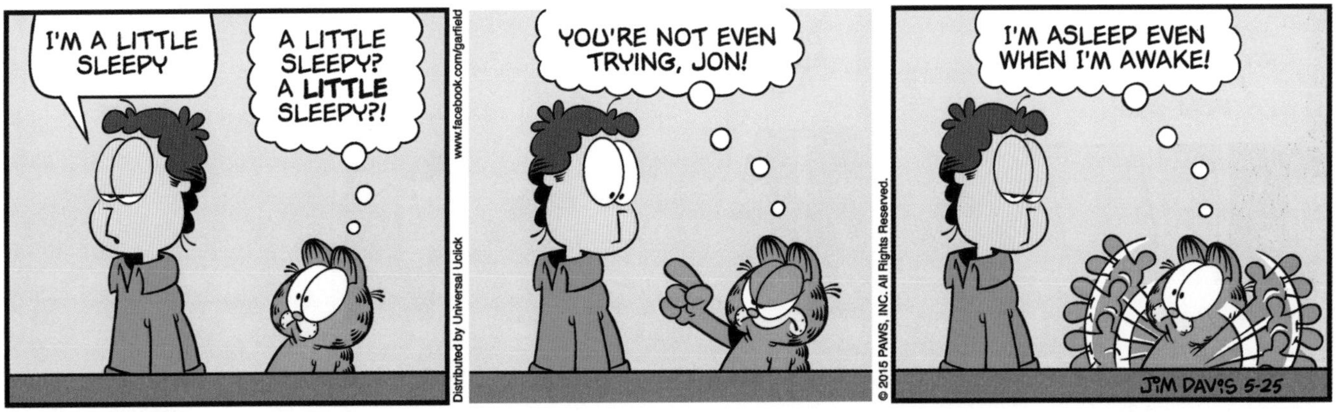
I'M A LITTLE SLEEPY
A LITTLE SLEEPY? A **LITTLE** SLEEPY?!
YOU'RE NOT EVEN TRYING, JON!
I'M ASLEEP EVEN WHEN I'M AWAKE!
JIM DAVIS 5-25
Distributed by Universal Uclick www.facebook.com/garfield
© 2015 PAWS, INC. All Rights Reserved.

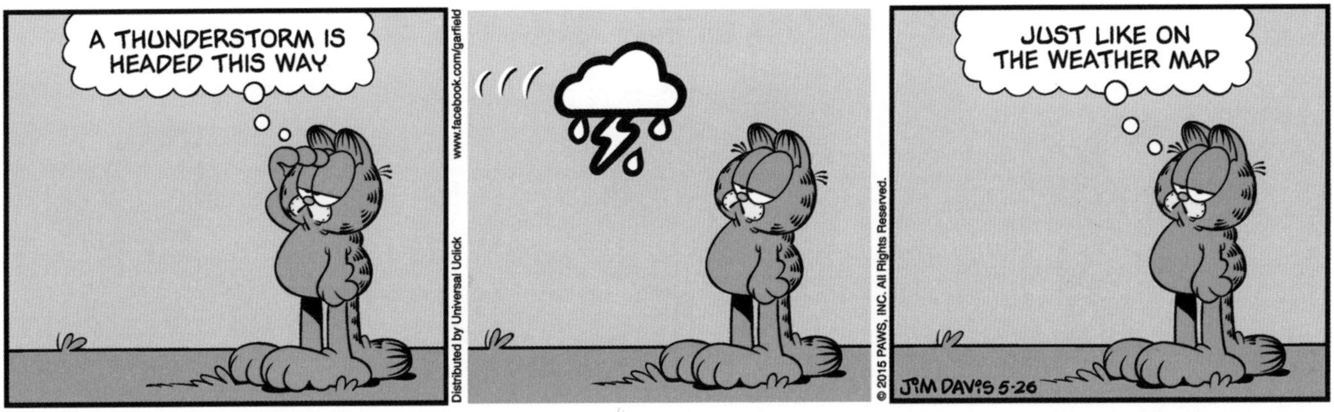
A THUNDERSTORM IS HEADED THIS WAY
JUST LIKE ON THE WEATHER MAP
JIM DAVIS 5-26
Distributed by Universal Uclick www.facebook.com/garfield
© 2015 PAWS, INC. All Rights Reserved.

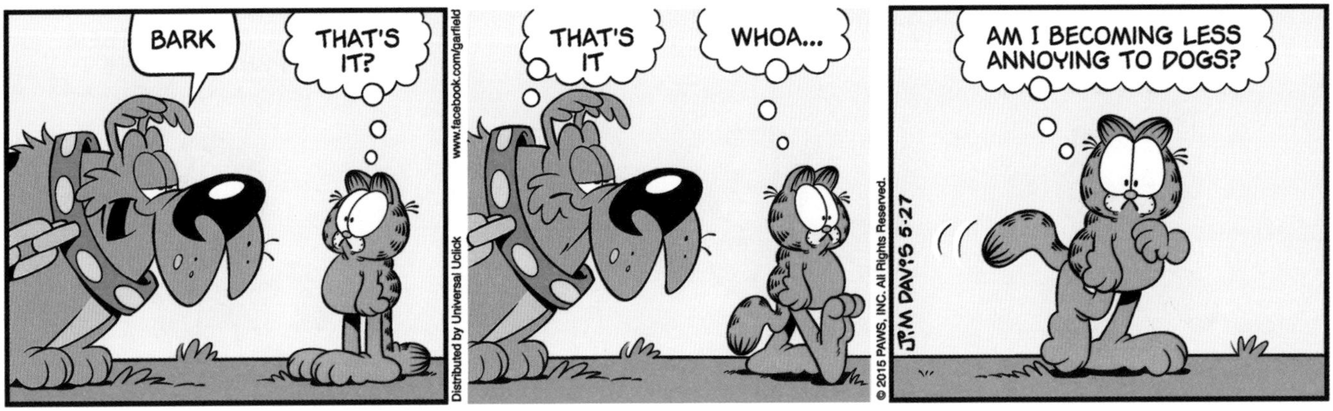
BARK
THAT'S IT?
THAT'S IT
WHOA...
AM I BECOMING LESS ANNOYING TO DOGS?
JIM DAVIS 5-27
Distributed by Universal Uclick www.facebook.com/garfield
© 2015 PAWS, INC. All Rights Reserved.

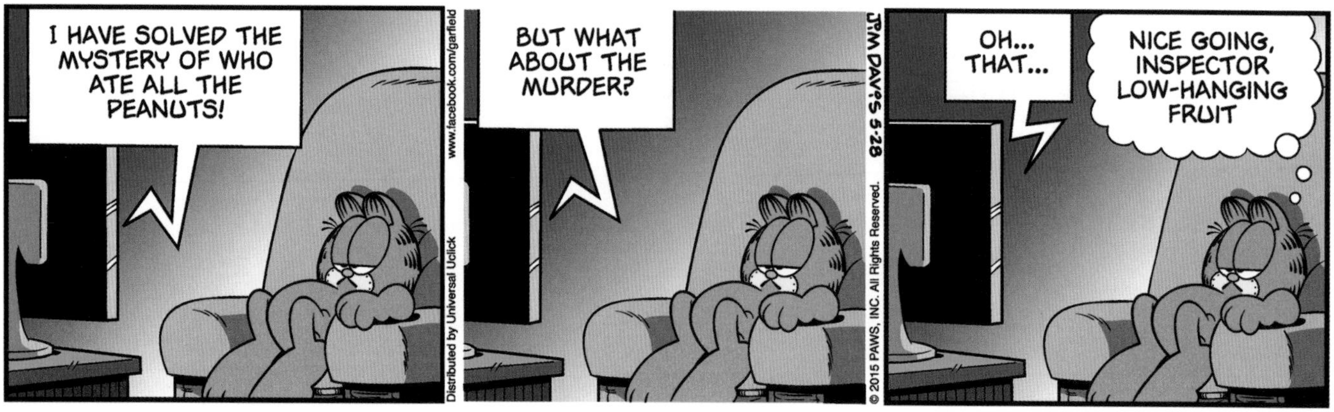
I HAVE SOLVED THE MYSTERY OF WHO ATE ALL THE PEANUTS!
BUT WHAT ABOUT THE MURDER?
OH... THAT...
NICE GOING, INSPECTOR LOW-HANGING FRUIT
JIM DAVIS 5-28

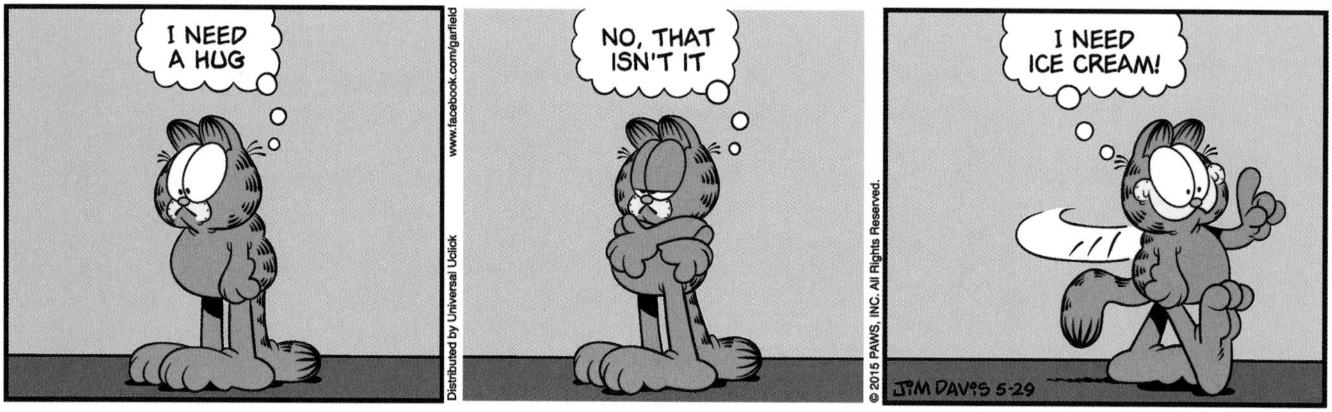
I NEED A HUG
NO, THAT ISN'T IT
I NEED ICE CREAM!
JIM DAVIS 5-29

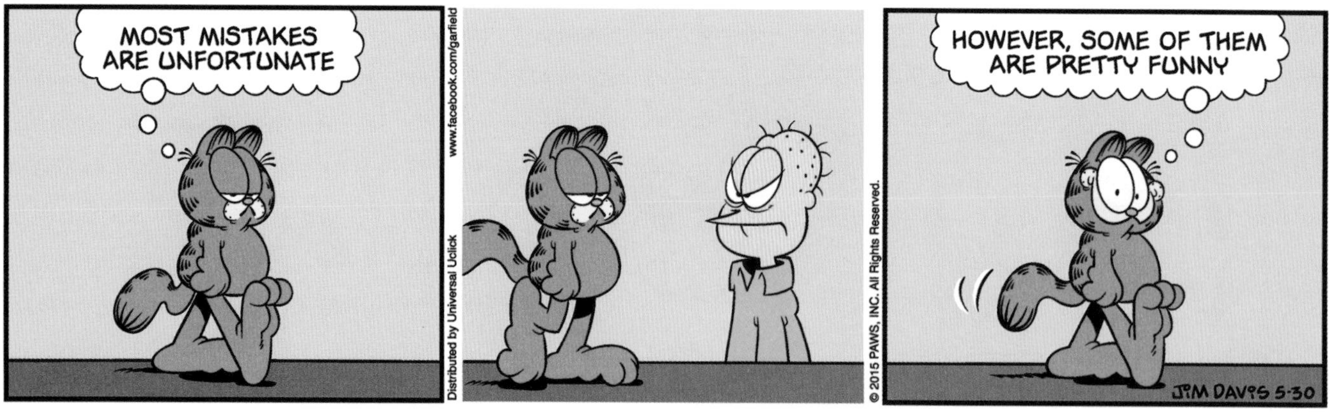
MOST MISTAKES ARE UNFORTUNATE
HOWEVER, SOME OF THEM ARE PRETTY FUNNY
JIM DAVIS 5-30

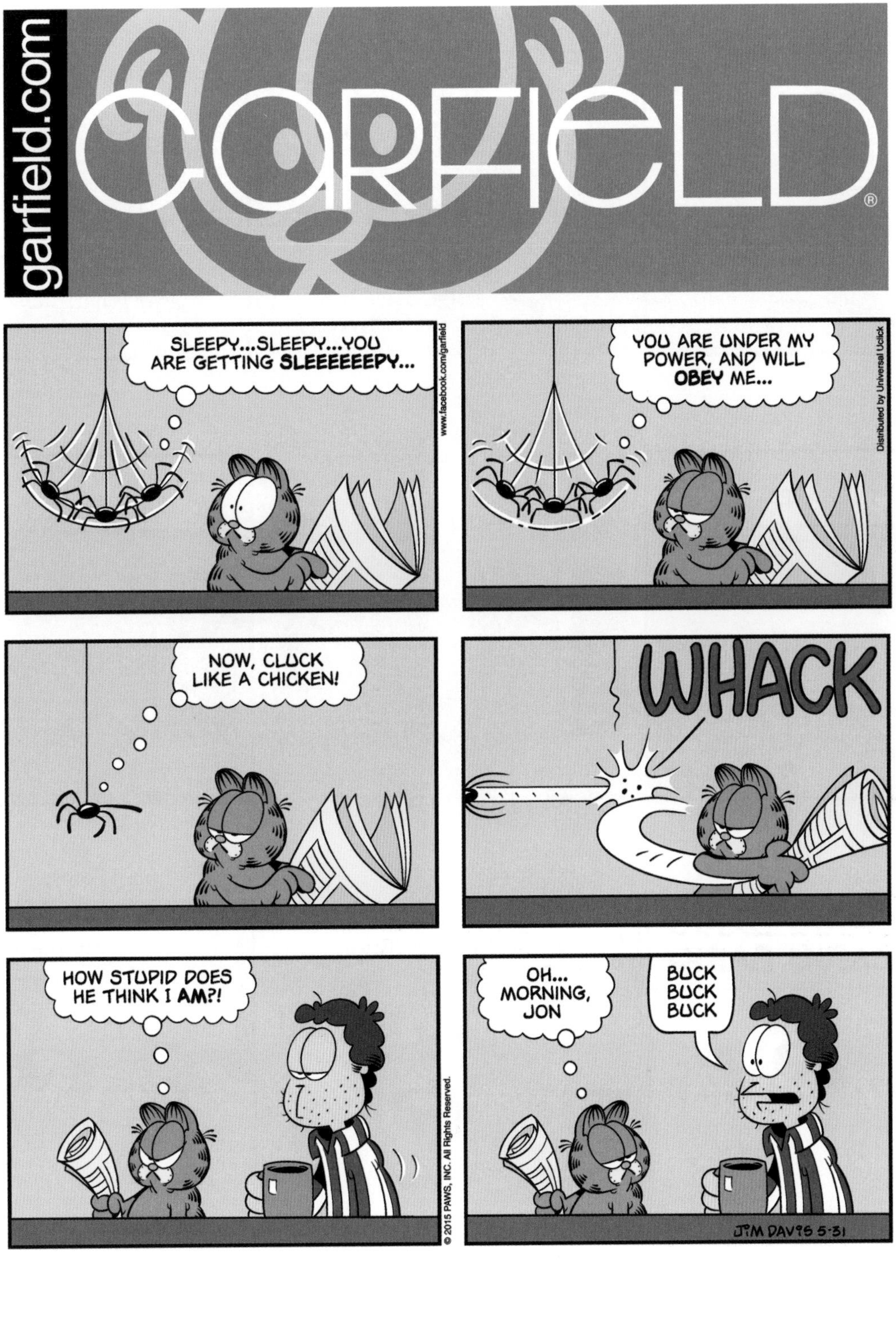
garfield.com
GARFIELD
SLEEPY...SLEEPY...YOU ARE GETTING SLEEEEEEPY...
www.facebook.com/garfield
YOU ARE UNDER MY POWER, AND WILL OBEY ME...
Distributed by Universal Uclick
NOW, CLUCK LIKE A CHICKEN!
WHACK
HOW STUPID DOES HE THINK I AM?!
© 2015 PAWS, INC. All Rights Reserved.
OH... MORNING, JON
BUCK BUCK BUCK
JIM DAVIS 5-31

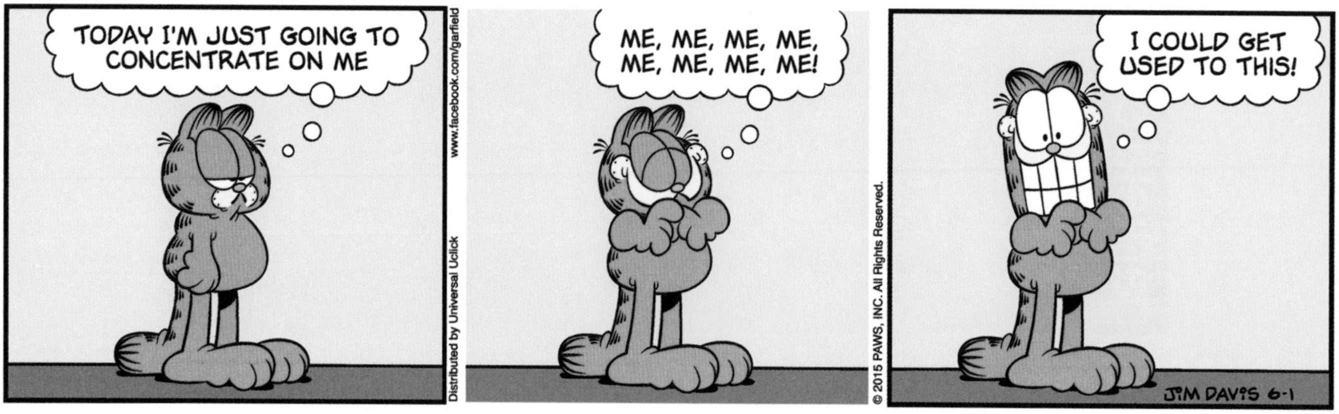
TODAY I'M JUST GOING TO CONCENTRATE ON ME
ME, ME, ME, ME, ME, ME, ME, ME!
I COULD GET USED TO THIS!
JIM DAVIS 6-1
www.facebook.com/garfield
Distributed by Universal Uclick
© 2015 PAWS, INC. All Rights Reserved.

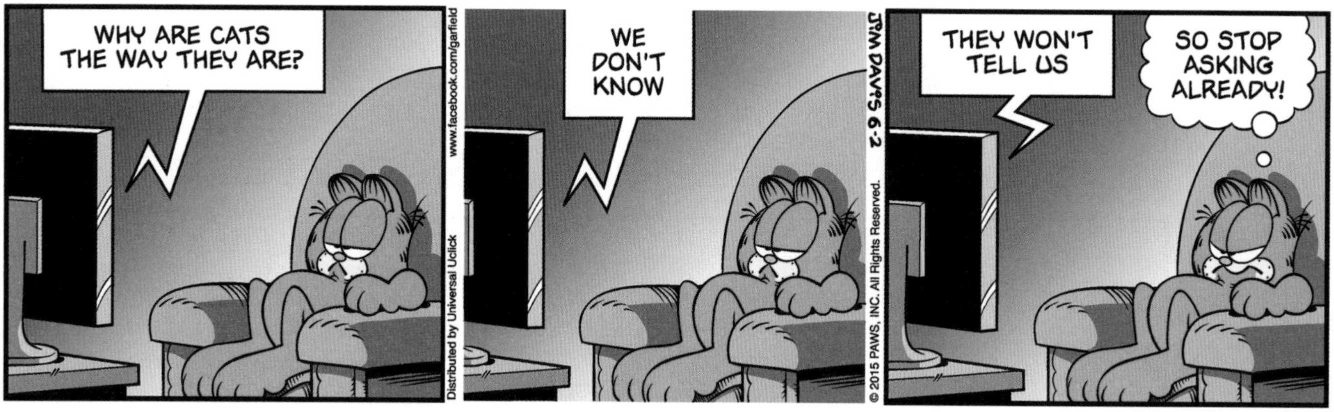
WHY ARE CATS THE WAY THEY ARE?
WE DON'T KNOW
THEY WON'T TELL US
SO STOP ASKING ALREADY!
JIM DAVIS 6-2
www.facebook.com/garfield
Distributed by Universal Uclick
© 2015 PAWS, INC. All Rights Reserved.

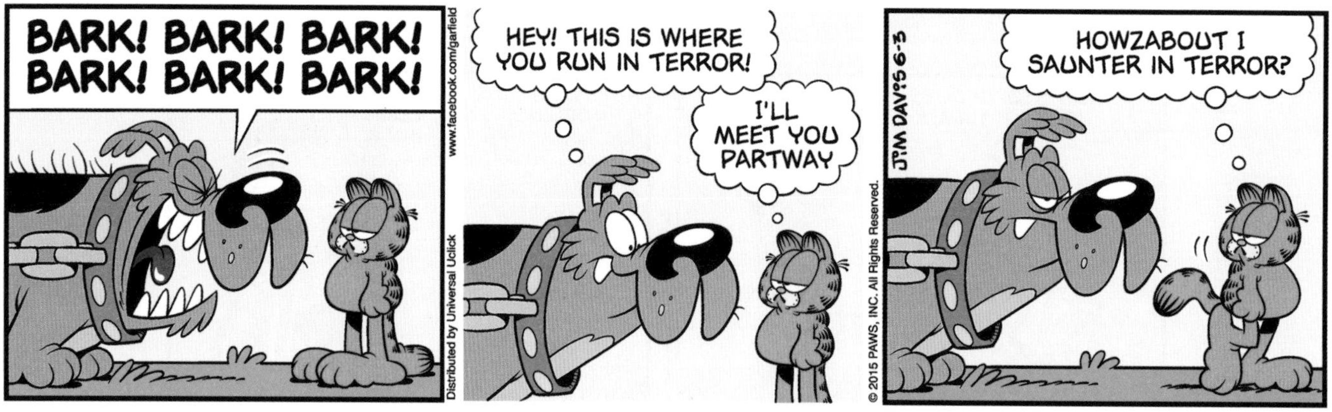
BARK! BARK! BARK! BARK! BARK! BARK!
HEY! THIS IS WHERE YOU RUN IN TERROR!
I'LL MEET YOU PARTWAY
HOWZABOUT I SAUNTER IN TERROR?
JIM DAVIS 6-3
www.facebook.com/garfield
Distributed by Universal Uclick
© 2015 PAWS, INC. All Rights Reserved.

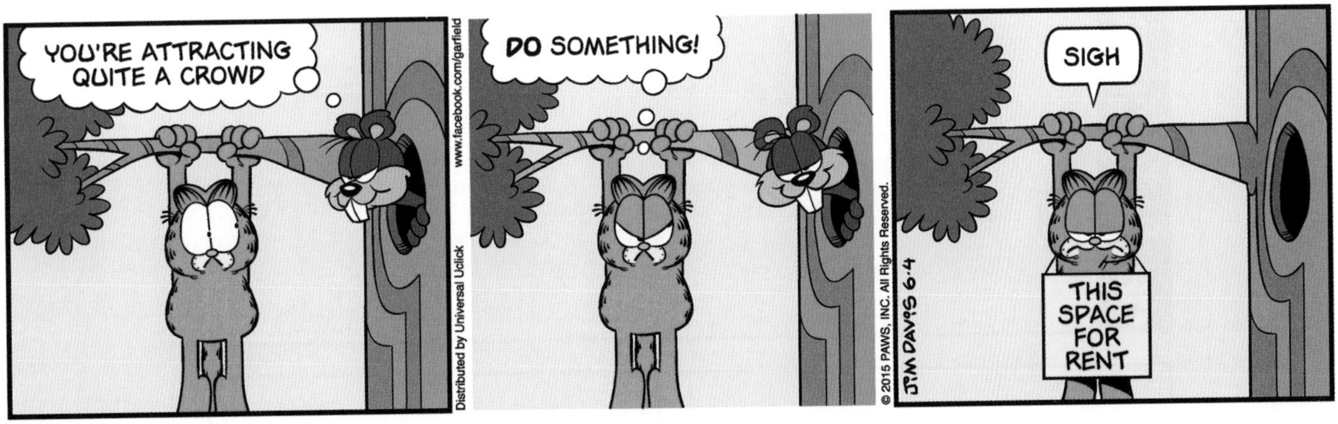
YOU'RE ATTRACTING QUITE A CROWD
www.facebook.com/garfield
Distributed by Universal Uclick
DO SOMETHING!
SIGH
THIS SPACE FOR RENT
© 2015 PAWS, INC. All Rights Reserved.
JIM DAVIS 6-4

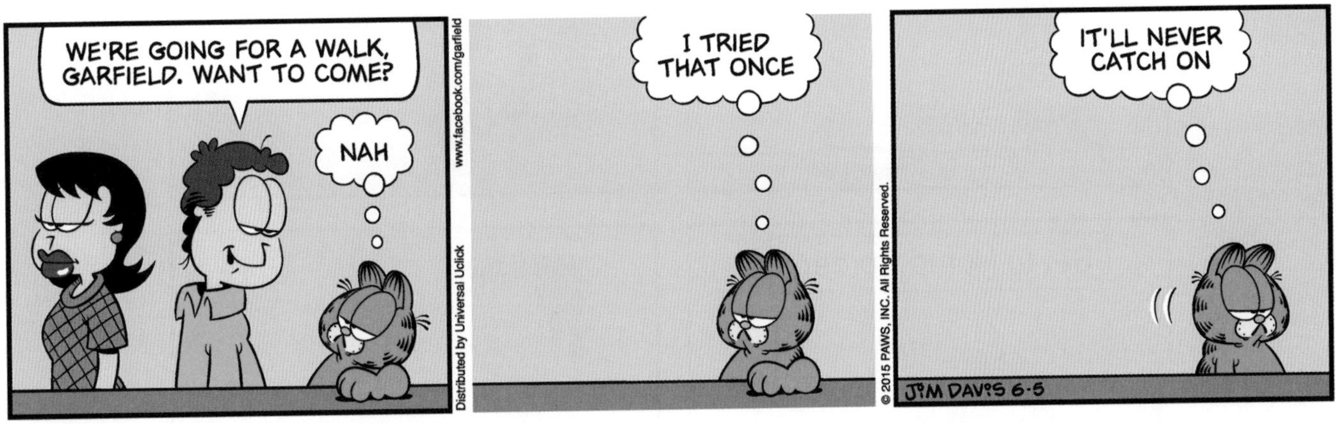
WE'RE GOING FOR A WALK, GARFIELD. WANT TO COME?
NAH
www.facebook.com/garfield
Distributed by Universal Uclick
I TRIED THAT ONCE
IT'LL NEVER CATCH ON
© 2015 PAWS, INC. All Rights Reserved.
JIM DAVIS 6-5

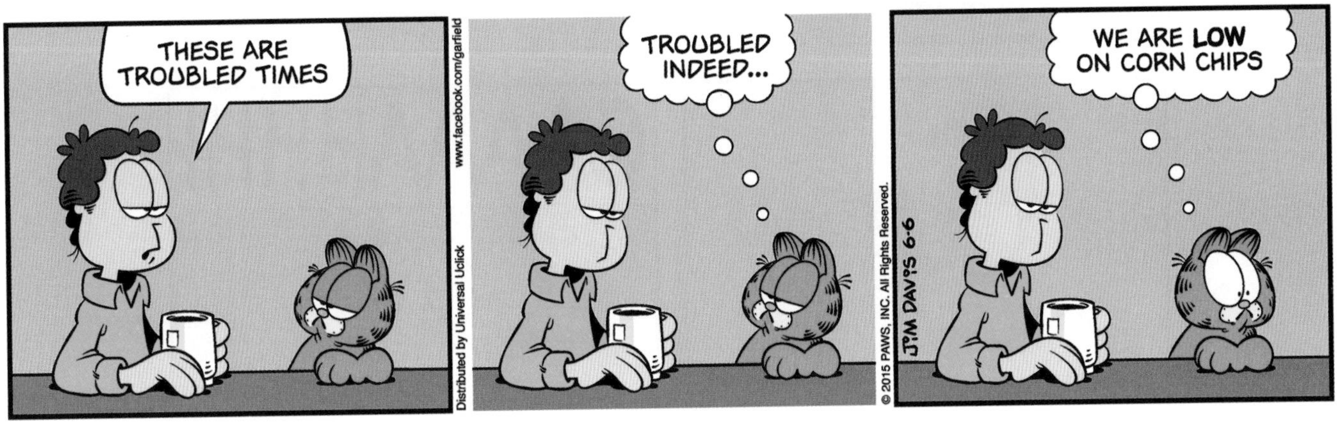
THESE ARE TROUBLED TIMES
www.facebook.com/garfield
Distributed by Universal Uclick
TROUBLED INDEED...
WE ARE **LOW** ON CORN CHIPS
© 2015 PAWS, INC. All Rights Reserved.
JIM DAVIS 6-6

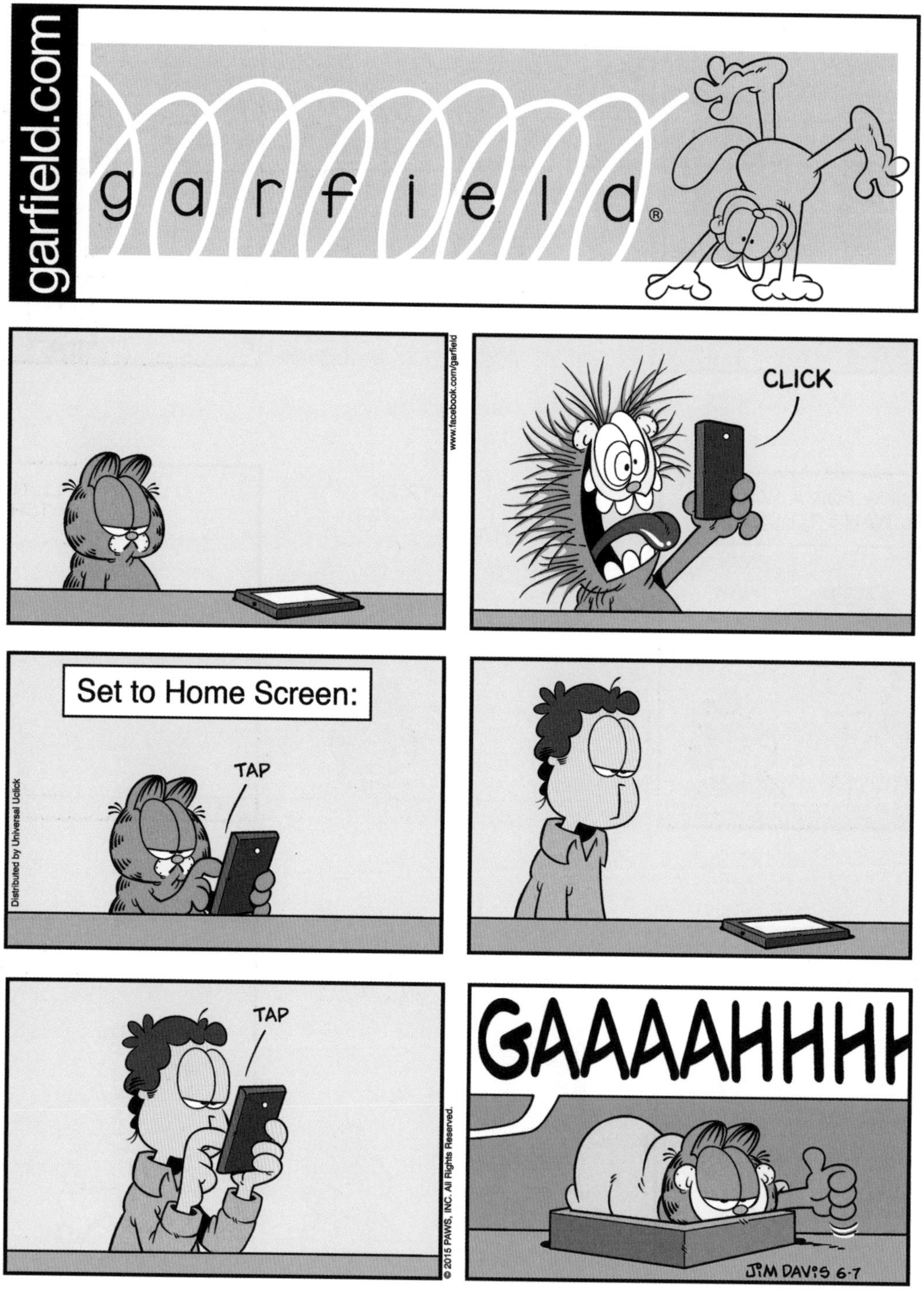
garfield.com
garfield®
www.facebook.com/garfield
CLICK
Set to Home Screen:
TAP
Distributed by Universal Uclick
TAP
© 2015 PAWS, INC. All Rights Reserved.
GAAAAHHHH
JIM DAVIS 6-7

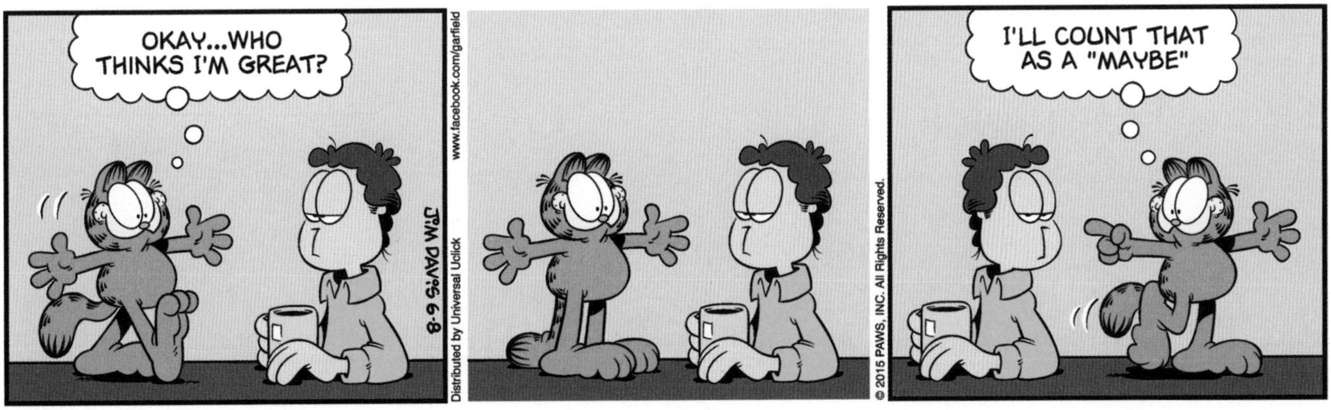
OKAY...WHO THINKS I'M GREAT?
I'LL COUNT THAT AS A "MAYBE"
JIM DAVIS 6-8
Distributed by Universal Uclick www.facebook.com/garfield
© 2015 PAWS, INC. All Rights Reserved.

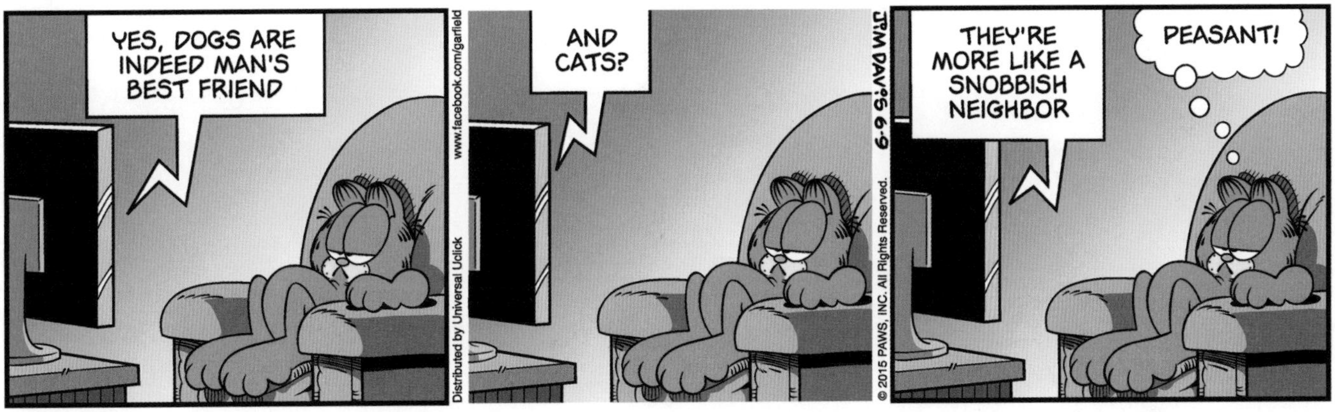
YES, DOGS ARE INDEED MAN'S BEST FRIEND
AND CATS?
THEY'RE MORE LIKE A SNOBBISH NEIGHBOR
PEASANT!
JIM DAVIS 6-9
Distributed by Universal Uclick www.facebook.com/garfield
© 2015 PAWS, INC. All Rights Reserved.

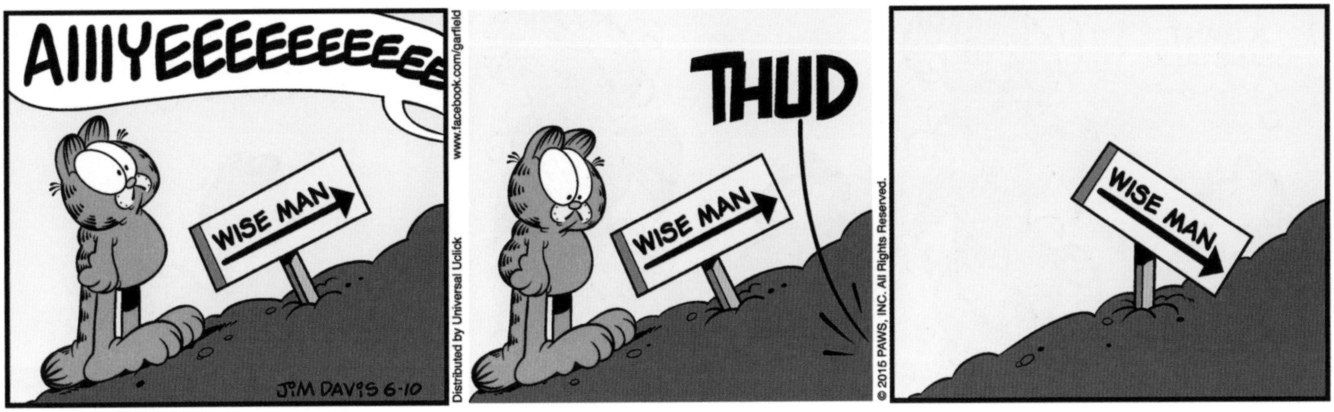
AIIIYEEEEEEEEEE
WISE MAN
WISE MAN
THUD
WISE MAN
JIM DAVIS 6-10
Distributed by Universal Uclick www.facebook.com/garfield
© 2015 PAWS, INC. All Rights Reserved.

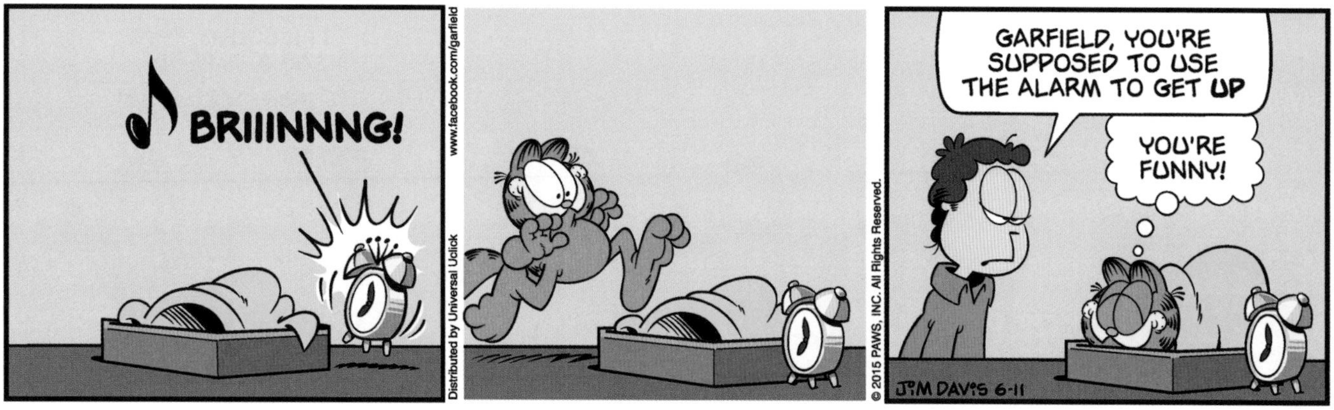
BRIIINNNG!
GARFIELD, YOU'RE SUPPOSED TO USE THE ALARM TO GET UP
YOU'RE FUNNY!
JIM DAVIS 6-11
Distributed by Universal Uclick www.facebook.com/garfield
© 2015 PAWS, INC. All Rights Reserved.

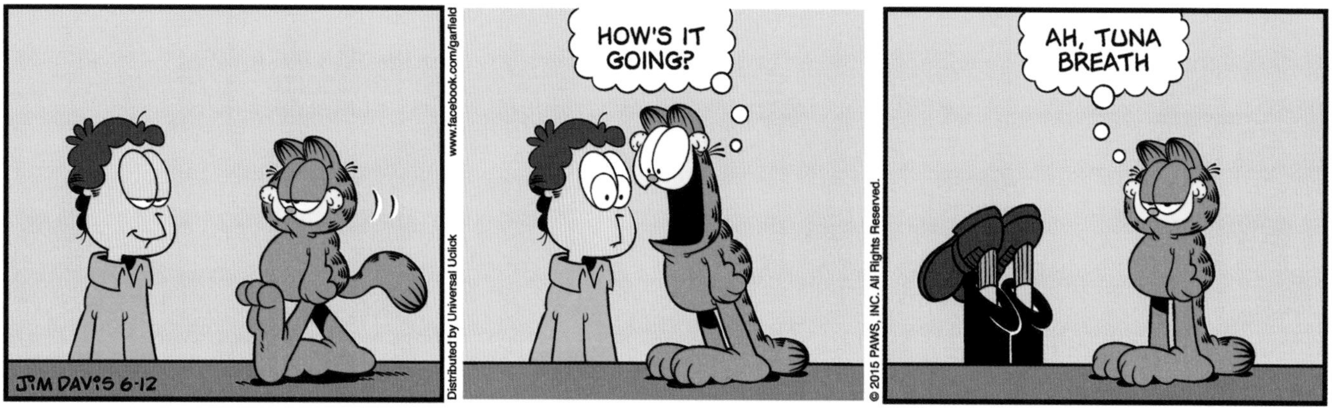
JIM DAVIS 6-12
HOW'S IT GOING?
AH, TUNA BREATH
Distributed by Universal Uclick www.facebook.com/garfield
© 2015 PAWS, INC. All Rights Reserved.

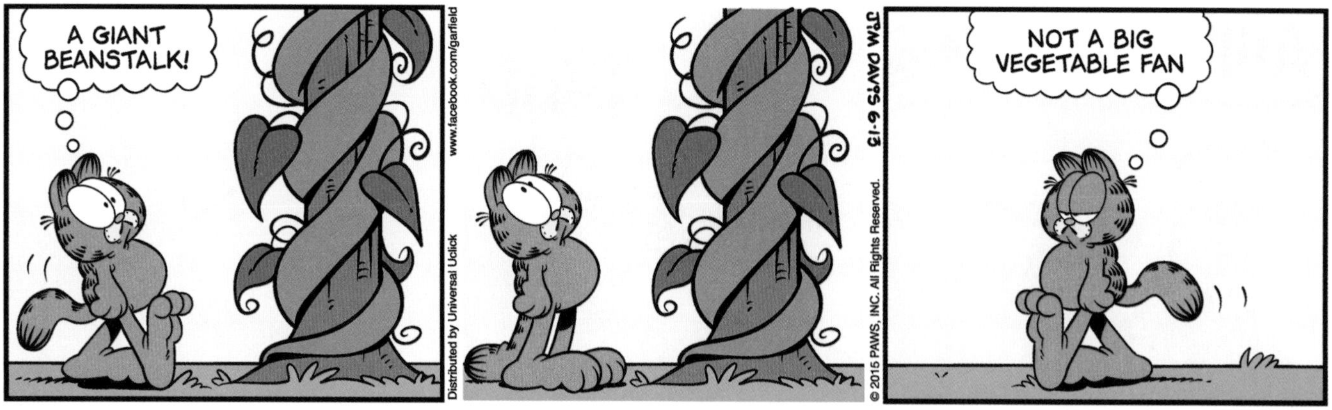
A GIANT BEANSTALK!
JIM DAVIS 6-13
NOT A BIG VEGETABLE FAN
Distributed by Universal Uclick www.facebook.com/garfield
© 2015 PAWS, INC. All Rights Reserved.

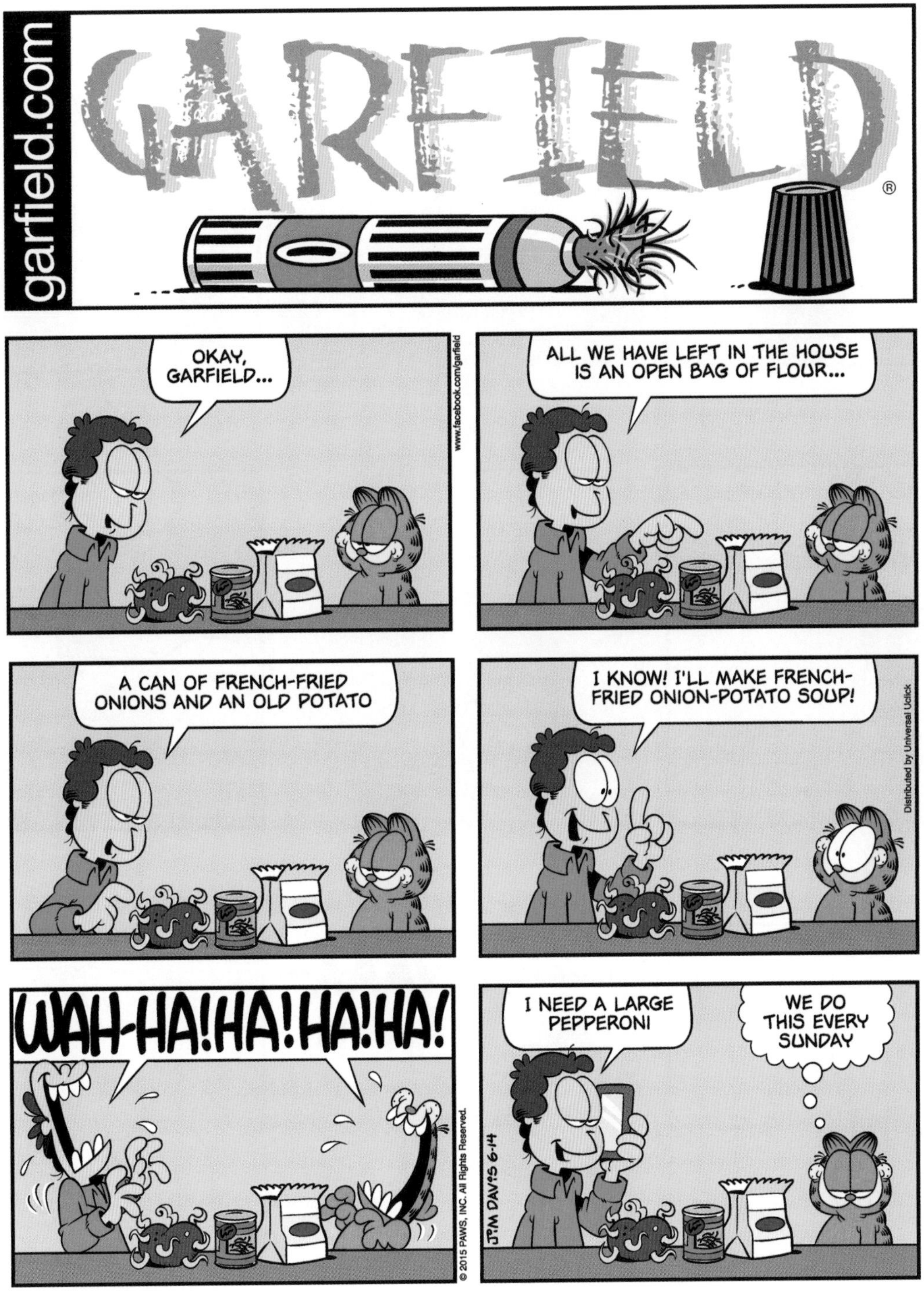
garfield.com
GARFIELD
OKAY, GARFIELD...
www.facebook.com/garfield
ALL WE HAVE LEFT IN THE HOUSE IS AN OPEN BAG OF FLOUR...
A CAN OF FRENCH-FRIED ONIONS AND AN OLD POTATO
I KNOW! I'LL MAKE FRENCH-FRIED ONION-POTATO SOUP!
Distributed by Universal Uclick
WAH-HA!HA!HA!HA!
© 2015 PAWS, INC. All Rights Reserved.
JPM DAVIS 6-14
I NEED A LARGE PEPPERONI
WE DO THIS EVERY SUNDAY

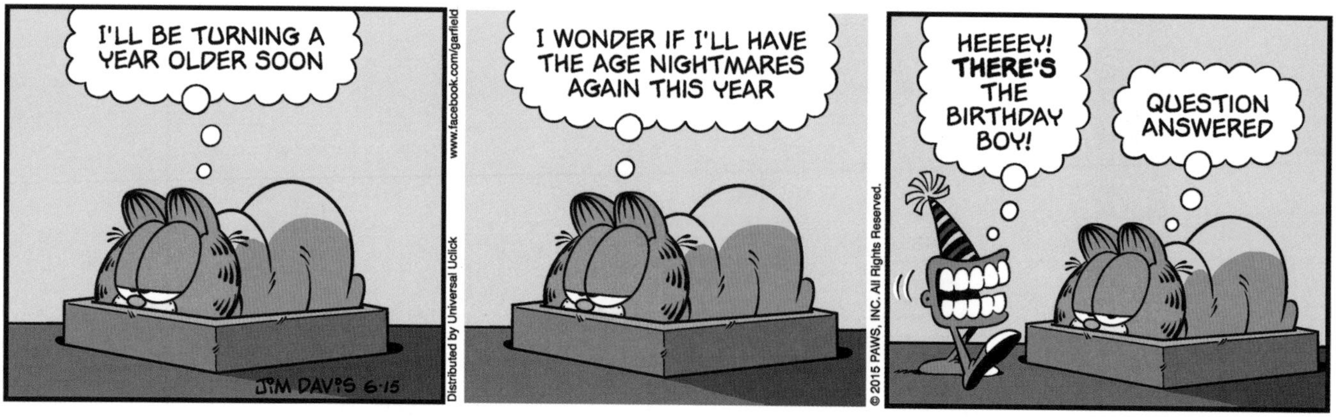
I'LL BE TURNING A YEAR OLDER SOON
JIM DAVIS 6-15
Distributed by Universal Uclick www.facebook.com/garfield
I WONDER IF I'LL HAVE THE AGE NIGHTMARES AGAIN THIS YEAR
© 2015 PAWS, INC. All Rights Reserved.
HEEEEY! **THERE'S** THE BIRTHDAY BOY!
QUESTION ANSWERED

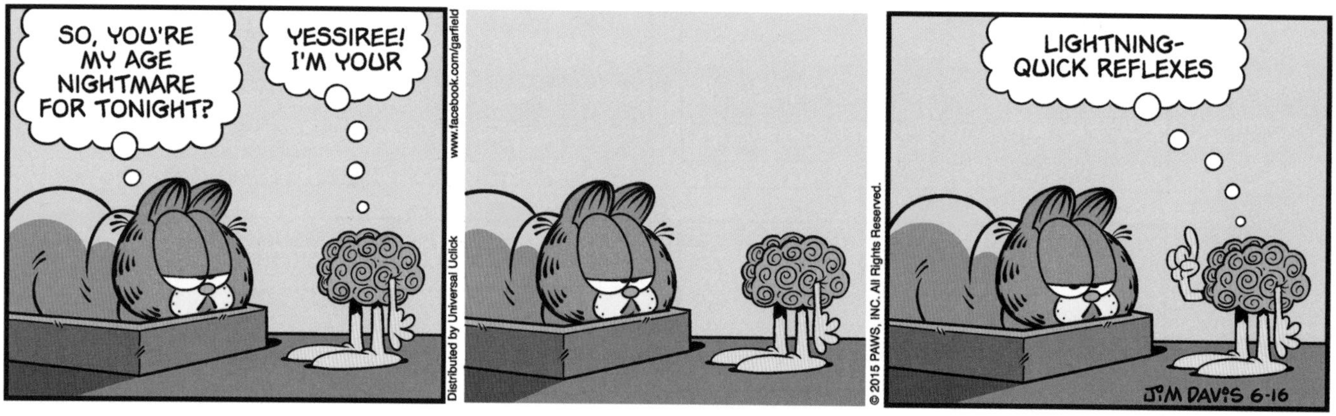
SO, YOU'RE MY AGE NIGHTMARE FOR TONIGHT?
YESSIREE! I'M YOUR
Distributed by Universal Uclick www.facebook.com/garfield
© 2015 PAWS, INC. All Rights Reserved.
LIGHTNING-QUICK REFLEXES
JIM DAVIS 6-16

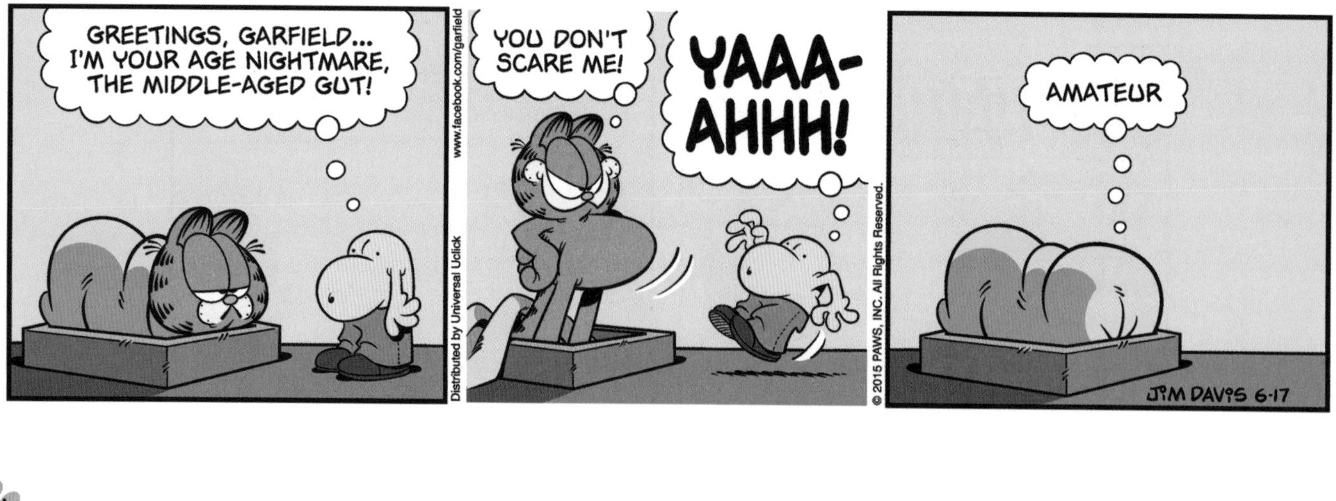
GREETINGS, GARFIELD... I'M YOUR AGE NIGHTMARE, THE MIDDLE-AGED GUT!
Distributed by Universal Uclick www.facebook.com/garfield
YOU DON'T SCARE ME!
YAAA-AHHH!
© 2015 PAWS, INC. All Rights Reserved.
AMATEUR
JIM DAVIS 6-17

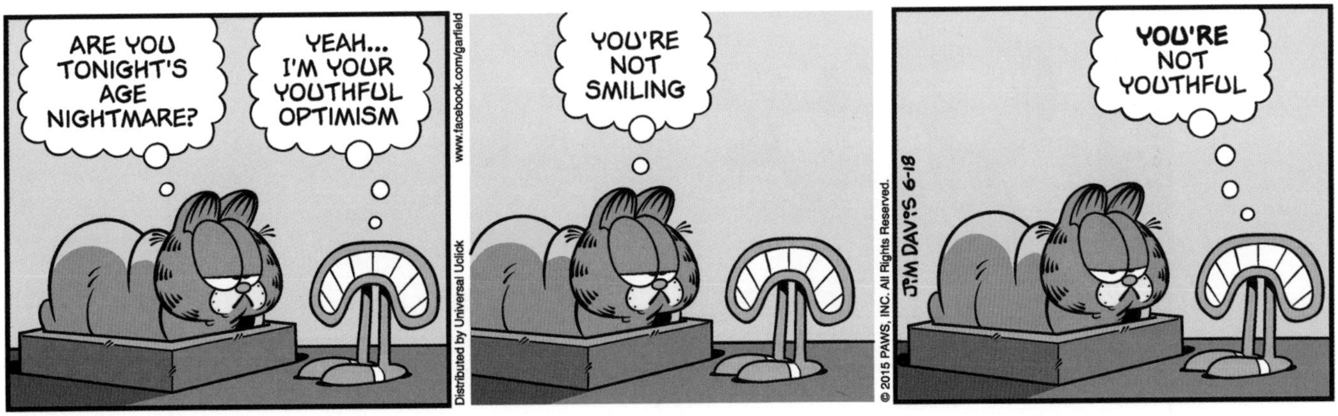
ARE YOU TONIGHT'S AGE NIGHTMARE?
YEAH... I'M YOUR YOUTHFUL OPTIMISM
YOU'RE NOT SMILING
YOU'RE NOT YOUTHFUL
JIM DAVIS 6-18
Distributed by Universal Uclick www.facebook.com/garfield
© 2015 PAWS, INC. All Rights Reserved.

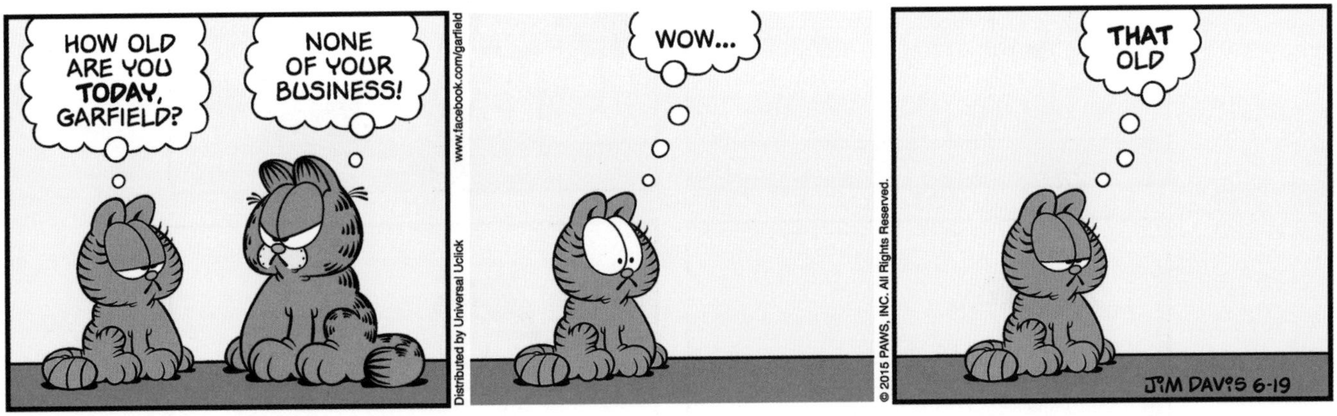
HOW OLD ARE YOU TODAY, GARFIELD?
NONE OF YOUR BUSINESS!
WOW...
THAT OLD
JIM DAVIS 6-19
Distributed by Universal Uclick www.facebook.com/garfield
© 2015 PAWS, INC. All Rights Reserved.

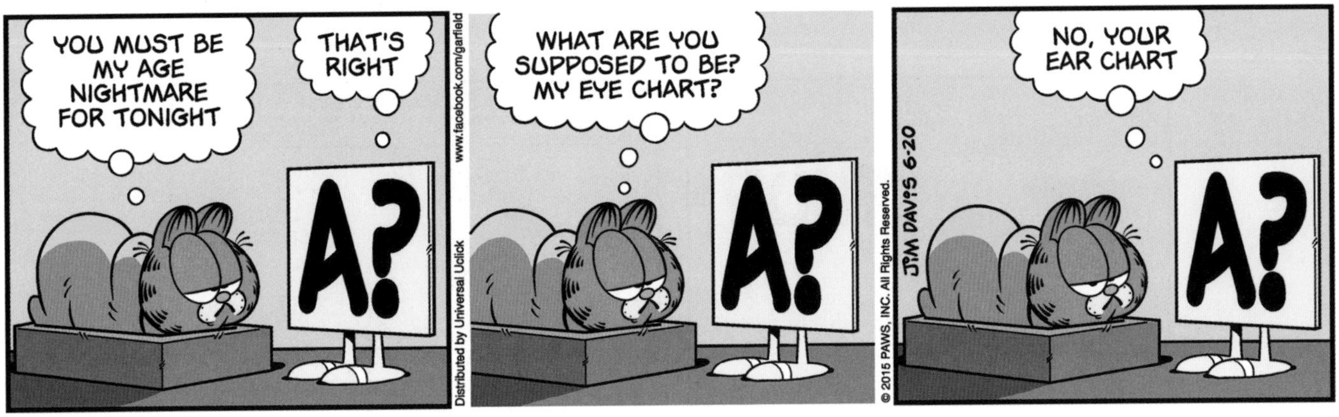
YOU MUST BE MY AGE NIGHTMARE FOR TONIGHT
THAT'S RIGHT
WHAT ARE YOU SUPPOSED TO BE? MY EYE CHART?
NO, YOUR EAR CHART
A?
JIM DAVIS 6-20
Distributed by Universal Uclick www.facebook.com/garfield
© 2015 PAWS, INC. All Rights Reserved.

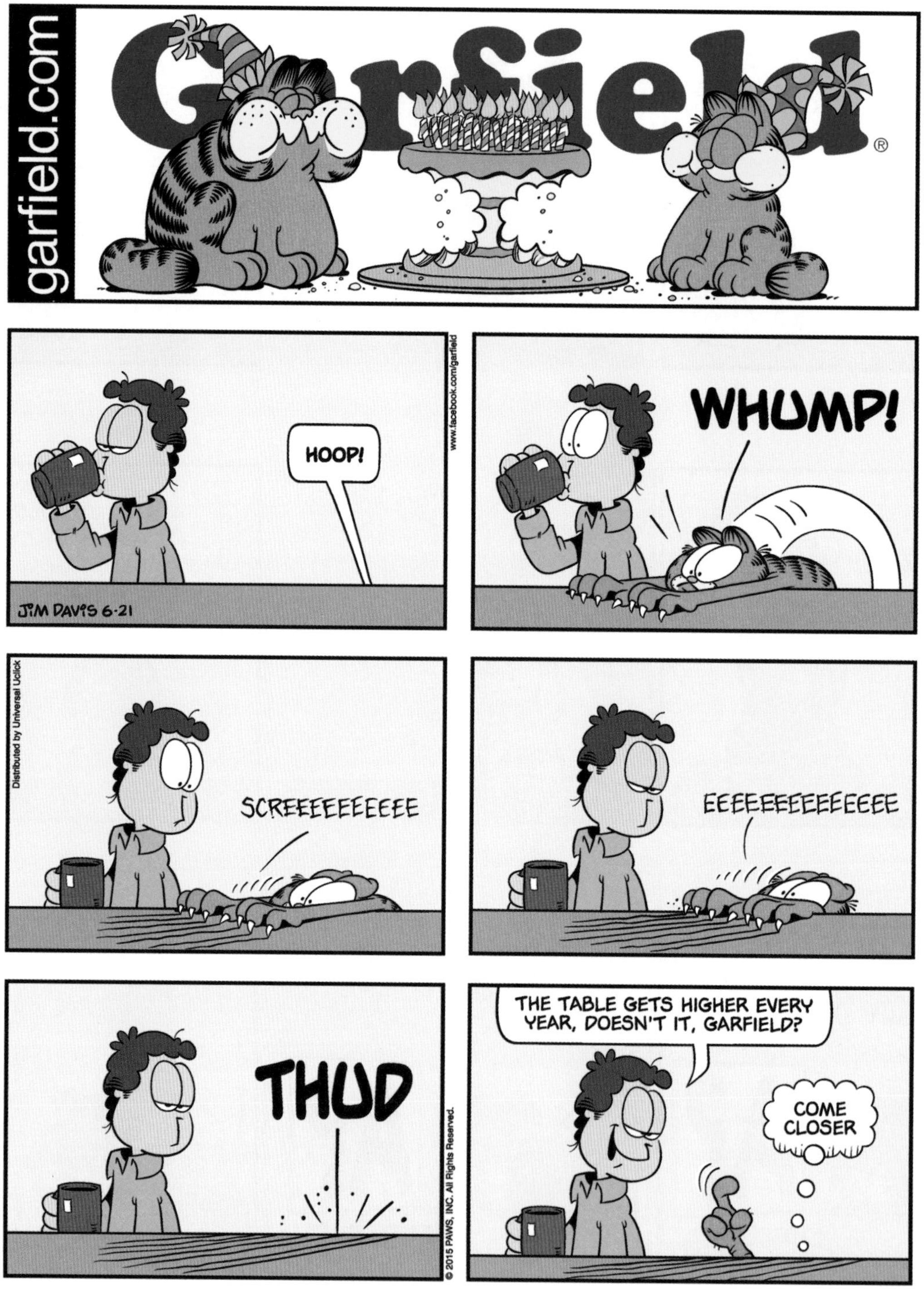
garfield.com
Garfield®
JIM DAVIS 6-21
HOOP!
www.facebook.com/garfield
WHUMP!
Distributed by Universal Uclick
SCREEEEEEEEEE
EEEEEEEEEEEEE
THUD
© 2015 PAWS, INC. All Rights Reserved.
THE TABLE GETS HIGHER EVERY YEAR, DOESN'T IT, GARFIELD?
COME CLOSER

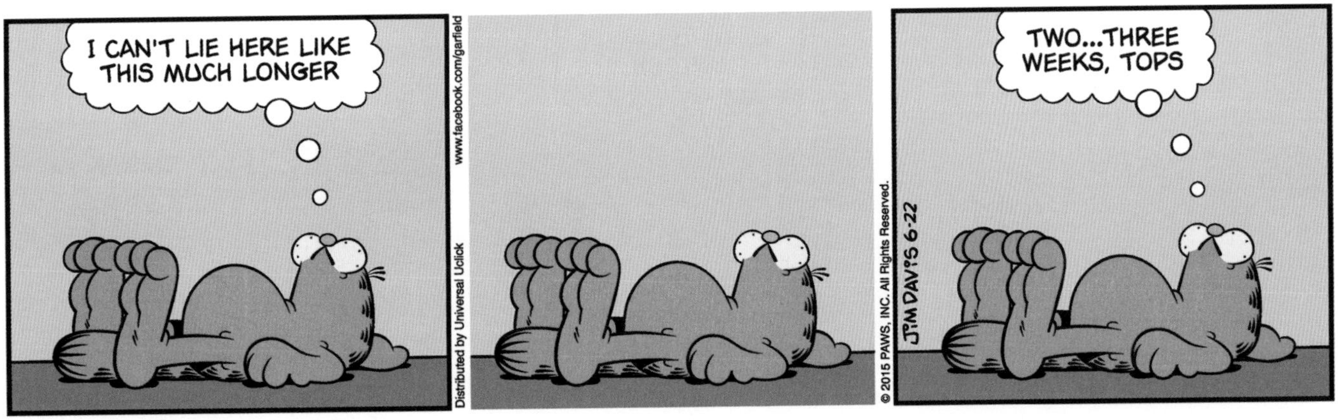
I CAN'T LIE HERE LIKE THIS MUCH LONGER
TWO...THREE WEEKS, TOPS
JIM DAVIS 6-22
© 2015 PAWS, INC. All Rights Reserved.
Distributed by Universal Uclick www.facebook.com/garfield

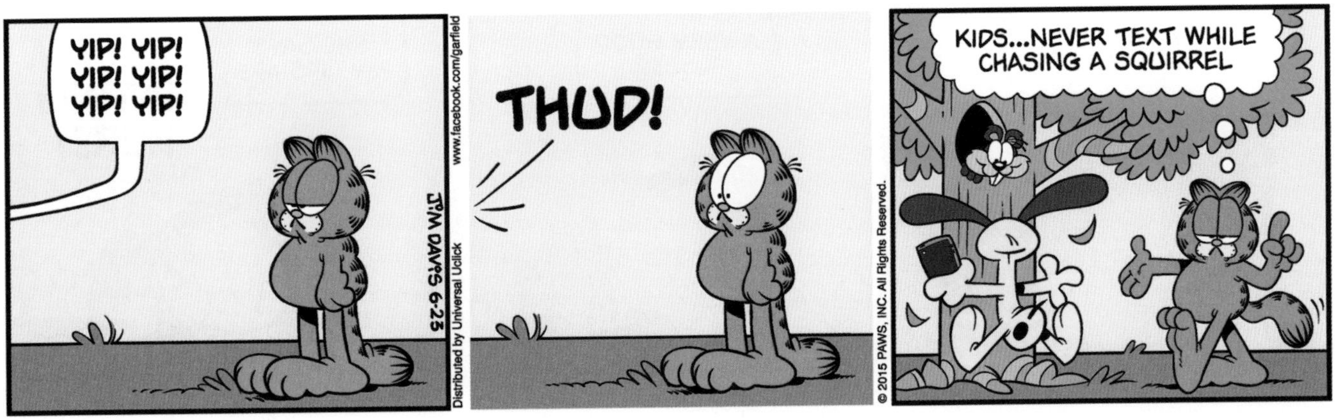
YIP! YIP! YIP! YIP! YIP! YIP!
JIM DAVIS 6-23
THUD!
KIDS...NEVER TEXT WHILE CHASING A SQUIRREL
© 2015 PAWS, INC. All Rights Reserved.
Distributed by Universal Uclick www.facebook.com/garfield

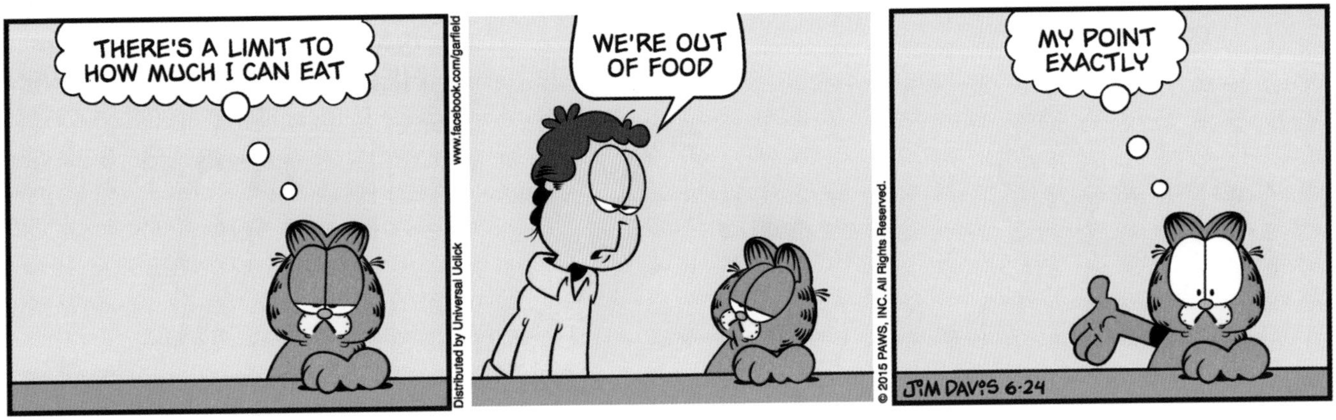
THERE'S A LIMIT TO HOW MUCH I CAN EAT
WE'RE OUT OF FOOD
MY POINT EXACTLY
JIM DAVIS 6-24
© 2015 PAWS, INC. All Rights Reserved.
Distributed by Universal Uclick www.facebook.com/garfield

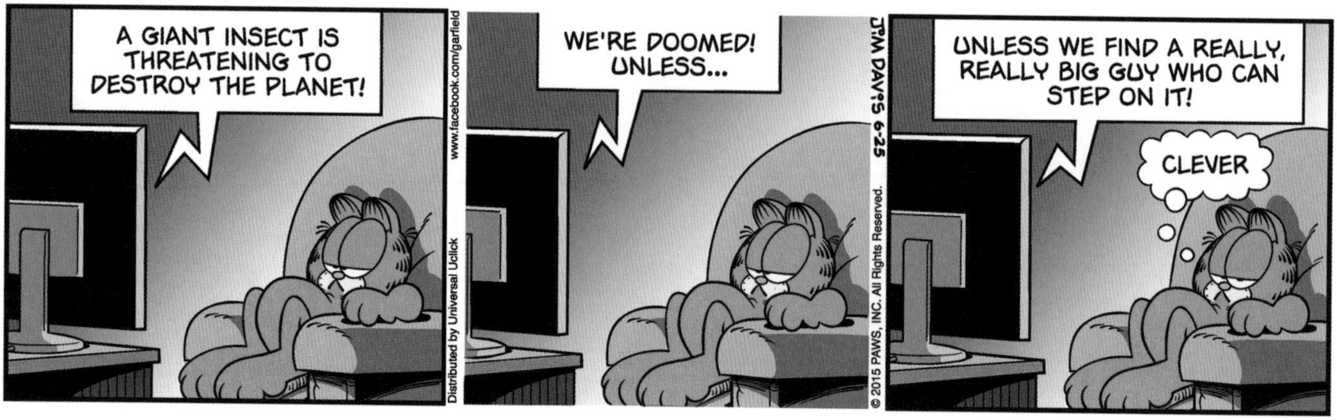
A GIANT INSECT IS THREATENING TO DESTROY THE PLANET!
WE'RE DOOMED! UNLESS...
UNLESS WE FIND A REALLY, REALLY BIG GUY WHO CAN STEP ON IT!
CLEVER
JIM DAVIS 6-25
www.facebook.com/garfield
Distributed by Universal Uclick
© 2015 PAWS, INC. All Rights Reserved.

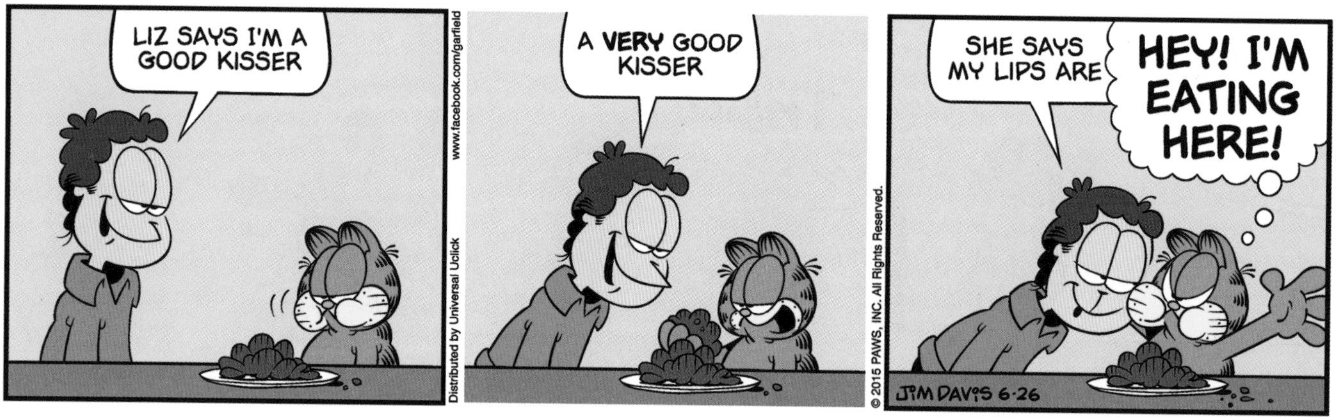
LIZ SAYS I'M A GOOD KISSER
A **VERY** GOOD KISSER
SHE SAYS MY LIPS ARE
HEY! I'M EATING HERE!
JIM DAVIS 6-26
www.facebook.com/garfield
Distributed by Universal Uclick
© 2015 PAWS, INC. All Rights Reserved.

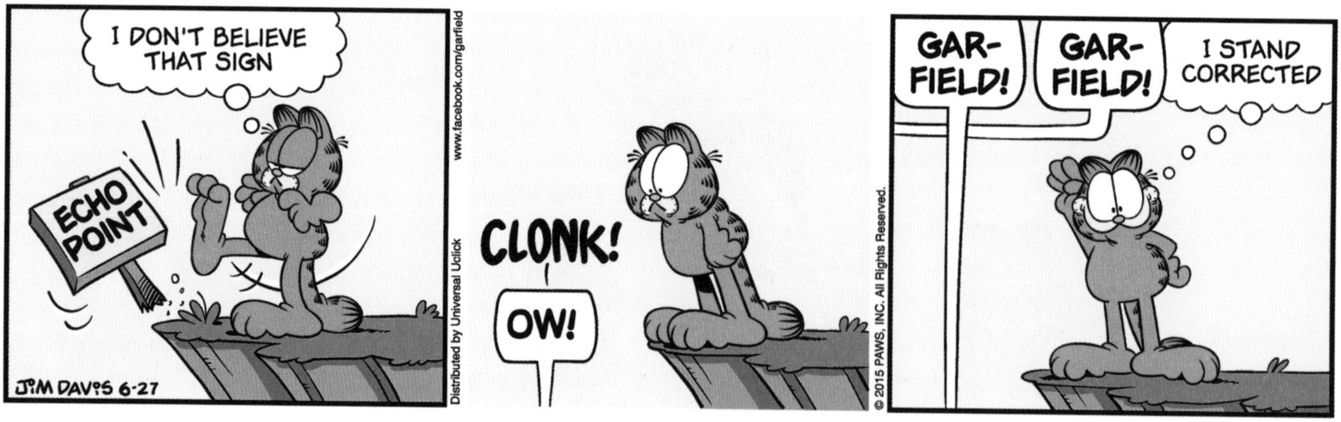
I DON'T BELIEVE THAT SIGN
ECHO POINT
JIM DAVIS 6-27
CLONK!
OW!
GAR-FIELD!
GAR-FIELD!
I STAND CORRECTED
www.facebook.com/garfield
Distributed by Universal Uclick
© 2015 PAWS, INC. All Rights Reserved.

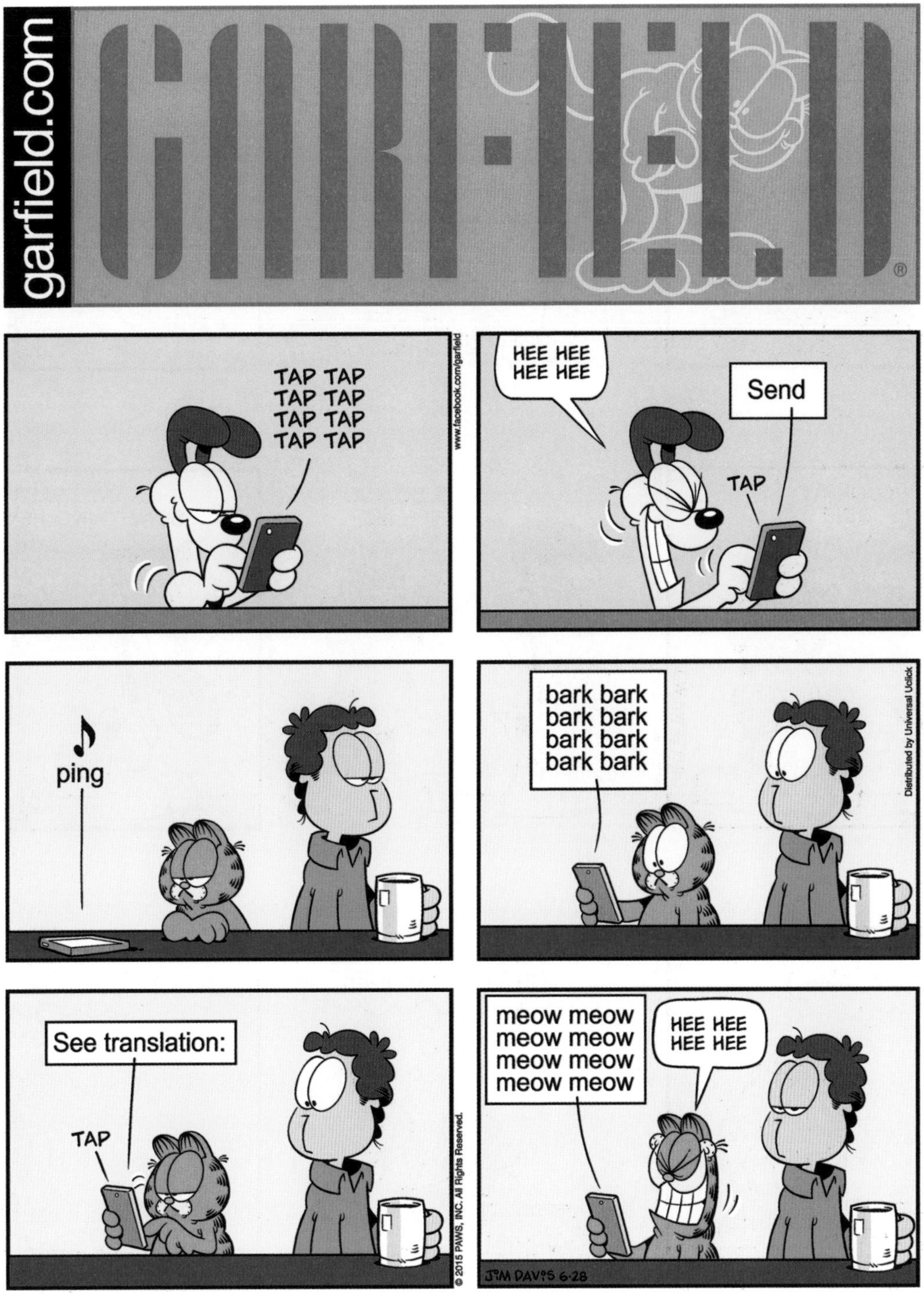
garfield.com
TAP TAP TAP TAP TAP TAP TAP TAP
www.facebook.com/garfield
HEE HEE HEE HEE
Send
TAP
ping
bark bark bark bark bark bark bark bark
Distributed by Universal Uclick
See translation:
TAP
© 2015 PAWS, INC. All Rights Reserved.
meow meow meow meow meow meow meow meow
HEE HEE HEE HEE
JIM DAVIS 6-28

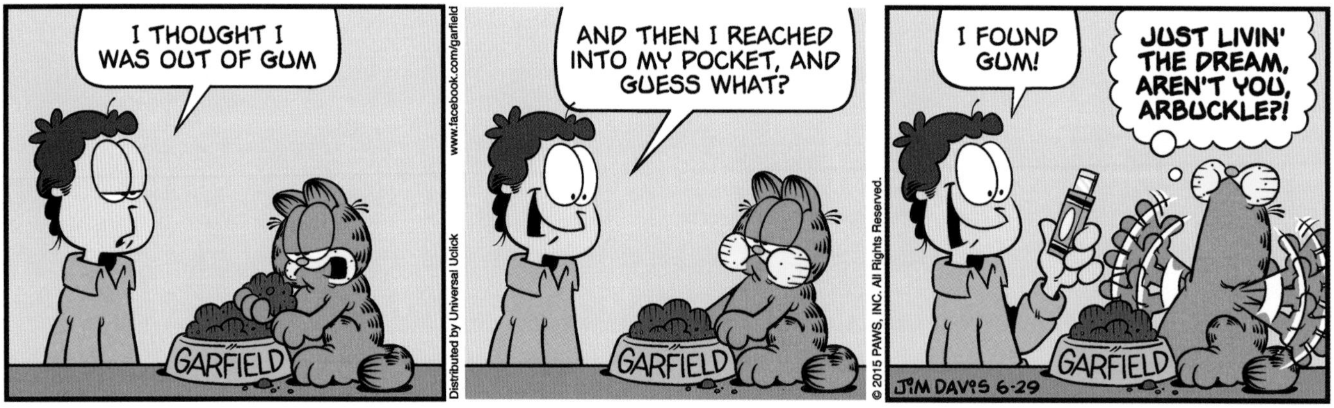
I THOUGHT I WAS OUT OF GUM
AND THEN I REACHED INTO MY POCKET, AND GUESS WHAT?
I FOUND GUM!
JUST LIVIN' THE DREAM, AREN'T YOU, ARBUCKLE?!
GARFIELD
JIM DAVIS 6-29
Distributed by Universal Uclick www.facebook.com/garfield
© 2015 PAWS, INC. All Rights Reserved.

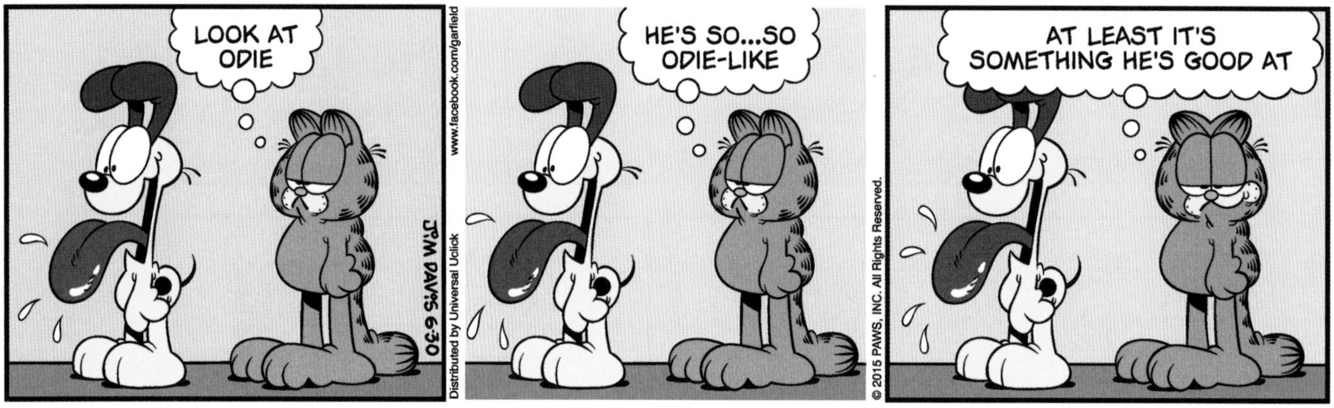
LOOK AT ODIE
HE'S SO...SO ODIE-LIKE
AT LEAST IT'S SOMETHING HE'S GOOD AT
JIM DAVIS 6-30
Distributed by Universal Uclick www.facebook.com/garfield
© 2015 PAWS, INC. All Rights Reserved.

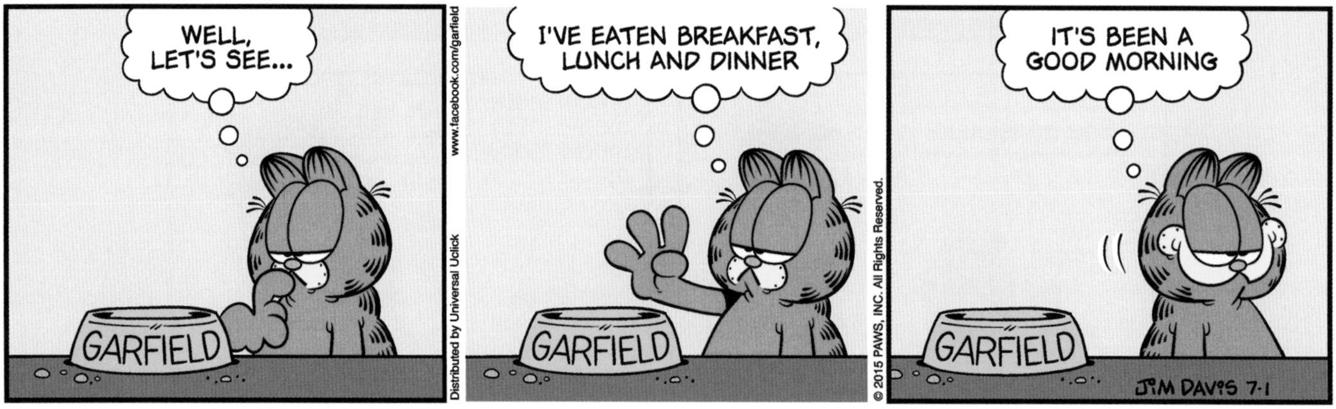
WELL, LET'S SEE...
I'VE EATEN BREAKFAST, LUNCH AND DINNER
IT'S BEEN A GOOD MORNING
GARFIELD
JIM DAVIS 7-1
Distributed by Universal Uclick www.facebook.com/garfield
© 2015 PAWS, INC. All Rights Reserved.

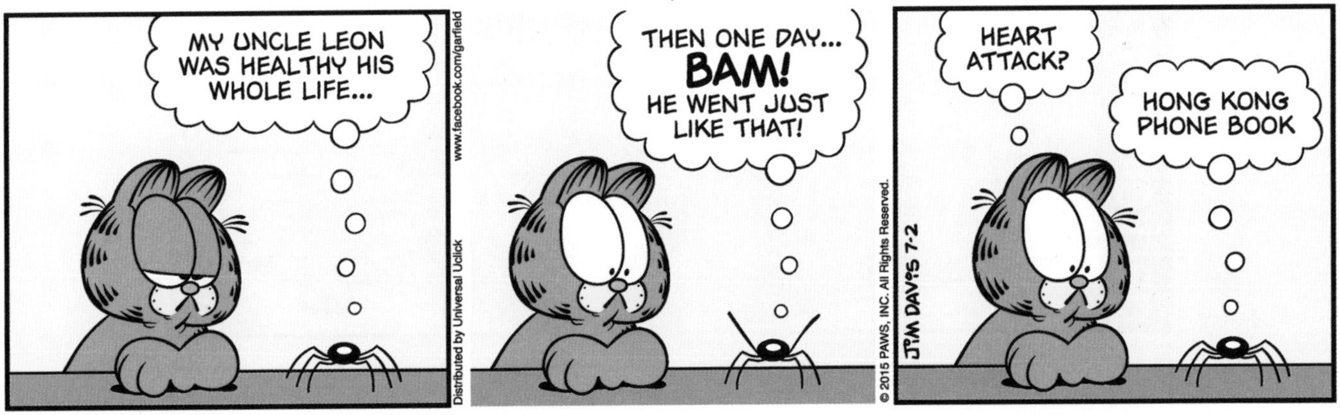
MY UNCLE LEON WAS HEALTHY HIS WHOLE LIFE...
Distributed by Universal Uclick
www.facebook.com/garfield
THEN ONE DAY... BAM! HE WENT JUST LIKE THAT!
© 2015 PAWS, INC. All Rights Reserved.
JIM DAVIS 7-2
HEART ATTACK?
HONG KONG PHONE BOOK

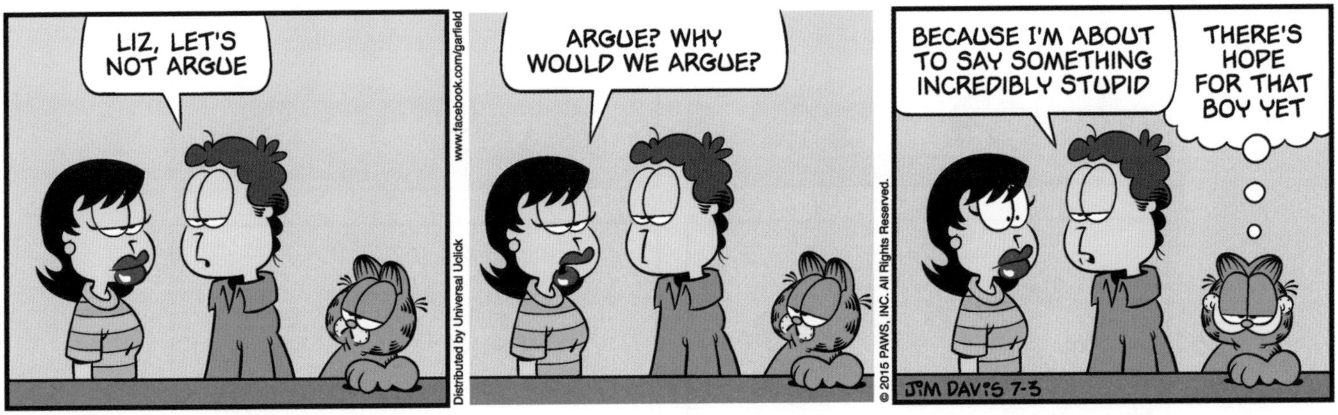
LIZ, LET'S NOT ARGUE
Distributed by Universal Uclick
www.facebook.com/garfield
ARGUE? WHY WOULD WE ARGUE?
© 2015 PAWS, INC. All Rights Reserved.
BECAUSE I'M ABOUT TO SAY SOMETHING INCREDIBLY STUPID
THERE'S HOPE FOR THAT BOY YET
JIM DAVIS 7-3

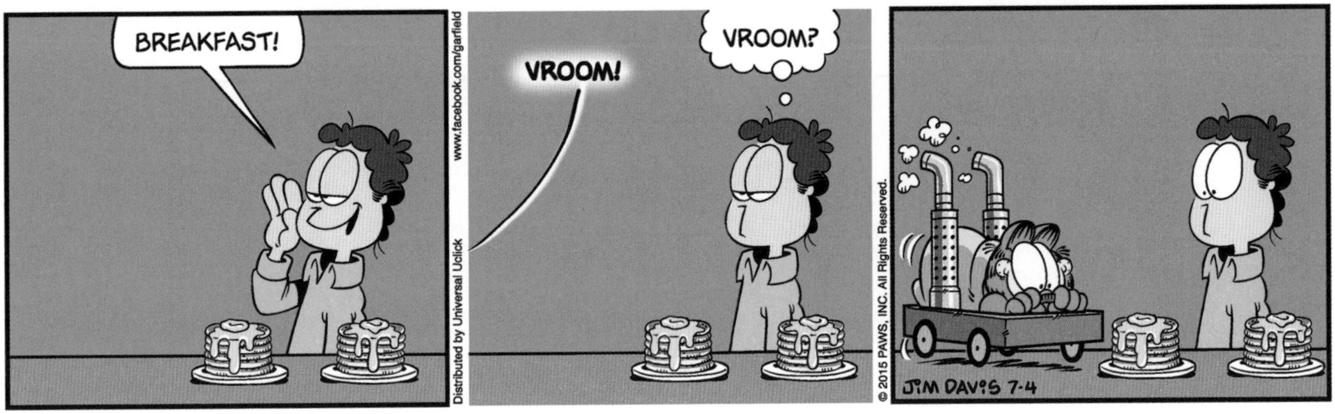
BREAKFAST!
Distributed by Universal Uclick
www.facebook.com/garfield
VROOM!
VROOM?
© 2015 PAWS, INC. All Rights Reserved.
JIM DAVIS 7-4

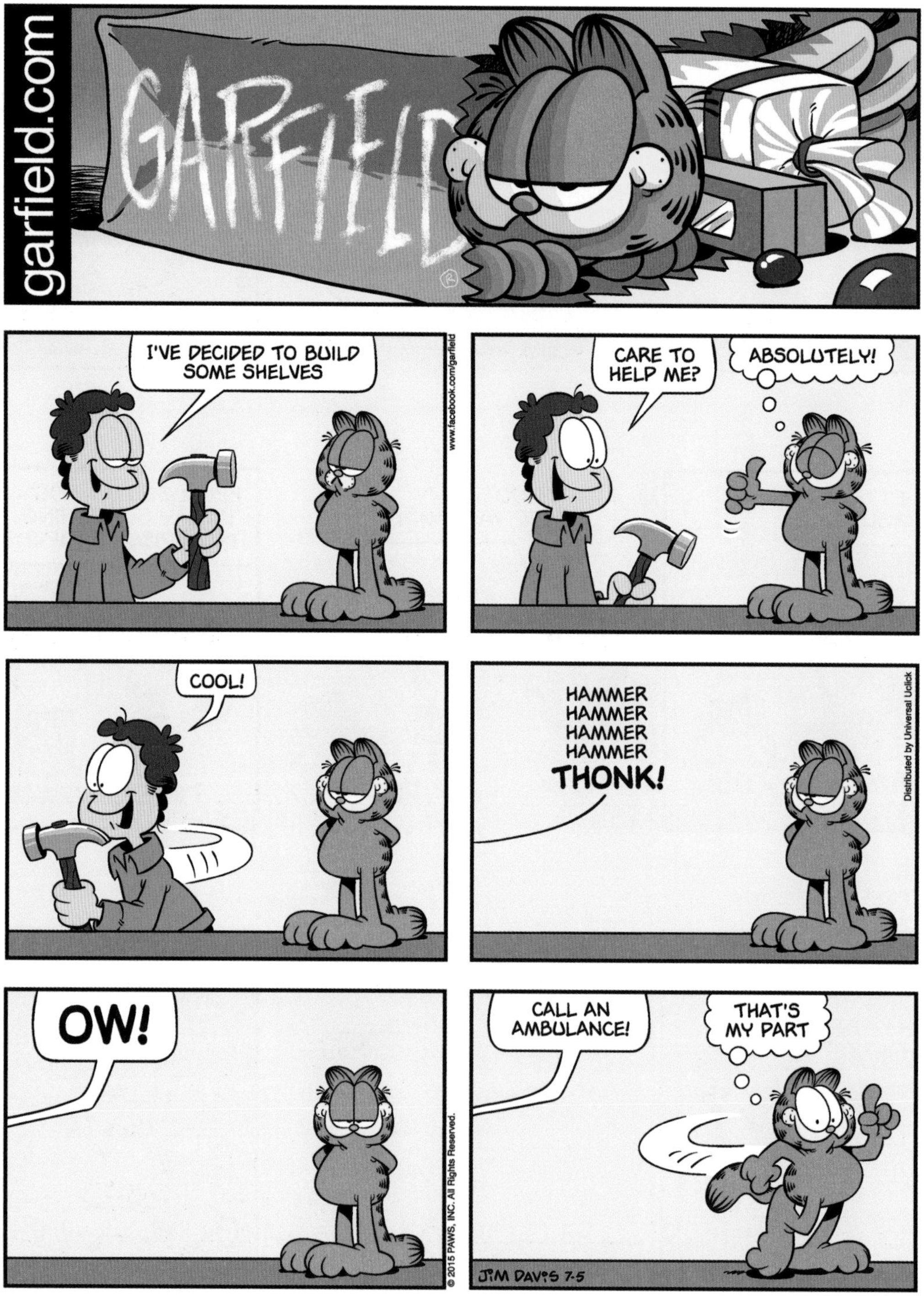
garfield.com
GARFIELD
I'VE DECIDED TO BUILD SOME SHELVES
www.facebook.com/garfield
CARE TO HELP ME?
ABSOLUTELY!
COOL!
HAMMER
HAMMER
HAMMER
HAMMER
THONK!
Distributed by Universal Uclick
OW!
© 2015 PAWS, INC. All Rights Reserved.
CALL AN AMBULANCE!
THAT'S MY PART
JIM DAVIS 7-5

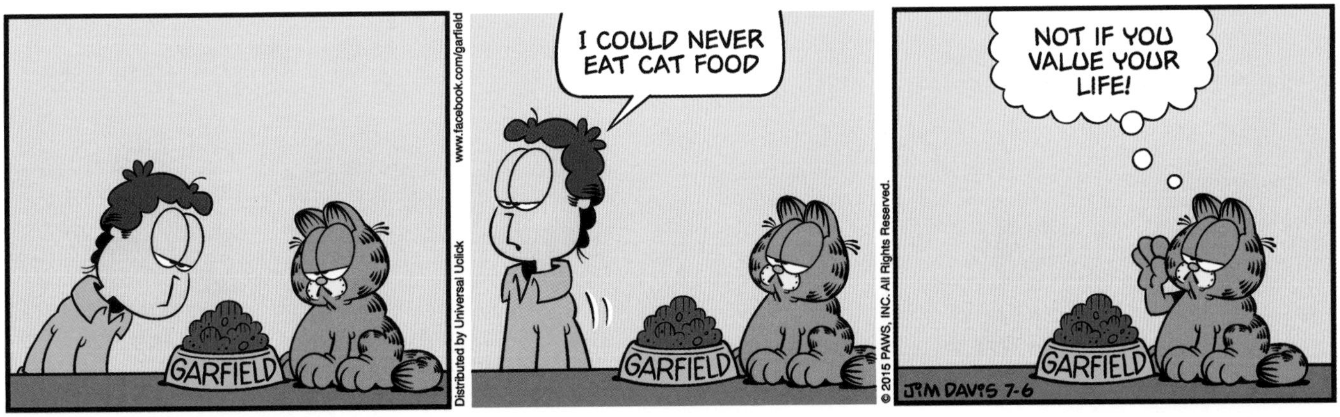
www.facebook.com/garfield
Distributed by Universal Uclick
I COULD NEVER EAT CAT FOOD
© 2015 PAWS, INC. All Rights Reserved.
NOT IF YOU VALUE YOUR LIFE!
JIM DAVIS 7-6

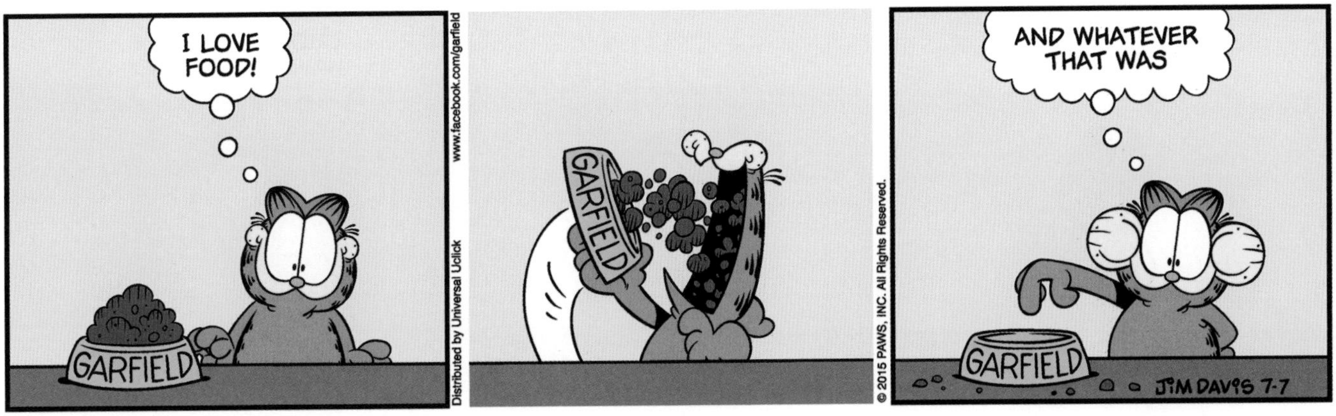
I LOVE FOOD!
www.facebook.com/garfield
Distributed by Universal Uclick
© 2015 PAWS, INC. All Rights Reserved.
AND WHATEVER THAT WAS
JIM DAVIS 7-7

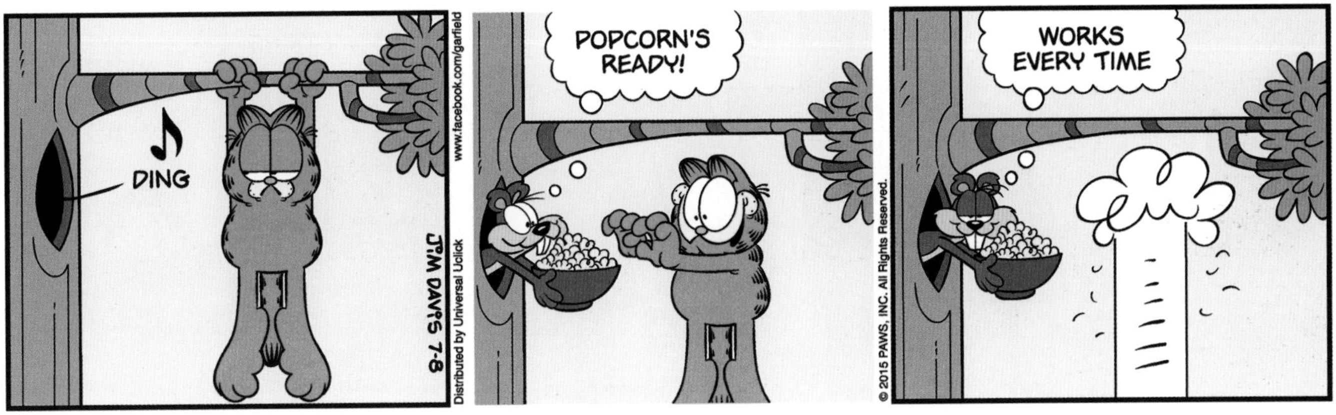
DING
JIM DAVIS 7-8
www.facebook.com/garfield
Distributed by Universal Uclick
POPCORN'S READY!
© 2015 PAWS, INC. All Rights Reserved.
WORKS EVERY TIME

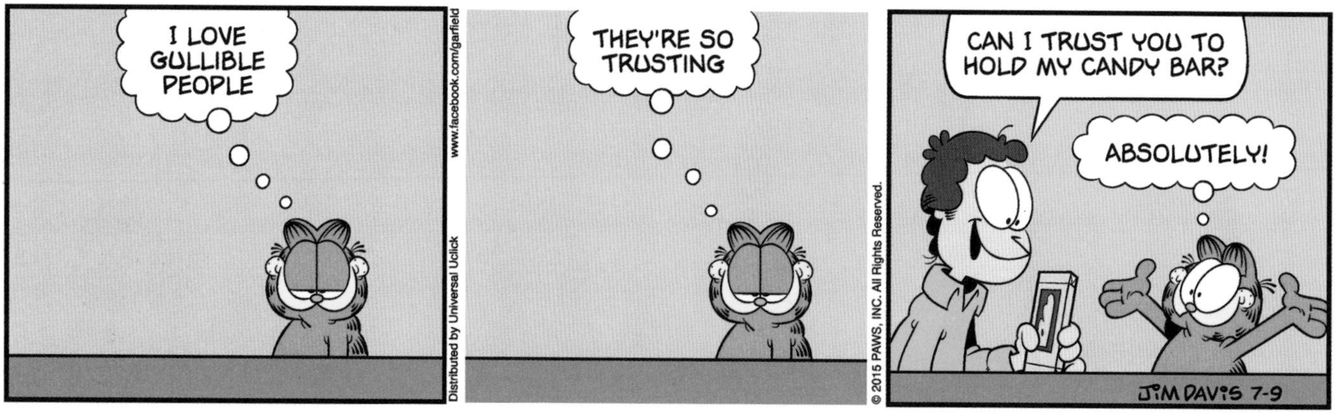
I LOVE GULLIBLE PEOPLE
THEY'RE SO TRUSTING
CAN I TRUST YOU TO HOLD MY CANDY BAR?
ABSOLUTELY!
Distributed by Universal Uclick www.facebook.com/garfield
© 2015 PAWS, INC. All Rights Reserved.
JIM DAVIS 7-9

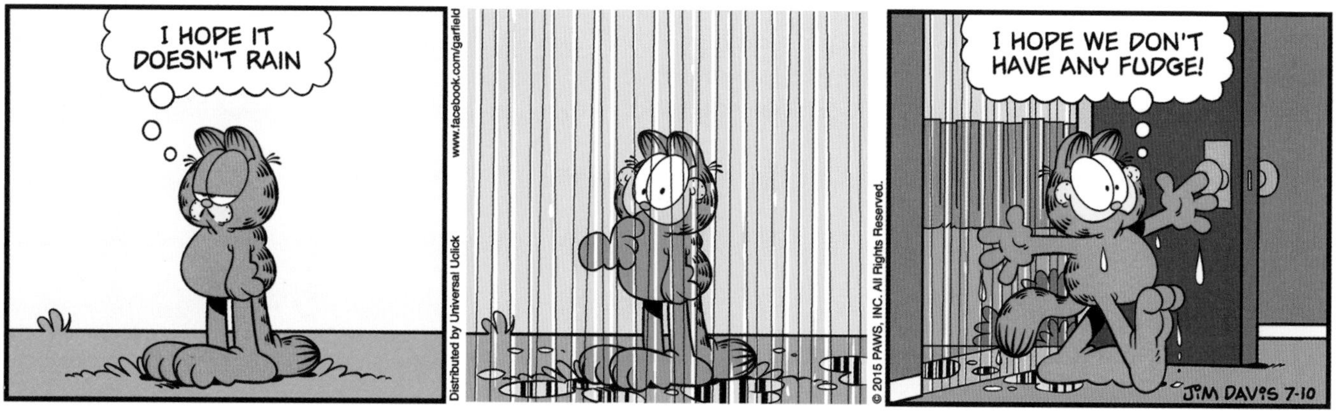
I HOPE IT DOESN'T RAIN
I HOPE WE DON'T HAVE ANY FUDGE!
Distributed by Universal Uclick www.facebook.com/garfield
© 2015 PAWS, INC. All Rights Reserved.
JIM DAVIS 7-10

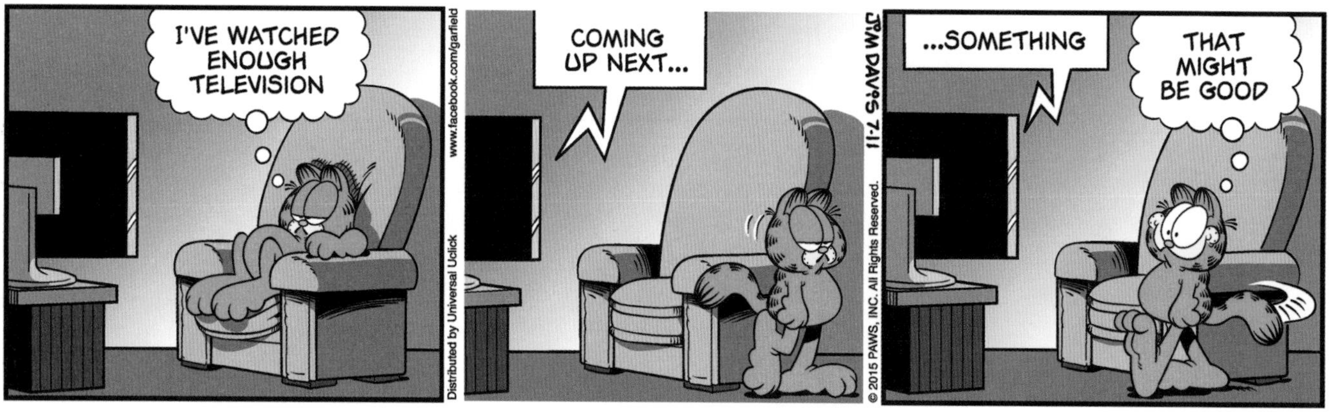
I'VE WATCHED ENOUGH TELEVISION
COMING UP NEXT...
...SOMETHING
THAT MIGHT BE GOOD
Distributed by Universal Uclick www.facebook.com/garfield
JIM DAVIS 7-11
© 2015 PAWS, INC. All Rights Reserved.

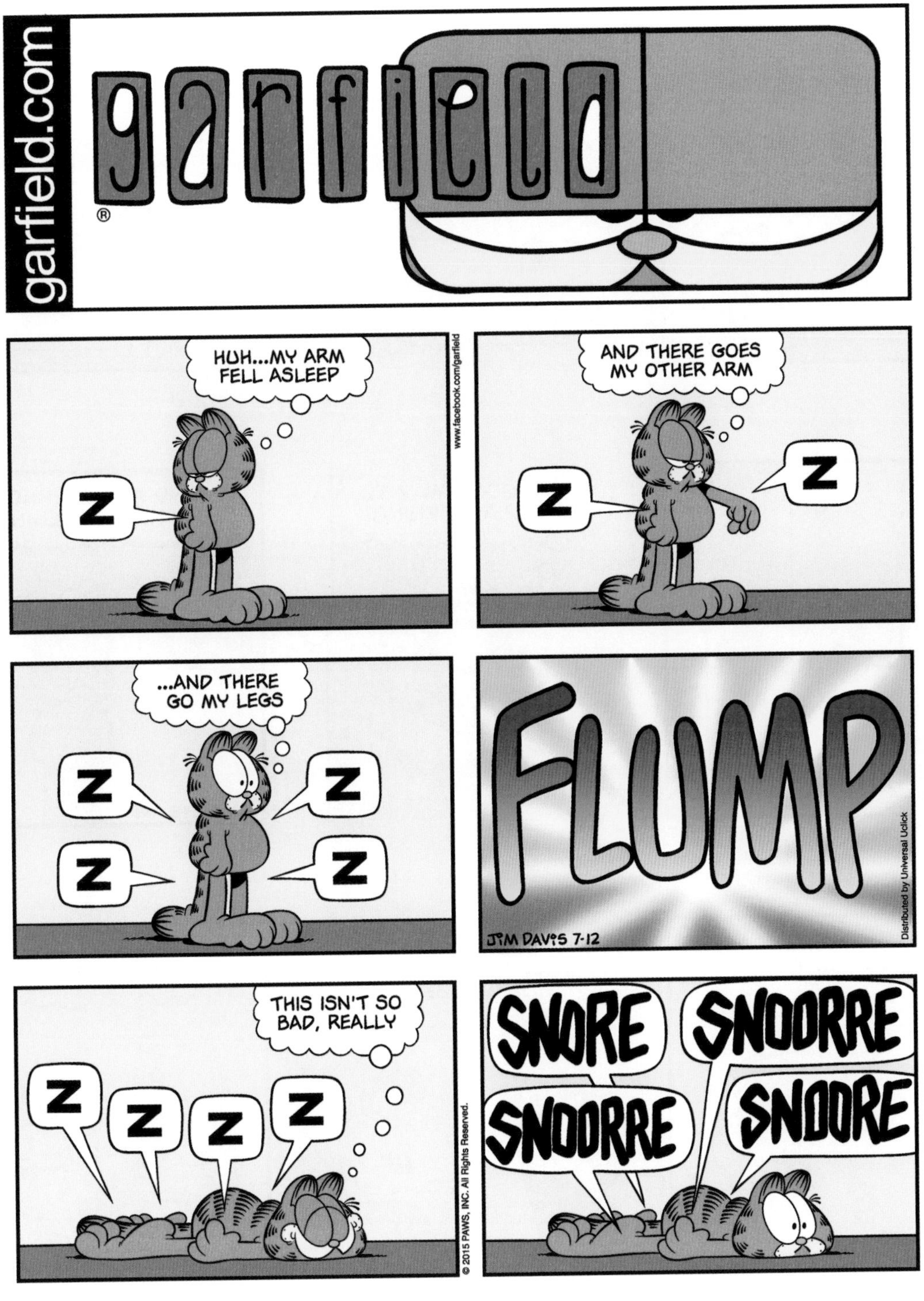
garfield.com
garfield
®
HUH...MY ARM FELL ASLEEP
Z
www.facebook.com/garfield
AND THERE GOES MY OTHER ARM
Z
Z
...AND THERE GO MY LEGS
Z
Z
Z
Z
FLUMP
JIM DAVIS 7-12
Distributed by Universal Uclick
THIS ISN'T SO BAD, REALLY
Z
Z
Z
Z
© 2015 PAWS, INC. All Rights Reserved.
SNORE
SNOORRE
SNOORRE
SNOORE

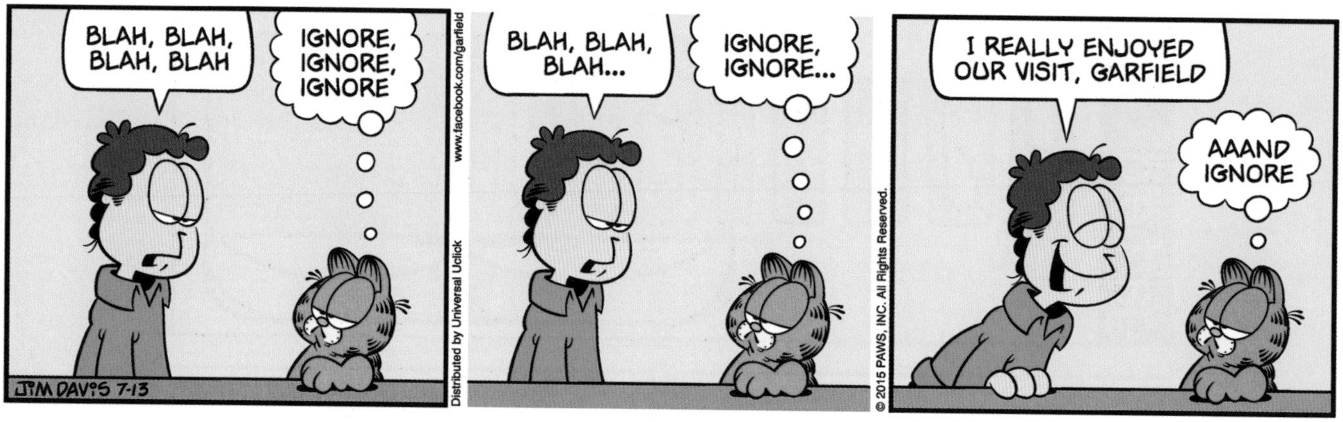
BLAH, BLAH, BLAH, BLAH
IGNORE, IGNORE, IGNORE
JIM DAVIS 7-13
Distributed by Universal Uclick www.facebook.com/garfield
BLAH, BLAH, BLAH...
IGNORE, IGNORE...
© 2015 PAWS, INC. All Rights Reserved.
I REALLY ENJOYED OUR VISIT, GARFIELD
AAAND IGNORE

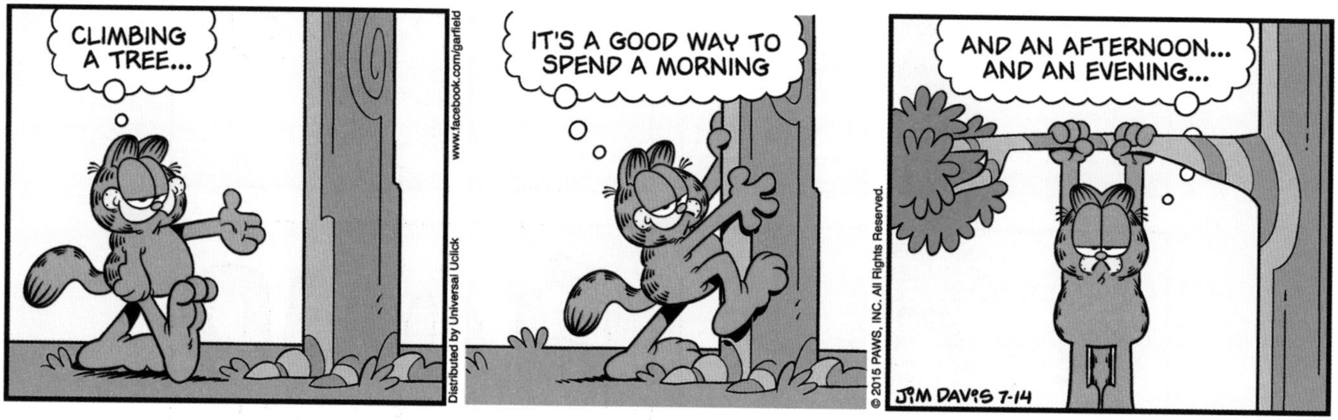
CLIMBING A TREE...
Distributed by Universal Uclick www.facebook.com/garfield
IT'S A GOOD WAY TO SPEND A MORNING
© 2015 PAWS, INC. All Rights Reserved.
AND AN AFTERNOON... AND AN EVENING...
JIM DAVIS 7-14

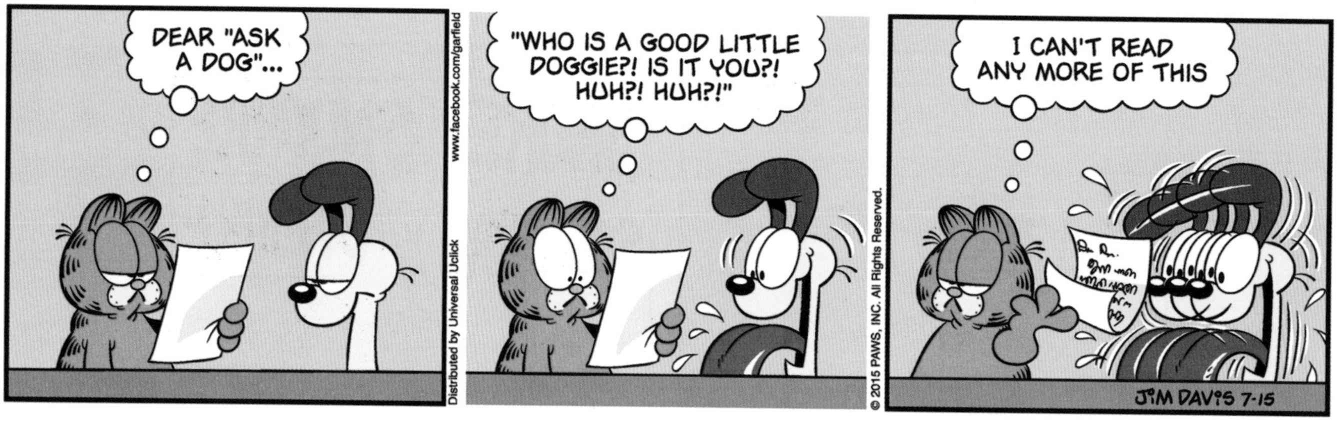
DEAR "ASK A DOG"...
Distributed by Universal Uclick www.facebook.com/garfield
"WHO IS A GOOD LITTLE DOGGIE?! IS IT YOU?! HUH?! HUH?!"
© 2015 PAWS, INC. All Rights Reserved.
I CAN'T READ ANY MORE OF THIS
JIM DAVIS 7-15

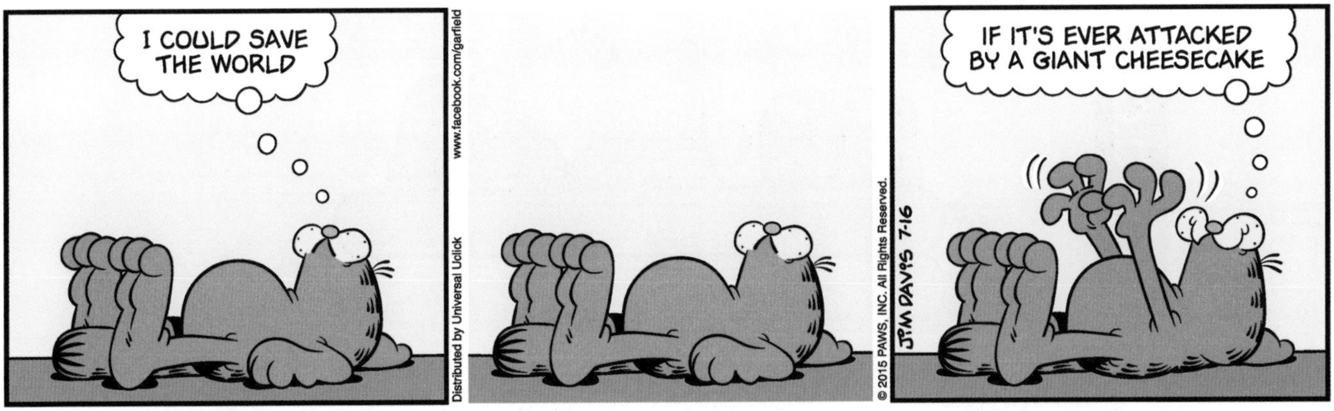
I COULD SAVE THE WORLD
IF IT'S EVER ATTACKED BY A GIANT CHEESECAKE
JIM DAVIS 7-16
Distributed by Universal Uclick www.facebook.com/garfield
© 2015 PAWS, INC. All Rights Reserved.

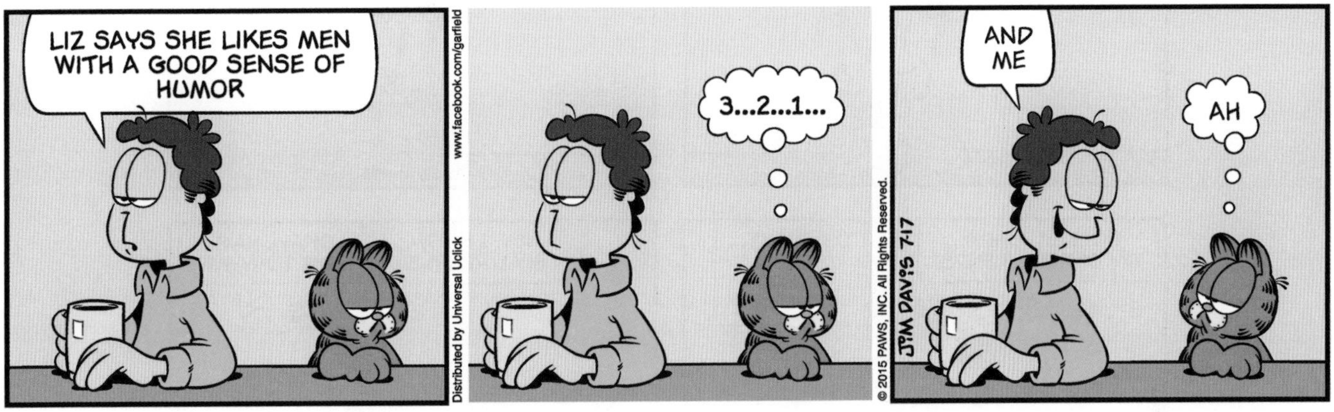
LIZ SAYS SHE LIKES MEN WITH A GOOD SENSE OF HUMOR
3...2...1...
AND ME
AH
JIM DAVIS 7-17
Distributed by Universal Uclick www.facebook.com/garfield
© 2015 PAWS, INC. All Rights Reserved.

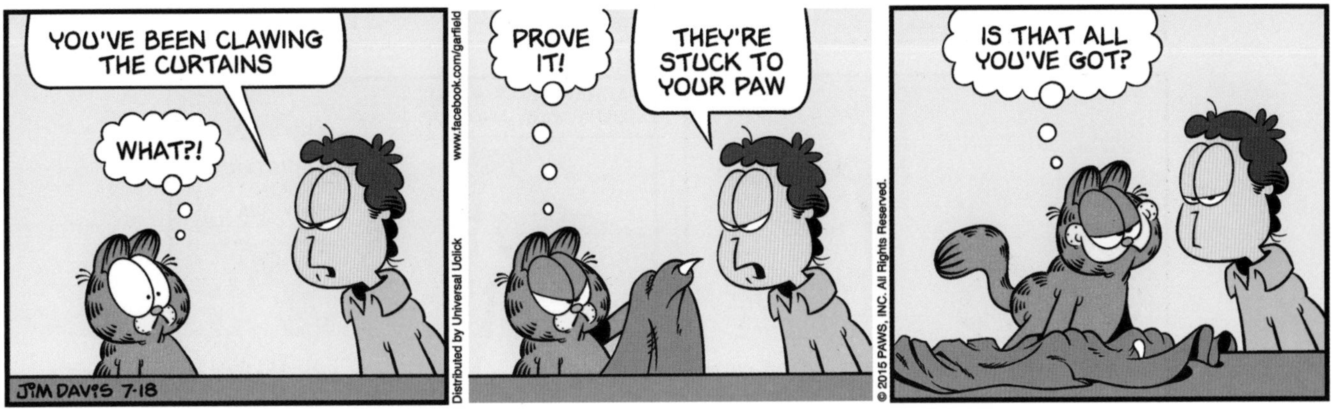
YOU'VE BEEN CLAWING THE CURTAINS
WHAT?!
PROVE IT!
THEY'RE STUCK TO YOUR PAW
IS THAT ALL YOU'VE GOT?
JIM DAVIS 7-18
Distributed by Universal Uclick www.facebook.com/garfield
© 2015 PAWS, INC. All Rights Reserved.

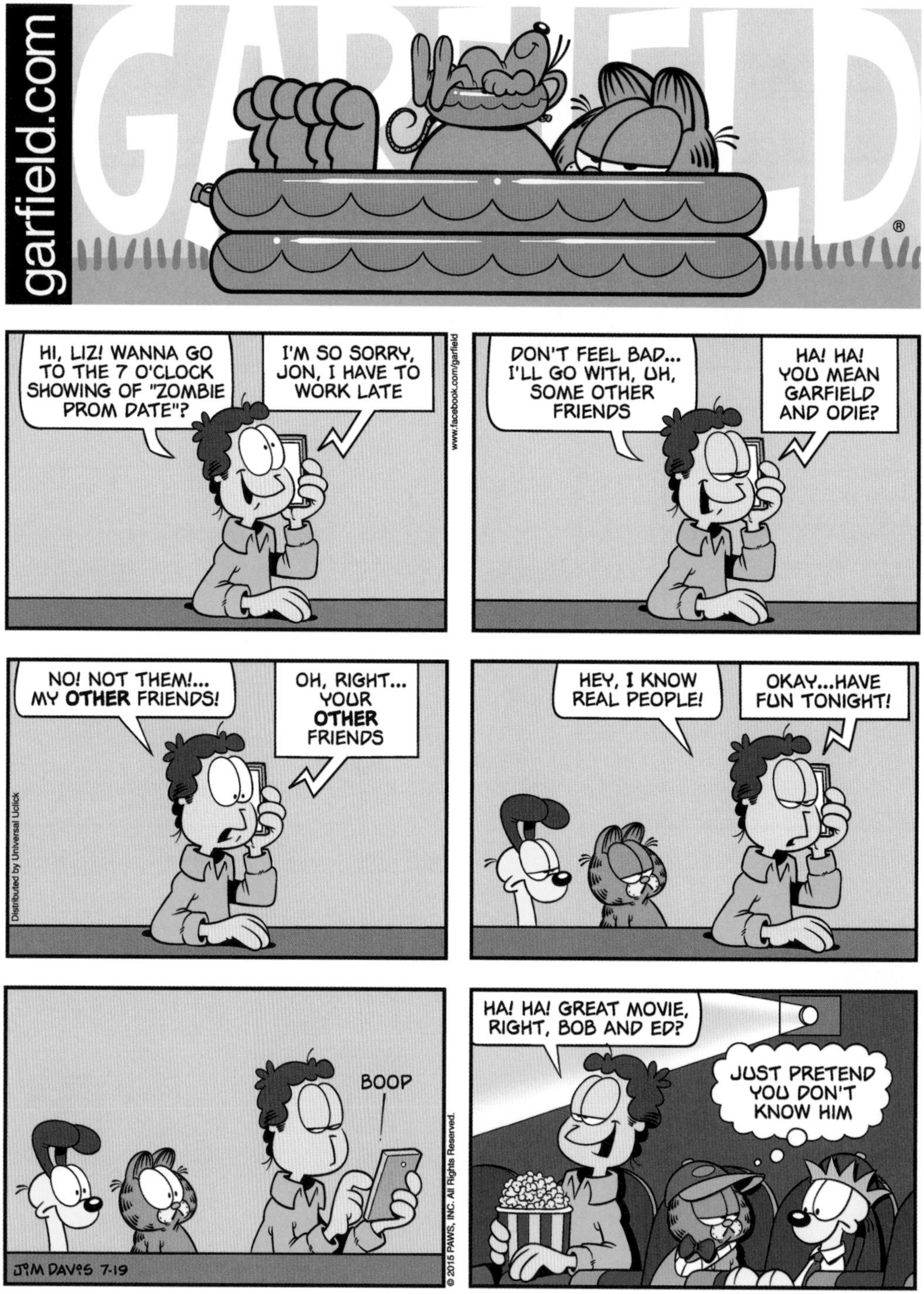
garfield.com
GARFIELD®
HI, LIZ! WANNA GO TO THE 7 O'CLOCK SHOWING OF "ZOMBIE PROM DATE"?
I'M SO SORRY, JON, I HAVE TO WORK LATE
www.facebook.com/garfield
DON'T FEEL BAD... I'LL GO WITH, UH, SOME OTHER FRIENDS
HA! HA! YOU MEAN GARFIELD AND ODIE?
NO! NOT THEM!... MY **OTHER** FRIENDS!
OH, RIGHT... YOUR **OTHER** FRIENDS
Distributed by Universal Uclick
HEY, I KNOW REAL PEOPLE!
OKAY...HAVE FUN TONIGHT!
BOOP
JIM DAVIS 7-19
© 2015 PAWS, INC. All Rights Reserved.
HA! HA! GREAT MOVIE, RIGHT, BOB AND ED?
JUST PRETEND YOU DON'T KNOW HIM

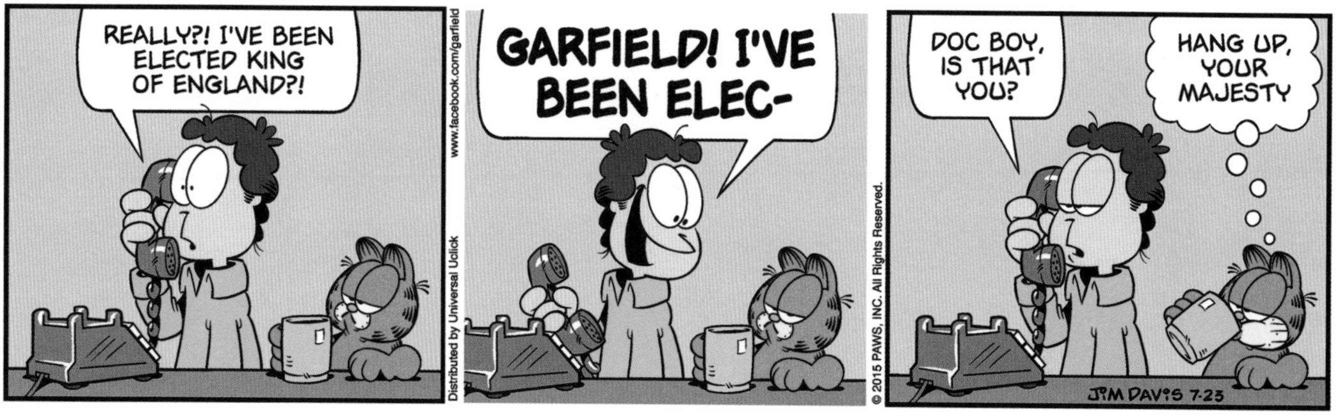
REALLY?! I'VE BEEN ELECTED KING OF ENGLAND?!
GARFIELD! I'VE BEEN ELEC-
DOC BOY, IS THAT YOU?
HANG UP, YOUR MAJESTY
Distributed by Universal Uclick
www.facebook.com/garfield
© 2015 PAWS, INC. All Rights Reserved.
JIM DAVIS 7-23

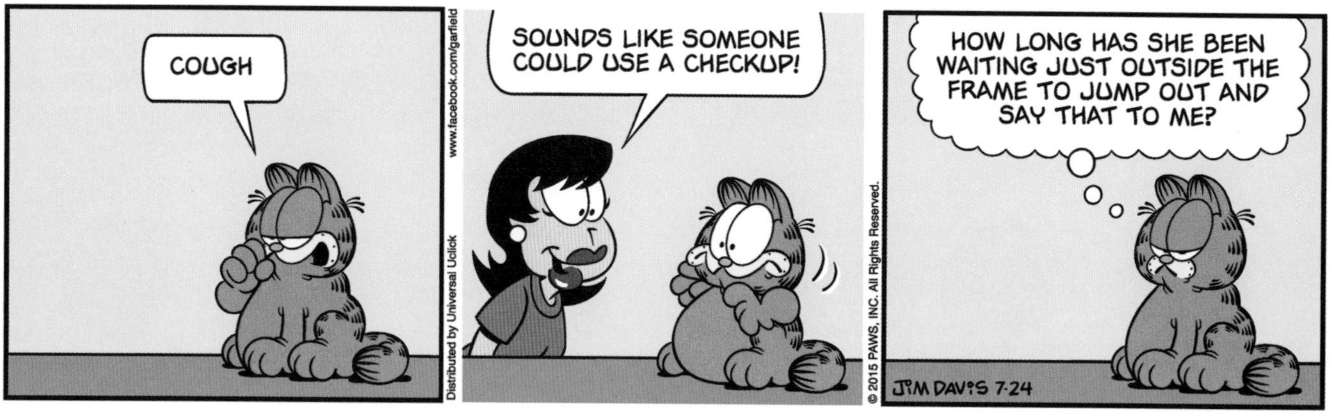
COUGH
SOUNDS LIKE SOMEONE COULD USE A CHECKUP!
HOW LONG HAS SHE BEEN WAITING JUST OUTSIDE THE FRAME TO JUMP OUT AND SAY THAT TO ME?
Distributed by Universal Uclick
www.facebook.com/garfield
© 2015 PAWS, INC. All Rights Reserved.
JIM DAVIS 7-24

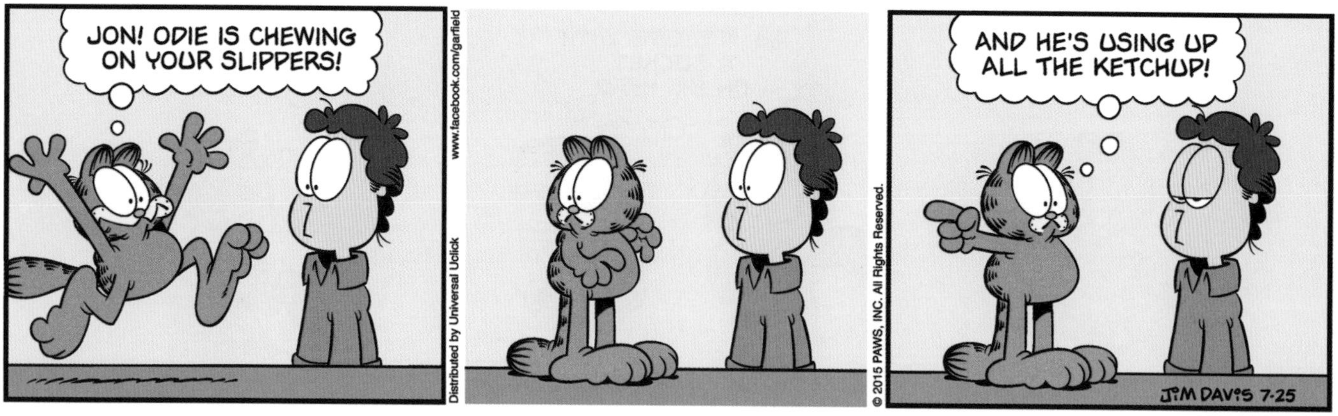
JON! ODIE IS CHEWING ON YOUR SLIPPERS!
AND HE'S USING UP ALL THE KETCHUP!
Distributed by Universal Uclick
www.facebook.com/garfield
© 2015 PAWS, INC. All Rights Reserved.
JIM DAVIS 7-25

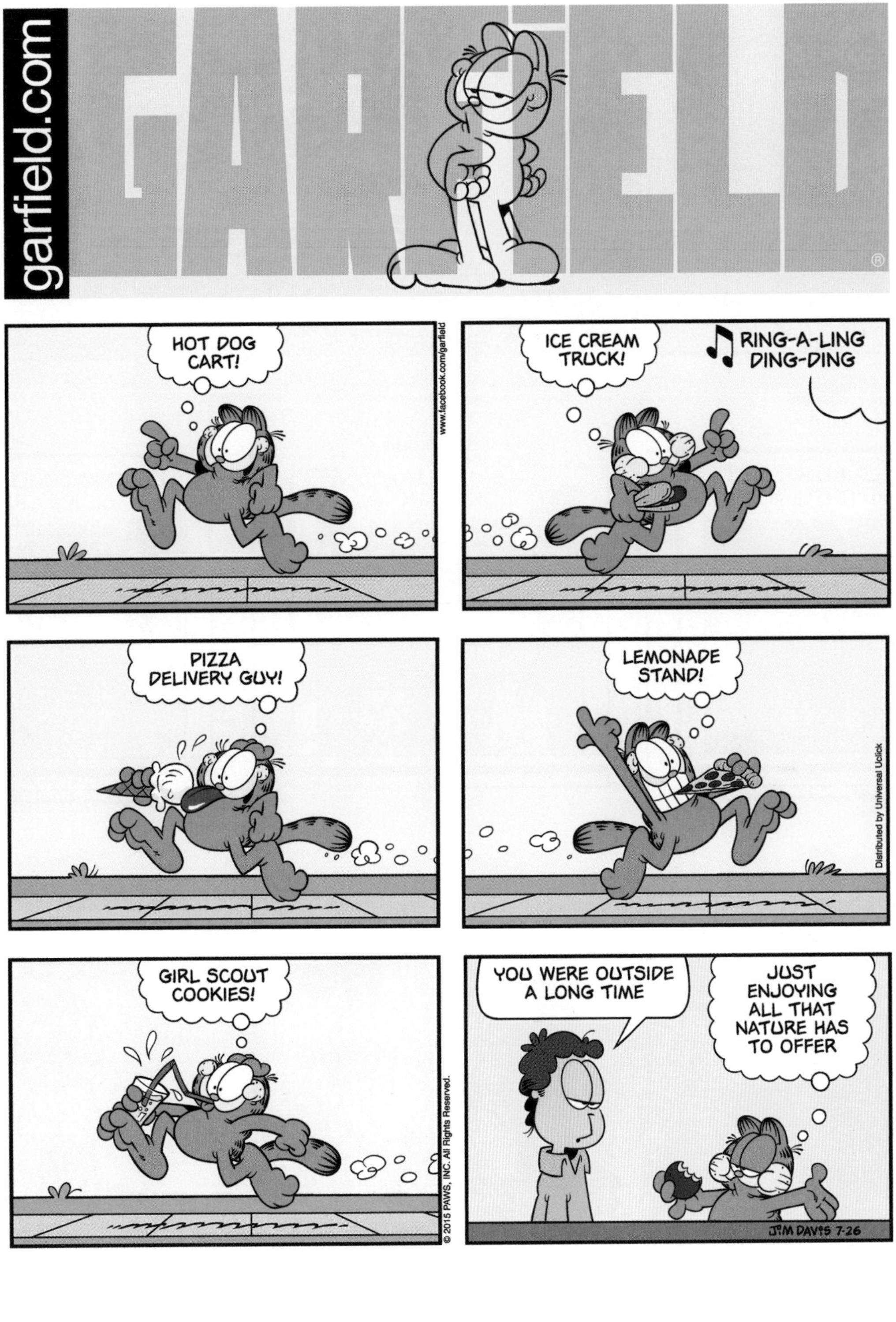
garfield.com
GARFIELD®
www.facebook.com/garfield
HOT DOG CART!
ICE CREAM TRUCK!
RING-A-LING DING-DING
PIZZA DELIVERY GUY!
LEMONADE STAND!
Distributed by Universal Uclick
GIRL SCOUT COOKIES!
© 2015 PAWS, INC. All Rights Reserved.
YOU WERE OUTSIDE A LONG TIME
JUST ENJOYING ALL THAT NATURE HAS TO OFFER
JIM DAVIS 7-26

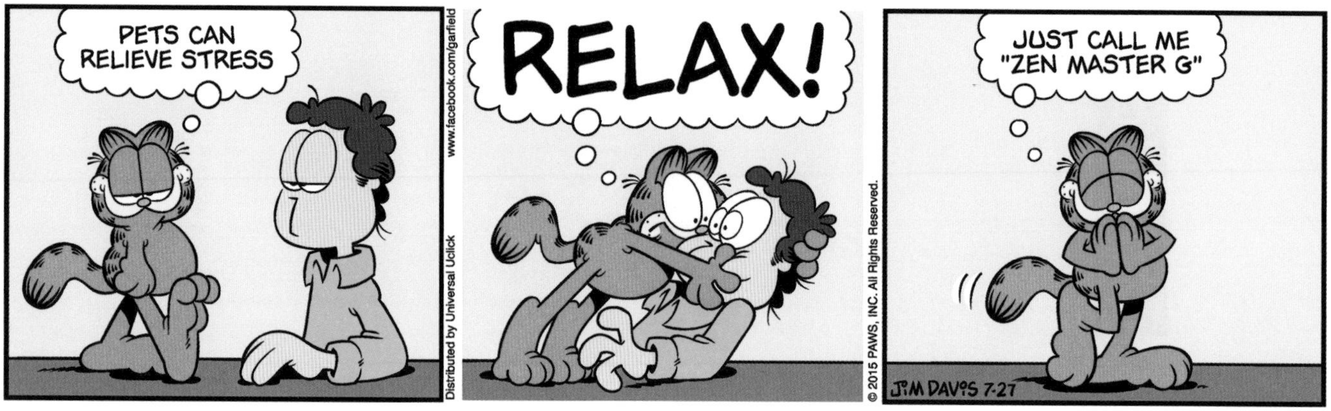
PETS CAN RELIEVE STRESS
RELAX!
JUST CALL ME "ZEN MASTER G"
JIM DAVIS 7-27
Distributed by Universal Uclick
www.facebook.com/garfield
© 2015 PAWS, INC. All Rights Reserved.

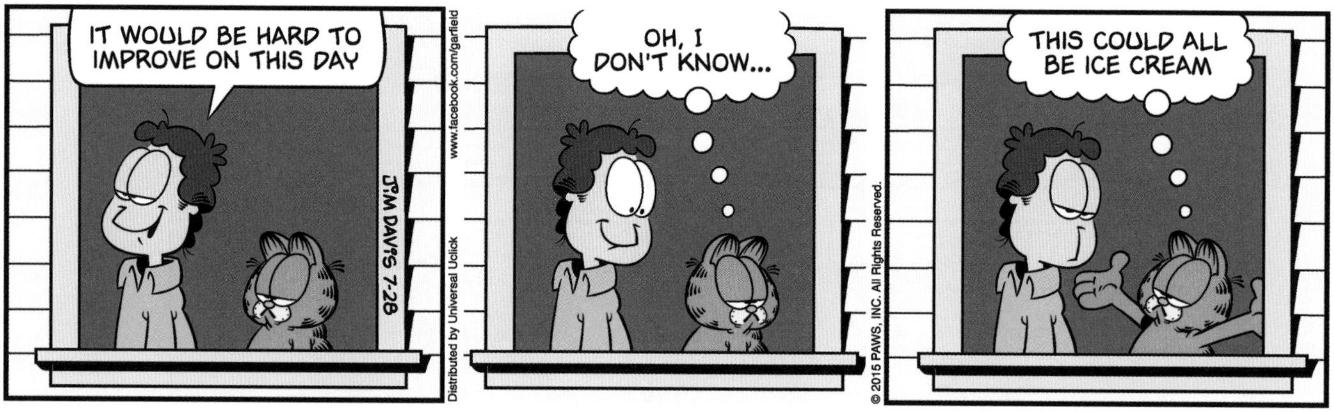
IT WOULD BE HARD TO IMPROVE ON THIS DAY
JIM DAVIS 7-28
OH, I DON'T KNOW...
THIS COULD ALL BE ICE CREAM
Distributed by Universal Uclick
www.facebook.com/garfield
© 2015 PAWS, INC. All Rights Reserved.

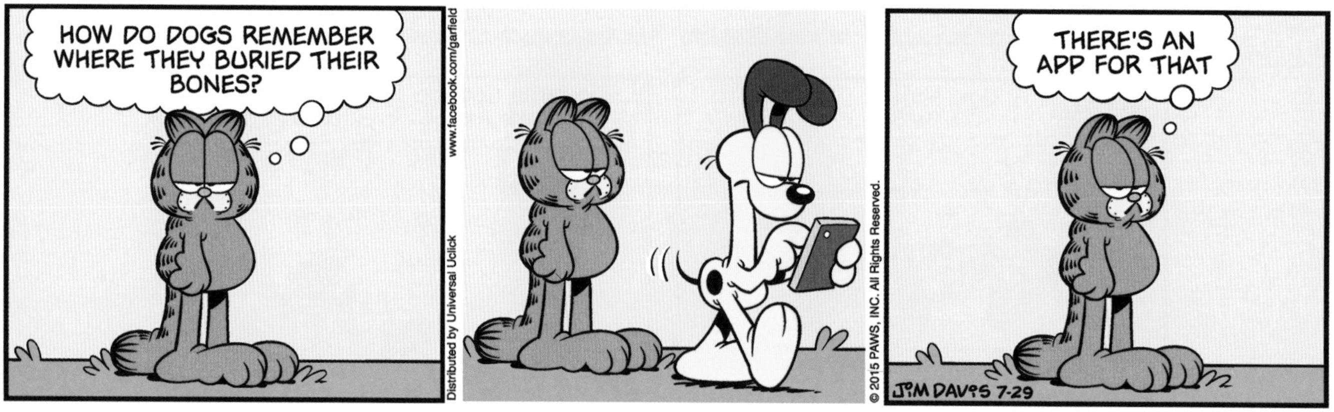
HOW DO DOGS REMEMBER WHERE THEY BURIED THEIR BONES?
THERE'S AN APP FOR THAT
JIM DAVIS 7-29
Distributed by Universal Uclick
www.facebook.com/garfield
© 2015 PAWS, INC. All Rights Reserved.

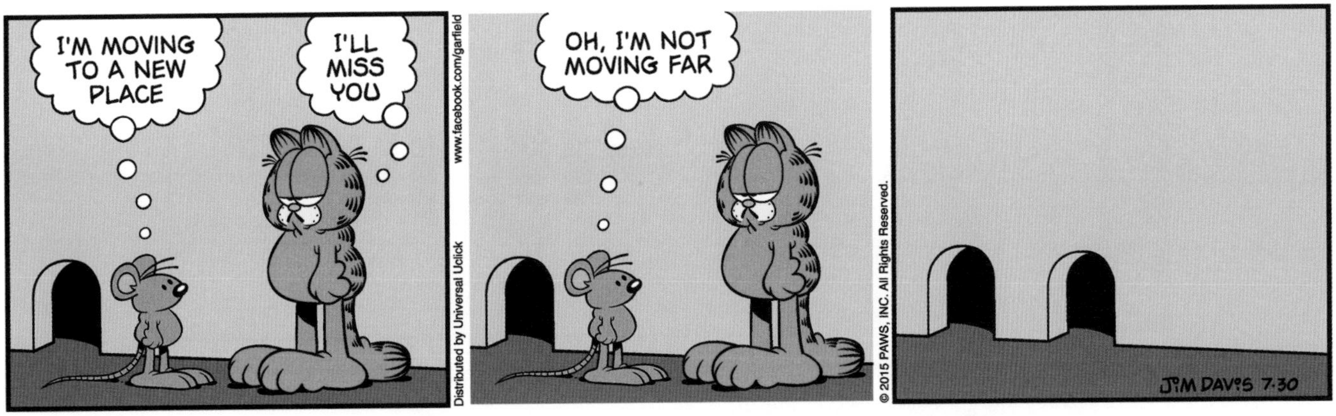
I'M MOVING TO A NEW PLACE
I'LL MISS YOU
OH, I'M NOT MOVING FAR
JIM DAVIS 7-30
Distributed by Universal Uclick www.facebook.com/garfield
© 2015 PAWS, INC. All Rights Reserved.

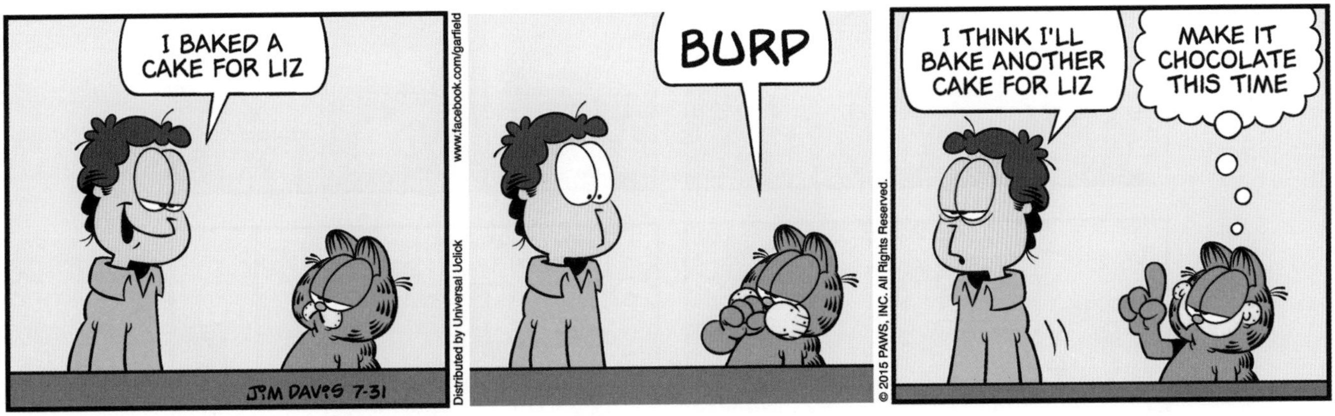
I BAKED A CAKE FOR LIZ
JIM DAVIS 7-31
BURP
I THINK I'LL BAKE ANOTHER CAKE FOR LIZ
MAKE IT CHOCOLATE THIS TIME
Distributed by Universal Uclick www.facebook.com/garfield
© 2015 PAWS, INC. All Rights Reserved.

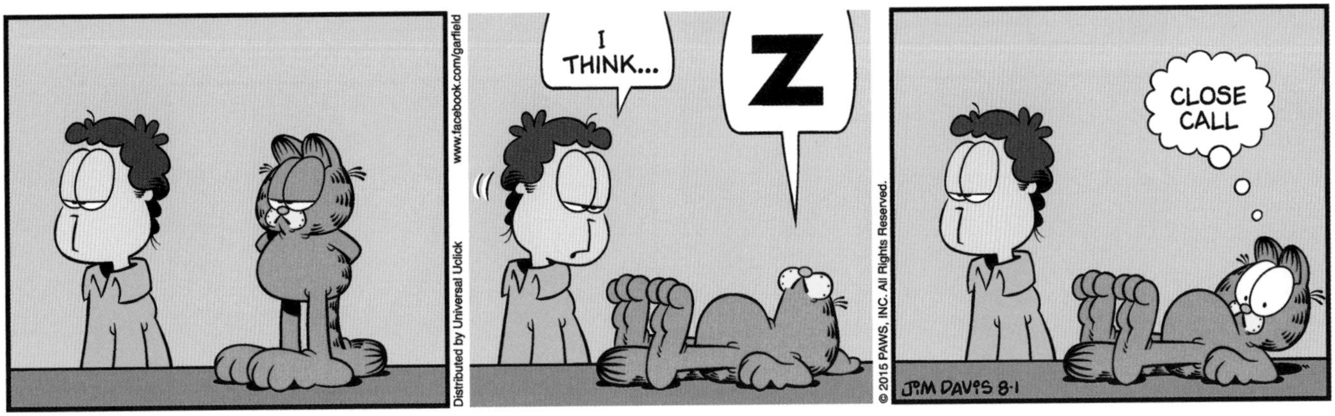
I THINK...
Z
CLOSE CALL
JIM DAVIS 8-1
Distributed by Universal Uclick www.facebook.com/garfield
© 2015 PAWS, INC. All Rights Reserved.

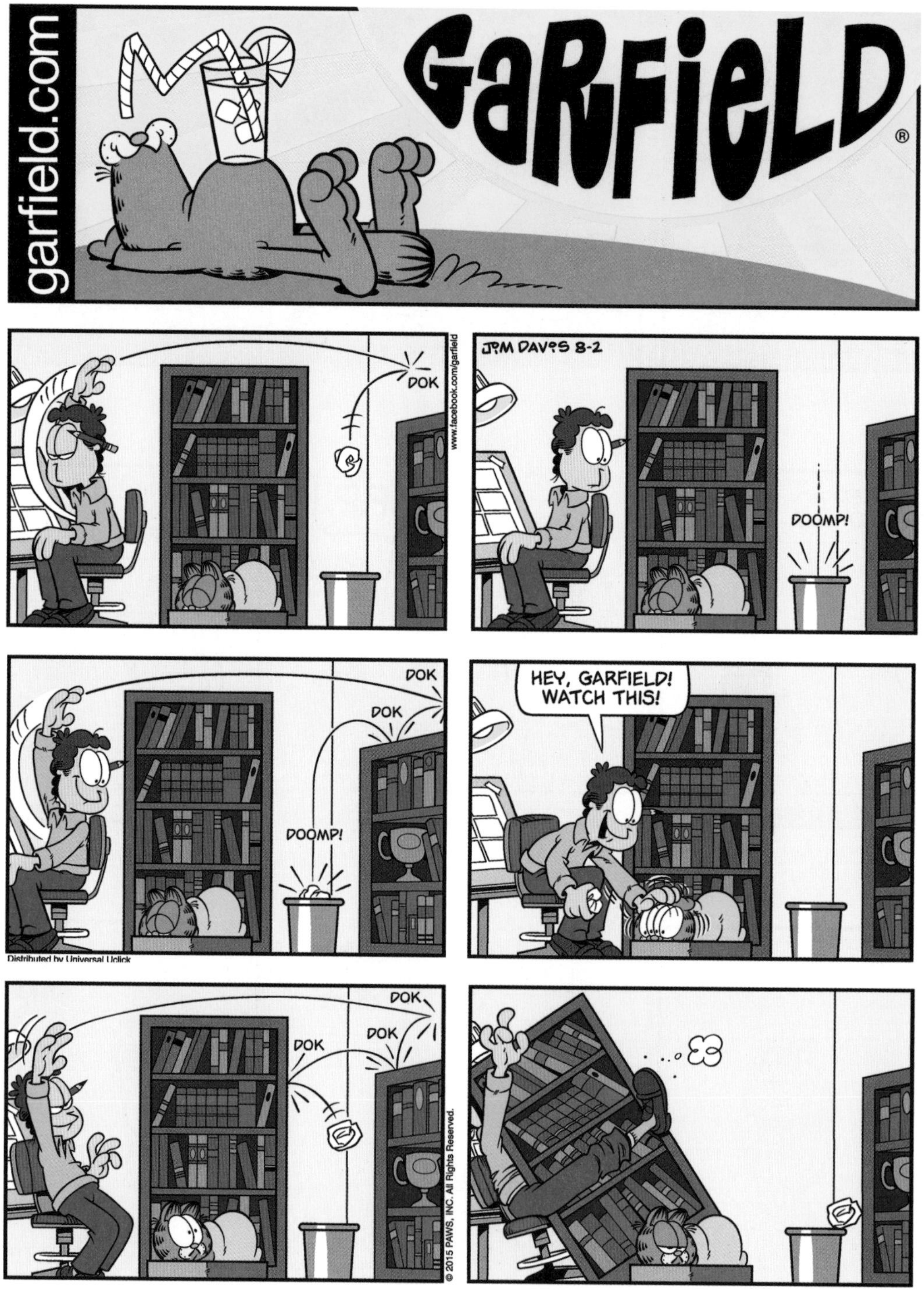
garfield.com
GARFIELD®
www.facebook.com/garfield
DOK
JIM DAVIS 8-2
DOOMP!
DOK
DOK
DOOMP!
HEY, GARFIELD! WATCH THIS!
Distributed by Universal Uclick
DOK
DOK
DOK

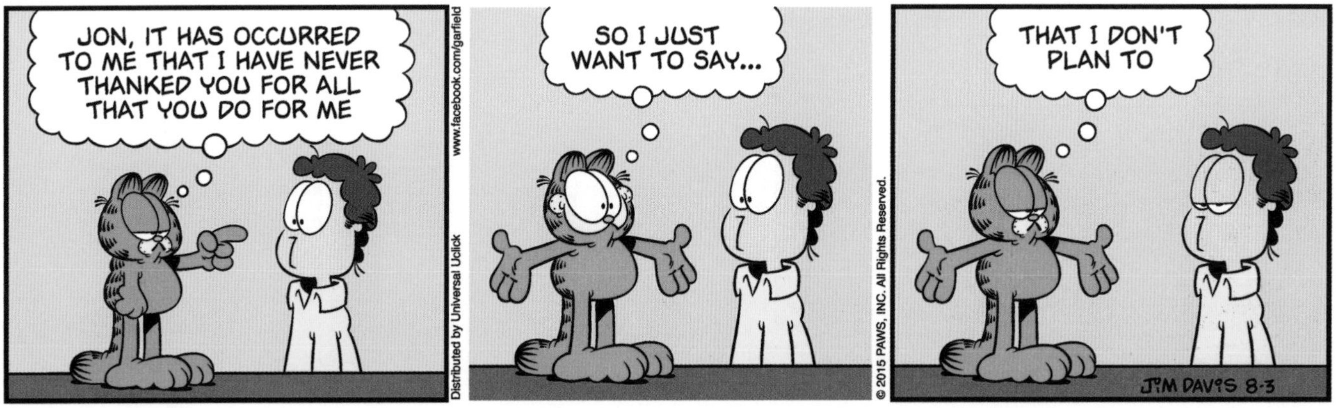
JON, IT HAS OCCURRED TO ME THAT I HAVE NEVER THANKED YOU FOR ALL THAT YOU DO FOR ME
SO I JUST WANT TO SAY...
THAT I DON'T PLAN TO
JIM DAVIS 8-3
Distributed by Universal Uclick www.facebook.com/garfield
© 2015 PAWS, INC. All Rights Reserved.

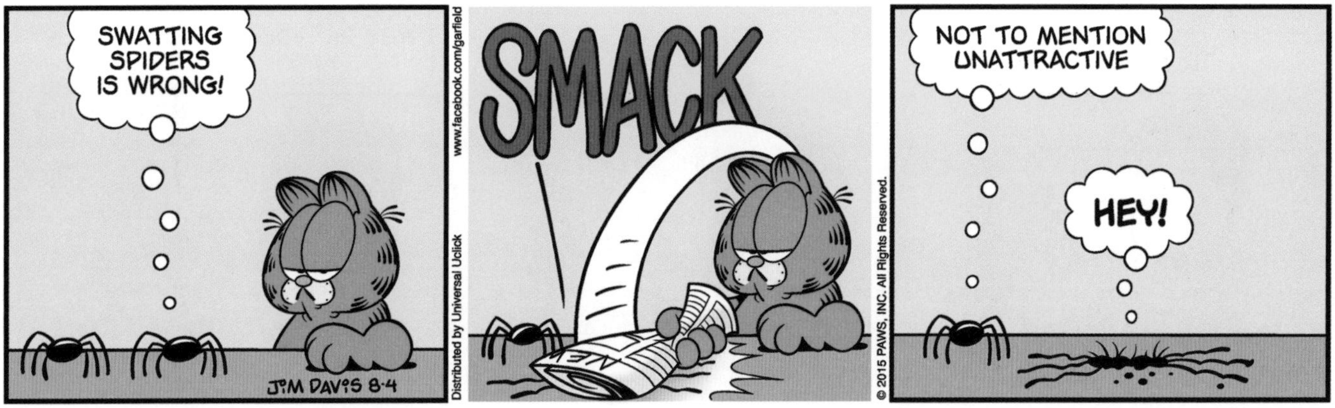
SWATTING SPIDERS IS WRONG!
JIM DAVIS 8-4
SMACK
NOT TO MENTION UNATTRACTIVE
HEY!
Distributed by Universal Uclick www.facebook.com/garfield
© 2015 PAWS, INC. All Rights Reserved.

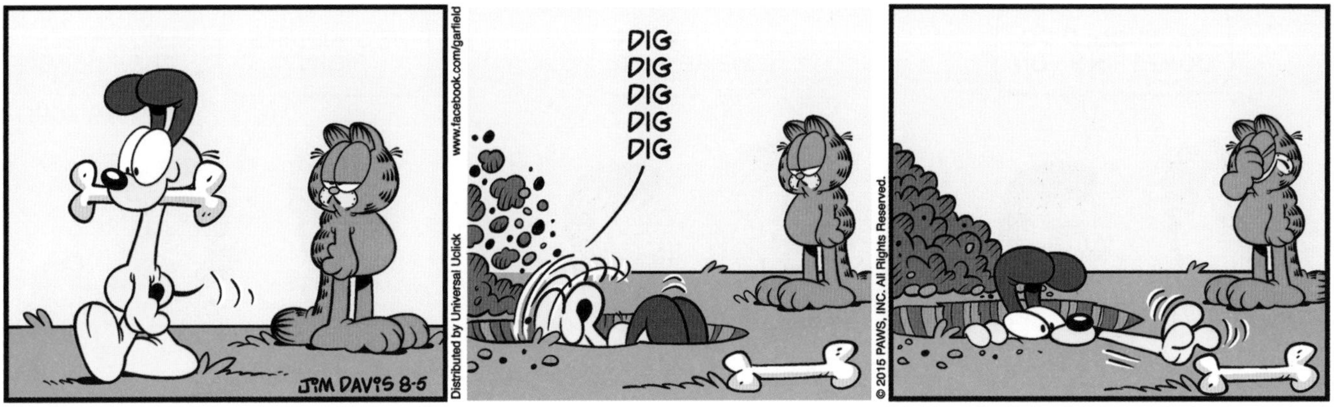
JIM DAVIS 8-5
DIG
DIG
DIG
DIG
DIG
Distributed by Universal Uclick www.facebook.com/garfield
© 2015 PAWS, INC. All Rights Reserved.

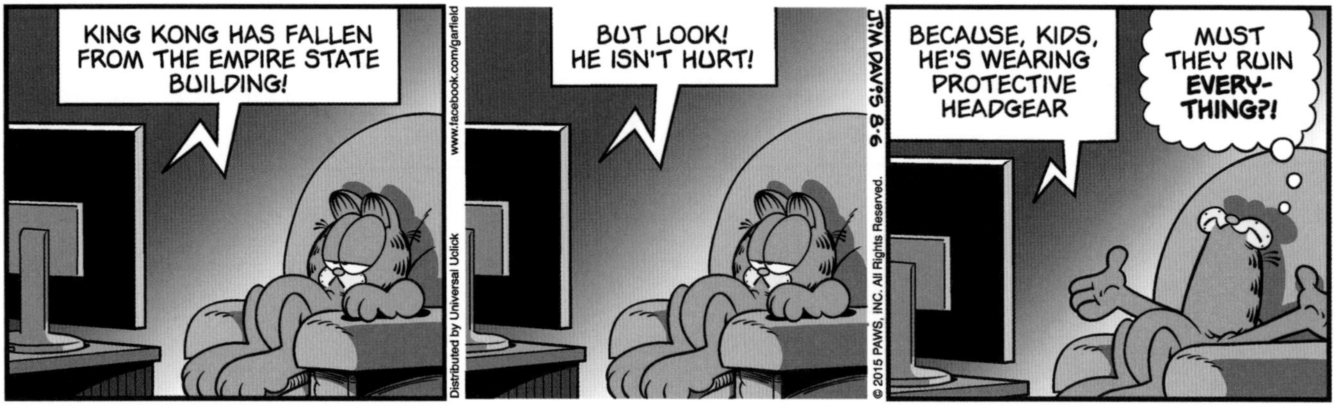
KING KONG HAS FALLEN FROM THE EMPIRE STATE BUILDING!
BUT LOOK! HE ISN'T HURT!
JIM DAVIS 8-6
BECAUSE, KIDS, HE'S WEARING PROTECTIVE HEADGEAR
MUST THEY RUIN **EVERY-THING?!**
www.facebook.com/garfield
Distributed by Universal Uclick
© 2015 PAWS, INC. All Rights Reserved.

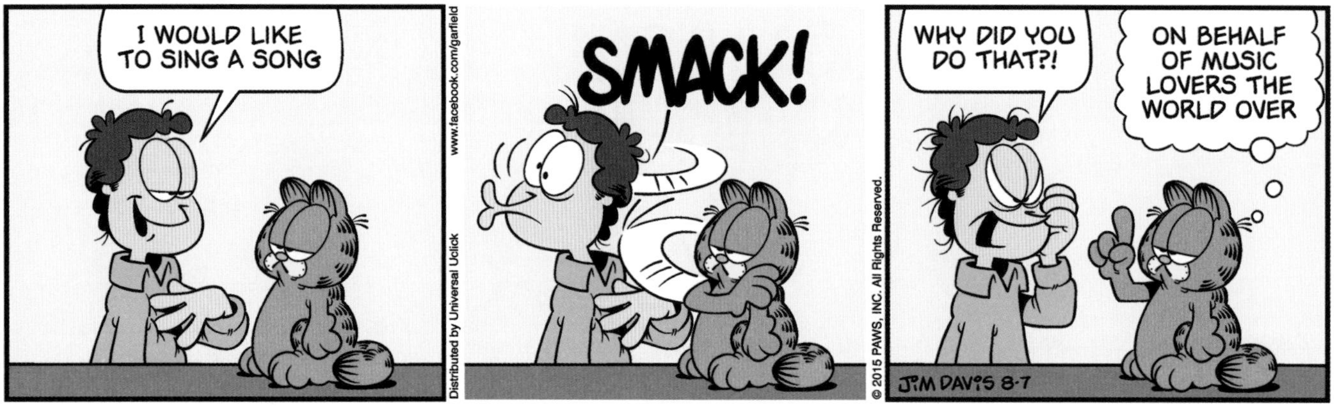
I WOULD LIKE TO SING A SONG
SMACK!
WHY DID YOU DO THAT?!
ON BEHALF OF MUSIC LOVERS THE WORLD OVER
JIM DAVIS 8-7
www.facebook.com/garfield
Distributed by Universal Uclick
© 2015 PAWS, INC. All Rights Reserved.

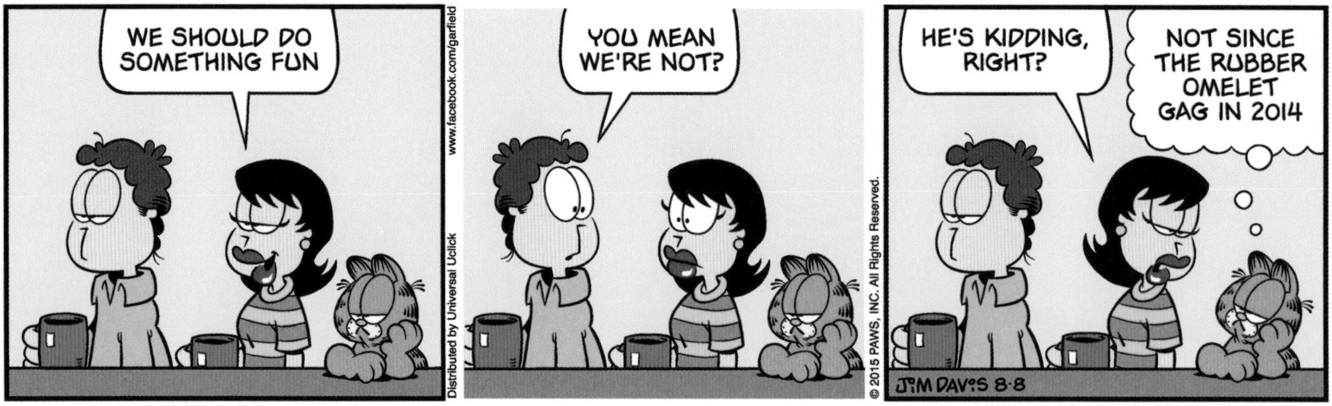
WE SHOULD DO SOMETHING FUN
YOU MEAN WE'RE NOT?
HE'S KIDDING, RIGHT?
NOT SINCE THE RUBBER OMELET GAG IN 2014
JIM DAVIS 8-8
www.facebook.com/garfield
Distributed by Universal Uclick
© 2015 PAWS, INC. All Rights Reserved.

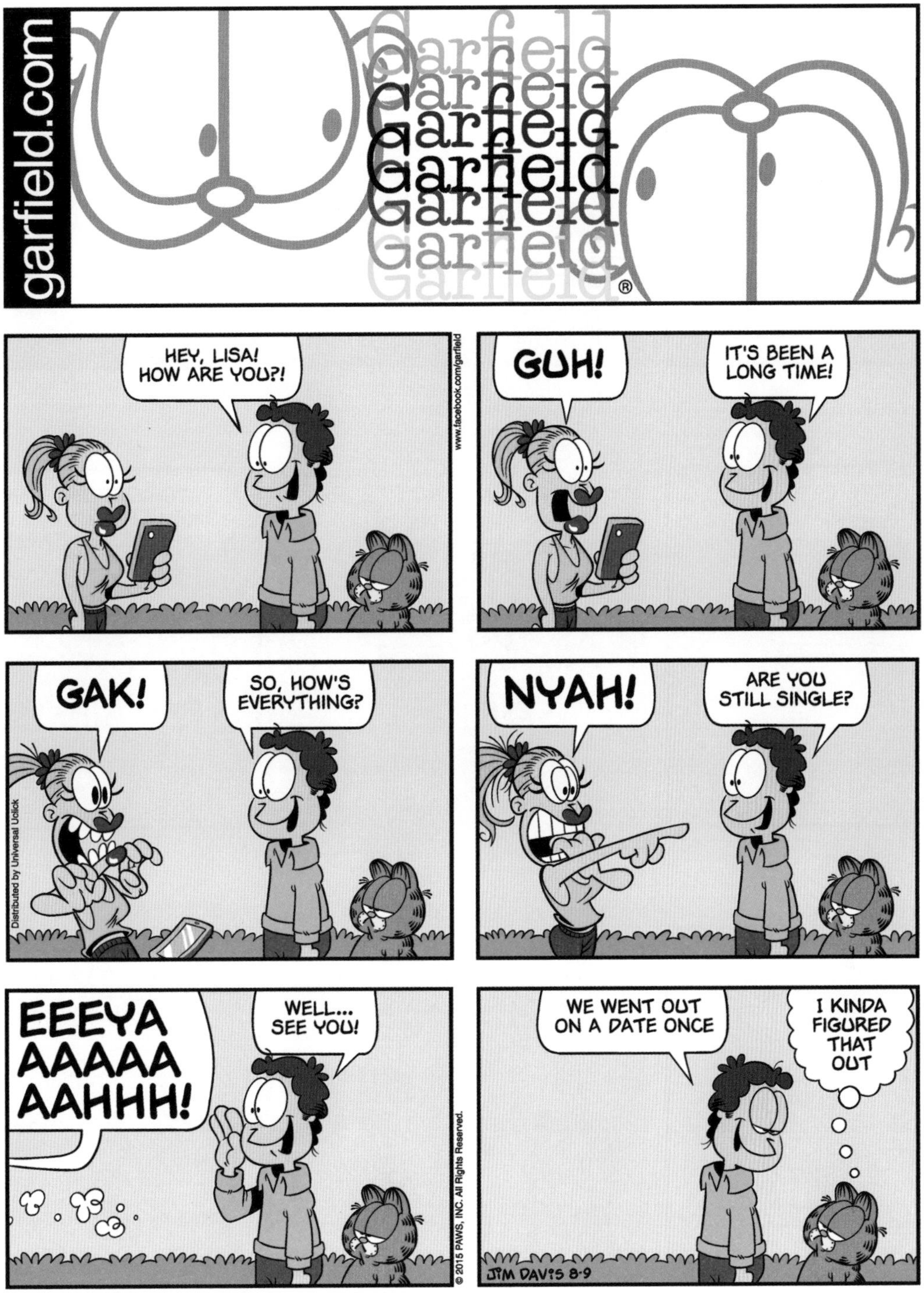
garfield.com
Garfield®
HEY, LISA! HOW ARE YOU?!
www.facebook.com/garfield
GUH!
IT'S BEEN A LONG TIME!
GAK!
SO, HOW'S EVERYTHING?
Distributed by Universal Uclick
NYAH!
ARE YOU STILL SINGLE?
EEEYA AAAAA AAHHH!
WELL... SEE YOU!
© 2015 PAWS, INC. All Rights Reserved.
WE WENT OUT ON A DATE ONCE
I KINDA FIGURED THAT OUT
JIM DAVIS 8-9

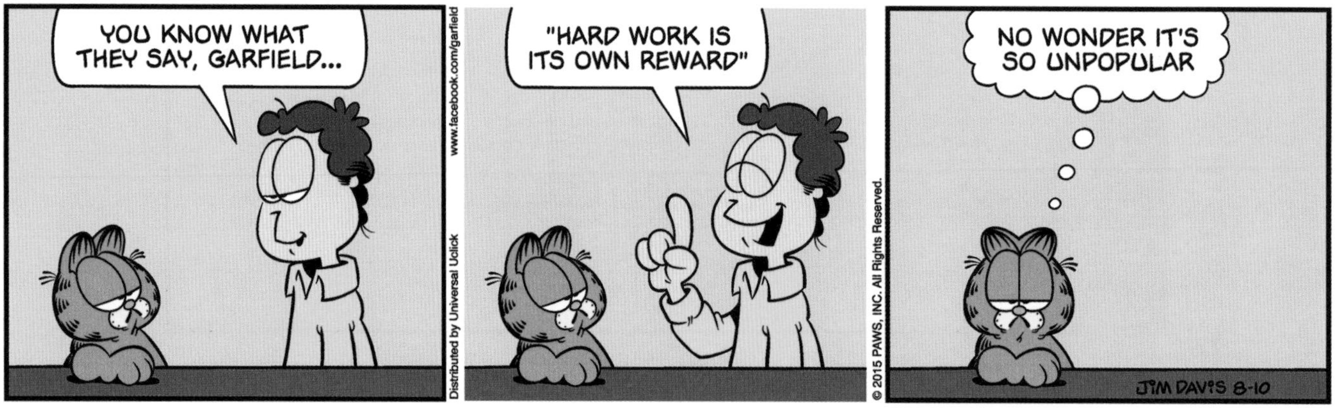
YOU KNOW WHAT THEY SAY, GARFIELD...
"HARD WORK IS ITS OWN REWARD"
NO WONDER IT'S SO UNPOPULAR
JIM DAVIS 8-10
www.facebook.com/garfield
Distributed by Universal Uclick
© 2015 PAWS, INC. All Rights Reserved.

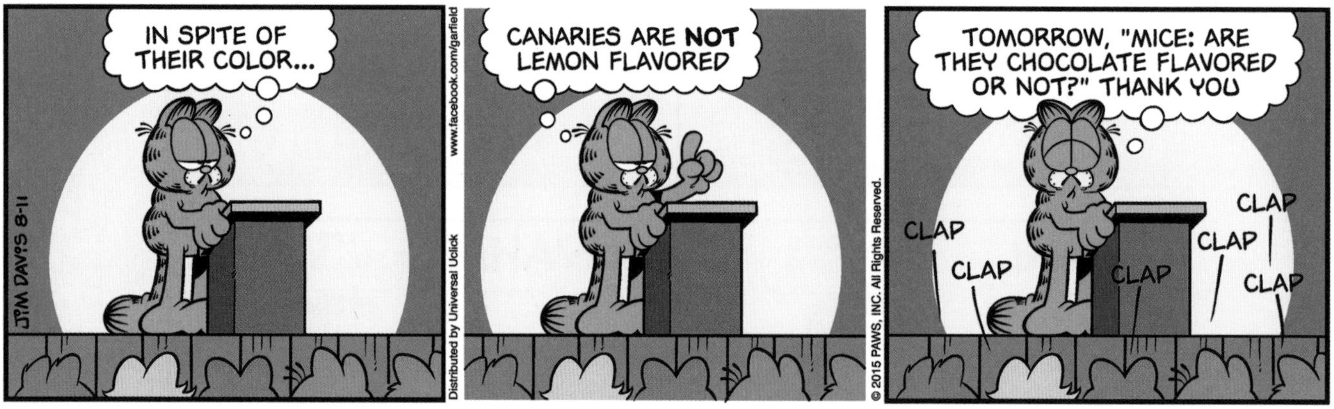
IN SPITE OF THEIR COLOR...
JIM DAVIS 8-11
CANARIES ARE **NOT** LEMON FLAVORED
TOMORROW, "MICE: ARE THEY CHOCOLATE FLAVORED OR NOT?" THANK YOU
CLAP
CLAP
CLAP
CLAP
CLAP
CLAP
www.facebook.com/garfield
Distributed by Universal Uclick
© 2015 PAWS, INC. All Rights Reserved.

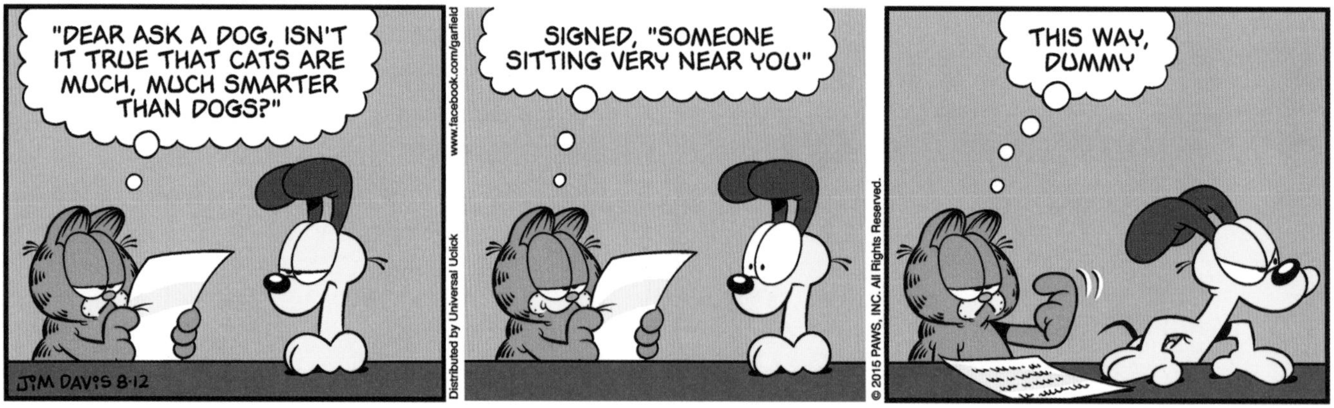
"DEAR ASK A DOG, ISN'T IT TRUE THAT CATS ARE MUCH, MUCH SMARTER THAN DOGS?"
JIM DAVIS 8-12
SIGNED, "SOMEONE SITTING VERY NEAR YOU"
THIS WAY, DUMMY
www.facebook.com/garfield
Distributed by Universal Uclick
© 2015 PAWS, INC. All Rights Reserved.

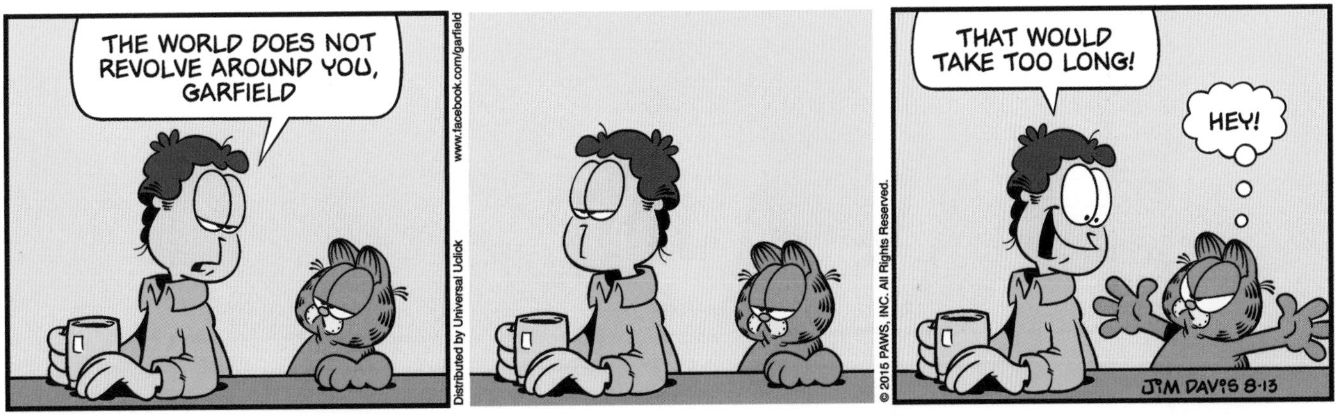
THE WORLD DOES NOT REVOLVE AROUND YOU, GARFIELD
www.facebook.com/garfield
Distributed by Universal Uclick
THAT WOULD TAKE TOO LONG!
HEY!
© 2015 PAWS, INC. All Rights Reserved.
JIM DAVIS 8-13

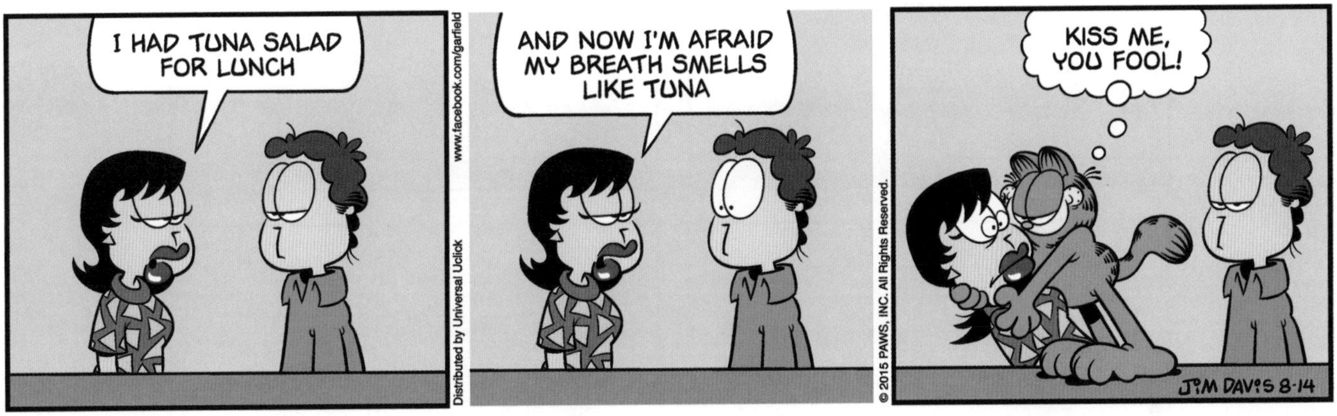
I HAD TUNA SALAD FOR LUNCH
www.facebook.com/garfield
Distributed by Universal Uclick
AND NOW I'M AFRAID MY BREATH SMELLS LIKE TUNA
KISS ME, YOU FOOL!
© 2015 PAWS, INC. All Rights Reserved.
JIM DAVIS 8-14

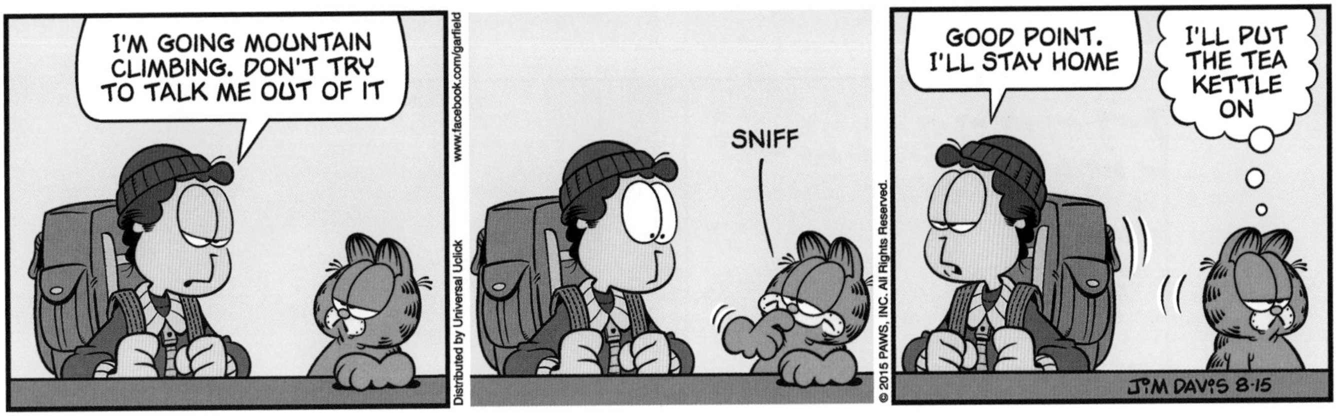
I'M GOING MOUNTAIN CLIMBING. DON'T TRY TO TALK ME OUT OF IT
www.facebook.com/garfield
Distributed by Universal Uclick
SNIFF
GOOD POINT. I'LL STAY HOME
I'LL PUT THE TEA KETTLE ON
© 2015 PAWS, INC. All Rights Reserved.
JIM DAVIS 8-15

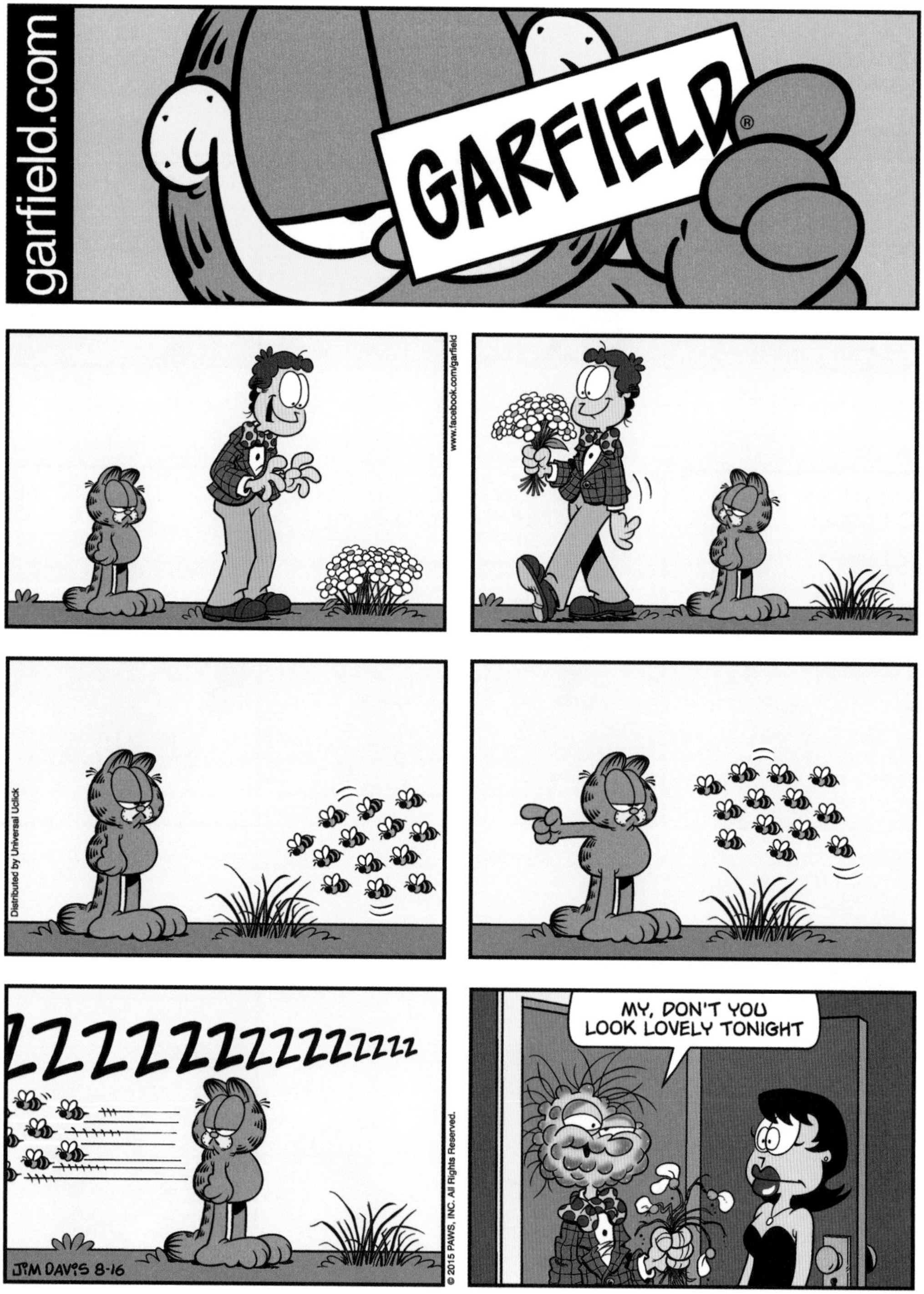
garfield.com
GARFIELD®
www.facebook.com/garfield
Distributed by Universal Uclick
ZZZZZZZZZZZZzzzz
JIM DAVIS 8-16
© 2015 PAWS, INC. All Rights Reserved.
MY, DON'T YOU LOOK LOVELY TONIGHT

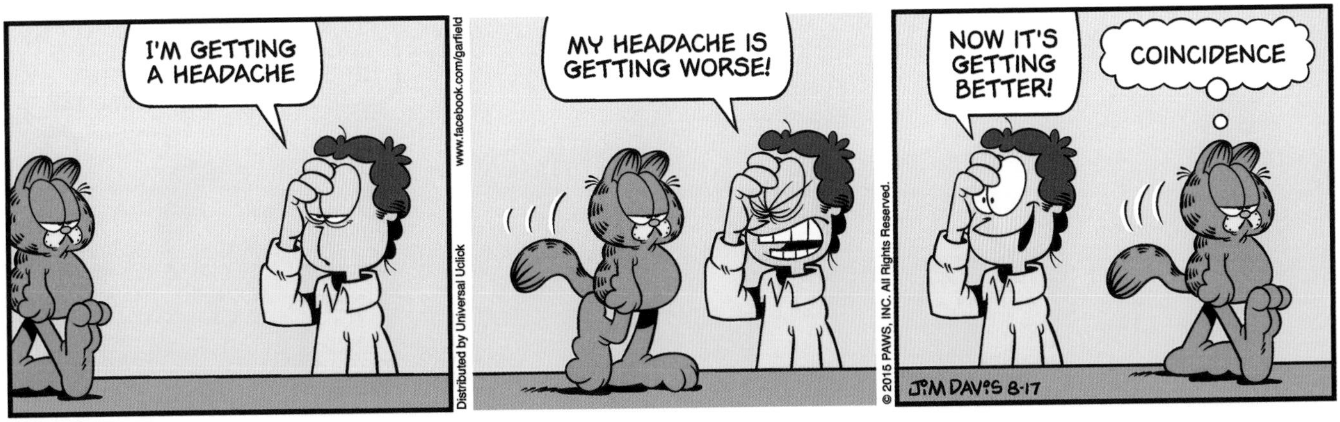
I'M GETTING A HEADACHE
www.facebook.com/garfield
Distributed by Universal Uclick
MY HEADACHE IS GETTING WORSE!
© 2015 PAWS, INC. All Rights Reserved.
NOW IT'S GETTING BETTER!
COINCIDENCE
JIM DAVIS 8-17

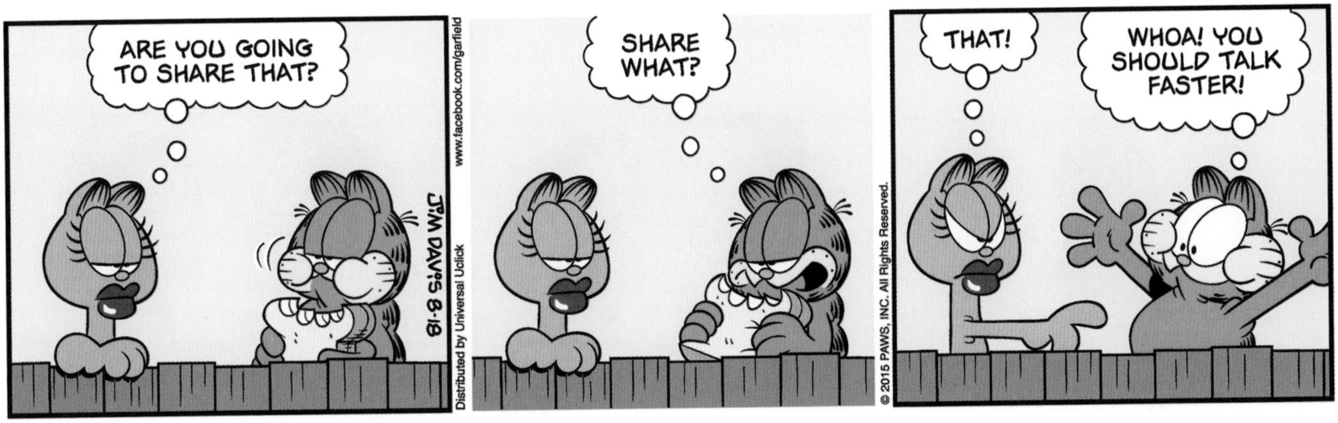
ARE YOU GOING TO SHARE THAT?
JIM DAVIS 8-18
www.facebook.com/garfield
Distributed by Universal Uclick
SHARE WHAT?
© 2015 PAWS, INC. All Rights Reserved.
THAT!
WHOA! YOU SHOULD TALK FASTER!

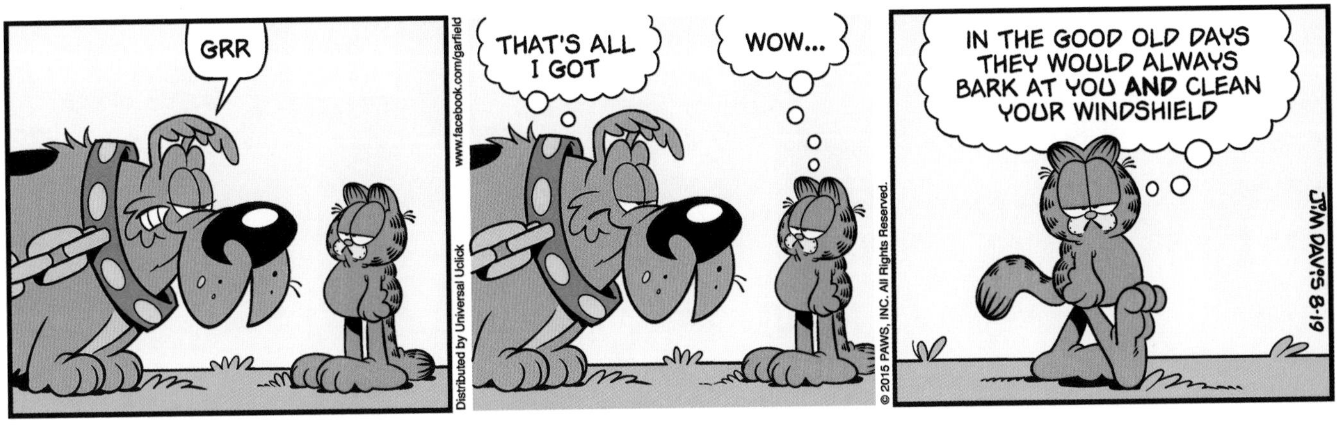
GRR
www.facebook.com/garfield
Distributed by Universal Uclick
THAT'S ALL I GOT
WOW...
© 2015 PAWS, INC. All Rights Reserved.
IN THE GOOD OLD DAYS THEY WOULD ALWAYS BARK AT YOU AND CLEAN YOUR WINDSHIELD
JIM DAVIS 8-19

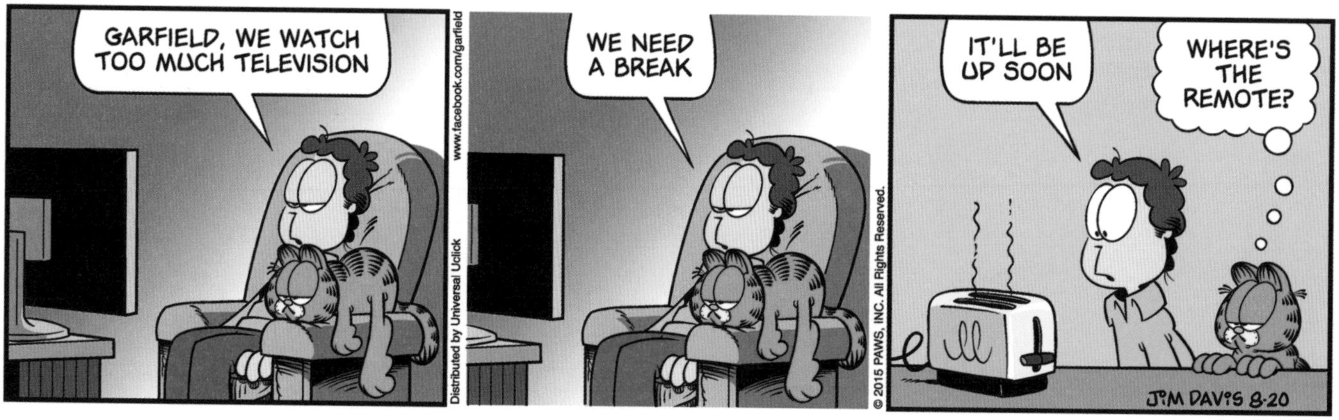
GARFIELD, WE WATCH TOO MUCH TELEVISION
WE NEED A BREAK
IT'LL BE UP SOON
WHERE'S THE REMOTE?
www.facebook.com/garfield Distributed by Universal Uclick
© 2015 PAWS, INC. All Rights Reserved.
JIM DAVIS 8-20

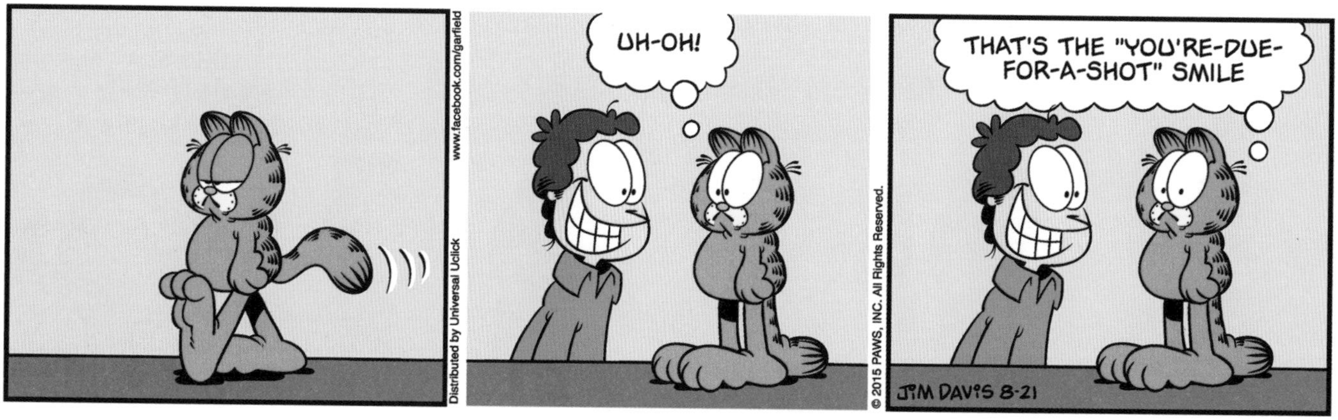
UH-OH!
THAT'S THE "YOU'RE-DUE-FOR-A-SHOT" SMILE
www.facebook.com/garfield Distributed by Universal Uclick
© 2015 PAWS, INC. All Rights Reserved.
JIM DAVIS 8-21

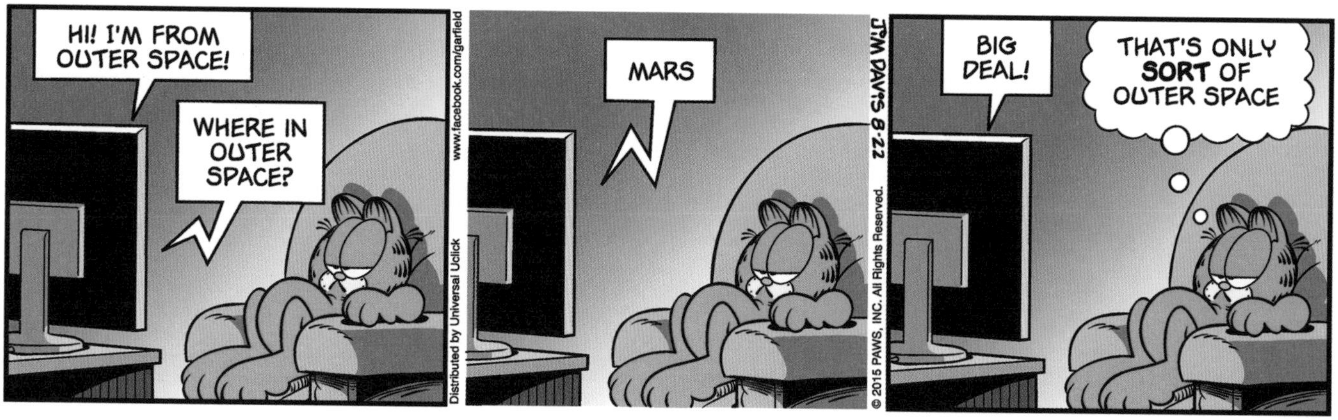
HI! I'M FROM OUTER SPACE!
WHERE IN OUTER SPACE?
MARS
BIG DEAL!
THAT'S ONLY **SORT** OF OUTER SPACE
www.facebook.com/garfield Distributed by Universal Uclick
© 2015 PAWS, INC. All Rights Reserved.
JIM DAVIS 8-22

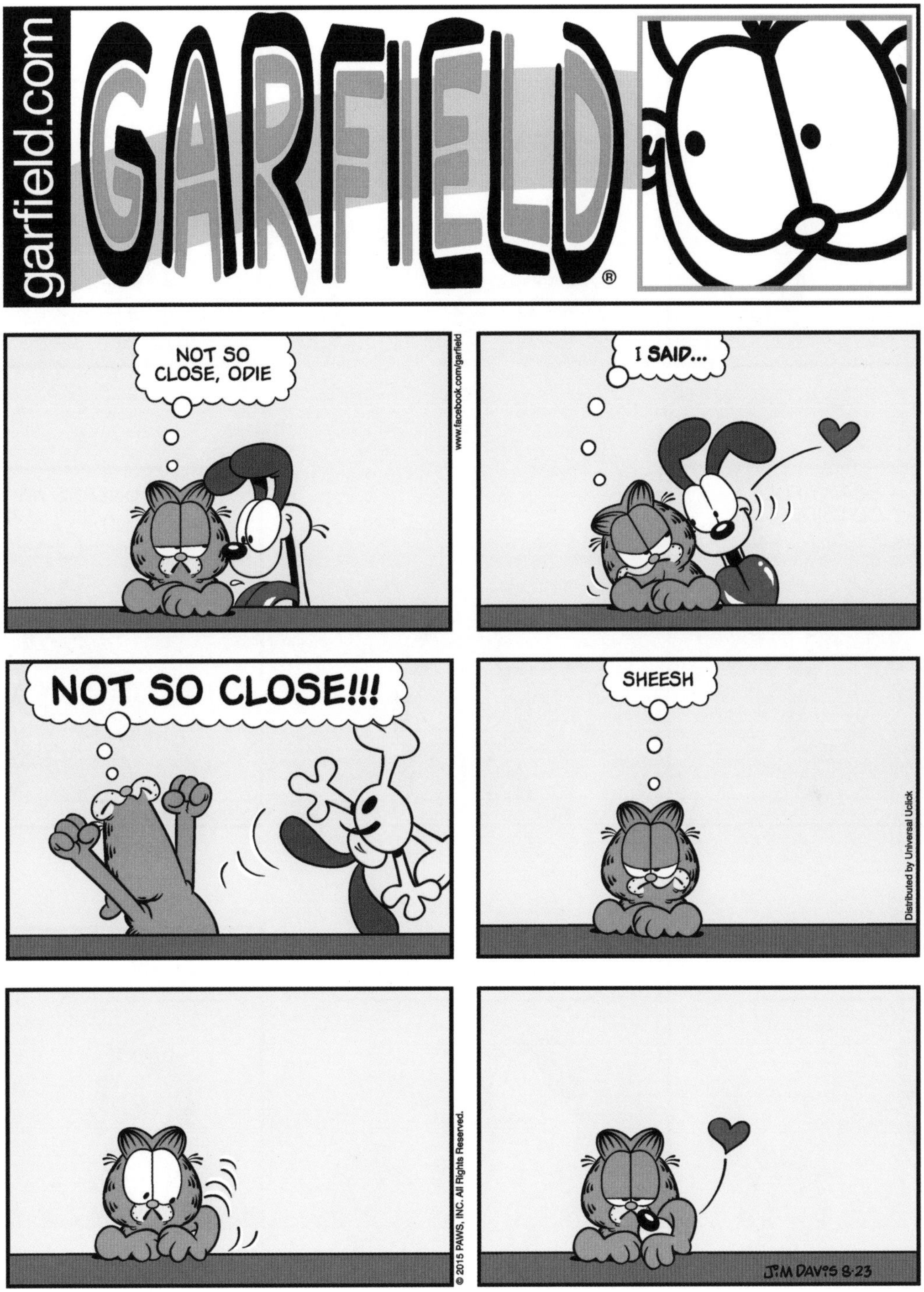
garfield.com
GARFIELD®
www.facebook.com/garfield
NOT SO CLOSE, ODIE
I SAID...
NOT SO CLOSE!!!
SHEESH
Distributed by Universal Uclick
© 2015 PAWS, INC. All Rights Reserved.
JIM DAVIS 8-23

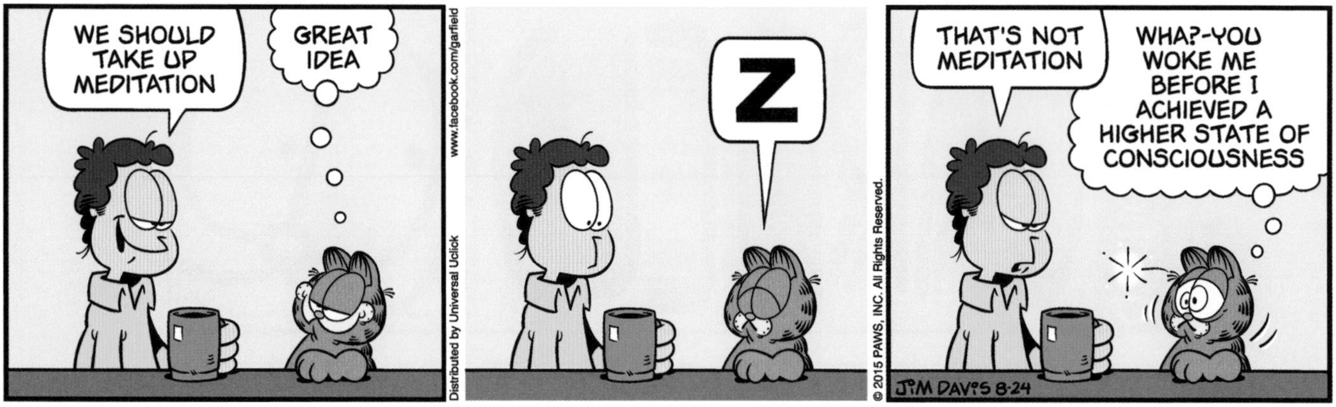
WE SHOULD TAKE UP MEDITATION
GREAT IDEA
Z
THAT'S NOT MEDITATION
WHA?-YOU WOKE ME BEFORE I ACHIEVED A HIGHER STATE OF CONSCIOUSNESS
JIM DAVIS 8-24
Distributed by Universal Uclick www.facebook.com/garfield
© 2015 PAWS, INC. All Rights Reserved.

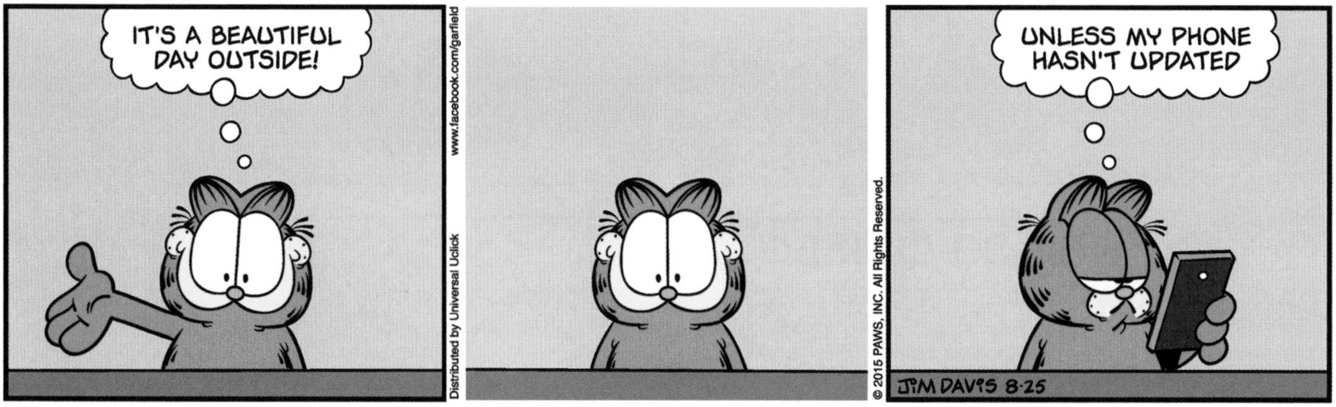
IT'S A BEAUTIFUL DAY OUTSIDE!
UNLESS MY PHONE HASN'T UPDATED
JIM DAVIS 8-25
Distributed by Universal Uclick www.facebook.com/garfield
© 2015 PAWS, INC. All Rights Reserved.

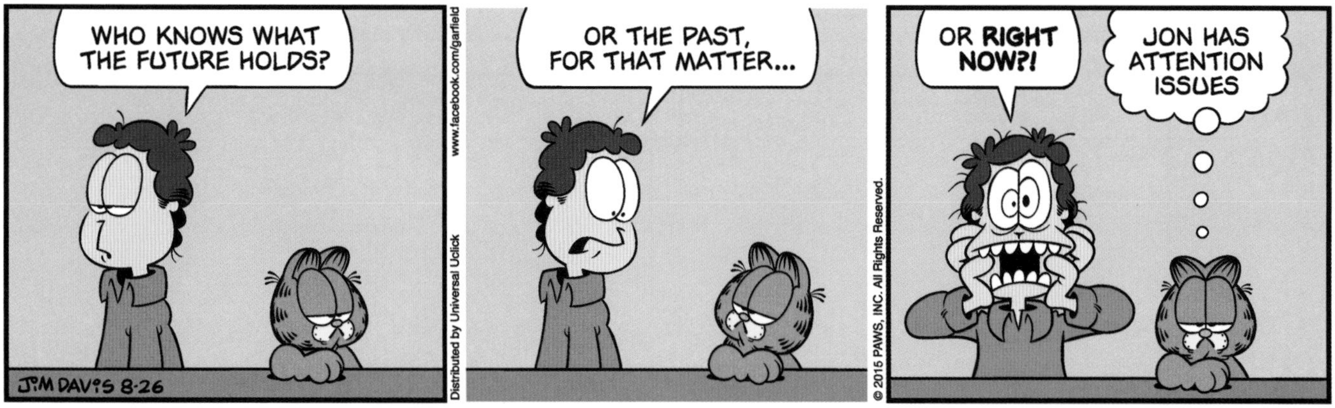
WHO KNOWS WHAT THE FUTURE HOLDS?
OR THE PAST, FOR THAT MATTER...
OR **RIGHT NOW?!**
JON HAS ATTENTION ISSUES
JIM DAVIS 8-26
Distributed by Universal Uclick www.facebook.com/garfield
© 2015 PAWS, INC. All Rights Reserved.

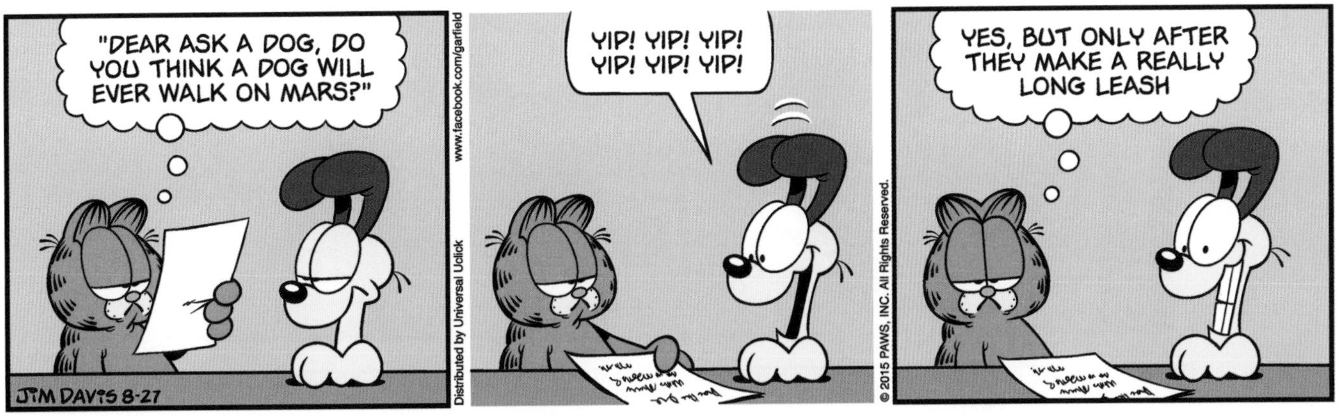
"DEAR ASK A DOG, DO YOU THINK A DOG WILL EVER WALK ON MARS?"
JIM DAVIS 8-27
YIP! YIP! YIP! YIP! YIP! YIP!
YES, BUT ONLY AFTER THEY MAKE A REALLY LONG LEASH
Distributed by Universal Uclick www.facebook.com/garfield
© 2015 PAWS, INC. All Rights Reserved.

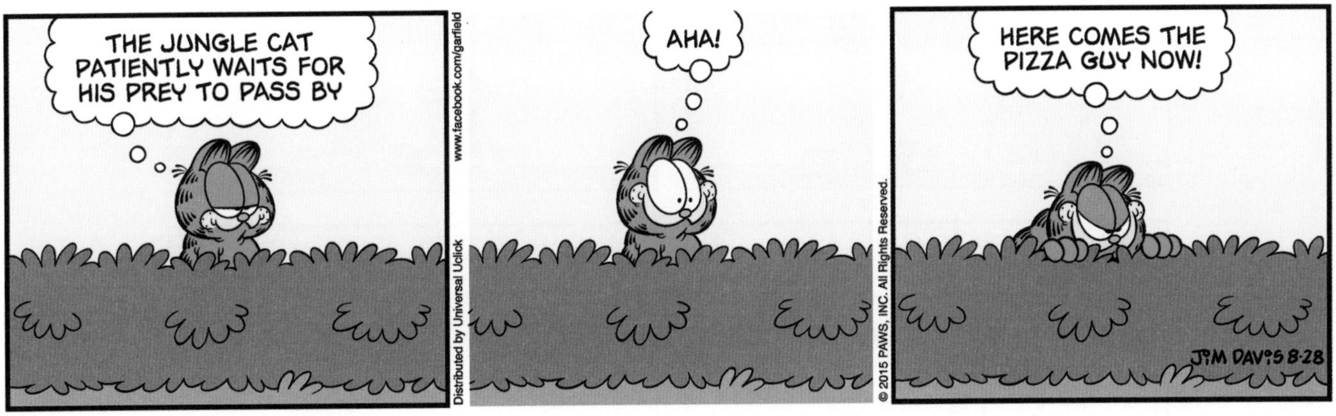
THE JUNGLE CAT PATIENTLY WAITS FOR HIS PREY TO PASS BY
AHA!
HERE COMES THE PIZZA GUY NOW!
JIM DAVIS 8-28
Distributed by Universal Uclick www.facebook.com/garfield
© 2015 PAWS, INC. All Rights Reserved.

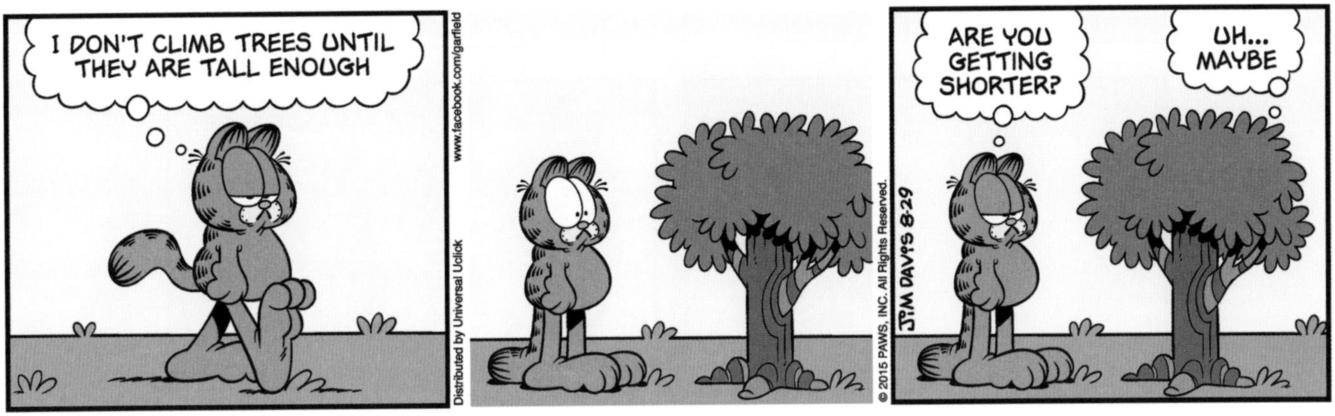
I DON'T CLIMB TREES UNTIL THEY ARE TALL ENOUGH
ARE YOU GETTING SHORTER?
UH... MAYBE
JIM DAVIS 8-29
Distributed by Universal Uclick www.facebook.com/garfield
© 2015 PAWS, INC. All Rights Reserved.

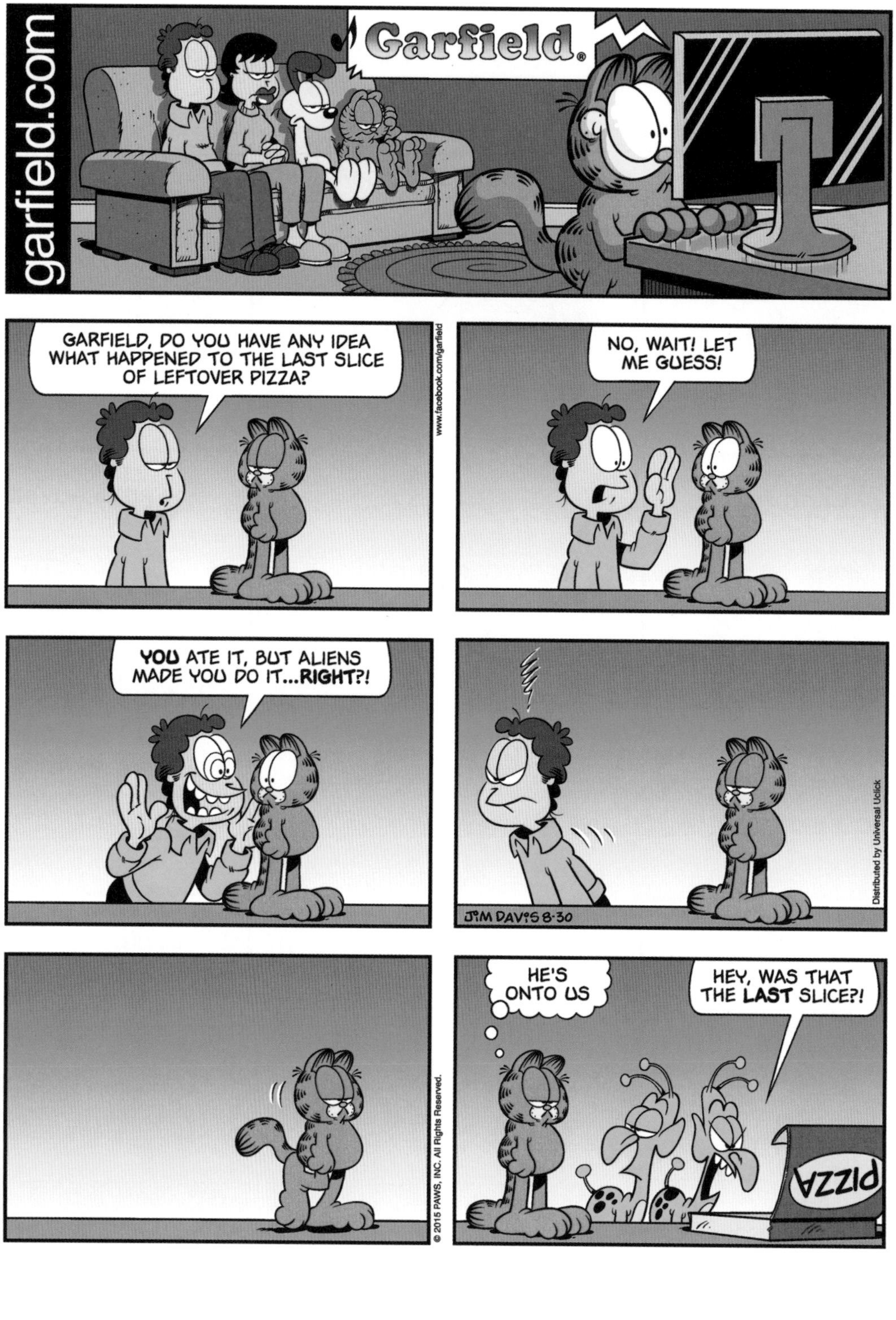

garfield.com
Garfield
GARFIELD, DO YOU HAVE ANY IDEA WHAT HAPPENED TO THE LAST SLICE OF LEFTOVER PIZZA?
www.facebook.com/garfield
NO, WAIT! LET ME GUESS!
YOU ATE IT, BUT ALIENS MADE YOU DO IT...RIGHT?!
JIM DAVIS 8-30
Distributed by Universal Uclick
© 2015 PAWS, INC. All Rights Reserved.
HE'S ONTO US
HEY, WAS THAT THE LAST SLICE?!
PIZZA

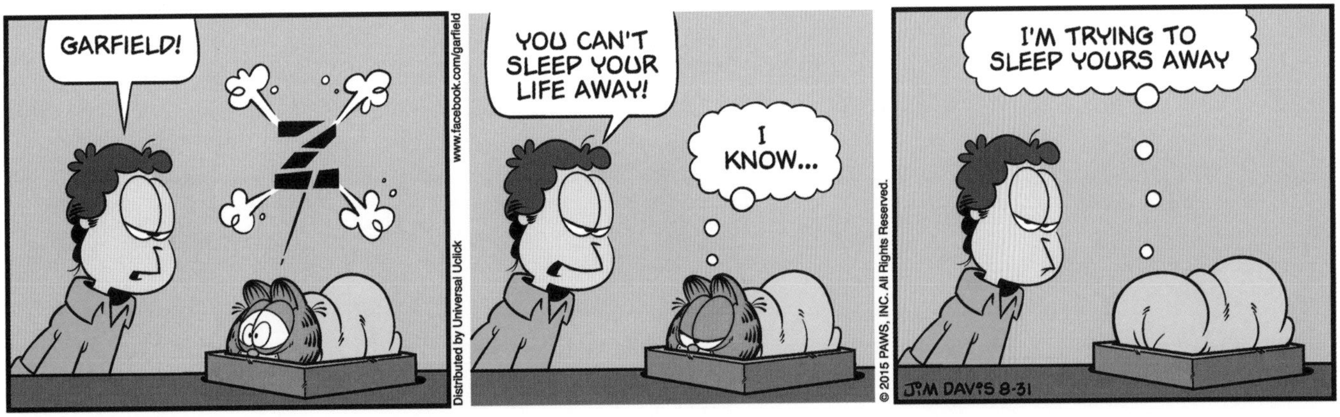
GARFIELD!
Z
YOU CAN'T SLEEP YOUR LIFE AWAY!
I KNOW...
I'M TRYING TO SLEEP YOURS AWAY
www.facebook.com/garfield
Distributed by Universal Uclick
© 2015 PAWS, INC. All Rights Reserved.
JIM DAVIS 8-31

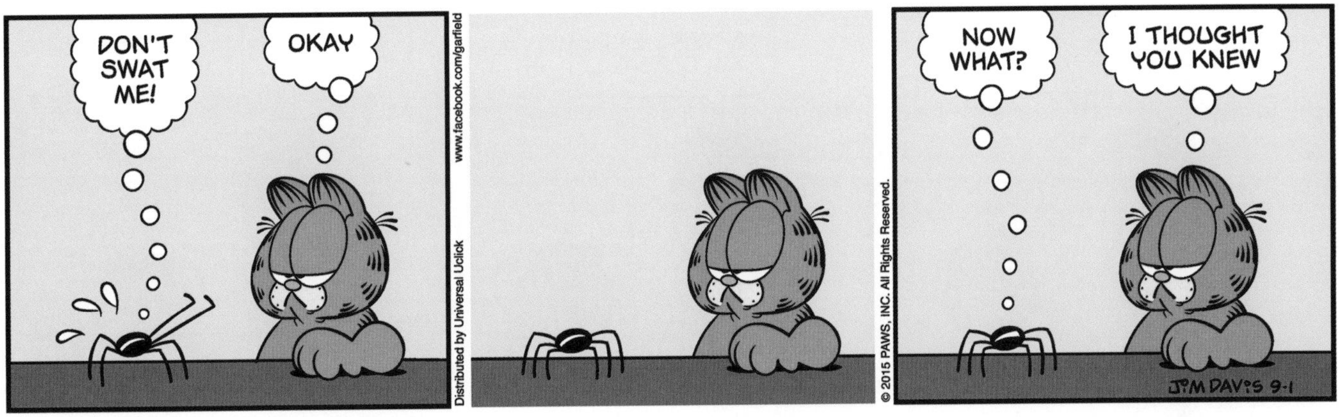
DON'T SWAT ME!
OKAY
NOW WHAT?
I THOUGHT YOU KNEW
www.facebook.com/garfield
Distributed by Universal Uclick
© 2015 PAWS, INC. All Rights Reserved.
JIM DAVIS 9-1

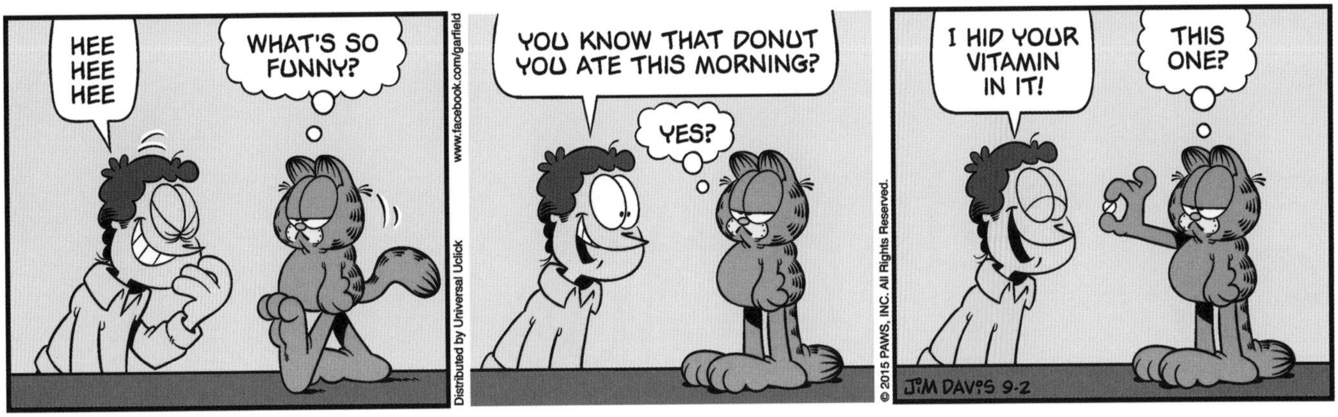
HEE HEE HEE
WHAT'S SO FUNNY?
YOU KNOW THAT DONUT YOU ATE THIS MORNING?
YES?
I HID YOUR VITAMIN IN IT!
THIS ONE?
www.facebook.com/garfield
Distributed by Universal Uclick
© 2015 PAWS, INC. All Rights Reserved.
JIM DAVIS 9-2

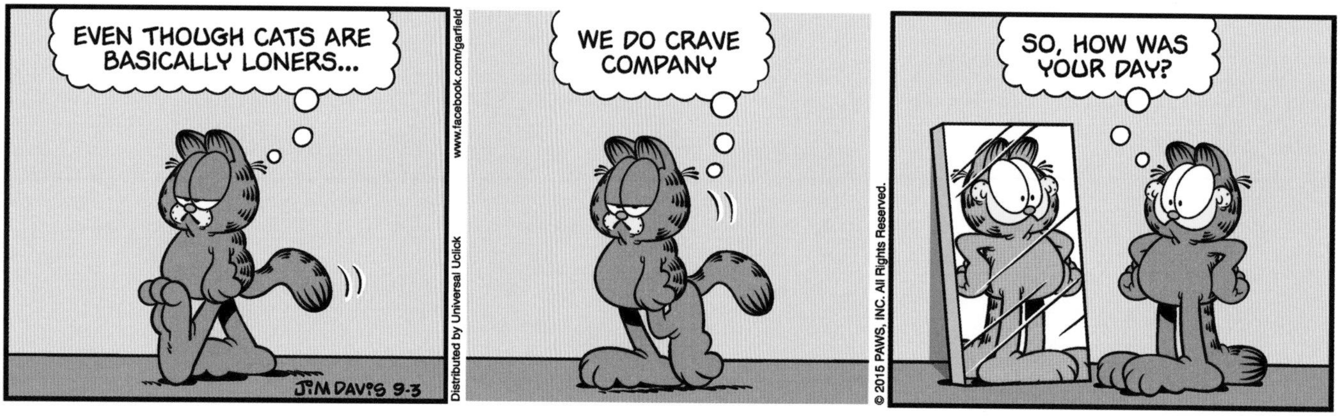
EVEN THOUGH CATS ARE BASICALLY LONERS...
JIM DAVIS 9-3
Distributed by Universal Uclick
www.facebook.com/garfield
WE DO CRAVE COMPANY
© 2015 PAWS, INC. All Rights Reserved.
SO, HOW WAS YOUR DAY?

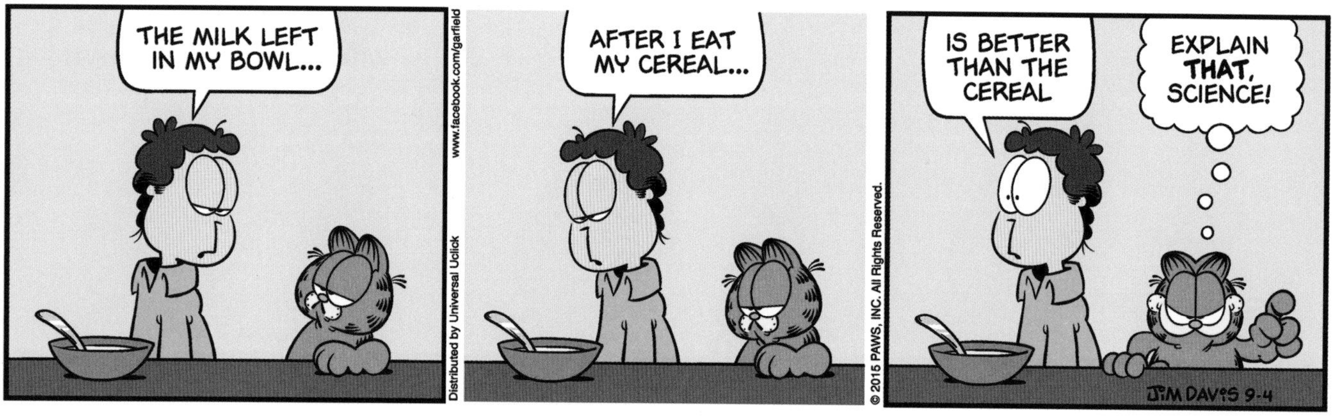
THE MILK LEFT IN MY BOWL...
Distributed by Universal Uclick
www.facebook.com/garfield
AFTER I EAT MY CEREAL...
© 2015 PAWS, INC. All Rights Reserved.
IS BETTER THAN THE CEREAL
EXPLAIN **THAT**, SCIENCE!
JIM DAVIS 9-4

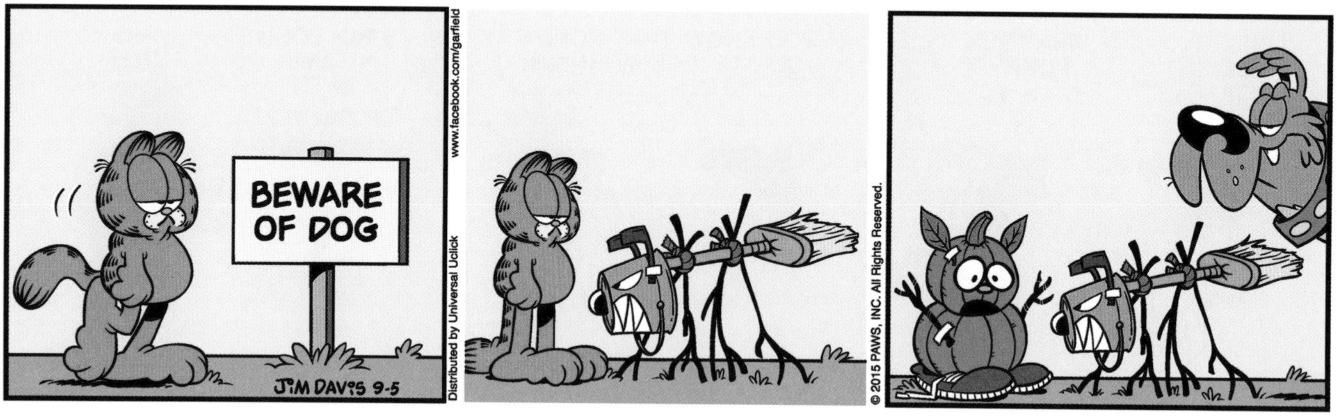
BEWARE OF DOG
JIM DAVIS 9-5
Distributed by Universal Uclick
www.facebook.com/garfield
© 2015 PAWS, INC. All Rights Reserved.

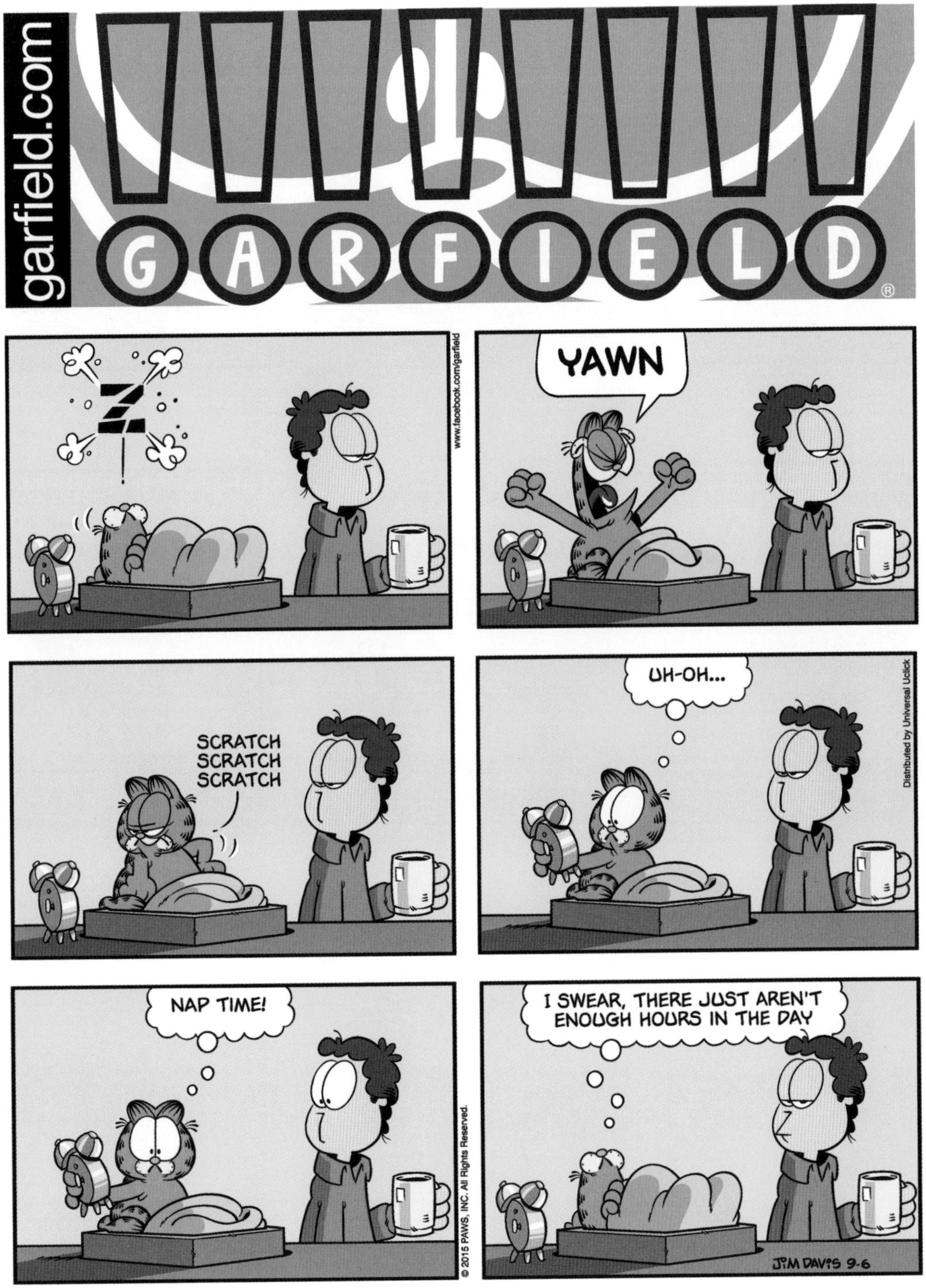
garfield.com
GARFIELD
www.facebook.com/garfield
YAWN
SCRATCH
SCRATCH
SCRATCH
UH-OH...
Distributed by Universal Uclick
NAP TIME!
© 2015 PAWS, INC. All Rights Reserved.
I SWEAR, THERE JUST AREN'T ENOUGH HOURS IN THE DAY
JIM DAVIS 9-6

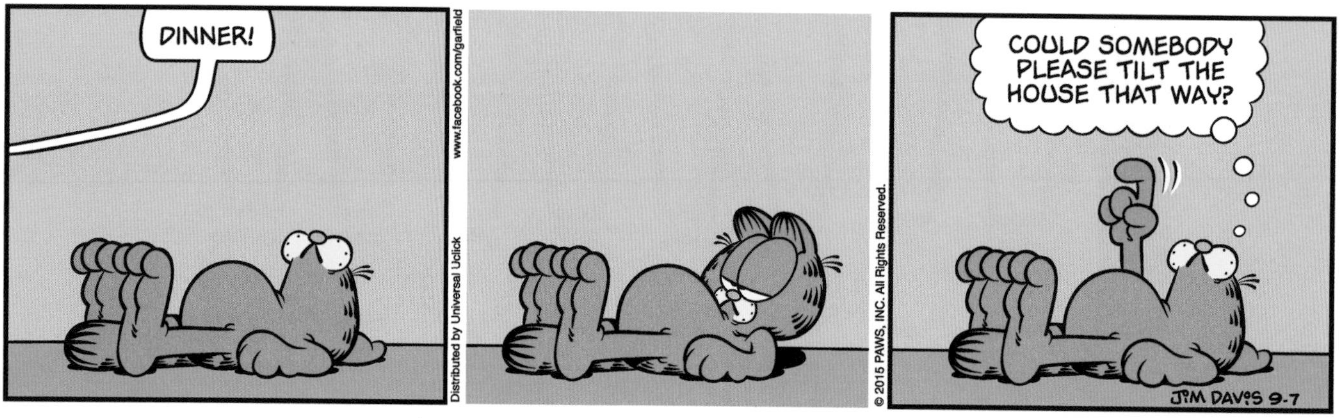
DINNER!
www.facebook.com/garfield
Distributed by Universal Uclick
© 2015 PAWS, INC. All Rights Reserved.
COULD SOMEBODY PLEASE TILT THE HOUSE THAT WAY?
JIM DAVIS 9-7

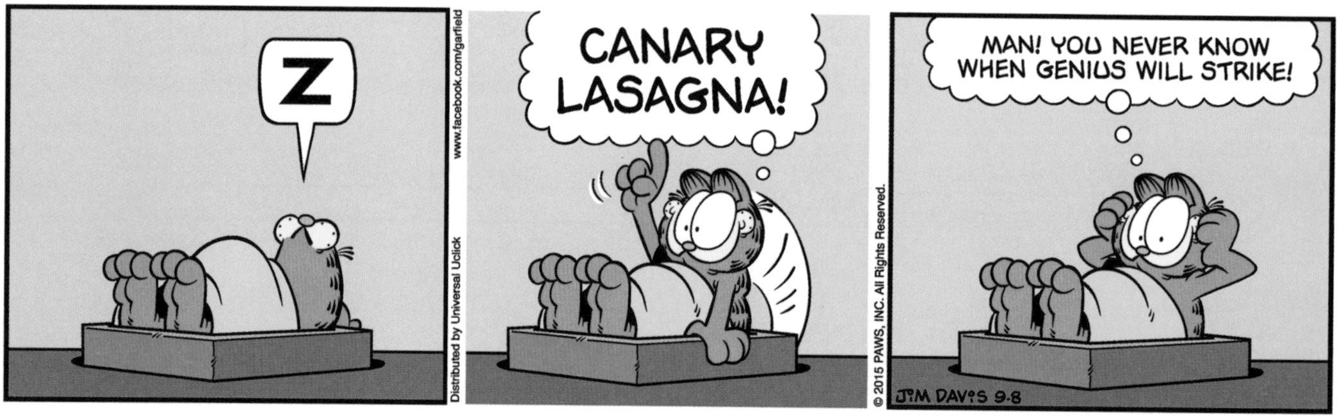
Z
www.facebook.com/garfield
Distributed by Universal Uclick
CANARY LASAGNA!
© 2015 PAWS, INC. All Rights Reserved.
MAN! YOU NEVER KNOW WHEN GENIUS WILL STRIKE!
JIM DAVIS 9-8

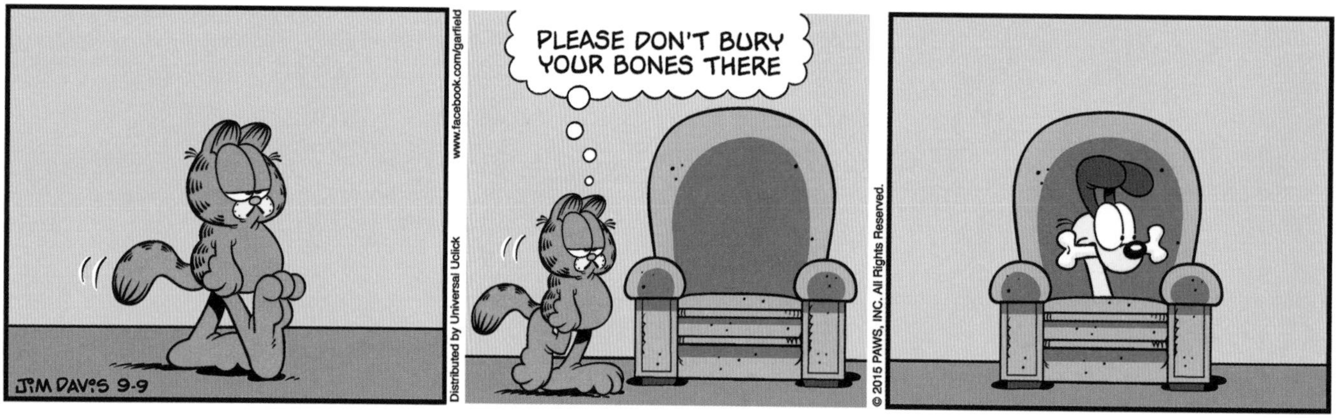
JIM DAVIS 9-9
www.facebook.com/garfield
Distributed by Universal Uclick
PLEASE DON'T BURY YOUR BONES THERE
© 2015 PAWS, INC. All Rights Reserved.

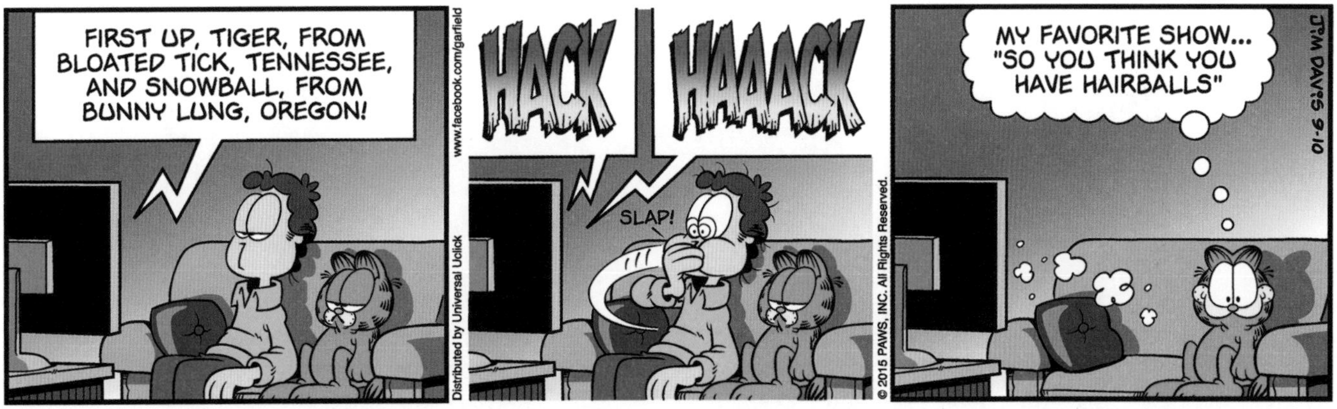
FIRST UP, TIGER, FROM BLOATED TICK, TENNESSEE, AND SNOWBALL, FROM BUNNY LUNG, OREGON!
www.facebook.com/garfield
Distributed by Universal Uclick
HACK
HAAACK
SLAP!
© 2015 PAWS, INC. All Rights Reserved.
MY FAVORITE SHOW... "SO YOU THINK YOU HAVE HAIRBALLS"
JIM DAVIS 9-10

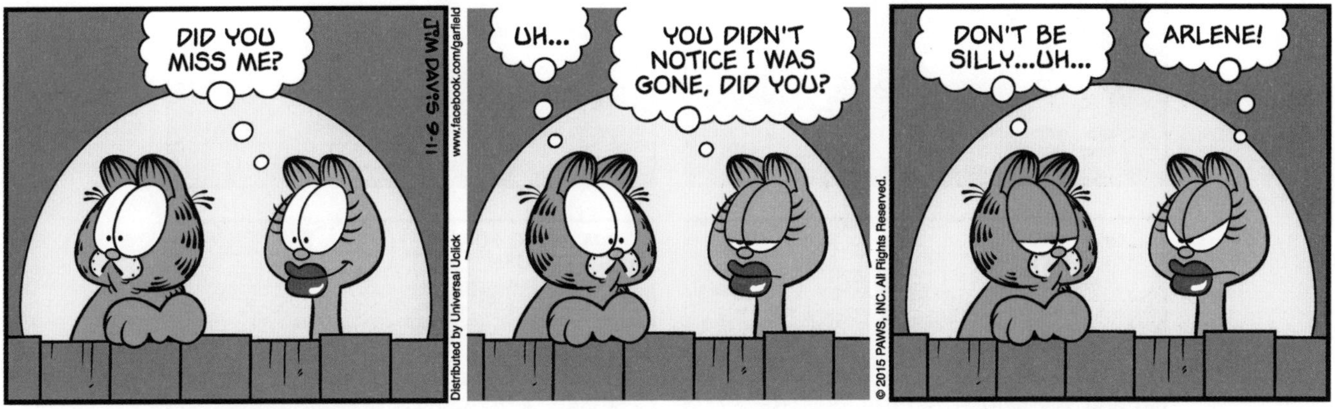
DID YOU MISS ME?
JIM DAVIS 9-11
www.facebook.com/garfield
Distributed by Universal Uclick
UH...
YOU DIDN'T NOTICE I WAS GONE, DID YOU?
© 2015 PAWS, INC. All Rights Reserved.
DON'T BE SILLY...UH...
ARLENE!

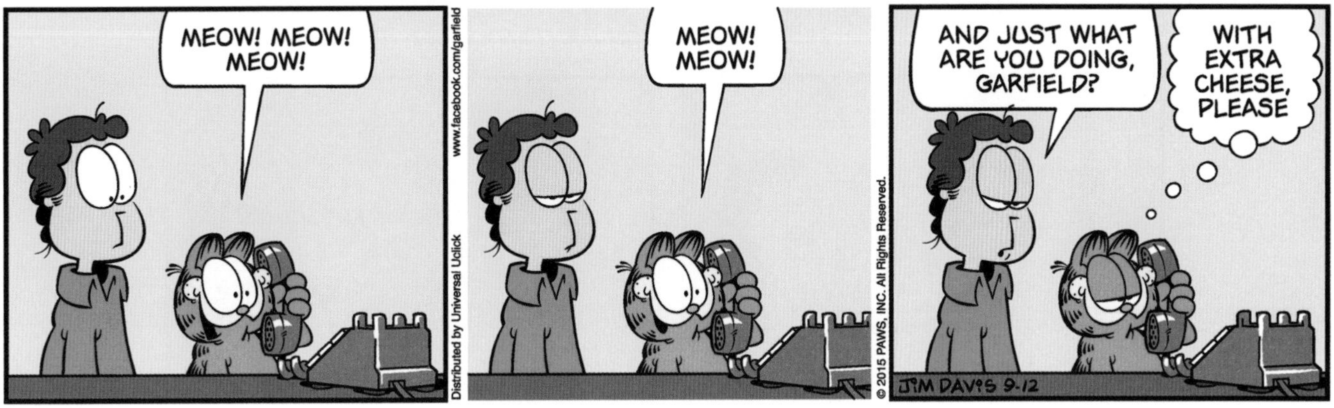
MEOW! MEOW! MEOW!
www.facebook.com/garfield
Distributed by Universal Uclick
MEOW! MEOW!
© 2015 PAWS, INC. All Rights Reserved.
AND JUST WHAT ARE YOU DOING, GARFIELD?
WITH EXTRA CHEESE, PLEASE
JIM DAVIS 9-12

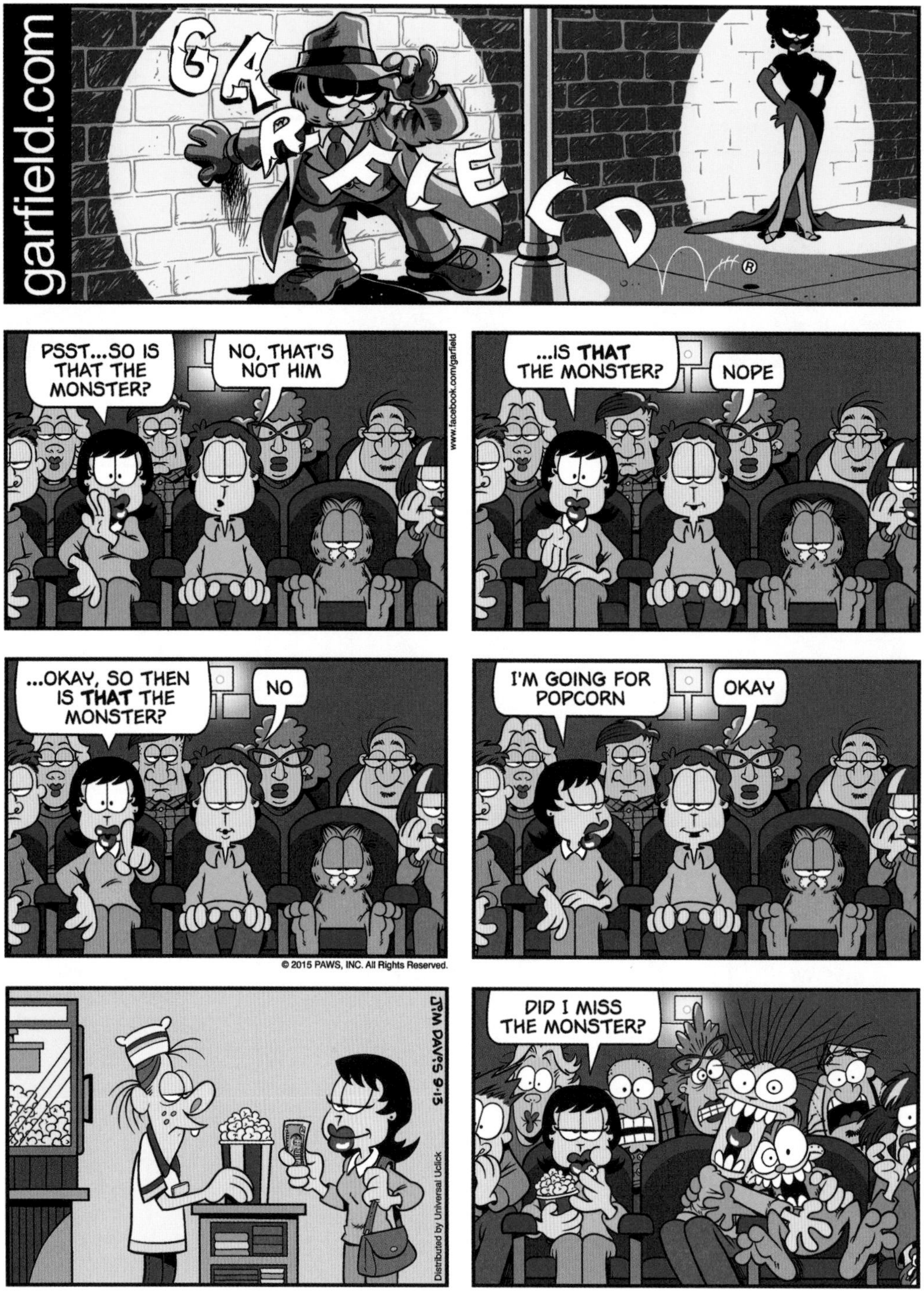
garfield.com
GARFIELD
PSST...SO IS THAT THE MONSTER?
NO, THAT'S NOT HIM
www.facebook.com/garfield
...IS THAT THE MONSTER?
NOPE
...OKAY, SO THEN IS THAT THE MONSTER?
NO
I'M GOING FOR POPCORN
OKAY
© 2015 PAWS, INC. All Rights Reserved.
JPM DAVIS 9-13
Distributed by Universal Uclick
DID I MISS THE MONSTER?

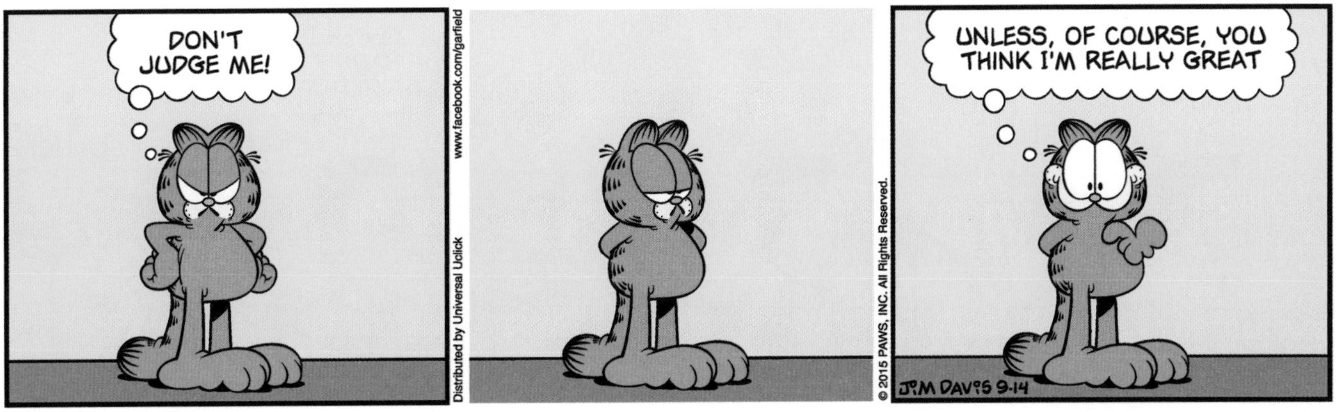
DON'T JUDGE ME!
Distributed by Universal Uclick www.facebook.com/garfield
UNLESS, OF COURSE, YOU THINK I'M REALLY GREAT
© 2015 PAWS, INC. All Rights Reserved.
JIM DAVIS 9-14

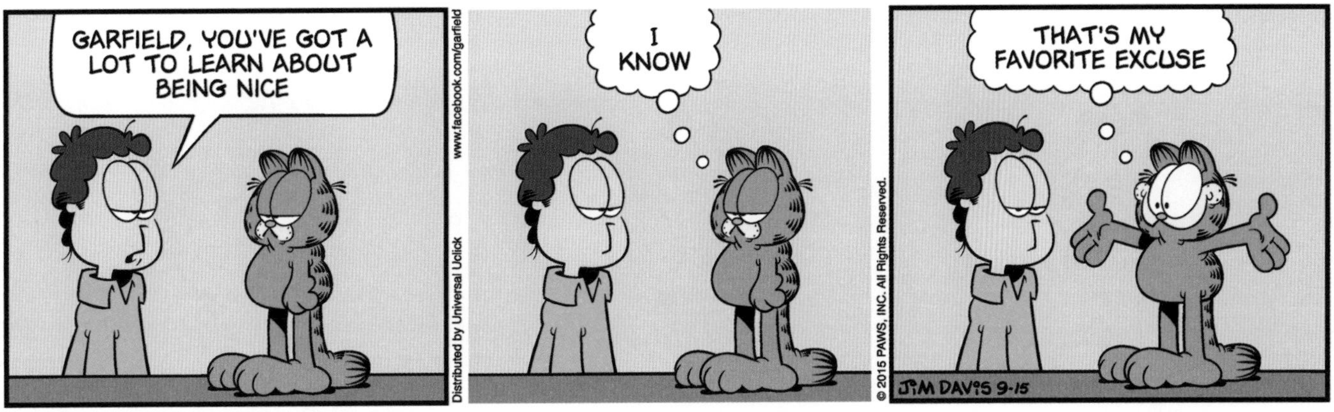
GARFIELD, YOU'VE GOT A LOT TO LEARN ABOUT BEING NICE
Distributed by Universal Uclick www.facebook.com/garfield
I KNOW
© 2015 PAWS, INC. All Rights Reserved.
THAT'S MY FAVORITE EXCUSE
JIM DAVIS 9-15

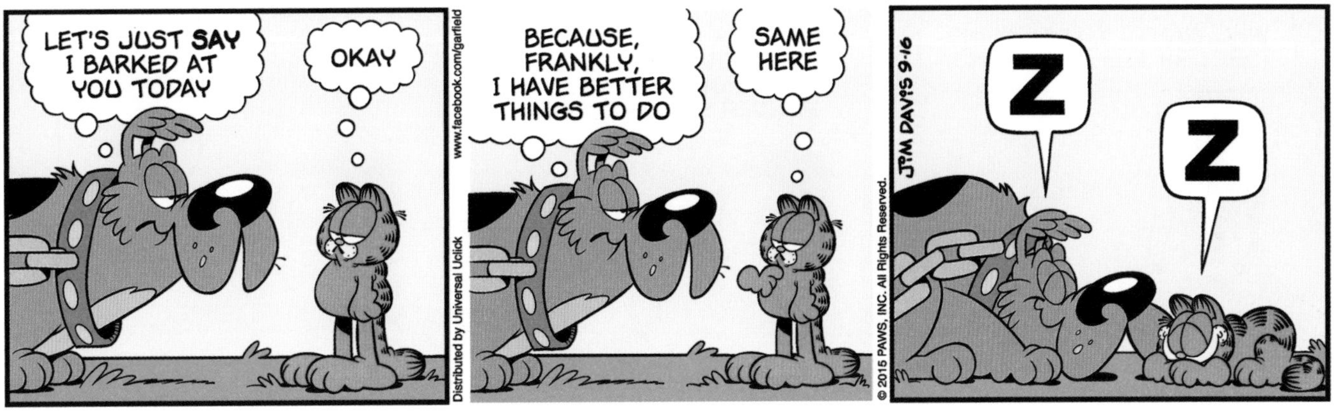
LET'S JUST **SAY** I BARKED AT YOU TODAY
OKAY
Distributed by Universal Uclick www.facebook.com/garfield
BECAUSE, FRANKLY, I HAVE BETTER THINGS TO DO
SAME HERE
© 2015 PAWS, INC. All Rights Reserved.
JIM DAVIS 9-16
Z
Z

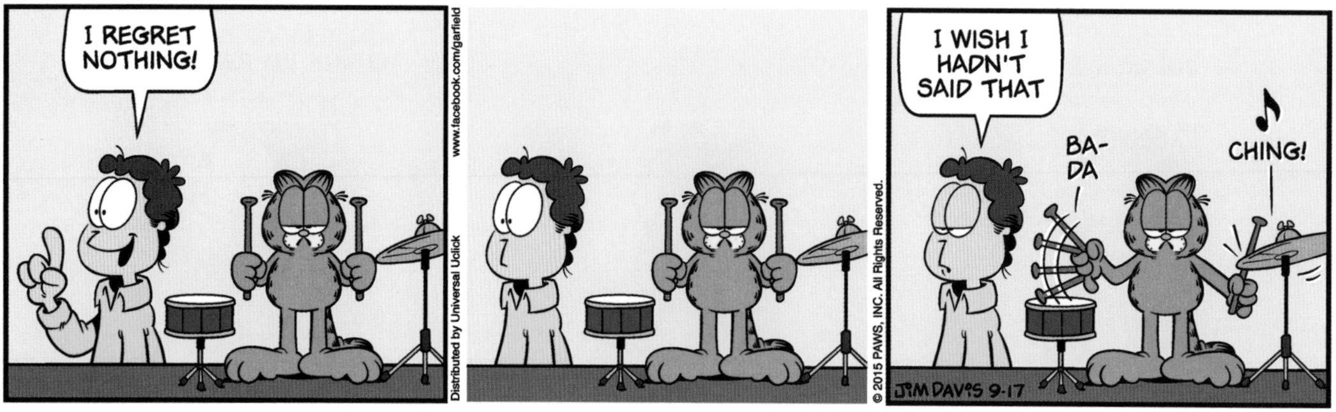
I REGRET NOTHING!
Distributed by Universal Uclick www.facebook.com/garfield
I WISH I HADN'T SAID THAT
BA-DA
CHING!
© 2015 PAWS, INC. All Rights Reserved.
JIM DAVIS 9-17

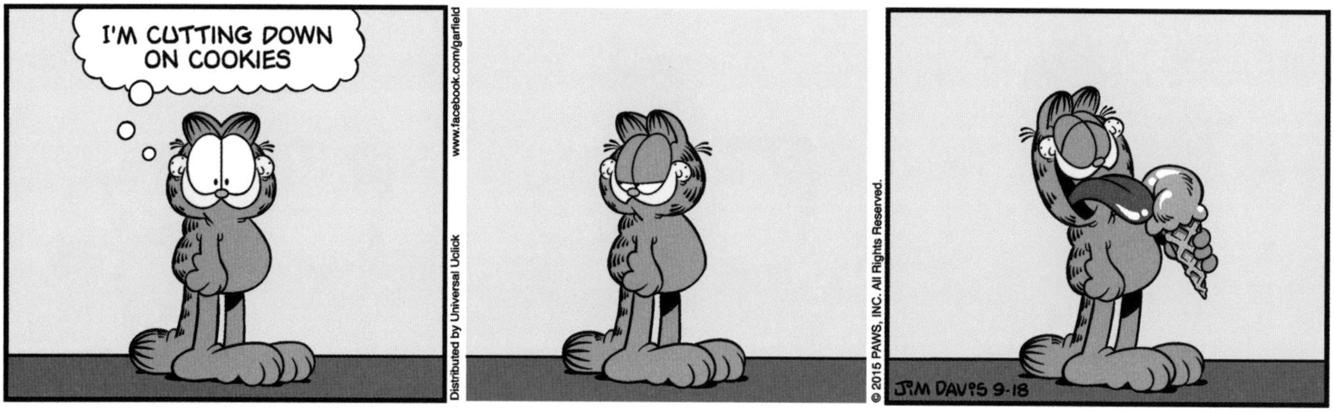
I'M CUTTING DOWN ON COOKIES
Distributed by Universal Uclick www.facebook.com/garfield
© 2015 PAWS, INC. All Rights Reserved.
JIM DAVIS 9-18

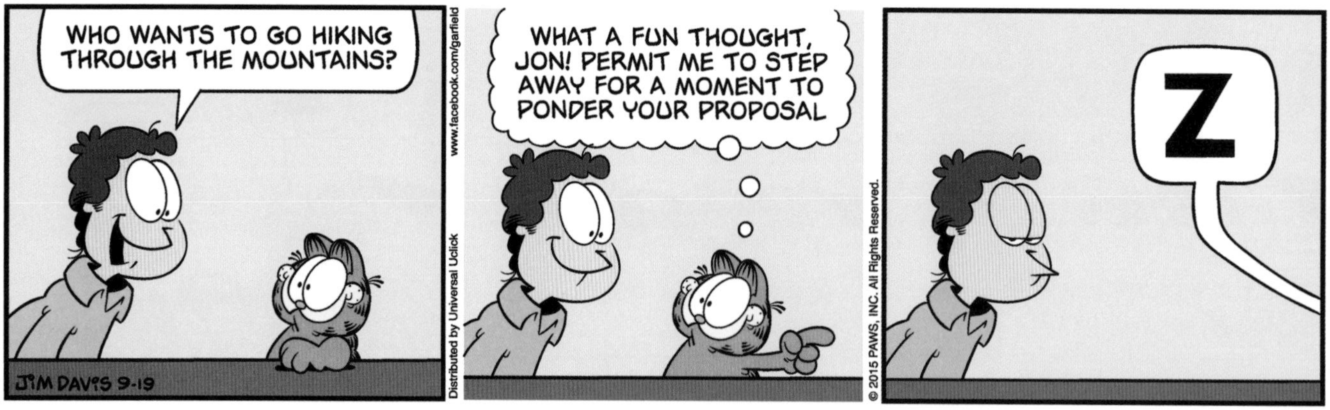
WHO WANTS TO GO HIKING THROUGH THE MOUNTAINS?
JIM DAVIS 9-19
Distributed by Universal Uclick www.facebook.com/garfield
WHAT A FUN THOUGHT, JON! PERMIT ME TO STEP AWAY FOR A MOMENT TO PONDER YOUR PROPOSAL
© 2015 PAWS, INC. All Rights Reserved.
Z

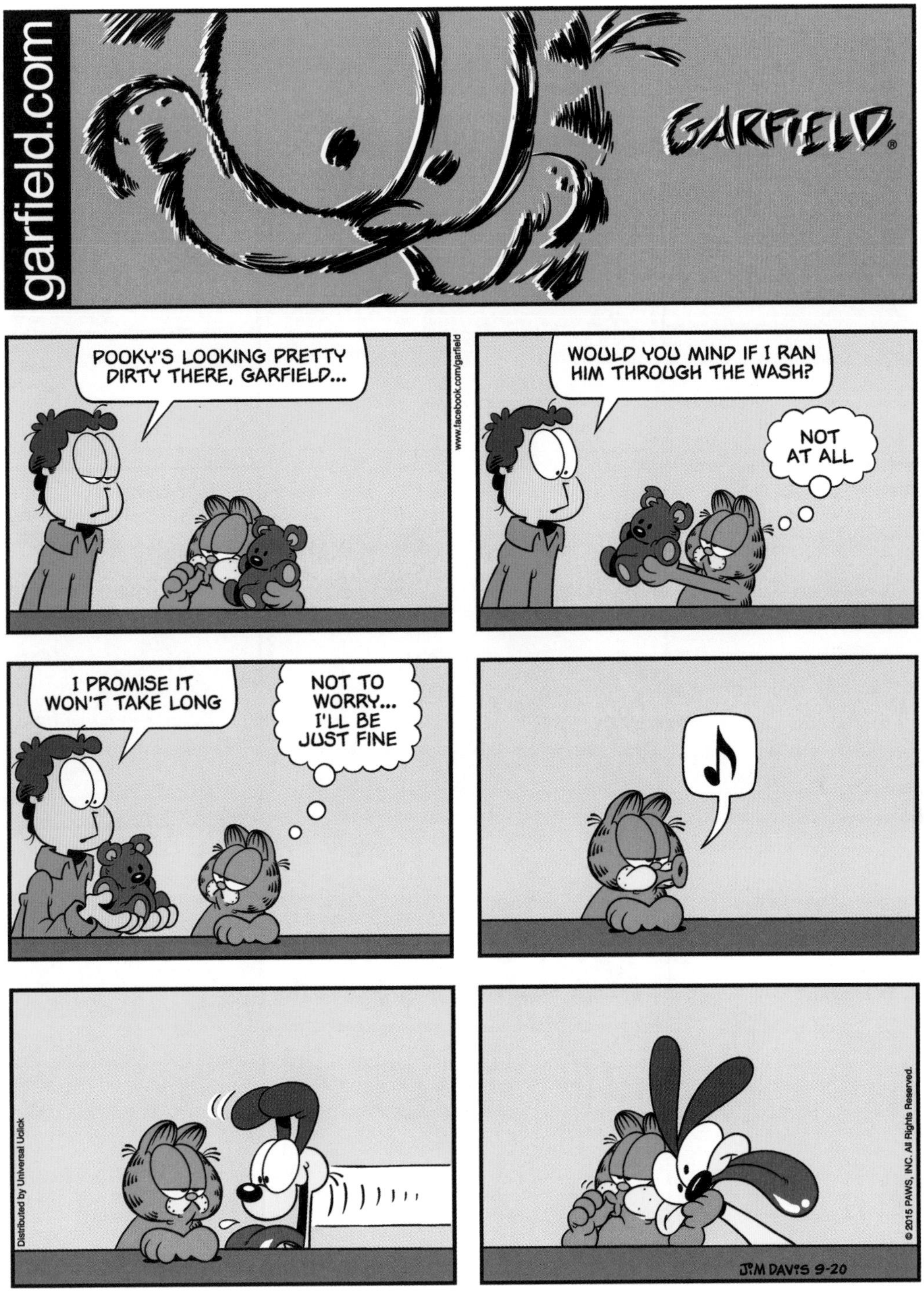
garfield.com
GARFIELD®
POOKY'S LOOKING PRETTY DIRTY THERE, GARFIELD...
www.facebook.com/garfield
WOULD YOU MIND IF I RAN HIM THROUGH THE WASH?
NOT AT ALL
I PROMISE IT WON'T TAKE LONG
NOT TO WORRY... I'LL BE JUST FINE
♪
Distributed by Universal Uclick
© 2015 PAWS, INC. All Rights Reserved.
JIM DAVIS 9-20

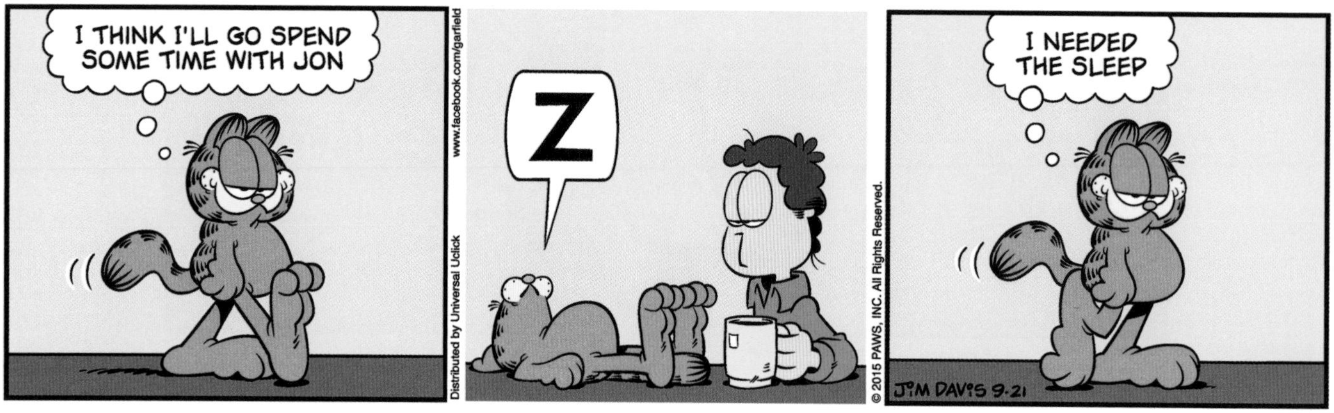
I THINK I'LL GO SPEND SOME TIME WITH JON
Distributed by Universal Uclick
www.facebook.com/garfield
Z
© 2015 PAWS, INC. All Rights Reserved.
I NEEDED THE SLEEP
JIM DAVIS 9-21

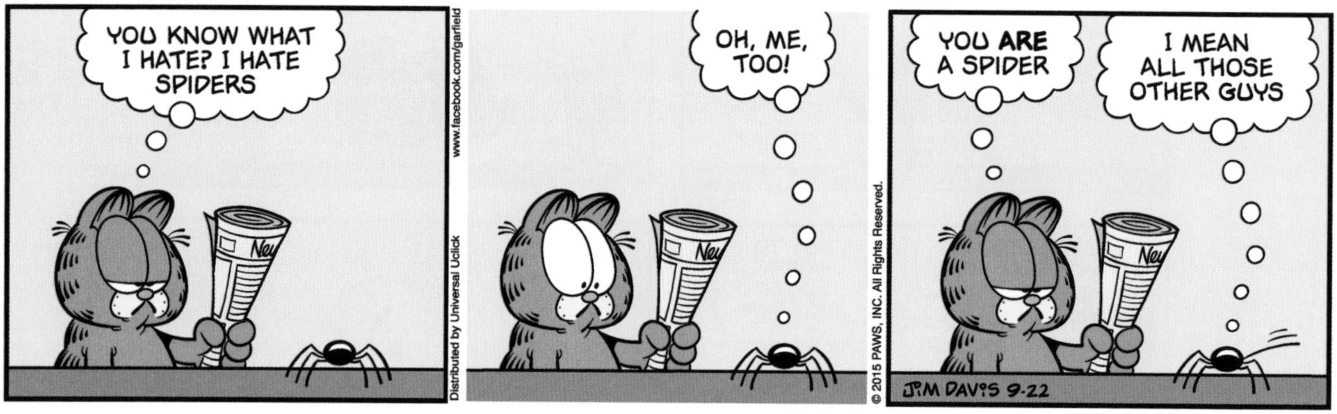
YOU KNOW WHAT I HATE? I HATE SPIDERS
Distributed by Universal Uclick
www.facebook.com/garfield
OH, ME, TOO!
© 2015 PAWS, INC. All Rights Reserved.
YOU **ARE** A SPIDER
I MEAN ALL THOSE OTHER GUYS
JIM DAVIS 9-22

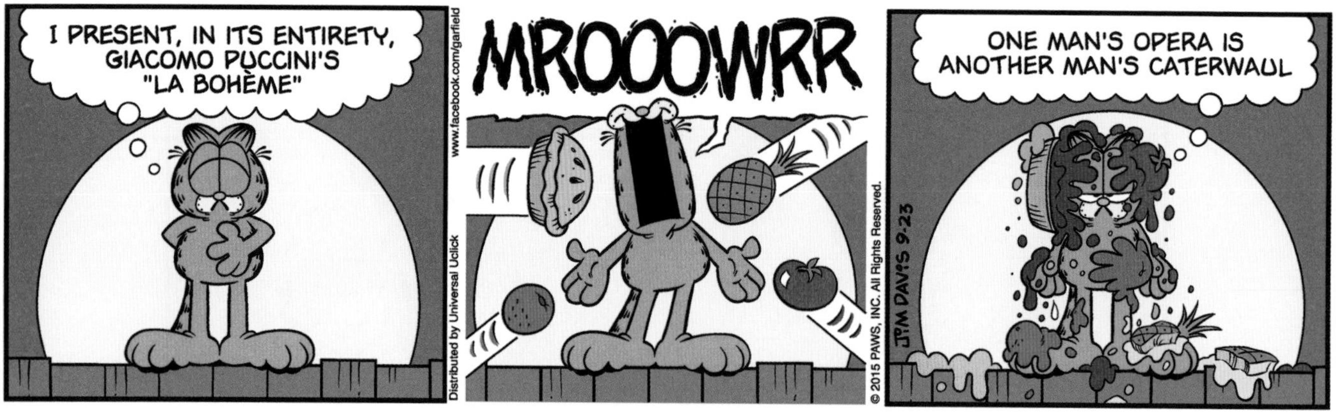
I PRESENT, IN ITS ENTIRETY, GIACOMO PUCCINI'S "LA BOHÈME"
Distributed by Universal Uclick
www.facebook.com/garfield
MROOOWRR
© 2015 PAWS, INC. All Rights Reserved.
JIM DAVIS 9-23
ONE MAN'S OPERA IS ANOTHER MAN'S CATERWAUL

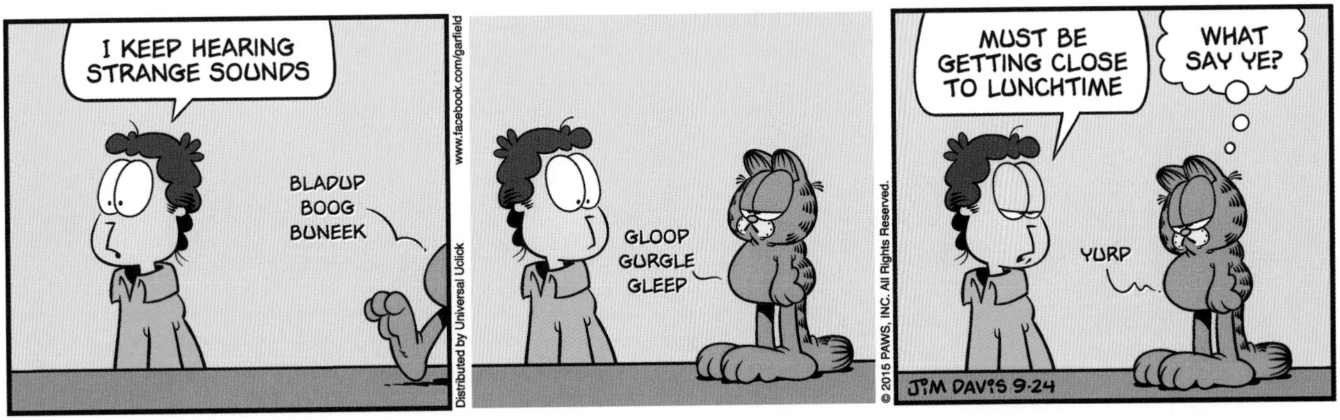
I KEEP HEARING STRANGE SOUNDS
BLADUP BOOG BUNEEK
www.facebook.com/garfield
Distributed by Universal Uclick
GLOOP GURGLE GLEEP
© 2015 PAWS, INC. All Rights Reserved.
MUST BE GETTING CLOSE TO LUNCHTIME
WHAT SAY YE?
YURP
JIM DAVIS 9-24

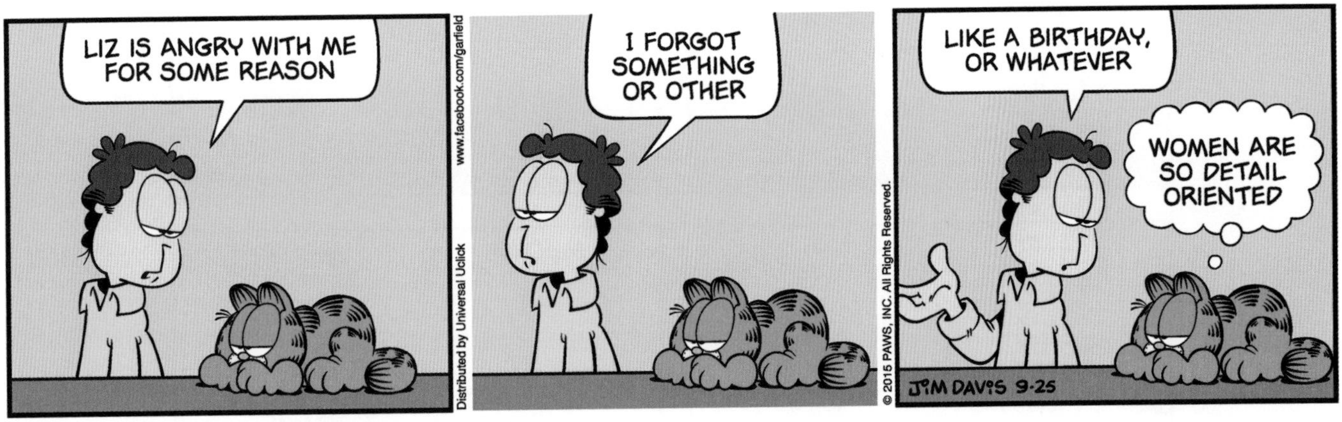
LIZ IS ANGRY WITH ME FOR SOME REASON
www.facebook.com/garfield
Distributed by Universal Uclick
I FORGOT SOMETHING OR OTHER
© 2015 PAWS, INC. All Rights Reserved.
LIKE A BIRTHDAY, OR WHATEVER
WOMEN ARE SO DETAIL ORIENTED
JIM DAVIS 9-25

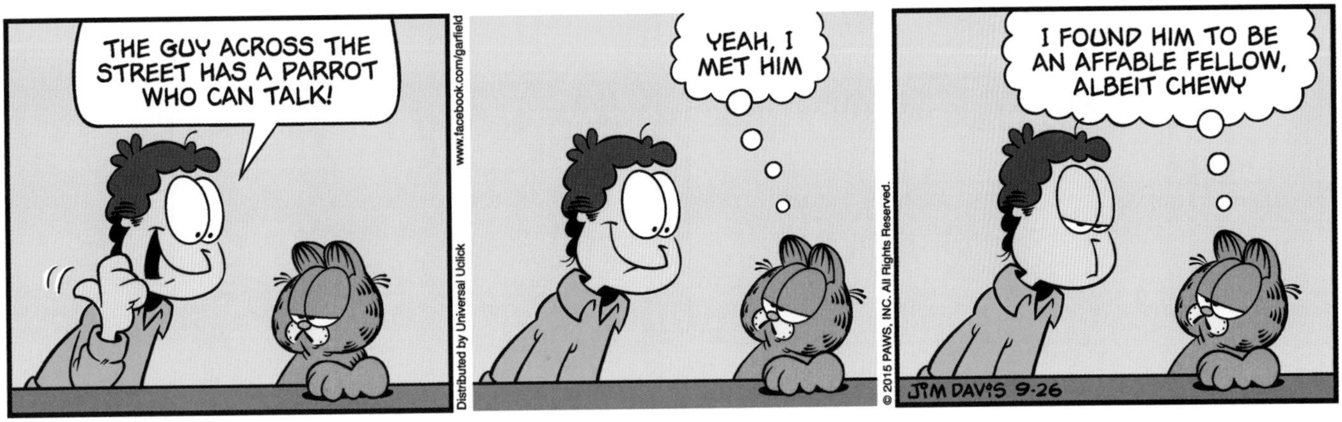
THE GUY ACROSS THE STREET HAS A PARROT WHO CAN TALK!
www.facebook.com/garfield
Distributed by Universal Uclick
YEAH, I MET HIM
© 2015 PAWS, INC. All Rights Reserved.
I FOUND HIM TO BE AN AFFABLE FELLOW, ALBEIT CHEWY
JIM DAVIS 9-26

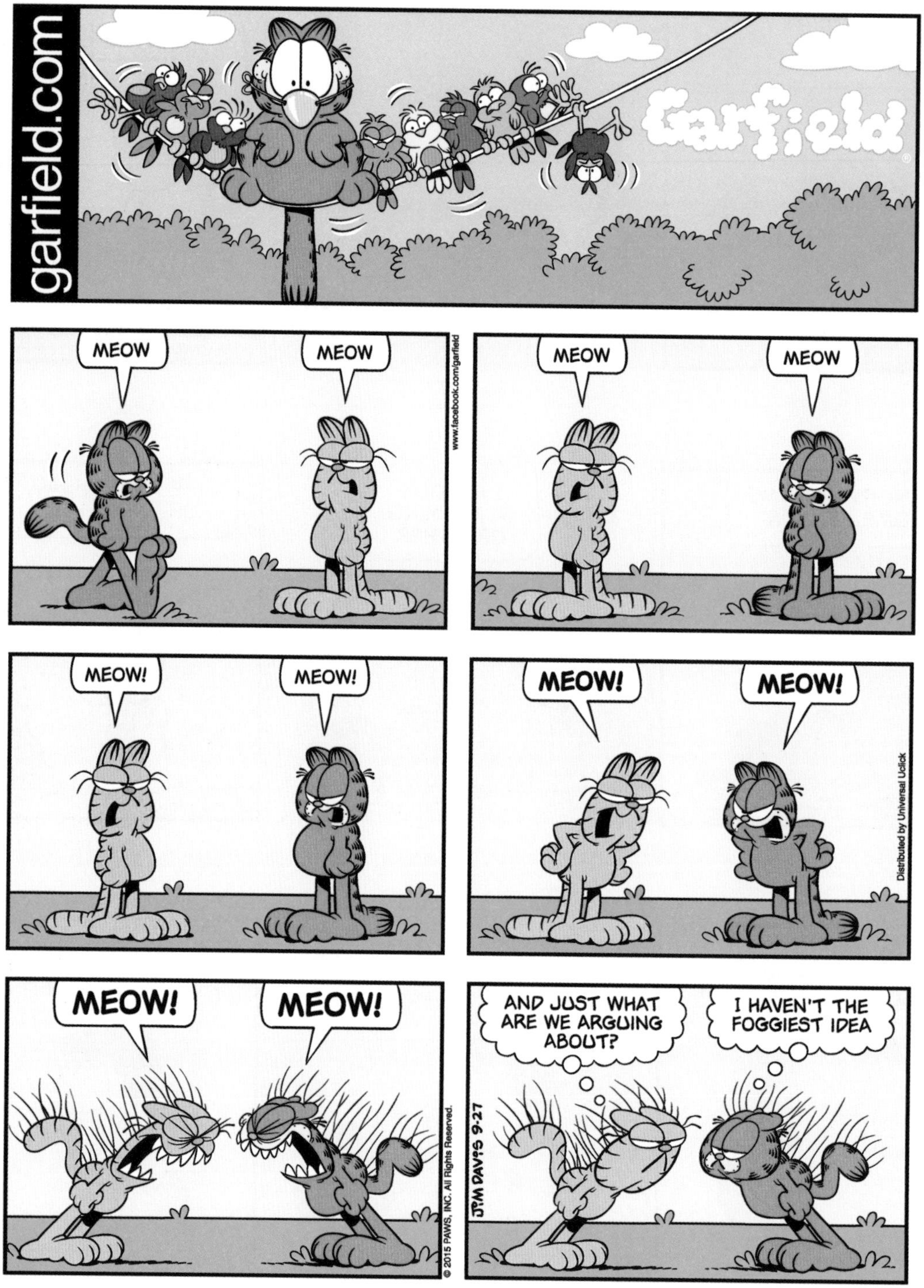
garfield.com
Garfield
MEOW
MEOW
www.facebook.com/garfield
MEOW
MEOW
MEOW!
MEOW!
MEOW!
MEOW!
Distributed by Universal Uclick
MEOW!
MEOW!
© 2015 PAWS, INC. All Rights Reserved.
JIM DAVIS 9-27
AND JUST WHAT ARE WE ARGUING ABOUT?
I HAVEN'T THE FOGGIEST IDEA

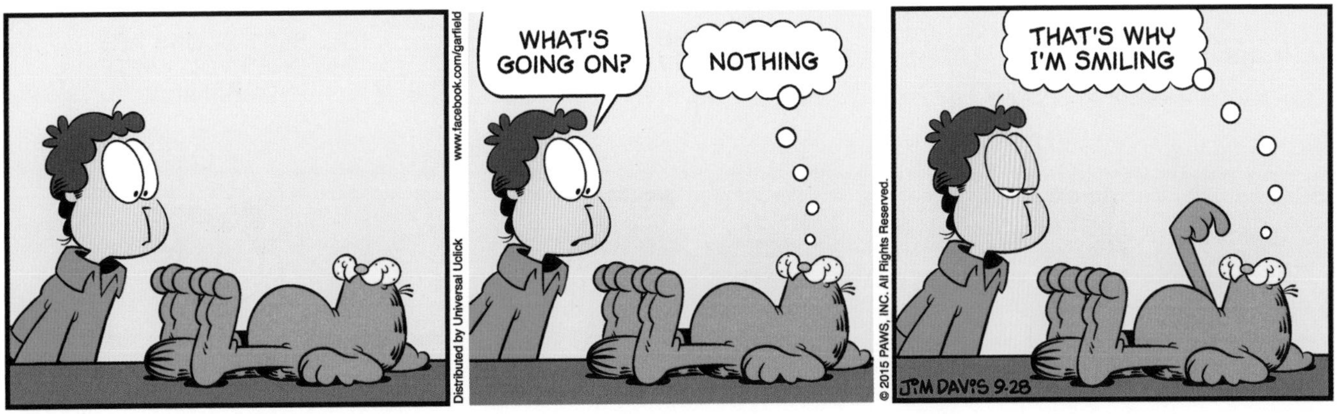
WHAT'S GOING ON?
NOTHING
THAT'S WHY I'M SMILING

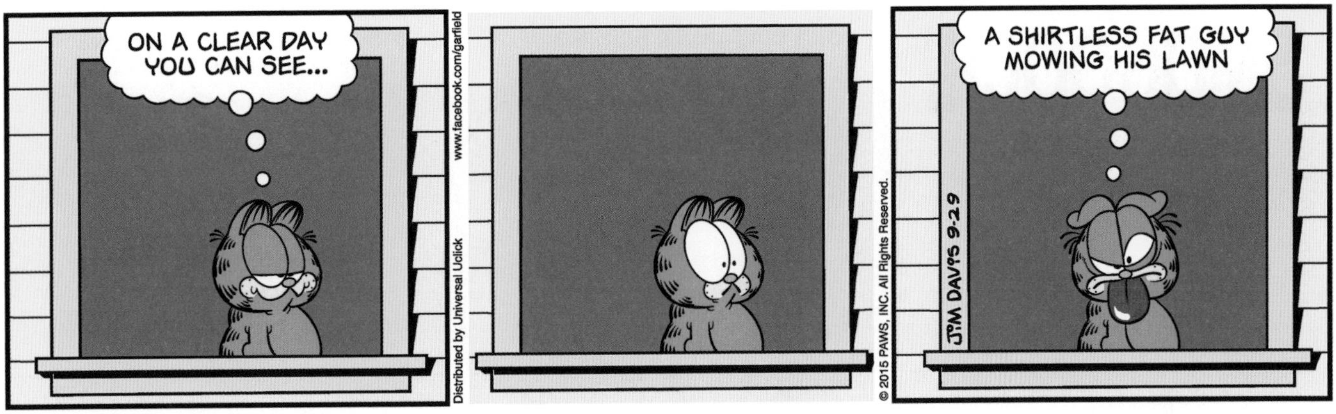
ON A CLEAR DAY YOU CAN SEE...
A SHIRTLESS FAT GUY MOWING HIS LAWN

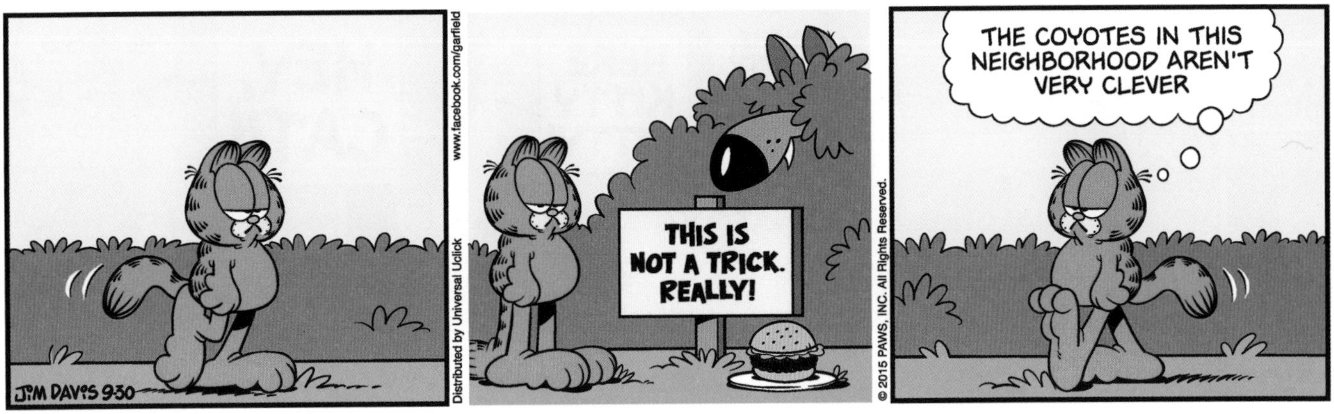
THIS IS NOT A TRICK. REALLY!
THE COYOTES IN THIS NEIGHBORHOOD AREN'T VERY CLEVER

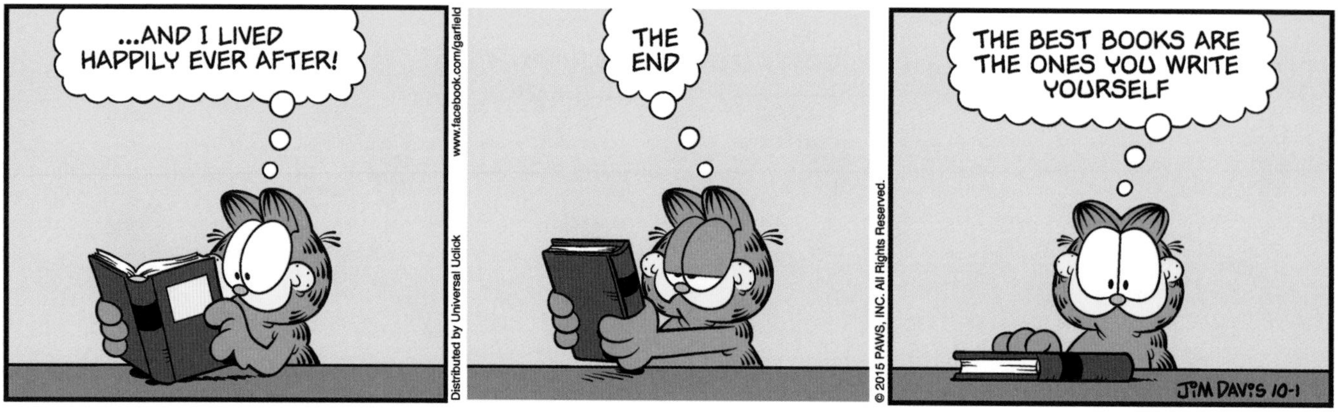
...AND I LIVED HAPPILY EVER AFTER!
THE END
THE BEST BOOKS ARE THE ONES YOU WRITE YOURSELF
JIM DAVIS 10-1
Distributed by Universal Uclick www.facebook.com/garfield
© 2015 PAWS, INC. All Rights Reserved.

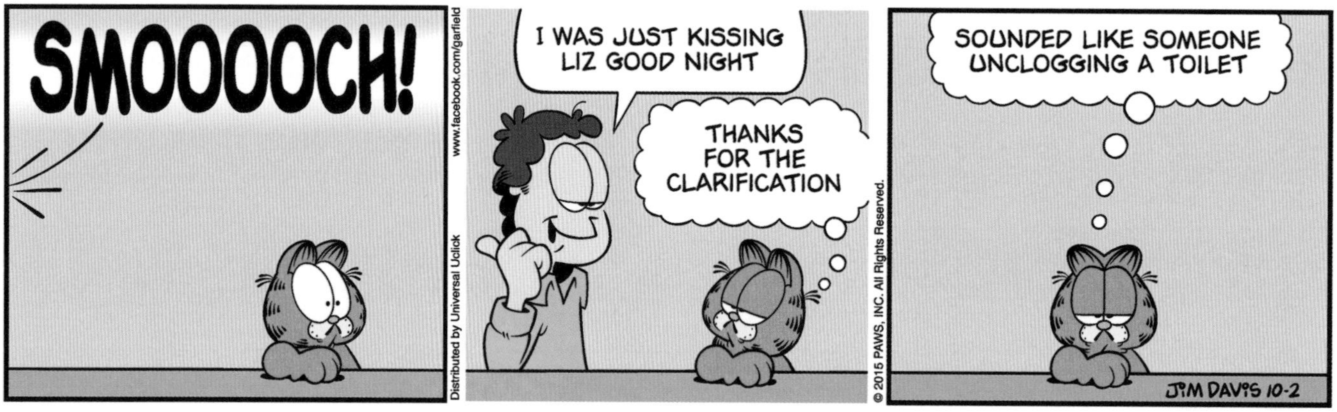
SMOOOOCH!
I WAS JUST KISSING LIZ GOOD NIGHT
THANKS FOR THE CLARIFICATION
SOUNDED LIKE SOMEONE UNCLOGGING A TOILET
JIM DAVIS 10-2
Distributed by Universal Uclick www.facebook.com/garfield
© 2015 PAWS, INC. All Rights Reserved.

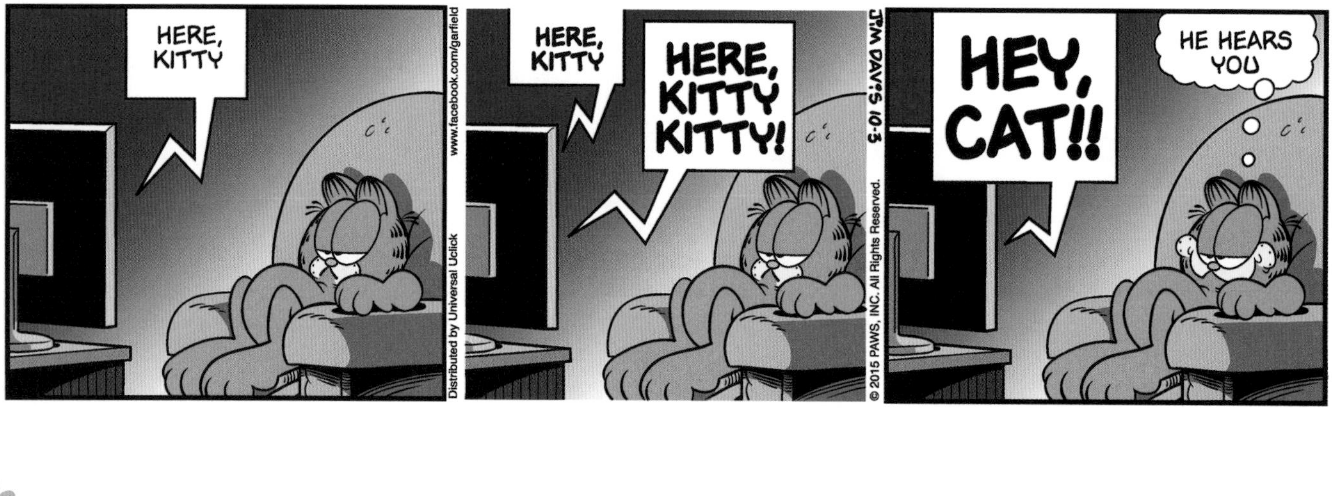
HERE, KITTY
HERE, KITTY
HERE, KITTY KITTY!
HEY, CAT!!
HE HEARS YOU
JIM DAVIS 10-3
Distributed by Universal Uclick www.facebook.com/garfield
© 2015 PAWS, INC. All Rights Reserved.

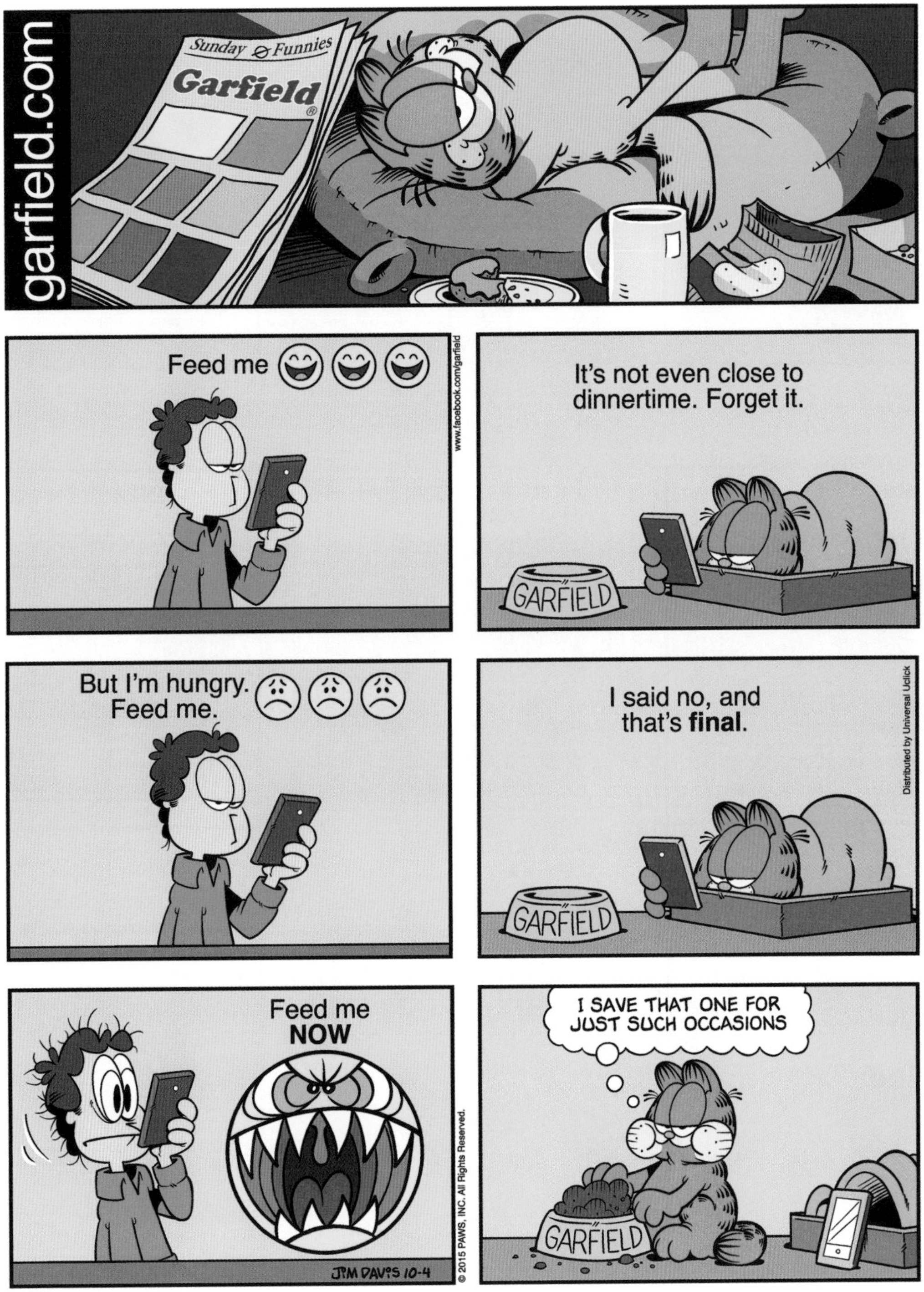
garfield.com
Sunday Funnies
Garfield
Feed me
www.facebook.com/garfield
It's not even close to dinnertime. Forget it.
GARFIELD
But I'm hungry. Feed me.
I said no, and that's **final**.
Distributed by Universal Uclick
GARFIELD
Feed me **NOW**
JIM DAVIS 10-4
© 2015 PAWS, INC. All Rights Reserved.
I SAVE THAT ONE FOR JUST SUCH OCCASIONS
GARFIELD

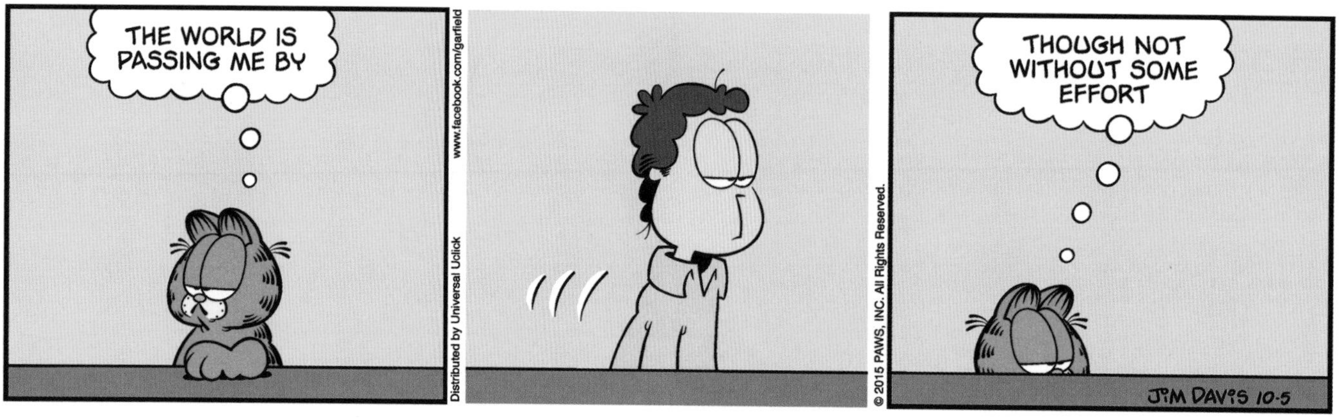
THE WORLD IS PASSING ME BY
THOUGH NOT WITHOUT SOME EFFORT
www.facebook.com/garfield
Distributed by Universal Uclick
© 2015 PAWS, INC. All Rights Reserved.
JIM DAVIS 10-5

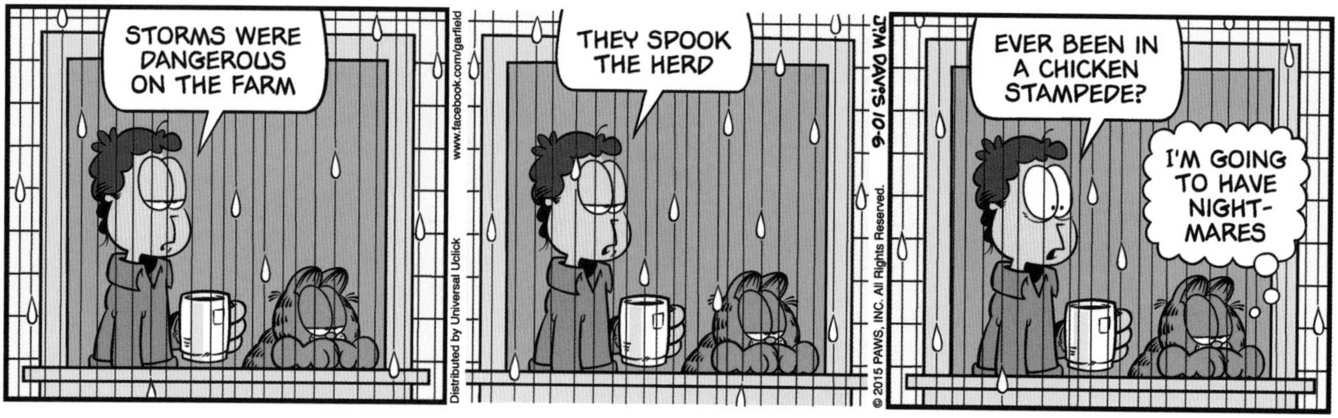
STORMS WERE DANGEROUS ON THE FARM
THEY SPOOK THE HERD
EVER BEEN IN A CHICKEN STAMPEDE?
I'M GOING TO HAVE NIGHT-MARES
www.facebook.com/garfield
Distributed by Universal Uclick
JIM DAVIS 10-6
© 2015 PAWS, INC. All Rights Reserved.

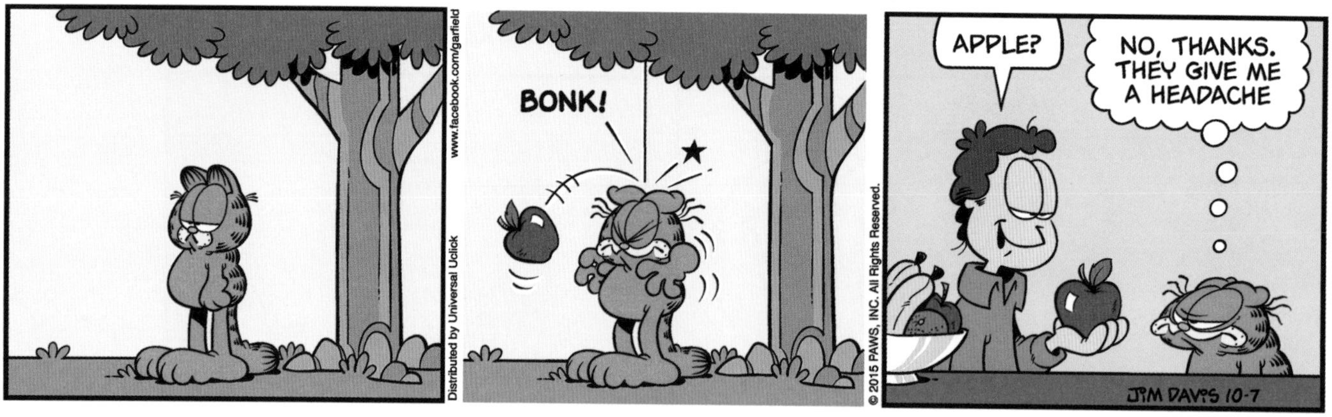
BONK!
APPLE?
NO, THANKS. THEY GIVE ME A HEADACHE
www.facebook.com/garfield
Distributed by Universal Uclick
© 2015 PAWS, INC. All Rights Reserved.
JIM DAVIS 10-7

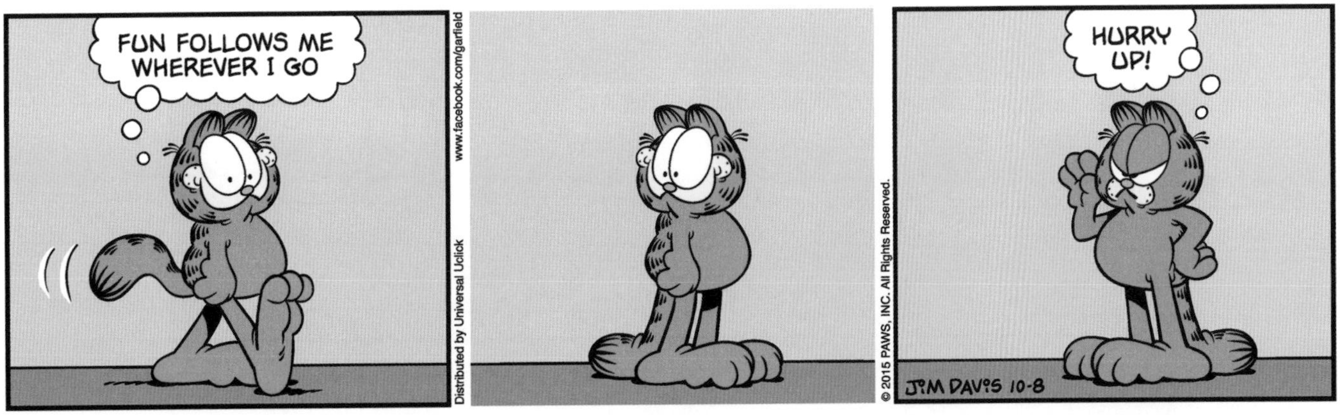
FUN FOLLOWS ME WHEREVER I GO
HURRY UP!
Distributed by Universal Uclick www.facebook.com/garfield
© 2015 PAWS, INC. All Rights Reserved.
JIM DAVIS 10-8

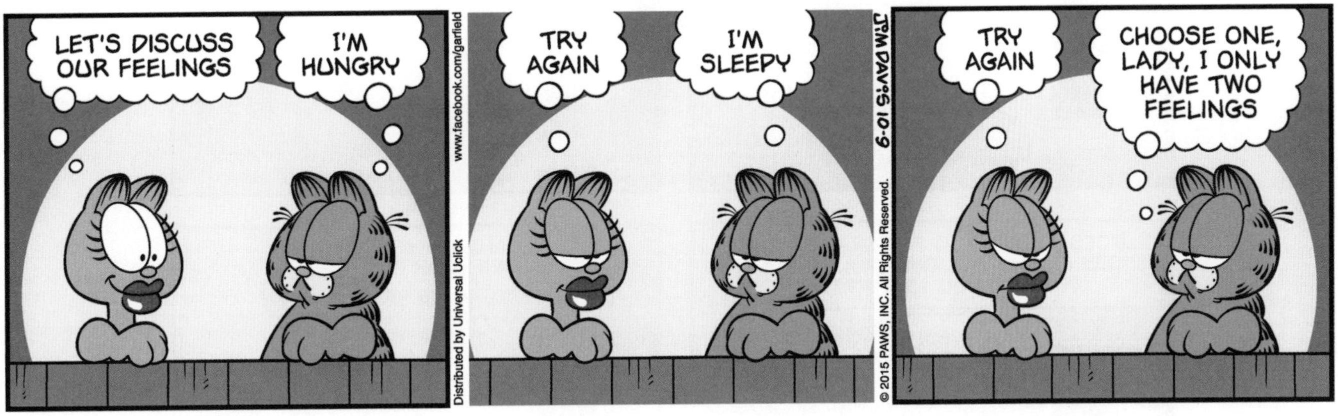
LET'S DISCUSS OUR FEELINGS
I'M HUNGRY
TRY AGAIN
I'M SLEEPY
TRY AGAIN
CHOOSE ONE, LADY, I ONLY HAVE TWO FEELINGS
Distributed by Universal Uclick www.facebook.com/garfield
© 2015 PAWS, INC. All Rights Reserved.
JIM DAVIS 10-9

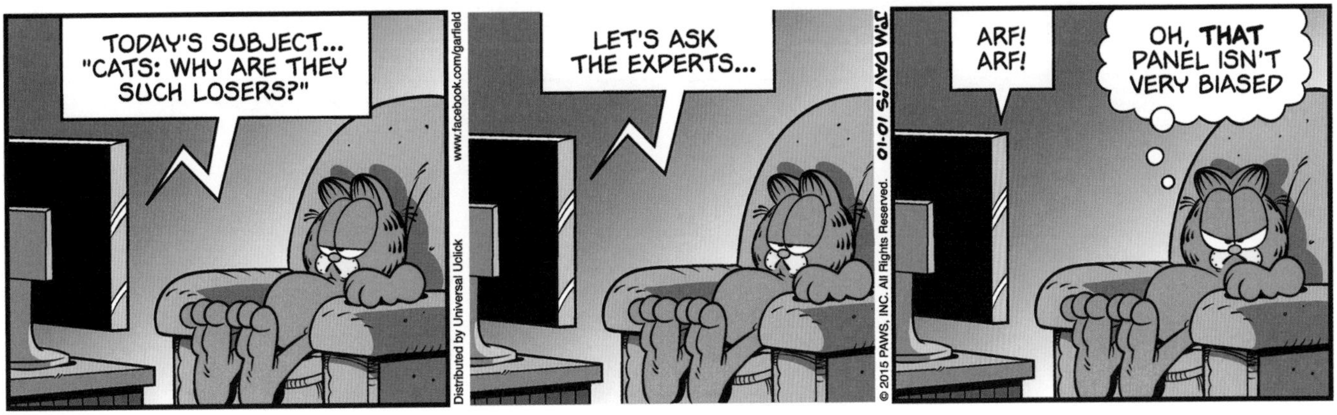
TODAY'S SUBJECT... "CATS: WHY ARE THEY SUCH LOSERS?"
LET'S ASK THE EXPERTS...
ARF! ARF!
OH, THAT PANEL ISN'T VERY BIASED
Distributed by Universal Uclick www.facebook.com/garfield
© 2015 PAWS, INC. All Rights Reserved.
JIM DAVIS 10-10

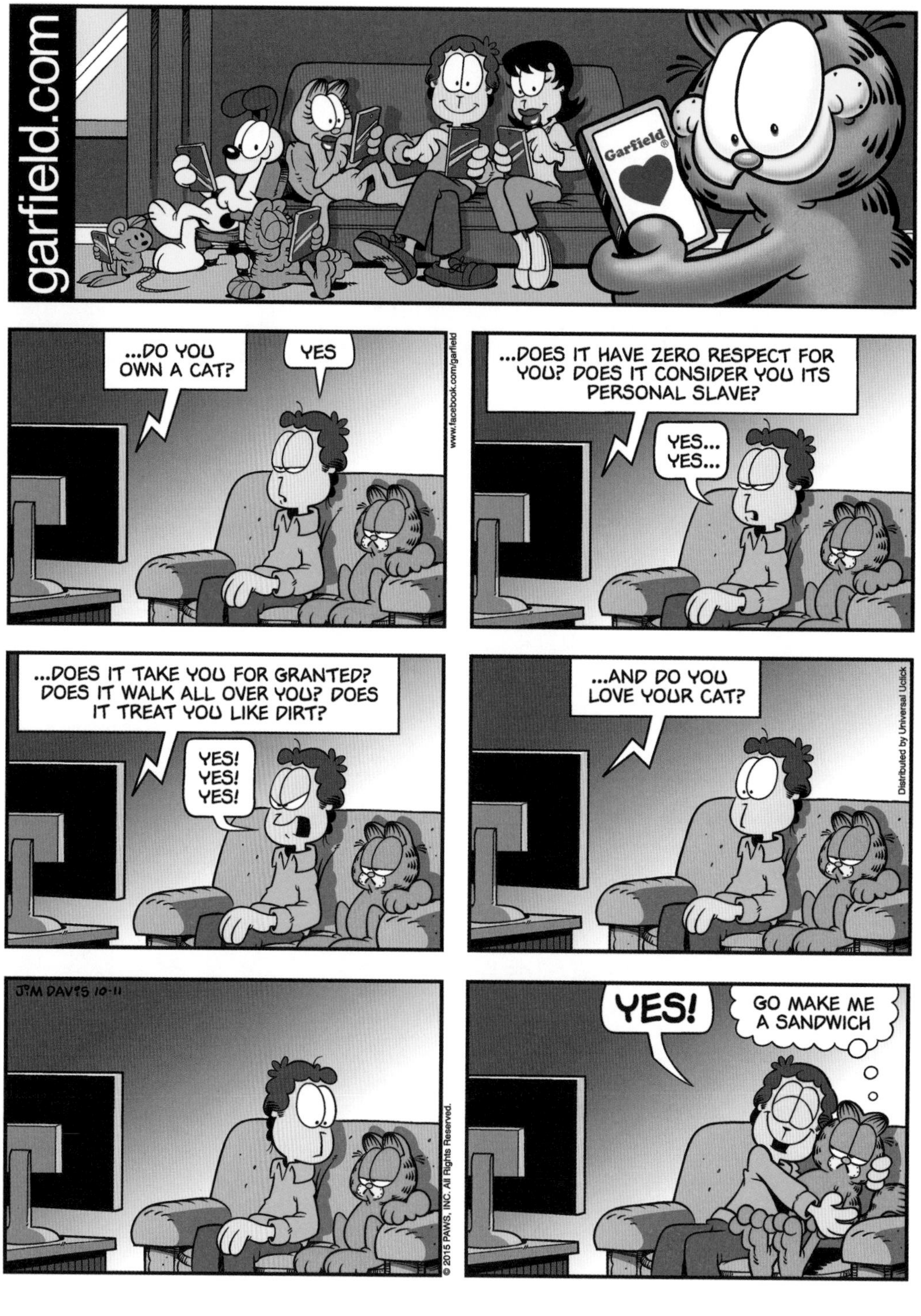
garfield.com
Garfield
...DO YOU OWN A CAT?
YES
www.facebook.com/garfield
...DOES IT HAVE ZERO RESPECT FOR YOU? DOES IT CONSIDER YOU ITS PERSONAL SLAVE?
YES... YES...
...DOES IT TAKE YOU FOR GRANTED? DOES IT WALK ALL OVER YOU? DOES IT TREAT YOU LIKE DIRT?
YES! YES! YES!
...AND DO YOU LOVE YOUR CAT?
Distributed by Universal Uclick
JIM DAVIS 10-11
© 2015 PAWS, INC. All Rights Reserved.
YES!
GO MAKE ME A SANDWICH

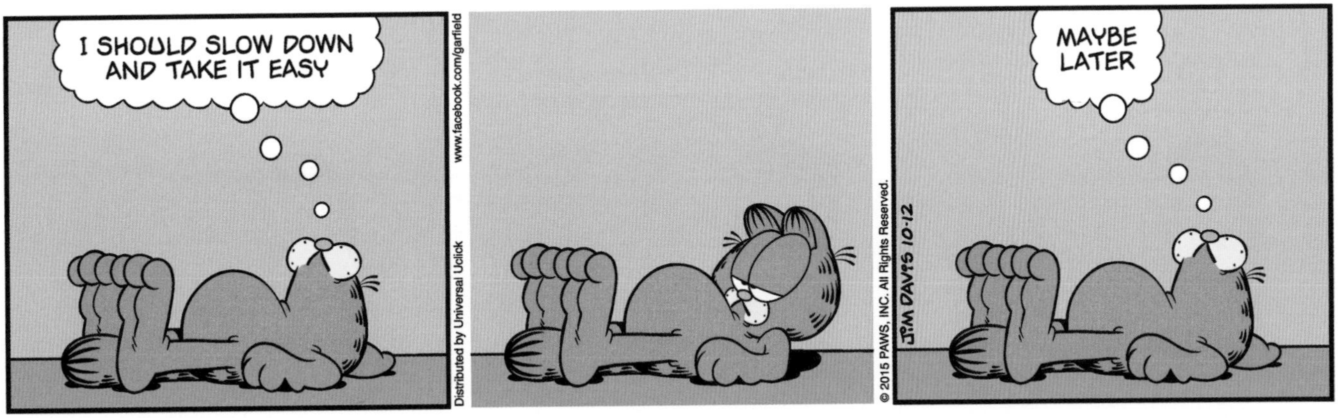
I SHOULD SLOW DOWN AND TAKE IT EASY
www.facebook.com/garfield
Distributed by Universal Uclick
© 2015 PAWS, INC. All Rights Reserved.
JIM DAVIS 10-12
MAYBE LATER

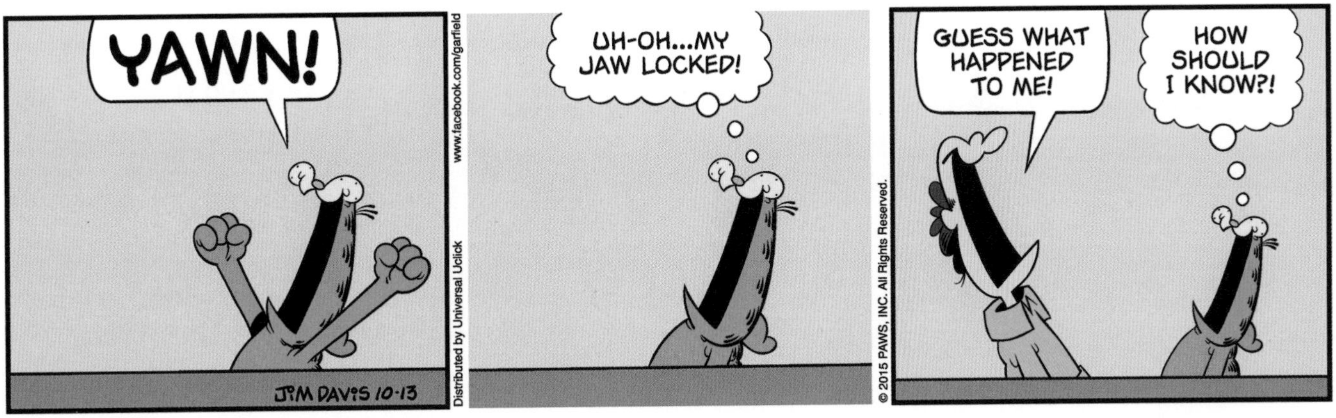
YAWN!
JIM DAVIS 10-13
www.facebook.com/garfield
Distributed by Universal Uclick
UH-OH...MY JAW LOCKED!
© 2015 PAWS, INC. All Rights Reserved.
GUESS WHAT HAPPENED TO ME!
HOW SHOULD I KNOW?!

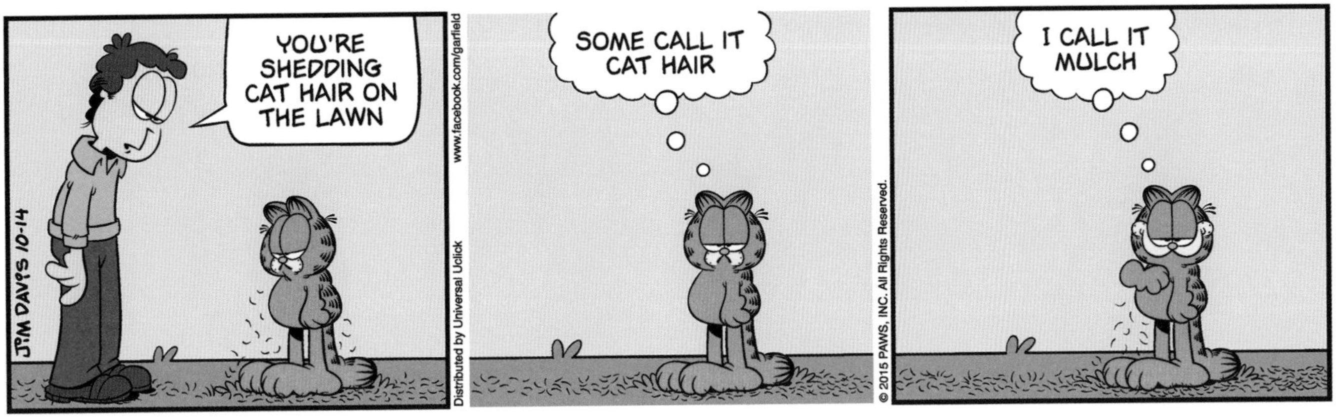
JIM DAVIS 10-14
YOU'RE SHEDDING CAT HAIR ON THE LAWN
www.facebook.com/garfield
Distributed by Universal Uclick
SOME CALL IT CAT HAIR
© 2015 PAWS, INC. All Rights Reserved.
I CALL IT MULCH

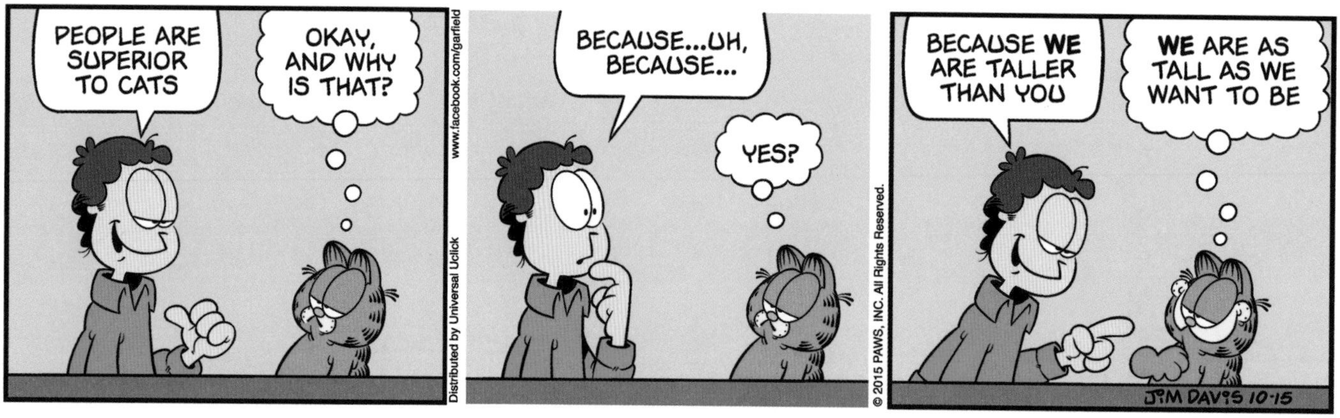
PEOPLE ARE SUPERIOR TO CATS
OKAY, AND WHY IS THAT?
Distributed by Universal Uclick www.facebook.com/garfield
BECAUSE...UH, BECAUSE...
YES?
© 2015 PAWS, INC. All Rights Reserved.
BECAUSE **WE** ARE TALLER THAN YOU
WE ARE AS TALL AS WE WANT TO BE
JIM DAVIS 10-15

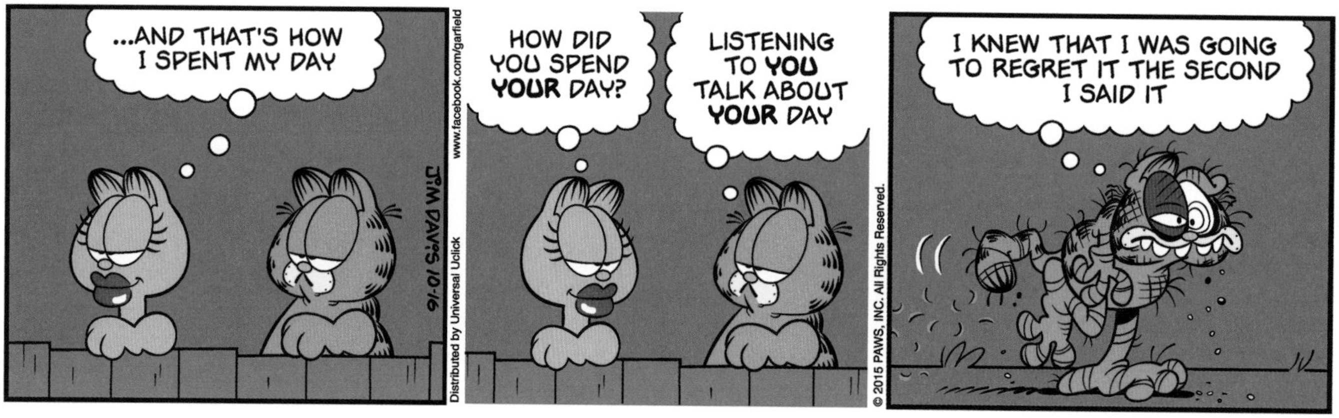
...AND THAT'S HOW I SPENT MY DAY
JIM DAVIS 10-16
Distributed by Universal Uclick www.facebook.com/garfield
HOW DID YOU SPEND **YOUR** DAY?
LISTENING TO **YOU** TALK ABOUT **YOUR** DAY
© 2015 PAWS, INC. All Rights Reserved.
I KNEW THAT I WAS GOING TO REGRET IT THE SECOND I SAID IT

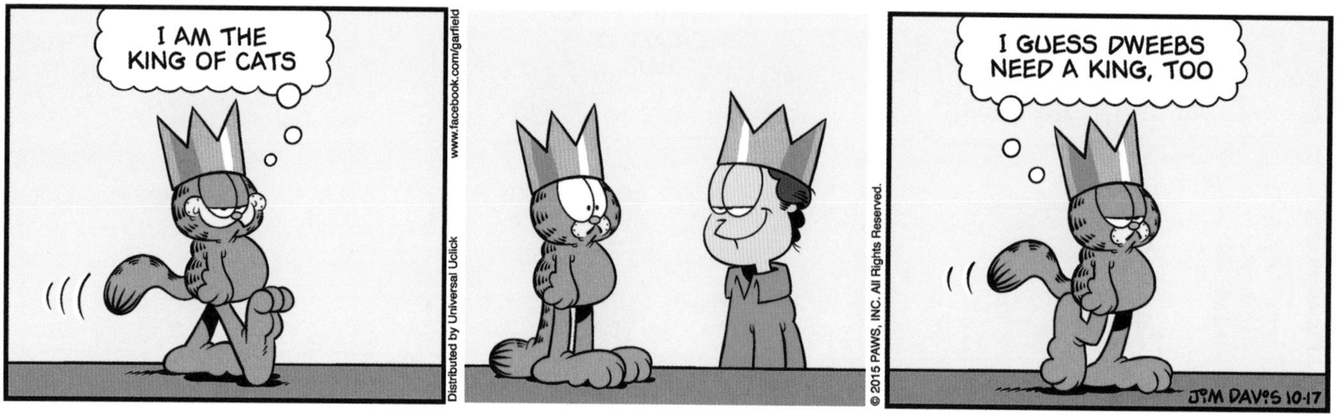
I AM THE KING OF CATS
Distributed by Universal Uclick www.facebook.com/garfield
© 2015 PAWS, INC. All Rights Reserved.
I GUESS DWEEBS NEED A KING, TOO
JIM DAVIS 10-17

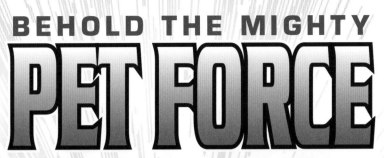

BEHOLD THE MIGHTY

PET FORCE

FOUR SUPERPOWERED PETS FROM A PARALLEL UNIVERSE!

GARZOOKA

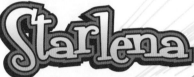

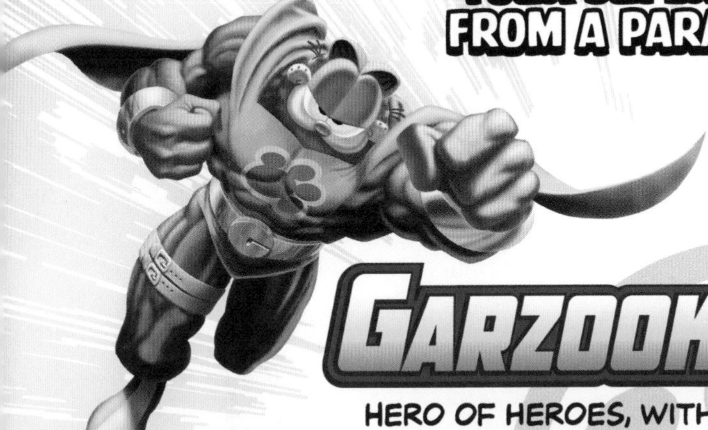

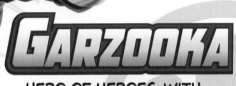

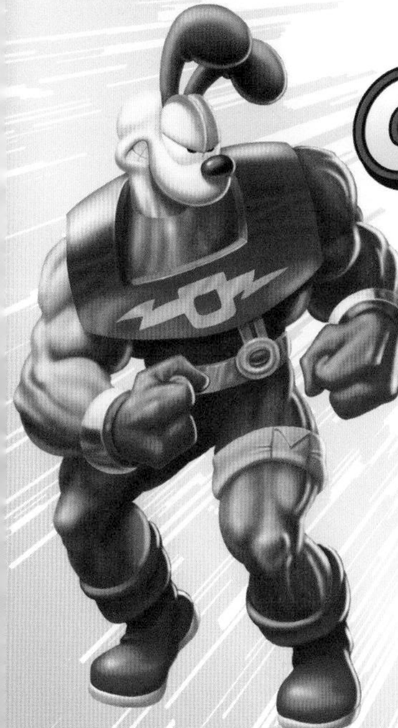

HERO OF HEROES, WITH THE ABILITY TO FIRE GAMMA-RADIATED HAIRBALLS

Starlena

HER ICY STARE FREEZES ALL BAD GUYS IN THEIR TRACKS

ODIOUS

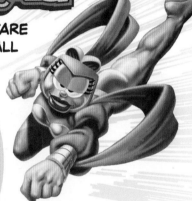

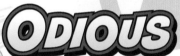

A POTENT STUN TONGUE, AND A BLACK HOLE WHERE HIS BRAIN SHOULD BE

ABNERMAL

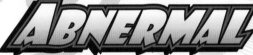

QUICK AS A BLINK, WITH PESTER-POWER OF COSMIC PROPORTIONS

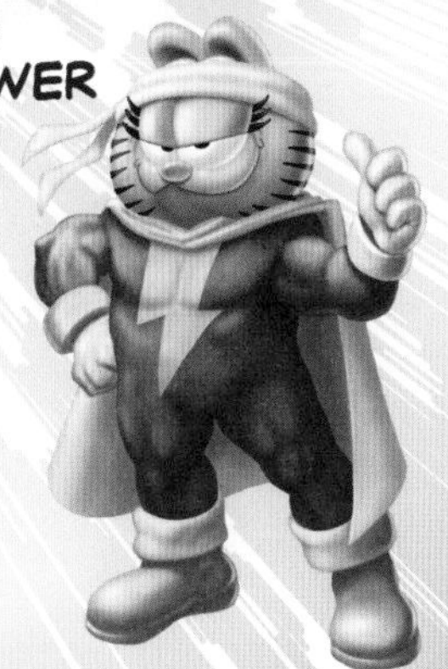

TOGETHER, THESE DEFENDERS OF JUSTICE ARE THE GALAXY'S MIGHTIEST - AND HUNGRIEST - HEROES!

Let the fur fly!

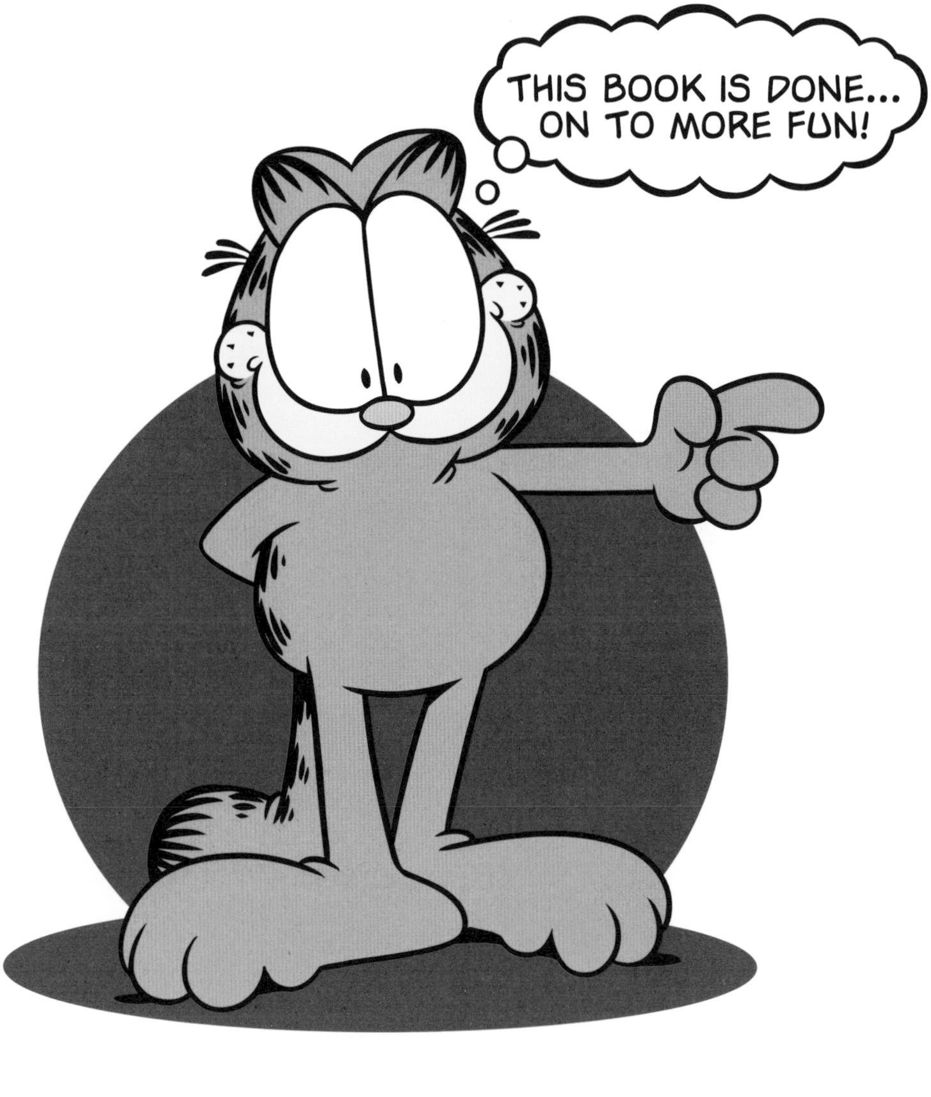
THIS BOOK IS DONE... ON TO MORE FUN!

Garfield
EATS AND RUNS

BY JIM DAVIS

Ballantine Books • New York

GARFIELD'S 40TH BIRTHDAY EXTRAVAGANZA!

SPECIAL NEW BOOK CELEBRATING GARFIELD'S EPIC 40TH BIRTHDAY! JUNE 19, 2018

The big year is finally here! Garfield, the original party animal, is aging disgracefully and celebrating wildly! Hey, what do you expect from the mischievous fat cat who is so good at being bad?

Join the party, as celebrity cartoonists and fans alike pay homage to the famous feline. Even Broadway legend Lin-Manuel Miranda, a lifelong Garfield lover, gets into the act by composing the book's foreword.

This commemorative collection of birthday comic strips—plus a ton of other festive fun—is a gift for Garfield fans of all ages!

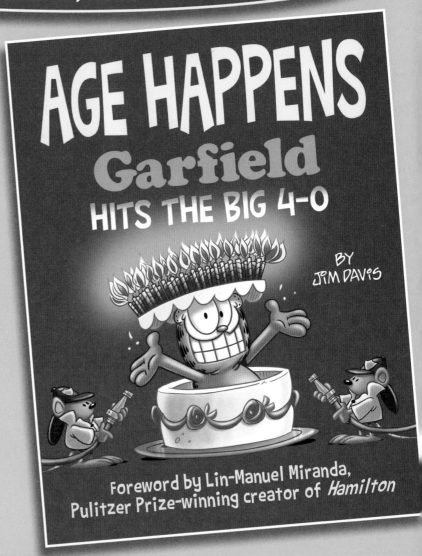

AGE HAPPENS

Garfield

HITS THE BIG 4-0

BY JIM DAVIS

Foreword by Lin-Manuel Miranda, Pulitzer Prize-winning creator of *Hamilton*

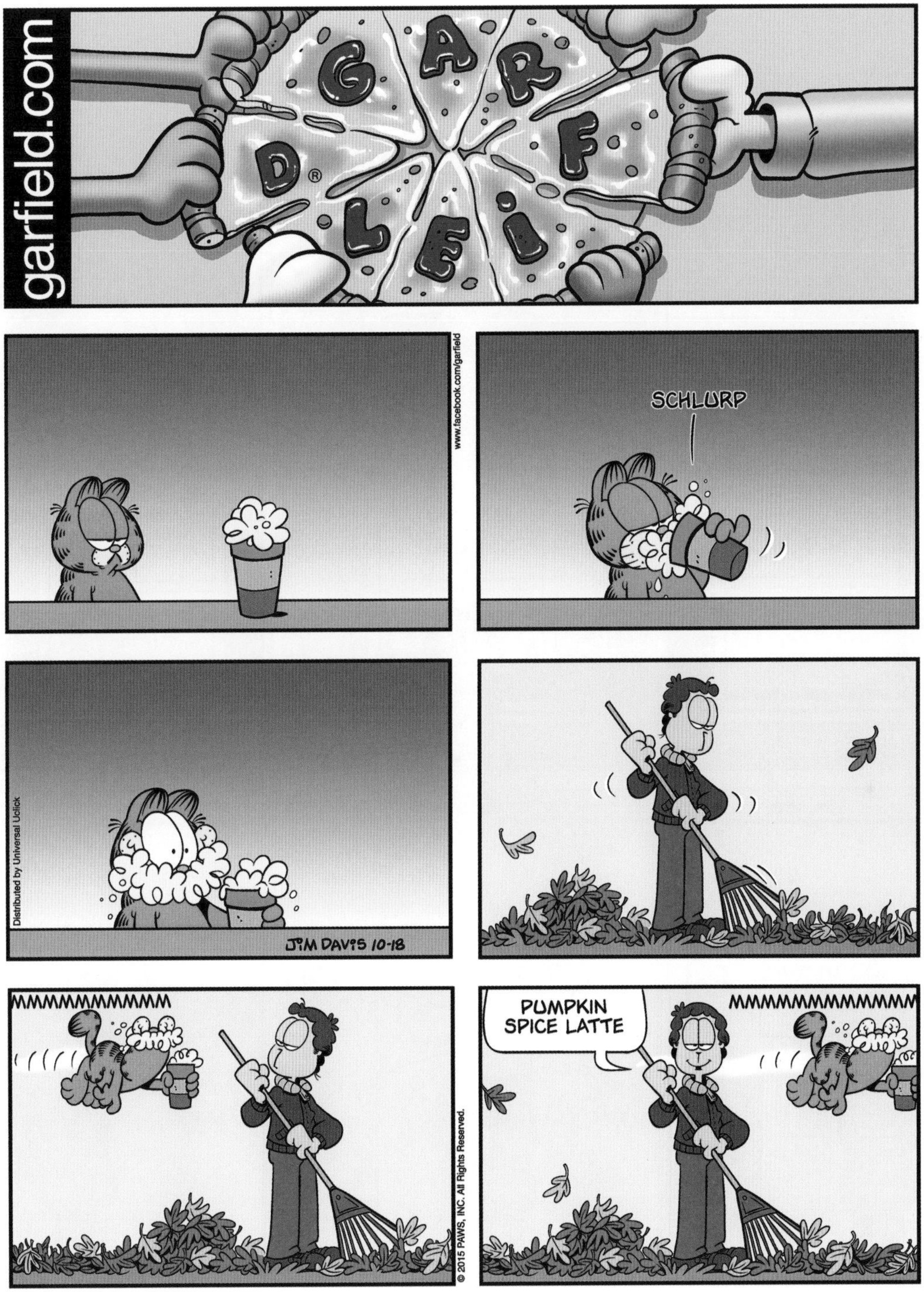
garfield.com
GARFIELD®
www.facebook.com/garfield
SCHLURP
Distributed by Universal Uclick
JIM DAVIS 10-18
MMMMMMMMMMM
© 2015 PAWS, INC. All Rights Reserved.
PUMPKIN SPICE LATTE
MMMMMMMMMMMM

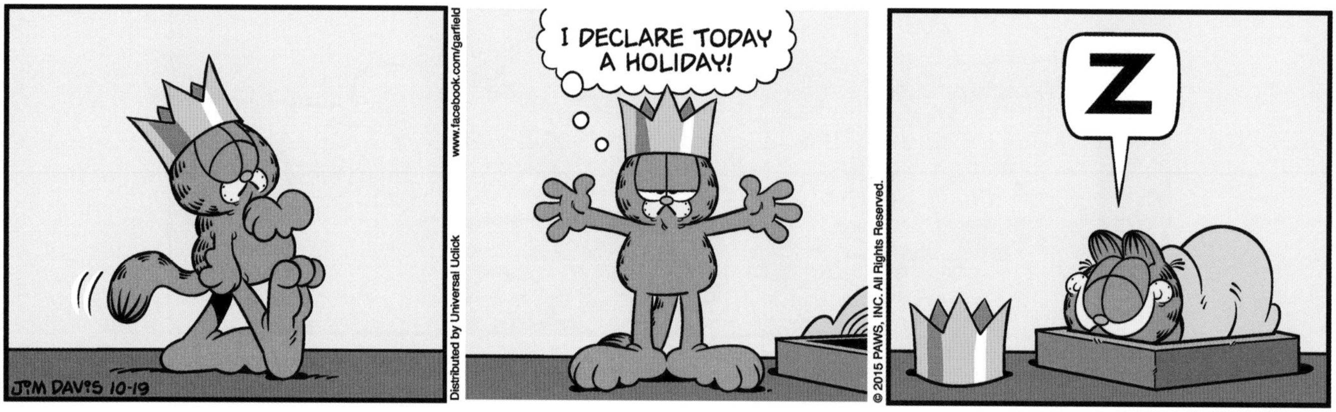
JIM DAVIS 10-19
Distributed by Universal Uclick
www.facebook.com/garfield
I DECLARE TODAY A HOLIDAY!
© 2015 PAWS, INC. All Rights Reserved.
Z

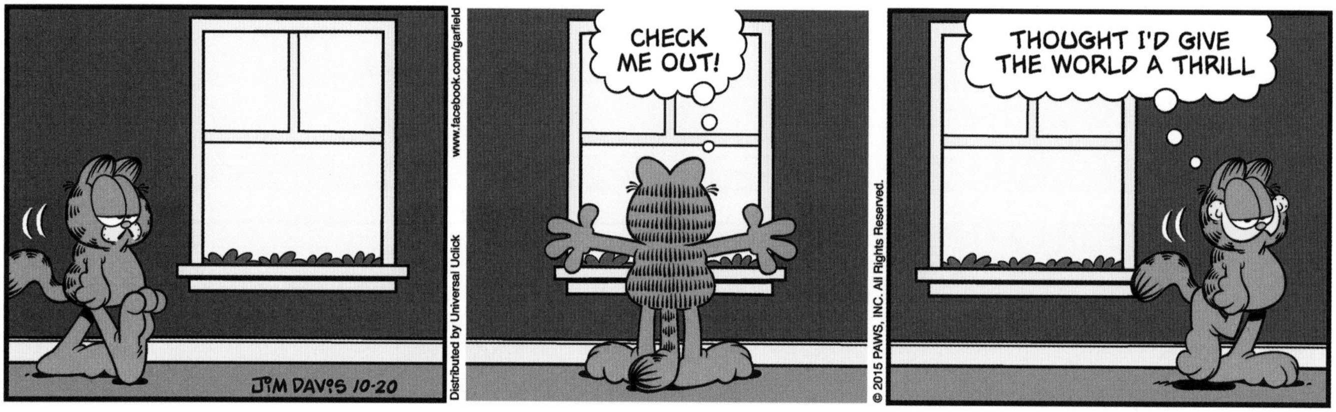
JIM DAVIS 10-20
Distributed by Universal Uclick
www.facebook.com/garfield
CHECK ME OUT!
© 2015 PAWS, INC. All Rights Reserved.
THOUGHT I'D GIVE THE WORLD A THRILL

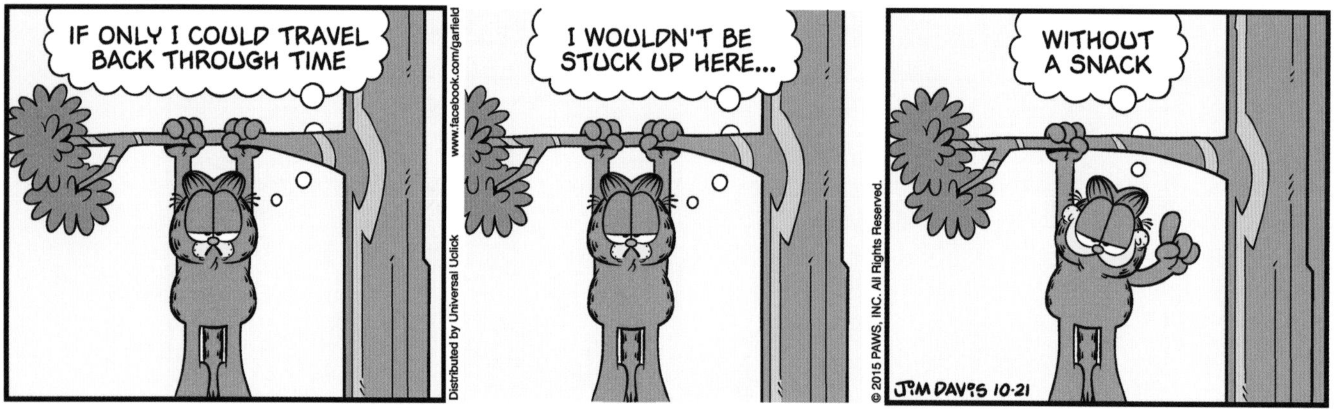
IF ONLY I COULD TRAVEL BACK THROUGH TIME
Distributed by Universal Uclick
www.facebook.com/garfield
I WOULDN'T BE STUCK UP HERE...
© 2015 PAWS, INC. All Rights Reserved.
WITHOUT A SNACK
JIM DAVIS 10-21

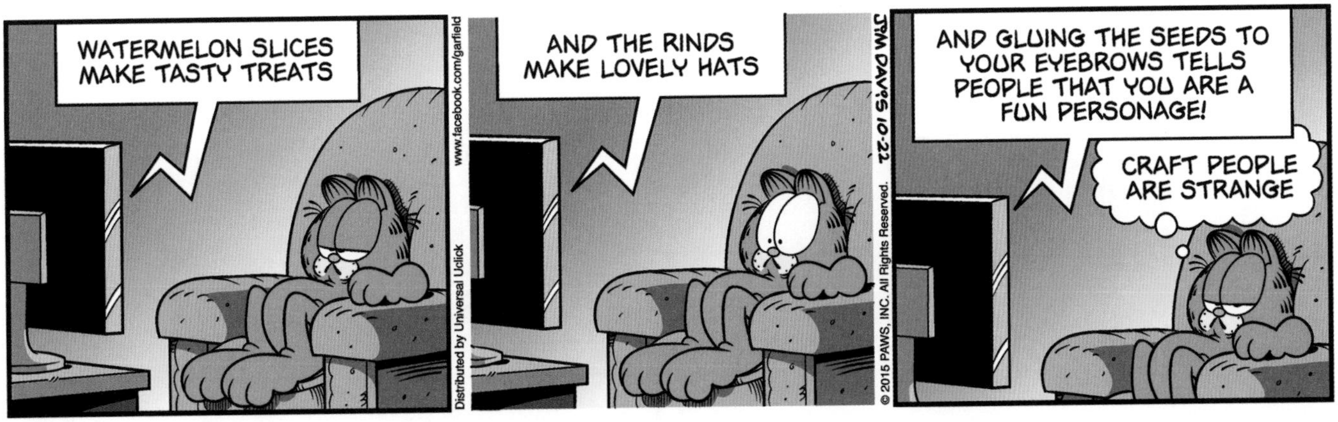
WATERMELON SLICES MAKE TASTY TREATS
AND THE RINDS MAKE LOVELY HATS
AND GLUING THE SEEDS TO YOUR EYEBROWS TELLS PEOPLE THAT YOU ARE A FUN PERSONAGE!
CRAFT PEOPLE ARE STRANGE
www.facebook.com/garfield
Distributed by Universal Uclick
JIM DAVIS 10-22
© 2015 PAWS, INC. All Rights Reserved.

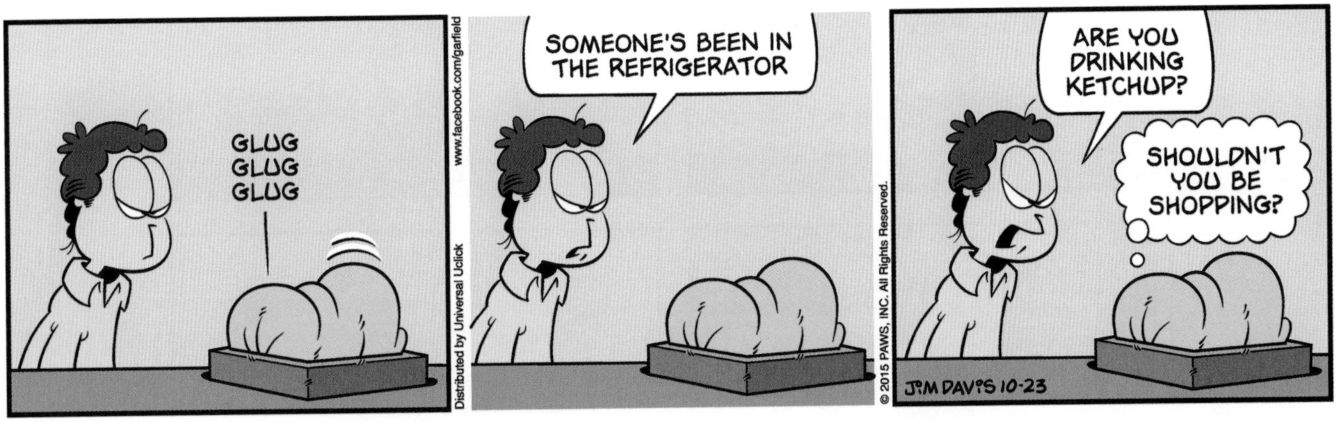
GLUG GLUG GLUG
SOMEONE'S BEEN IN THE REFRIGERATOR
ARE YOU DRINKING KETCHUP?
SHOULDN'T YOU BE SHOPPING?
www.facebook.com/garfield
Distributed by Universal Uclick
© 2015 PAWS, INC. All Rights Reserved.
JIM DAVIS 10-23

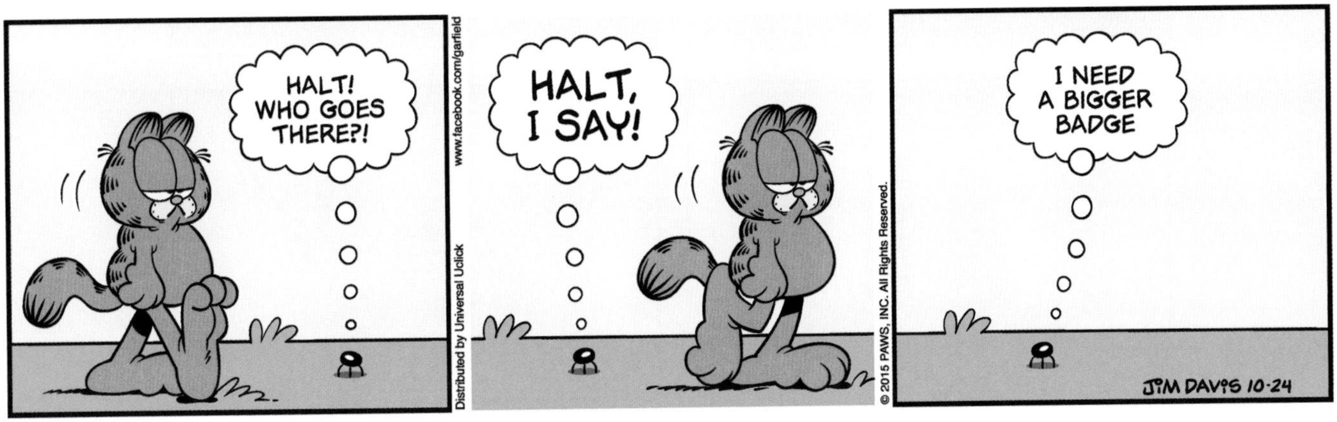
HALT! WHO GOES THERE?!
HALT, I SAY!
I NEED A BIGGER BADGE
www.facebook.com/garfield
Distributed by Universal Uclick
© 2015 PAWS, INC. All Rights Reserved.
JIM DAVIS 10-24

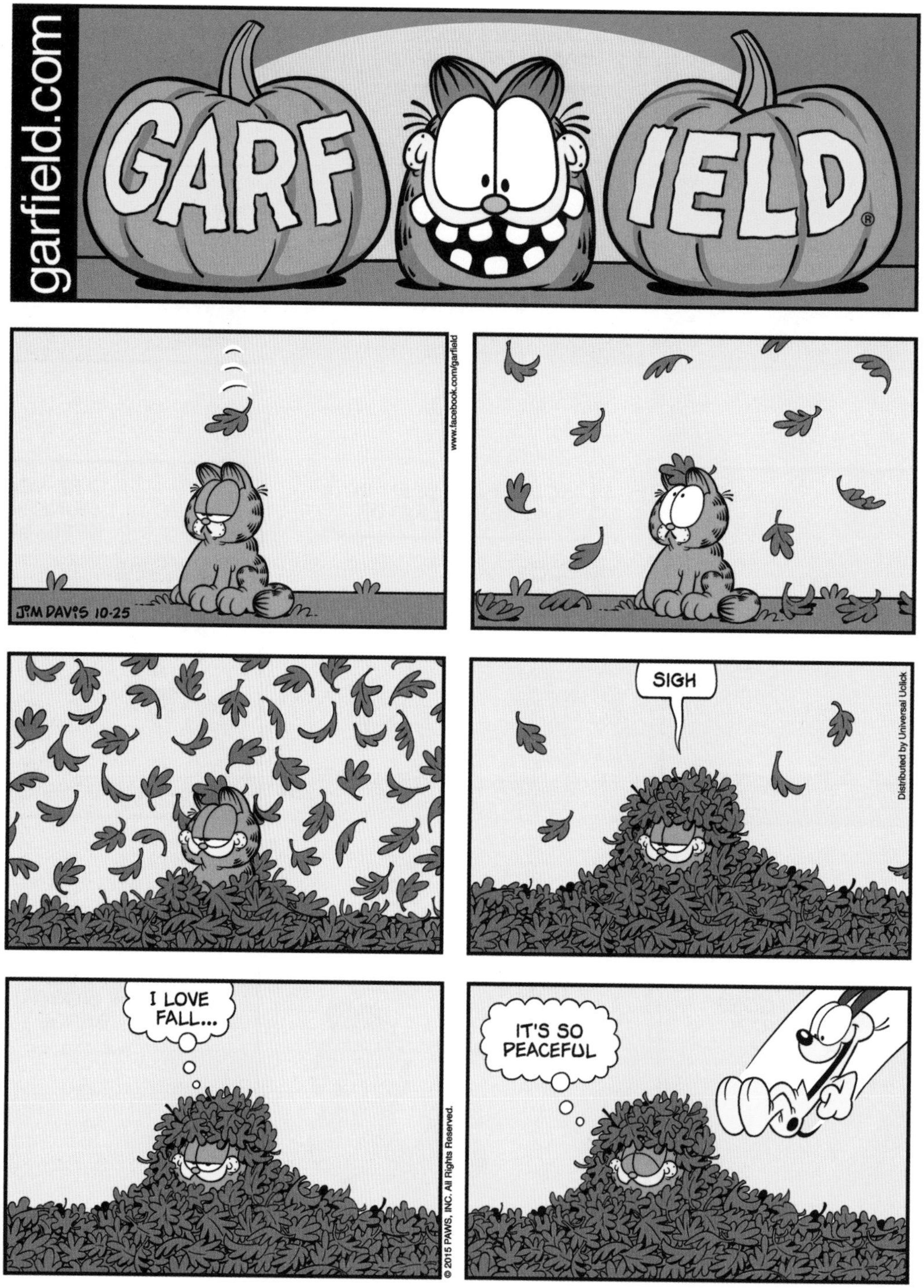
garfield.com
GARF
IELD
www.facebook.com/garfield
JIM DAVIS 10-25
SIGH
Distributed by Universal Uclick
I LOVE FALL...
© 2015 PAWS, INC. All Rights Reserved.
IT'S SO PEACEFUL

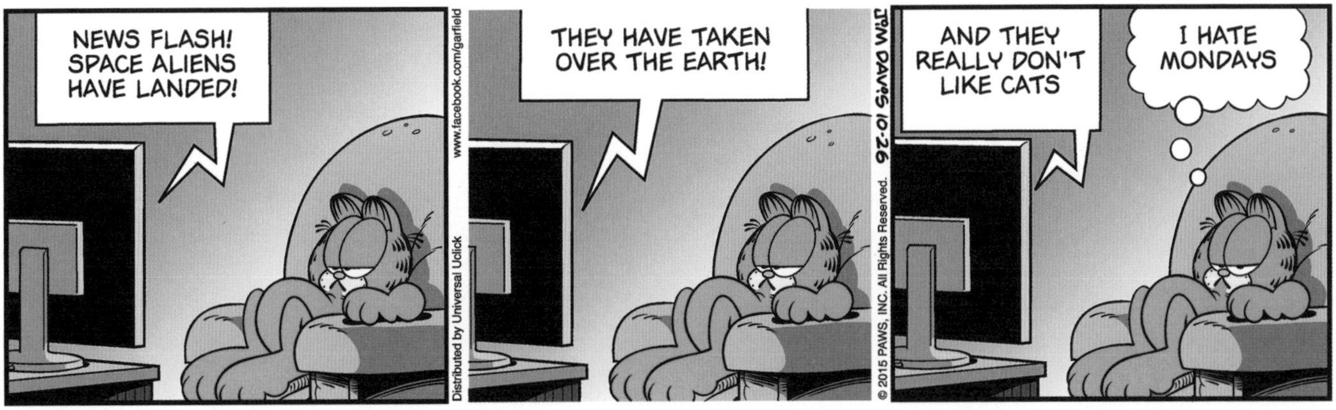
NEWS FLASH! SPACE ALIENS HAVE LANDED!
THEY HAVE TAKEN OVER THE EARTH!
AND THEY REALLY DON'T LIKE CATS
I HATE MONDAYS
JIM DAVIS 10-26
www.facebook.com/garfield
Distributed by Universal Uclick
© 2015 PAWS, INC. All Rights Reserved.

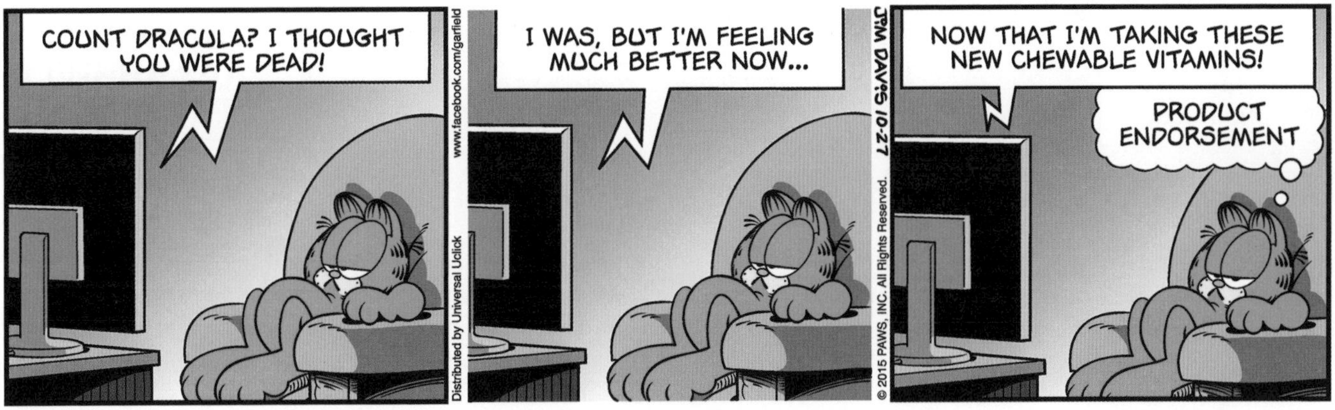
COUNT DRACULA? I THOUGHT YOU WERE DEAD!
I WAS, BUT I'M FEELING MUCH BETTER NOW...
NOW THAT I'M TAKING THESE NEW CHEWABLE VITAMINS!
PRODUCT ENDORSEMENT
JIM DAVIS 10-27
www.facebook.com/garfield
Distributed by Universal Uclick
© 2015 PAWS, INC. All Rights Reserved.

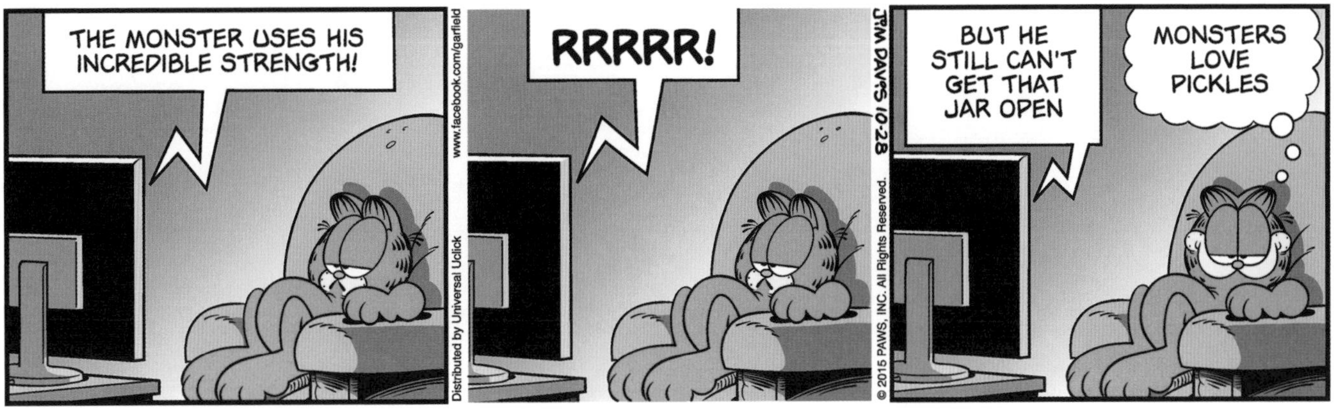
THE MONSTER USES HIS INCREDIBLE STRENGTH!
RRRRR!
BUT HE STILL CAN'T GET THAT JAR OPEN
MONSTERS LOVE PICKLES
JIM DAVIS 10-28
www.facebook.com/garfield
Distributed by Universal Uclick
© 2015 PAWS, INC. All Rights Reserved.

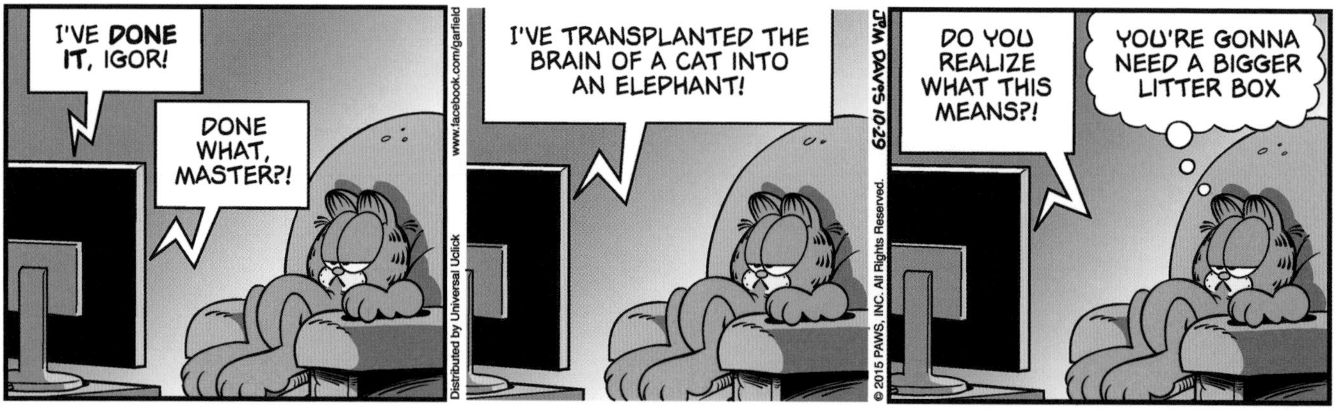
I'VE **DONE IT**, IGOR!
DONE WHAT, MASTER?!
I'VE TRANSPLANTED THE BRAIN OF A CAT INTO AN ELEPHANT!
JIM DAVIS 10-29
DO YOU REALIZE WHAT THIS MEANS?!
YOU'RE GONNA NEED A BIGGER LITTER BOX
Distributed by Universal Uclick www.facebook.com/garfield
© 2015 PAWS, INC. All Rights Reserved.

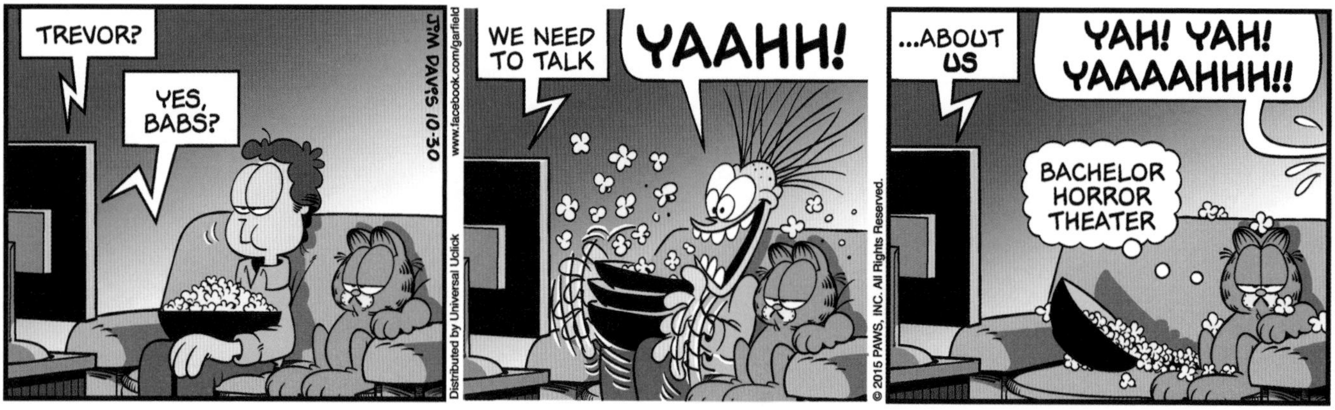
TREVOR?
YES, BABS?
JIM DAVIS 10-30
WE NEED TO TALK
YAAHH!
...ABOUT **US**
YAH! YAH! YAAAAHHH!!
BACHELOR HORROR THEATER
Distributed by Universal Uclick www.facebook.com/garfield
© 2015 PAWS, INC. All Rights Reserved.

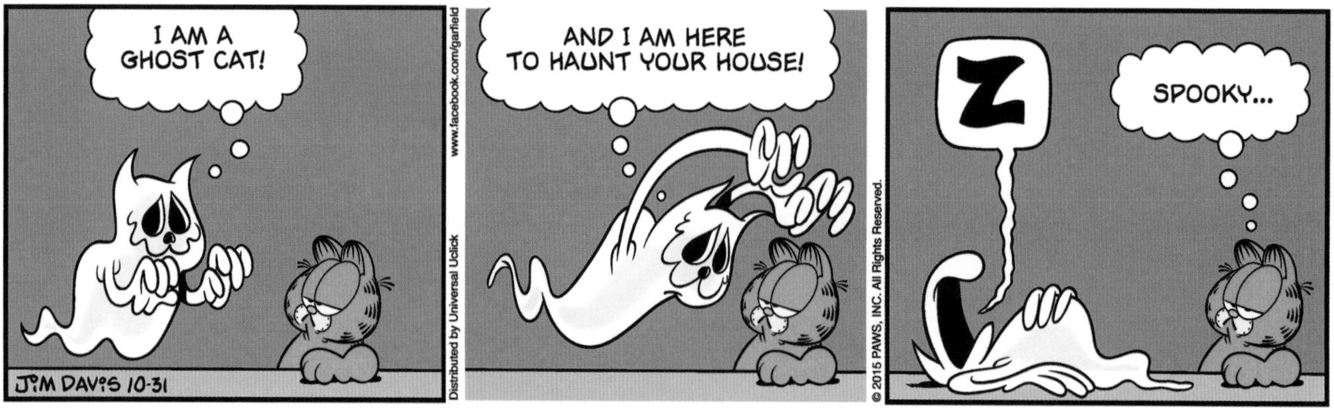
I AM A GHOST CAT!
JIM DAVIS 10-31
AND I AM HERE TO HAUNT YOUR HOUSE!
Z
SPOOKY...
Distributed by Universal Uclick www.facebook.com/garfield
© 2015 PAWS, INC. All Rights Reserved.

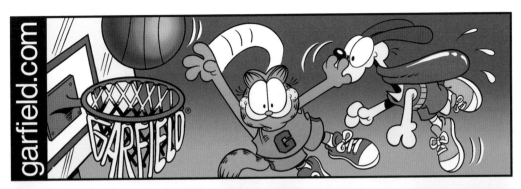

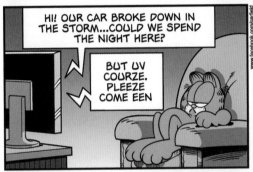

garfield.com
GARFIELD®
www.facebook.com/garfield
JIM DAVIS 11-1
HI! OUR CAR BROKE DOWN IN THE STORM...COULD WE SPEND THE NIGHT HERE?
BUT UV COURZE. PLEEZE COME EEN
I'M CYNDI, AND THIS IS TIFFANY!
AND YOU CAN CALL ME "COUNT"
Distributed by Universal Uclick
WHAT DO YOU DO, MR. COUNT?!
I'M A...VEB DESIGNER. AND YOU?
WE'RE PROFESSIONAL NECK MODELS!
...SAY VAT?
NECK MODELS! WATCH, WE'LL POSE FOR YOU!
© 2015 PAWS, INC. All Rights Reserved.
ZIS IS ZEE GREATEST NIGHT OF MY LIFE!
I LOVE MOVIES WITH HAPPY ENDINGS

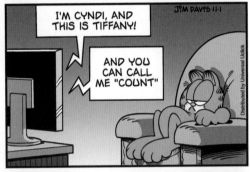

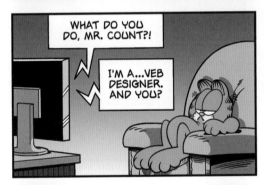

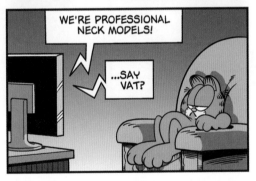

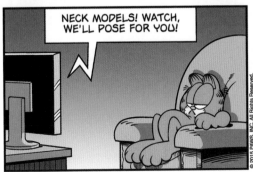

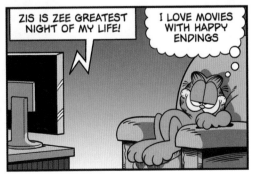

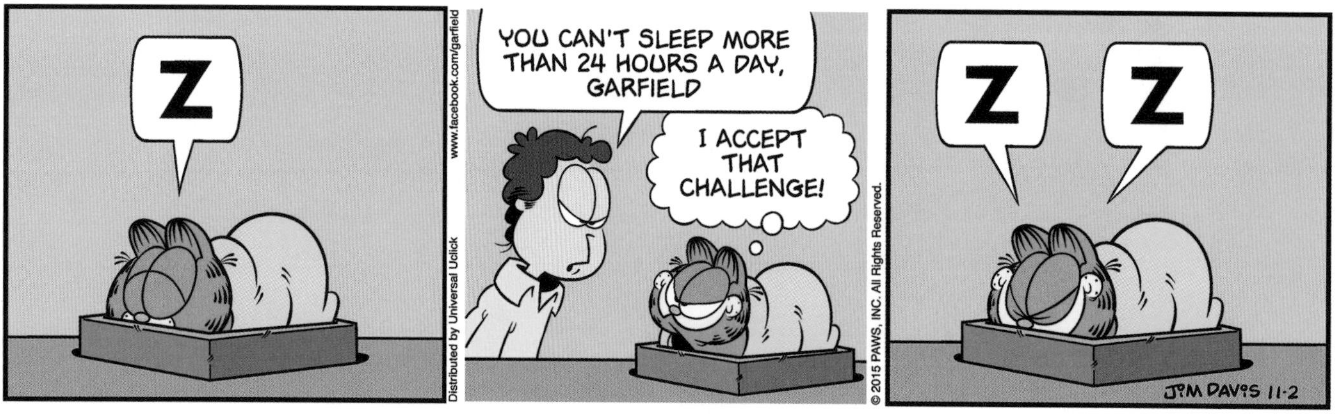
Z
YOU CAN'T SLEEP MORE THAN 24 HOURS A DAY, GARFIELD
I ACCEPT THAT CHALLENGE!
Z
Z
JIM DAVIS 11-2
Distributed by Universal Uclick
www.facebook.com/garfield
© 2015 PAWS, INC. All Rights Reserved.

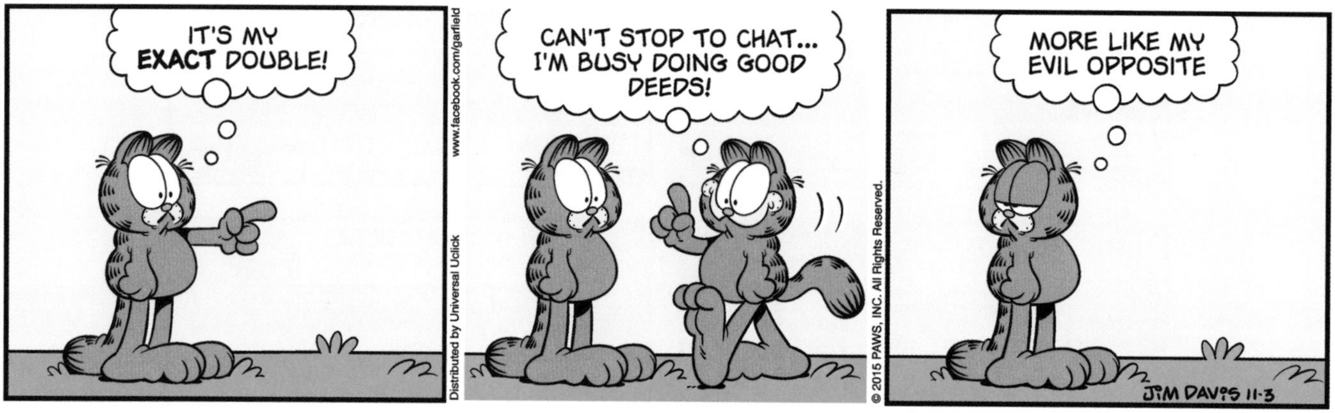
IT'S MY **EXACT** DOUBLE!
CAN'T STOP TO CHAT... I'M BUSY DOING GOOD DEEDS!
MORE LIKE MY EVIL OPPOSITE
JIM DAVIS 11-3
Distributed by Universal Uclick
www.facebook.com/garfield
© 2015 PAWS, INC. All Rights Reserved.

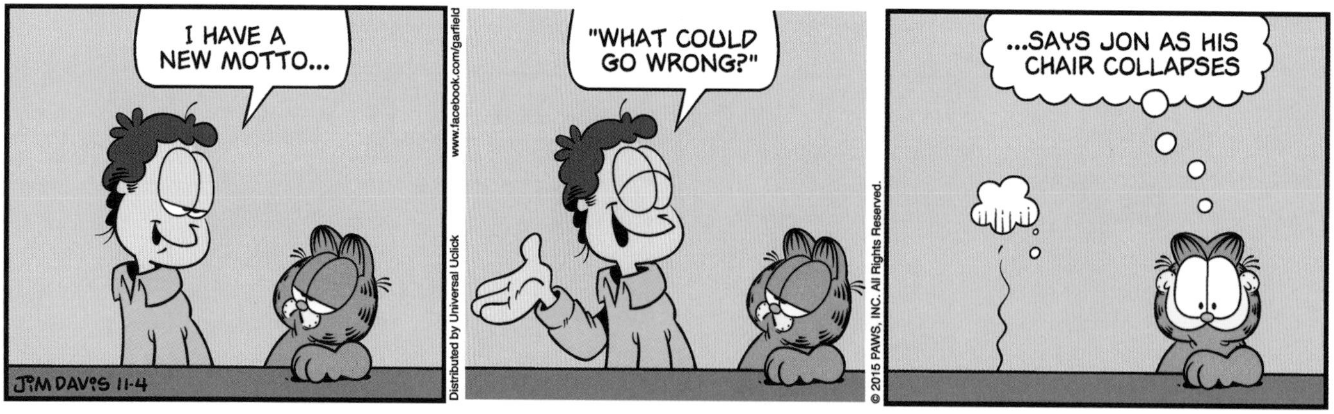
I HAVE A NEW MOTTO...
"WHAT COULD GO WRONG?"
...SAYS JON AS HIS CHAIR COLLAPSES
JIM DAVIS 11-4
Distributed by Universal Uclick
www.facebook.com/garfield
© 2015 PAWS, INC. All Rights Reserved.

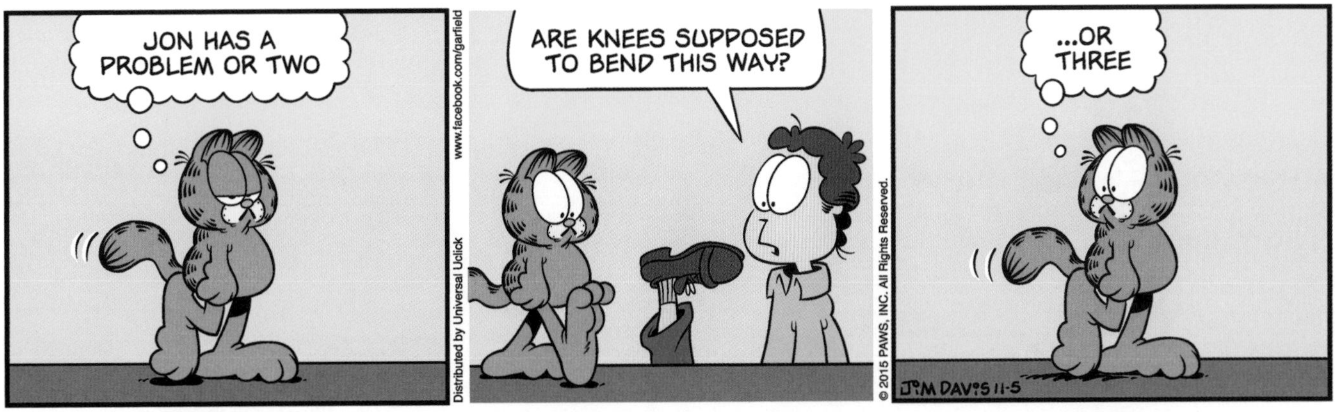
JON HAS A PROBLEM OR TWO
ARE KNEES SUPPOSED TO BEND THIS WAY?
...OR THREE
www.facebook.com/garfield
Distributed by Universal Uclick
© 2015 PAWS, INC. All Rights Reserved.
JIM DAVIS 11-5

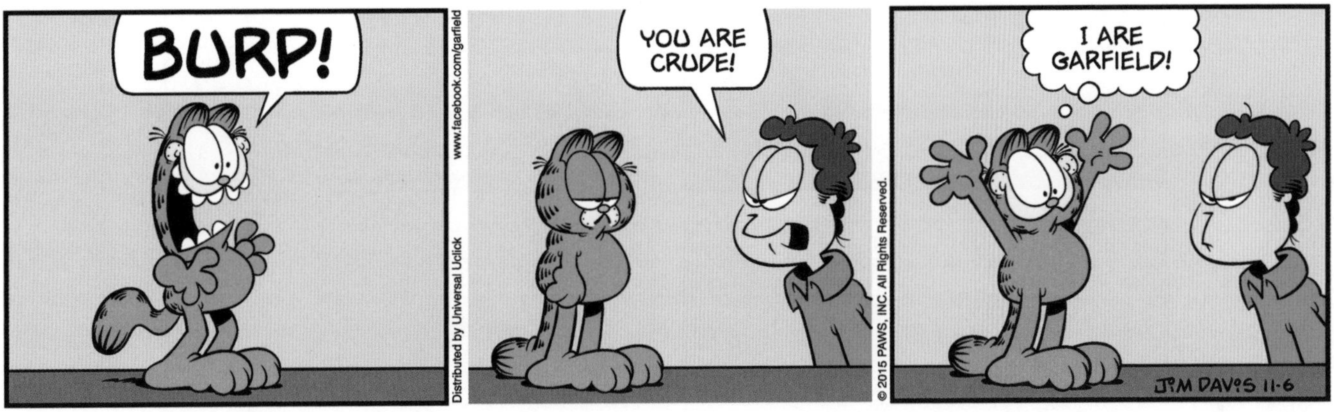
BURP!
YOU ARE CRUDE!
I ARE GARFIELD!
www.facebook.com/garfield
Distributed by Universal Uclick
© 2015 PAWS, INC. All Rights Reserved.
JIM DAVIS 11-6

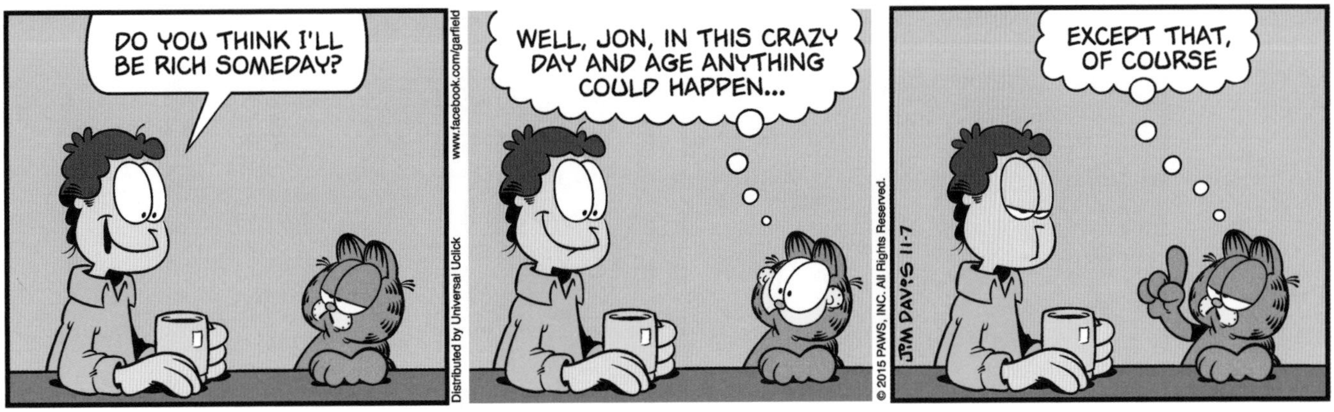
DO YOU THINK I'LL BE RICH SOMEDAY?
WELL, JON, IN THIS CRAZY DAY AND AGE ANYTHING COULD HAPPEN...
EXCEPT THAT, OF COURSE
www.facebook.com/garfield
Distributed by Universal Uclick
© 2015 PAWS, INC. All Rights Reserved.
JIM DAVIS 11-7

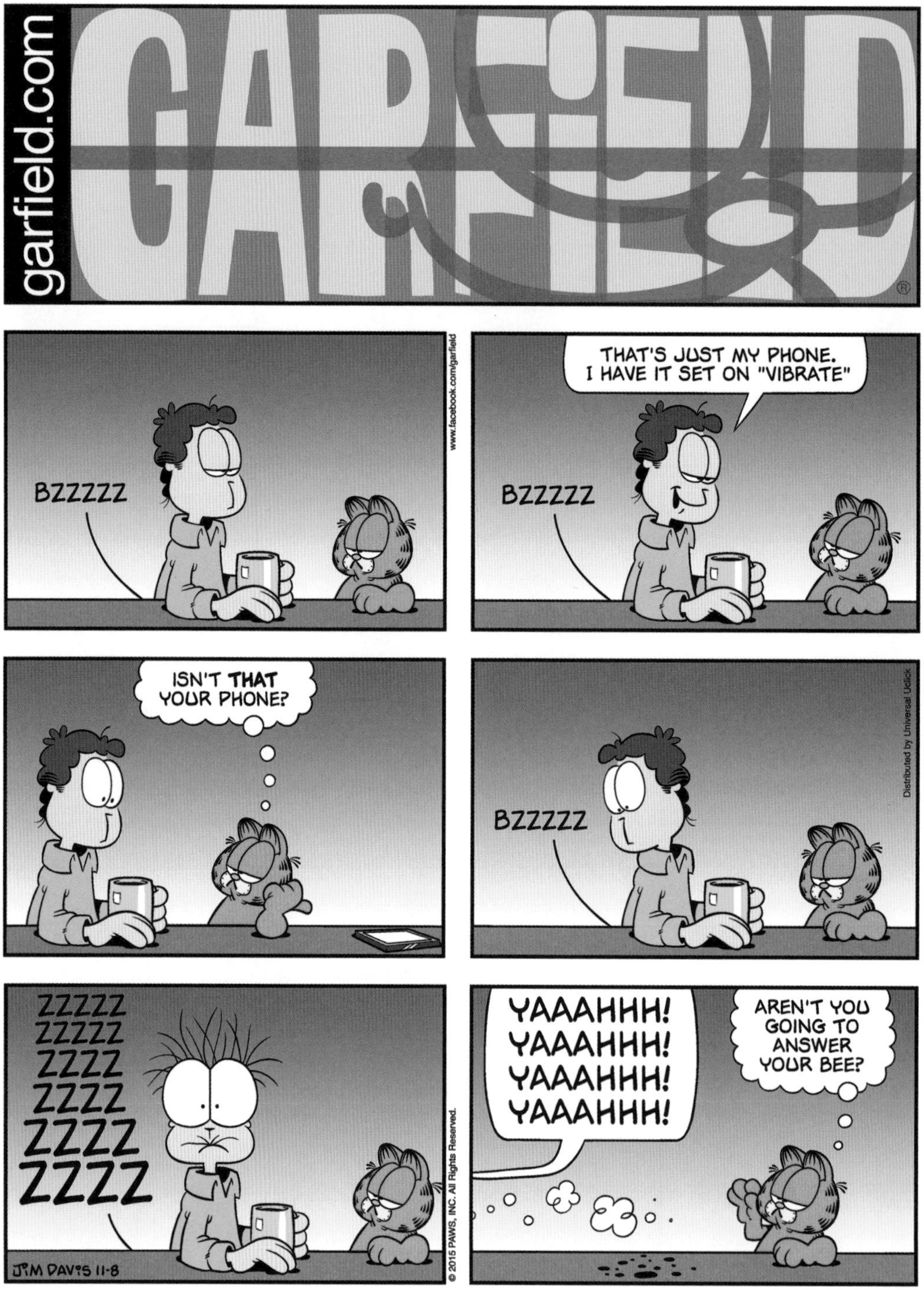
garfield.com
GARFIELD
www.facebook.com/garfield
BZZZZZ
THAT'S JUST MY PHONE. I HAVE IT SET ON "VIBRATE"
BZZZZZ
ISN'T THAT YOUR PHONE?
Distributed by Universal Uclick
BZZZZZ
ZZZZZ ZZZZZ ZZZZ ZZZZ ZZZZ ZZZZ
JIM DAVIS 11-8
© 2015 PAWS, INC. All Rights Reserved.
YAAAHHH! YAAAHHH! YAAAHHH! YAAAHHH!
AREN'T YOU GOING TO ANSWER YOUR BEE?

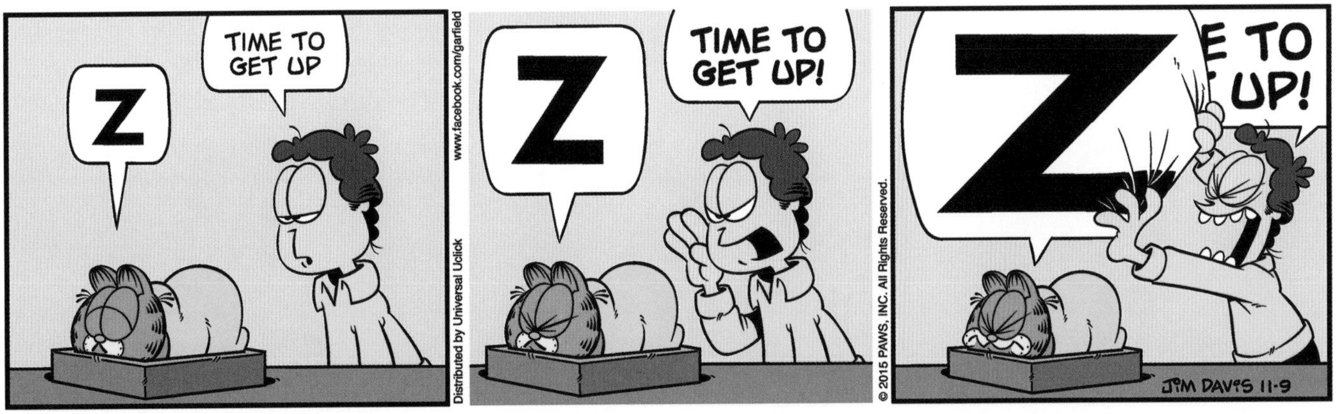
Z
TIME TO GET UP
www.facebook.com/garfield
Distributed by Universal Uclick
Z
TIME TO GET UP!
© 2015 PAWS, INC. All Rights Reserved.
Z
E TO
UP!
JIM DAVIS 11-9

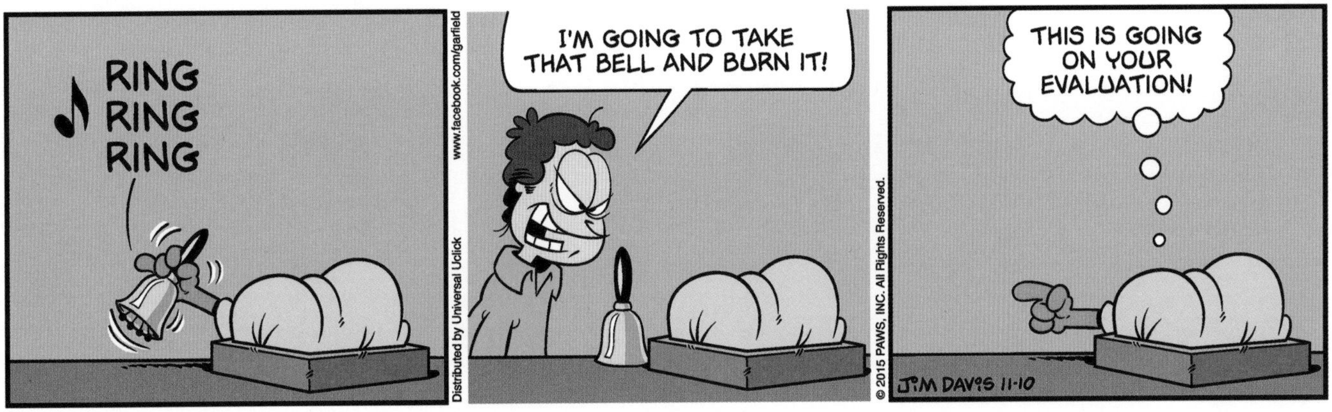
RING
RING
RING
www.facebook.com/garfield
Distributed by Universal Uclick
I'M GOING TO TAKE THAT BELL AND BURN IT!
© 2015 PAWS, INC. All Rights Reserved.
THIS IS GOING ON YOUR EVALUATION!
JIM DAVIS 11-10

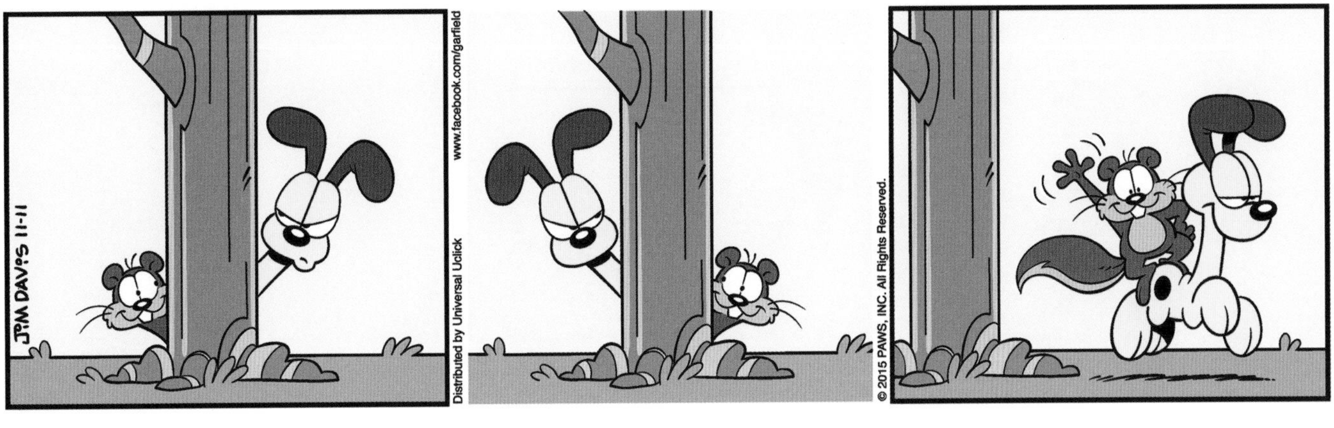
JIM DAVIS 11-11
www.facebook.com/garfield
Distributed by Universal Uclick
© 2015 PAWS, INC. All Rights Reserved.

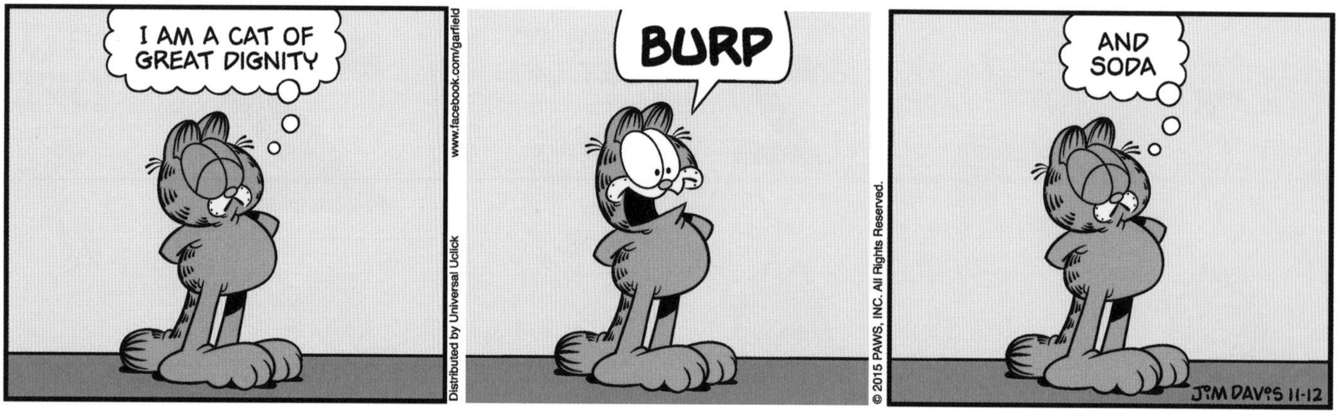
I AM A CAT OF GREAT DIGNITY
Distributed by Universal Uclick
www.facebook.com/garfield
BURP
© 2015 PAWS, INC. All Rights Reserved.
AND SODA
JIM DAVIS 11-12

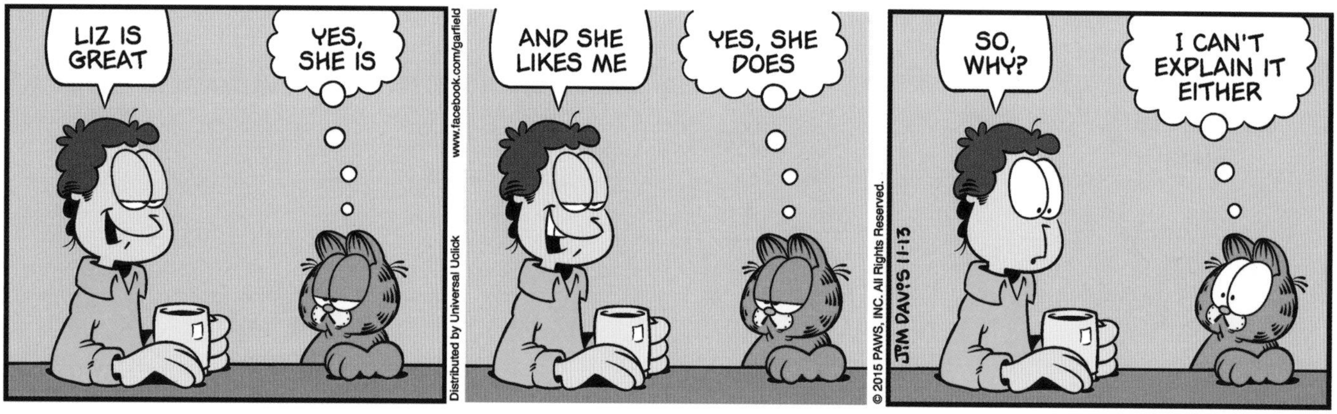
LIZ IS GREAT
YES, SHE IS
Distributed by Universal Uclick
www.facebook.com/garfield
AND SHE LIKES ME
YES, SHE DOES
© 2015 PAWS, INC. All Rights Reserved.
JIM DAVIS 11-13
SO, WHY?
I CAN'T EXPLAIN IT EITHER

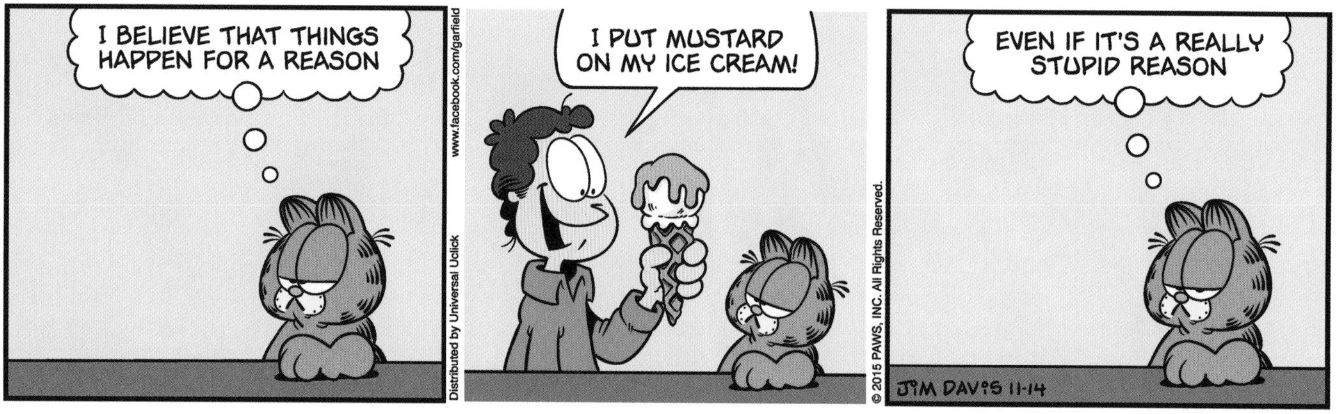
I BELIEVE THAT THINGS HAPPEN FOR A REASON
Distributed by Universal Uclick
www.facebook.com/garfield
I PUT MUSTARD ON MY ICE CREAM!
© 2015 PAWS, INC. All Rights Reserved.
JIM DAVIS 11-14
EVEN IF IT'S A REALLY STUPID REASON

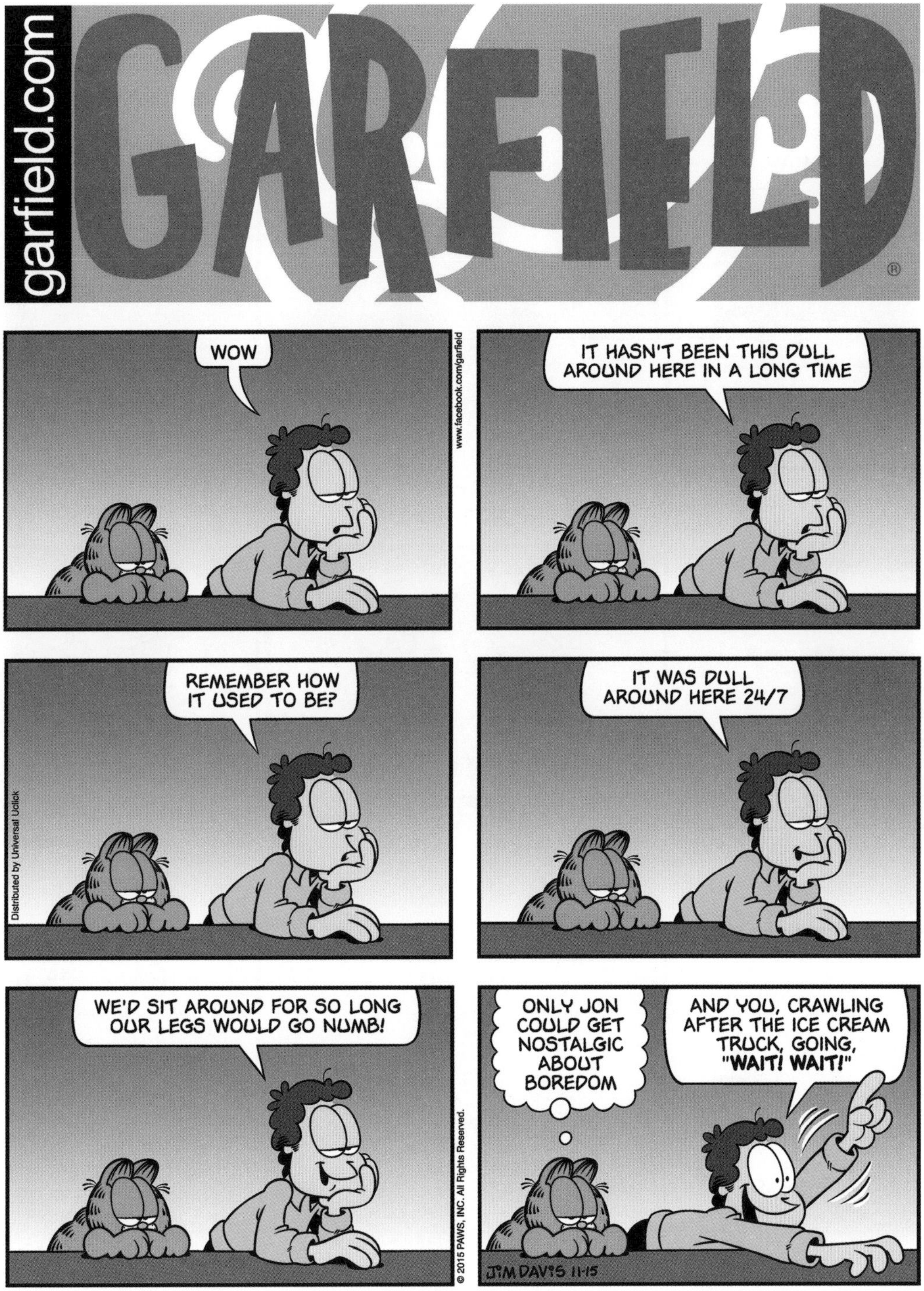
garfield.com
GARFIELD
WOW
IT HASN'T BEEN THIS DULL AROUND HERE IN A LONG TIME
www.facebook.com/garfield
REMEMBER HOW IT USED TO BE?
IT WAS DULL AROUND HERE 24/7
Distributed by Universal Uclick
WE'D SIT AROUND FOR SO LONG OUR LEGS WOULD GO NUMB!
ONLY JON COULD GET NOSTALGIC ABOUT BOREDOM
AND YOU, CRAWLING AFTER THE ICE CREAM TRUCK, GOING, "WAIT! WAIT!"
© 2015 PAWS, INC. All Rights Reserved.
JIM DAVIS 11-15

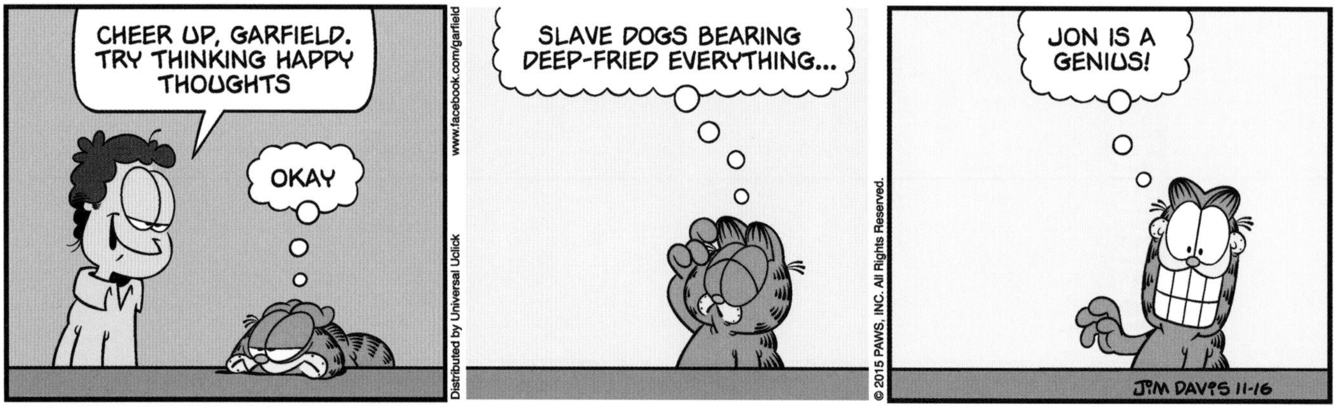
CHEER UP, GARFIELD. TRY THINKING HAPPY THOUGHTS
OKAY
Distributed by Universal Uclick www.facebook.com/garfield
SLAVE DOGS BEARING DEEP-FRIED EVERYTHING...
© 2015 PAWS, INC. All Rights Reserved.
JON IS A GENIUS!
JIM DAVIS 11-16

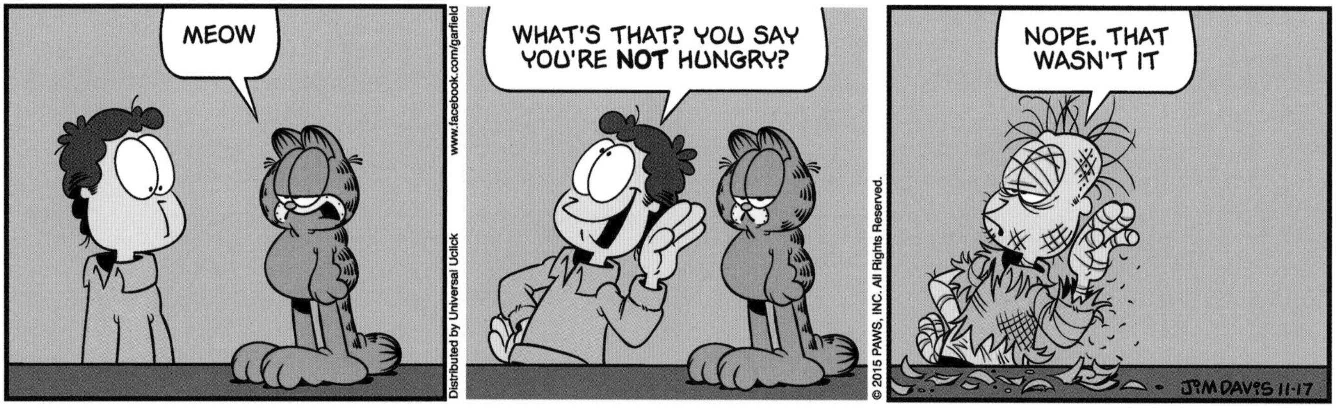
MEOW
Distributed by Universal Uclick www.facebook.com/garfield
WHAT'S THAT? YOU SAY YOU'RE **NOT** HUNGRY?
© 2015 PAWS, INC. All Rights Reserved.
NOPE. THAT WASN'T IT
JIM DAVIS 11-17

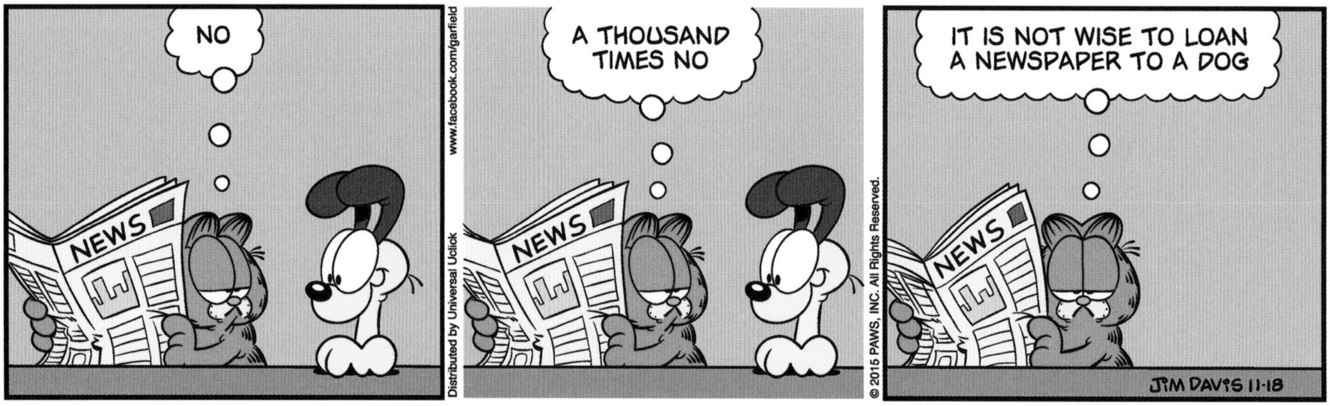
NO
NEWS
Distributed by Universal Uclick www.facebook.com/garfield
A THOUSAND TIMES NO
NEWS
© 2015 PAWS, INC. All Rights Reserved.
IT IS NOT WISE TO LOAN A NEWSPAPER TO A DOG
NEWS
JIM DAVIS 11-18

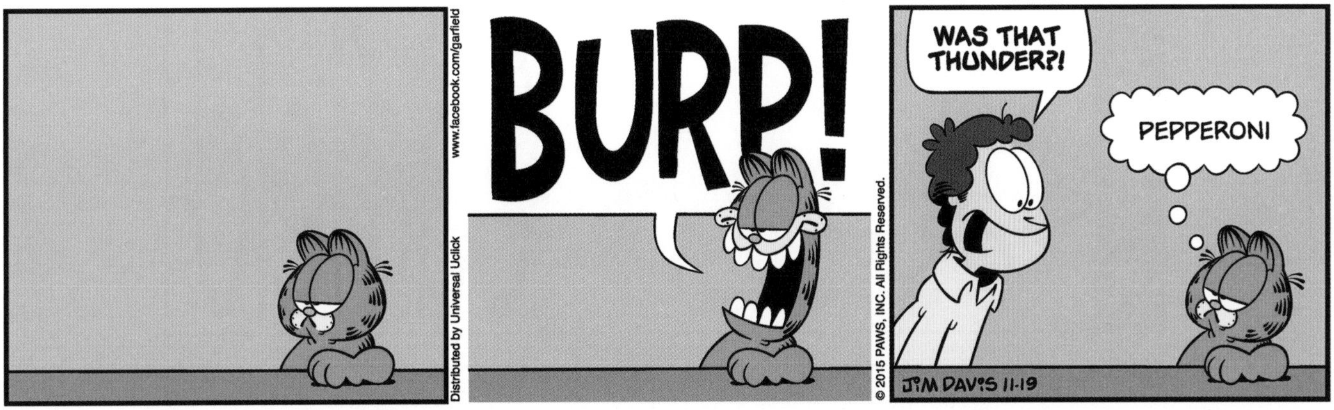
BURP!
WAS THAT THUNDER?!
PEPPERONI
JIM DAVIS 11-19
Distributed by Universal Uclick
www.facebook.com/garfield
© 2015 PAWS, INC. All Rights Reserved.

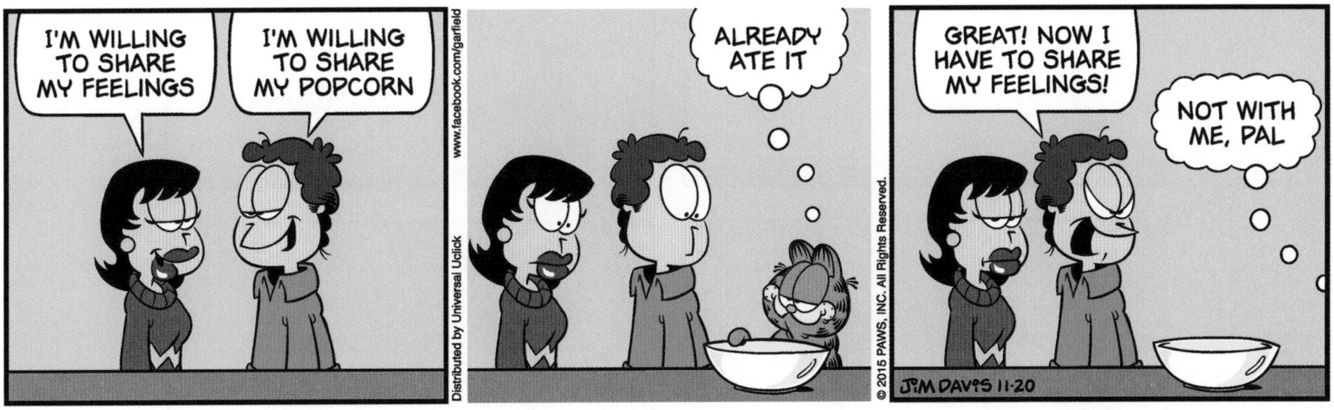
I'M WILLING TO SHARE MY FEELINGS
I'M WILLING TO SHARE MY POPCORN
ALREADY ATE IT
GREAT! NOW I HAVE TO SHARE MY FEELINGS!
NOT WITH ME, PAL
JIM DAVIS 11-20
Distributed by Universal Uclick
www.facebook.com/garfield
© 2015 PAWS, INC. All Rights Reserved.

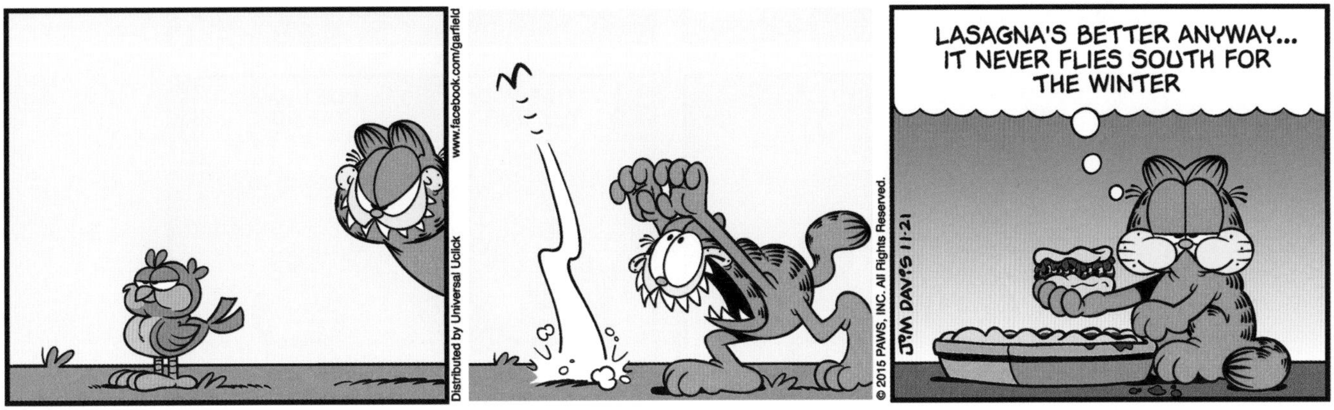
LASAGNA'S BETTER ANYWAY... IT NEVER FLIES SOUTH FOR THE WINTER
JIM DAVIS 11-21
Distributed by Universal Uclick
www.facebook.com/garfield
© 2015 PAWS, INC. All Rights Reserved.

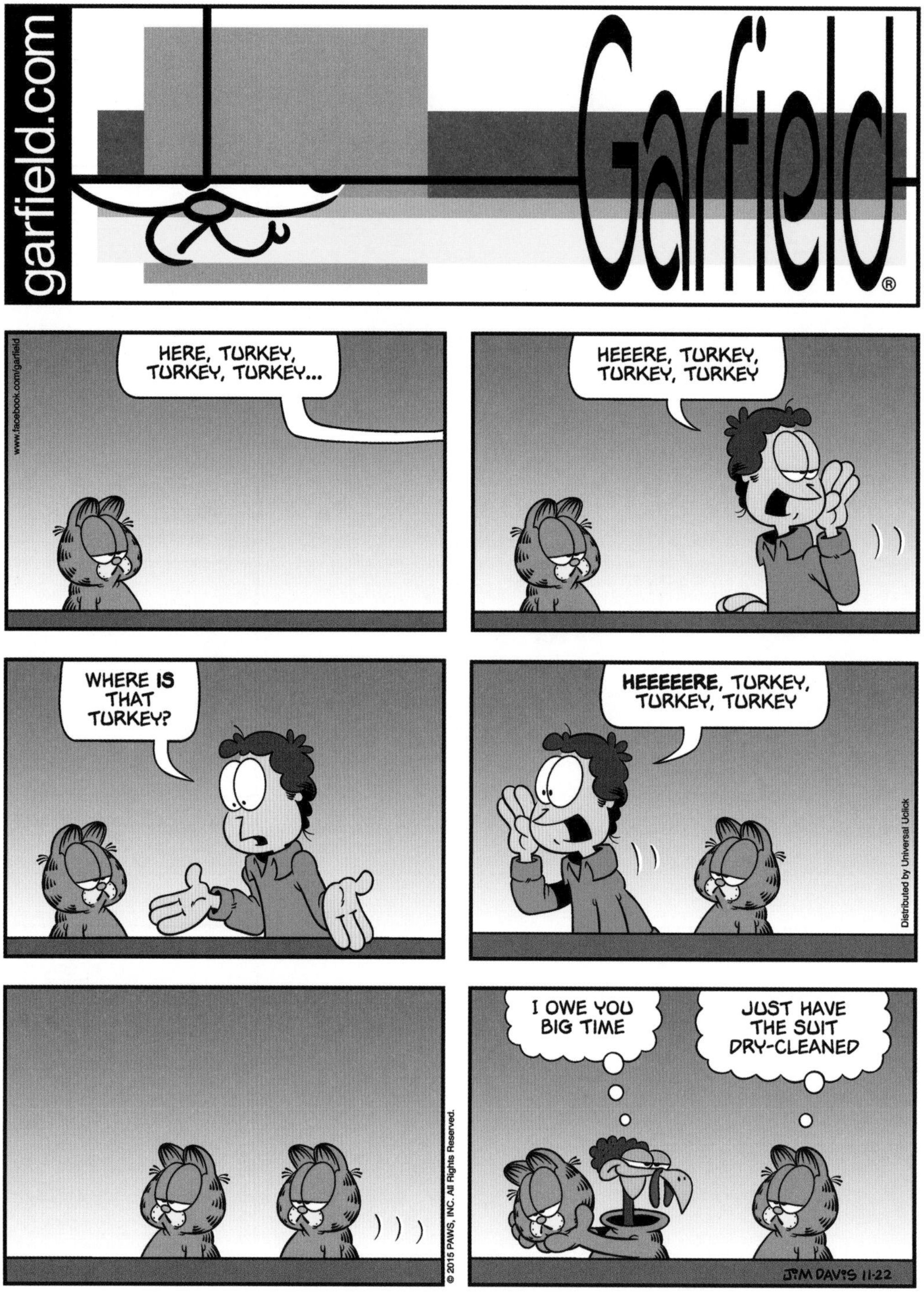
garfield.com
Garfield®
www.facebook.com/garfield
HERE, TURKEY, TURKEY, TURKEY...
HEEERE, TURKEY, TURKEY, TURKEY
WHERE **IS** THAT TURKEY?
HEEEEERE, TURKEY, TURKEY, TURKEY
Distributed by Universal Uclick
© 2015 PAWS, INC. All Rights Reserved.
I OWE YOU BIG TIME
JUST HAVE THE SUIT DRY-CLEANED
JIM DAVIS 11-22

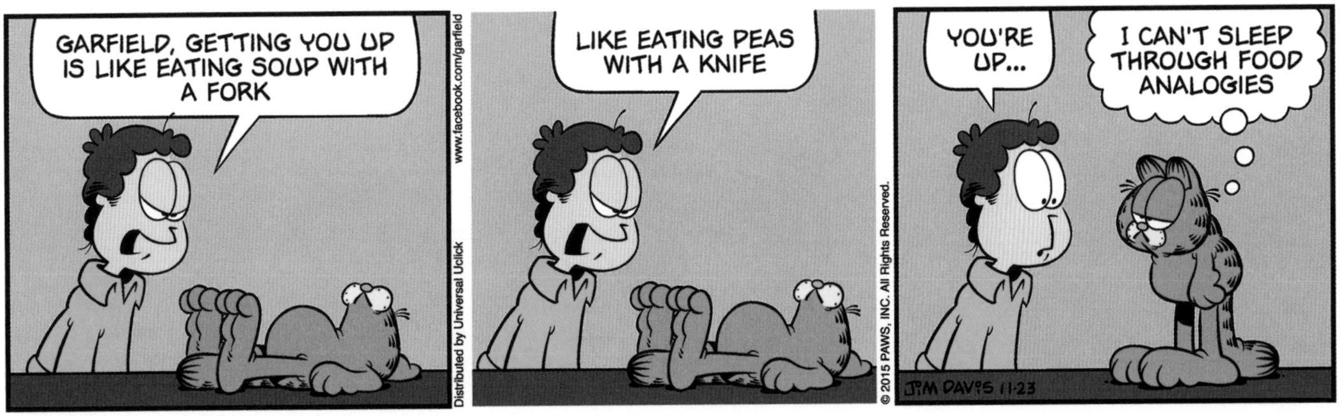
GARFIELD, GETTING YOU UP IS LIKE EATING SOUP WITH A FORK
www.facebook.com/garfield
Distributed by Universal Uclick
LIKE EATING PEAS WITH A KNIFE
© 2015 PAWS, INC. All Rights Reserved.
YOU'RE UP...
I CAN'T SLEEP THROUGH FOOD ANALOGIES
JIM DAVIS 11-23

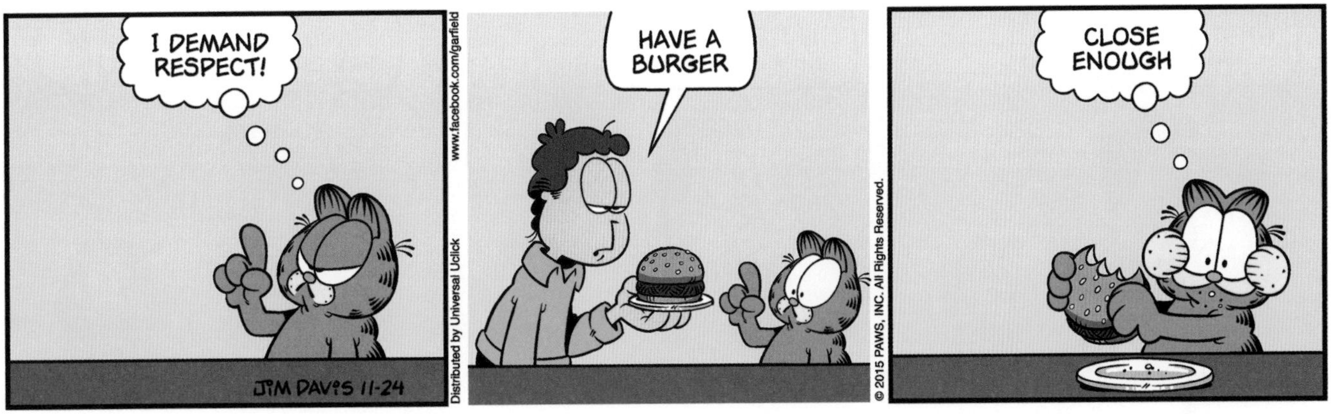
I DEMAND RESPECT!
JIM DAVIS 11-24
www.facebook.com/garfield
Distributed by Universal Uclick
HAVE A BURGER
© 2015 PAWS, INC. All Rights Reserved.
CLOSE ENOUGH

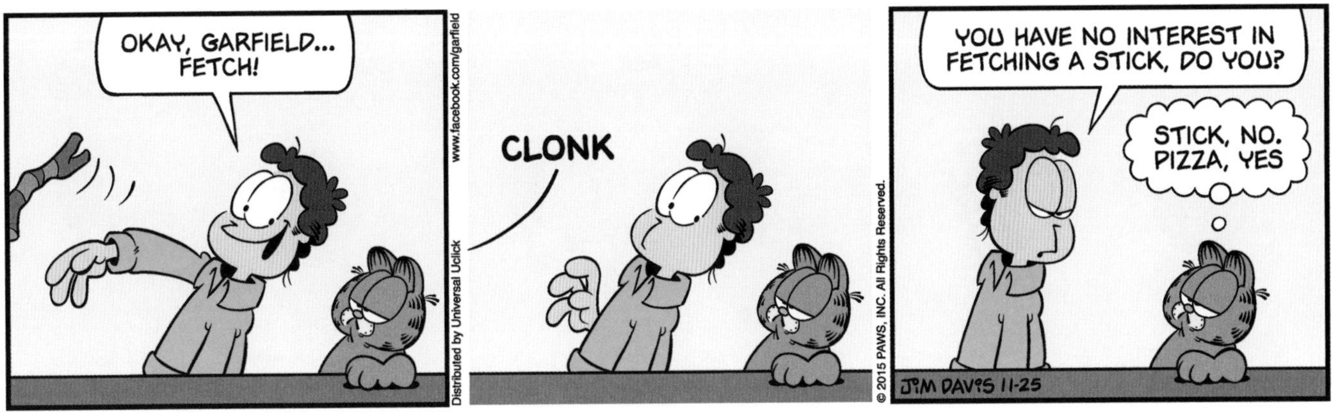
OKAY, GARFIELD... FETCH!
www.facebook.com/garfield
Distributed by Universal Uclick
CLONK
© 2015 PAWS, INC. All Rights Reserved.
YOU HAVE NO INTEREST IN FETCHING A STICK, DO YOU?
STICK, NO. PIZZA, YES
JIM DAVIS 11-25

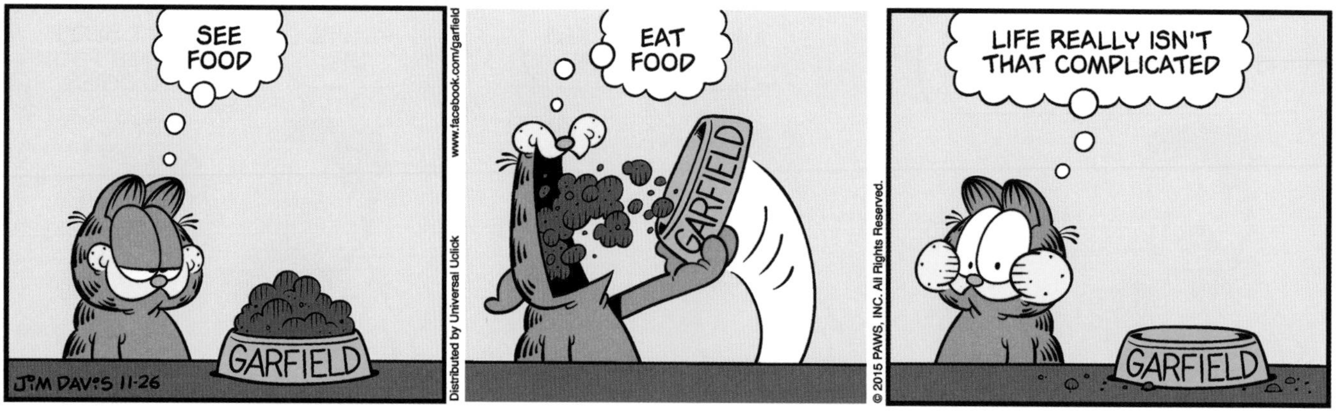
SEE FOOD
JIM DAVIS 11-26
GARFIELD
www.facebook.com/garfield
Distributed by Universal Uclick
EAT FOOD
GARFIELD
© 2015 PAWS, INC. All Rights Reserved.
LIFE REALLY ISN'T THAT COMPLICATED
GARFIELD

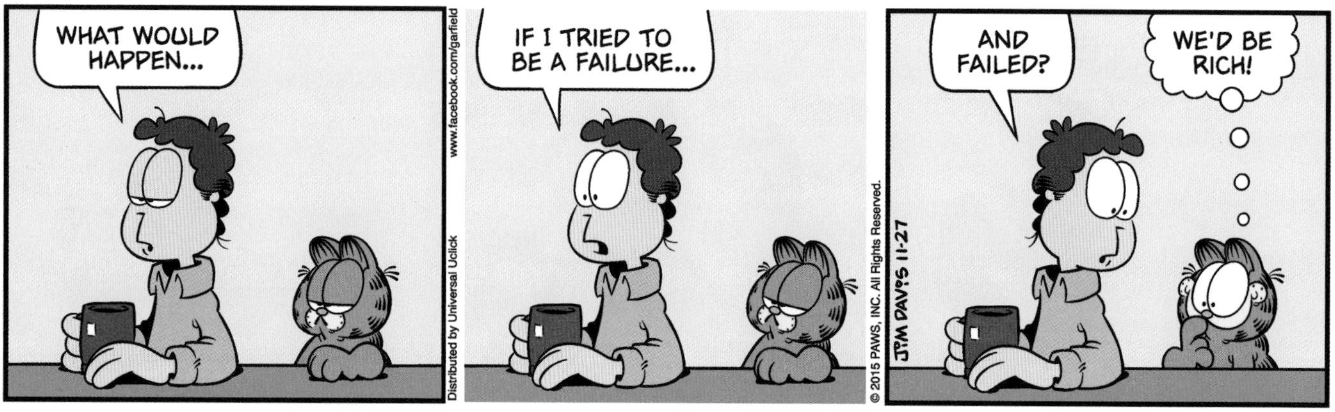
WHAT WOULD HAPPEN...
www.facebook.com/garfield
Distributed by Universal Uclick
IF I TRIED TO BE A FAILURE...
© 2015 PAWS, INC. All Rights Reserved.
JIM DAVIS 11-27
AND FAILED?
WE'D BE RICH!

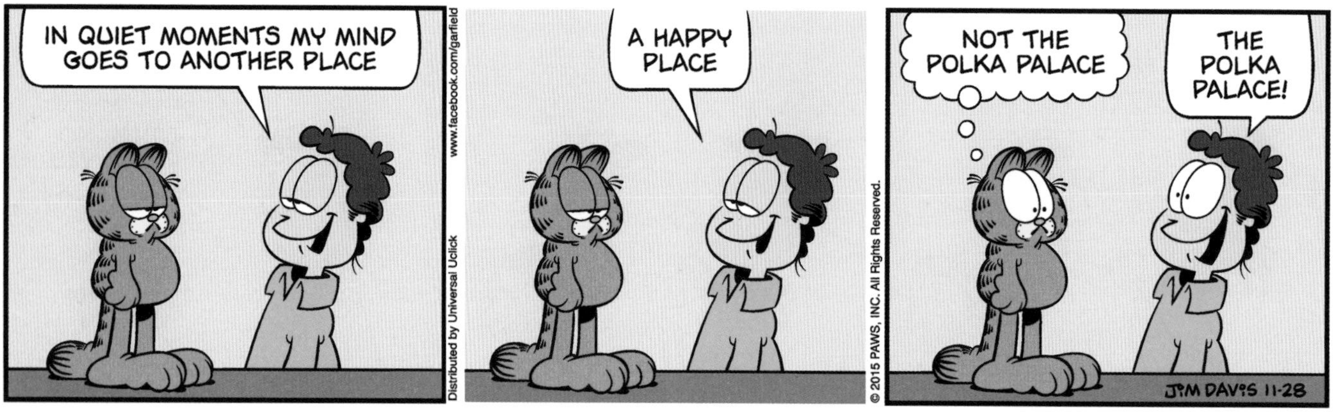
IN QUIET MOMENTS MY MIND GOES TO ANOTHER PLACE
www.facebook.com/garfield
Distributed by Universal Uclick
A HAPPY PLACE
© 2015 PAWS, INC. All Rights Reserved.
NOT THE POLKA PALACE
THE POLKA PALACE!
JIM DAVIS 11-28

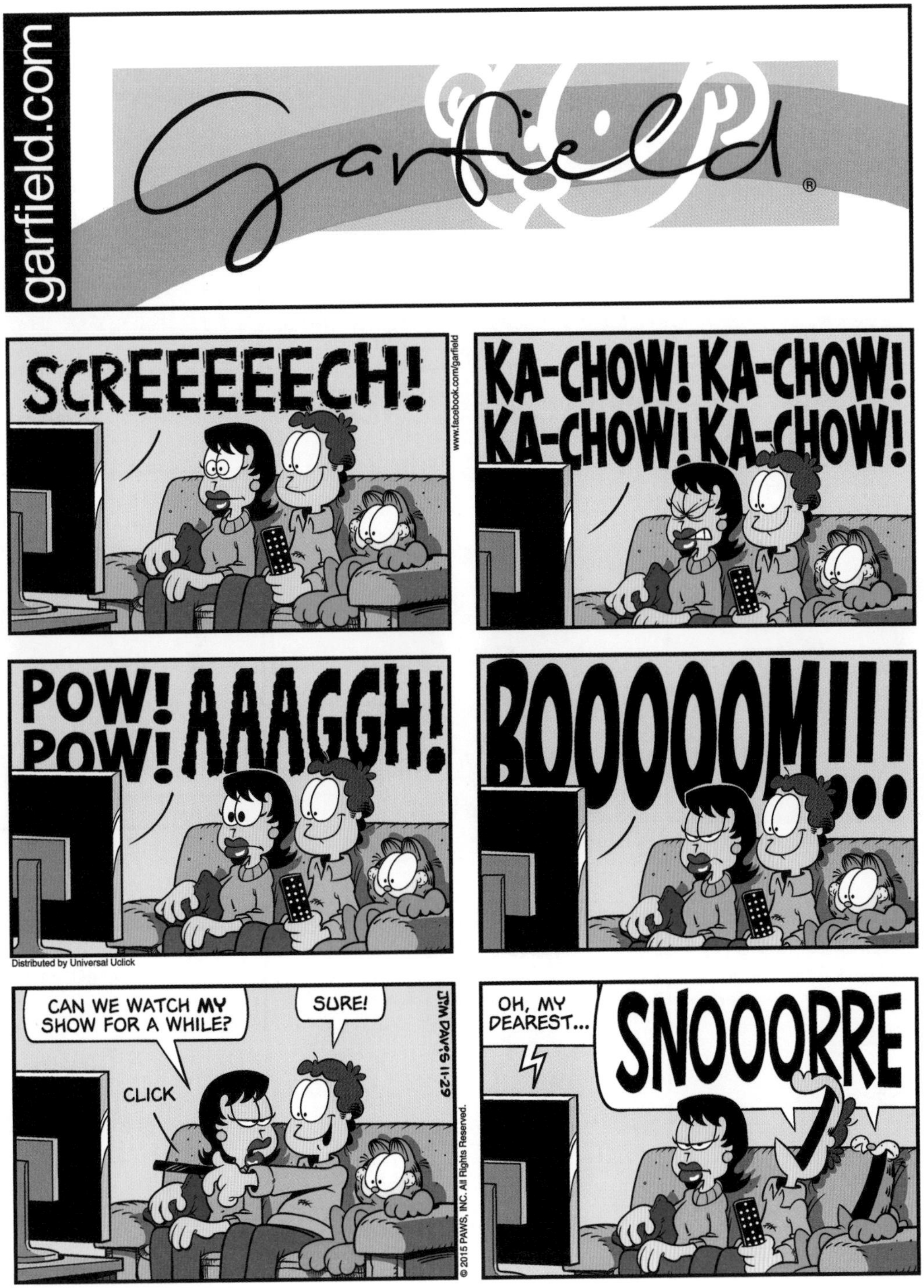
garfield.com
Garfield®
SCREEEEEECH!
www.facebook.com/garfield
KA-CHOW! KA-CHOW!
KA-CHOW! KA-CHOW!
POW! POW!
AAAGGH!
BOOOOOM!!!
Distributed by Universal Uclick
CAN WE WATCH MY SHOW FOR A WHILE?
SURE!
CLICK
JIM DAVIS 11-29
© 2015 PAWS, INC. All Rights Reserved.
OH, MY DEAREST...
SNOOORRE

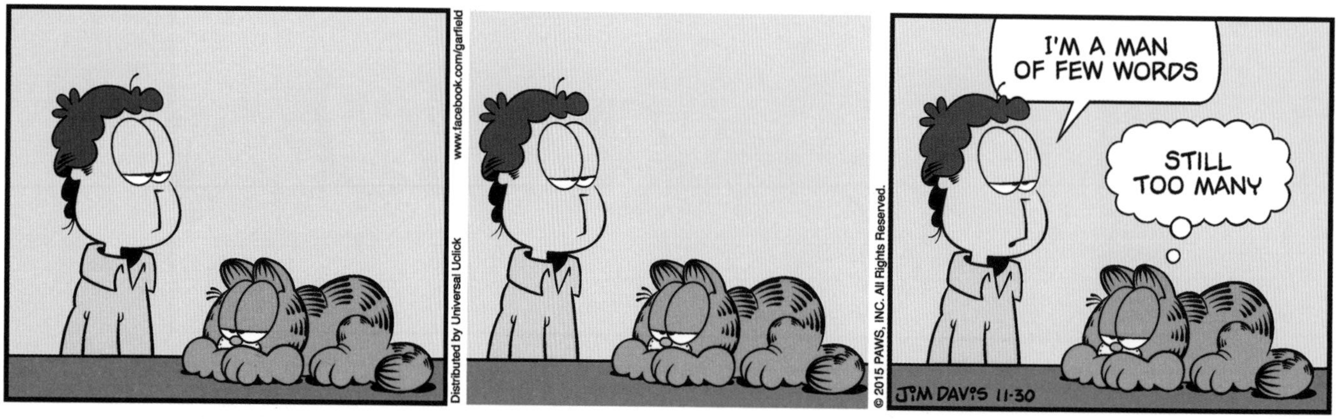
Distributed by Universal Uclick www.facebook.com/garfield
© 2015 PAWS, INC. All Rights Reserved.
I'M A MAN OF FEW WORDS
STILL TOO MANY
JIM DAVIS 11-30

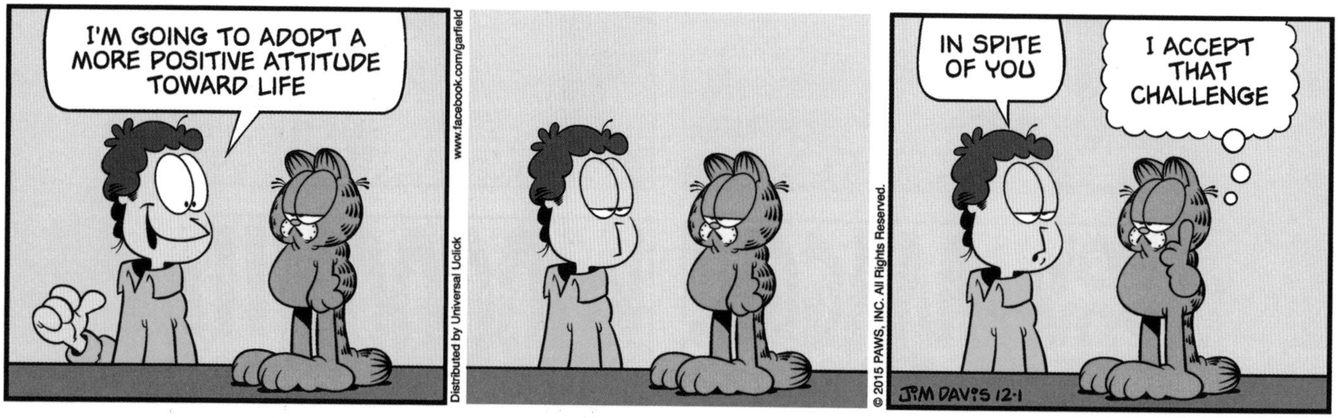
I'M GOING TO ADOPT A MORE POSITIVE ATTITUDE TOWARD LIFE
Distributed by Universal Uclick www.facebook.com/garfield
© 2015 PAWS, INC. All Rights Reserved.
IN SPITE OF YOU
I ACCEPT THAT CHALLENGE
JIM DAVIS 12-1

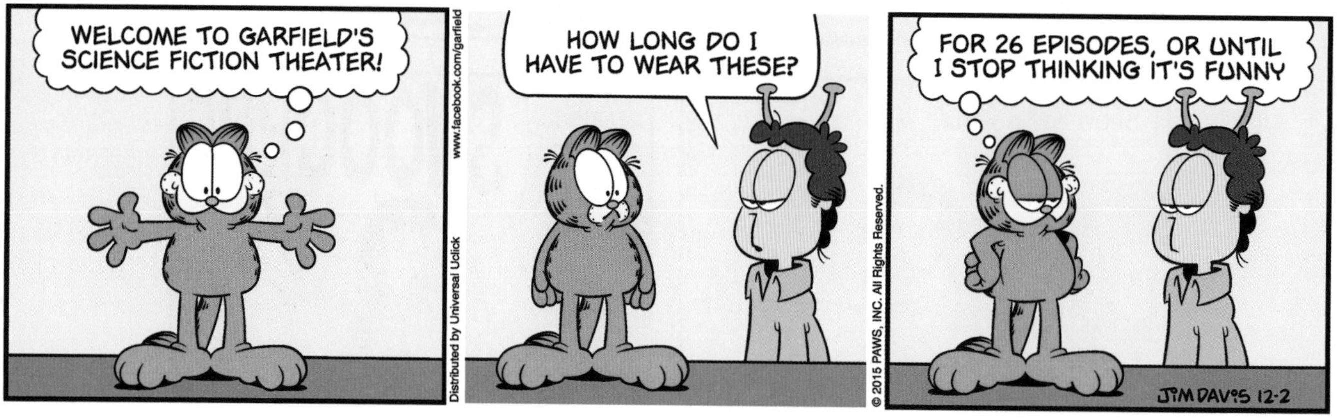
WELCOME TO GARFIELD'S SCIENCE FICTION THEATER!
Distributed by Universal Uclick www.facebook.com/garfield
HOW LONG DO I HAVE TO WEAR THESE?
© 2015 PAWS, INC. All Rights Reserved.
FOR 26 EPISODES, OR UNTIL I STOP THINKING IT'S FUNNY
JIM DAVIS 12-2

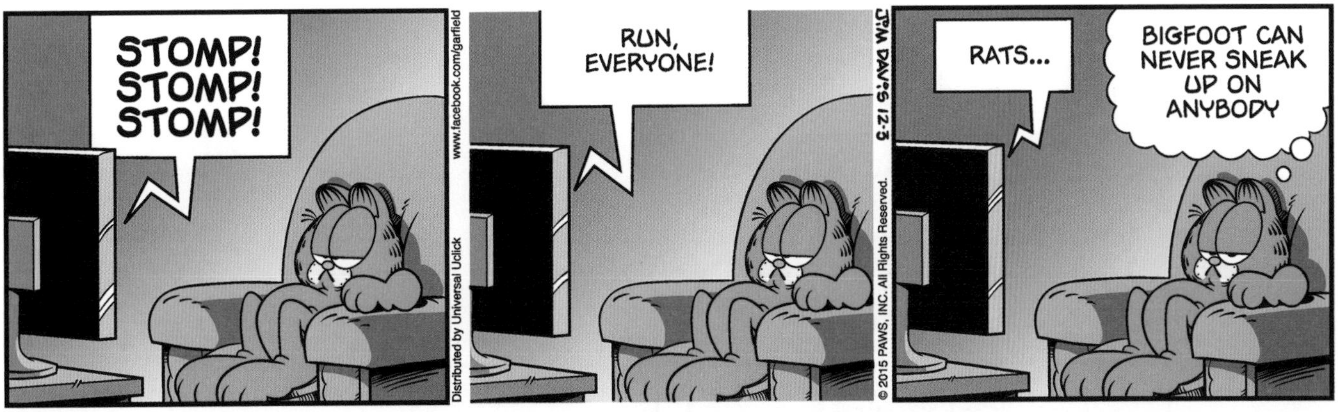
STOMP! STOMP! STOMP!
Distributed by Universal Uclick www.facebook.com/garfield
RUN, EVERYONE!
JIM DAVIS 12-3
© 2015 PAWS, INC. All Rights Reserved.
RATS...
BIGFOOT CAN NEVER SNEAK UP ON ANYBODY

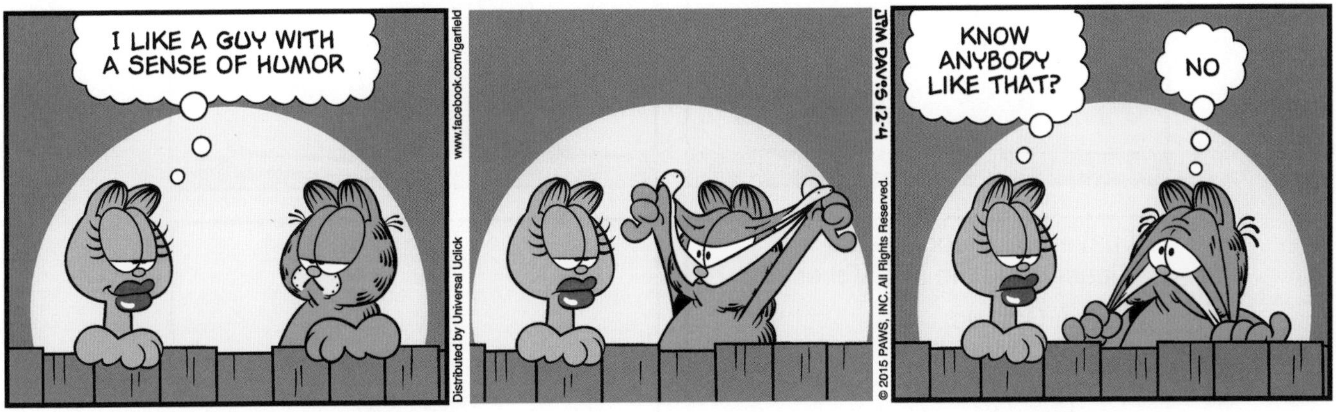
I LIKE A GUY WITH A SENSE OF HUMOR
Distributed by Universal Uclick www.facebook.com/garfield
JIM DAVIS 12-4
© 2015 PAWS, INC. All Rights Reserved.
KNOW ANYBODY LIKE THAT?
NO

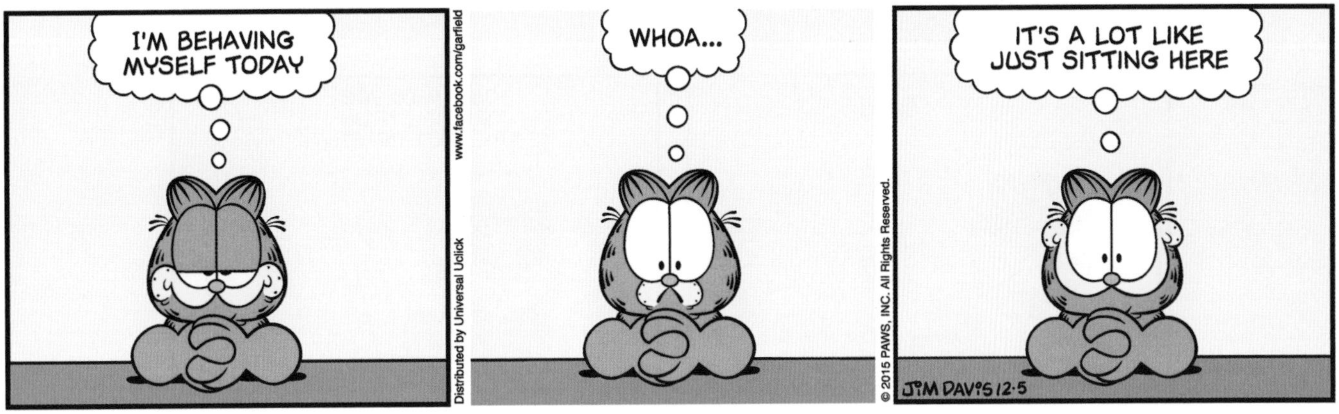
I'M BEHAVING MYSELF TODAY
Distributed by Universal Uclick www.facebook.com/garfield
WHOA...
© 2015 PAWS, INC. All Rights Reserved.
IT'S A LOT LIKE JUST SITTING HERE
JIM DAVIS 12-5

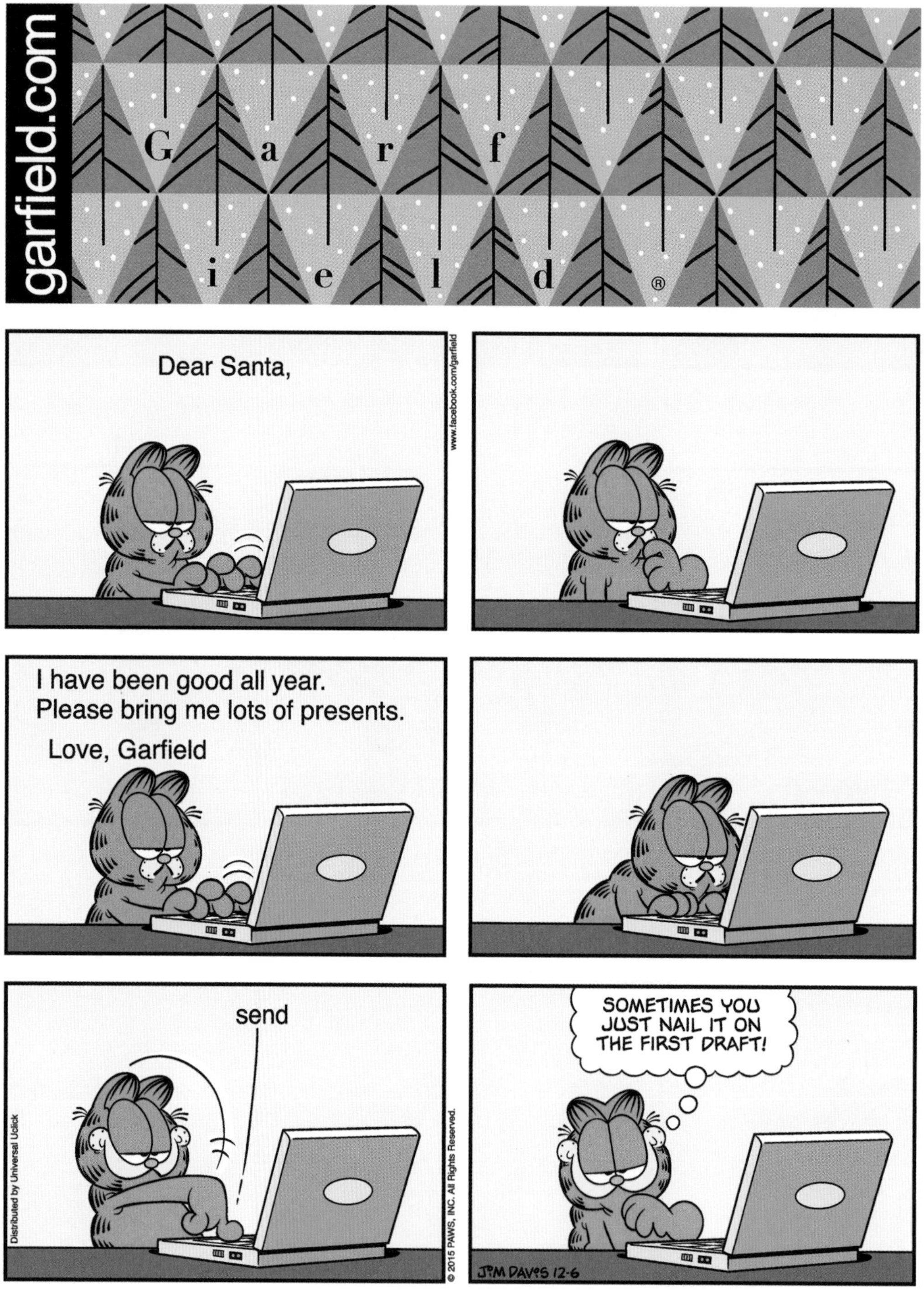
garfield.com
Garfield®
Dear Santa,
www.facebook.com/garfield
I have been good all year.
Please bring me lots of presents.
Love, Garfield
send
Distributed by Universal Uclick
© 2015 PAWS, INC. All Rights Reserved.
SOMETIMES YOU JUST NAIL IT ON THE FIRST DRAFT!
JIM DAVIS 12-6

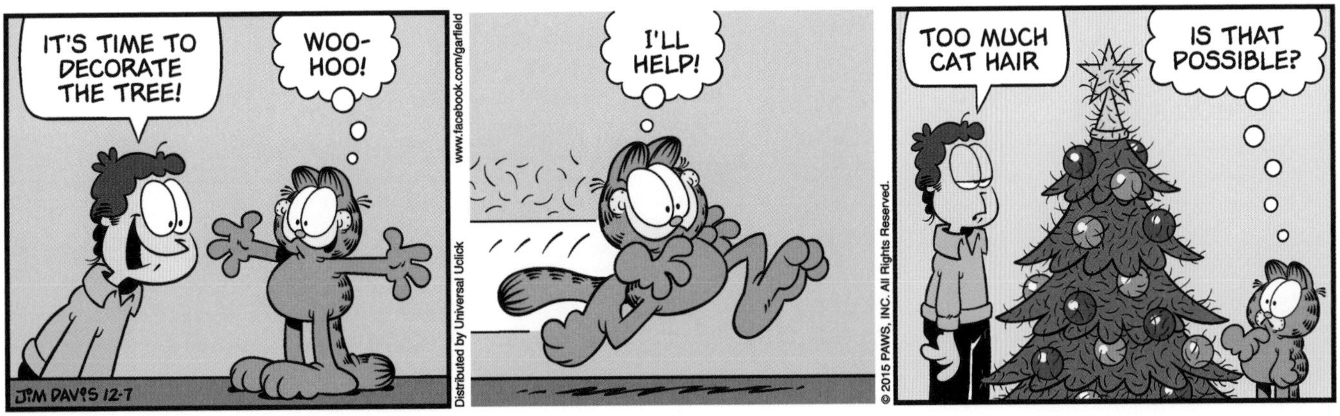
IT'S TIME TO DECORATE THE TREE!
WOO-HOO!
I'LL HELP!
TOO MUCH CAT HAIR
IS THAT POSSIBLE?
JIM DAVIS 12-7
Distributed by Universal Uclick
www.facebook.com/garfield
© 2015 PAWS, INC. All Rights Reserved.

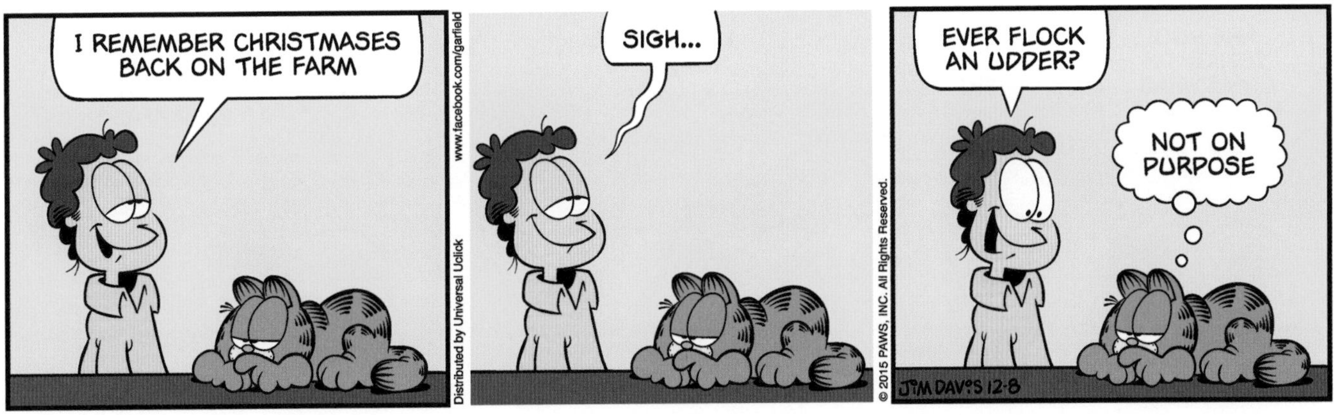
I REMEMBER CHRISTMASES BACK ON THE FARM
SIGH...
EVER FLOCK AN UDDER?
NOT ON PURPOSE
JIM DAVIS 12-8
Distributed by Universal Uclick
www.facebook.com/garfield
© 2015 PAWS, INC. All Rights Reserved.

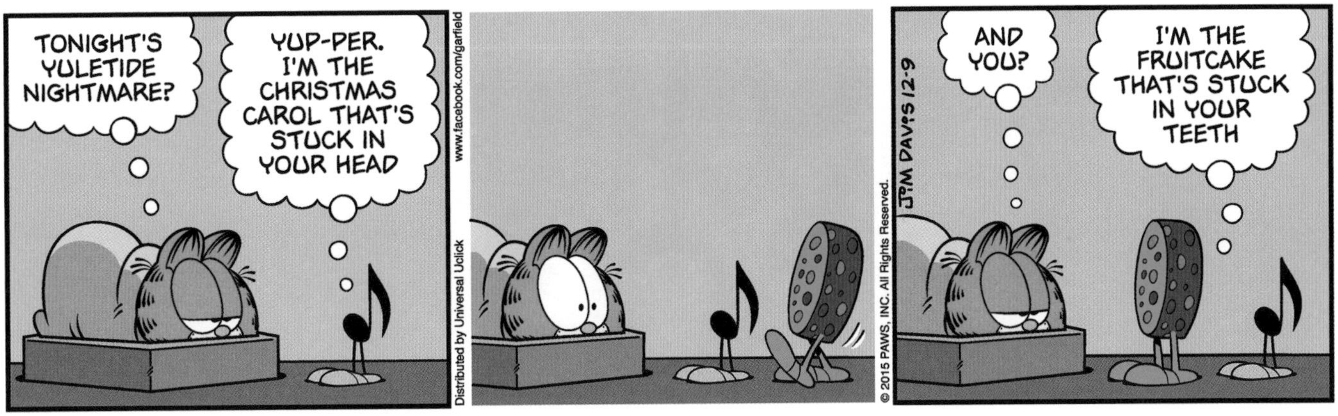
TONIGHT'S YULETIDE NIGHTMARE?
YUP-PER. I'M THE CHRISTMAS CAROL THAT'S STUCK IN YOUR HEAD
AND YOU?
I'M THE FRUITCAKE THAT'S STUCK IN YOUR TEETH
JIM DAVIS 12-9
Distributed by Universal Uclick
www.facebook.com/garfield
© 2015 PAWS, INC. All Rights Reserved.

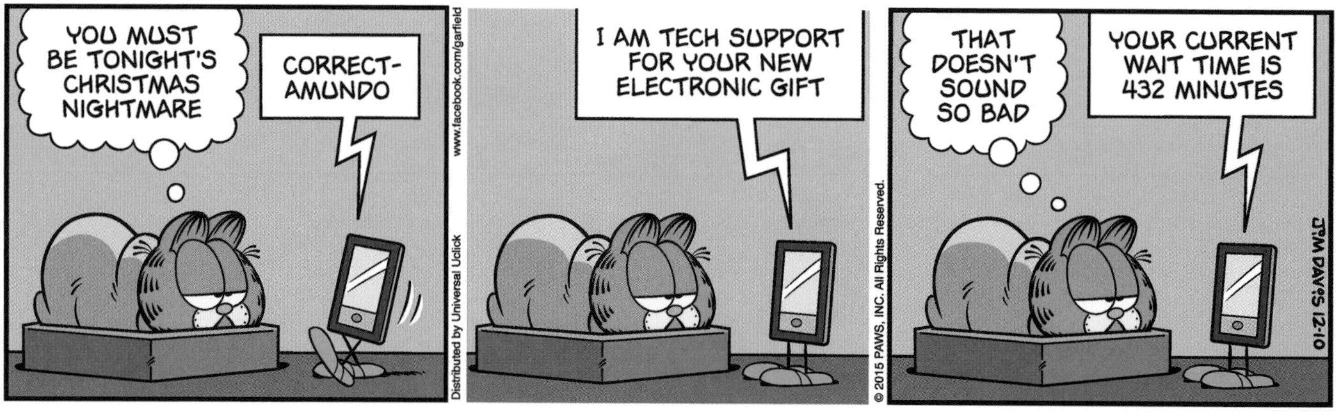
YOU MUST BE TONIGHT'S CHRISTMAS NIGHTMARE
CORRECT-AMUNDO
www.facebook.com/garfield
Distributed by Universal Uclick
I AM TECH SUPPORT FOR YOUR NEW ELECTRONIC GIFT
© 2015 PAWS, INC. All Rights Reserved.
THAT DOESN'T SOUND SO BAD
YOUR CURRENT WAIT TIME IS 432 MINUTES
JIM DAVIS 12-10

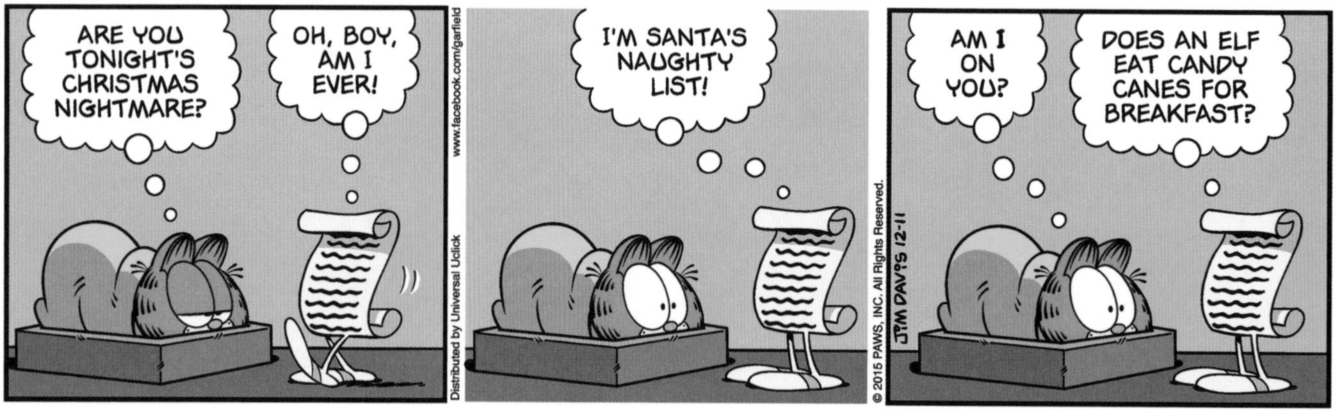
ARE YOU TONIGHT'S CHRISTMAS NIGHTMARE?
OH, BOY, AM I EVER!
www.facebook.com/garfield
Distributed by Universal Uclick
I'M SANTA'S NAUGHTY LIST!
© 2015 PAWS, INC. All Rights Reserved.
JIM DAVIS 12-11
AM I ON YOU?
DOES AN ELF EAT CANDY CANES FOR BREAKFAST?

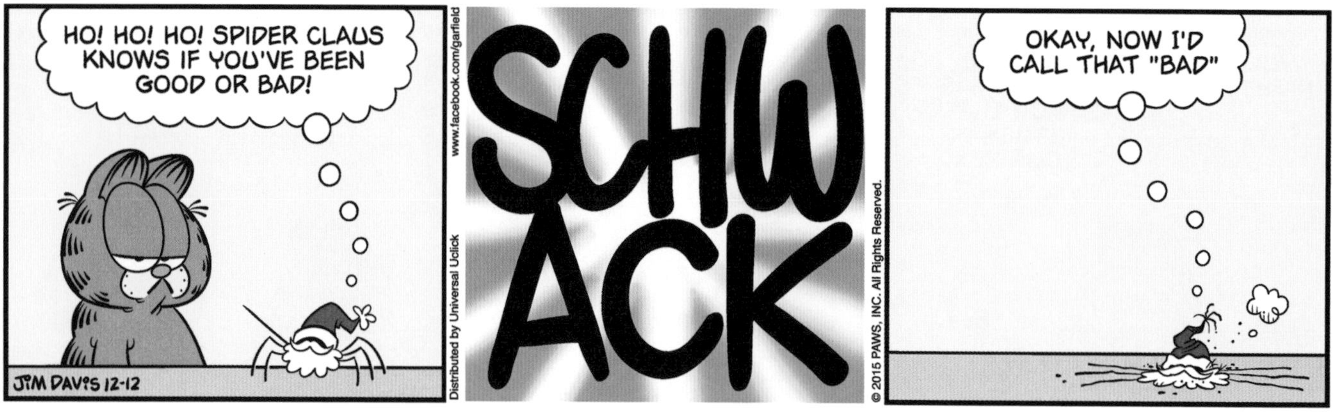
HO! HO! HO! SPIDER CLAUS KNOWS IF YOU'VE BEEN GOOD OR BAD!
JIM DAVIS 12-12
www.facebook.com/garfield
Distributed by Universal Uclick
SCHWACK
© 2015 PAWS, INC. All Rights Reserved.
OKAY, NOW I'D CALL THAT "BAD"

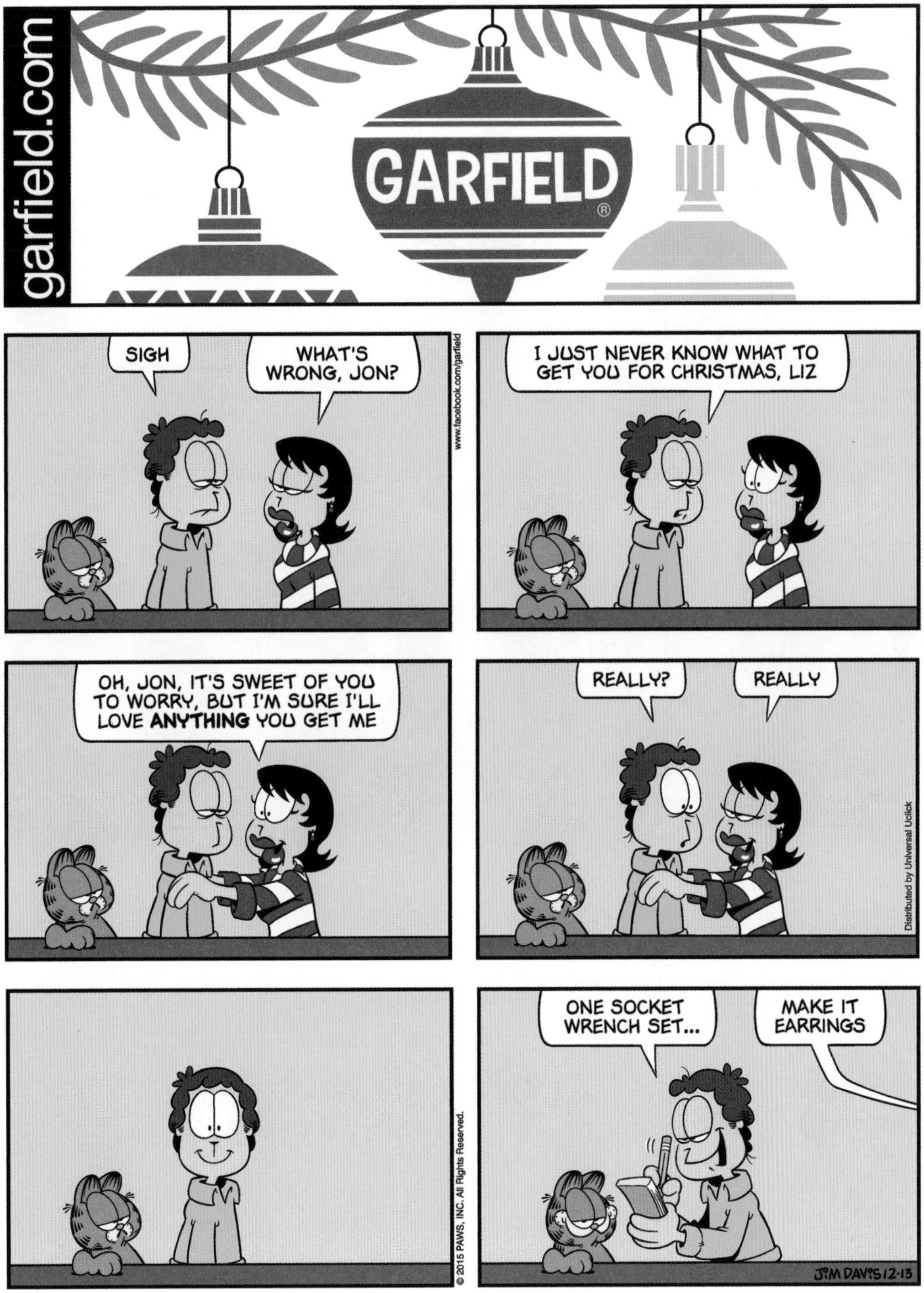
garfield.com
GARFIELD
SIGH
WHAT'S WRONG, JON?
www.facebook.com/garfield
I JUST NEVER KNOW WHAT TO GET YOU FOR CHRISTMAS, LIZ
OH, JON, IT'S SWEET OF YOU TO WORRY, BUT I'M SURE I'LL LOVE **ANYTHING** YOU GET ME
REALLY?
REALLY
Distributed by Universal Uclick
© 2015 PAWS, INC. All Rights Reserved.
ONE SOCKET WRENCH SET...
MAKE IT EARRINGS
JIM DAVIS 12-13

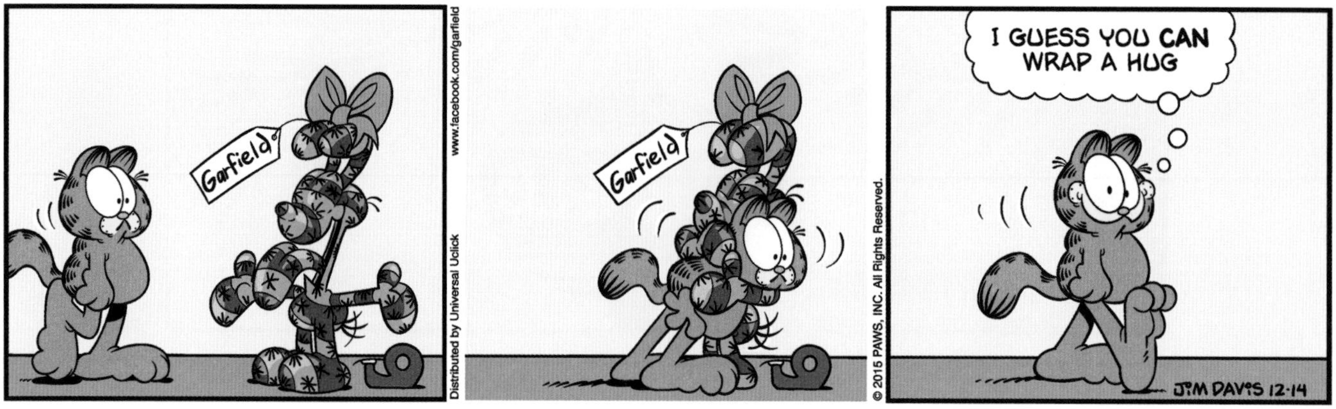
Garfield
Distributed by Universal Uclick
www.facebook.com/garfield
Garfield
© 2015 PAWS, INC. All Rights Reserved.
I GUESS YOU CAN WRAP A HUG
JIM DAVIS 12-14

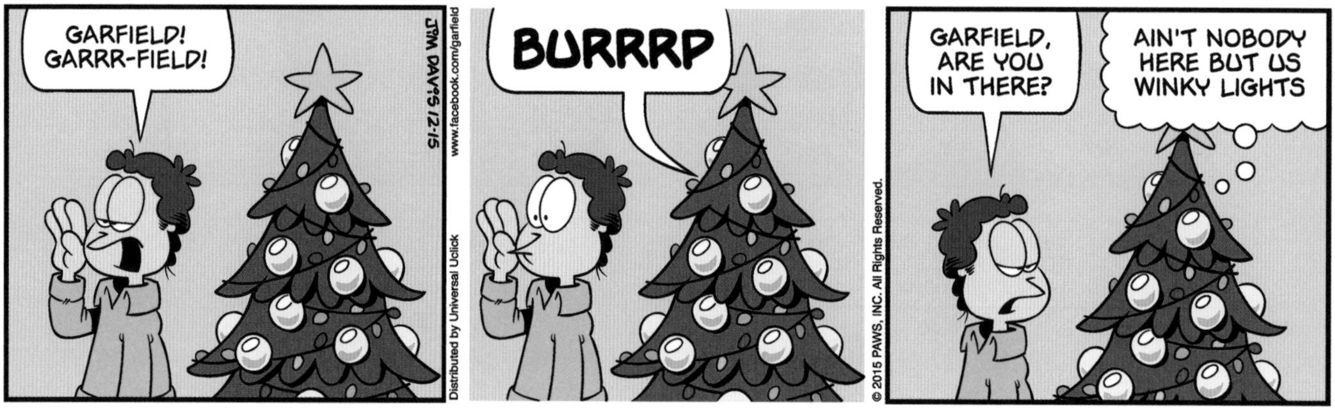
GARFIELD! GARRR-FIELD!
JIM DAVIS 12-15
Distributed by Universal Uclick
www.facebook.com/garfield
BURRRP
© 2015 PAWS, INC. All Rights Reserved.
GARFIELD, ARE YOU IN THERE?
AIN'T NOBODY HERE BUT US WINKY LIGHTS

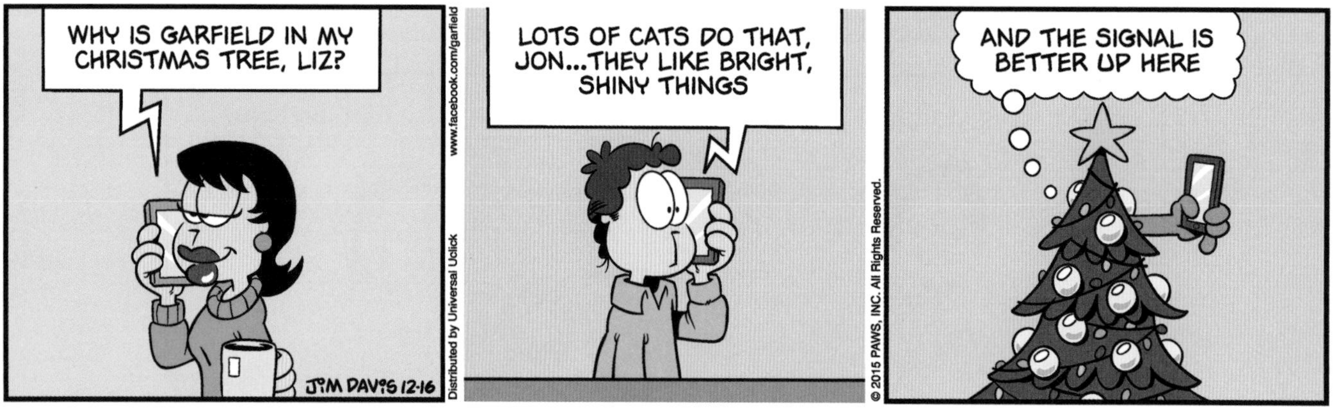
WHY IS GARFIELD IN MY CHRISTMAS TREE, LIZ?
JIM DAVIS 12-16
Distributed by Universal Uclick
www.facebook.com/garfield
LOTS OF CATS DO THAT, JON...THEY LIKE BRIGHT, SHINY THINGS
© 2015 PAWS, INC. All Rights Reserved.
AND THE SIGNAL IS BETTER UP HERE

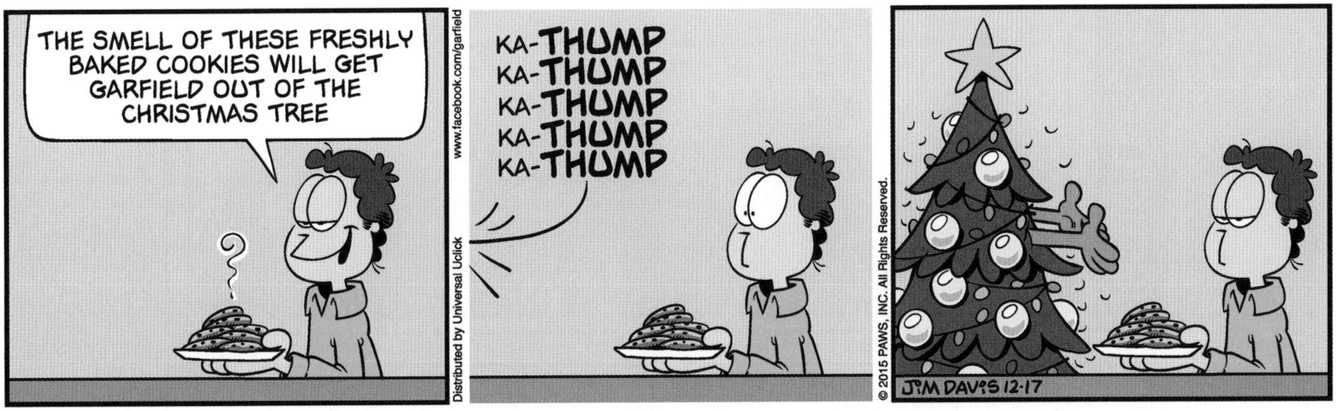
THE SMELL OF THESE FRESHLY BAKED COOKIES WILL GET GARFIELD OUT OF THE CHRISTMAS TREE
Distributed by Universal Uclick www.facebook.com/garfield
KA-THUMP
KA-THUMP
KA-THUMP
KA-THUMP
KA-THUMP
© 2015 PAWS, INC. All Rights Reserved.
JIM DAVIS 12-17

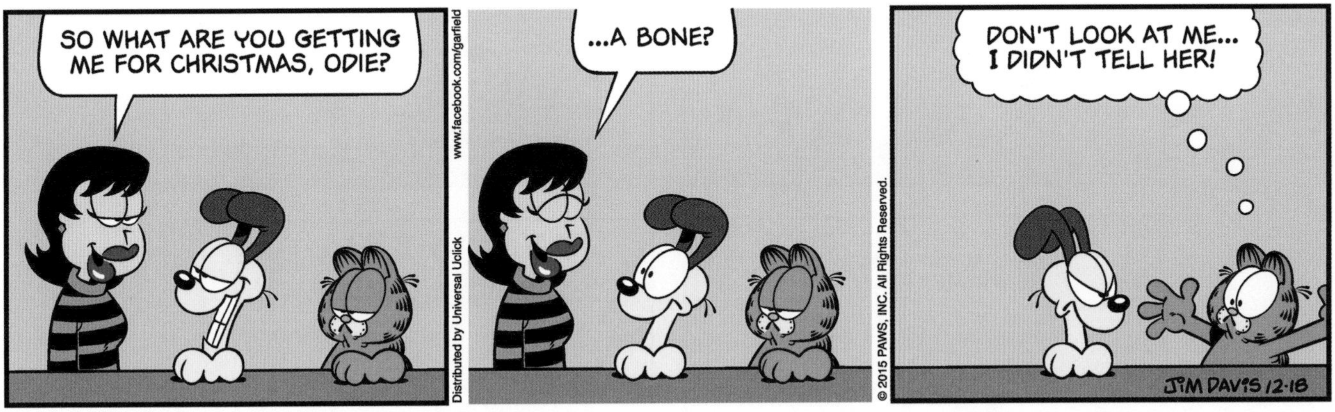
SO WHAT ARE YOU GETTING ME FOR CHRISTMAS, ODIE?
Distributed by Universal Uclick www.facebook.com/garfield
...A BONE?
© 2015 PAWS, INC. All Rights Reserved.
DON'T LOOK AT ME... I DIDN'T TELL HER!
JIM DAVIS 12-18

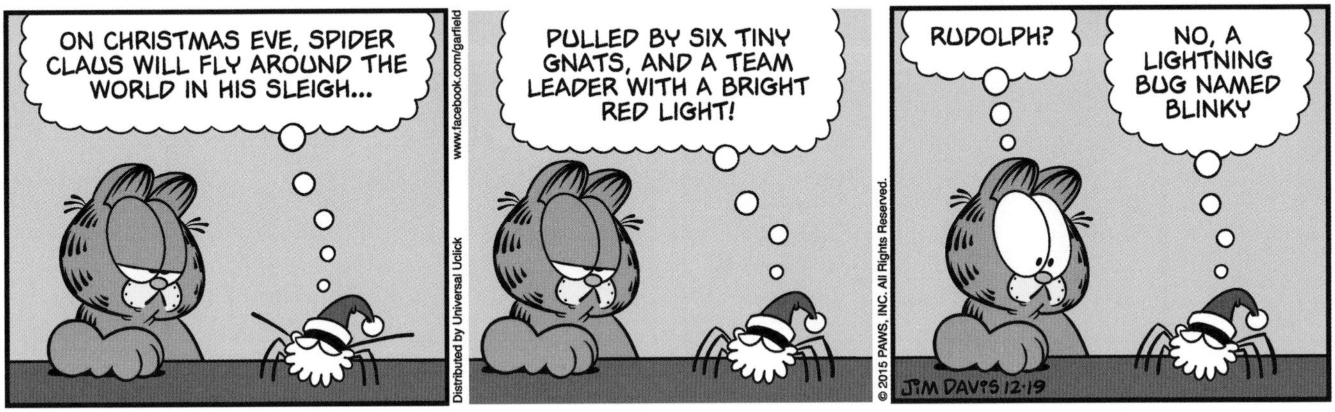
ON CHRISTMAS EVE, SPIDER CLAUS WILL FLY AROUND THE WORLD IN HIS SLEIGH...
Distributed by Universal Uclick www.facebook.com/garfield
PULLED BY SIX TINY GNATS, AND A TEAM LEADER WITH A BRIGHT RED LIGHT!
© 2015 PAWS, INC. All Rights Reserved.
RUDOLPH?
NO, A LIGHTNING BUG NAMED BLINKY
JIM DAVIS 12-19

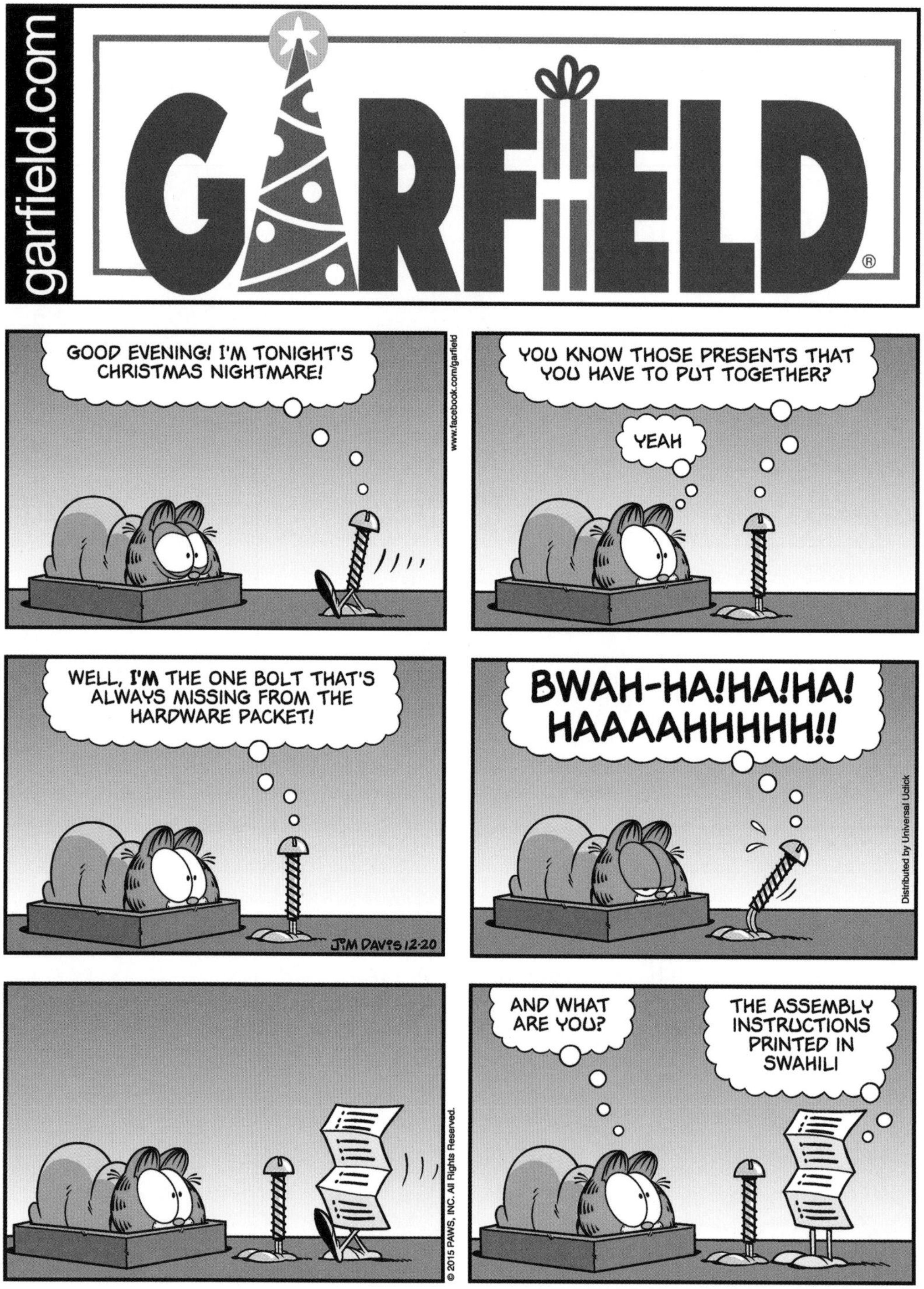
garfield.com
GARFIELD
GOOD EVENING! I'M TONIGHT'S CHRISTMAS NIGHTMARE!
www.facebook.com/garfield
YOU KNOW THOSE PRESENTS THAT YOU HAVE TO PUT TOGETHER?
YEAH
WELL, I'M THE ONE BOLT THAT'S ALWAYS MISSING FROM THE HARDWARE PACKET!
JIM DAVIS 12-20
BWAH-HA!HA!HA! HAAAAHHHHH!!
Distributed by Universal Uclick
© 2015 PAWS, INC. All Rights Reserved.
AND WHAT ARE YOU?
THE ASSEMBLY INSTRUCTIONS PRINTED IN SWAHILI

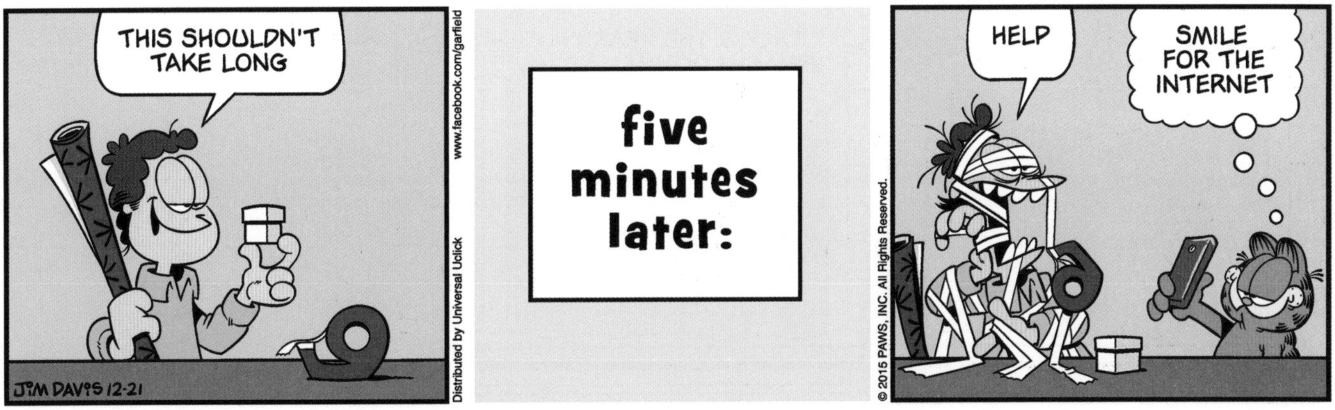
THIS SHOULDN'T TAKE LONG
JIM DAVIS 12-21
Distributed by Universal Uclick www.facebook.com/garfield
five minutes later:
© 2015 PAWS, INC. All Rights Reserved.
HELP
SMILE FOR THE INTERNET

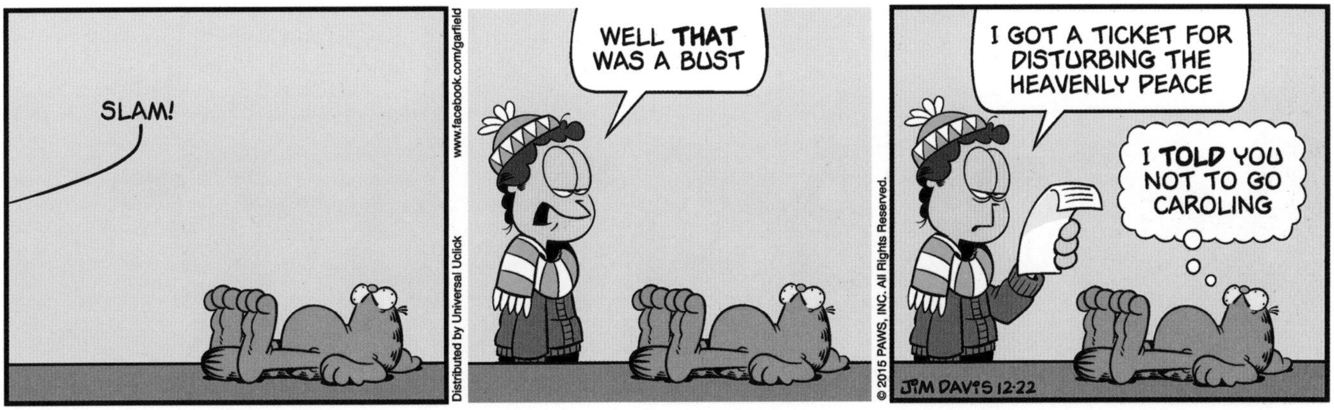
SLAM!
Distributed by Universal Uclick www.facebook.com/garfield
WELL THAT WAS A BUST
© 2015 PAWS, INC. All Rights Reserved.
I GOT A TICKET FOR DISTURBING THE HEAVENLY PEACE
I TOLD YOU NOT TO GO CAROLING
JIM DAVIS 12-22

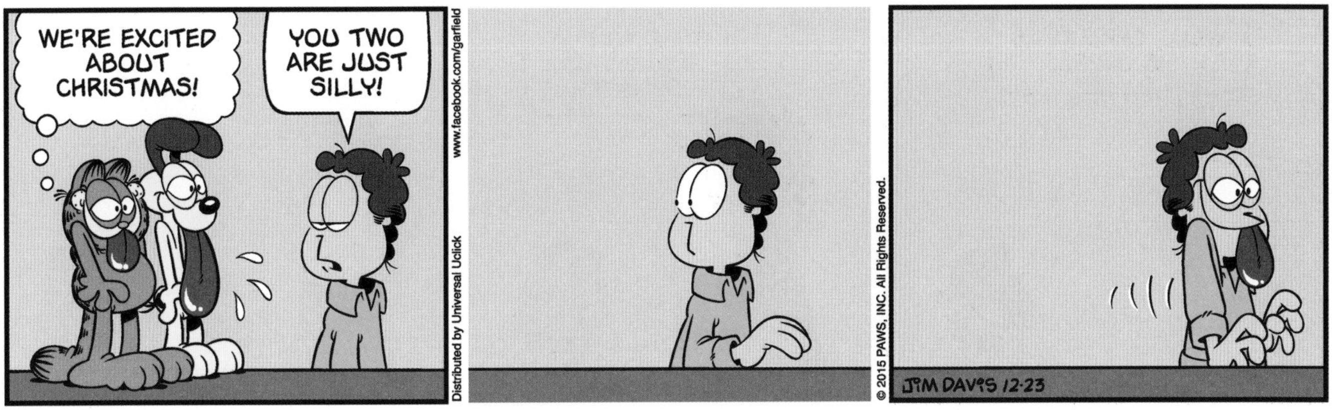
WE'RE EXCITED ABOUT CHRISTMAS!
YOU TWO ARE JUST SILLY!
Distributed by Universal Uclick www.facebook.com/garfield
© 2015 PAWS, INC. All Rights Reserved.
JIM DAVIS 12-23

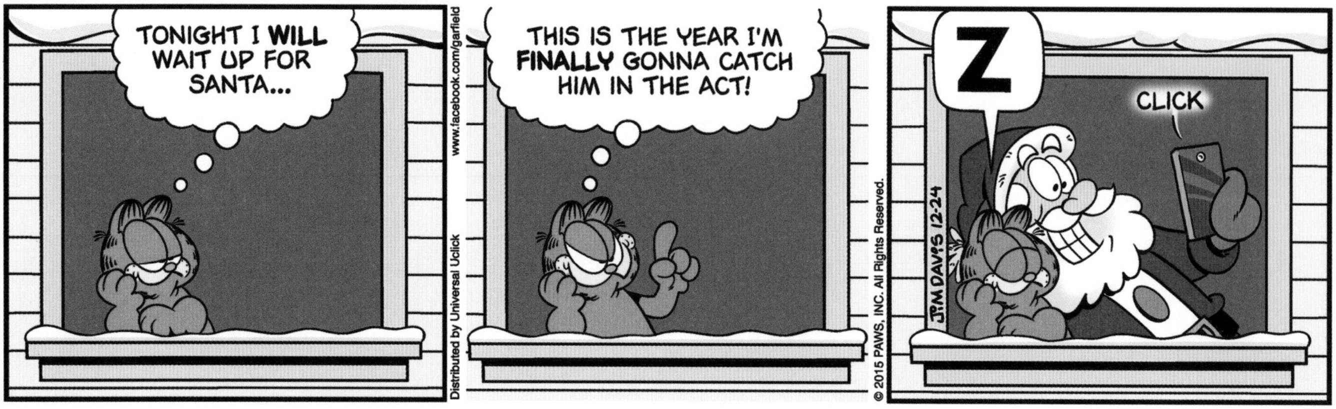
TONIGHT I **WILL** WAIT UP FOR SANTA...
THIS IS THE YEAR I'M **FINALLY** GONNA CATCH HIM IN THE ACT!
Z
CLICK
JIM DAVIS 12-24
Distributed by Universal Uclick www.facebook.com/garfield
© 2015 PAWS, INC. All Rights Reserved.

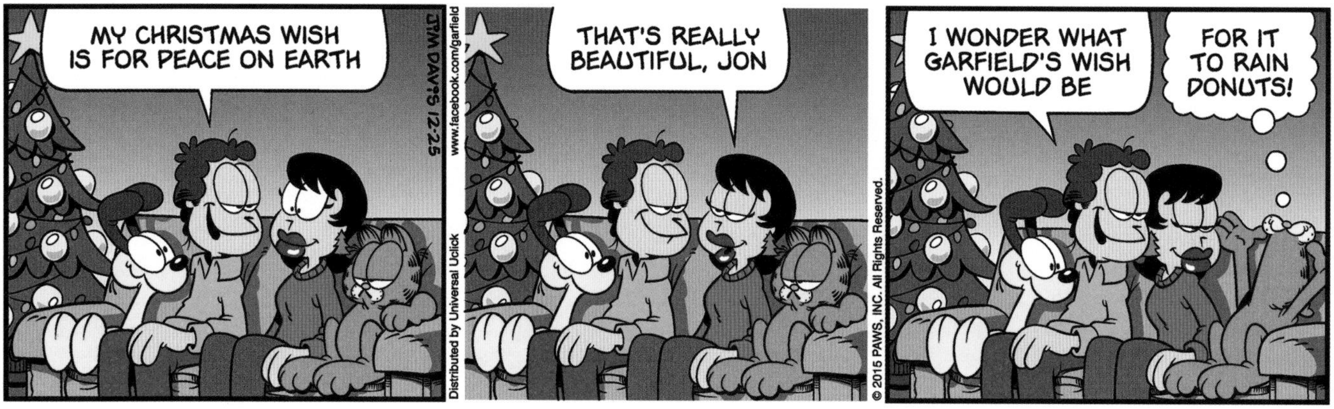
MY CHRISTMAS WISH IS FOR PEACE ON EARTH
JIM DAVIS 12-25
THAT'S REALLY BEAUTIFUL, JON
I WONDER WHAT GARFIELD'S WISH WOULD BE
FOR IT TO RAIN DONUTS!
Distributed by Universal Uclick www.facebook.com/garfield
© 2015 PAWS, INC. All Rights Reserved.

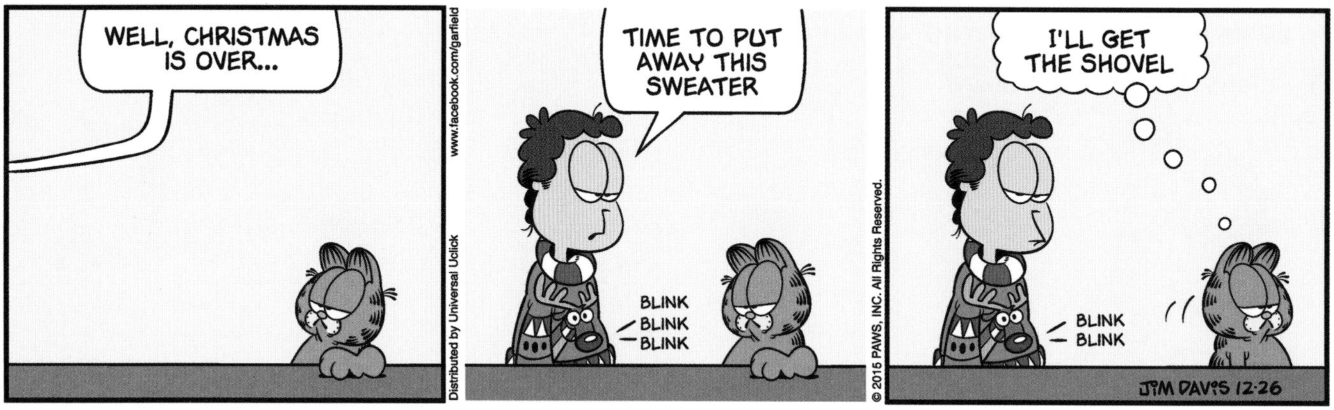
WELL, CHRISTMAS IS OVER...
TIME TO PUT AWAY THIS SWEATER
BLINK BLINK BLINK
I'LL GET THE SHOVEL
BLINK BLINK
JIM DAVIS 12-26
Distributed by Universal Uclick www.facebook.com/garfield
© 2015 PAWS, INC. All Rights Reserved.

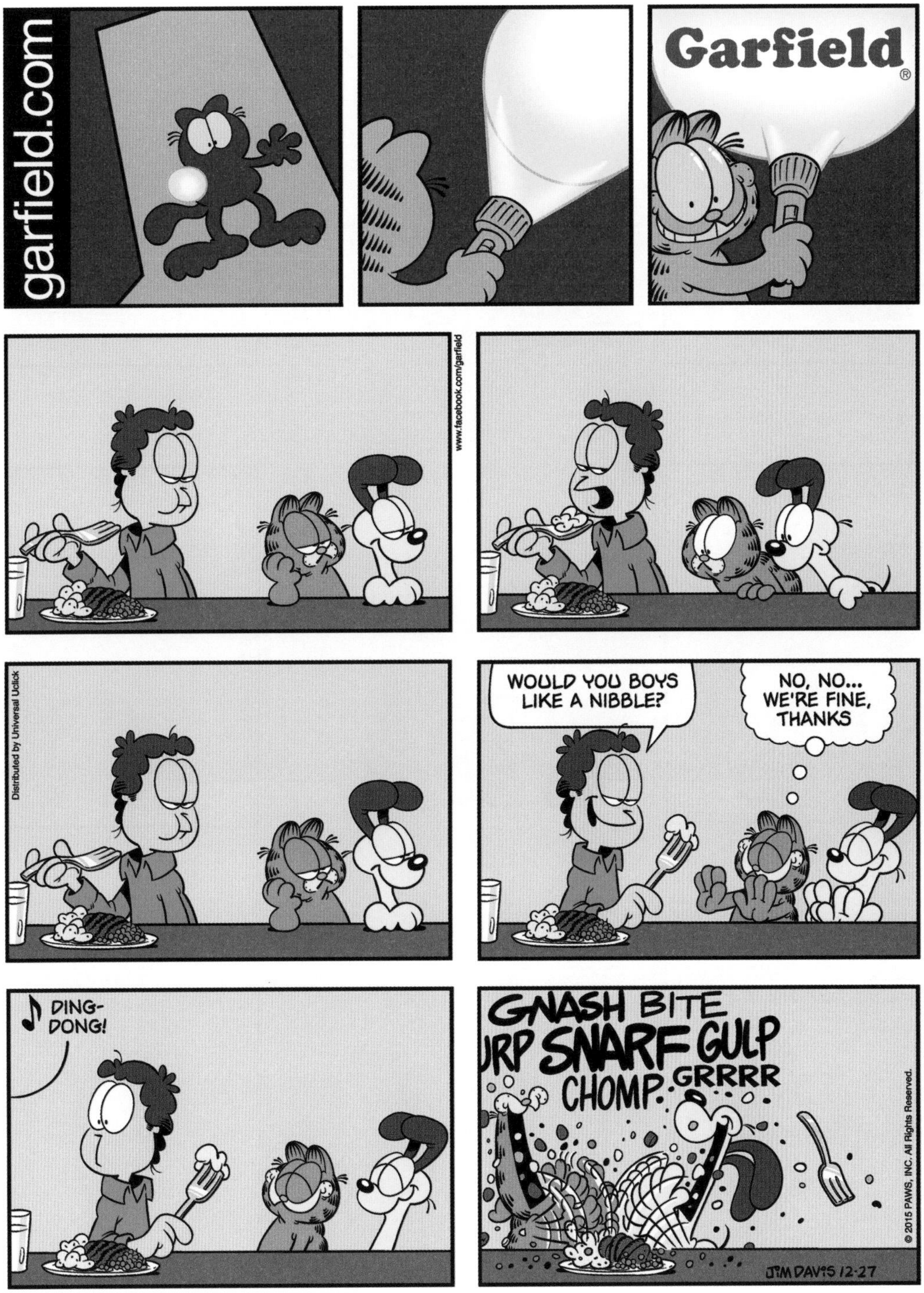
garfield.com
Garfield®
www.facebook.com/garfield
Distributed by Universal Uclick
WOULD YOU BOYS LIKE A NIBBLE?
NO, NO... WE'RE FINE, THANKS
DING-DONG!
GNASH BITE
SNARF GULP
CHOMP
GRRRR
© 2015 PAWS, INC. All Rights Reserved.
JIM DAVIS 12-27

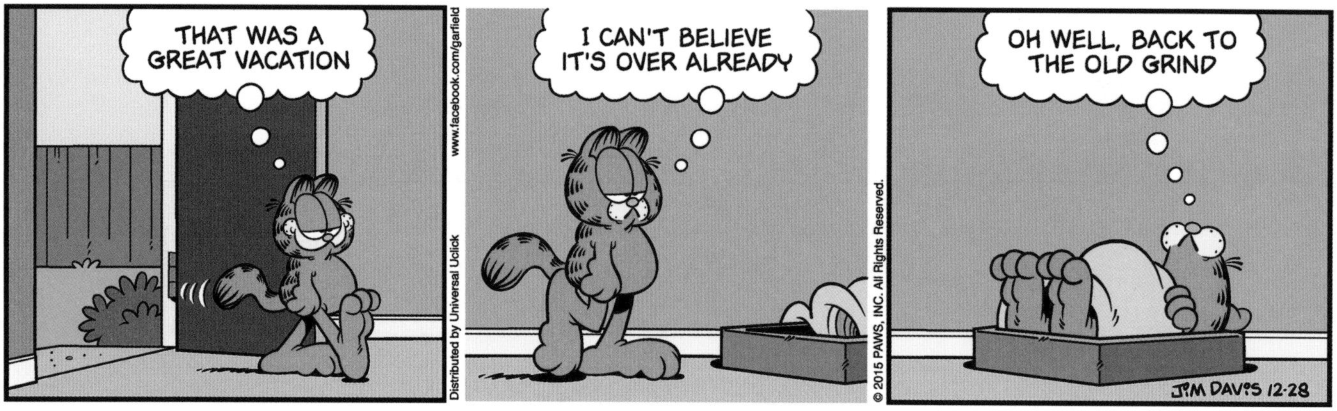
THAT WAS A GREAT VACATION
Distributed by Universal Uclick
www.facebook.com/garfield
I CAN'T BELIEVE IT'S OVER ALREADY
© 2015 PAWS, INC. All Rights Reserved.
OH WELL, BACK TO THE OLD GRIND
JIM DAVIS 12-28

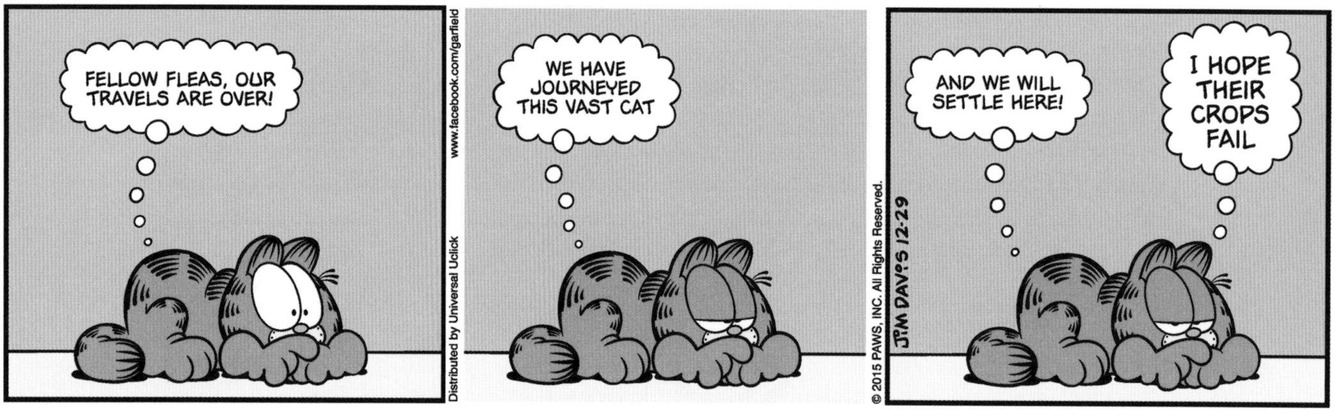
FELLOW FLEAS, OUR TRAVELS ARE OVER!
Distributed by Universal Uclick
www.facebook.com/garfield
WE HAVE JOURNEYED THIS VAST CAT
© 2015 PAWS, INC. All Rights Reserved.
JIM DAVIS 12-29
AND WE WILL SETTLE HERE!
I HOPE THEIR CROPS FAIL

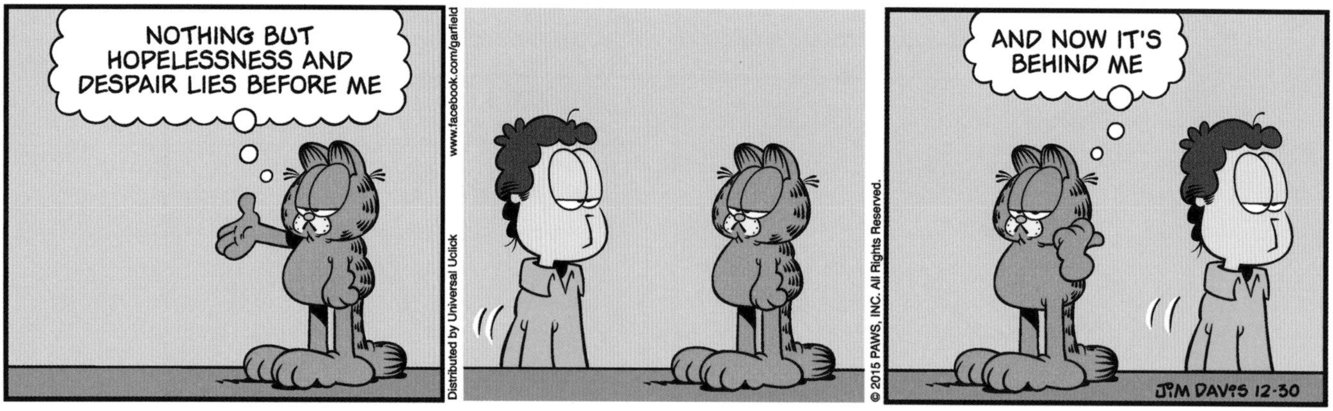
NOTHING BUT HOPELESSNESS AND DESPAIR LIES BEFORE ME
Distributed by Universal Uclick
www.facebook.com/garfield
© 2015 PAWS, INC. All Rights Reserved.
AND NOW IT'S BEHIND ME
JIM DAVIS 12-30

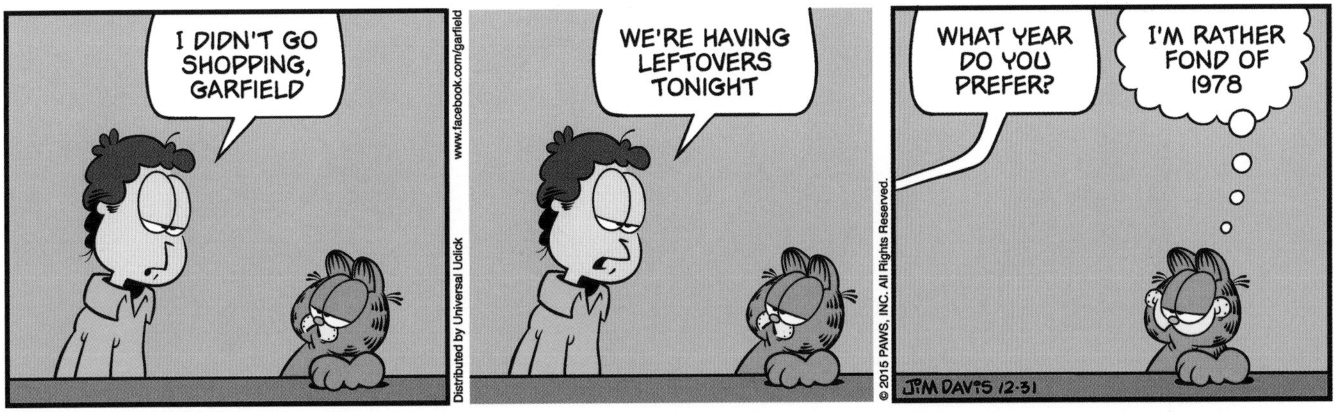
I DIDN'T GO SHOPPING, GARFIELD
WE'RE HAVING LEFTOVERS TONIGHT
WHAT YEAR DO YOU PREFER?
I'M RATHER FOND OF 1978
JIM DAVIS 12-31
www.facebook.com/garfield
Distributed by Universal Uclick
© 2015 PAWS, INC. All Rights Reserved.

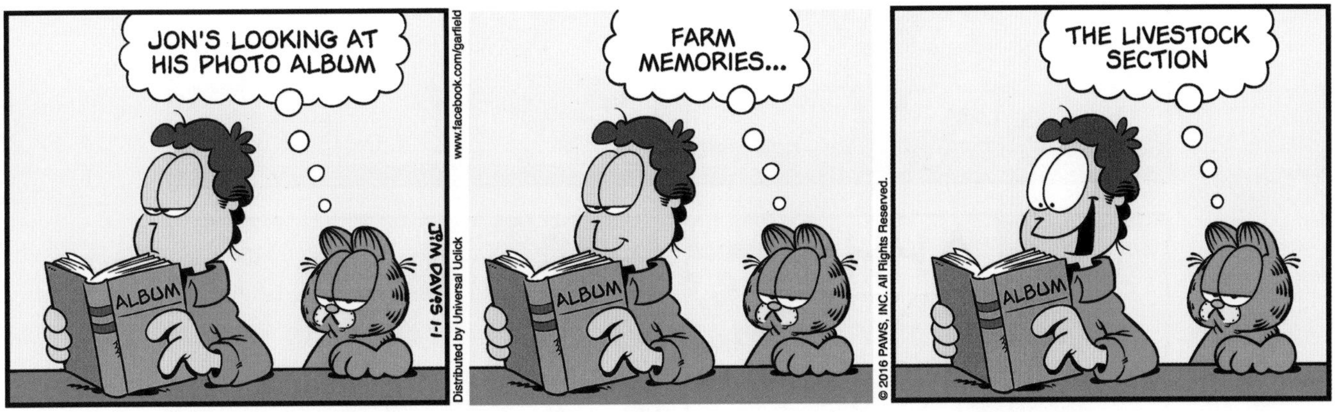
JON'S LOOKING AT HIS PHOTO ALBUM
ALBUM
JIM DAVIS 1-1
FARM MEMORIES...
THE LIVESTOCK SECTION
www.facebook.com/garfield
Distributed by Universal Uclick
© 2016 PAWS, INC. All Rights Reserved.

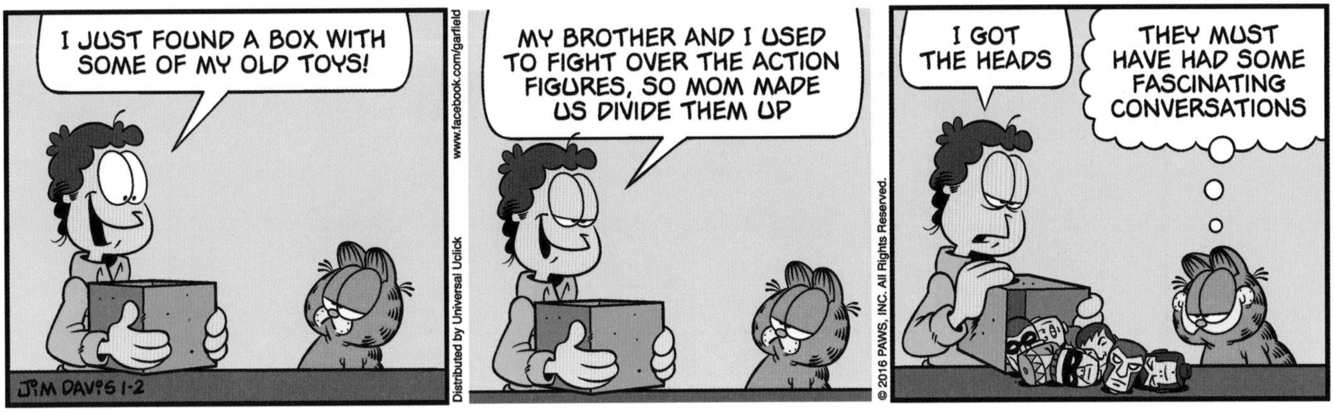
I JUST FOUND A BOX WITH SOME OF MY OLD TOYS!
JIM DAVIS 1-2
MY BROTHER AND I USED TO FIGHT OVER THE ACTION FIGURES, SO MOM MADE US DIVIDE THEM UP
I GOT THE HEADS
THEY MUST HAVE HAD SOME FASCINATING CONVERSATIONS
www.facebook.com/garfield
Distributed by Universal Uclick
© 2016 PAWS, INC. All Rights Reserved.

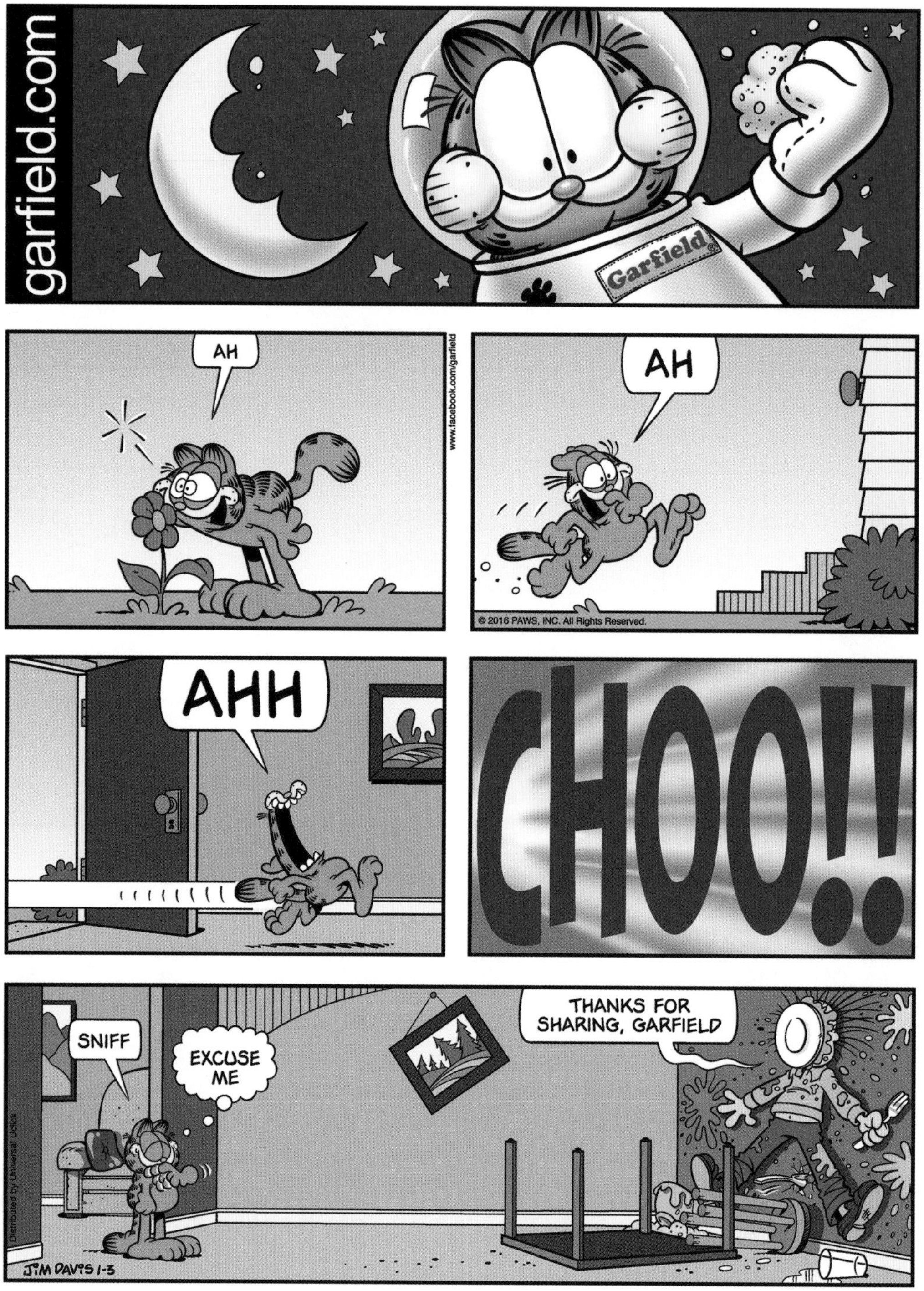
garfield.com
Garfield
AH
www.facebook.com/garfield
AH
© 2016 PAWS, INC. All Rights Reserved.
AHH
CHOO!!
SNIFF
EXCUSE ME
THANKS FOR SHARING, GARFIELD
Distributed by Universal Uclick
JIM DAVIS 1-3

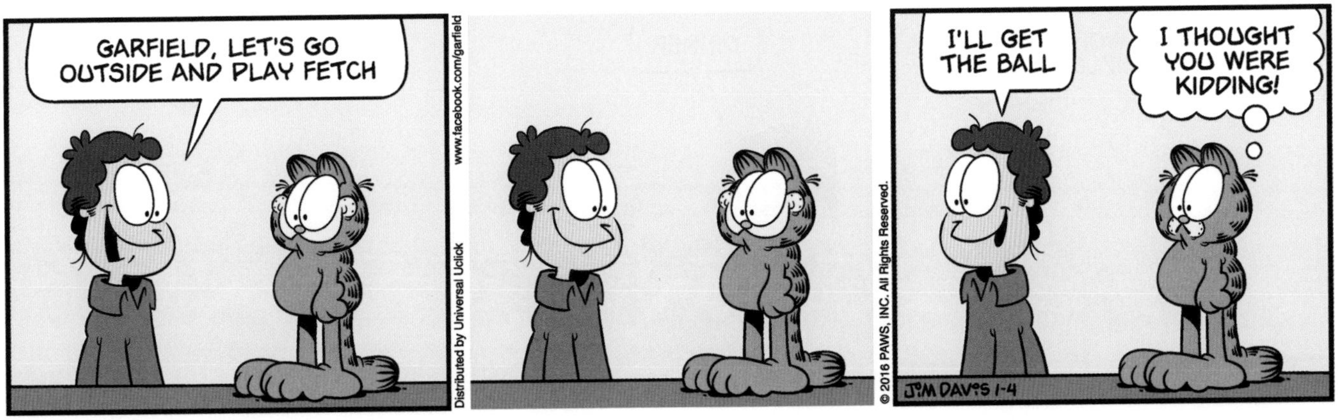
GARFIELD, LET'S GO OUTSIDE AND PLAY FETCH
www.facebook.com/garfield
Distributed by Universal Uclick
I'LL GET THE BALL
I THOUGHT YOU WERE KIDDING!
© 2016 PAWS, INC. All Rights Reserved.
JIM DAVIS 1-4

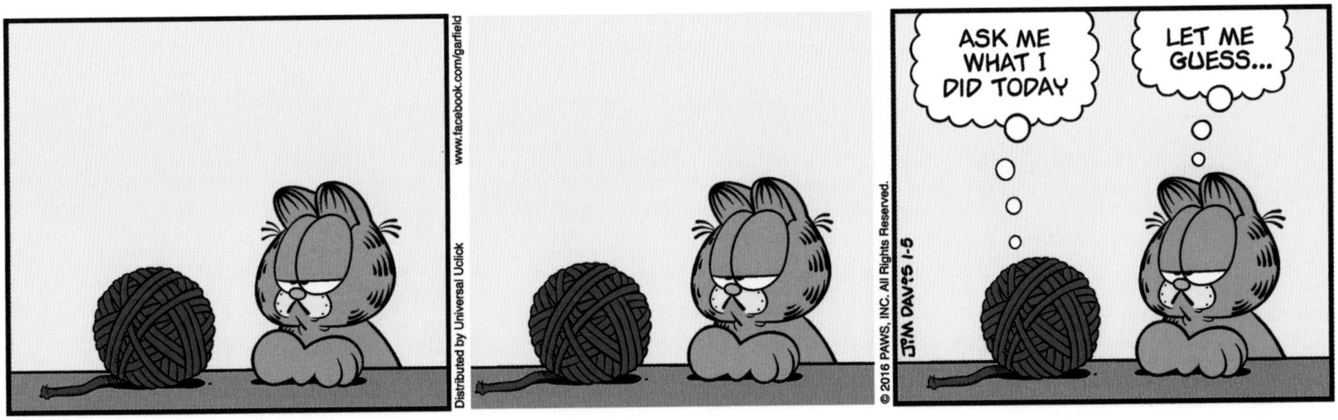
www.facebook.com/garfield
Distributed by Universal Uclick
ASK ME WHAT I DID TODAY
LET ME GUESS...
© 2016 PAWS, INC. All Rights Reserved.
JIM DAVIS 1-5

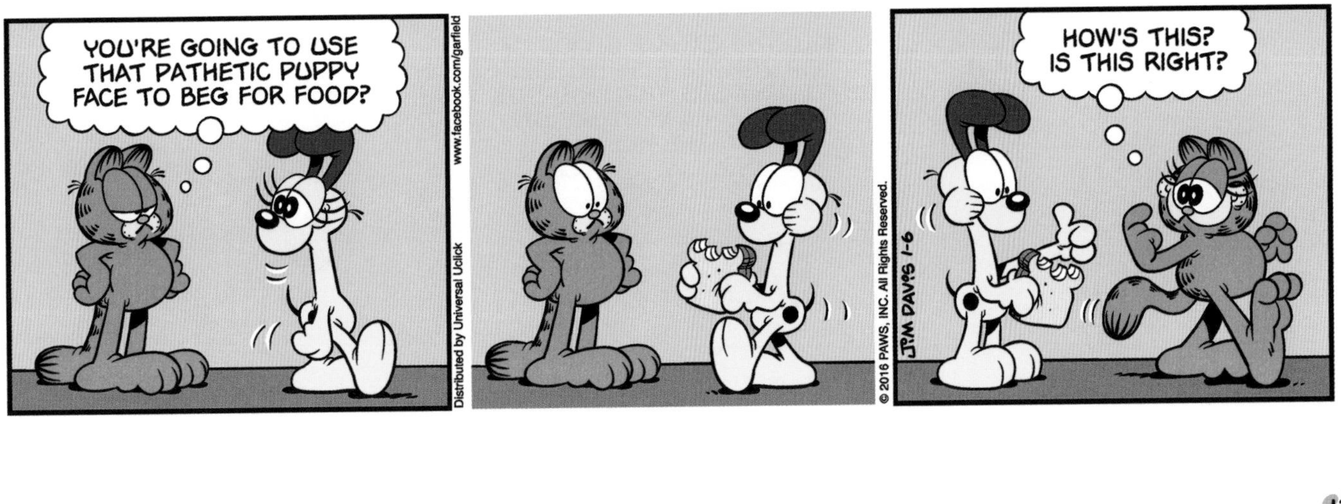
YOU'RE GOING TO USE THAT PATHETIC PUPPY FACE TO BEG FOR FOOD?
www.facebook.com/garfield
Distributed by Universal Uclick
HOW'S THIS? IS THIS RIGHT?
© 2016 PAWS, INC. All Rights Reserved.
JIM DAVIS 1-6

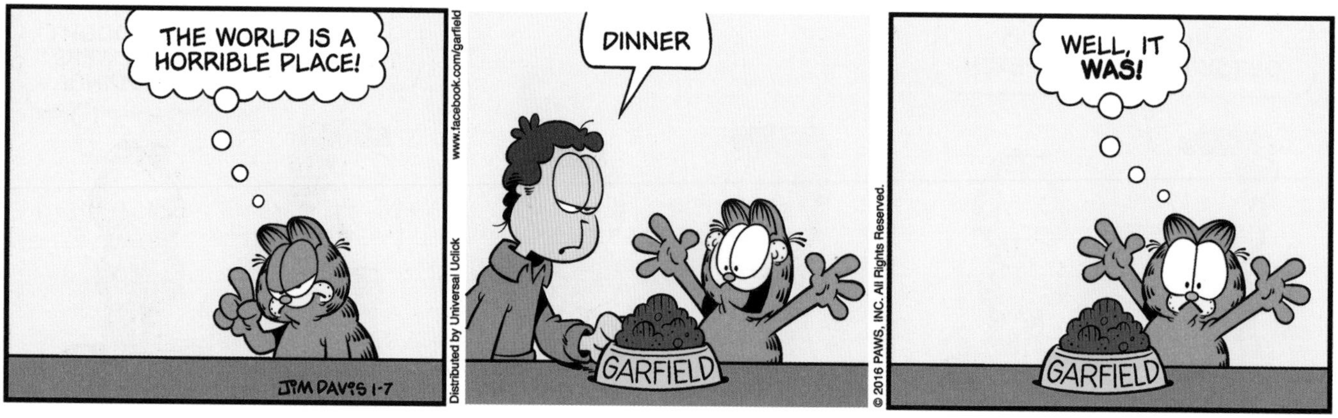
THE WORLD IS A HORRIBLE PLACE!
JIM DAVIS 1-7
Distributed by Universal Uclick
www.facebook.com/garfield
DINNER
GARFIELD
© 2016 PAWS, INC. All Rights Reserved.
WELL, IT WAS!
GARFIELD

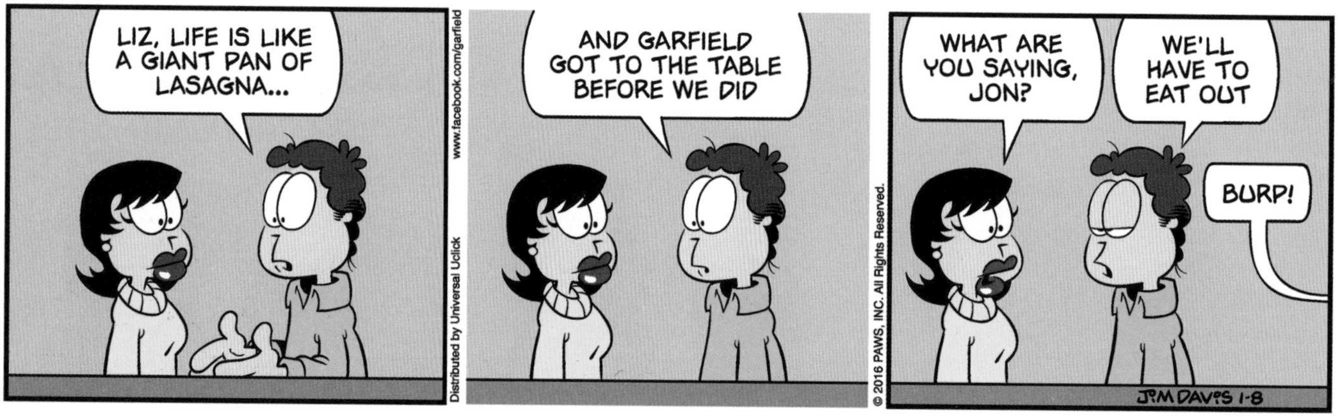
LIZ, LIFE IS LIKE A GIANT PAN OF LASAGNA...
Distributed by Universal Uclick
www.facebook.com/garfield
AND GARFIELD GOT TO THE TABLE BEFORE WE DID
© 2016 PAWS, INC. All Rights Reserved.
WHAT ARE YOU SAYING, JON?
WE'LL HAVE TO EAT OUT
BURP!
JIM DAVIS 1-8

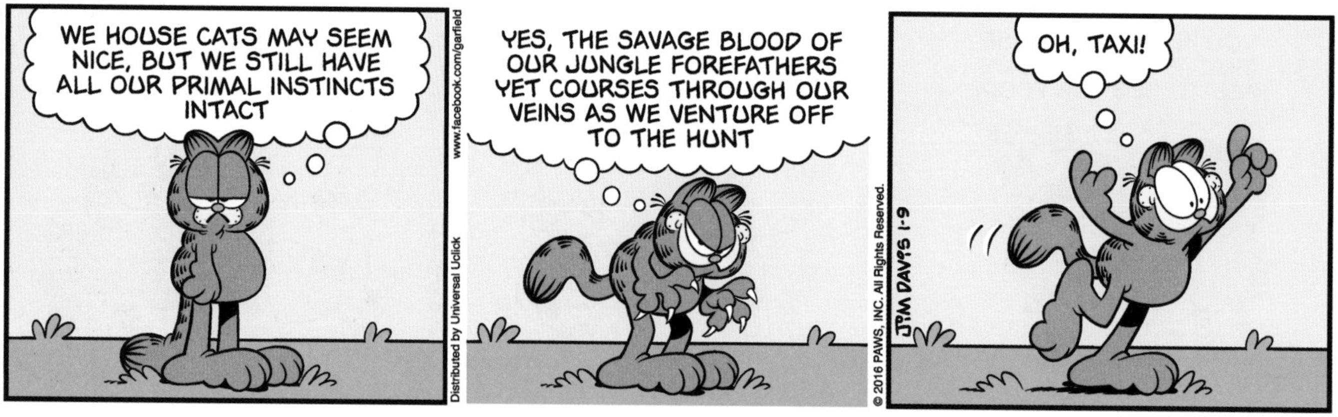
WE HOUSE CATS MAY SEEM NICE, BUT WE STILL HAVE ALL OUR PRIMAL INSTINCTS INTACT
Distributed by Universal Uclick
www.facebook.com/garfield
YES, THE SAVAGE BLOOD OF OUR JUNGLE FOREFATHERS YET COURSES THROUGH OUR VEINS AS WE VENTURE OFF TO THE HUNT
© 2016 PAWS, INC. All Rights Reserved.
JIM DAVIS 1-9
OH, TAXI!

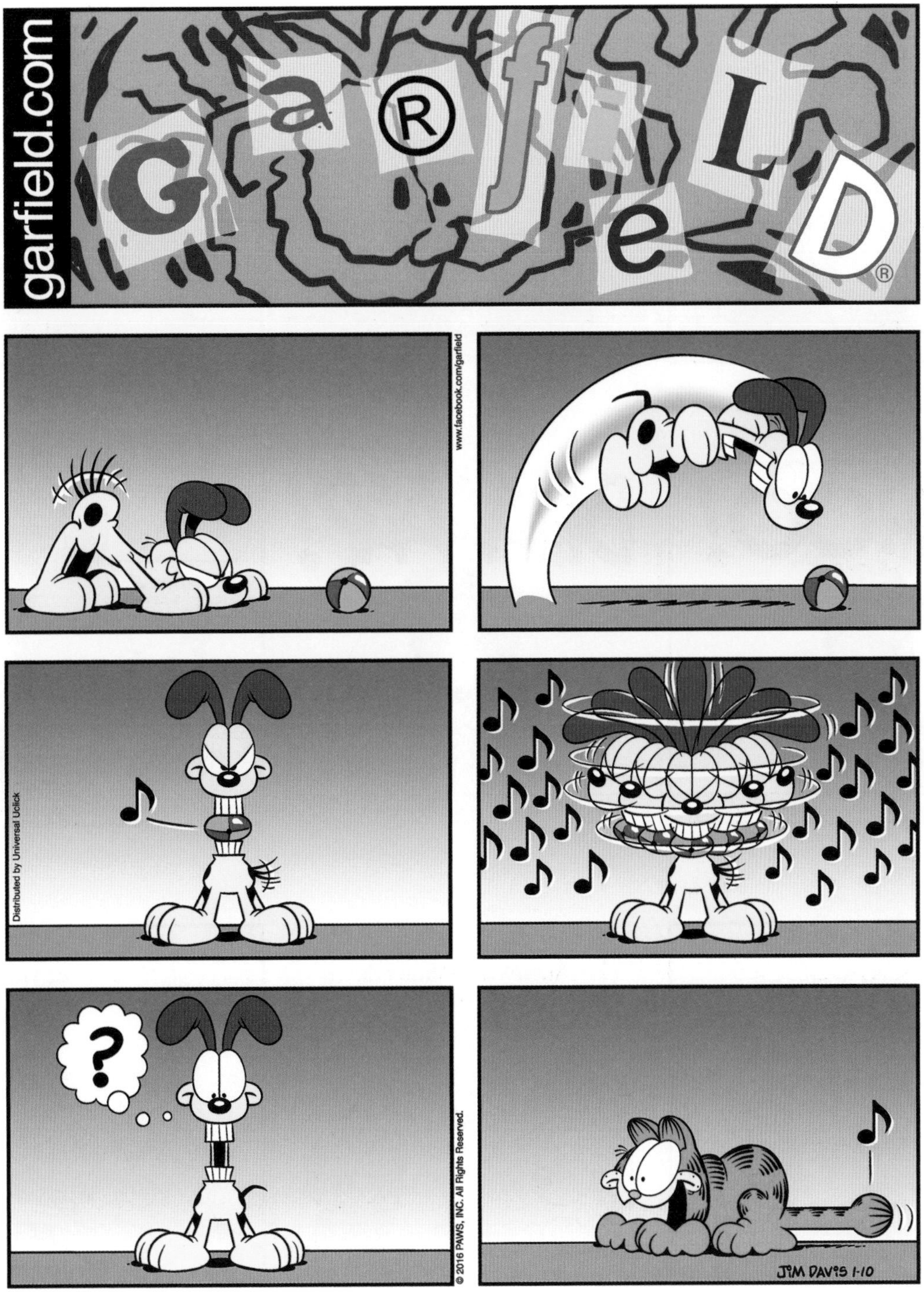
garfield.com
GaRfiELD
www.facebook.com/garfield
Distributed by Universal Uclick
?
© 2016 PAWS, INC. All Rights Reserved.
JIM DAVIS 1-10

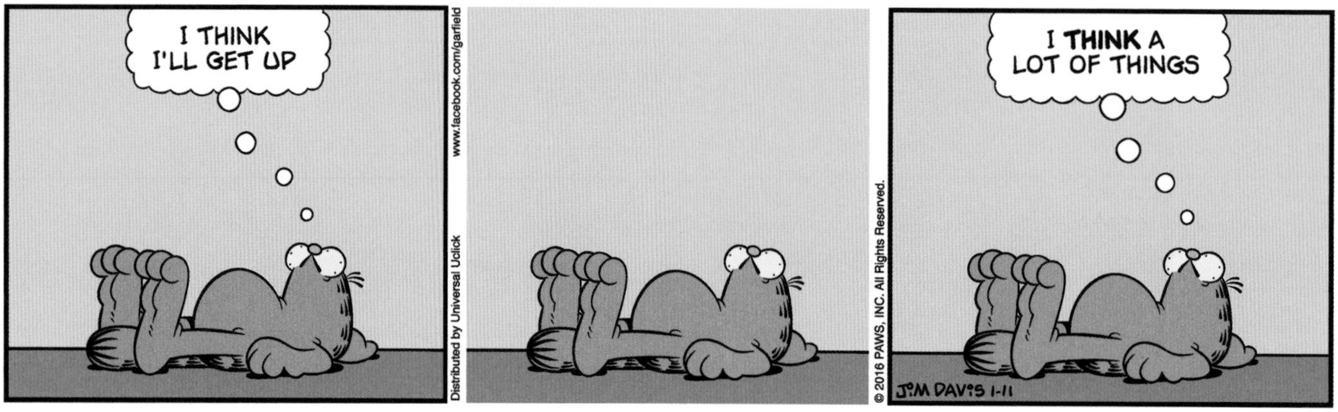
I THINK I'LL GET UP
I THINK A LOT OF THINGS
JIM DAVIS 1-11
Distributed by Universal Uclick www.facebook.com/garfield
© 2016 PAWS, INC. All Rights Reserved.

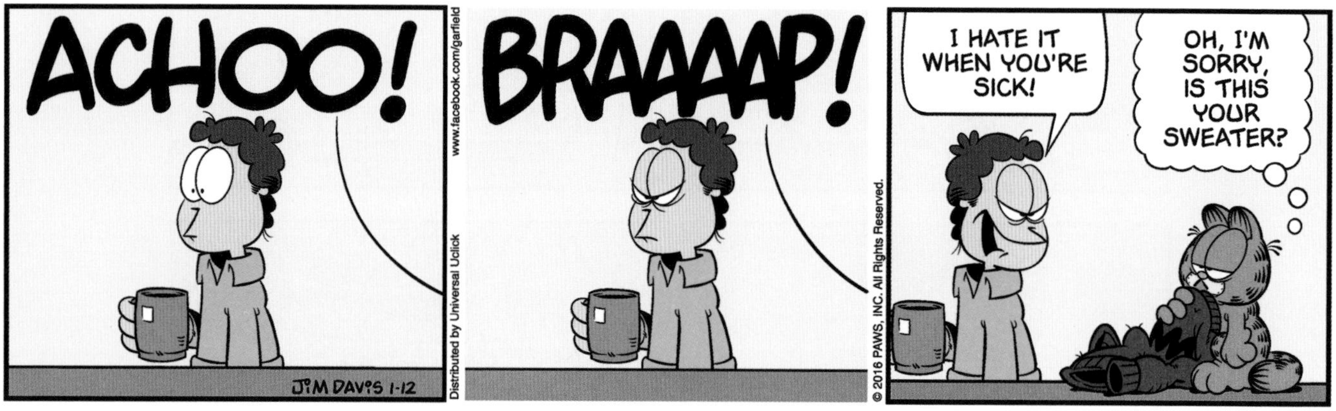
ACHOO!
BRAAAAP!
I HATE IT WHEN YOU'RE SICK!
OH, I'M SORRY, IS THIS YOUR SWEATER?
JIM DAVIS 1-12
Distributed by Universal Uclick www.facebook.com/garfield
© 2016 PAWS, INC. All Rights Reserved.

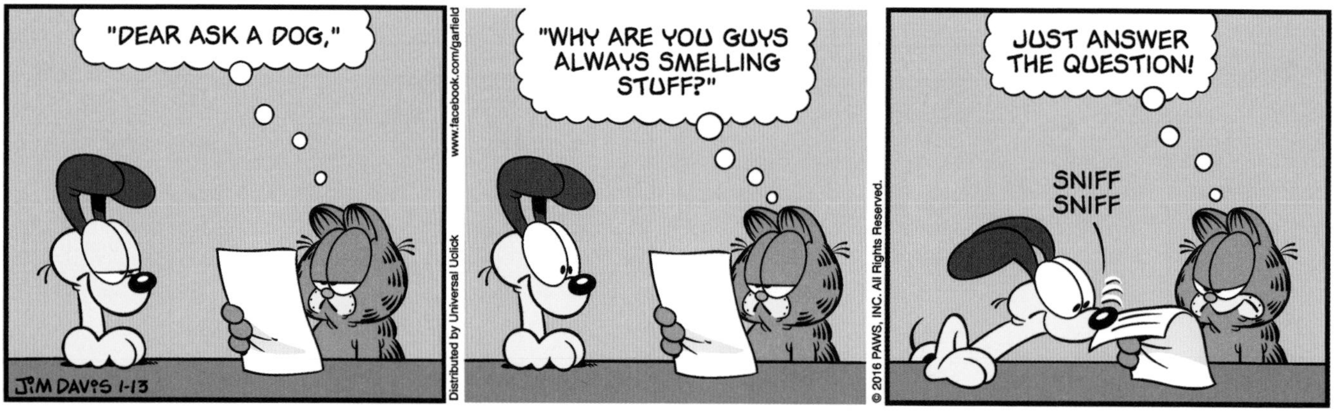
"DEAR ASK A DOG,"
"WHY ARE YOU GUYS ALWAYS SMELLING STUFF?"
JUST ANSWER THE QUESTION!
SNIFF SNIFF
JIM DAVIS 1-13
Distributed by Universal Uclick www.facebook.com/garfield
© 2016 PAWS, INC. All Rights Reserved.

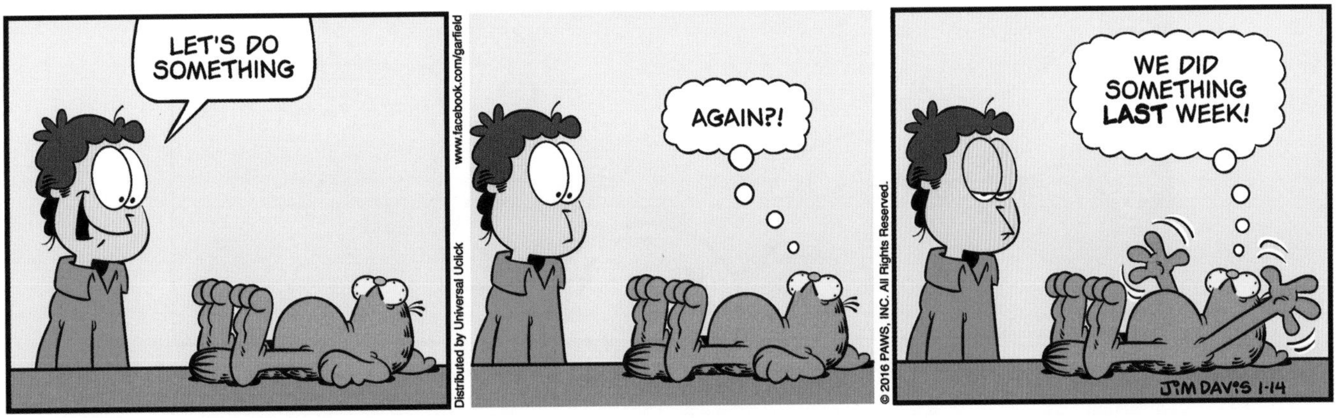
LET'S DO SOMETHING
AGAIN?!
WE DID SOMETHING LAST WEEK!
JIM DAVIS 1-14
www.facebook.com/garfield
Distributed by Universal Uclick
© 2016 PAWS, INC. All Rights Reserved.

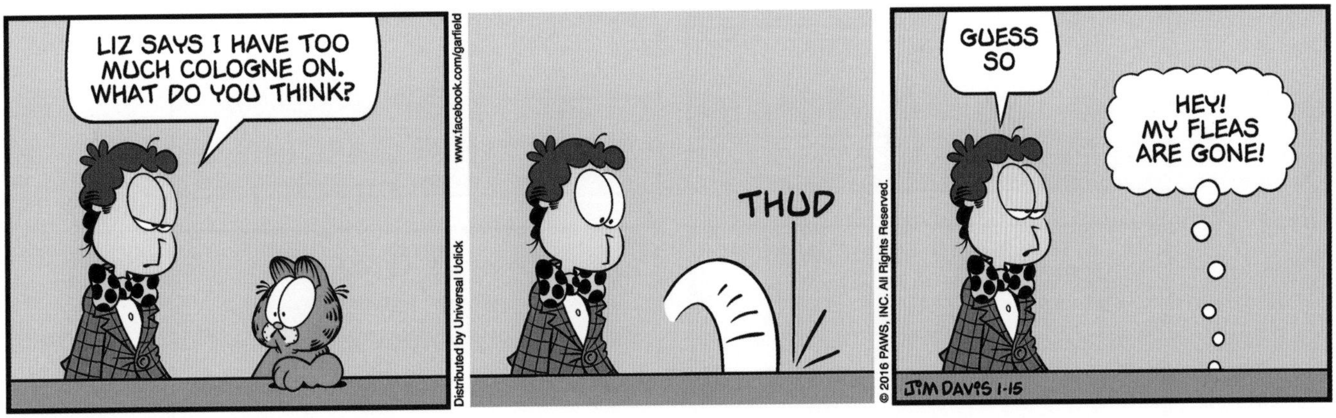
LIZ SAYS I HAVE TOO MUCH COLOGNE ON. WHAT DO YOU THINK?
THUD
GUESS SO
HEY! MY FLEAS ARE GONE!
JIM DAVIS 1-15
www.facebook.com/garfield
Distributed by Universal Uclick
© 2016 PAWS, INC. All Rights Reserved.

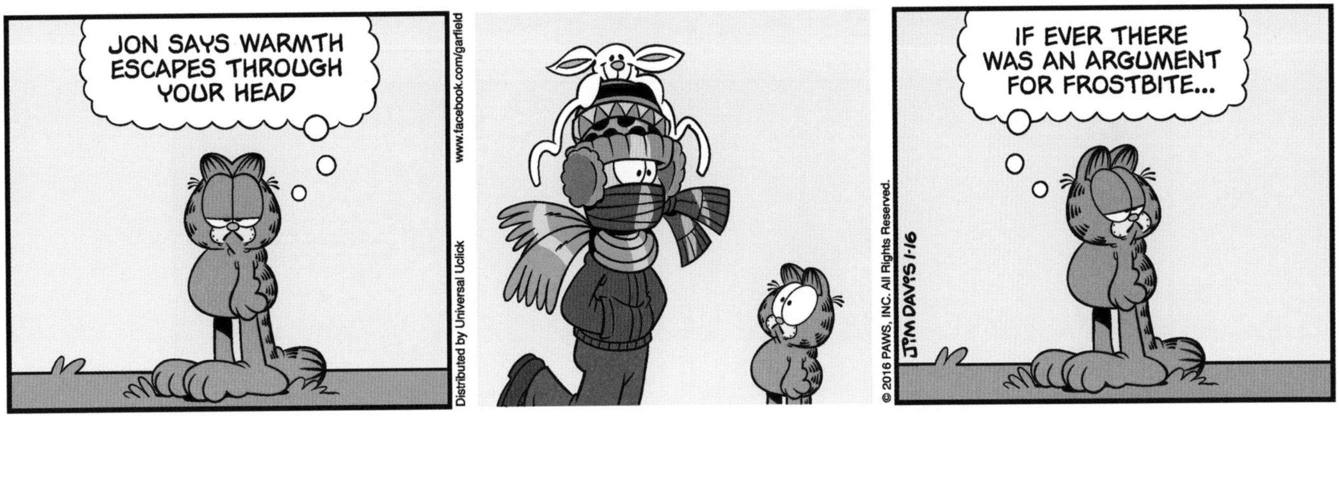
JON SAYS WARMTH ESCAPES THROUGH YOUR HEAD
IF EVER THERE WAS AN ARGUMENT FOR FROSTBITE...
JIM DAVIS 1-16
www.facebook.com/garfield
Distributed by Universal Uclick
© 2016 PAWS, INC. All Rights Reserved.

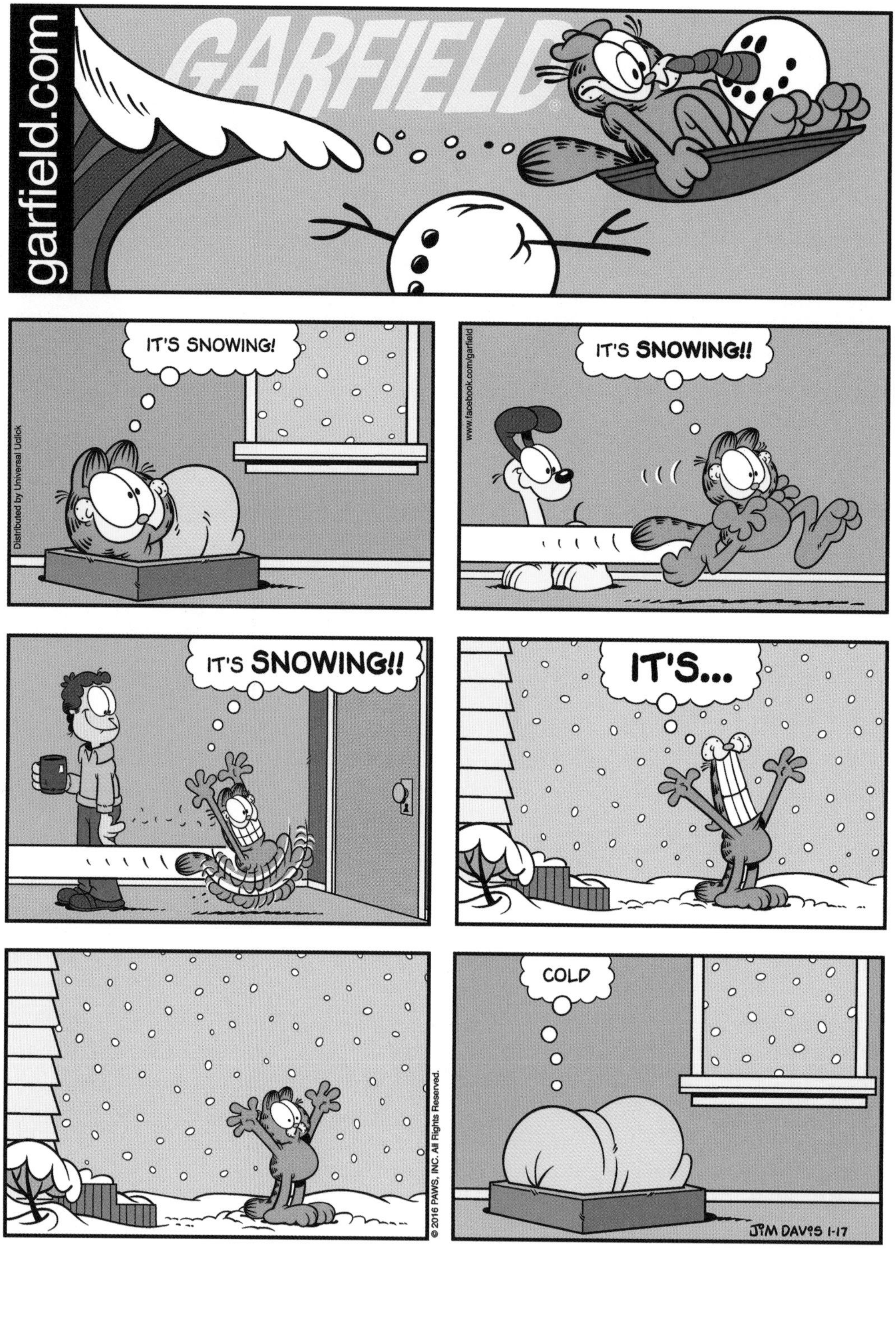
GARFIELD
garfield.com
Distributed by Universal Uclick
IT'S SNOWING!
www.facebook.com/garfield
IT'S SNOWING!!
IT'S SNOWING!!
IT'S...
© 2016 PAWS, INC. All Rights Reserved.
COLD
JIM DAVIS 1-17

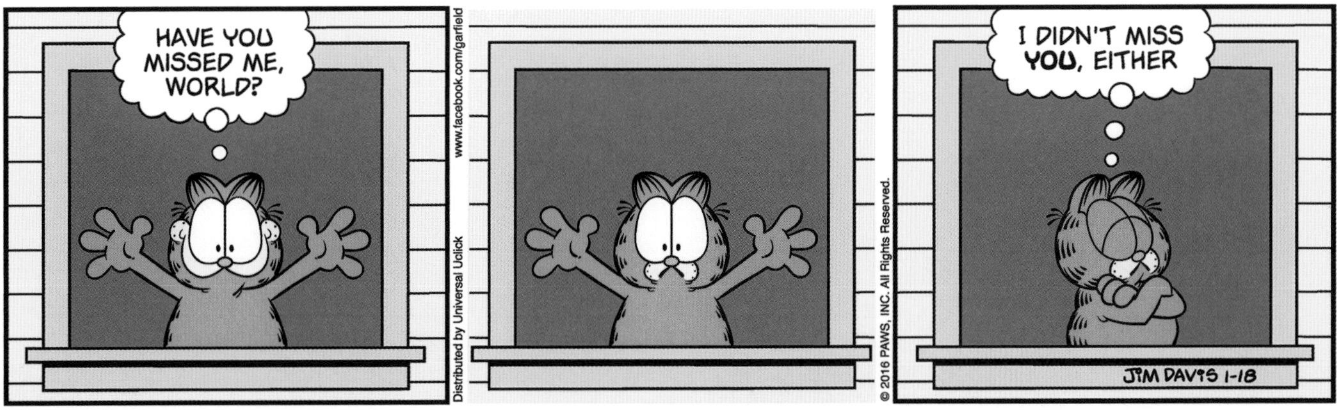
HAVE YOU MISSED ME, WORLD?
Distributed by Universal Uclick www.facebook.com/garfield
© 2016 PAWS, INC. All Rights Reserved.
I DIDN'T MISS YOU, EITHER
JIM DAVIS 1-18

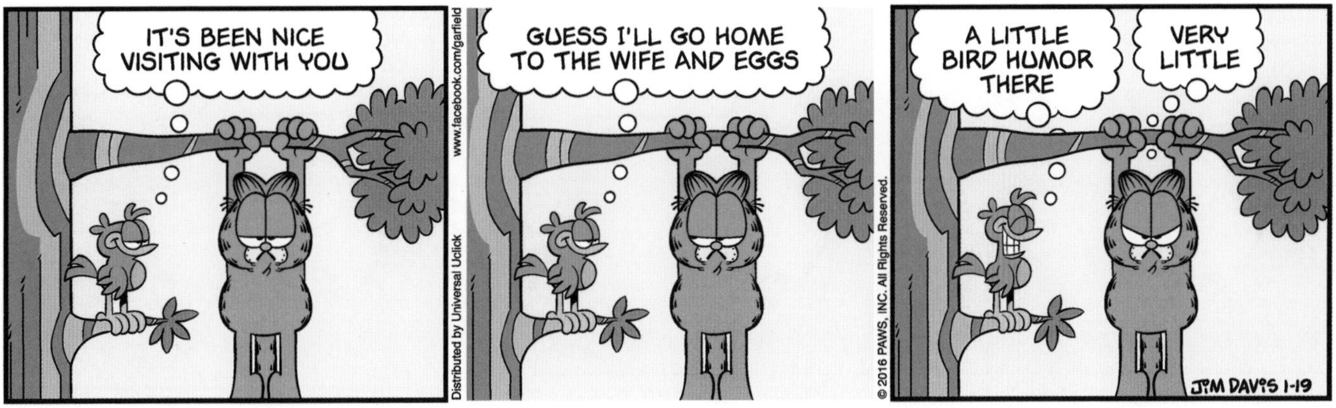
IT'S BEEN NICE VISITING WITH YOU
Distributed by Universal Uclick www.facebook.com/garfield
GUESS I'LL GO HOME TO THE WIFE AND EGGS
© 2016 PAWS, INC. All Rights Reserved.
A LITTLE BIRD HUMOR THERE
VERY LITTLE
JIM DAVIS 1-19

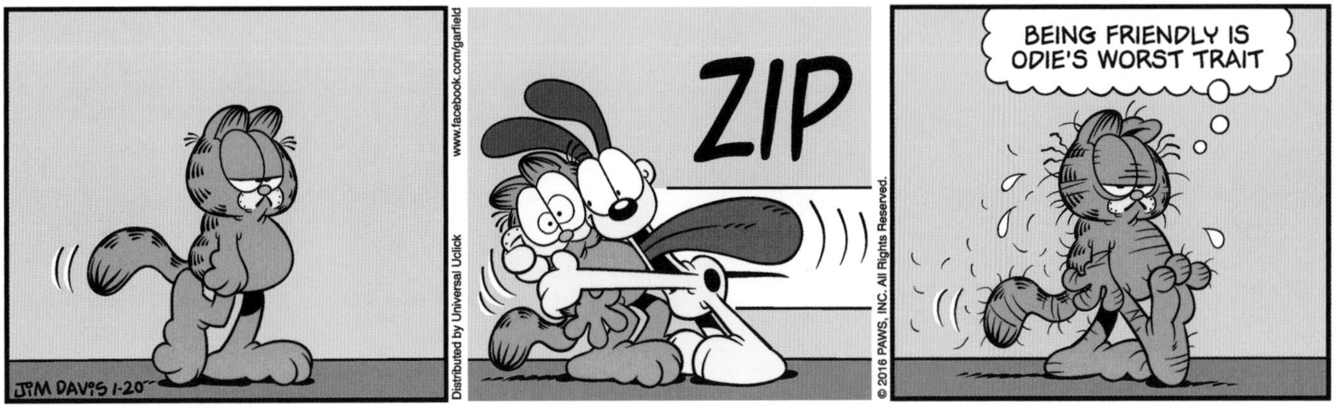
JIM DAVIS 1-20
Distributed by Universal Uclick www.facebook.com/garfield
ZIP
© 2016 PAWS, INC. All Rights Reserved.
BEING FRIENDLY IS ODIE'S WORST TRAIT

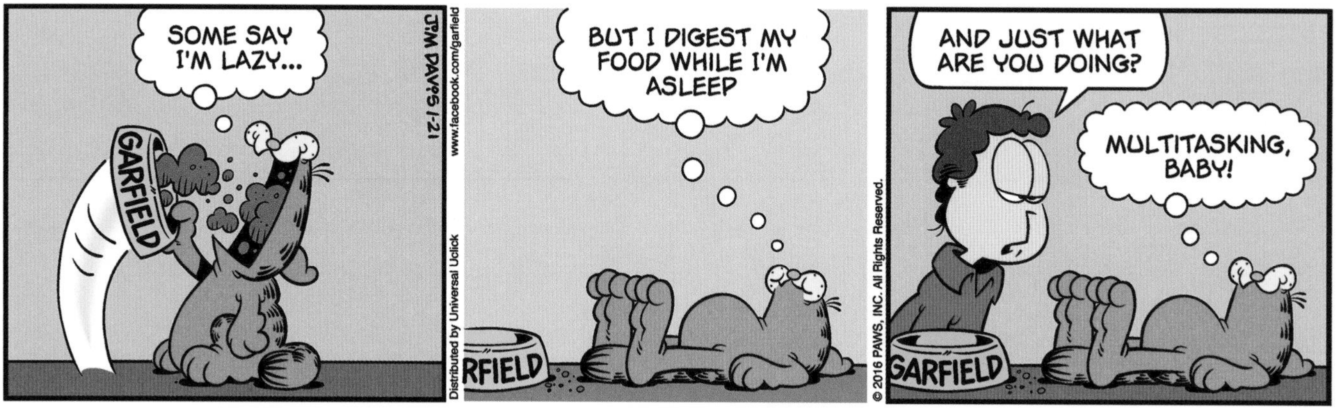
SOME SAY I'M LAZY...
BUT I DIGEST MY FOOD WHILE I'M ASLEEP
AND JUST WHAT ARE YOU DOING?
MULTITASKING, BABY!

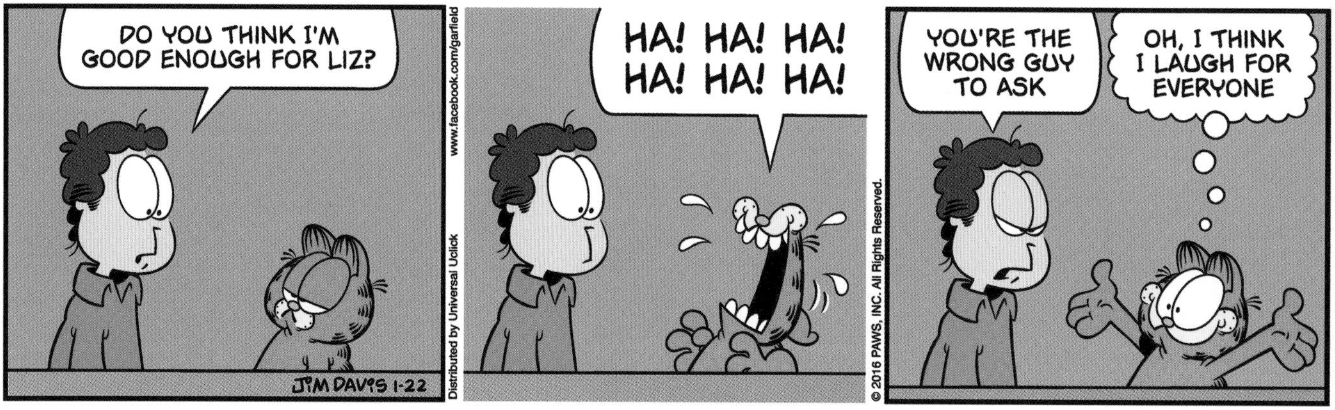
DO YOU THINK I'M GOOD ENOUGH FOR LIZ?
HA! HA! HA! HA! HA! HA!
YOU'RE THE WRONG GUY TO ASK
OH, I THINK I LAUGH FOR EVERYONE

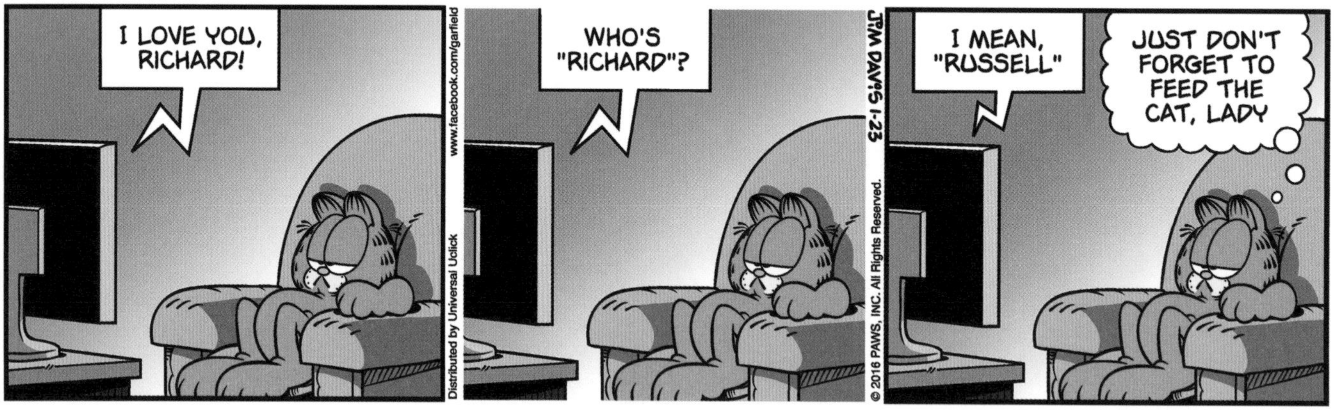
I LOVE YOU, RICHARD!
WHO'S "RICHARD"?
I MEAN, "RUSSELL"
JUST DON'T FORGET TO FEED THE CAT, LADY

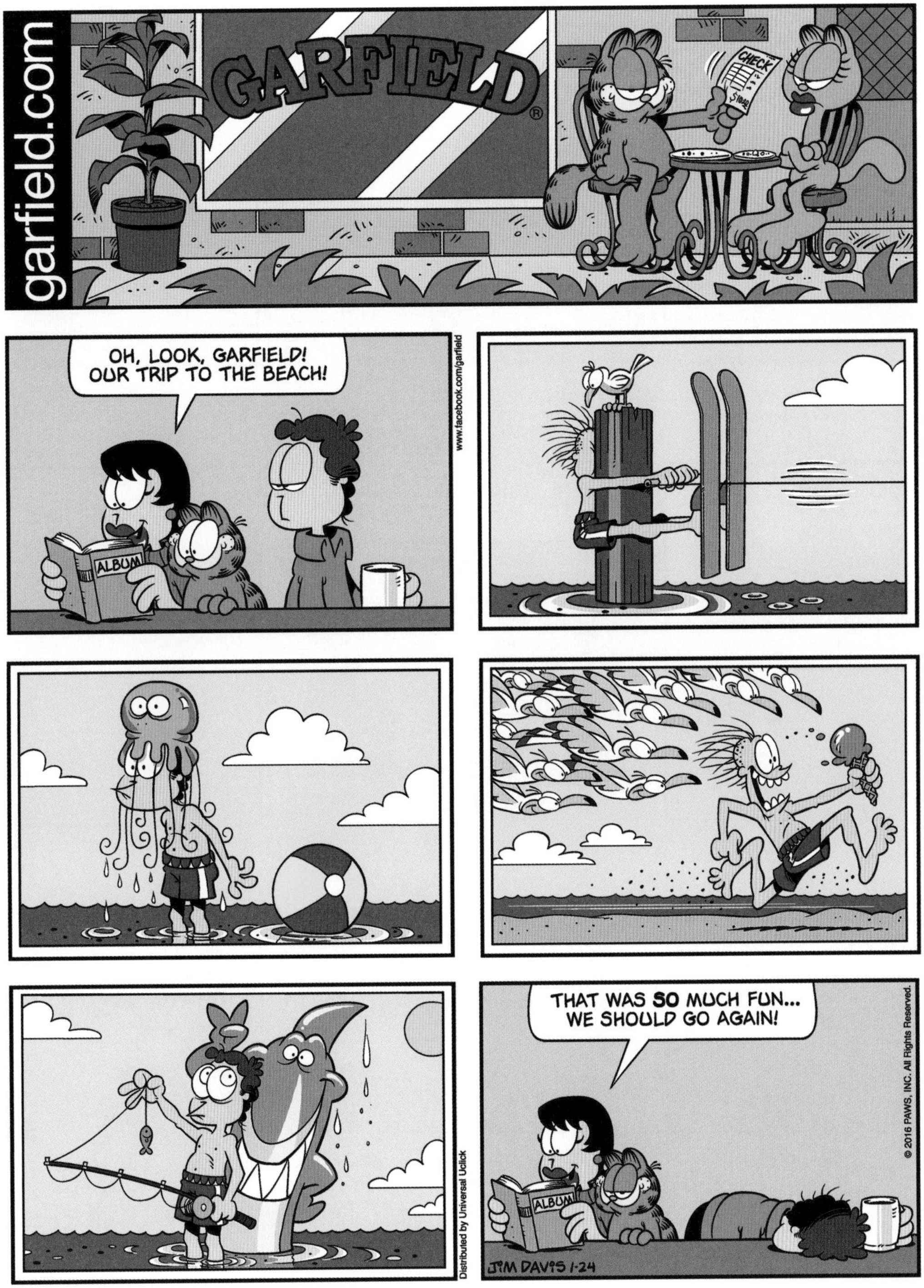
garfield.com
GARFIELD®
CHECK
OH, LOOK, GARFIELD! OUR TRIP TO THE BEACH!
ALBUM
www.facebook.com/garfield
THAT WAS SO MUCH FUN... WE SHOULD GO AGAIN!
ALBUM
JIM DAVIS 1-24
Distributed by Universal Uclick
© 2016 PAWS, INC. All Rights Reserved.

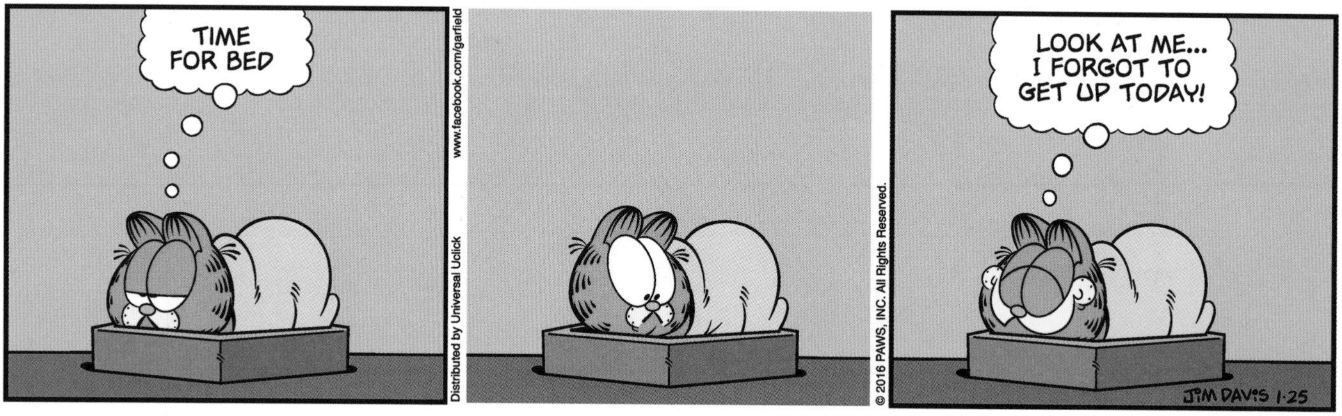
TIME FOR BED
LOOK AT ME... I FORGOT TO GET UP TODAY!
Distributed by Universal Uclick www.facebook.com/garfield
© 2016 PAWS, INC. All Rights Reserved.
JIM DAVIS 1-25

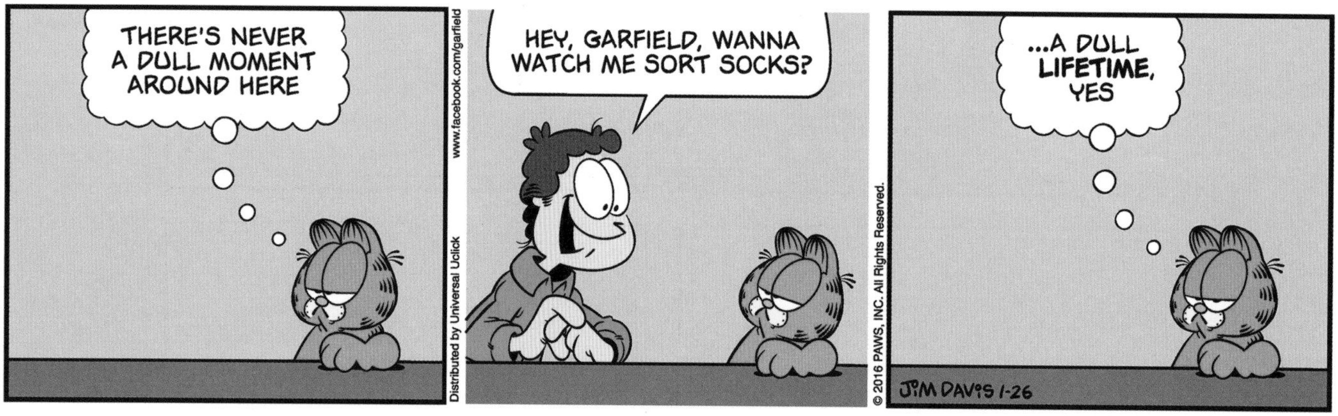
THERE'S NEVER A DULL MOMENT AROUND HERE
HEY, GARFIELD, WANNA WATCH ME SORT SOCKS?
...A DULL **LIFETIME**, YES
Distributed by Universal Uclick www.facebook.com/garfield
© 2016 PAWS, INC. All Rights Reserved.
JIM DAVIS 1-26

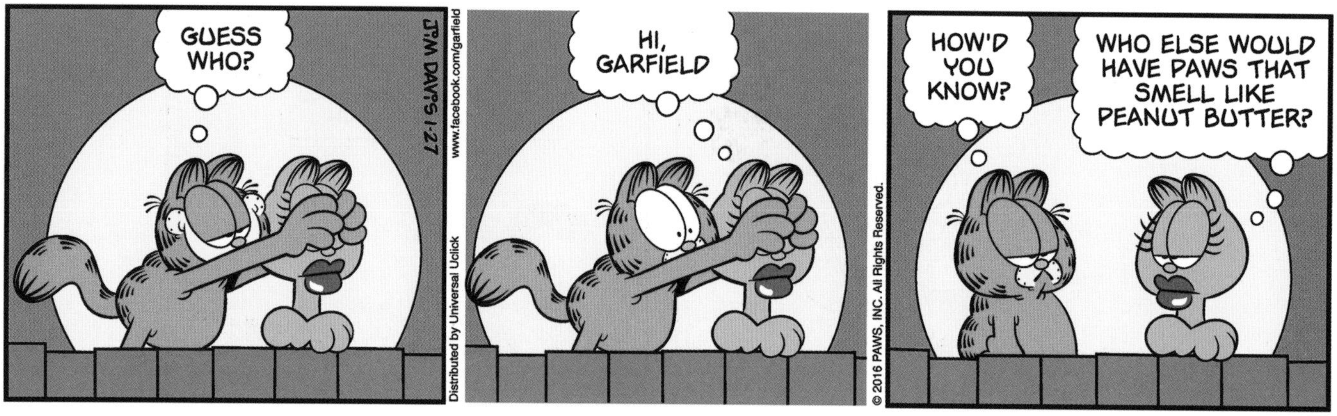
GUESS WHO?
JIM DAVIS 1-27
HI, GARFIELD
HOW'D YOU KNOW?
WHO ELSE WOULD HAVE PAWS THAT SMELL LIKE PEANUT BUTTER?
Distributed by Universal Uclick www.facebook.com/garfield
© 2016 PAWS, INC. All Rights Reserved.

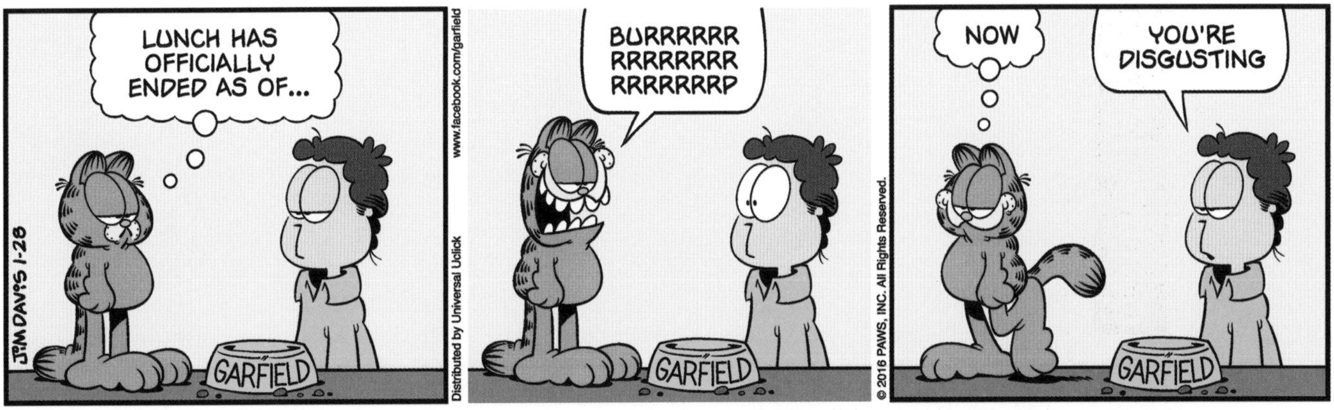
LUNCH HAS OFFICIALLY ENDED AS OF...
JIM DAVIS 1-28
GARFIELD
Distributed by Universal Uclick www.facebook.com/garfield
BURRRRRR RRRRRRRR RRRRRRRP
GARFIELD
© 2016 PAWS, INC. All Rights Reserved.
NOW
YOU'RE DISGUSTING
GARFIELD

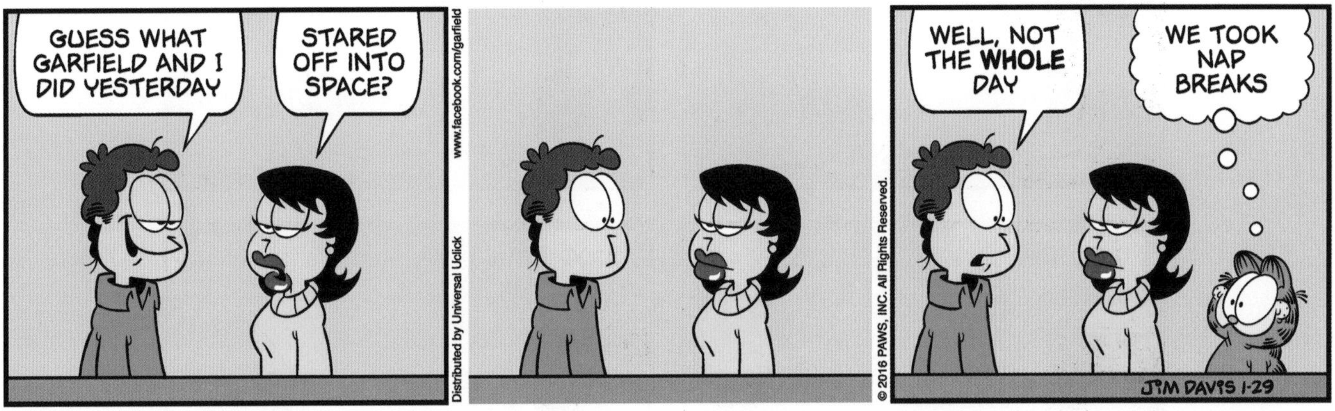
GUESS WHAT GARFIELD AND I DID YESTERDAY
STARED OFF INTO SPACE?
Distributed by Universal Uclick www.facebook.com/garfield
© 2016 PAWS, INC. All Rights Reserved.
WELL, NOT THE **WHOLE** DAY
WE TOOK NAP BREAKS
JIM DAVIS 1-29

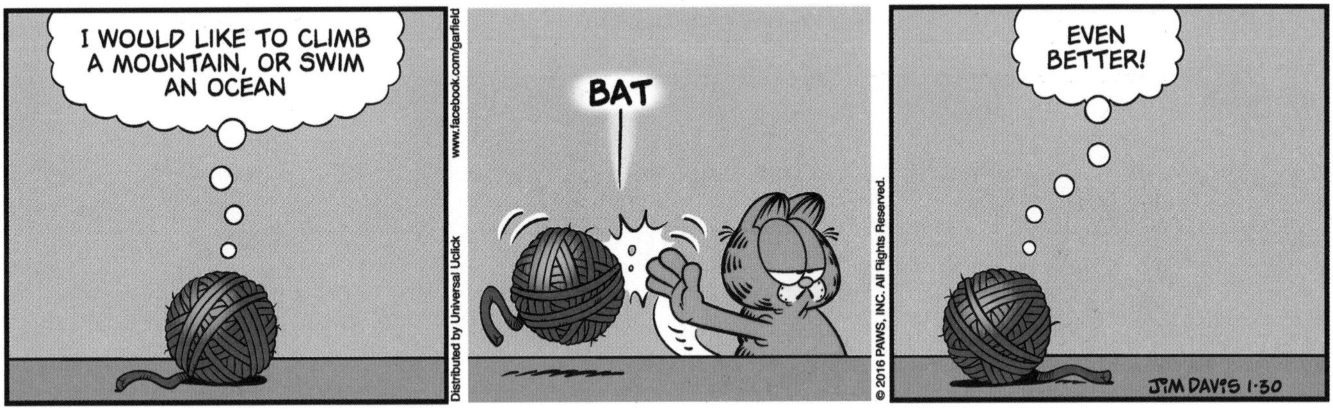
I WOULD LIKE TO CLIMB A MOUNTAIN, OR SWIM AN OCEAN
Distributed by Universal Uclick www.facebook.com/garfield
BAT
© 2016 PAWS, INC. All Rights Reserved.
EVEN BETTER!
JIM DAVIS 1-30

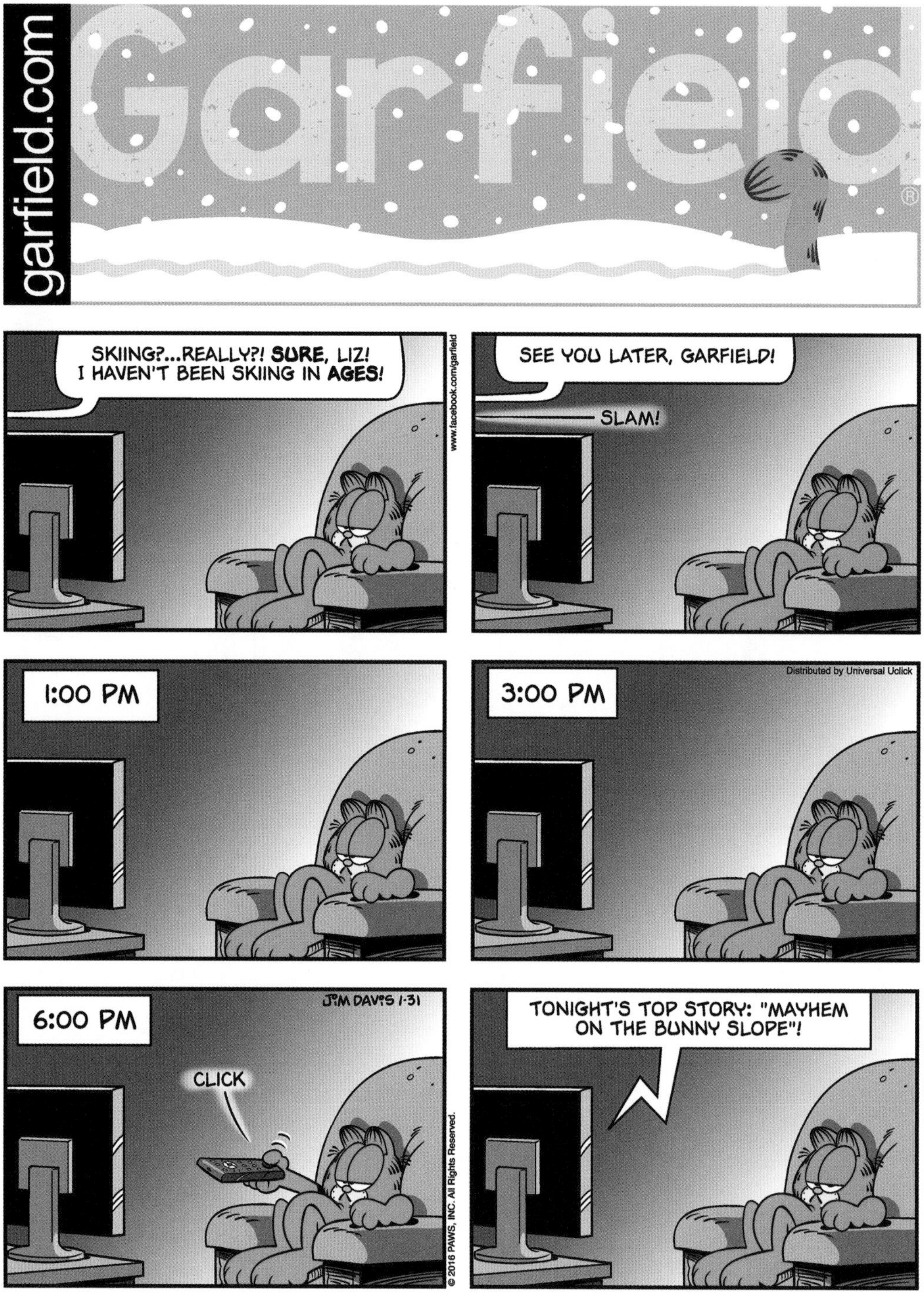
garfield.com
Garfield
SKIING?...REALLY?! SURE, LIZ! I HAVEN'T BEEN SKIING IN AGES!
www.facebook.com/garfield
SEE YOU LATER, GARFIELD!
SLAM!
1:00 PM
Distributed by Universal Uclick
3:00 PM
6:00 PM
JIM DAVIS 1-31
CLICK
© 2016 PAWS, INC. All Rights Reserved.
TONIGHT'S TOP STORY: "MAYHEM ON THE BUNNY SLOPE"!

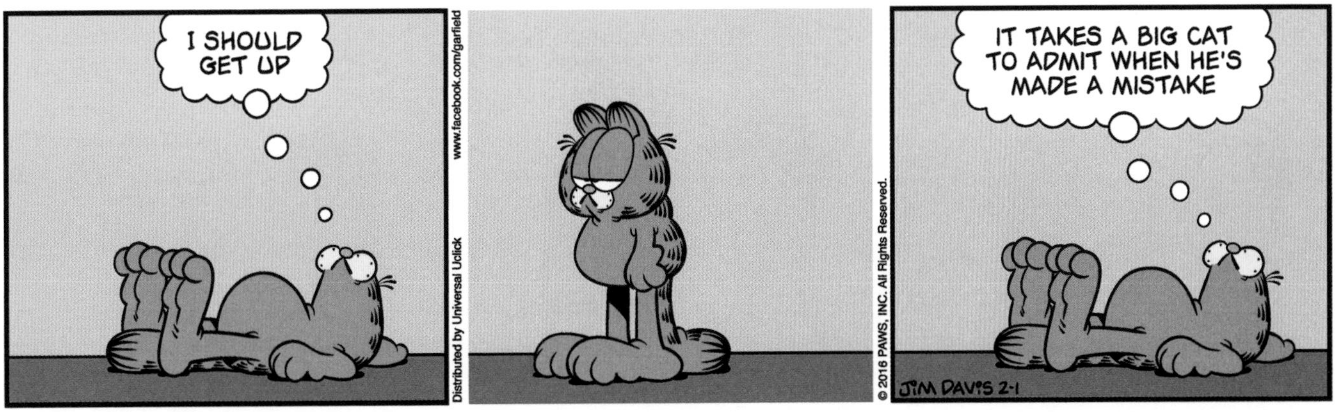
I SHOULD GET UP
Distributed by Universal Uclick www.facebook.com/garfield
IT TAKES A BIG CAT TO ADMIT WHEN HE'S MADE A MISTAKE
© 2016 PAWS, INC. All Rights Reserved.
JIM DAVIS 2-1

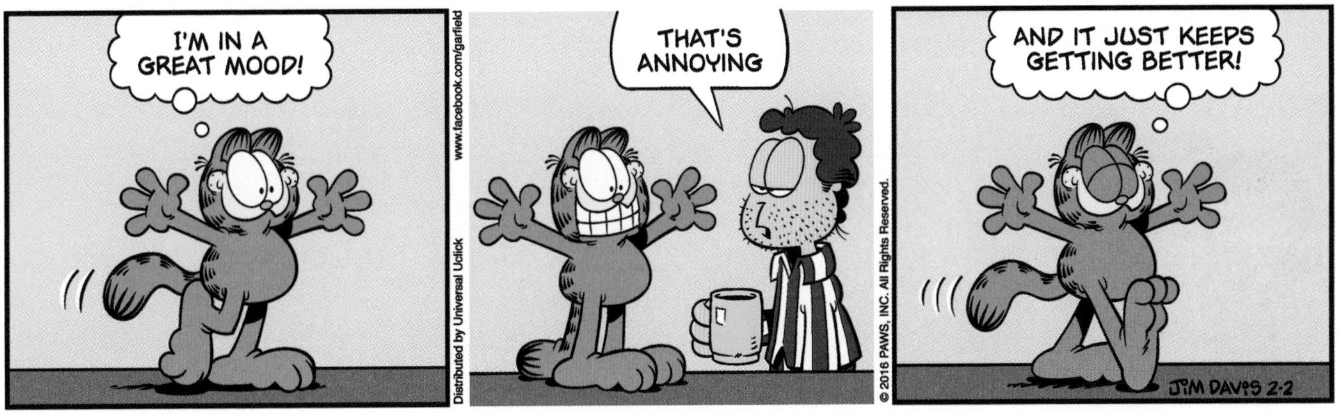
I'M IN A GREAT MOOD!
Distributed by Universal Uclick www.facebook.com/garfield
THAT'S ANNOYING
© 2016 PAWS, INC. All Rights Reserved.
AND IT JUST KEEPS GETTING BETTER!
JIM DAVIS 2-2

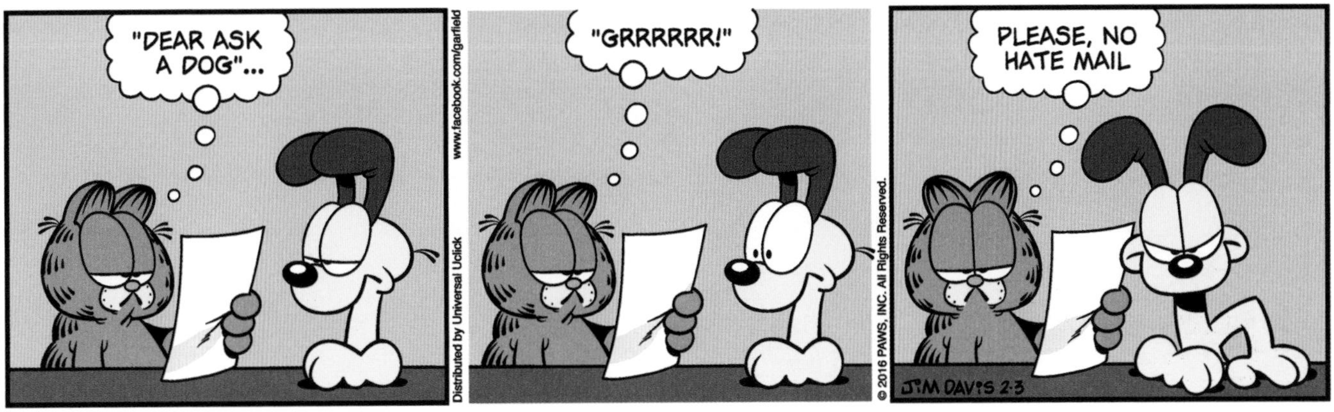
"DEAR ASK A DOG"...
Distributed by Universal Uclick www.facebook.com/garfield
"GRRRRRR!"
© 2016 PAWS, INC. All Rights Reserved.
PLEASE, NO HATE MAIL
JIM DAVIS 2-3

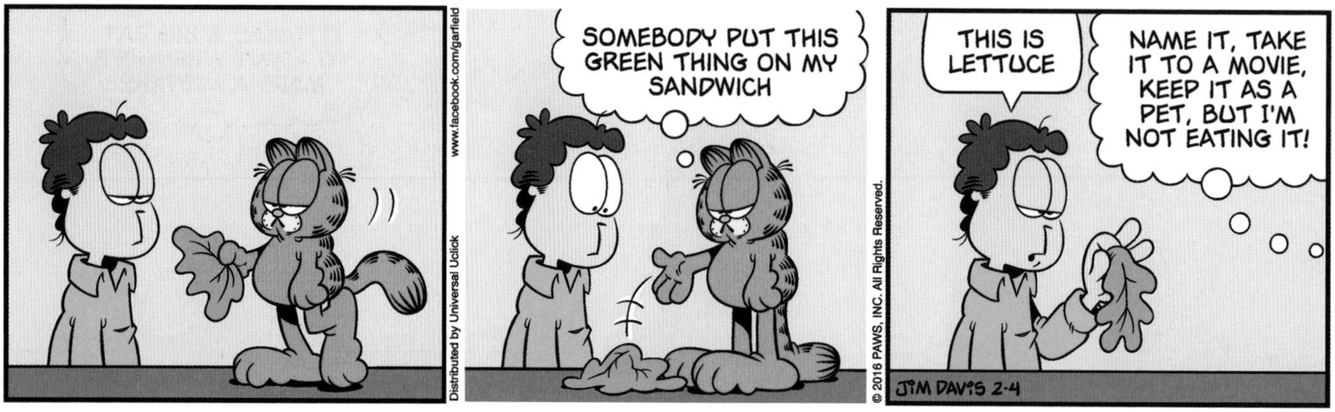
www.facebook.com/garfield
Distributed by Universal Uclick
SOMEBODY PUT THIS GREEN THING ON MY SANDWICH
© 2016 PAWS, INC. All Rights Reserved.
THIS IS LETTUCE
NAME IT, TAKE IT TO A MOVIE, KEEP IT AS A PET, BUT I'M NOT EATING IT!
JIM DAVIS 2-4

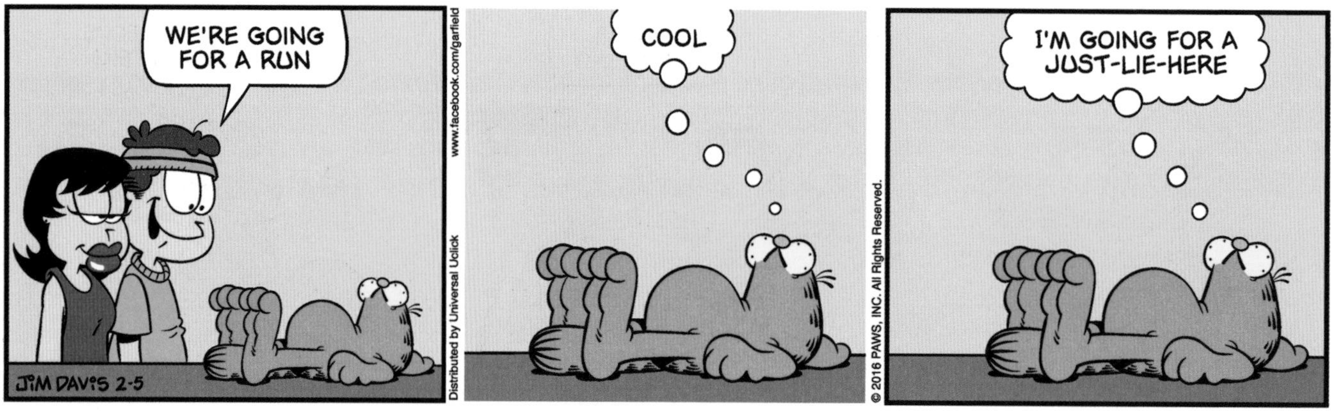
WE'RE GOING FOR A RUN
JIM DAVIS 2-5
www.facebook.com/garfield
Distributed by Universal Uclick
COOL
© 2016 PAWS, INC. All Rights Reserved.
I'M GOING FOR A JUST-LIE-HERE

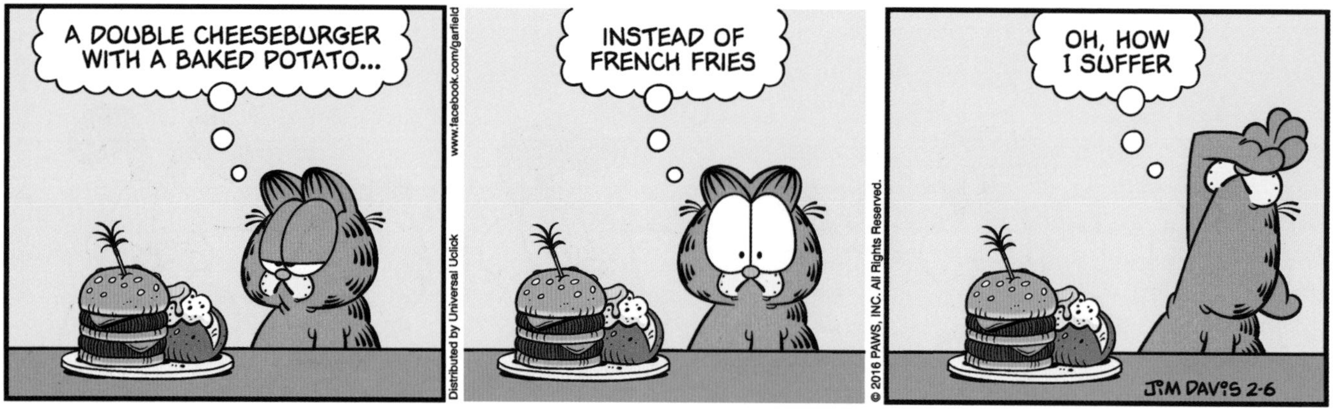
A DOUBLE CHEESEBURGER WITH A BAKED POTATO...
www.facebook.com/garfield
Distributed by Universal Uclick
INSTEAD OF FRENCH FRIES
© 2016 PAWS, INC. All Rights Reserved.
OH, HOW I SUFFER
JIM DAVIS 2-6

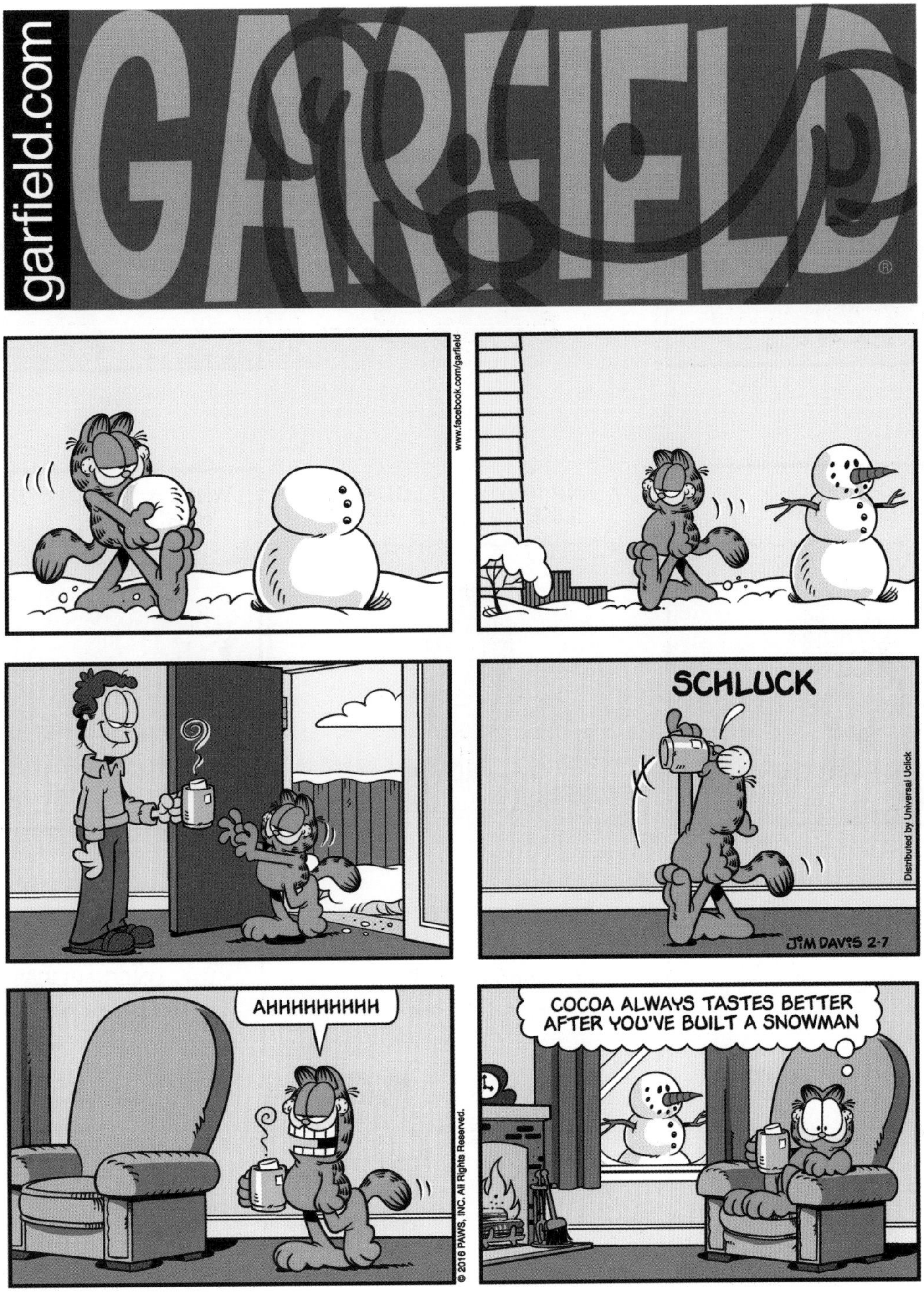
garfield.com
GARFIELD
www.facebook.com/garfield
SCHLUCK
Distributed by Universal Uclick
JIM DAVIS 2-7
AHHHHHHHHH
© 2016 PAWS, INC. All Rights Reserved.
COCOA ALWAYS TASTES BETTER AFTER YOU'VE BUILT A SNOWMAN

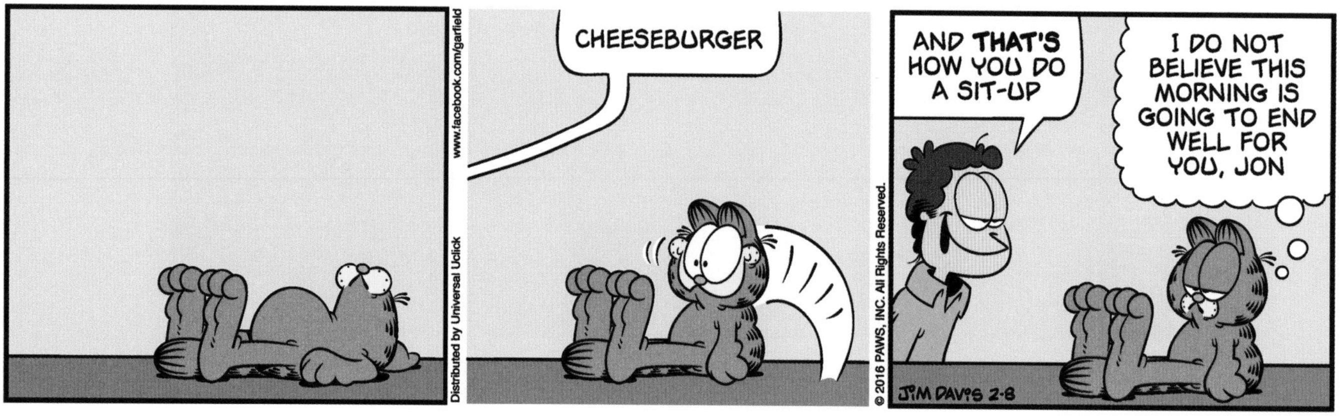
CHEESEBURGER
Distributed by Universal Uclick www.facebook.com/garfield
AND THAT'S HOW YOU DO A SIT-UP
I DO NOT BELIEVE THIS MORNING IS GOING TO END WELL FOR YOU, JON
© 2016 PAWS, INC. All Rights Reserved.
JIM DAVIS 2-8

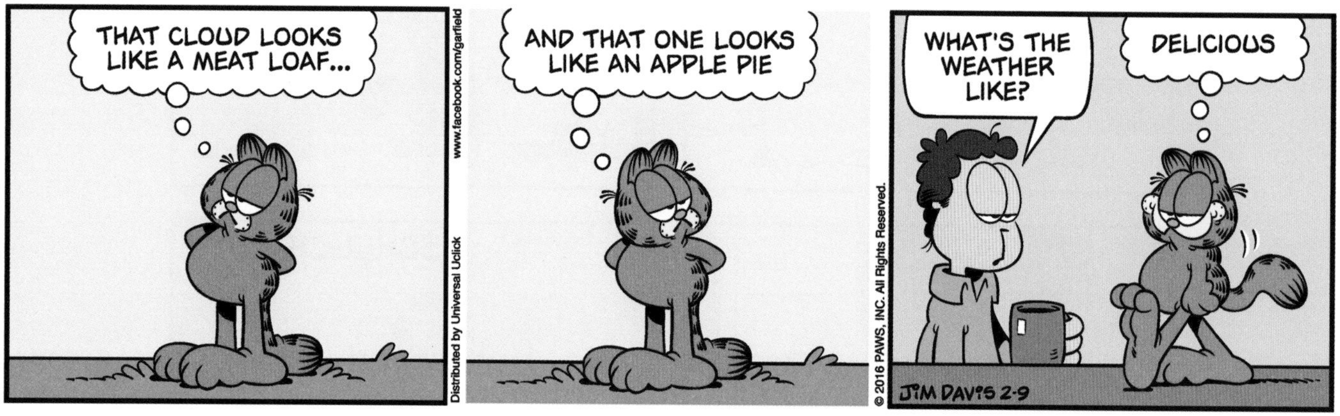
THAT CLOUD LOOKS LIKE A MEAT LOAF...
Distributed by Universal Uclick www.facebook.com/garfield
AND THAT ONE LOOKS LIKE AN APPLE PIE
WHAT'S THE WEATHER LIKE?
DELICIOUS
© 2016 PAWS, INC. All Rights Reserved.
JIM DAVIS 2-9

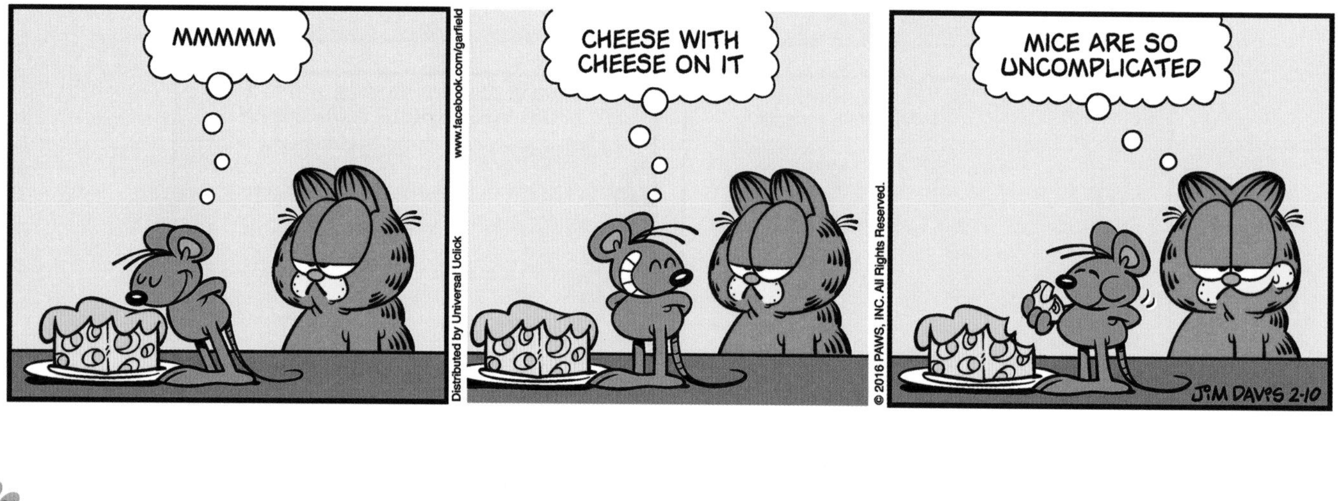
MMMMM
Distributed by Universal Uclick www.facebook.com/garfield
CHEESE WITH CHEESE ON IT
MICE ARE SO UNCOMPLICATED
© 2016 PAWS, INC. All Rights Reserved.
JIM DAVIS 2-10

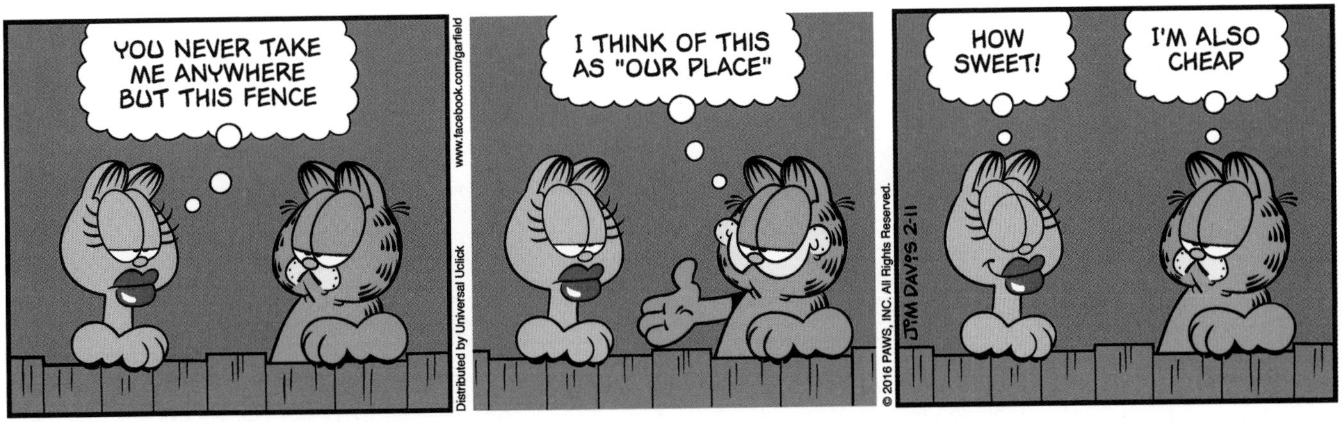

YOU NEVER TAKE ME ANYWHERE BUT THIS FENCE
I THINK OF THIS AS "OUR PLACE"
HOW SWEET!
I'M ALSO CHEAP
Distributed by Universal Uclick
www.facebook.com/garfield
© 2016 PAWS, INC. All Rights Reserved.
JIM DAVIS 2-11

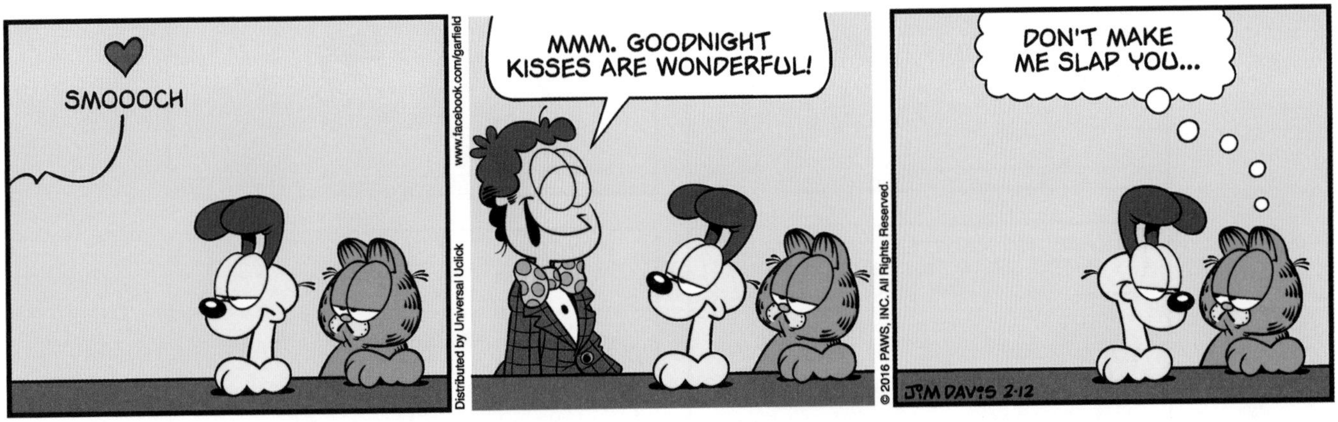

SMOOOCH
MMM. GOODNIGHT KISSES ARE WONDERFUL!
DON'T MAKE ME SLAP YOU...
Distributed by Universal Uclick
www.facebook.com/garfield
© 2016 PAWS, INC. All Rights Reserved.
JIM DAVIS 2-12

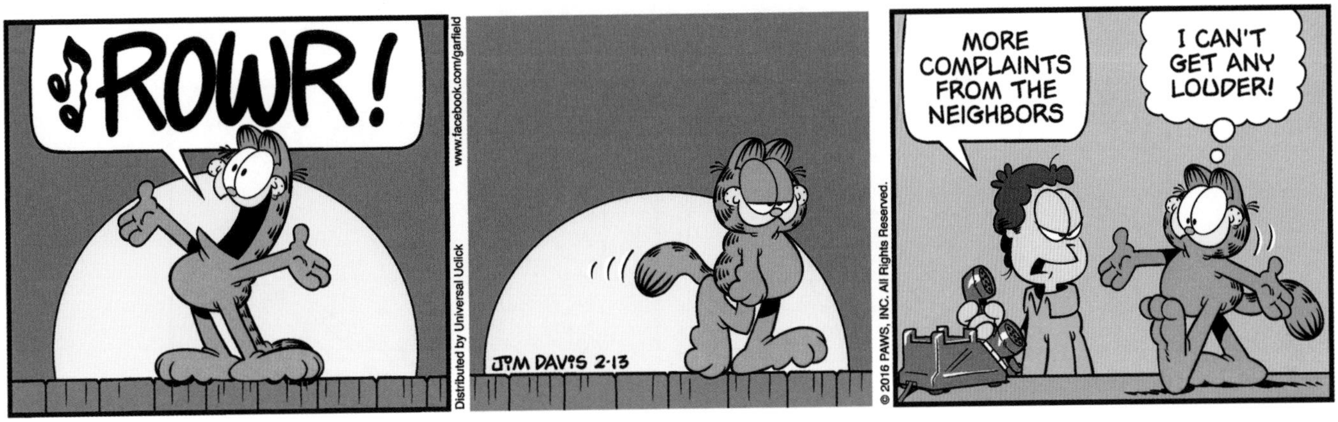

ROWR!
MORE COMPLAINTS FROM THE NEIGHBORS
I CAN'T GET ANY LOUDER!
Distributed by Universal Uclick
www.facebook.com/garfield
© 2016 PAWS, INC. All Rights Reserved.
JIM DAVIS 2-13

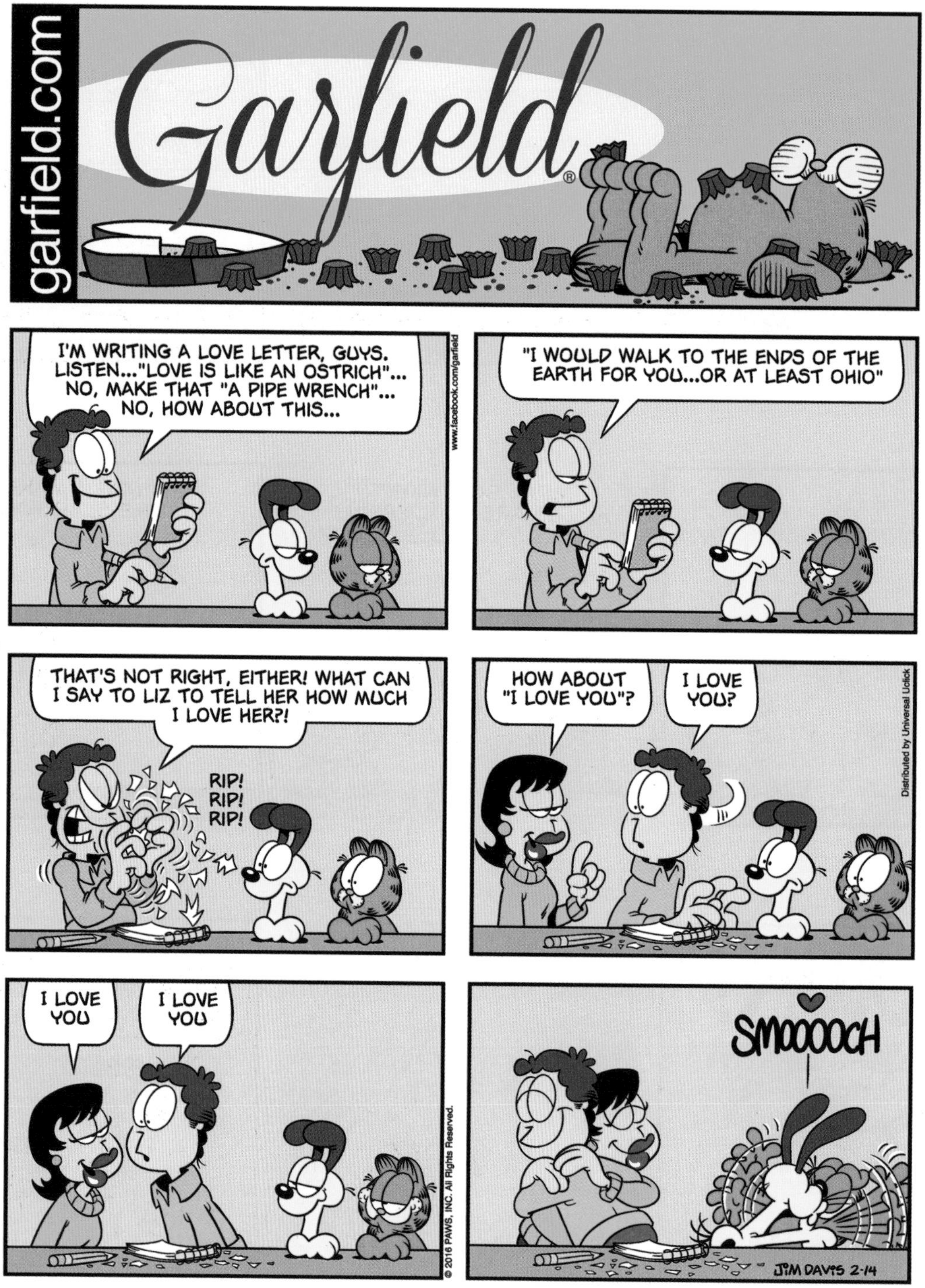

garfield.com
Garfield
I'M WRITING A LOVE LETTER, GUYS. LISTEN..."LOVE IS LIKE AN OSTRICH"... NO, MAKE THAT "A PIPE WRENCH"... NO, HOW ABOUT THIS...
www.facebook.com/garfield
"I WOULD WALK TO THE ENDS OF THE EARTH FOR YOU...OR AT LEAST OHIO"
THAT'S NOT RIGHT, EITHER! WHAT CAN I SAY TO LIZ TO TELL HER HOW MUCH I LOVE HER?!
RIP! RIP! RIP!
HOW ABOUT "I LOVE YOU"?
I LOVE YOU?
Distributed by Universal Uclick
I LOVE YOU
I LOVE YOU
© 2018 PAWS, INC. All Rights Reserved.
SMOOOOCH
JIM DAVIS 2-14

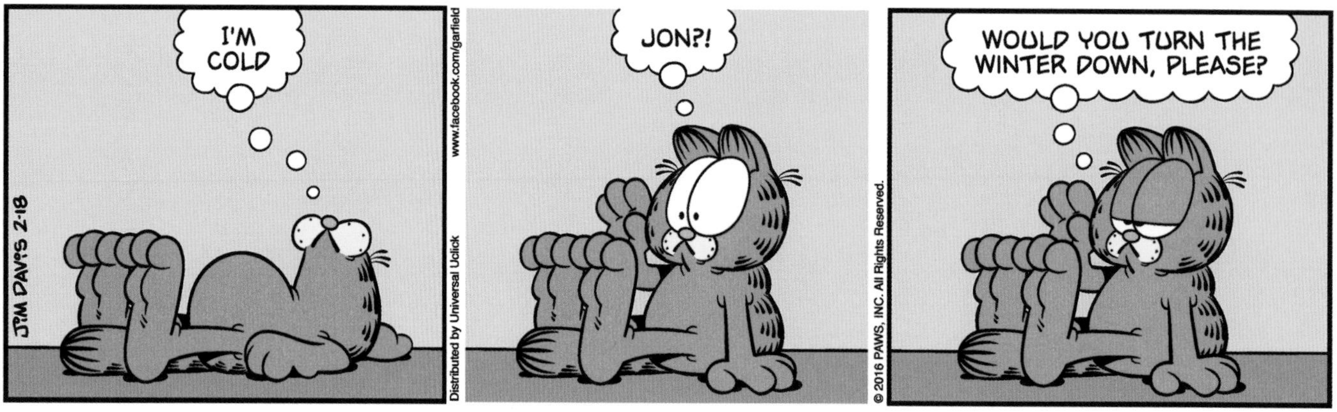
I'M COLD
JON?!
WOULD YOU TURN THE WINTER DOWN, PLEASE?
JIM DAVIS 2-18
Distributed by Universal Uclick www.facebook.com/garfield
© 2016 PAWS, INC. All Rights Reserved.

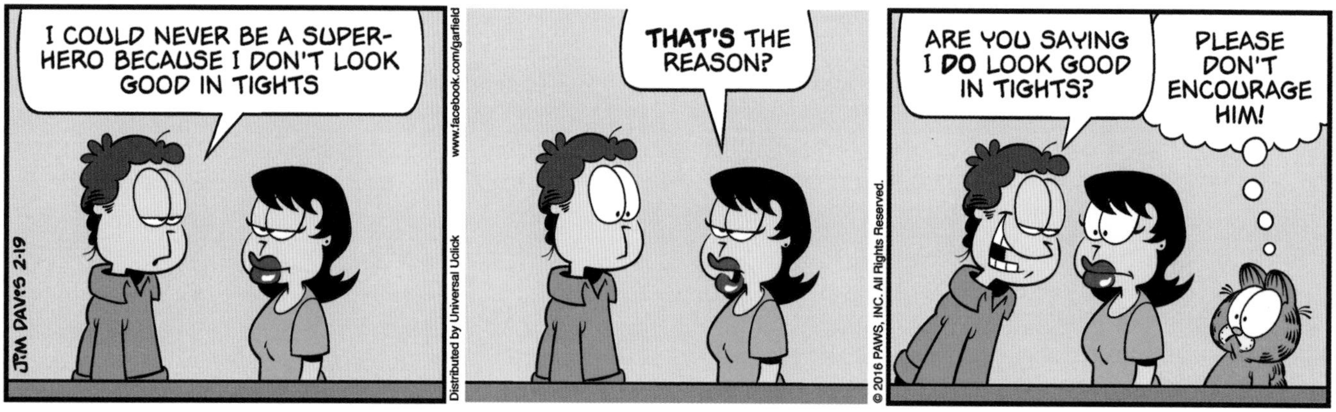
I COULD NEVER BE A SUPER-HERO BECAUSE I DON'T LOOK GOOD IN TIGHTS
THAT'S THE REASON?
ARE YOU SAYING I **DO** LOOK GOOD IN TIGHTS?
PLEASE DON'T ENCOURAGE HIM!
JIM DAVIS 2-19
Distributed by Universal Uclick www.facebook.com/garfield
© 2016 PAWS, INC. All Rights Reserved.

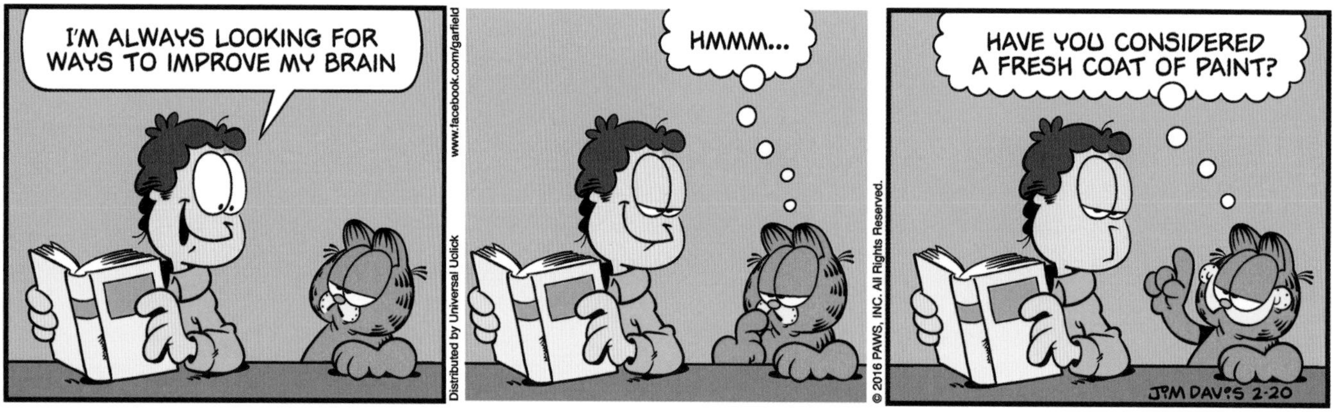
I'M ALWAYS LOOKING FOR WAYS TO IMPROVE MY BRAIN
HMMM...
HAVE YOU CONSIDERED A FRESH COAT OF PAINT?
JIM DAVIS 2-20
Distributed by Universal Uclick www.facebook.com/garfield
© 2016 PAWS, INC. All Rights Reserved.

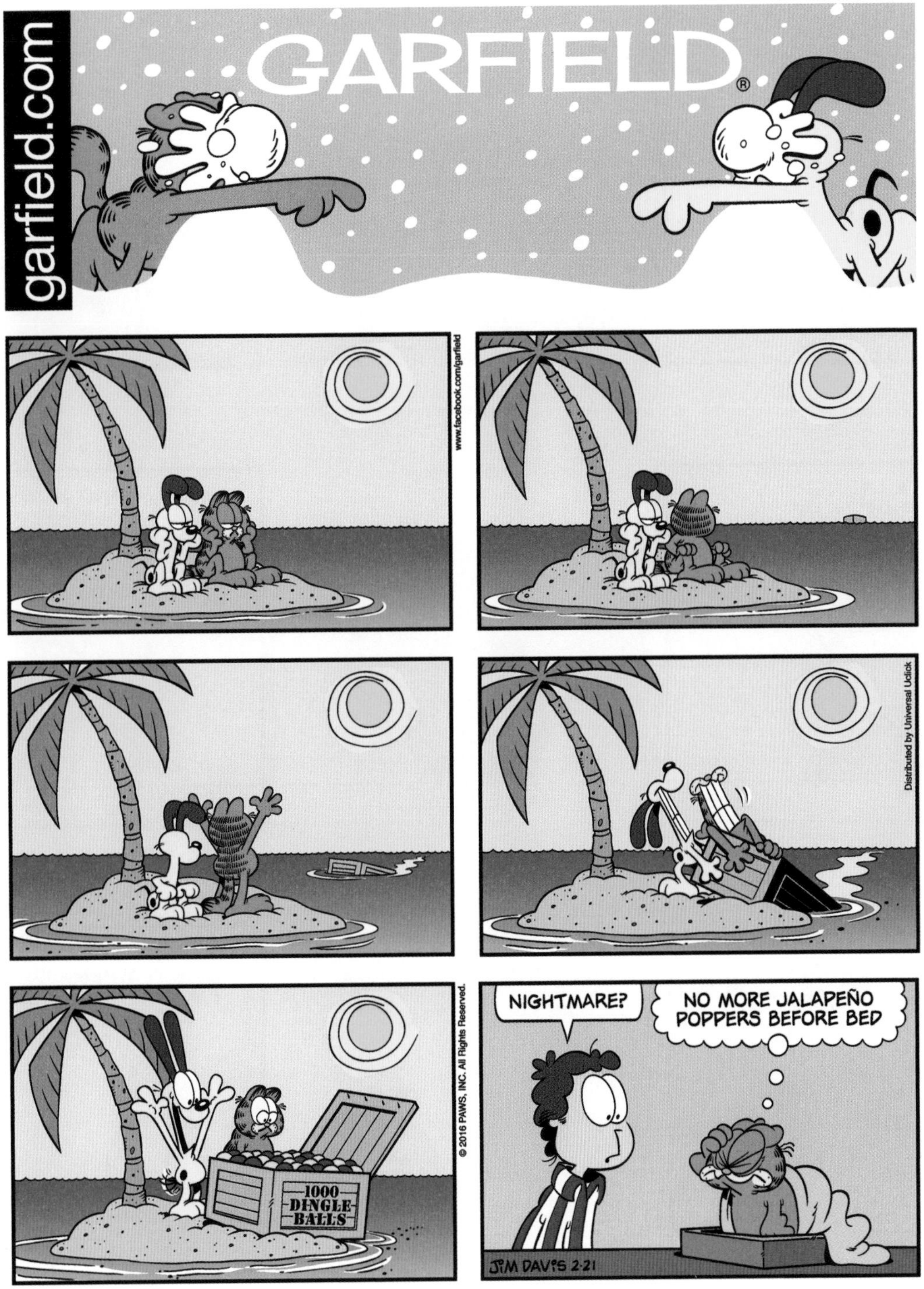
garfield.com
GARFIELD
www.facebook.com/garfield
Distributed by Universal Uclick
© 2016 PAWS, INC. All Rights Reserved.
1000 DINGLE BALLS
NIGHTMARE?
NO MORE JALAPEÑO POPPERS BEFORE BED
JIM DAVIS 2-21

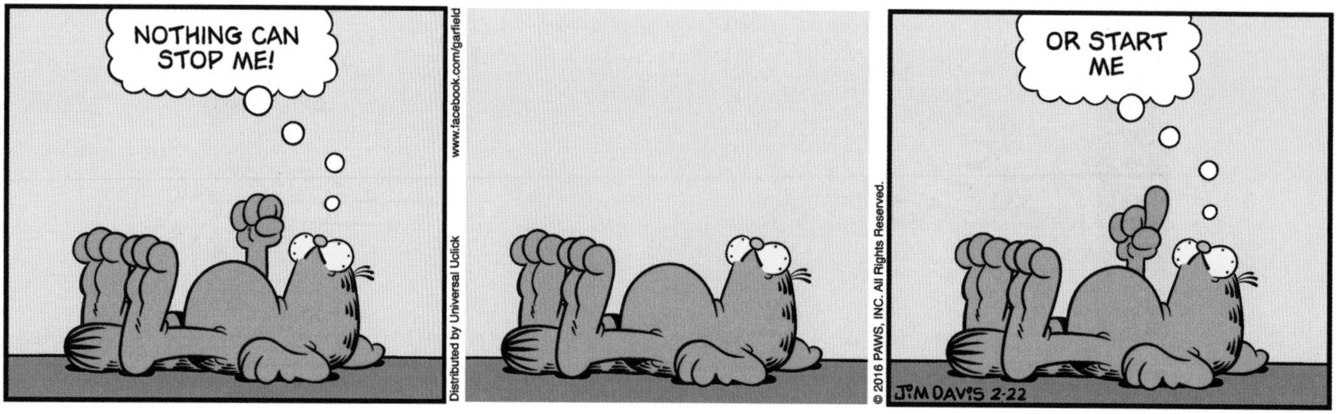
NOTHING CAN STOP ME!
OR START ME
Distributed by Universal Uclick www.facebook.com/garfield
© 2016 PAWS, INC. All Rights Reserved.
JIM DAVIS 2-22

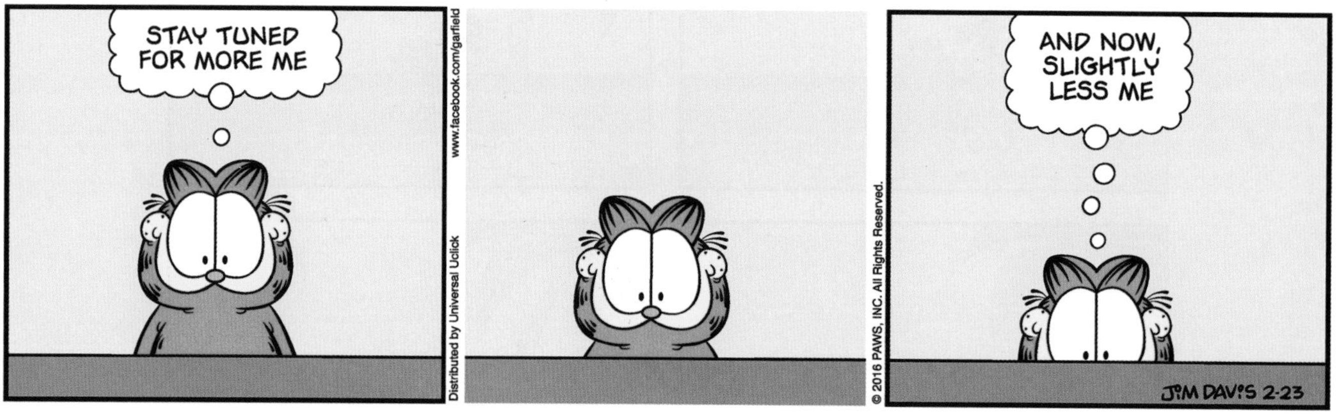
STAY TUNED FOR MORE ME
AND NOW, SLIGHTLY LESS ME
Distributed by Universal Uclick www.facebook.com/garfield
© 2016 PAWS, INC. All Rights Reserved.
JIM DAVIS 2-23

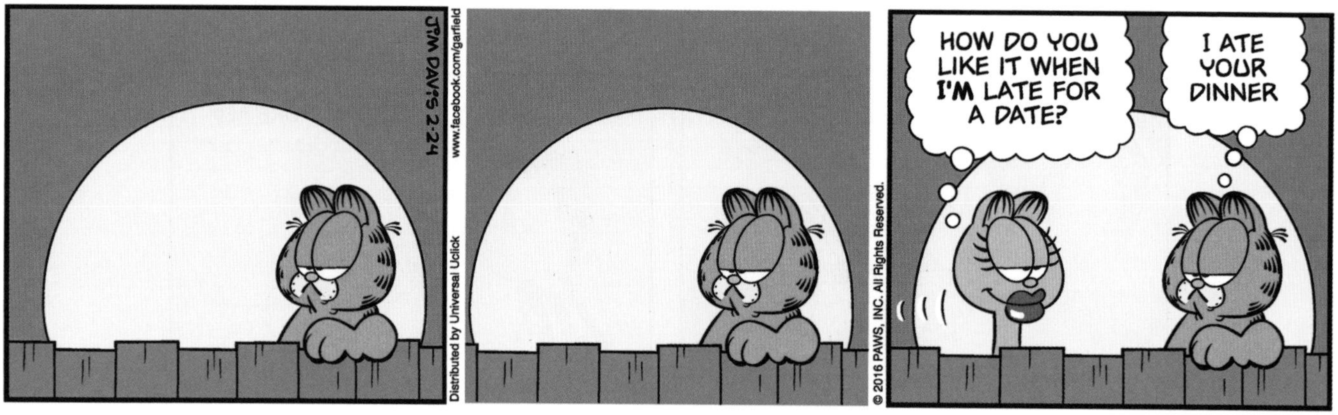
JIM DAVIS 2-24
Distributed by Universal Uclick www.facebook.com/garfield
© 2016 PAWS, INC. All Rights Reserved.
HOW DO YOU LIKE IT WHEN I'M LATE FOR A DATE?
I ATE YOUR DINNER

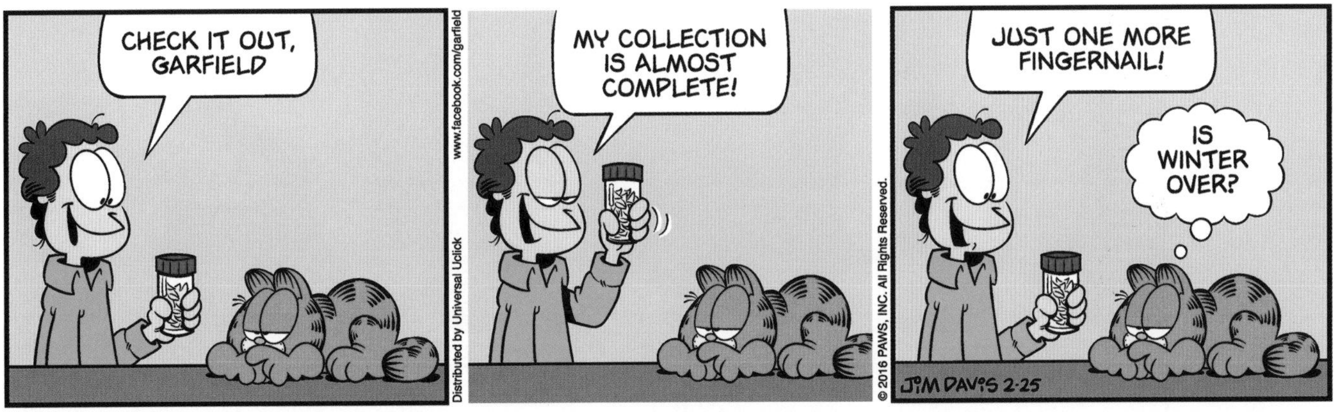
CHECK IT OUT, GARFIELD
MY COLLECTION IS ALMOST COMPLETE!
JUST ONE MORE FINGERNAIL!
IS WINTER OVER?
JIM DAVIS 2-25
www.facebook.com/garfield
Distributed by Universal Uclick
© 2016 PAWS, INC. All Rights Reserved.

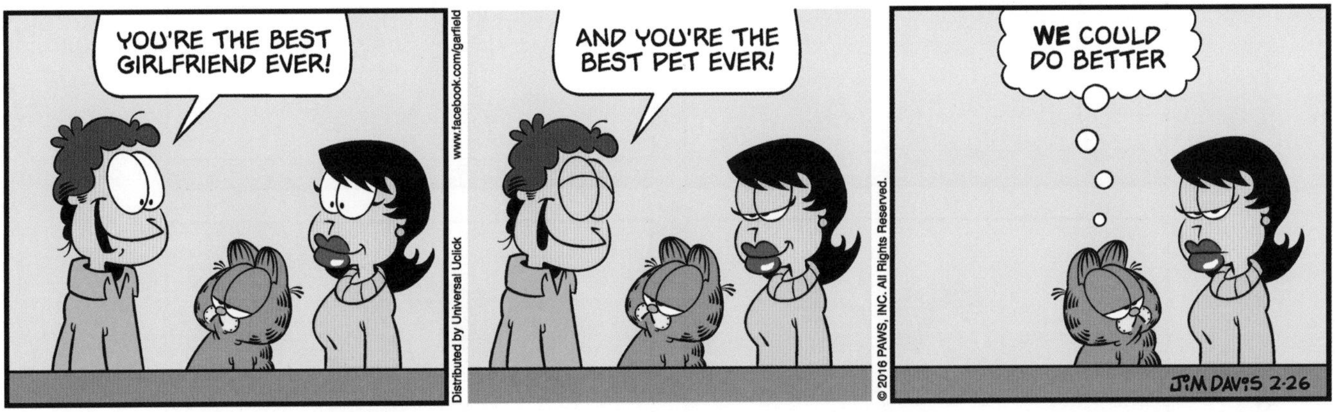
YOU'RE THE BEST GIRLFRIEND EVER!
AND YOU'RE THE BEST PET EVER!
WE COULD DO BETTER
JIM DAVIS 2-26
www.facebook.com/garfield
Distributed by Universal Uclick
© 2016 PAWS, INC. All Rights Reserved.

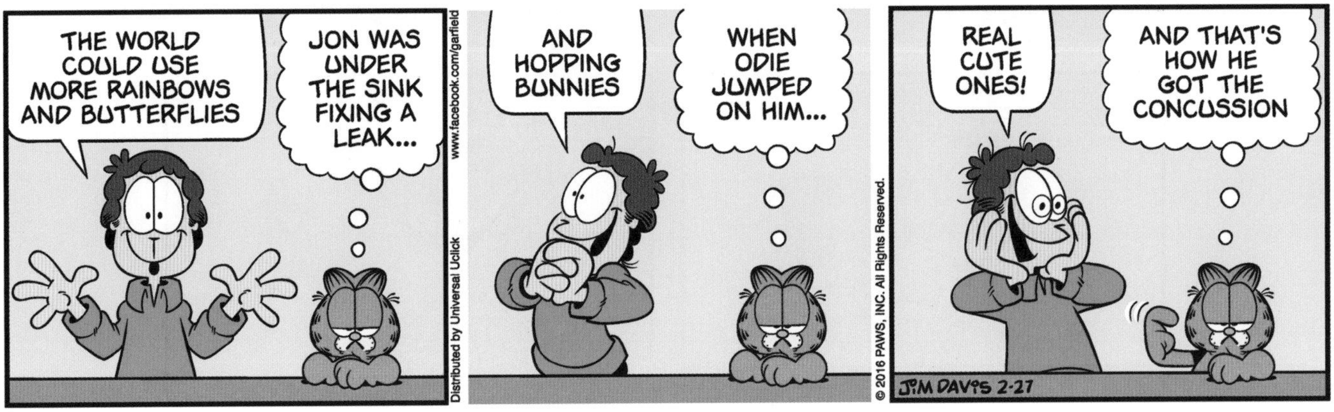
THE WORLD COULD USE MORE RAINBOWS AND BUTTERFLIES
JON WAS UNDER THE SINK FIXING A LEAK...
AND HOPPING BUNNIES
WHEN ODIE JUMPED ON HIM...
REAL CUTE ONES!
AND THAT'S HOW HE GOT THE CONCUSSION
JIM DAVIS 2-27
www.facebook.com/garfield
Distributed by Universal Uclick
© 2016 PAWS, INC. All Rights Reserved.

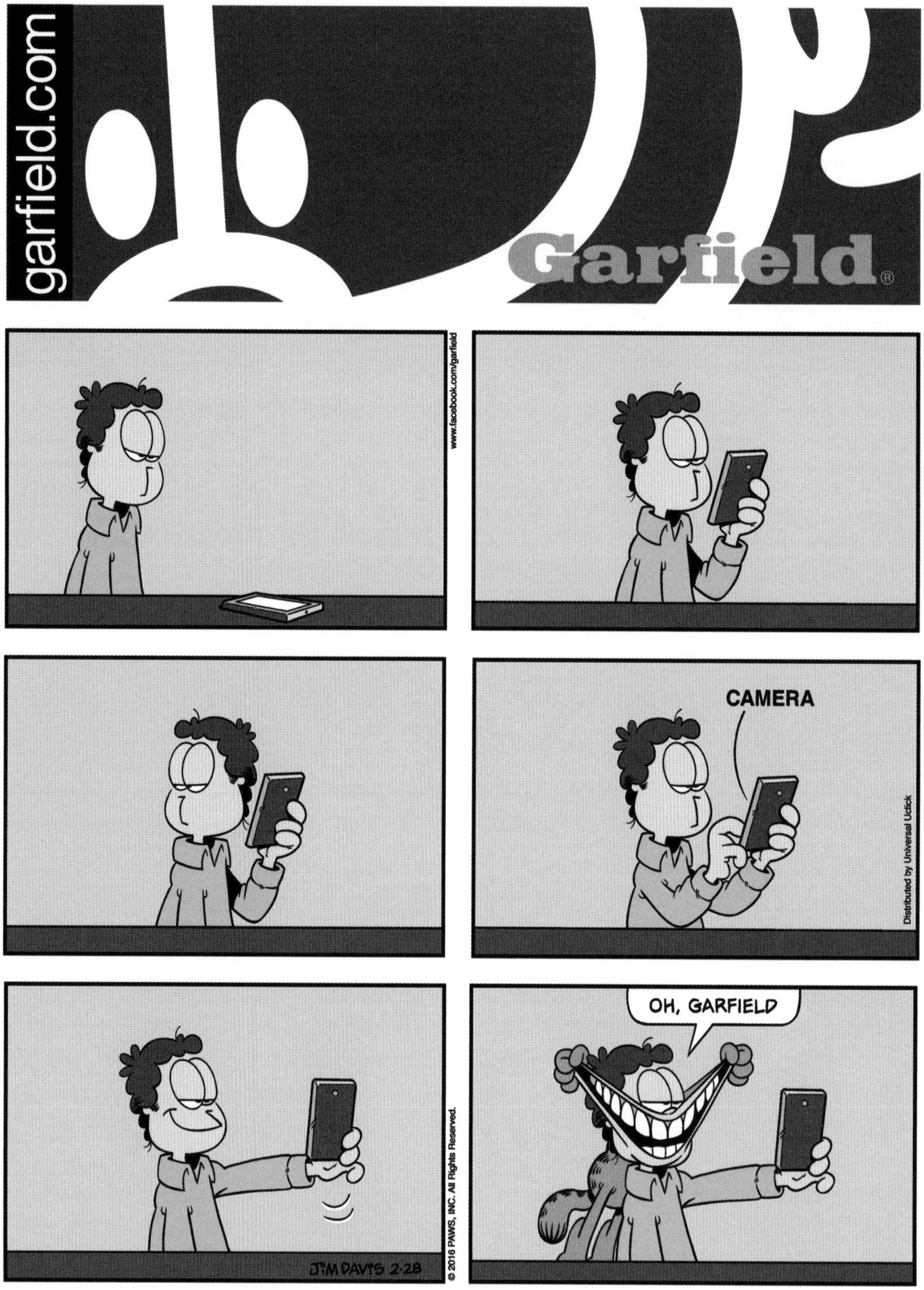
garfield.com
Garfield®
www.facebook.com/garfield
CAMERA
Distributed by Universal Uclick
JIM DAVIS 2-28
© 2016 PAWS, INC. All Rights Reserved.
OH, GARFIELD

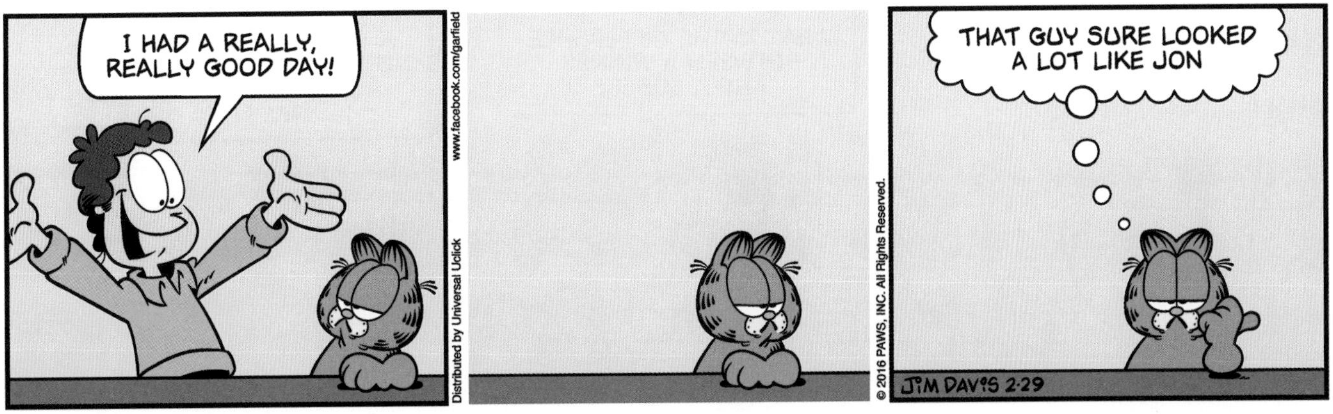
I HAD A REALLY, REALLY GOOD DAY!
www.facebook.com/garfield
Distributed by Universal Uclick
© 2016 PAWS, INC. All Rights Reserved.
THAT GUY SURE LOOKED A LOT LIKE JON
JIM DAVIS 2·29

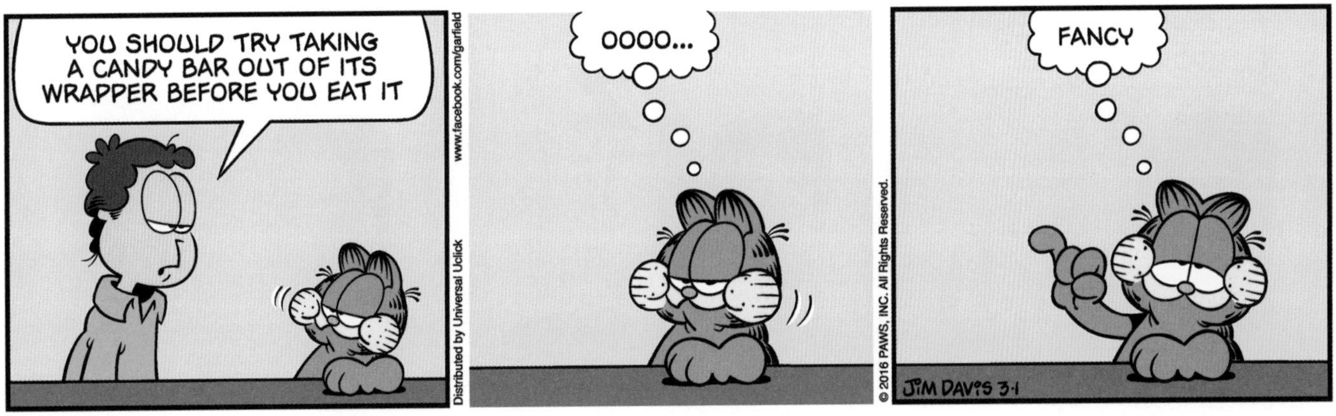
YOU SHOULD TRY TAKING A CANDY BAR OUT OF ITS WRAPPER BEFORE YOU EAT IT
www.facebook.com/garfield
Distributed by Universal Uclick
OOOO...
© 2016 PAWS, INC. All Rights Reserved.
FANCY
JIM DAVIS 3·1

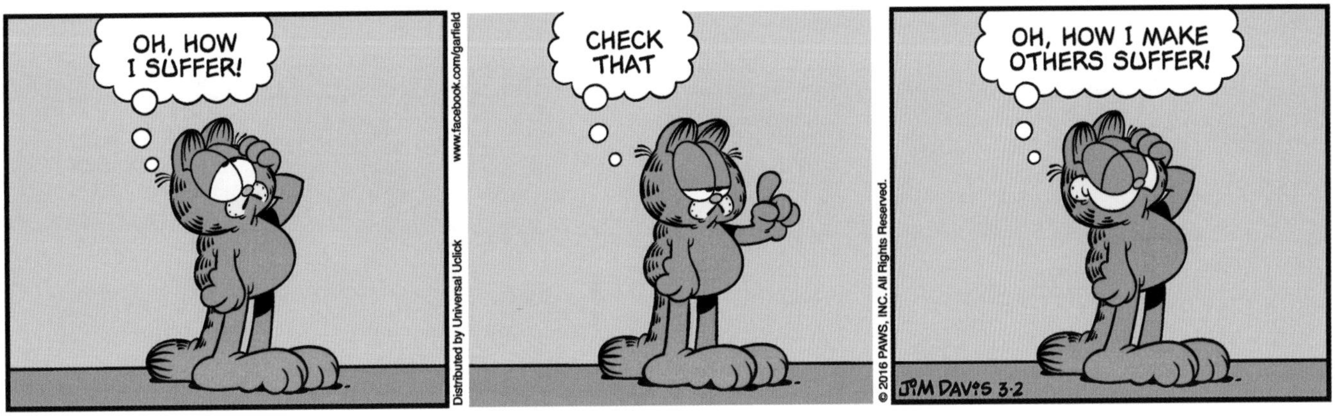
OH, HOW I SUFFER!
www.facebook.com/garfield
Distributed by Universal Uclick
CHECK THAT
© 2016 PAWS, INC. All Rights Reserved.
OH, HOW I MAKE OTHERS SUFFER!
JIM DAVIS 3·2

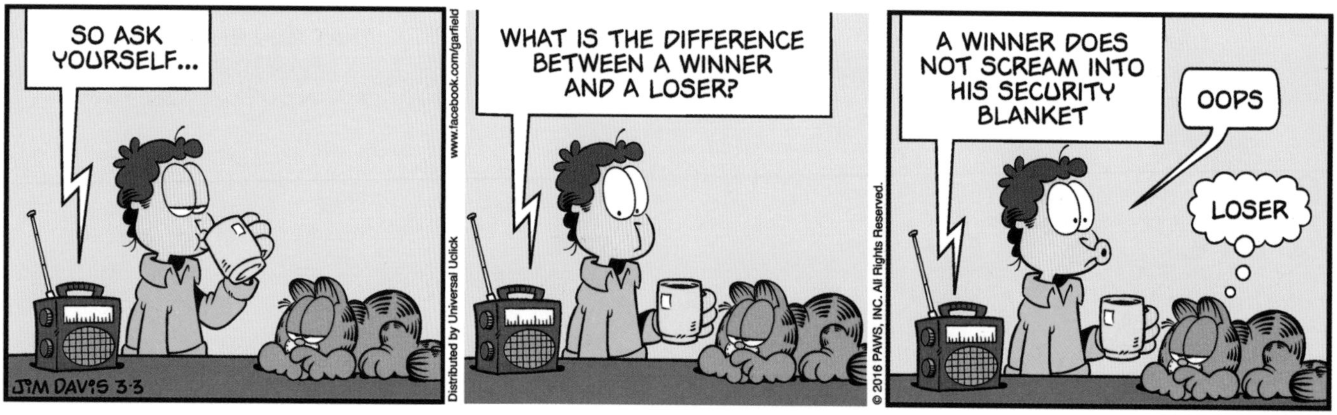
SO ASK YOURSELF...
JIM DAVIS 3-3
WHAT IS THE DIFFERENCE BETWEEN A WINNER AND A LOSER?
A WINNER DOES NOT SCREAM INTO HIS SECURITY BLANKET
OOPS
LOSER
www.facebook.com/garfield
Distributed by Universal Uclick
© 2016 PAWS, INC. All Rights Reserved.

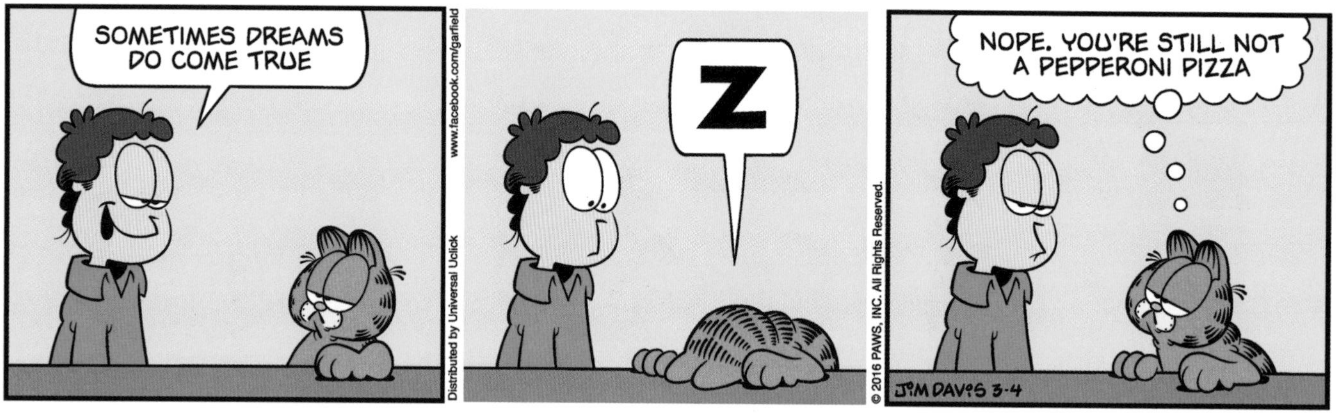
SOMETIMES DREAMS DO COME TRUE
Z
NOPE. YOU'RE STILL NOT A PEPPERONI PIZZA
JIM DAVIS 3-4
www.facebook.com/garfield
Distributed by Universal Uclick
© 2016 PAWS, INC. All Rights Reserved.

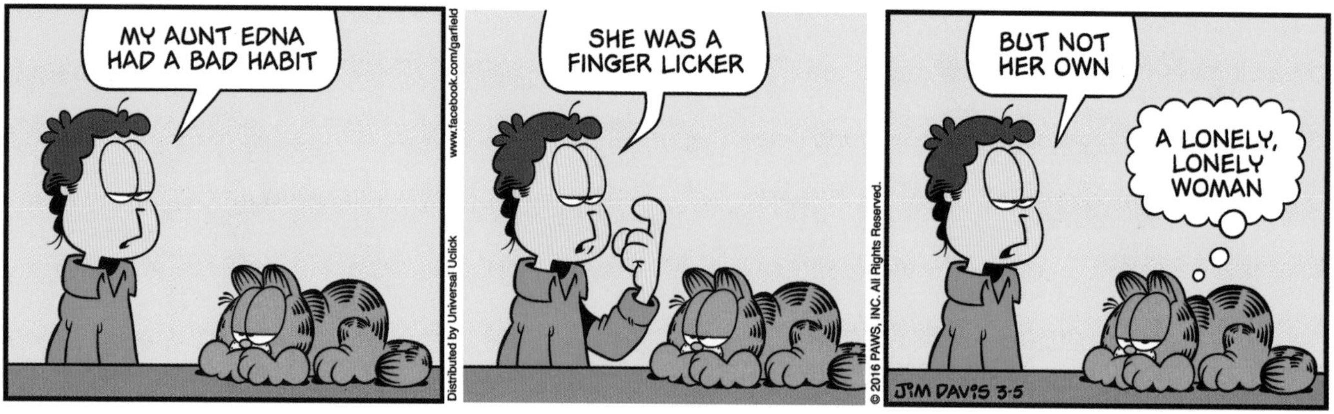
MY AUNT EDNA HAD A BAD HABIT
SHE WAS A FINGER LICKER
BUT NOT HER OWN
A LONELY, LONELY WOMAN
JIM DAVIS 3-5
www.facebook.com/garfield
Distributed by Universal Uclick
© 2016 PAWS, INC. All Rights Reserved.

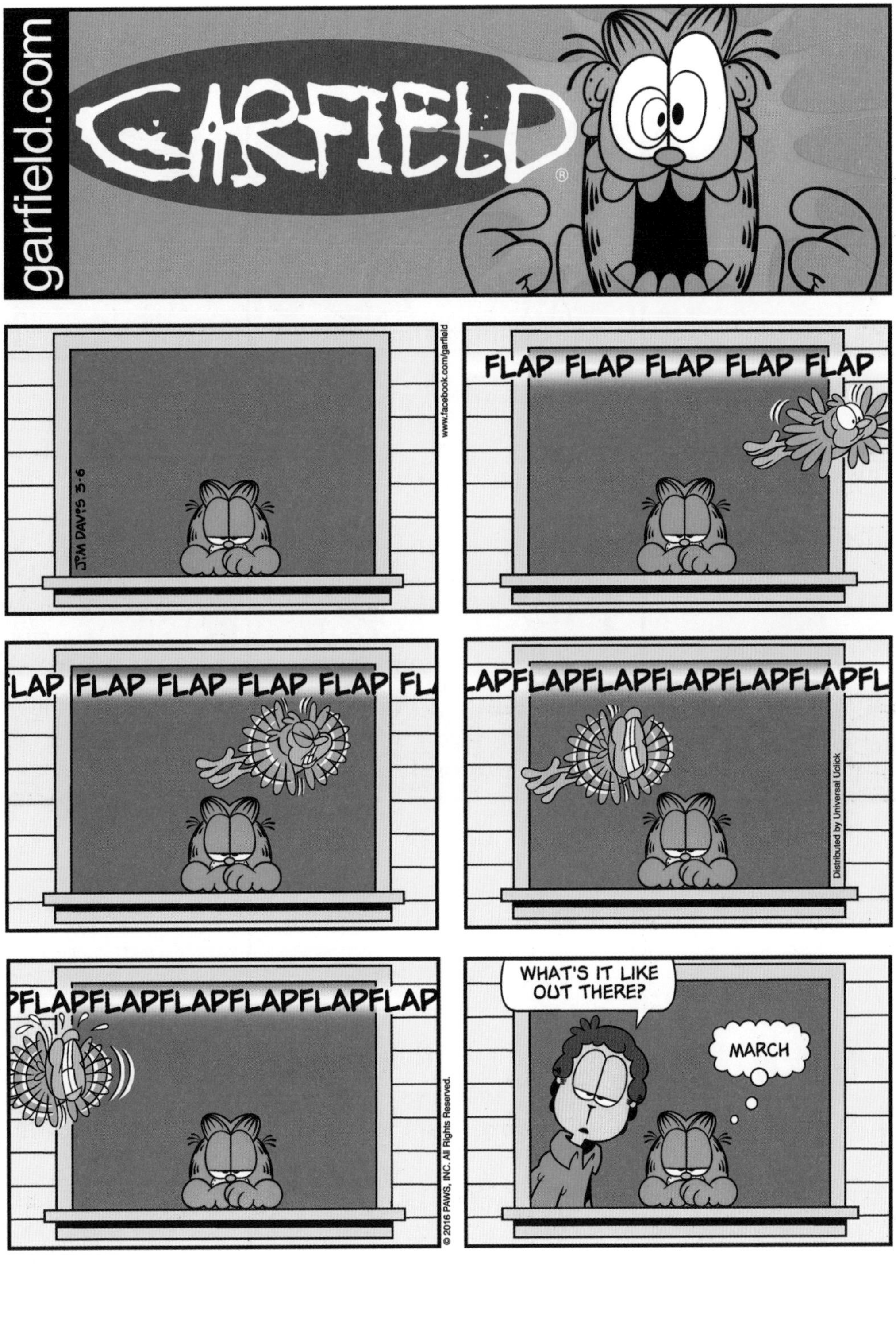
garfield.com
GARFIELD®
JPM DAVIS 3-6
www.facebook.com/garfield
FLAP FLAP FLAP FLAP FLAP
FLAP FLAP FLAP FLAP FLAP FL
LAPFLAPFLAPFLAPFLAPFLAPFL
Distributed by Universal Uclick
PFLAPFLAPFLAPFLAPFLAPFLAP
© 2016 PAWS, INC. All Rights Reserved.
WHAT'S IT LIKE OUT THERE?
MARCH

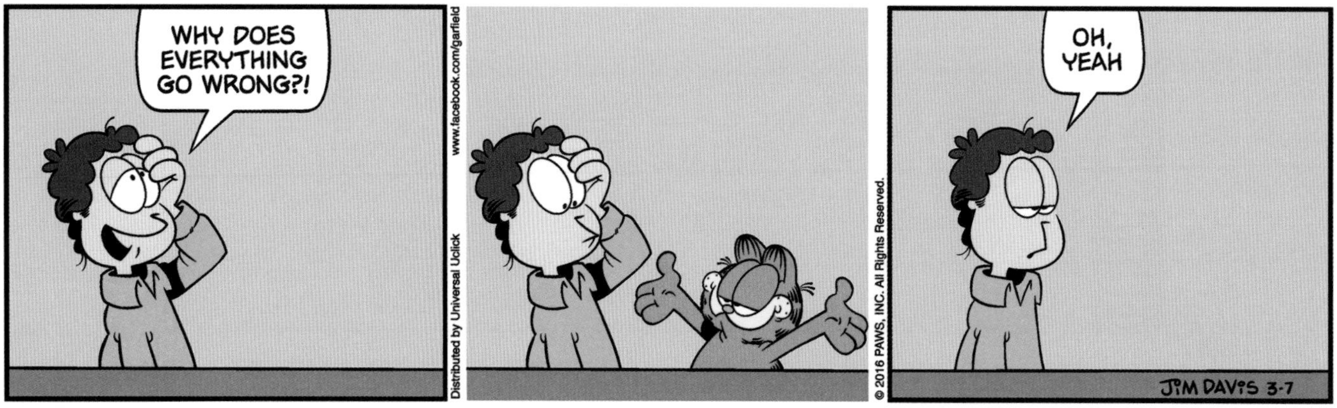
WHY DOES EVERYTHING GO WRONG?!
OH, YEAH
JIM DAVIS 3-7
Distributed by Universal Uclick www.facebook.com/garfield
© 2016 PAWS, INC. All Rights Reserved.

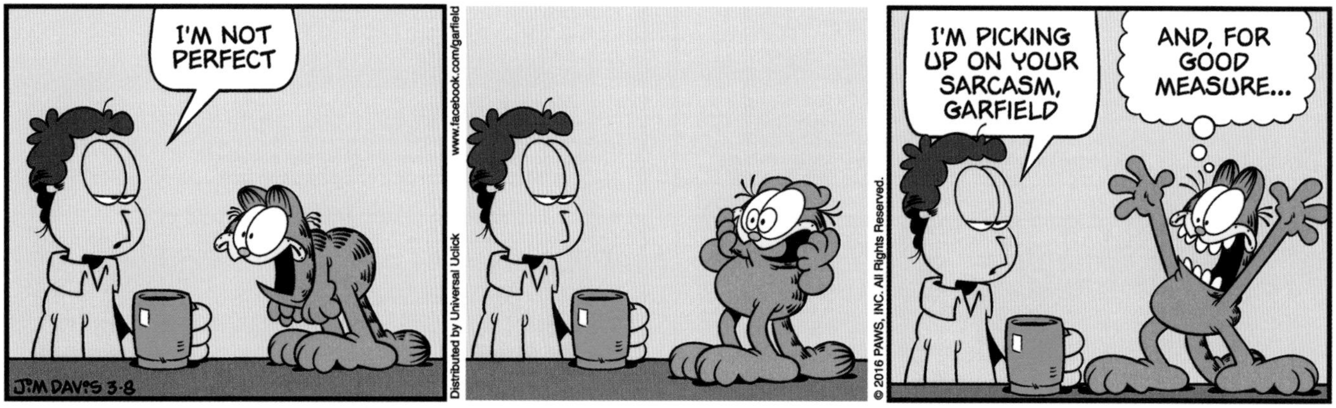
I'M NOT PERFECT
JIM DAVIS 3-8
I'M PICKING UP ON YOUR SARCASM, GARFIELD
AND, FOR GOOD MEASURE...
Distributed by Universal Uclick www.facebook.com/garfield
© 2016 PAWS, INC. All Rights Reserved.

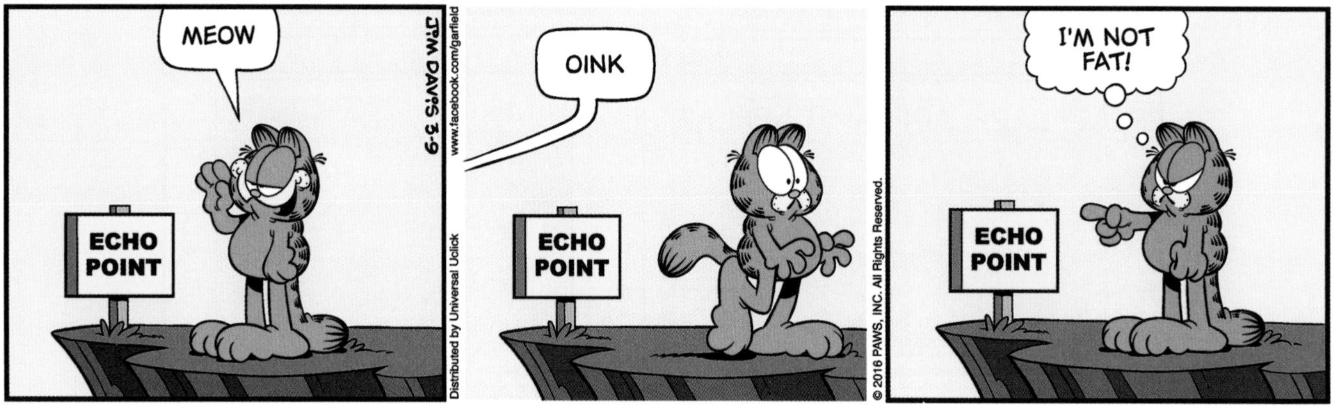
MEOW
ECHO POINT
JIM DAVIS 3-9
OINK
ECHO POINT
I'M NOT FAT!
ECHO POINT
Distributed by Universal Uclick www.facebook.com/garfield
© 2016 PAWS, INC. All Rights Reserved.

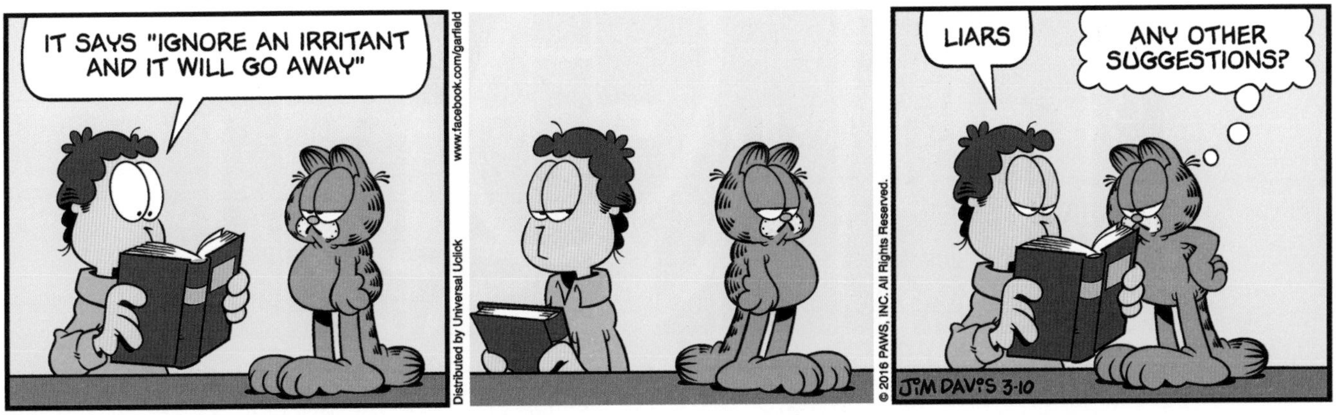
IT SAYS "IGNORE AN IRRITANT AND IT WILL GO AWAY"
LIARS
ANY OTHER SUGGESTIONS?
Distributed by Universal Uclick www.facebook.com/garfield
© 2016 PAWS, INC. All Rights Reserved.
JIM DAVIS 3-10

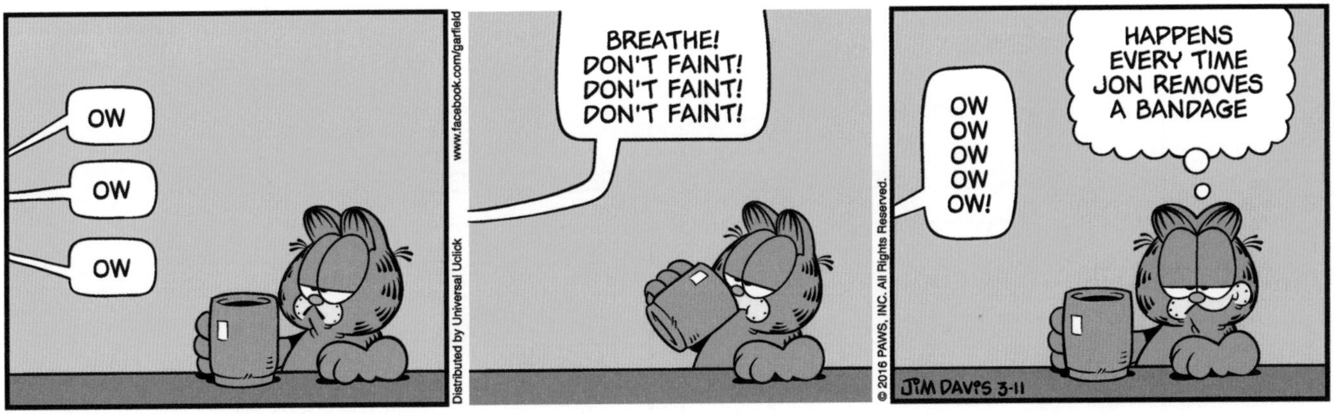
OW
OW
OW
BREATHE! DON'T FAINT! DON'T FAINT! DON'T FAINT!
OW OW OW OW OW!
HAPPENS EVERY TIME JON REMOVES A BANDAGE
Distributed by Universal Uclick www.facebook.com/garfield
© 2016 PAWS, INC. All Rights Reserved.
JIM DAVIS 3-11

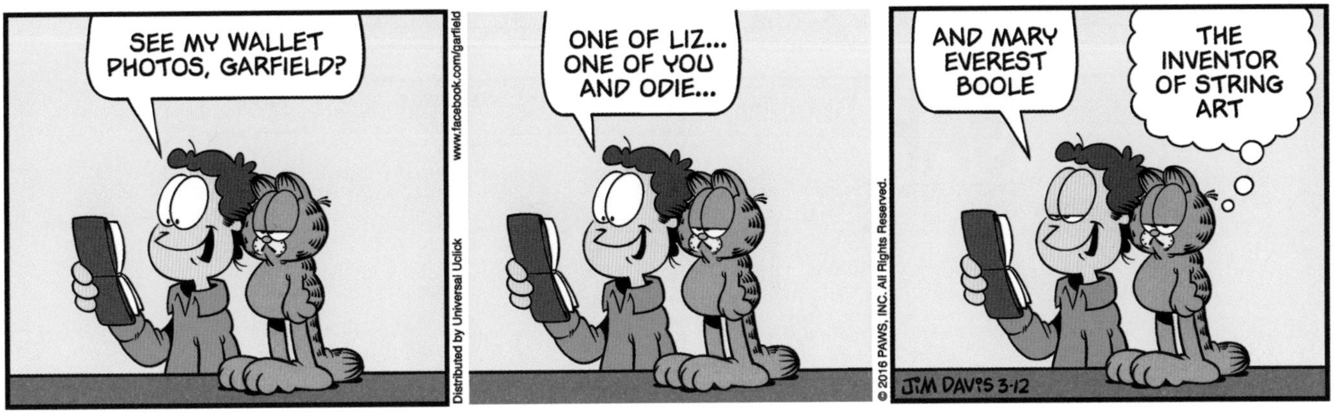
SEE MY WALLET PHOTOS, GARFIELD?
ONE OF LIZ... ONE OF YOU AND ODIE...
AND MARY EVEREST BOOLE
THE INVENTOR OF STRING ART
Distributed by Universal Uclick www.facebook.com/garfield
© 2016 PAWS, INC. All Rights Reserved.
JIM DAVIS 3-12

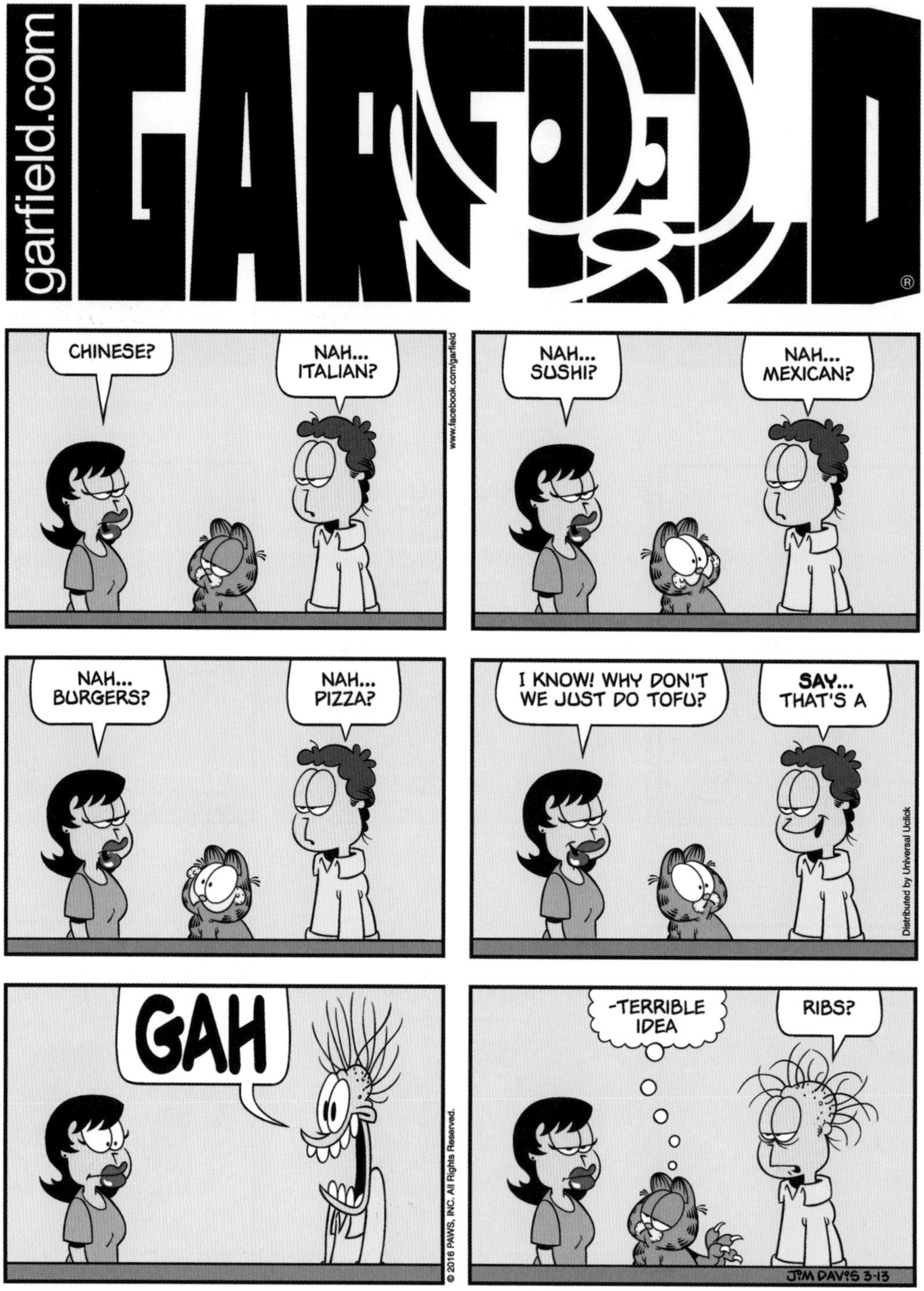
garfield.com
GARFIELD
CHINESE?
NAH... ITALIAN?
www.facebook.com/garfield
NAH... SUSHI?
NAH... MEXICAN?
NAH... BURGERS?
NAH... PIZZA?
I KNOW! WHY DON'T WE JUST DO TOFU?
SAY... THAT'S A
Distributed by Universal Uclick
GAH
© 2016 PAWS, INC. All Rights Reserved.
-TERRIBLE IDEA
RIBS?
JIM DAVIS 3-13

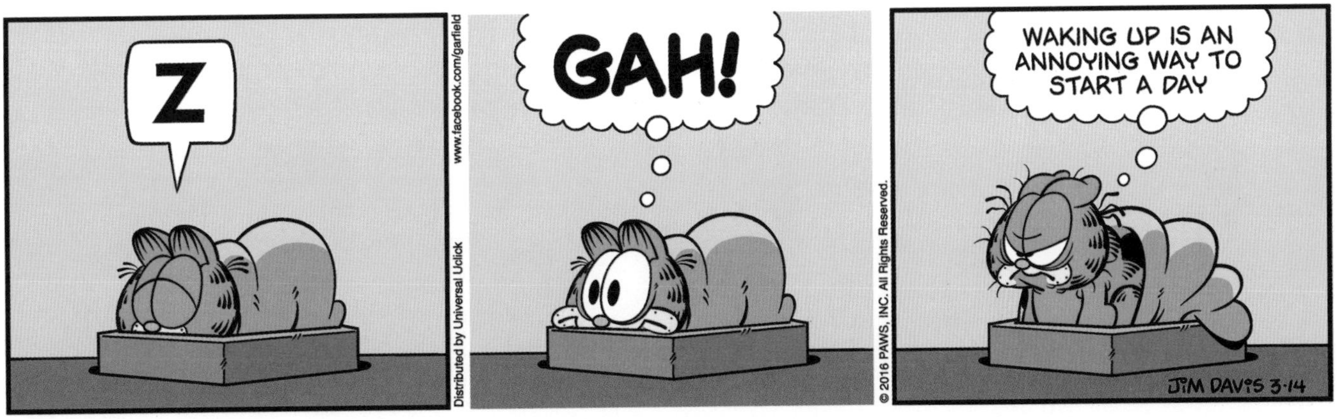
Z
GAH!
WAKING UP IS AN ANNOYING WAY TO START A DAY
JIM DAVIS 3-14
Distributed by Universal Uclick
www.facebook.com/garfield
© 2016 PAWS, INC. All Rights Reserved.

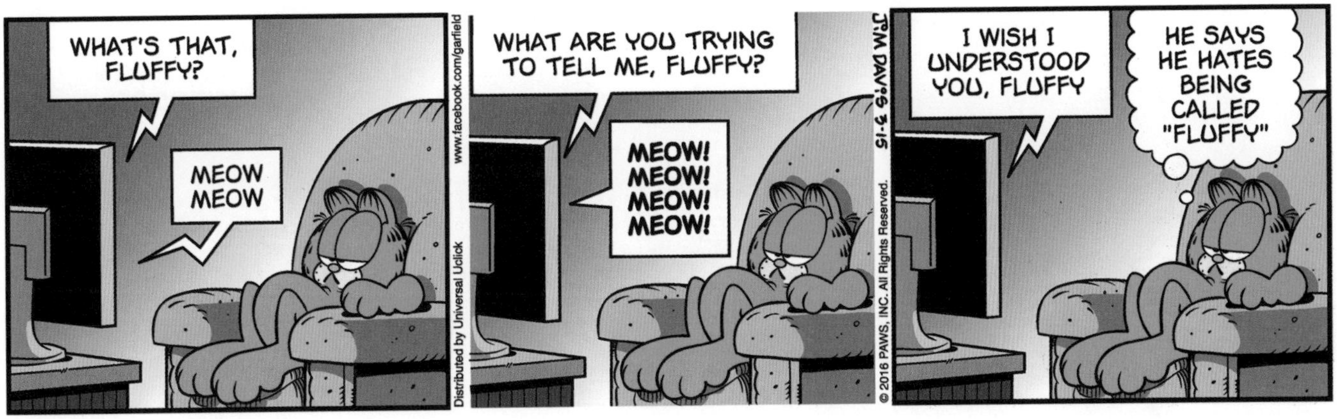
WHAT'S THAT, FLUFFY?
MEOW MEOW
WHAT ARE YOU TRYING TO TELL ME, FLUFFY?
MEOW! MEOW! MEOW! MEOW!
I WISH I UNDERSTOOD YOU, FLUFFY
HE SAYS HE HATES BEING CALLED "FLUFFY"
JIM DAVIS 3-15
Distributed by Universal Uclick
www.facebook.com/garfield
© 2016 PAWS, INC. All Rights Reserved.

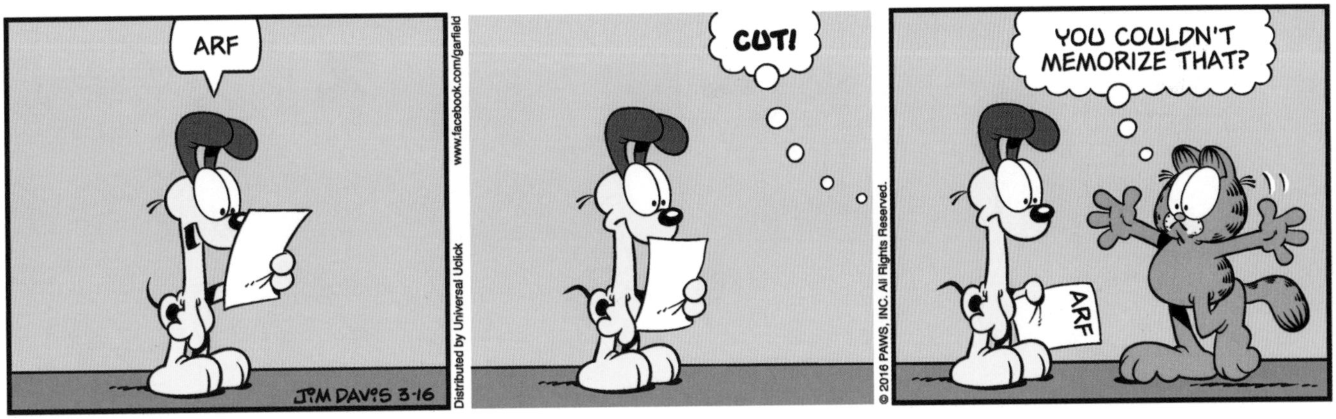
ARF
CUT!
YOU COULDN'T MEMORIZE THAT?
ARF
JIM DAVIS 3-16
Distributed by Universal Uclick
www.facebook.com/garfield
© 2016 PAWS, INC. All Rights Reserved.

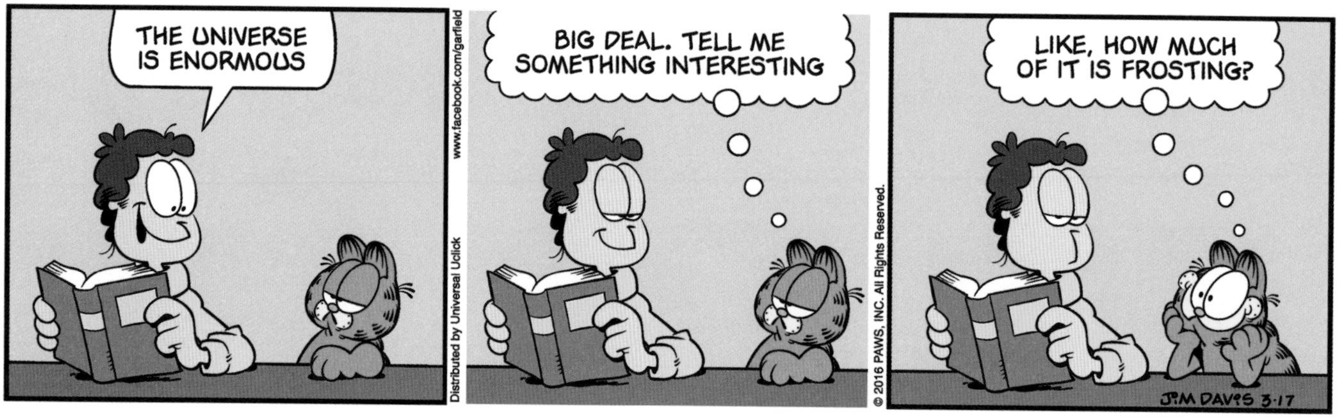
THE UNIVERSE IS ENORMOUS
www.facebook.com/garfield
Distributed by Universal Uclick
BIG DEAL. TELL ME SOMETHING INTERESTING
© 2016 PAWS, INC. All Rights Reserved.
LIKE, HOW MUCH OF IT IS FROSTING?
JIM DAVIS 3-17

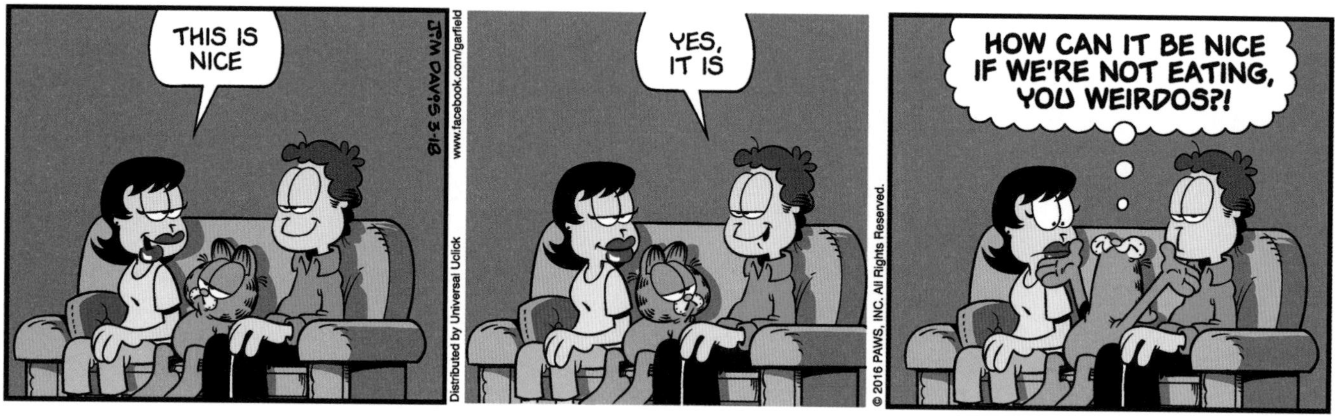
THIS IS NICE
JIM DAVIS 3-18
www.facebook.com/garfield
Distributed by Universal Uclick
YES, IT IS
© 2016 PAWS, INC. All Rights Reserved.
HOW CAN IT BE NICE IF WE'RE NOT EATING, YOU WEIRDOS?!

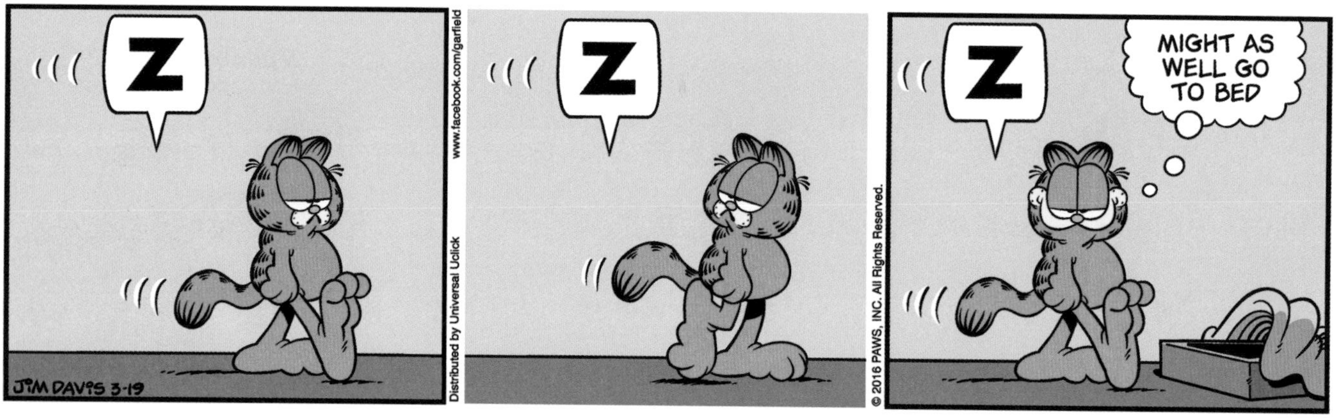
Z
JIM DAVIS 3-19
www.facebook.com/garfield
Distributed by Universal Uclick
Z
© 2016 PAWS, INC. All Rights Reserved.
Z
MIGHT AS WELL GO TO BED

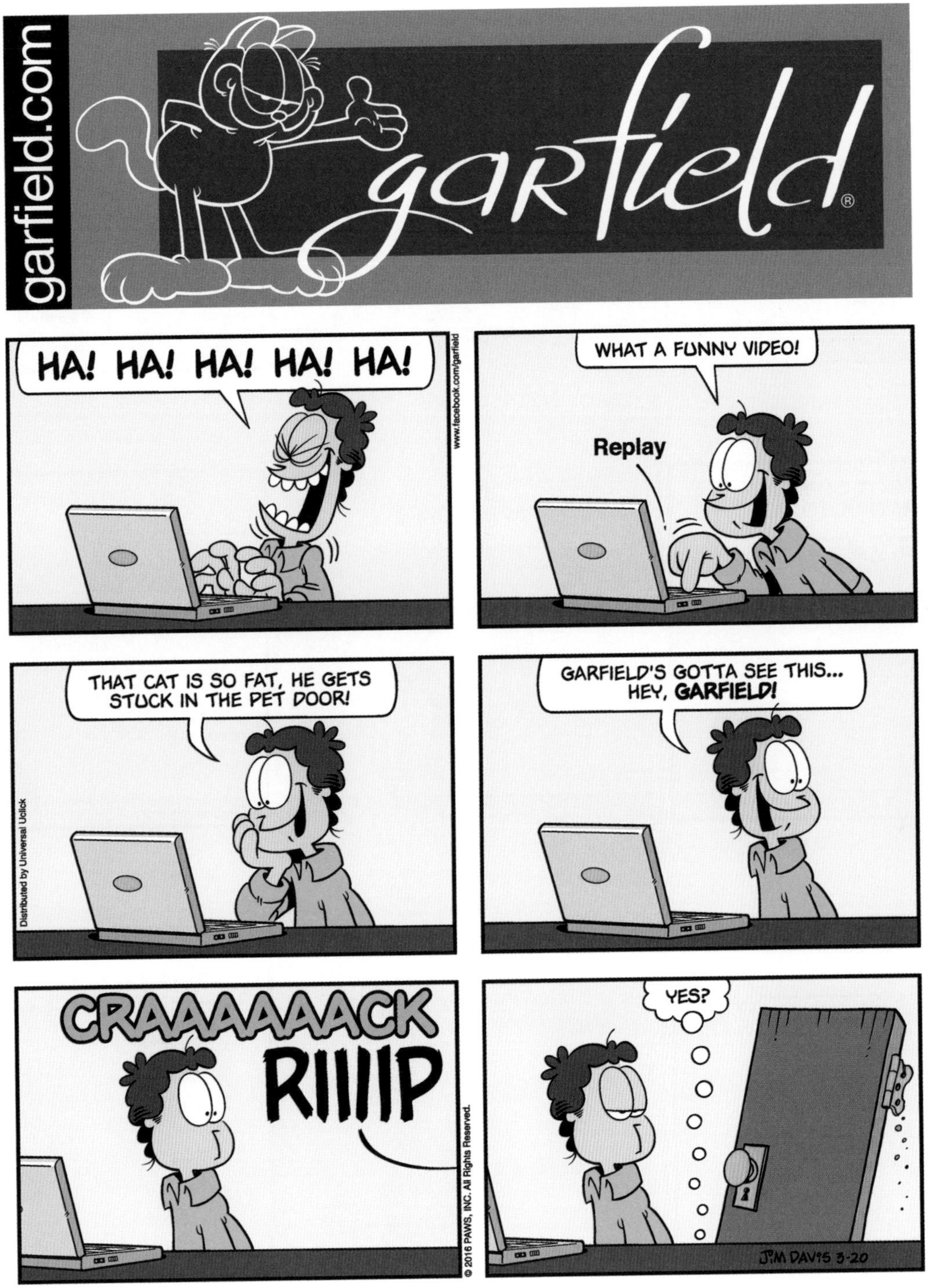
garfield.com
garfield
HA! HA! HA! HA! HA!
www.facebook.com/garfield
WHAT A FUNNY VIDEO!
Replay
THAT CAT IS SO FAT, HE GETS STUCK IN THE PET DOOR!
Distributed by Universal Uclick
GARFIELD'S GOTTA SEE THIS... HEY, GARFIELD!
CRAAAAAACK
RIIIP
© 2016 PAWS, INC. All Rights Reserved.
YES?
JIM DAVIS 3-20

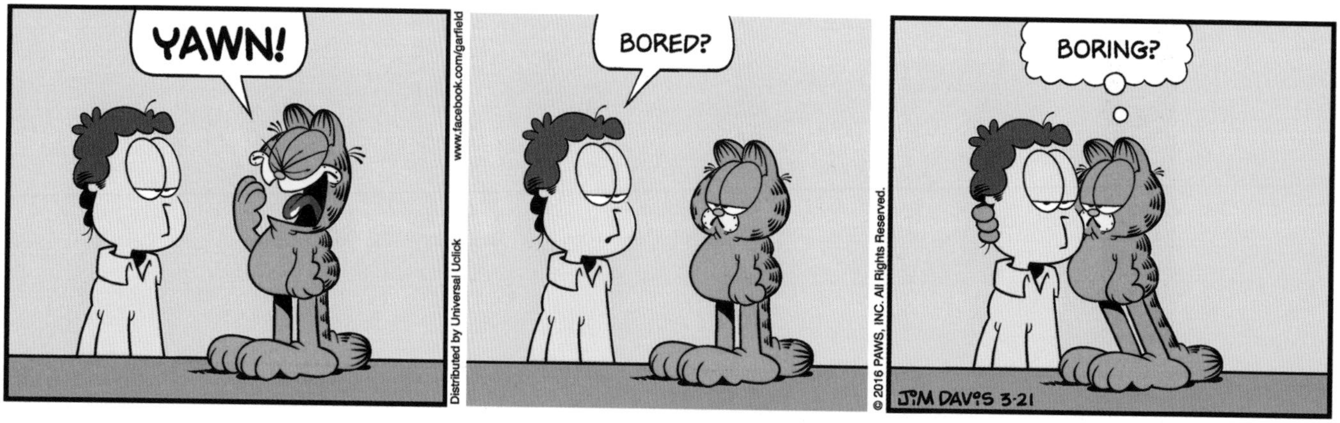
YAWN!
BORED?
BORING?
www.facebook.com/garfield
Distributed by Universal Uclick
© 2016 PAWS, INC. All Rights Reserved.
JIM DAVIS 3-21

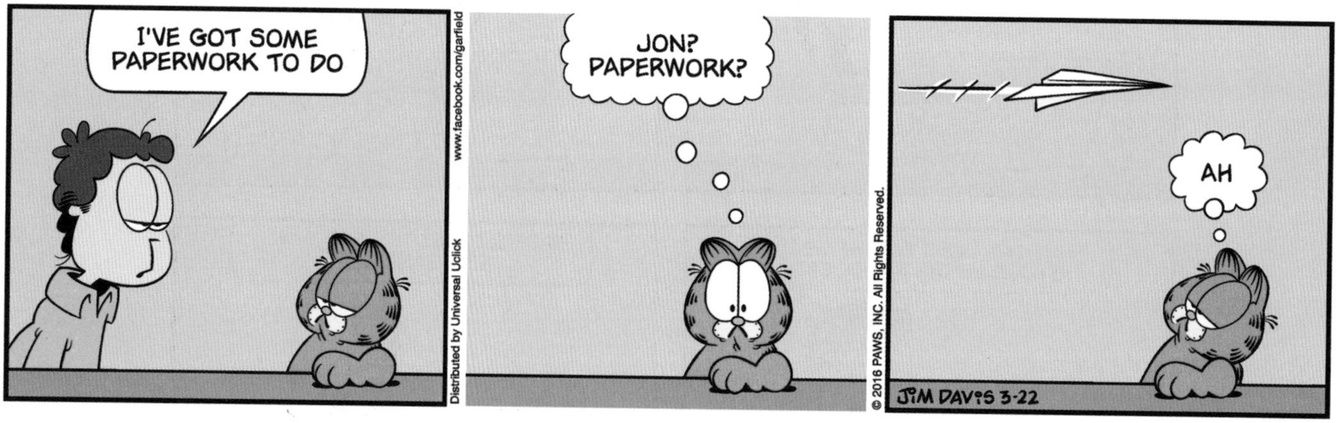
I'VE GOT SOME PAPERWORK TO DO
JON? PAPERWORK?
AH
www.facebook.com/garfield
Distributed by Universal Uclick
© 2016 PAWS, INC. All Rights Reserved.
JIM DAVIS 3-22

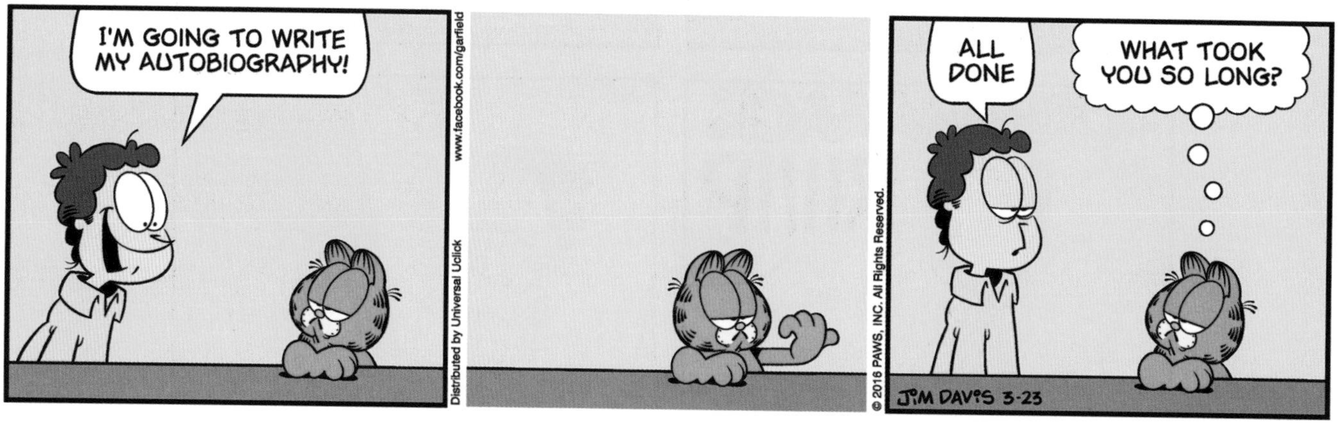
I'M GOING TO WRITE MY AUTOBIOGRAPHY!
ALL DONE
WHAT TOOK YOU SO LONG?
www.facebook.com/garfield
Distributed by Universal Uclick
© 2016 PAWS, INC. All Rights Reserved.
JIM DAVIS 3-23

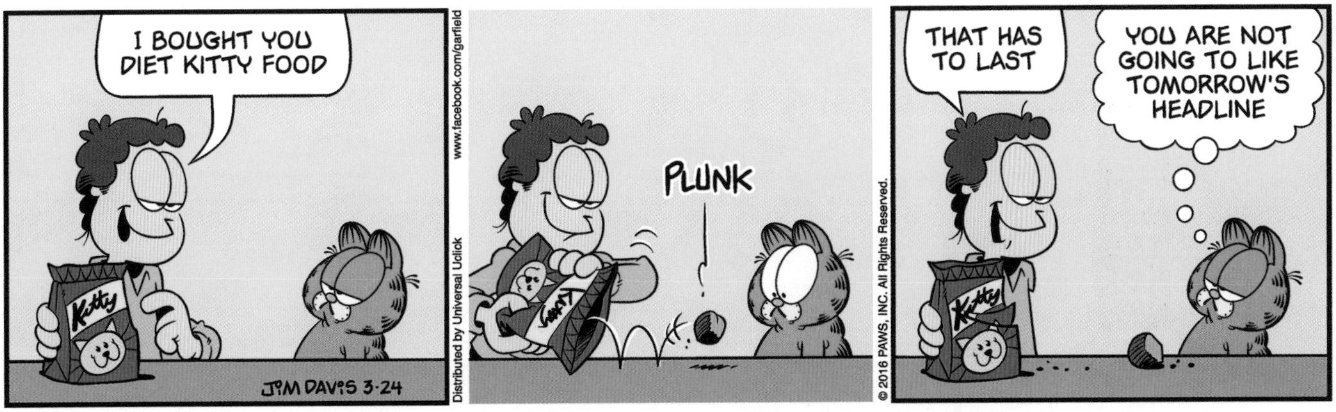
I BOUGHT YOU DIET KITTY FOOD
Kitty
JIM DAVIS 3-24
Distributed by Universal Uclick
www.facebook.com/garfield
PLUNK
© 2016 PAWS, INC. All Rights Reserved.
THAT HAS TO LAST
YOU ARE NOT GOING TO LIKE TOMORROW'S HEADLINE
Kitty

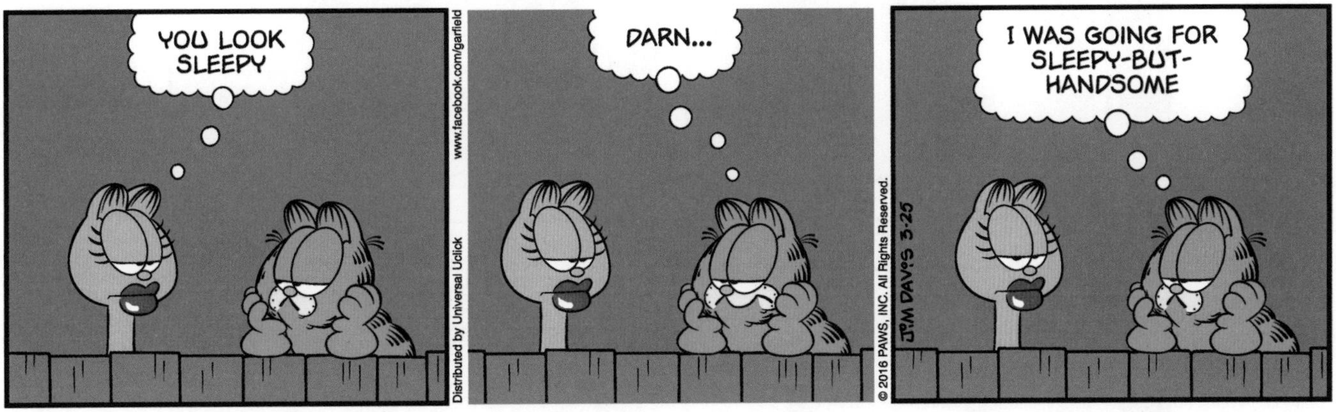
YOU LOOK SLEEPY
Distributed by Universal Uclick
www.facebook.com/garfield
DARN...
© 2016 PAWS, INC. All Rights Reserved.
JIM DAVIS 3-25
I WAS GOING FOR SLEEPY-BUT-HANDSOME

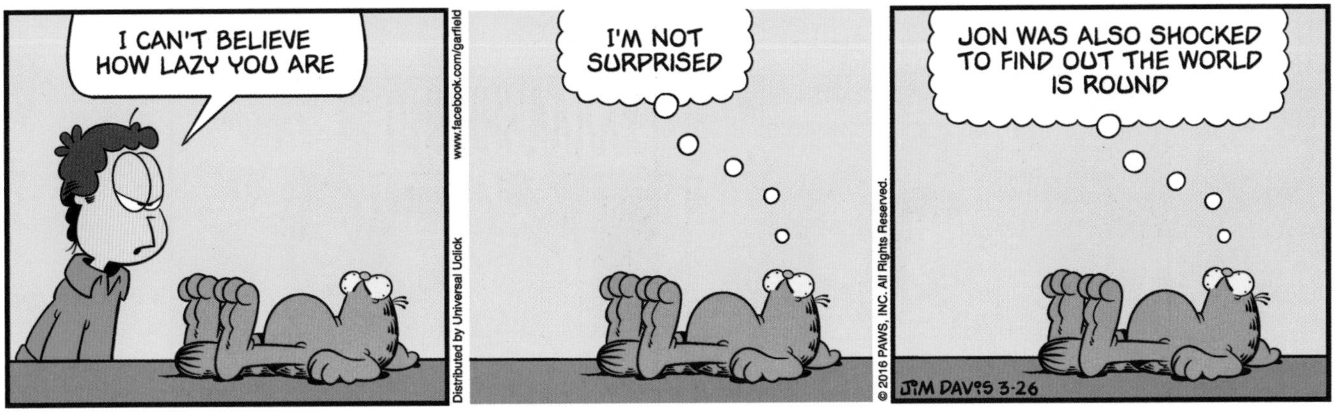
I CAN'T BELIEVE HOW LAZY YOU ARE
Distributed by Universal Uclick
www.facebook.com/garfield
I'M NOT SURPRISED
© 2016 PAWS, INC. All Rights Reserved.
JON WAS ALSO SHOCKED TO FIND OUT THE WORLD IS ROUND
JIM DAVIS 3-26

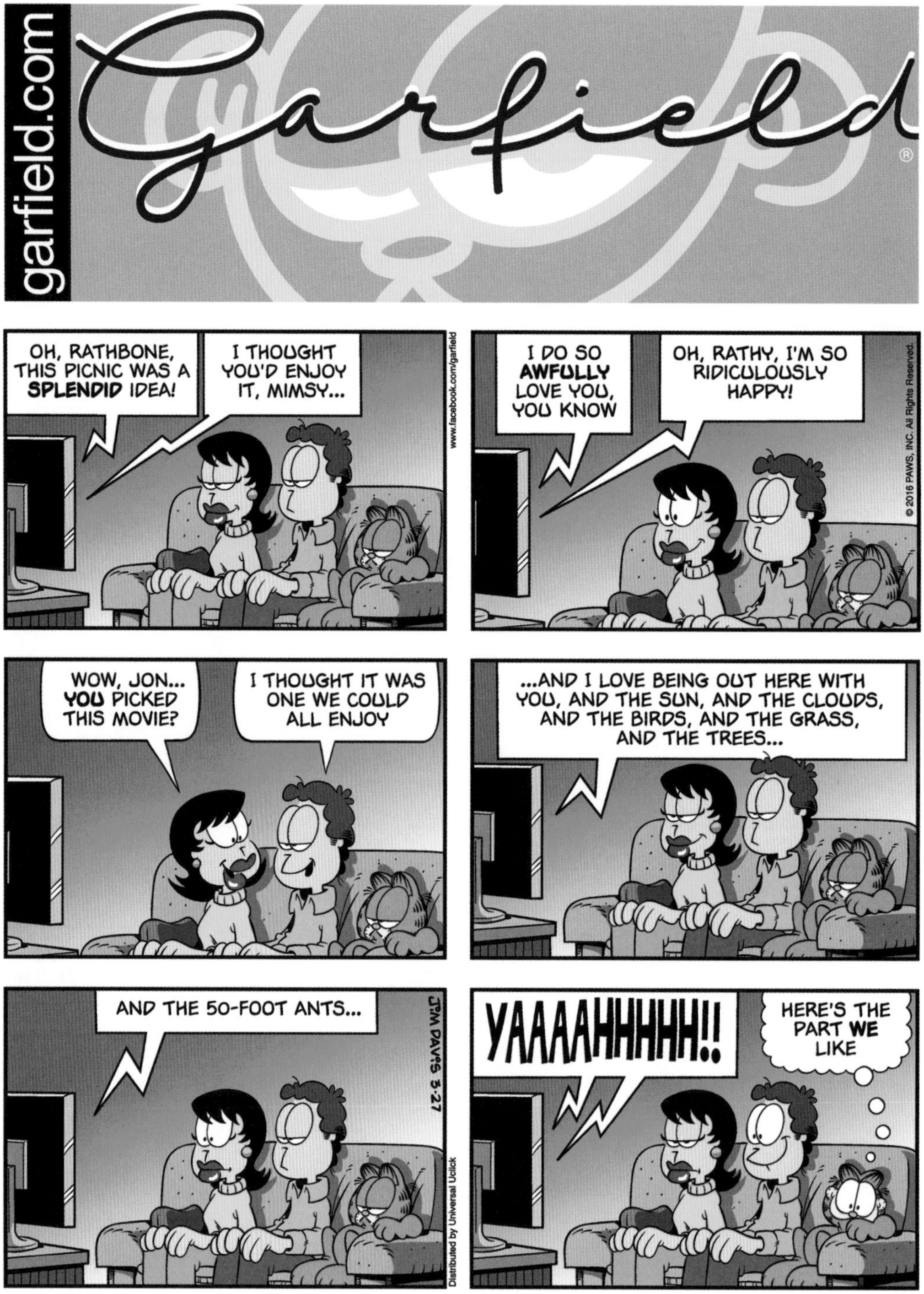
garfield.com
Garfield®
OH, RATHBONE, THIS PICNIC WAS A SPLENDID IDEA!
I THOUGHT YOU'D ENJOY IT, MIMSY...
www.facebook.com/garfield
I DO SO AWFULLY LOVE YOU, YOU KNOW
OH, RATHY, I'M SO RIDICULOUSLY HAPPY!
© 2016 PAWS, INC. All Rights Reserved.
WOW, JON... YOU PICKED THIS MOVIE?
I THOUGHT IT WAS ONE WE COULD ALL ENJOY
...AND I LOVE BEING OUT HERE WITH YOU, AND THE SUN, AND THE CLOUDS, AND THE BIRDS, AND THE GRASS, AND THE TREES...
AND THE 50-FOOT ANTS...
JIM DAVIS 3-27
Distributed by Universal Uclick
YAAAAHHHHH!!
HERE'S THE PART WE LIKE

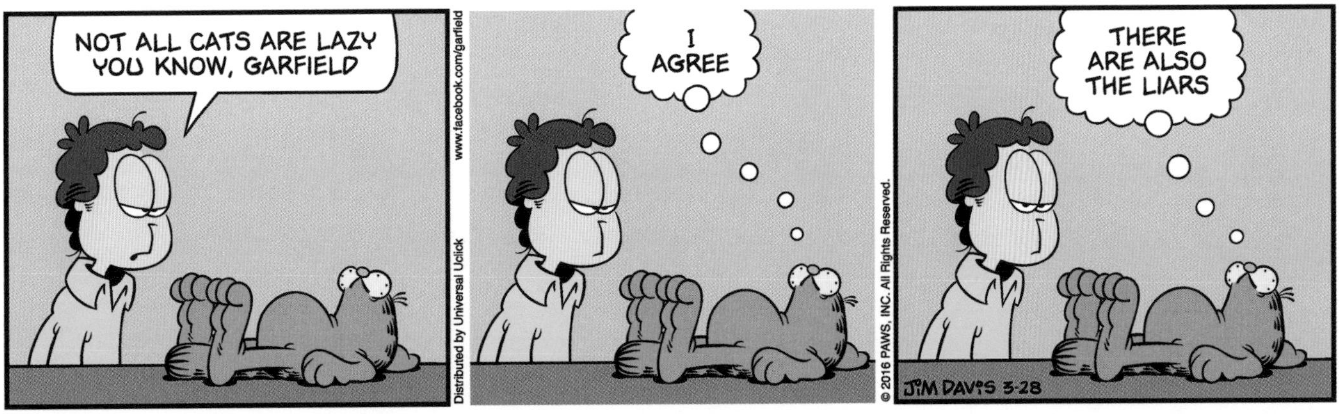
NOT ALL CATS ARE LAZY YOU KNOW, GARFIELD
I AGREE
THERE ARE ALSO THE LIARS
Distributed by Universal Uclick www.facebook.com/garfield
© 2016 PAWS, INC. All Rights Reserved.
JIM DAVIS 3-28

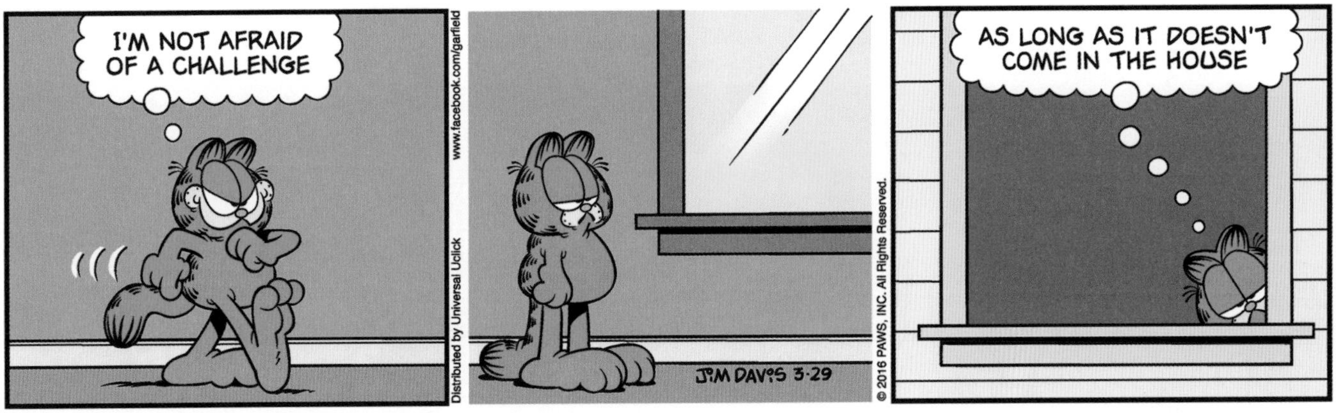
I'M NOT AFRAID OF A CHALLENGE
AS LONG AS IT DOESN'T COME IN THE HOUSE
Distributed by Universal Uclick www.facebook.com/garfield
© 2016 PAWS, INC. All Rights Reserved.
JIM DAVIS 3-29

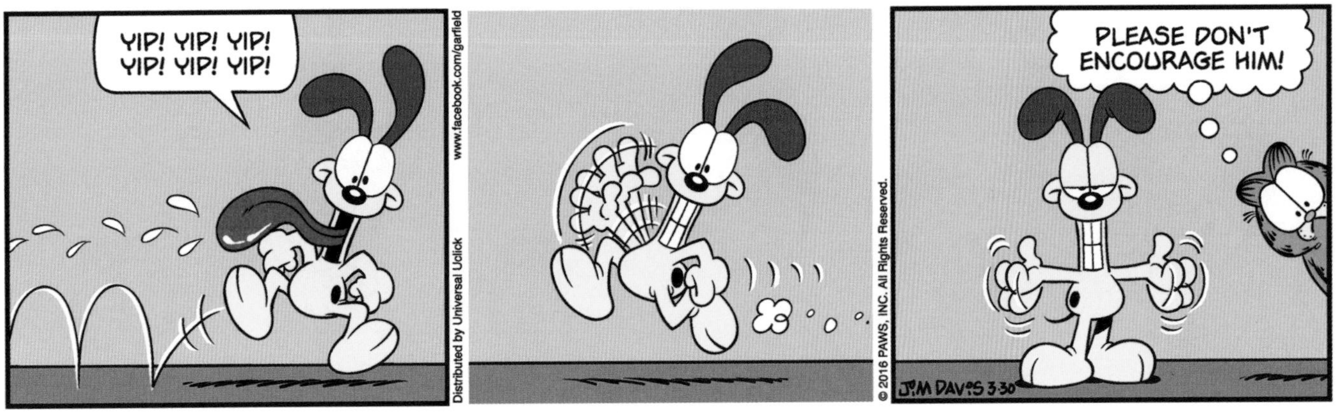
YIP! YIP! YIP! YIP! YIP! YIP!
PLEASE DON'T ENCOURAGE HIM!
Distributed by Universal Uclick www.facebook.com/garfield
© 2016 PAWS, INC. All Rights Reserved.
JIM DAVIS 3-30

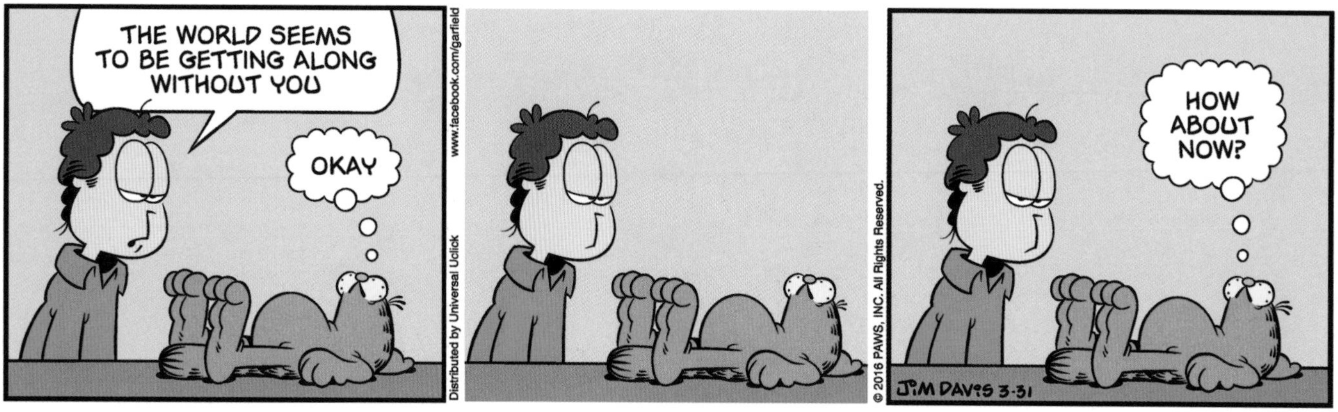
THE WORLD SEEMS TO BE GETTING ALONG WITHOUT YOU
OKAY
HOW ABOUT NOW?
Distributed by Universal Uclick www.facebook.com/garfield
© 2016 PAWS, INC. All Rights Reserved.
JIM DAVIS 3-31

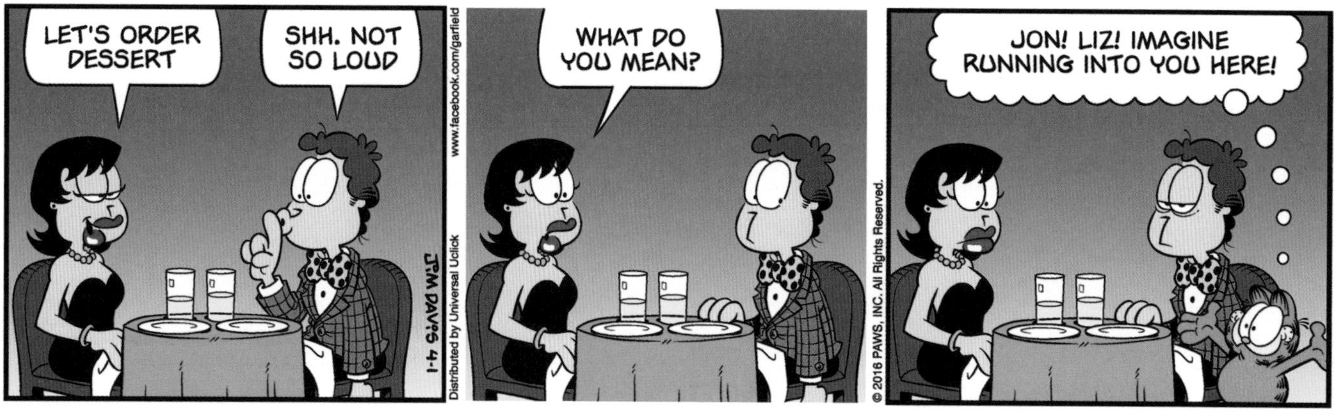
LET'S ORDER DESSERT
SHH. NOT SO LOUD
WHAT DO YOU MEAN?
JON! LIZ! IMAGINE RUNNING INTO YOU HERE!
JIM DAVIS 4-1
Distributed by Universal Uclick www.facebook.com/garfield
© 2016 PAWS, INC. All Rights Reserved.

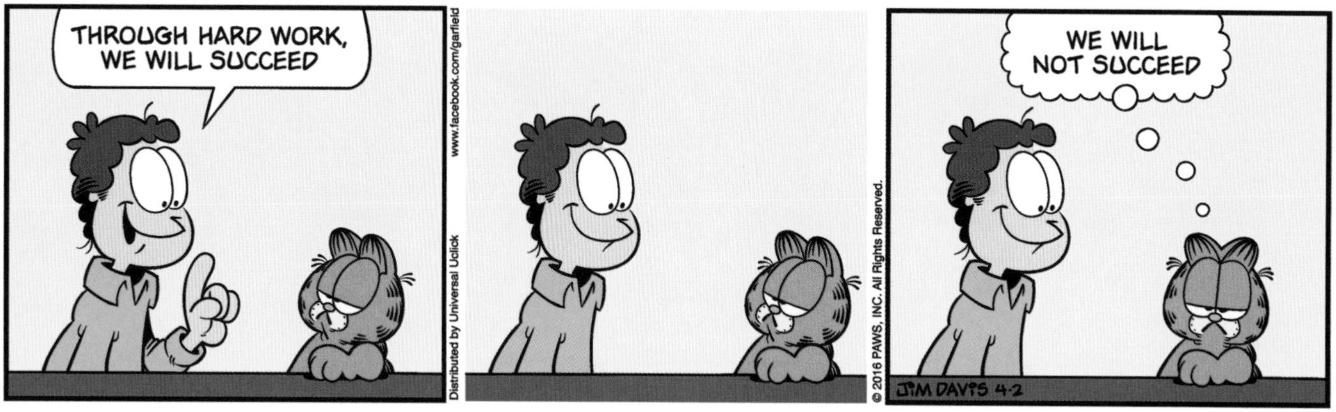
THROUGH HARD WORK, WE WILL SUCCEED
WE WILL NOT SUCCEED
Distributed by Universal Uclick www.facebook.com/garfield
© 2016 PAWS, INC. All Rights Reserved.
JIM DAVIS 4-2

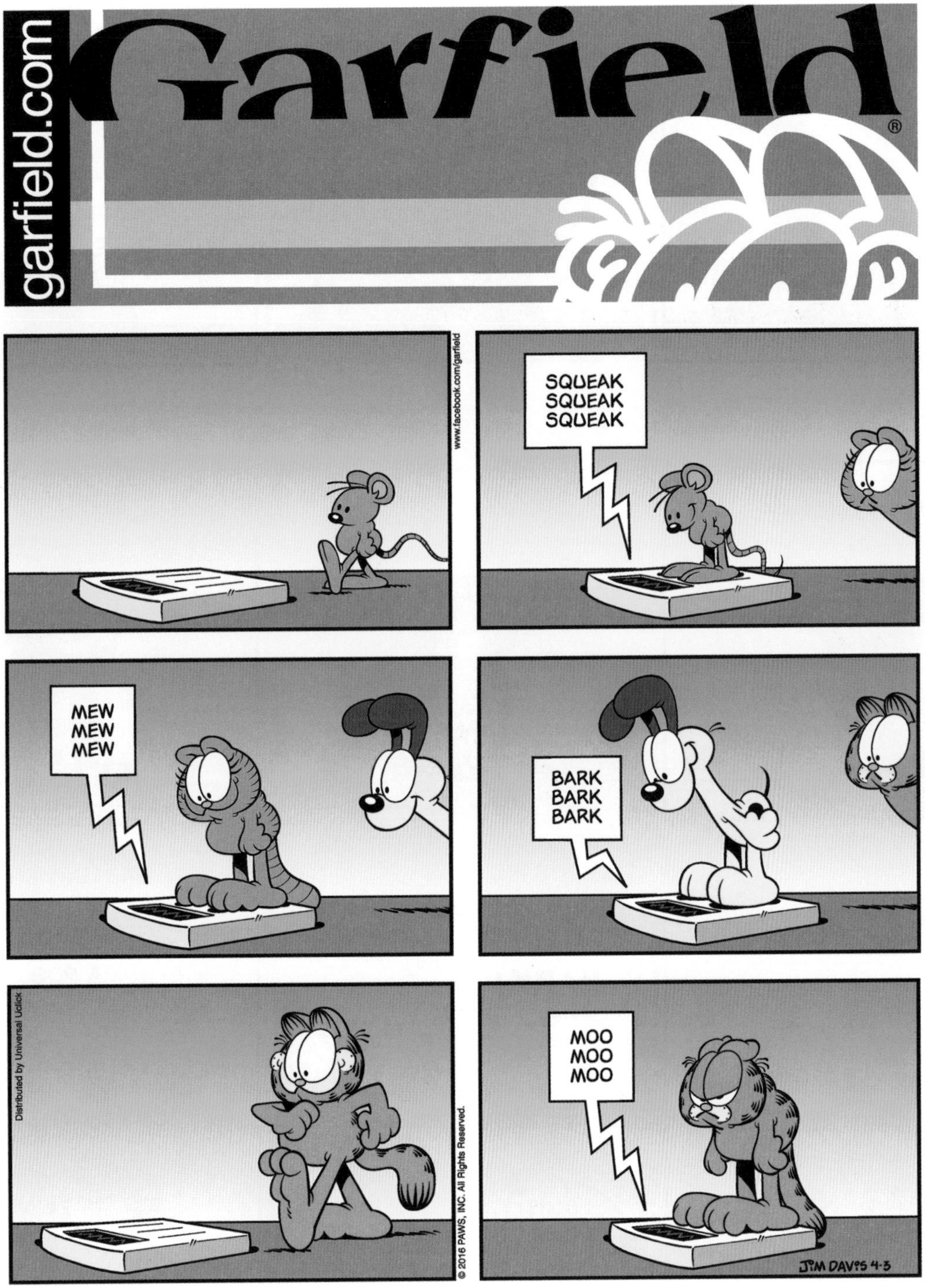
garfield.com
Garfield
www.facebook.com/garfield
SQUEAK SQUEAK SQUEAK
MEW MEW MEW
BARK BARK BARK
Distributed by Universal Uclick
© 2016 PAWS, INC. All Rights Reserved.
MOO MOO MOO
JIM DAVIS 4-3

YOU'RE MISSING OUT ON AN AWFUL LOT

THAT'S KIND OF THE IDEA

I DEMAND MY RIGHTS!

WITH CHOCOLATE SYRUP!

BARK!

THAT IS A DOG

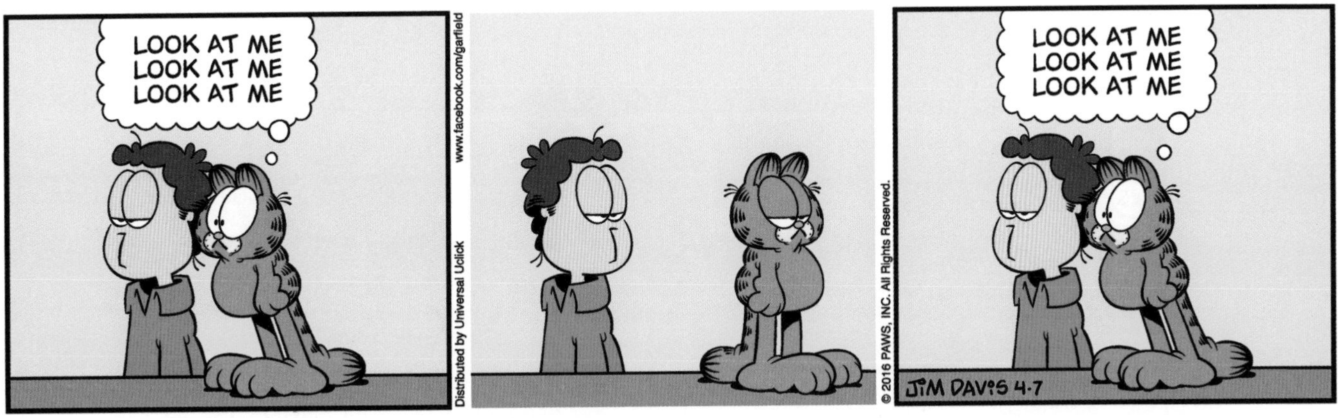
LOOK AT ME
LOOK AT ME
LOOK AT ME
Distributed by Universal Uclick www.facebook.com/garfield
© 2016 PAWS, INC. All Rights Reserved.
LOOK AT ME
LOOK AT ME
LOOK AT ME
JIM DAVIS 4-7

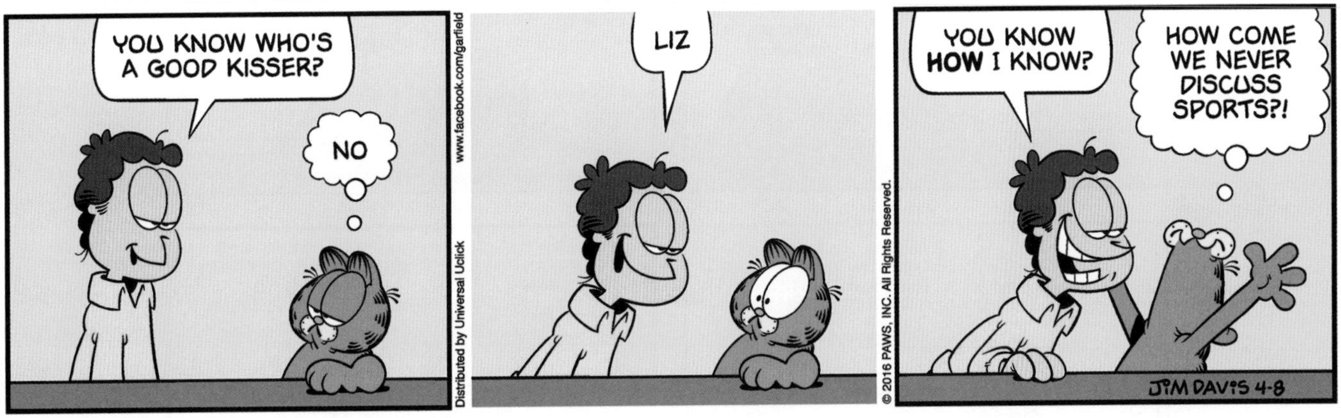
YOU KNOW WHO'S A GOOD KISSER?
NO
Distributed by Universal Uclick www.facebook.com/garfield
LIZ
© 2016 PAWS, INC. All Rights Reserved.
YOU KNOW **HOW** I KNOW?
HOW COME WE NEVER DISCUSS SPORTS?!
JIM DAVIS 4-8

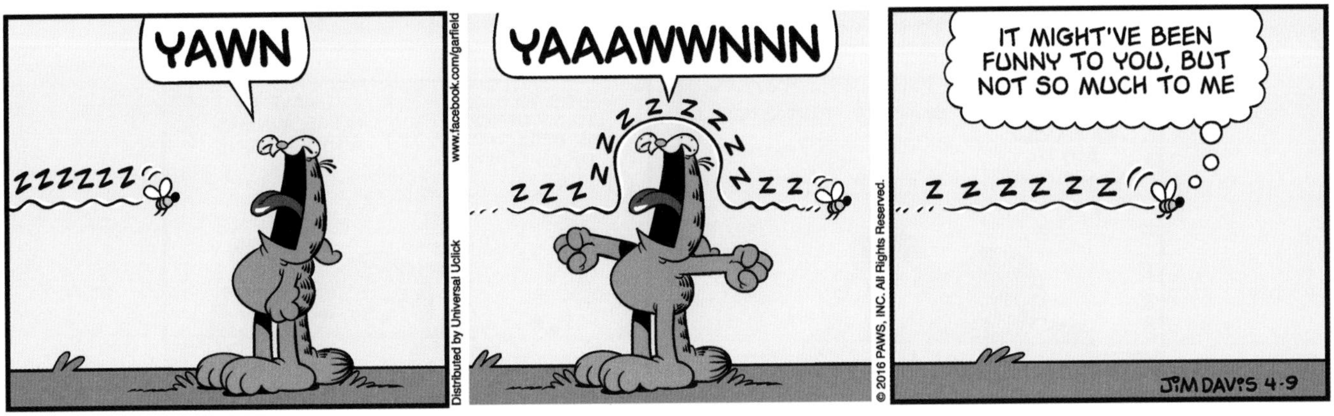
YAWN
ZZZZZZ
Distributed by Universal Uclick www.facebook.com/garfield
YAAAWWNNN
ZZZNZZZZZZNZZZ
© 2016 PAWS, INC. All Rights Reserved.
IT MIGHT'VE BEEN FUNNY TO YOU, BUT NOT SO MUCH TO ME
Z Z Z Z Z Z
JIM DAVIS 4-9

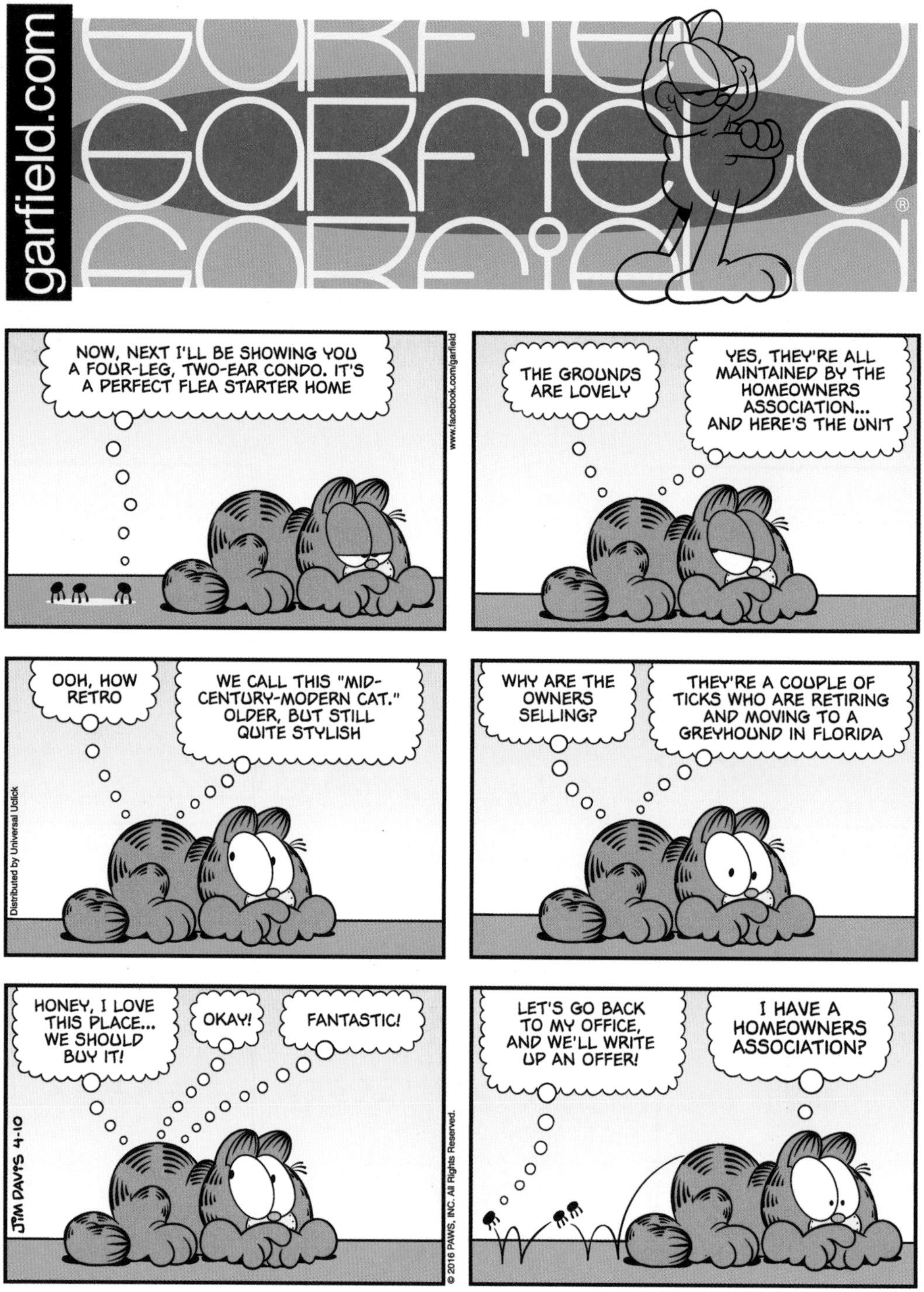
garfield.com
GARFIELD
NOW, NEXT I'LL BE SHOWING YOU A FOUR-LEG, TWO-EAR CONDO. IT'S A PERFECT FLEA STARTER HOME
www.facebook.com/garfield
THE GROUNDS ARE LOVELY
YES, THEY'RE ALL MAINTAINED BY THE HOMEOWNERS ASSOCIATION... AND HERE'S THE UNIT
OOH, HOW RETRO
WE CALL THIS "MID-CENTURY-MODERN CAT." OLDER, BUT STILL QUITE STYLISH
Distributed by Universal Uclick
WHY ARE THE OWNERS SELLING?
THEY'RE A COUPLE OF TICKS WHO ARE RETIRING AND MOVING TO A GREYHOUND IN FLORIDA
HONEY, I LOVE THIS PLACE... WE SHOULD BUY IT!
OKAY!
FANTASTIC!
JIM DAVIS 4-10
© 2016 PAWS, INC. All Rights Reserved.
LET'S GO BACK TO MY OFFICE, AND WE'LL WRITE UP AN OFFER!
I HAVE A HOMEOWNERS ASSOCIATION?

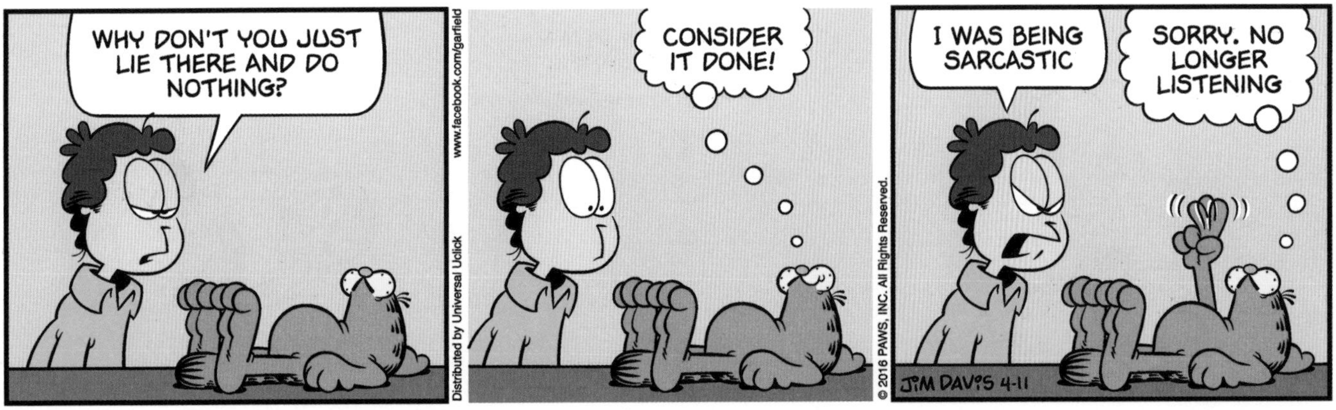
WHY DON'T YOU JUST LIE THERE AND DO NOTHING?
CONSIDER IT DONE!
I WAS BEING SARCASTIC
SORRY. NO LONGER LISTENING
JIM DAVIS 4-11
Distributed by Universal Uclick www.facebook.com/garfield
© 2016 PAWS, INC. All Rights Reserved.

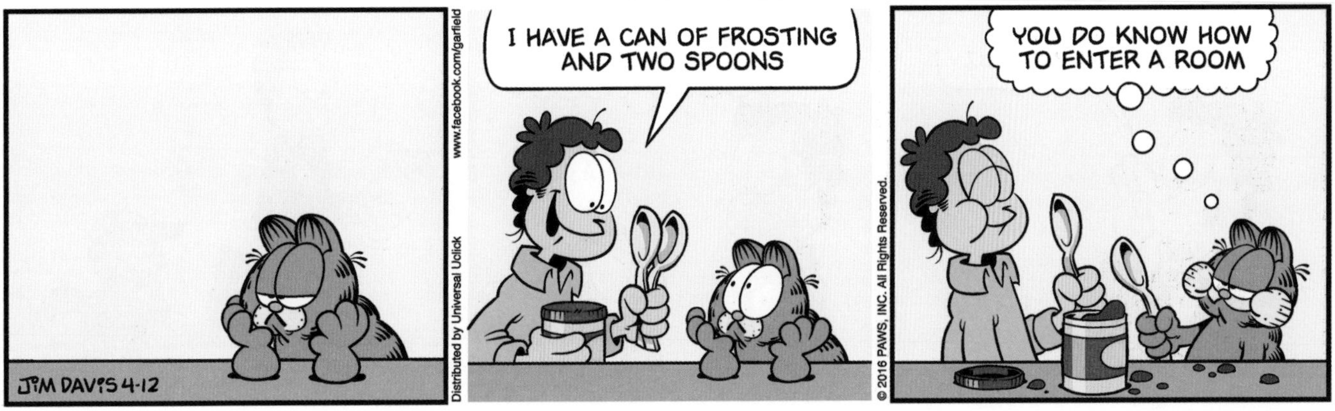
JIM DAVIS 4-12
I HAVE A CAN OF FROSTING AND TWO SPOONS
YOU DO KNOW HOW TO ENTER A ROOM
Distributed by Universal Uclick www.facebook.com/garfield
© 2016 PAWS, INC. All Rights Reserved.

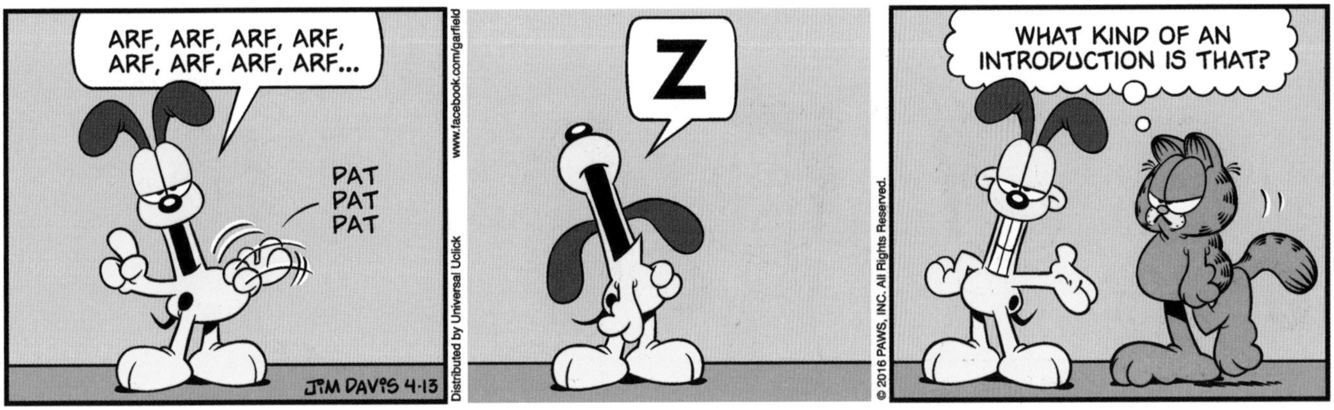
ARF, ARF, ARF, ARF, ARF, ARF, ARF, ARF...
PAT PAT PAT
JIM DAVIS 4-13
Z
WHAT KIND OF AN INTRODUCTION IS THAT?
Distributed by Universal Uclick www.facebook.com/garfield
© 2016 PAWS, INC. All Rights Reserved.

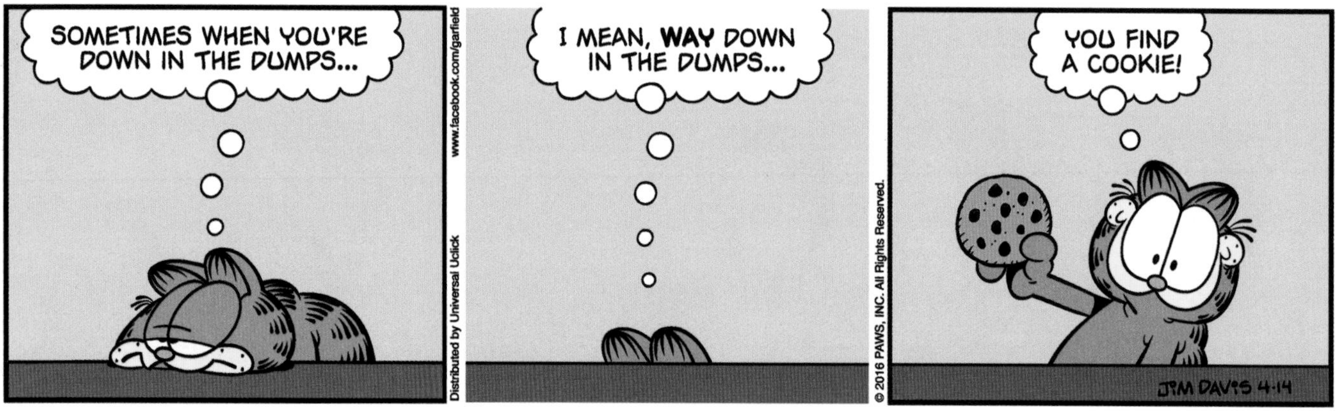
SOMETIMES WHEN YOU'RE DOWN IN THE DUMPS...
I MEAN, WAY DOWN IN THE DUMPS...
YOU FIND A COOKIE!
JIM DAVIS 4-14
Distributed by Universal Uclick www.facebook.com/garfield
© 2016 PAWS, INC. All Rights Reserved.

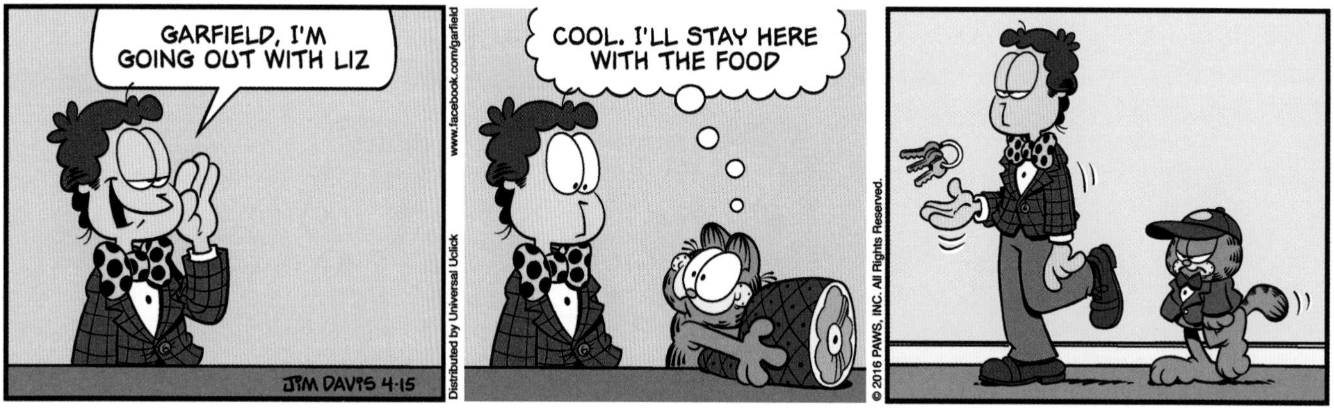
GARFIELD, I'M GOING OUT WITH LIZ
JIM DAVIS 4-15
COOL. I'LL STAY HERE WITH THE FOOD
Distributed by Universal Uclick www.facebook.com/garfield
© 2016 PAWS, INC. All Rights Reserved.

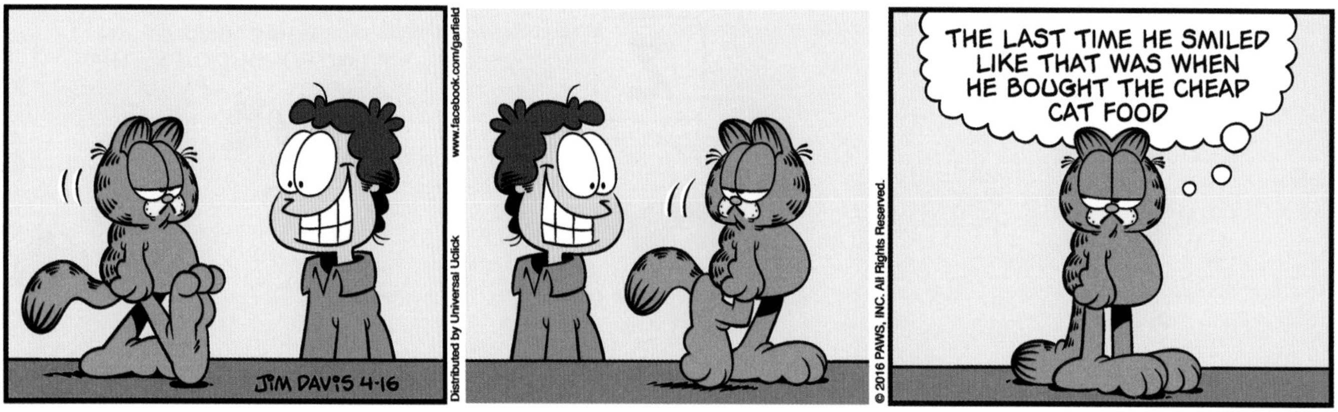
JIM DAVIS 4-16
THE LAST TIME HE SMILED LIKE THAT WAS WHEN HE BOUGHT THE CHEAP CAT FOOD
Distributed by Universal Uclick www.facebook.com/garfield
© 2016 PAWS, INC. All Rights Reserved.

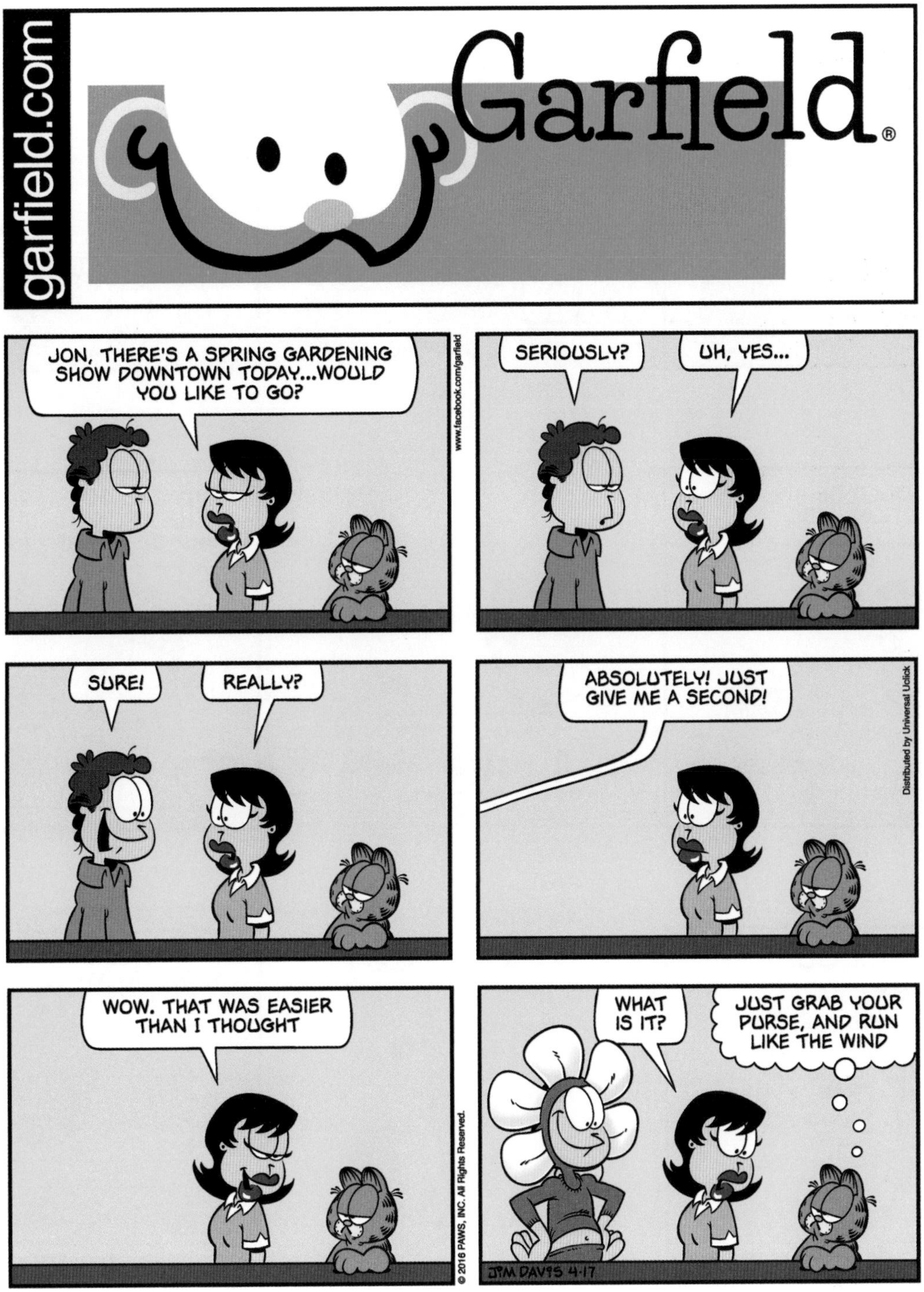
garfield.com
Garfield®
www.facebook.com/garfield
JON, THERE'S A SPRING GARDENING SHOW DOWNTOWN TODAY...WOULD YOU LIKE TO GO?
SERIOUSLY?
UH, YES...
SURE!
REALLY?
ABSOLUTELY! JUST GIVE ME A SECOND!
Distributed by Universal Uclick
WOW. THAT WAS EASIER THAN I THOUGHT
© 2016 PAWS, INC. All Rights Reserved.
WHAT IS IT?
JUST GRAB YOUR PURSE, AND RUN LIKE THE WIND
JIM DAVIS 4-17

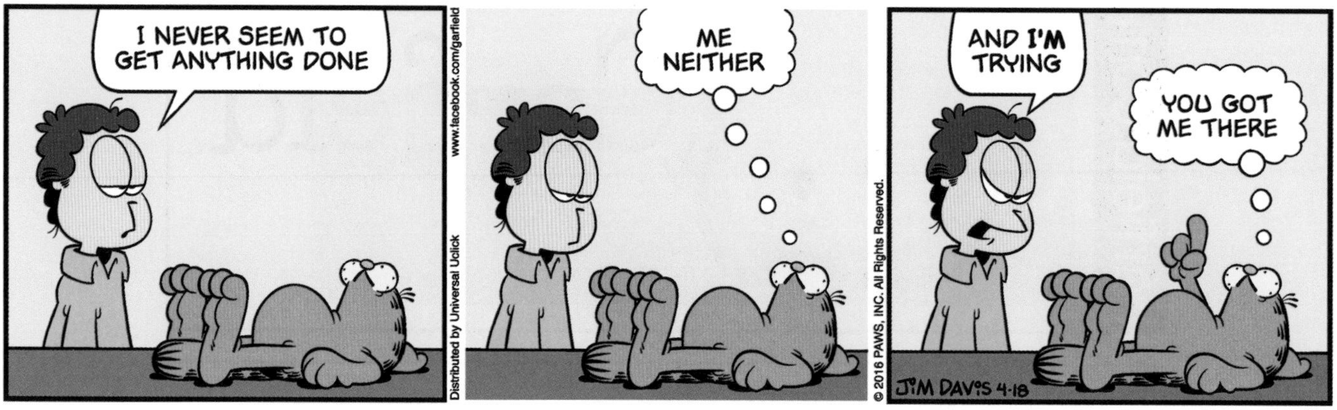
I NEVER SEEM TO GET ANYTHING DONE
ME NEITHER
AND I'M TRYING
YOU GOT ME THERE
JIM DAVIS 4-18
Distributed by Universal Uclick www.facebook.com/garfield
© 2016 PAWS, INC. All Rights Reserved.

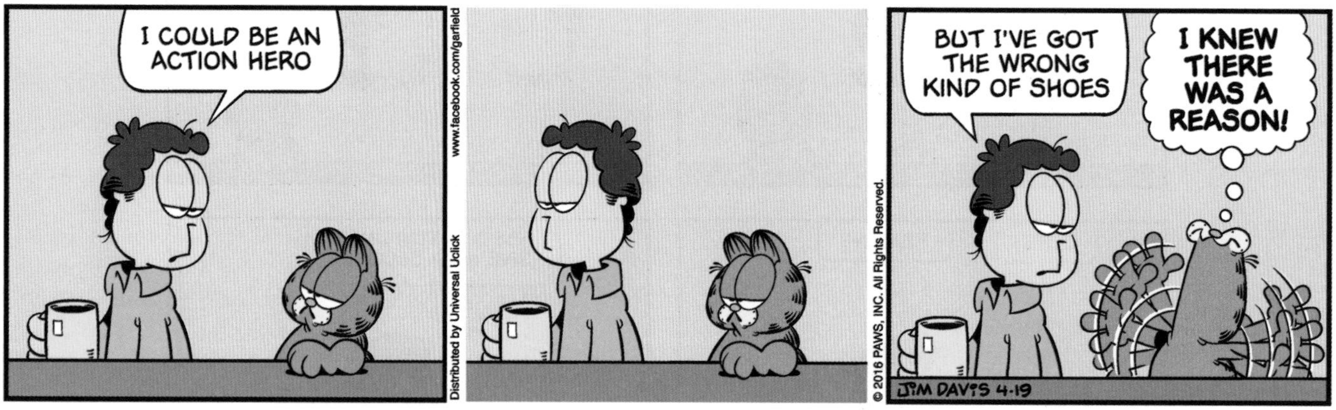
I COULD BE AN ACTION HERO
BUT I'VE GOT THE WRONG KIND OF SHOES
I KNEW THERE WAS A REASON!
JIM DAVIS 4-19
Distributed by Universal Uclick www.facebook.com/garfield
© 2016 PAWS, INC. All Rights Reserved.

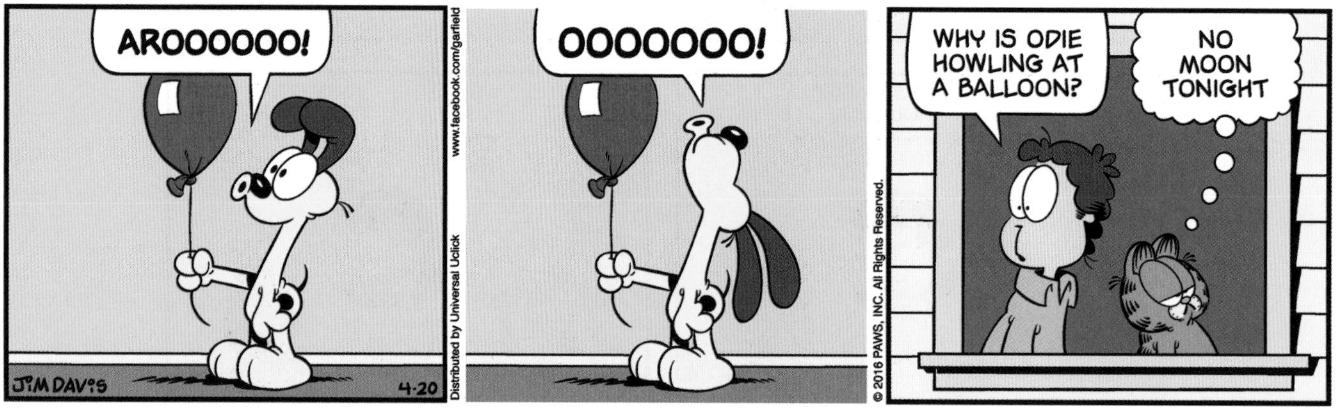
AROOOOOO!
OOOOOOO!
WHY IS ODIE HOWLING AT A BALLOON?
NO MOON TONIGHT
JIM DAVIS 4-20
Distributed by Universal Uclick www.facebook.com/garfield
© 2016 PAWS, INC. All Rights Reserved.

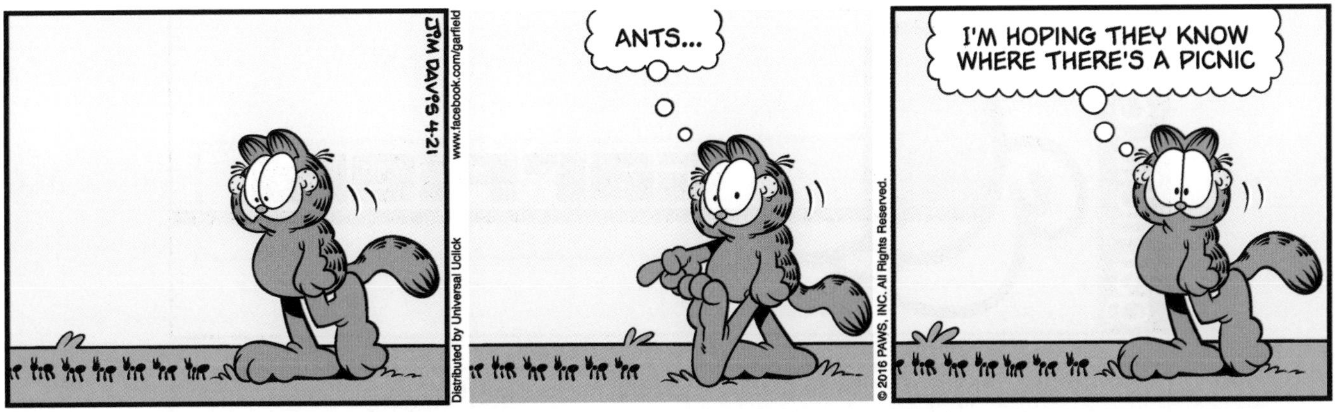
JIM DAVIS 4-21
www.facebook.com/garfield
Distributed by Universal Uclick
ANTS...
© 2016 PAWS, INC. All Rights Reserved.
I'M HOPING THEY KNOW WHERE THERE'S A PICNIC

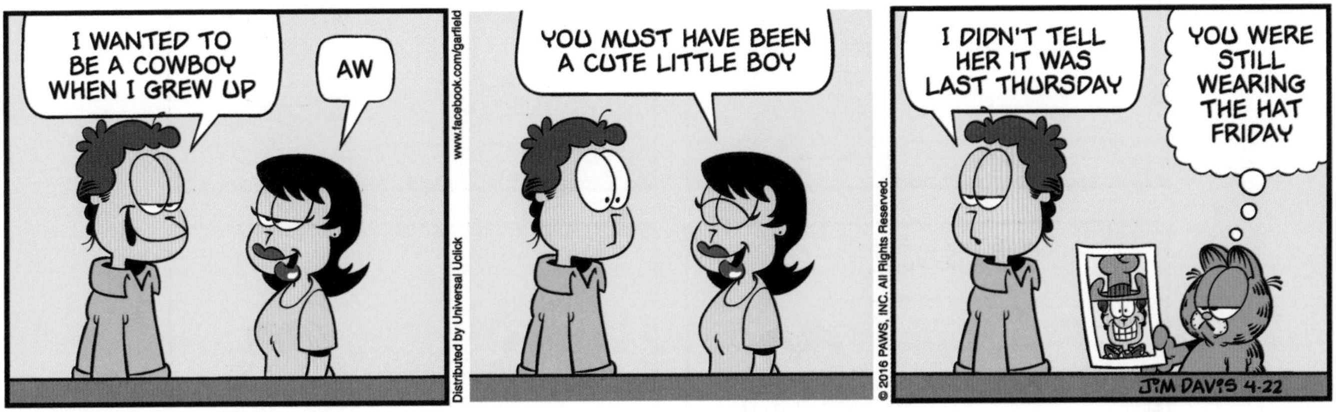
I WANTED TO BE A COWBOY WHEN I GREW UP
AW
www.facebook.com/garfield
Distributed by Universal Uclick
YOU MUST HAVE BEEN A CUTE LITTLE BOY
© 2016 PAWS, INC. All Rights Reserved.
I DIDN'T TELL HER IT WAS LAST THURSDAY
YOU WERE STILL WEARING THE HAT FRIDAY
JIM DAVIS 4-22

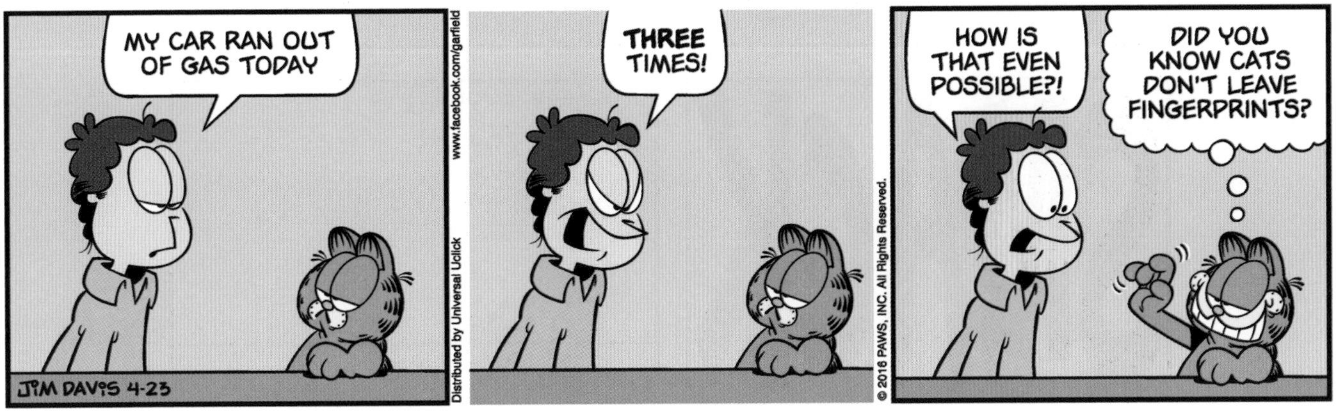
MY CAR RAN OUT OF GAS TODAY
JIM DAVIS 4-23
www.facebook.com/garfield
Distributed by Universal Uclick
THREE TIMES!
© 2016 PAWS, INC. All Rights Reserved.
HOW IS THAT EVEN POSSIBLE?!
DID YOU KNOW CATS DON'T LEAVE FINGERPRINTS?

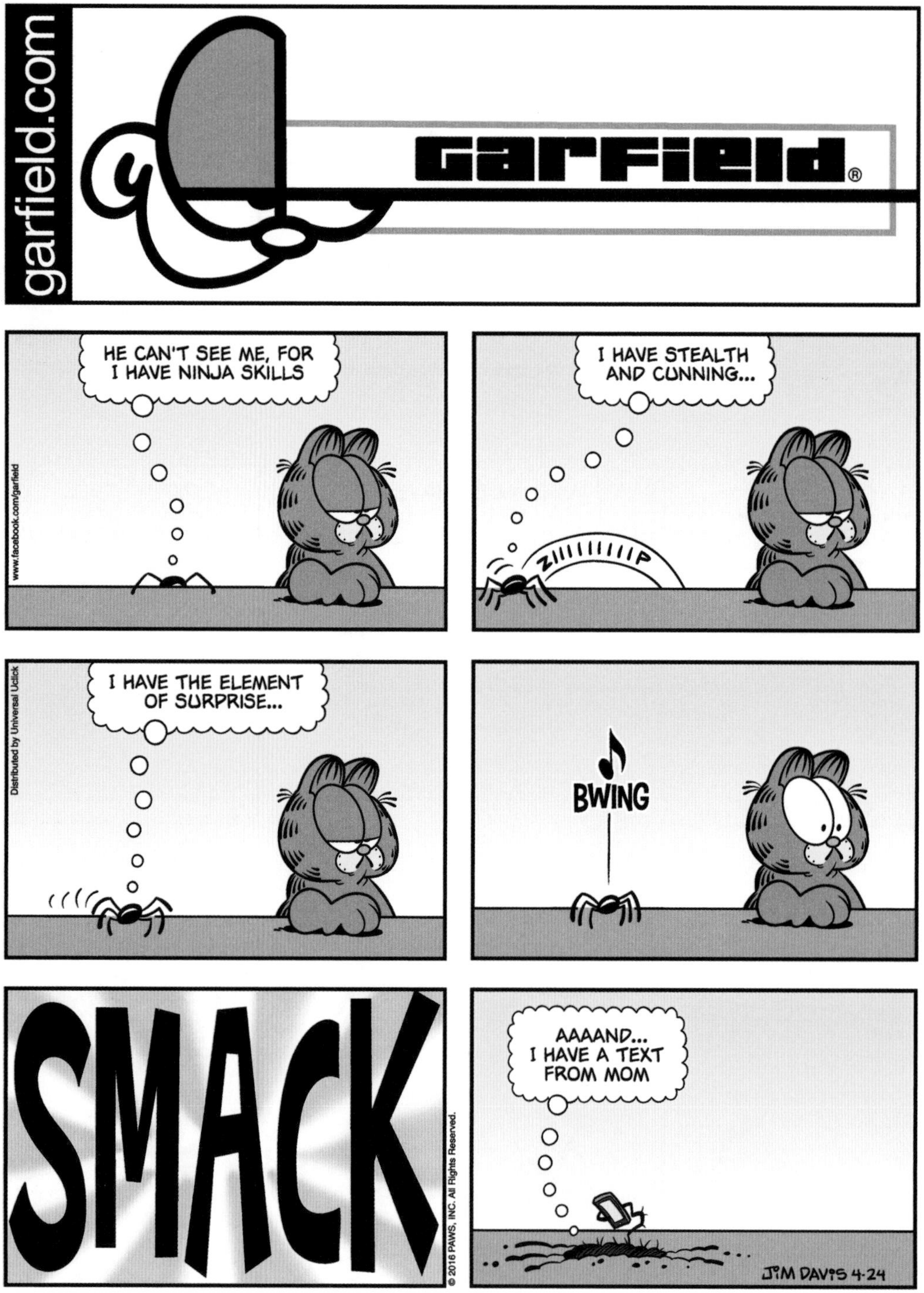
garfield.com
GARFIELD®
www.facebook.com/garfield
HE CAN'T SEE ME, FOR I HAVE NINJA SKILLS
I HAVE STEALTH AND CUNNING...
ZIIIIIIIIP
Distributed by Universal Uclick
I HAVE THE ELEMENT OF SURPRISE...
BWING
SMACK
© 2016 PAWS, INC. All Rights Reserved.
AAAAND... I HAVE A TEXT FROM MOM
JIM DAVIS 4-24

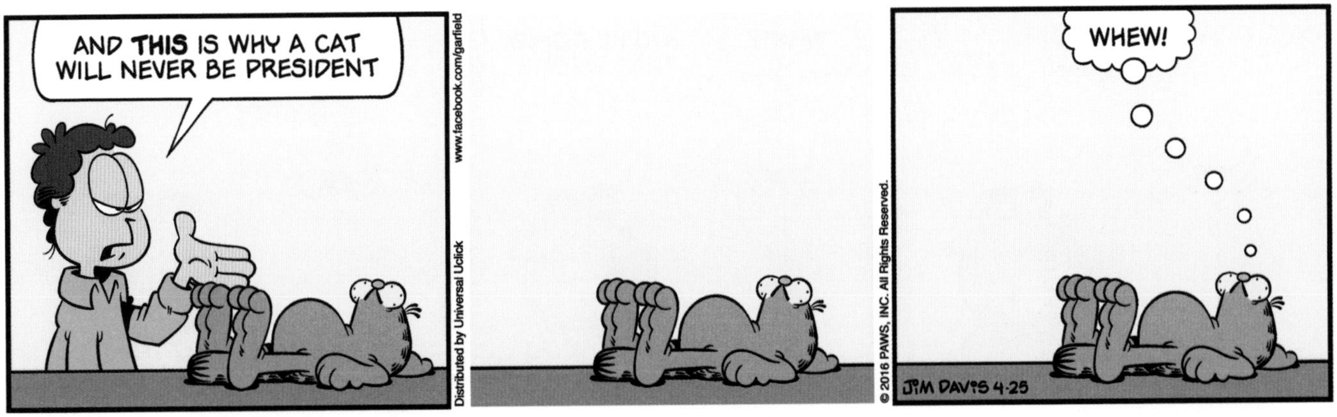
AND THIS IS WHY A CAT WILL NEVER BE PRESIDENT
Distributed by Universal Uclick www.facebook.com/garfield
WHEW!
© 2016 PAWS, INC. All Rights Reserved.
JIM DAVIS 4-25

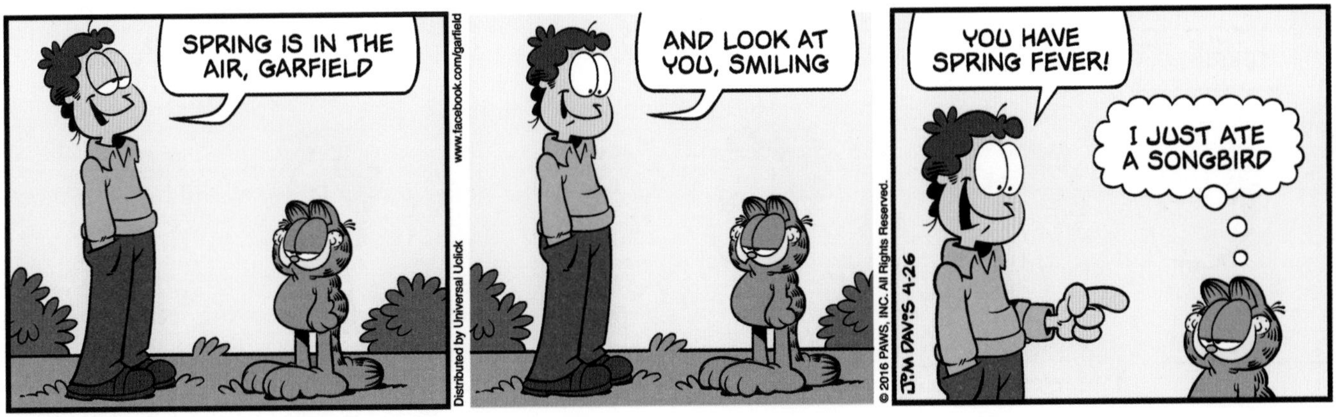
SPRING IS IN THE AIR, GARFIELD
Distributed by Universal Uclick www.facebook.com/garfield
AND LOOK AT YOU, SMILING
YOU HAVE SPRING FEVER!
I JUST ATE A SONGBIRD
© 2016 PAWS, INC. All Rights Reserved.
JIM DAVIS 4-26

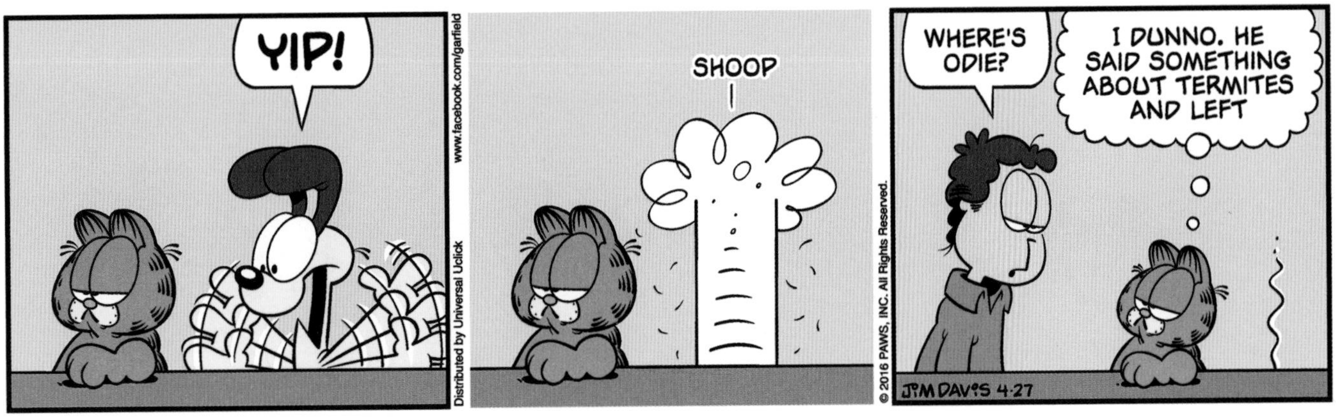
YIP!
Distributed by Universal Uclick www.facebook.com/garfield
SHOOP
WHERE'S ODIE?
I DUNNO. HE SAID SOMETHING ABOUT TERMITES AND LEFT
© 2016 PAWS, INC. All Rights Reserved.
JIM DAVIS 4-27

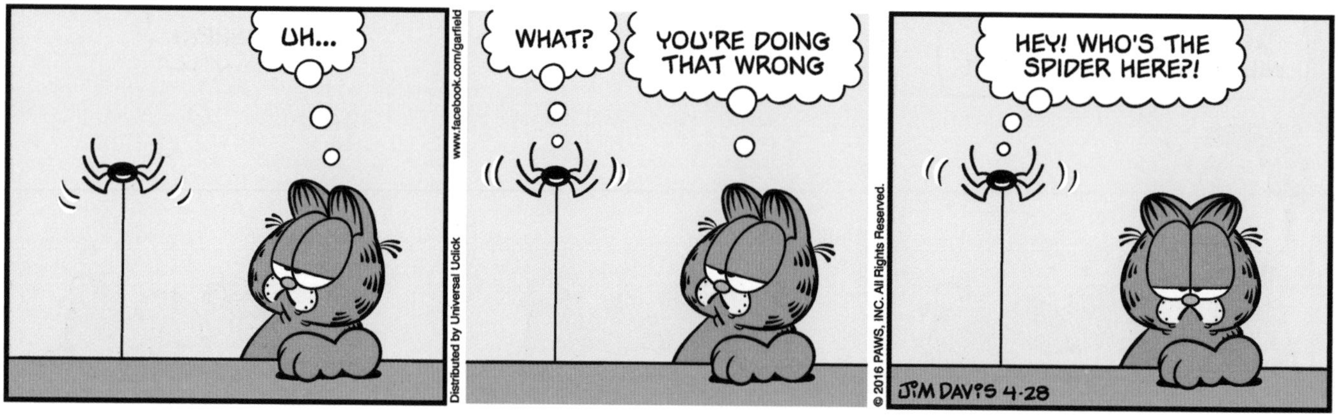
UH...
WHAT?
YOU'RE DOING THAT WRONG
HEY! WHO'S THE SPIDER HERE?!
JIM DAVIS 4-28
Distributed by Universal Uclick www.facebook.com/garfield
© 2016 PAWS, INC. All Rights Reserved.

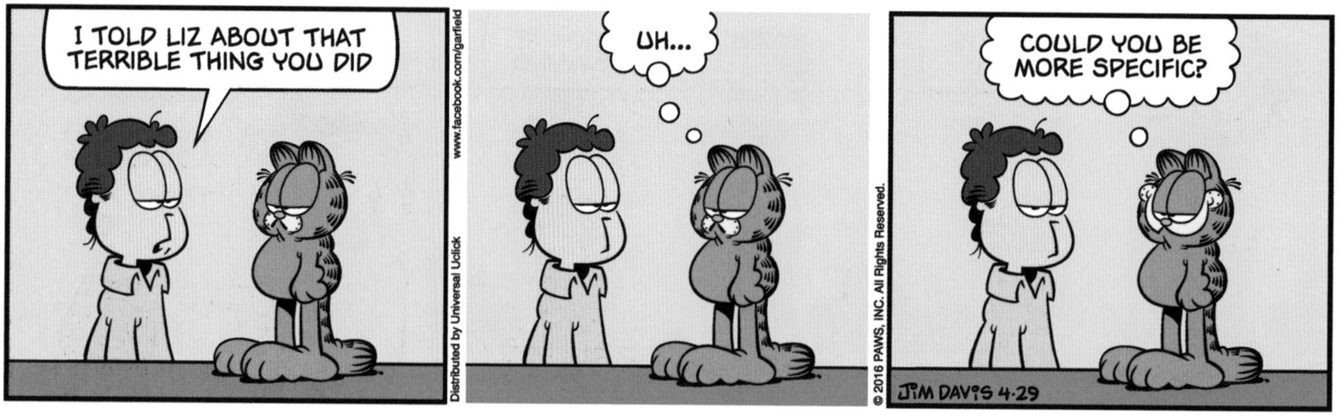
I TOLD LIZ ABOUT THAT TERRIBLE THING YOU DID
UH...
COULD YOU BE MORE SPECIFIC?
JIM DAVIS 4-29
Distributed by Universal Uclick www.facebook.com/garfield
© 2016 PAWS, INC. All Rights Reserved.

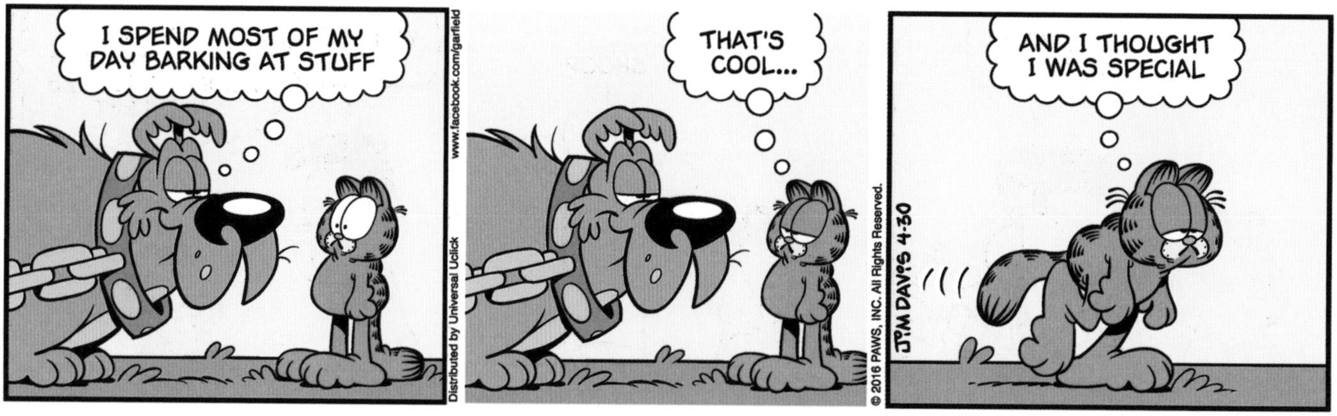
I SPEND MOST OF MY DAY BARKING AT STUFF
THAT'S COOL...
AND I THOUGHT I WAS SPECIAL
JIM DAVIS 4-30
Distributed by Universal Uclick www.facebook.com/garfield
© 2016 PAWS, INC. All Rights Reserved.

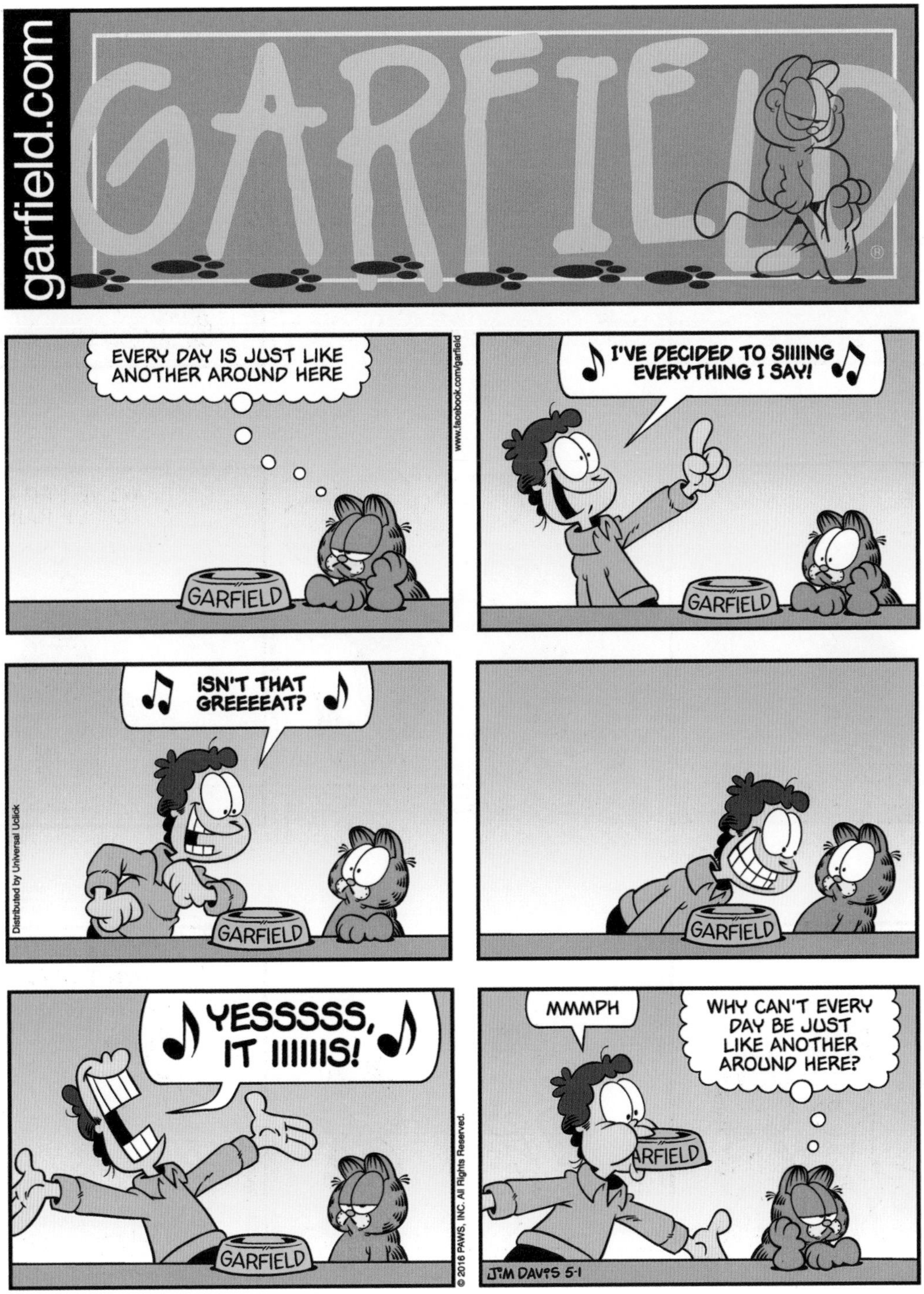
garfield.com
GARFIELD
EVERY DAY IS JUST LIKE ANOTHER AROUND HERE
www.facebook.com/garfield
I'VE DECIDED TO SIIIING EVERYTHING I SAY!
GARFIELD
ISN'T THAT GREEEEAT?
Distributed by Universal Uclick
YESSSSS, IT IIIIIIS!
© 2016 PAWS, INC. All Rights Reserved.
MMMPH
WHY CAN'T EVERY DAY BE JUST LIKE ANOTHER AROUND HERE?
JIM DAVIS 5-1

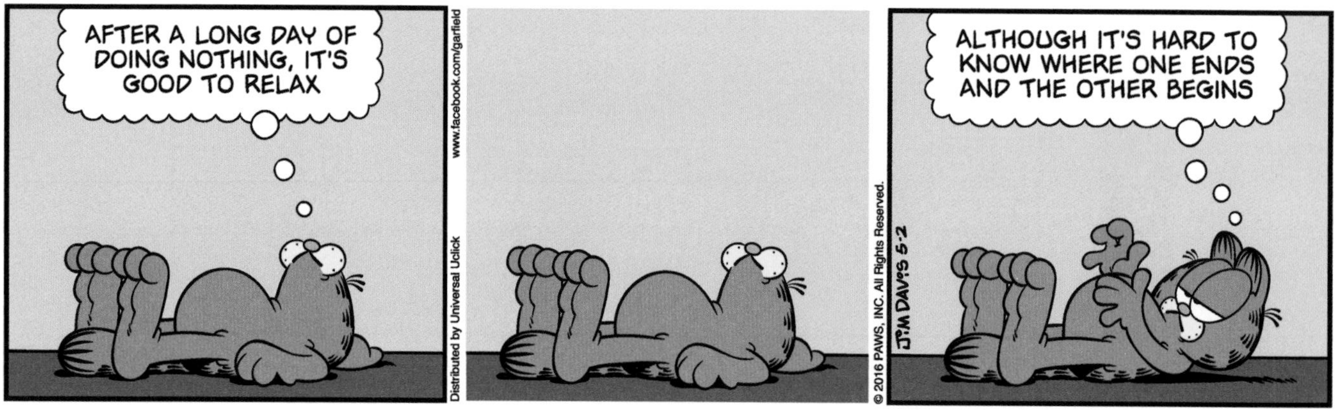
AFTER A LONG DAY OF DOING NOTHING, IT'S GOOD TO RELAX
www.facebook.com/garfield
Distributed by Universal Uclick
© 2016 PAWS, INC. All Rights Reserved.
JIM DAVIS 5-2
ALTHOUGH IT'S HARD TO KNOW WHERE ONE ENDS AND THE OTHER BEGINS

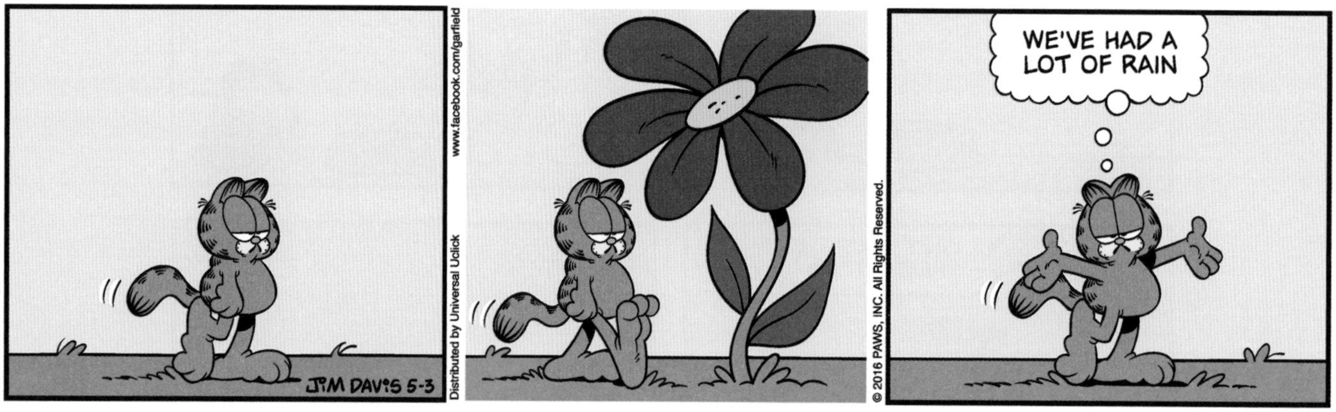
JIM DAVIS 5-3
www.facebook.com/garfield
Distributed by Universal Uclick
© 2016 PAWS, INC. All Rights Reserved.
WE'VE HAD A LOT OF RAIN

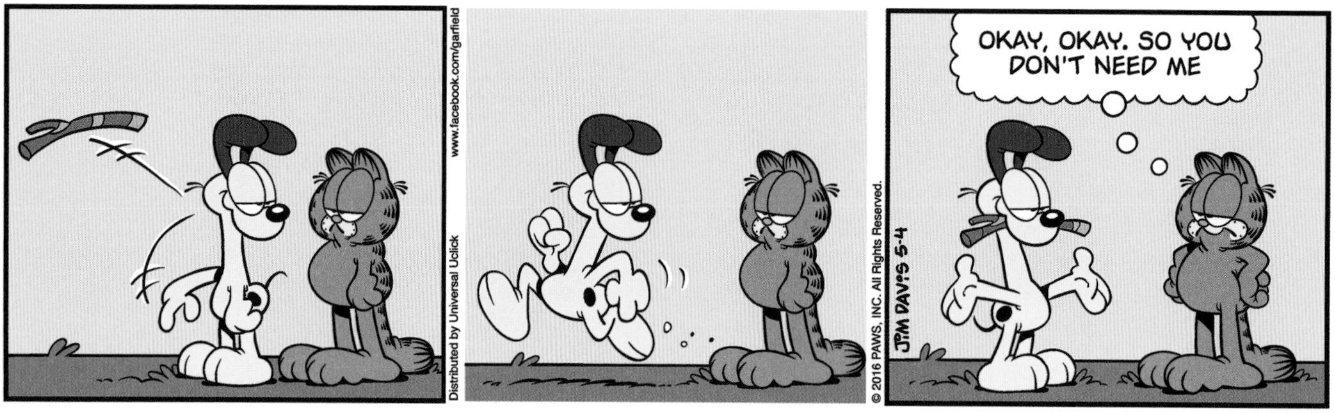
www.facebook.com/garfield
Distributed by Universal Uclick
© 2016 PAWS, INC. All Rights Reserved.
JIM DAVIS 5-4
OKAY, OKAY. SO YOU DON'T NEED ME

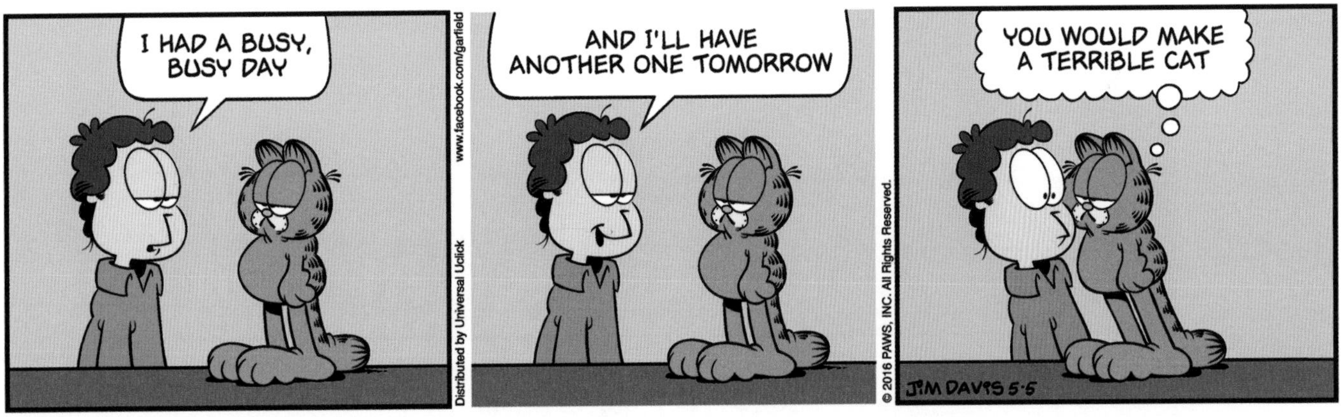
I HAD A BUSY, BUSY DAY
AND I'LL HAVE ANOTHER ONE TOMORROW
YOU WOULD MAKE A TERRIBLE CAT
JIM DAVIS 5-5
Distributed by Universal Uclick www.facebook.com/garfield
© 2016 PAWS, INC. All Rights Reserved.

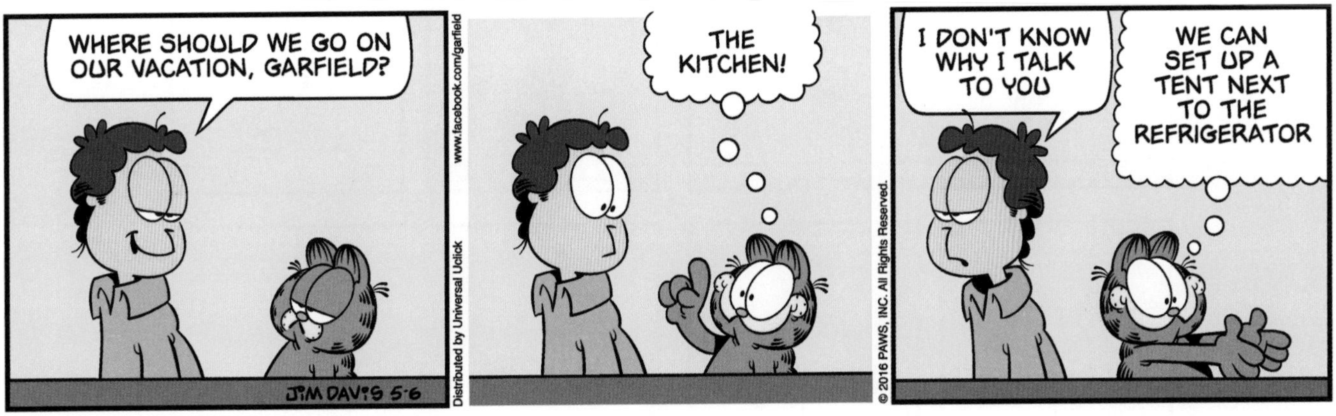
WHERE SHOULD WE GO ON OUR VACATION, GARFIELD?
JIM DAVIS 5-6
THE KITCHEN!
I DON'T KNOW WHY I TALK TO YOU
WE CAN SET UP A TENT NEXT TO THE REFRIGERATOR
Distributed by Universal Uclick www.facebook.com/garfield
© 2016 PAWS, INC. All Rights Reserved.

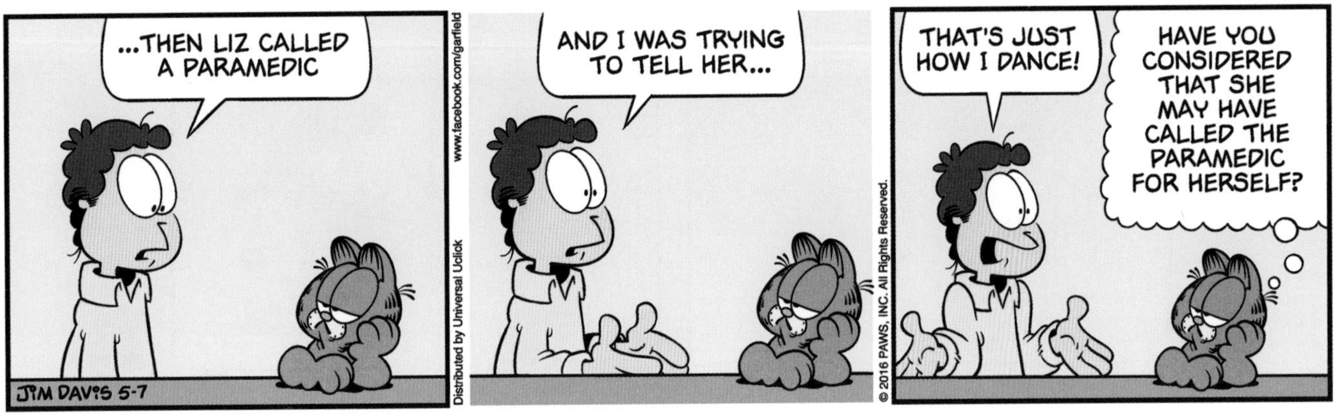
...THEN LIZ CALLED A PARAMEDIC
JIM DAVIS 5-7
AND I WAS TRYING TO TELL HER...
THAT'S JUST HOW I DANCE!
HAVE YOU CONSIDERED THAT SHE MAY HAVE CALLED THE PARAMEDIC FOR HERSELF?
Distributed by Universal Uclick www.facebook.com/garfield
© 2016 PAWS, INC. All Rights Reserved.

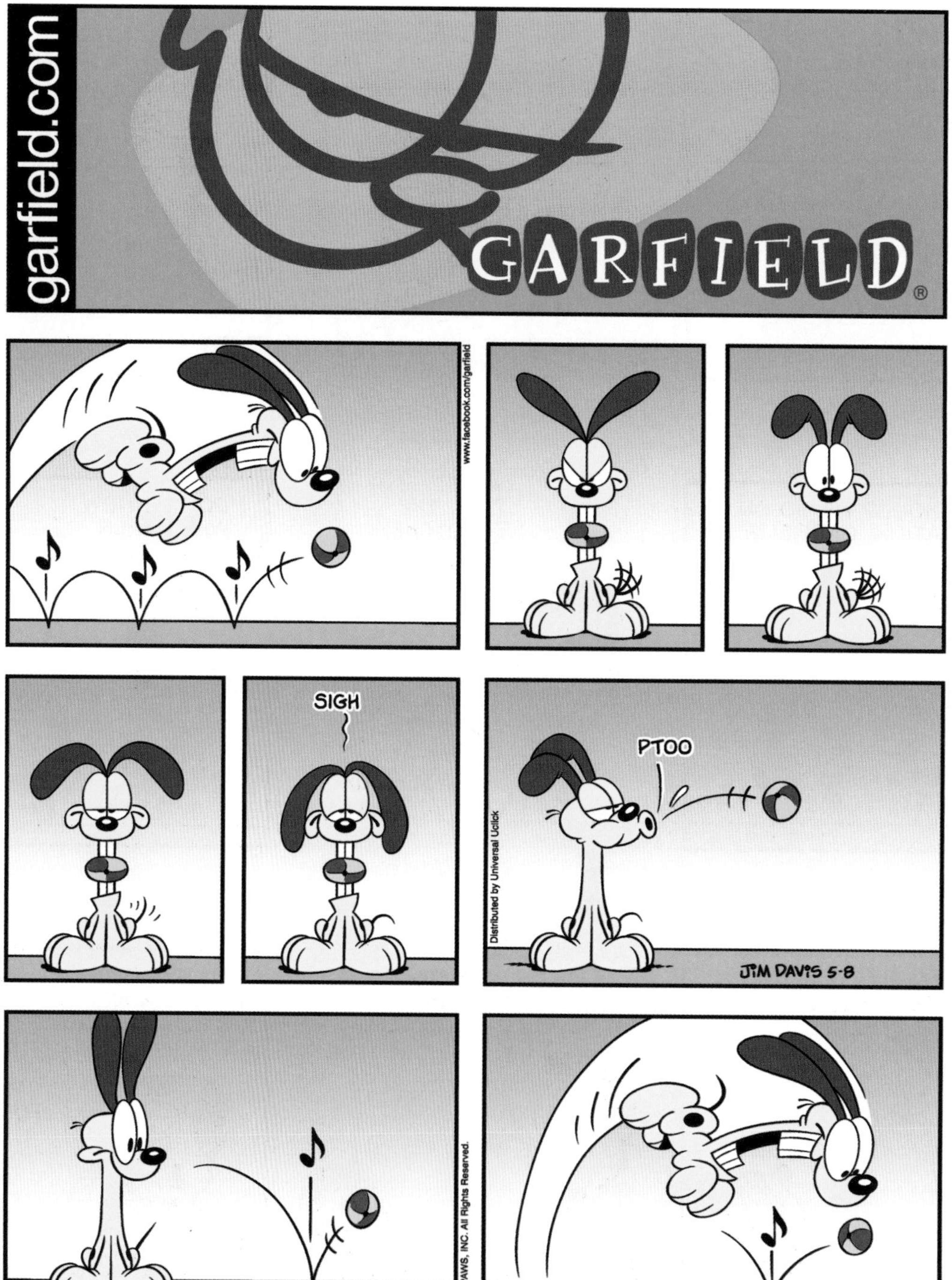
garfield.com
GARFIELD®
www.facebook.com/garfield
SIGH
PTOO
Distributed by Universal Uclick
JIM DAVIS 5-8
© 2016 PAWS, INC. All Rights Reserved.

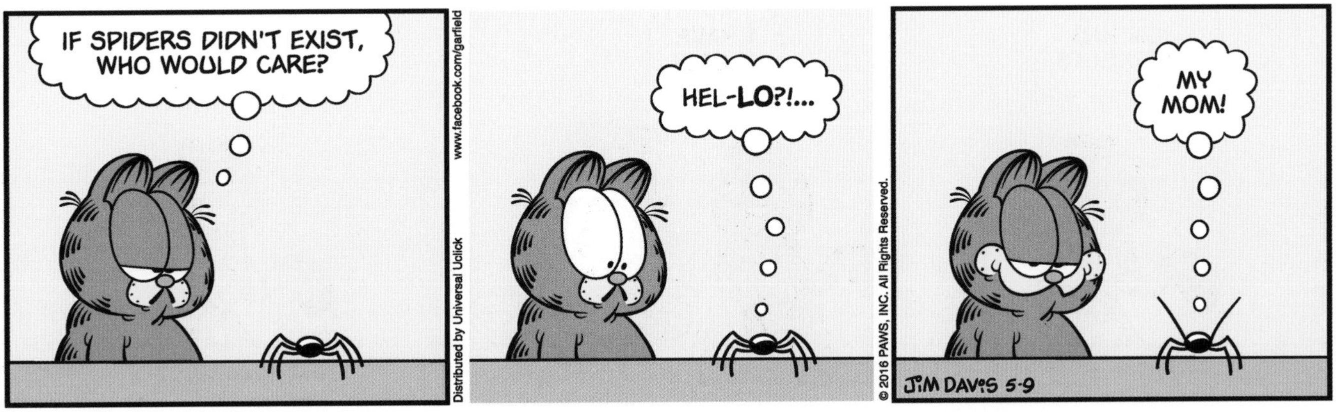
IF SPIDERS DIDN'T EXIST, WHO WOULD CARE?
www.facebook.com/garfield
Distributed by Universal Uclick
HEL-LO?!...
© 2016 PAWS, INC. All Rights Reserved.
MY MOM!
JIM DAVIS 5-9

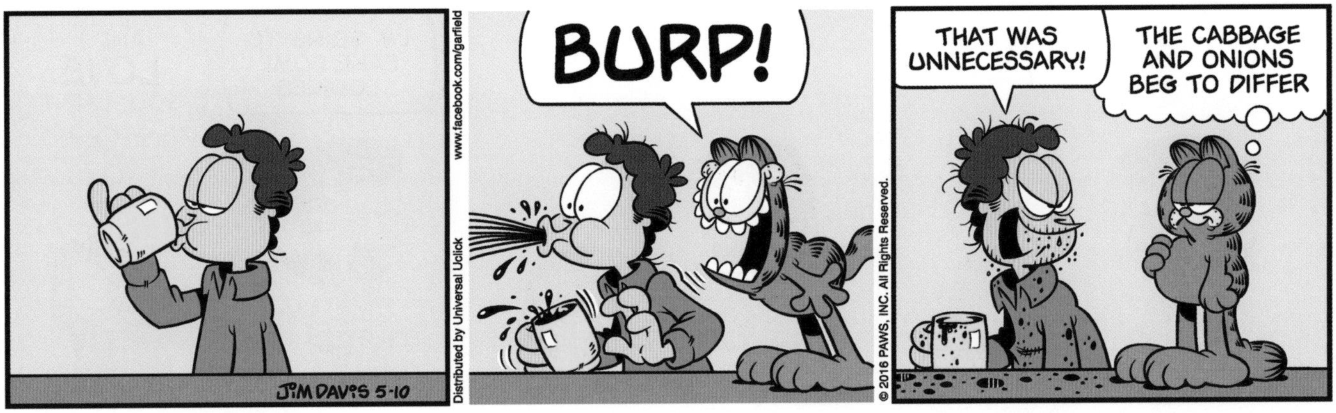
JIM DAVIS 5-10
www.facebook.com/garfield
Distributed by Universal Uclick
BURP!
© 2016 PAWS, INC. All Rights Reserved.
THAT WAS UNNECESSARY!
THE CABBAGE AND ONIONS BEG TO DIFFER

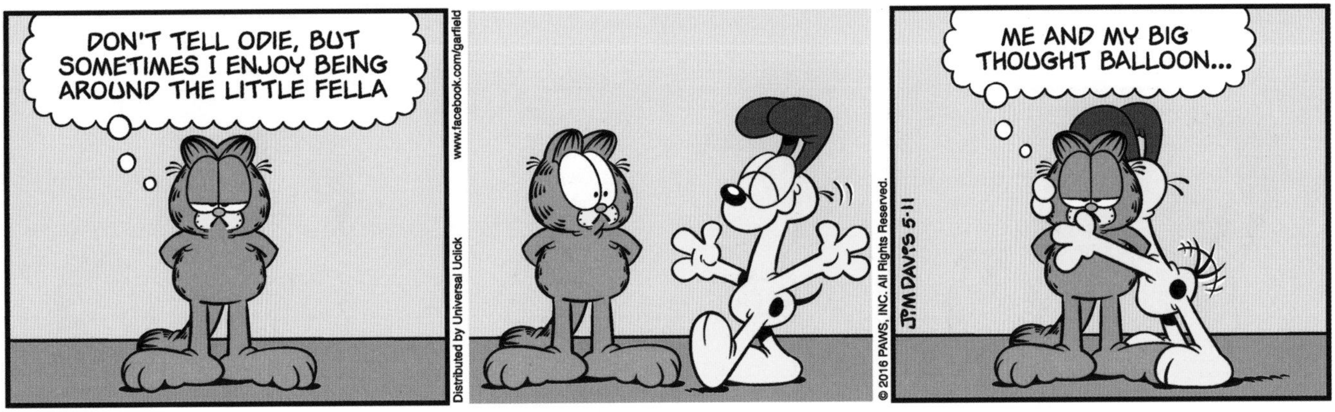
DON'T TELL ODIE, BUT SOMETIMES I ENJOY BEING AROUND THE LITTLE FELLA
www.facebook.com/garfield
Distributed by Universal Uclick
© 2016 PAWS, INC. All Rights Reserved.
JIM DAVIS 5-11
ME AND MY BIG THOUGHT BALLOON...

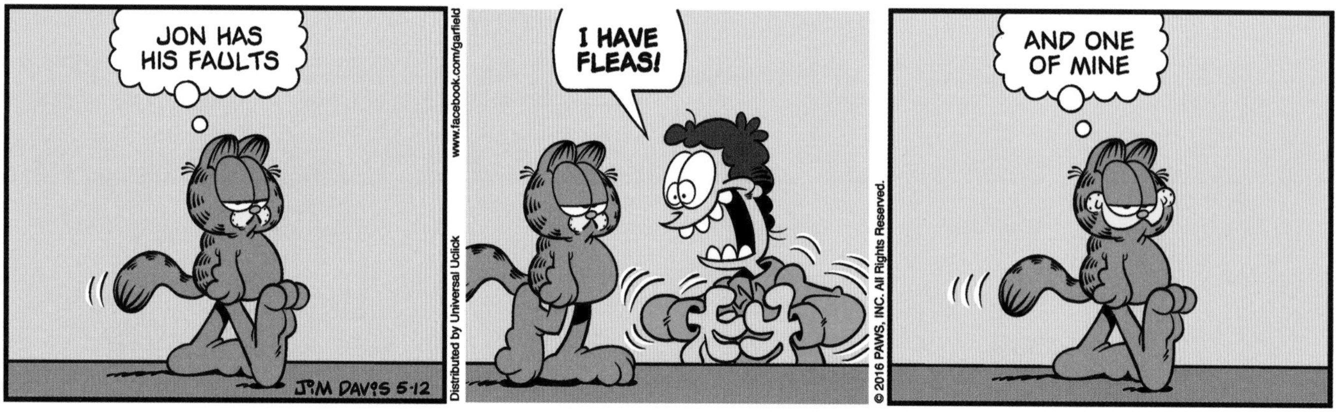
JON HAS HIS FAULTS
I HAVE FLEAS!
AND ONE OF MINE
JIM DAVIS 5-12
Distributed by Universal Uclick www.facebook.com/garfield
© 2016 PAWS, INC. All Rights Reserved.

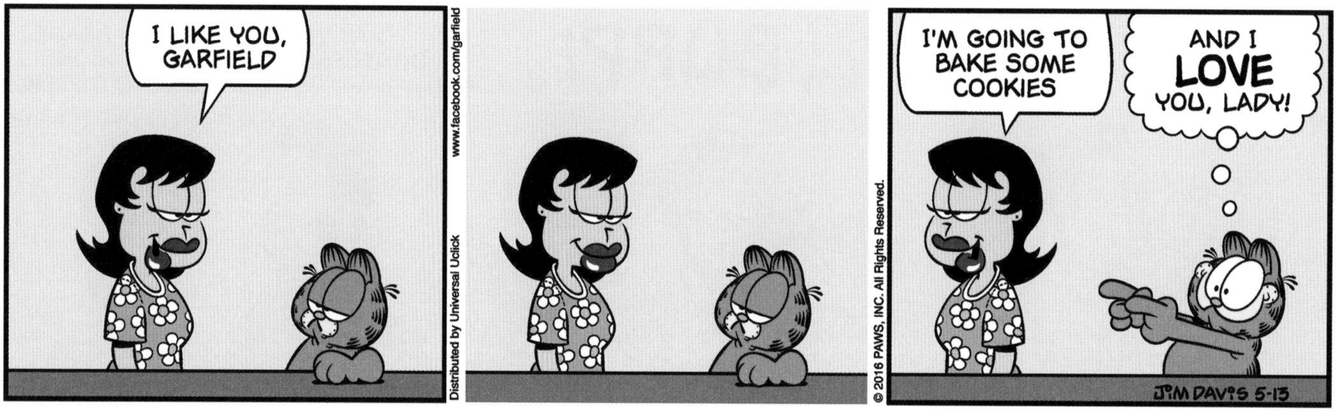
I LIKE YOU, GARFIELD
I'M GOING TO BAKE SOME COOKIES
AND I LOVE YOU, LADY!
JIM DAVIS 5-13
Distributed by Universal Uclick www.facebook.com/garfield
© 2016 PAWS, INC. All Rights Reserved.

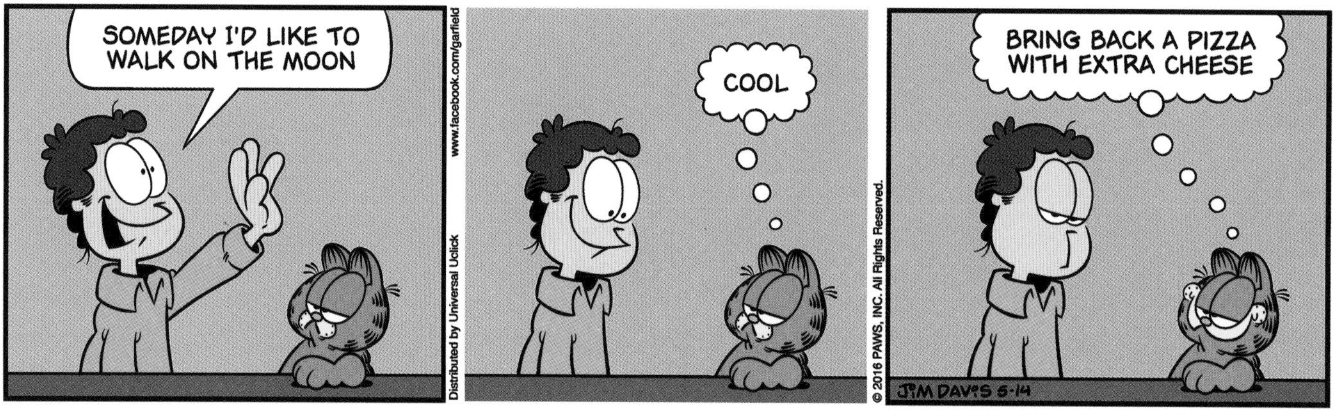
SOMEDAY I'D LIKE TO WALK ON THE MOON
COOL
BRING BACK A PIZZA WITH EXTRA CHEESE
JIM DAVIS 5-14
Distributed by Universal Uclick www.facebook.com/garfield
© 2016 PAWS, INC. All Rights Reserved.

WORKING HARD...

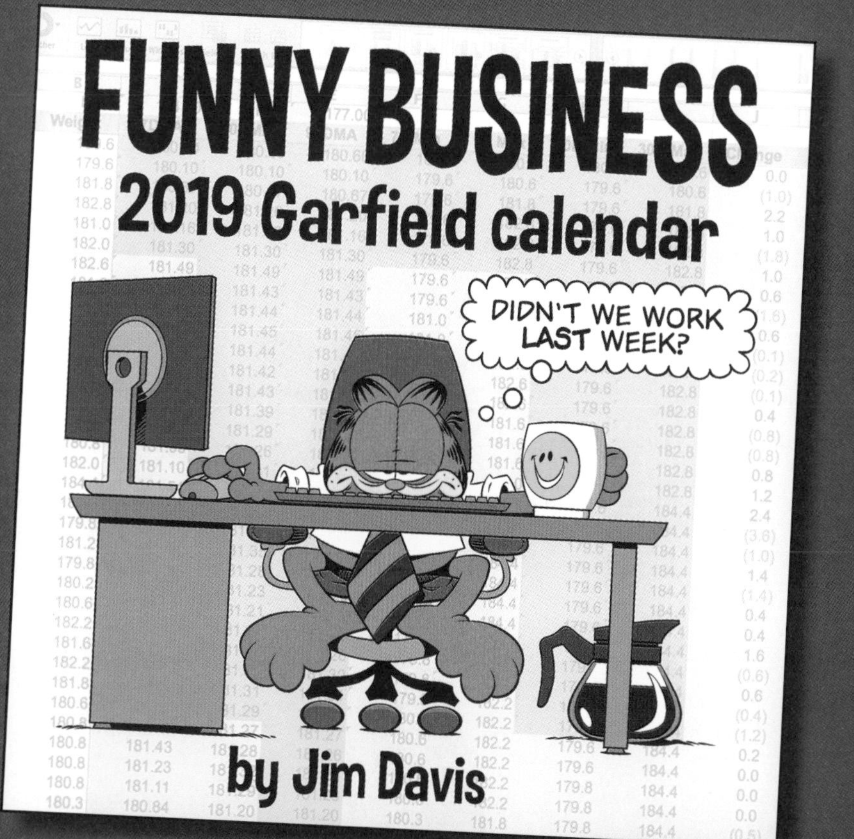
FUNNY BUSINESS
2019 Garfield calendar
DIDN'T WE WORK LAST WEEK?
by Jim Davis

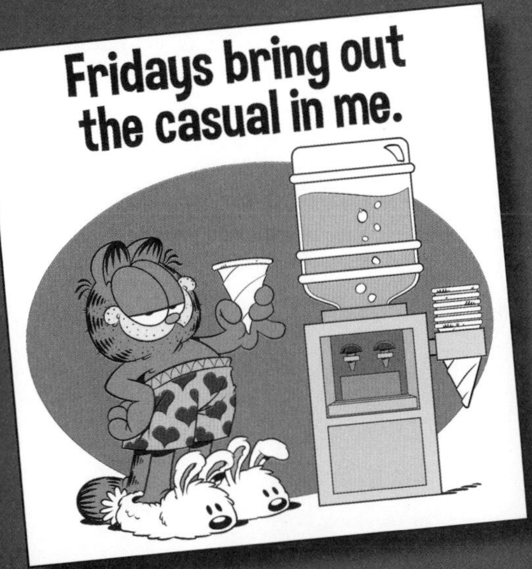
Fridays bring out the casual in me.

OR HARDLY WORKING?

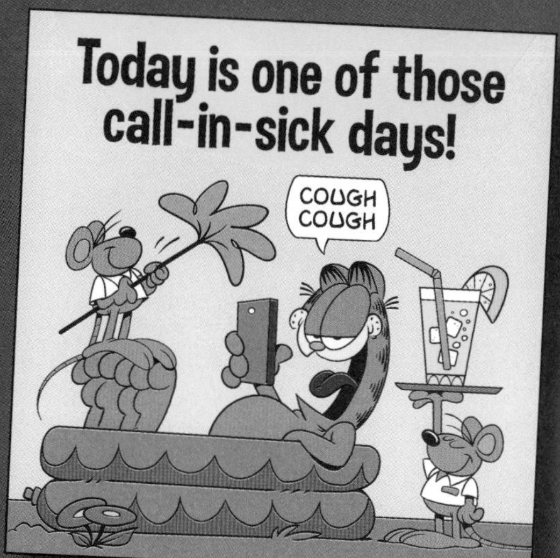
Today is one of those call-in-sick days!
COUGH COUGH

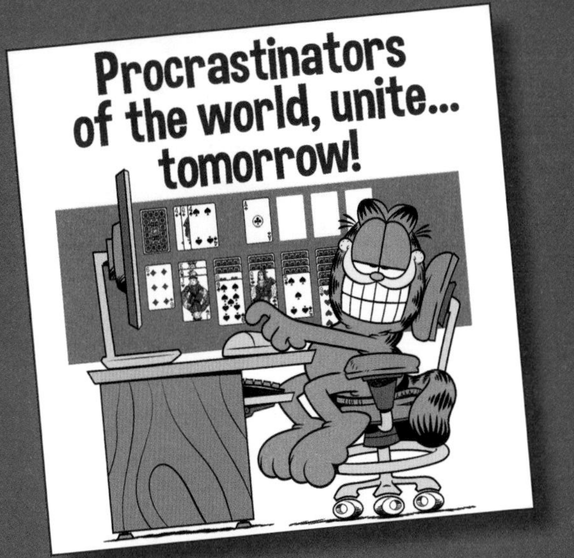
Procrastinators of the world, unite... tomorrow!

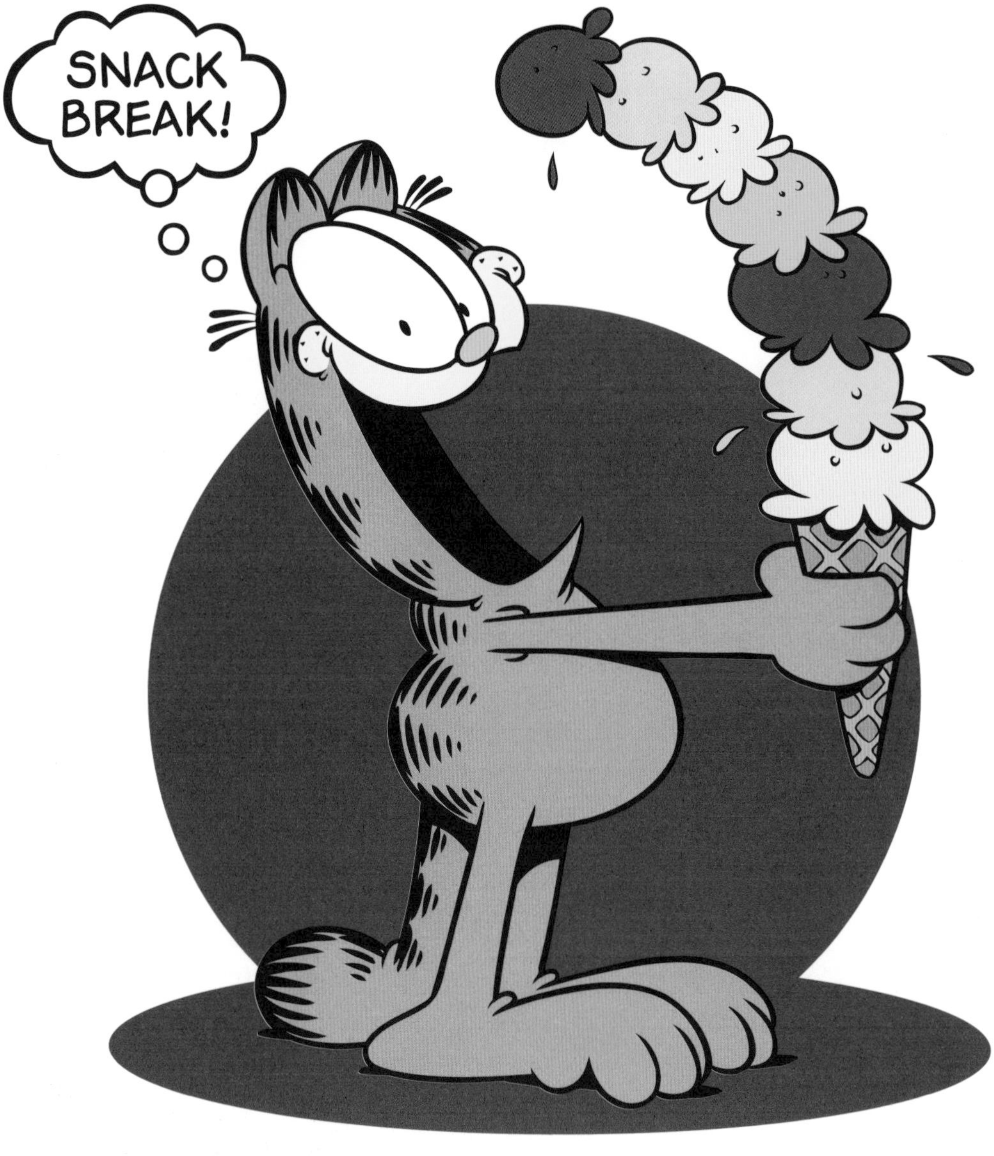
SNACK BREAK!

Garfield
NUTTY AS A FRUITCAKE

BY JIM DAVIS

Ballantine Books ● New York

Fat Cat
Fan Art

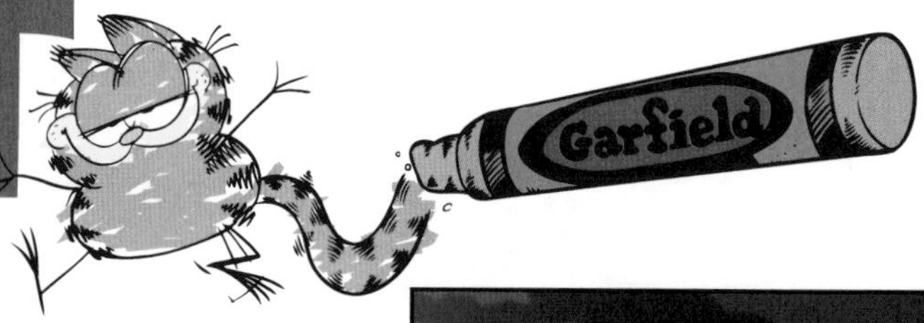
Garfield

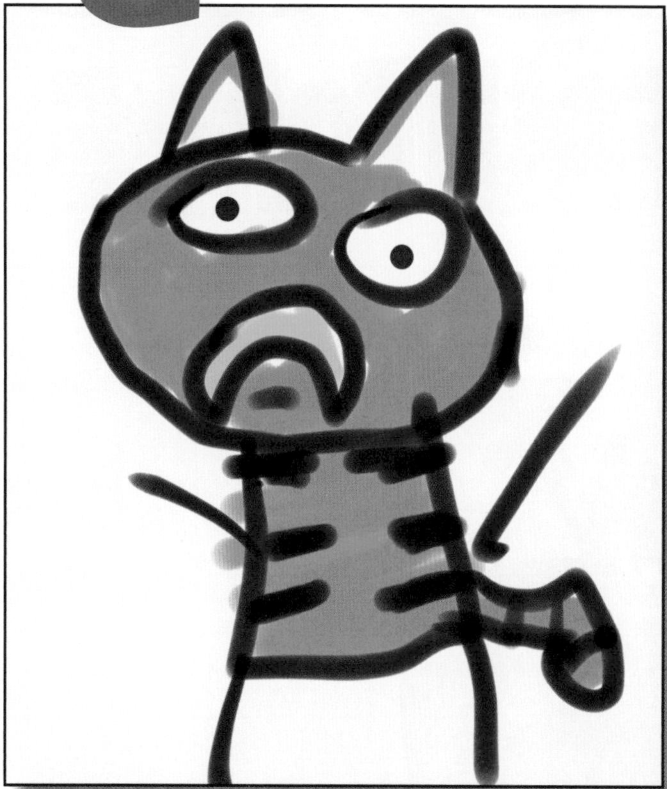

Jonathan G.
Age 17
Michigan

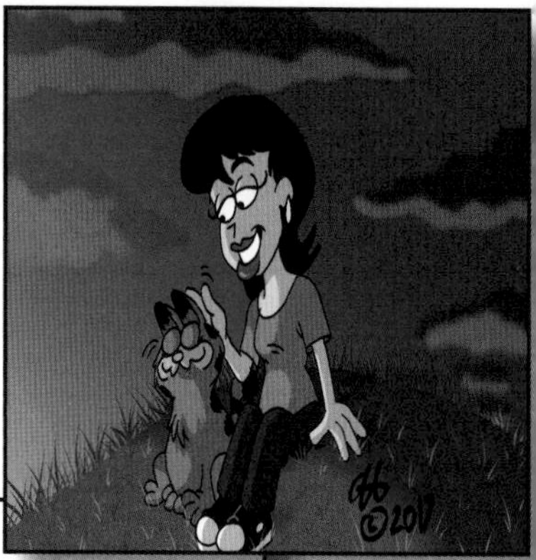

Clint H.
Age 24
Canada

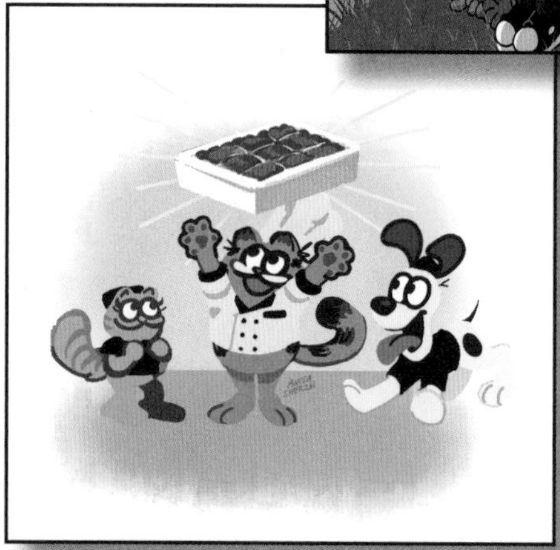

Anisa S.
Age 20
Massachusett

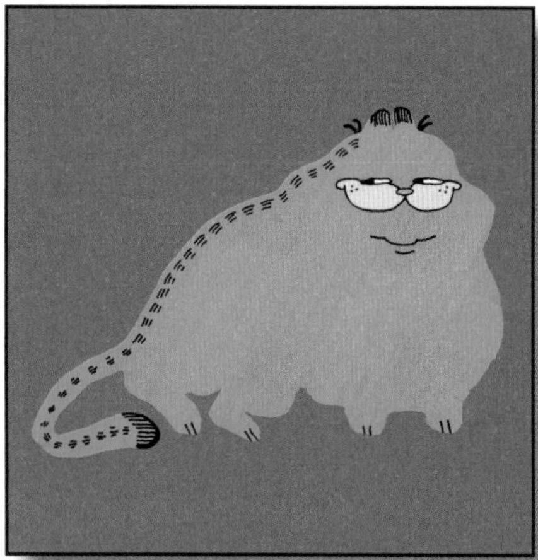

Zoe M.
Age 19
Texas

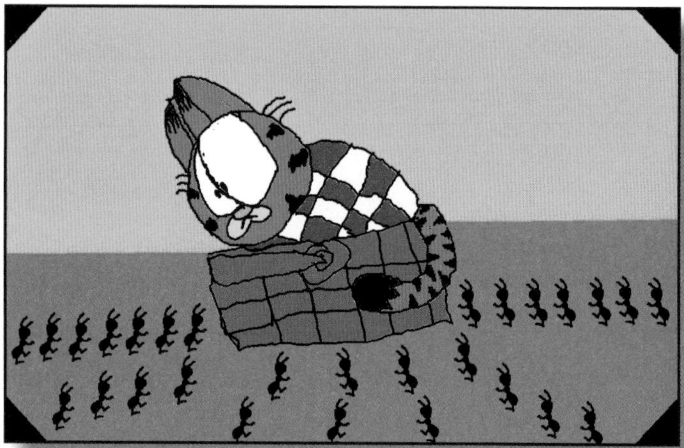

Elijah B.
Age 16
Ohio

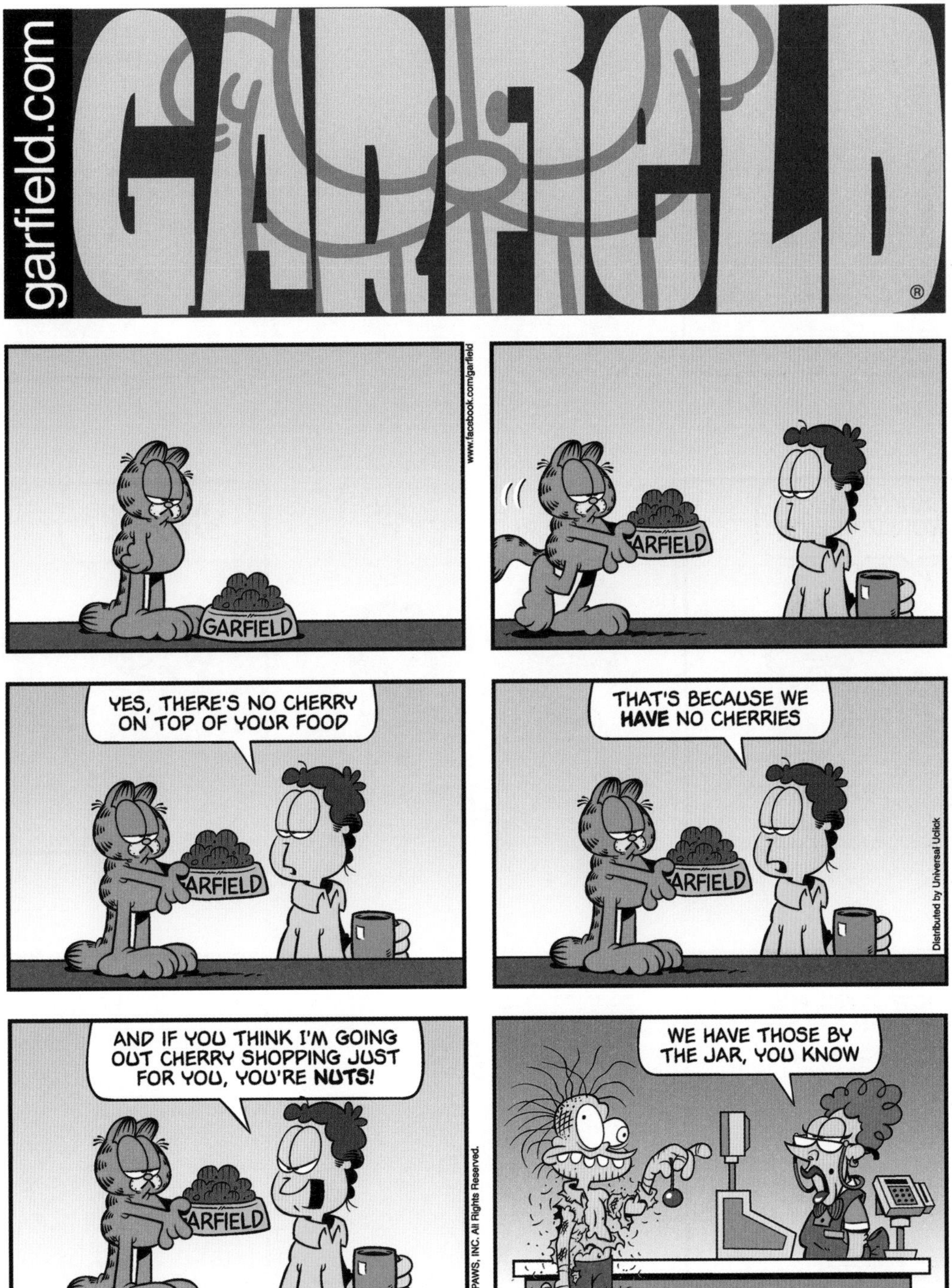
garfield.com
GARFIELD
www.facebook.com/garfield
GARFIELD
ARFIELD
YES, THERE'S NO CHERRY ON TOP OF YOUR FOOD
ARFIELD
THAT'S BECAUSE WE **HAVE** NO CHERRIES
ARFIELD
Distributed by Universal Uclick
AND IF YOU THINK I'M GOING OUT CHERRY SHOPPING JUST FOR YOU, YOU'RE **NUTS**!
ARFIELD
© 2016 PAWS, INC. All Rights Reserved.
WE HAVE THOSE BY THE JAR, YOU KNOW
JIM DAVIS 5-15

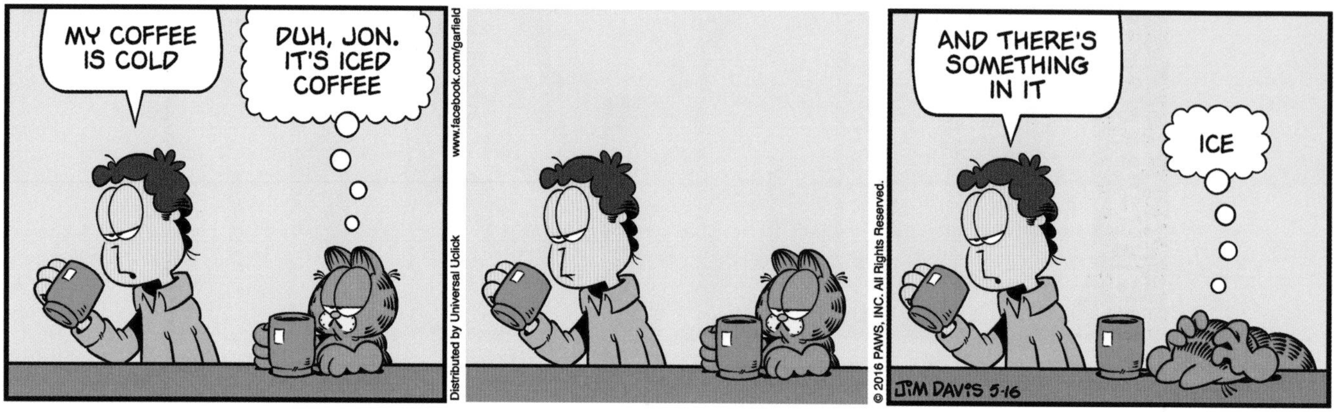
MY COFFEE IS COLD
DUH, JON. IT'S ICED COFFEE
Distributed by Universal Uclick www.facebook.com/garfield
AND THERE'S SOMETHING IN IT
ICE
© 2016 PAWS, INC. All Rights Reserved.
JIM DAVIS 5-16

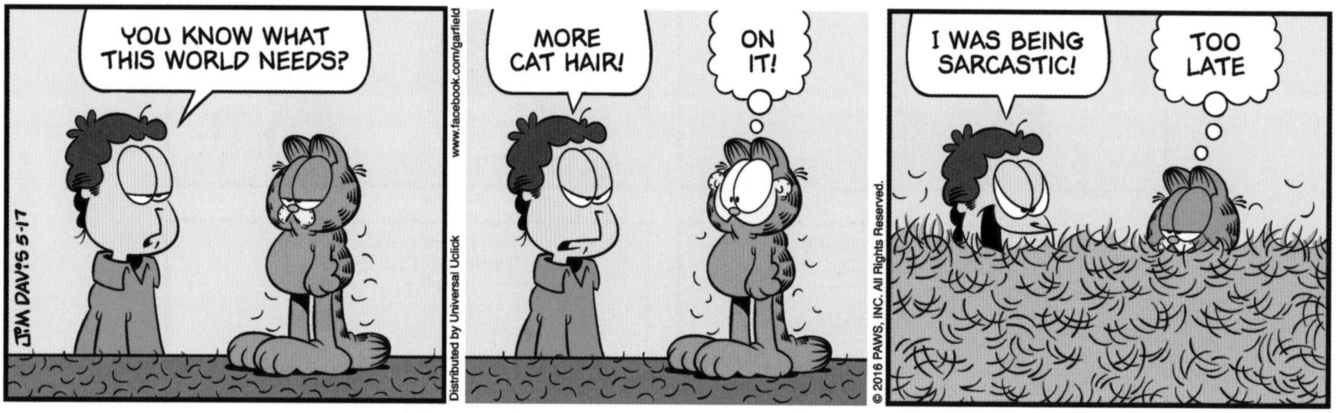
YOU KNOW WHAT THIS WORLD NEEDS?
JIM DAVIS 5-17
Distributed by Universal Uclick www.facebook.com/garfield
MORE CAT HAIR!
ON IT!
© 2016 PAWS, INC. All Rights Reserved.
I WAS BEING SARCASTIC!
TOO LATE

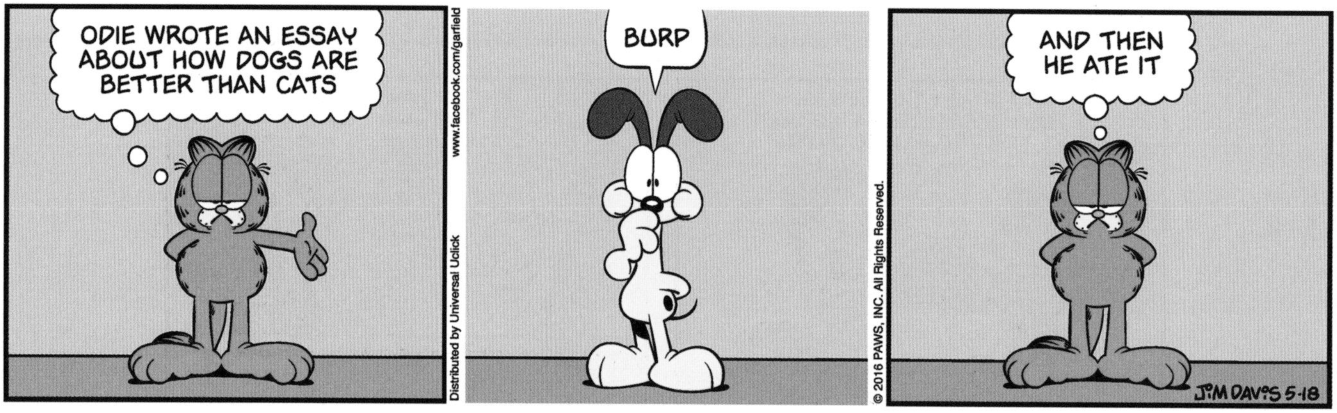
ODIE WROTE AN ESSAY ABOUT HOW DOGS ARE BETTER THAN CATS
Distributed by Universal Uclick www.facebook.com/garfield
BURP
© 2016 PAWS, INC. All Rights Reserved.
AND THEN HE ATE IT
JIM DAVIS 5-18

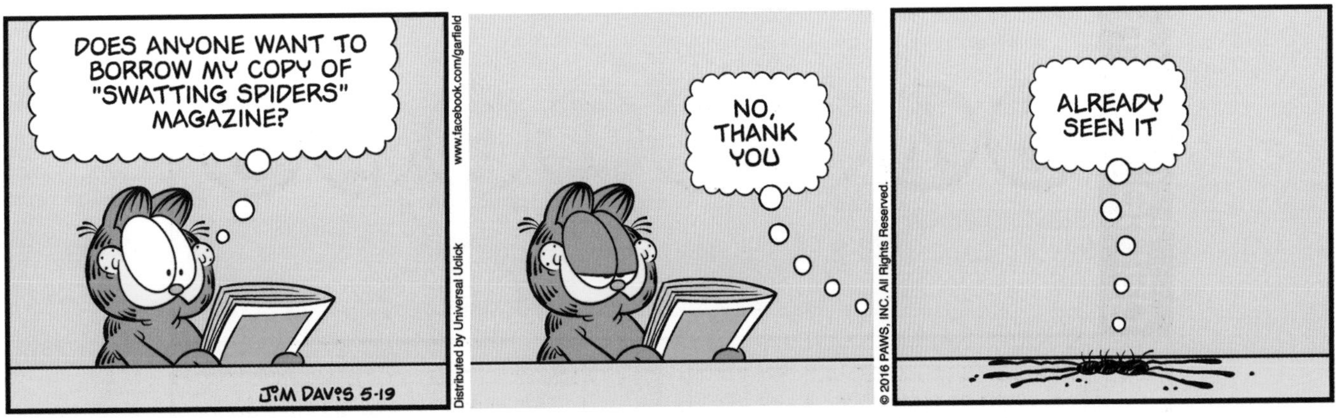
DOES ANYONE WANT TO BORROW MY COPY OF "SWATTING SPIDERS" MAGAZINE?
JIM DAVIS 5-19
www.facebook.com/garfield
Distributed by Universal Uclick
NO, THANK YOU
© 2016 PAWS, INC. All Rights Reserved.
ALREADY SEEN IT

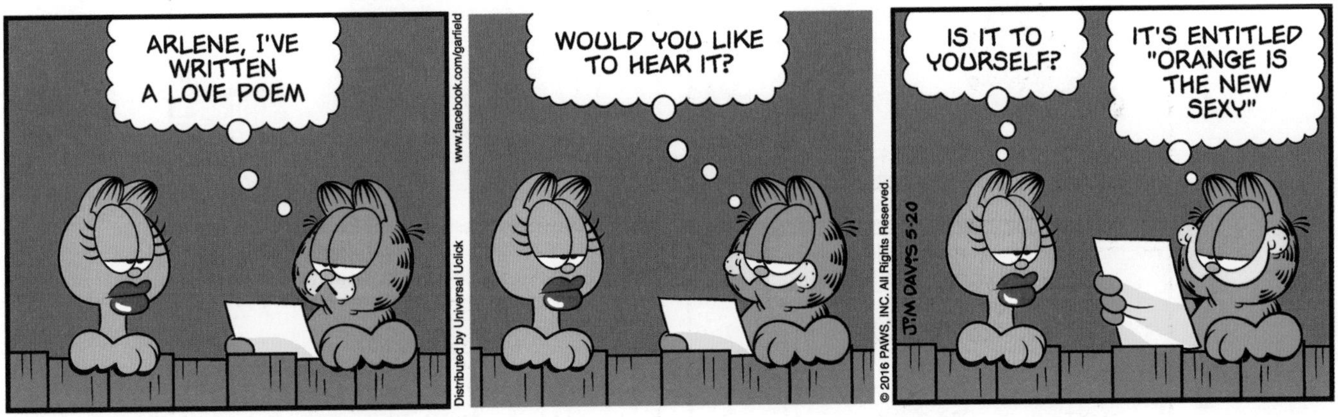
ARLENE, I'VE WRITTEN A LOVE POEM
www.facebook.com/garfield
Distributed by Universal Uclick
WOULD YOU LIKE TO HEAR IT?
© 2016 PAWS, INC. All Rights Reserved.
JIM DAVIS 5-20
IS IT TO YOURSELF?
IT'S ENTITLED "ORANGE IS THE NEW SEXY"

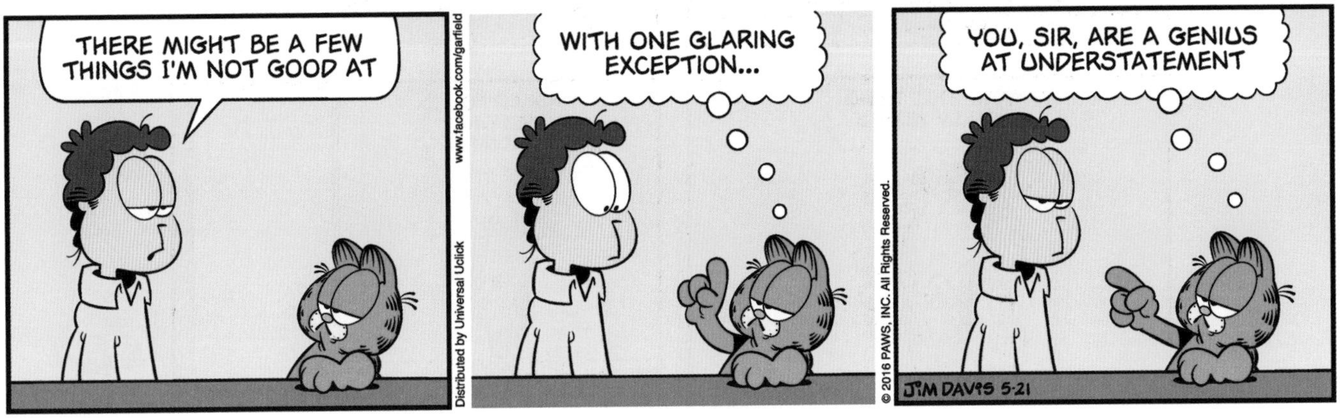
THERE MIGHT BE A FEW THINGS I'M NOT GOOD AT
www.facebook.com/garfield
Distributed by Universal Uclick
WITH ONE GLARING EXCEPTION...
© 2016 PAWS, INC. All Rights Reserved.
YOU, SIR, ARE A GENIUS AT UNDERSTATEMENT
JIM DAVIS 5-21

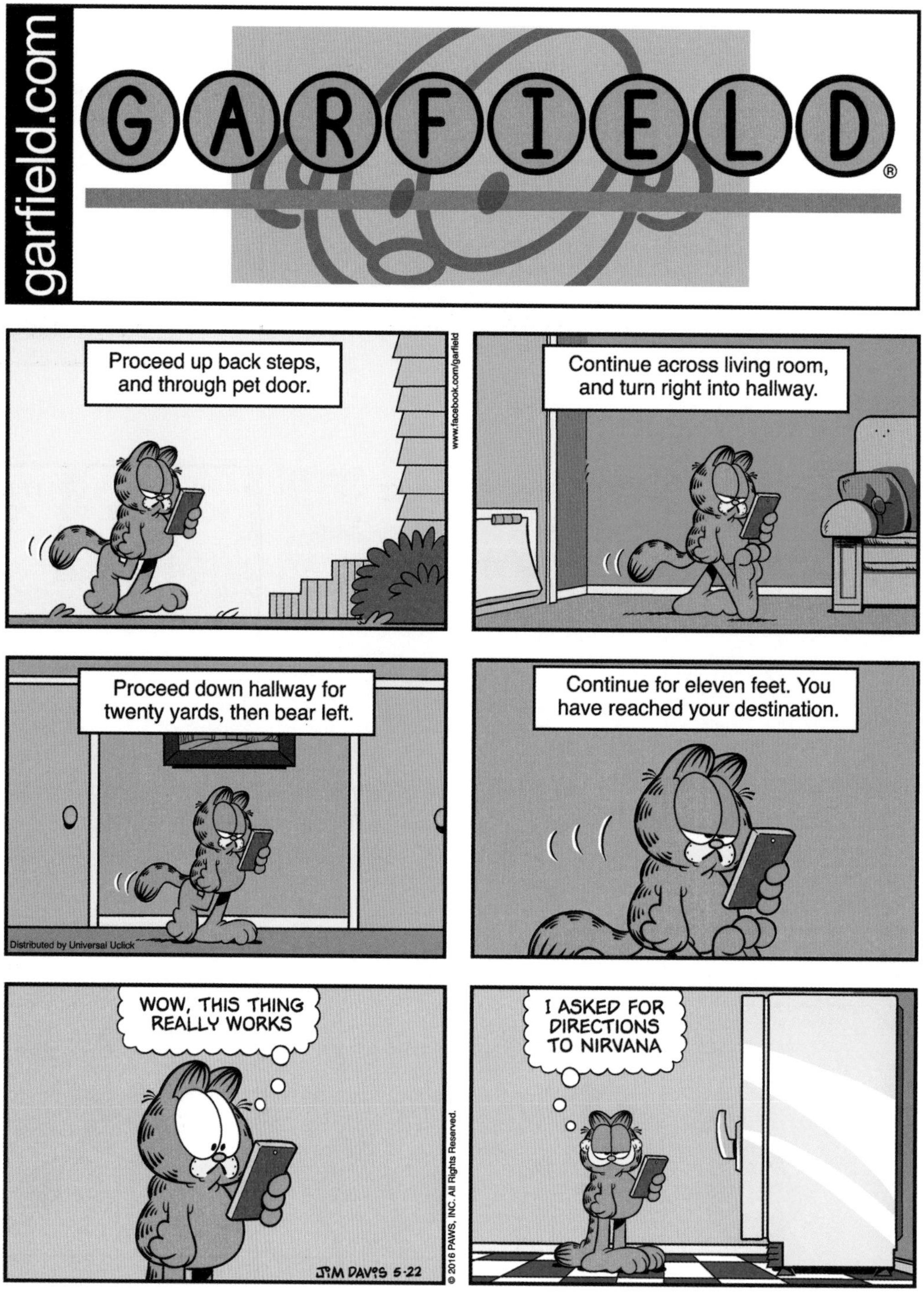
garfield.com
GARFIELD®
Proceed up back steps, and through pet door.
www.facebook.com/garfield
Continue across living room, and turn right into hallway.
Proceed down hallway for twenty yards, then bear left.
Distributed by Universal Uclick
Continue for eleven feet. You have reached your destination.
WOW, THIS THING REALLY WORKS
JIM DAVIS 5-22
© 2016 PAWS, INC. All Rights Reserved.
I ASKED FOR DIRECTIONS TO NIRVANA

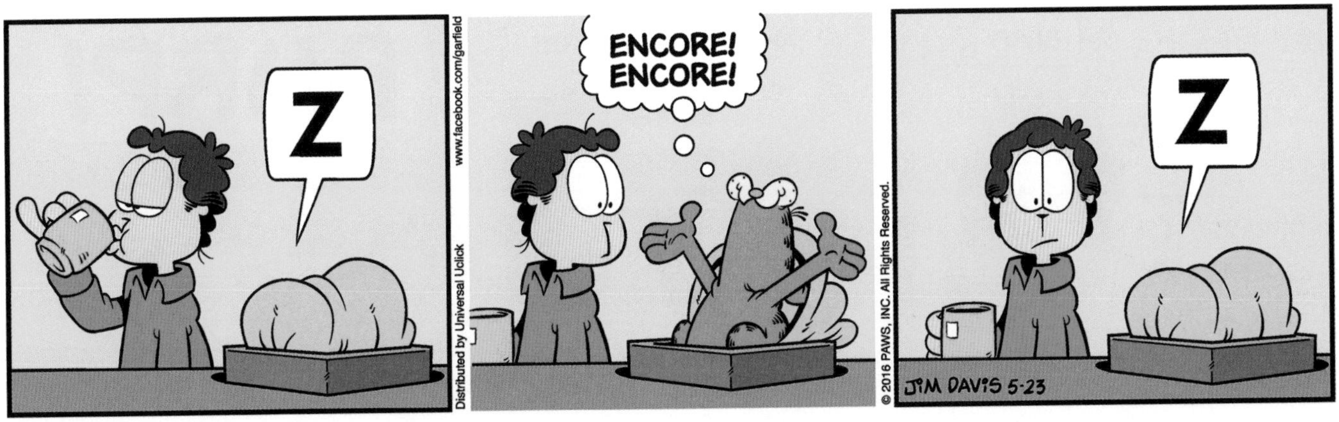
Z
www.facebook.com/garfield
Distributed by Universal Uclick
ENCORE! ENCORE!
© 2016 PAWS, INC. All Rights Reserved.
Z
JIM DAVIS 5-23

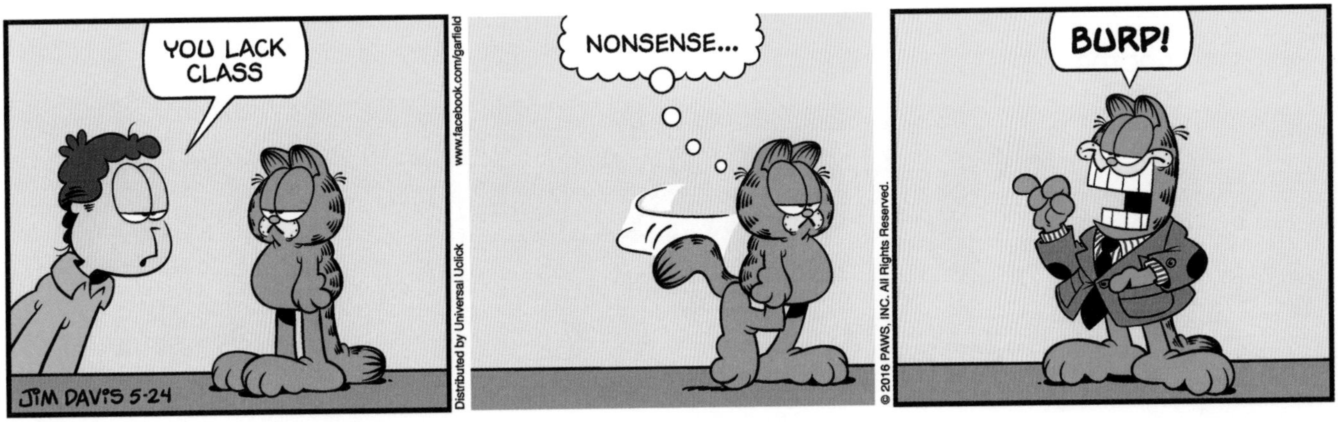
YOU LACK CLASS
JIM DAVIS 5-24
www.facebook.com/garfield
Distributed by Universal Uclick
NONSENSE...
© 2016 PAWS, INC. All Rights Reserved.
BURP!

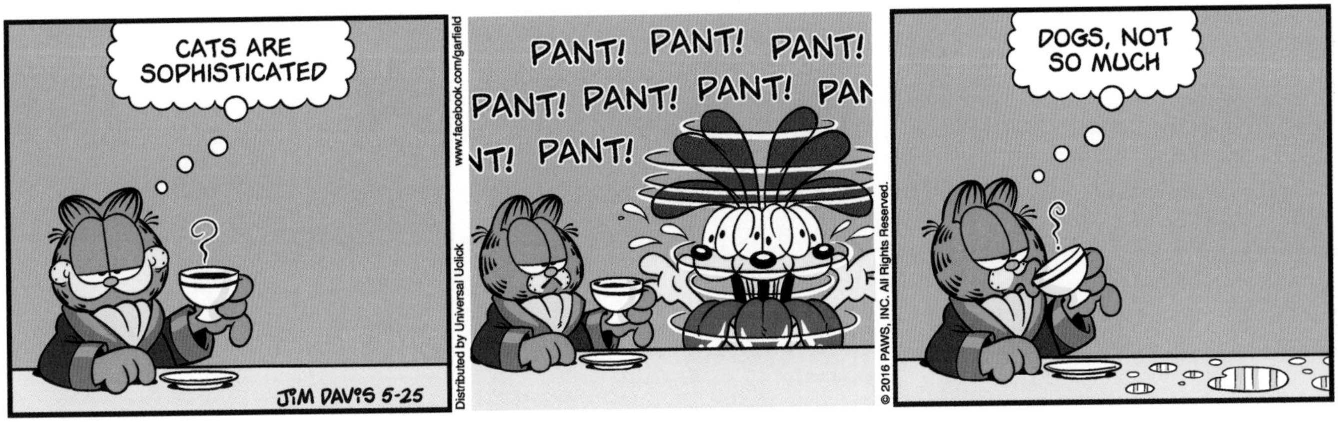
CATS ARE SOPHISTICATED
JIM DAVIS 5-25
www.facebook.com/garfield
Distributed by Universal Uclick
PANT! PANT! PANT!
PANT! PANT! PANT!
PANT!
© 2016 PAWS, INC. All Rights Reserved.
DOGS, NOT SO MUCH

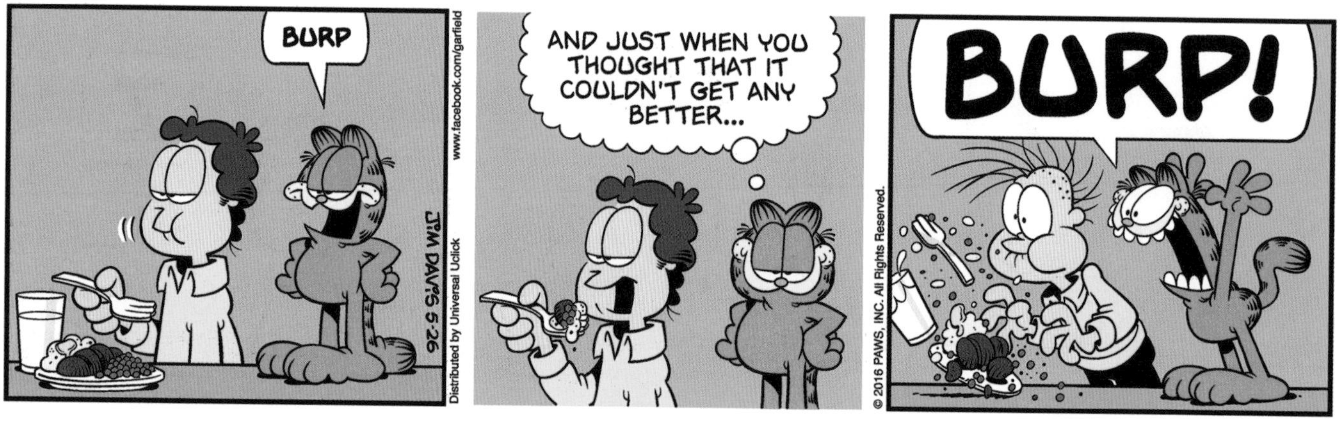
BURP
JIM DAVIS 5-26
Distributed by Universal Uclick
www.facebook.com/garfield
AND JUST WHEN YOU THOUGHT THAT IT COULDN'T GET ANY BETTER...
© 2016 PAWS, INC. All Rights Reserved.
BURP!

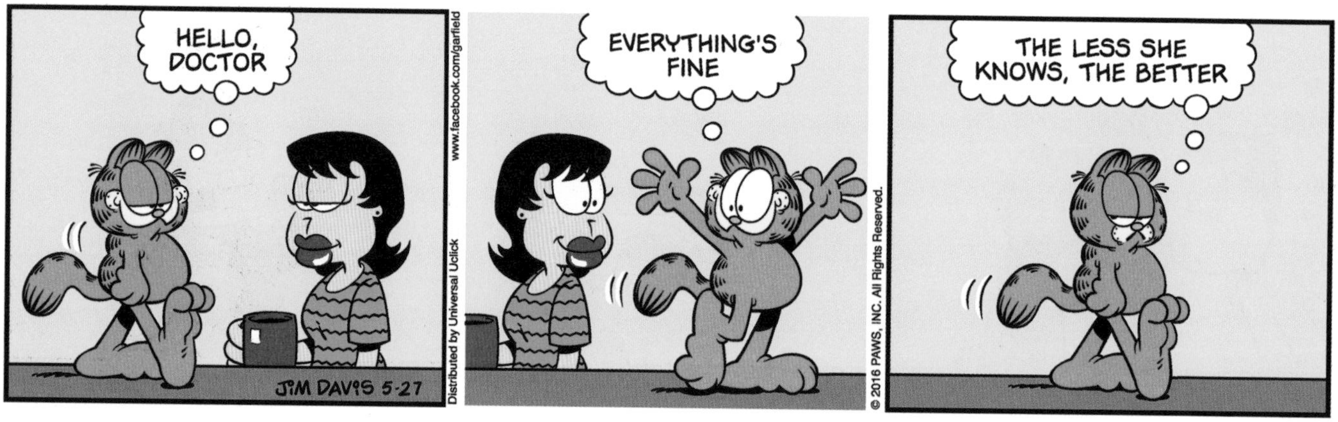
HELLO, DOCTOR
JIM DAVIS 5-27
Distributed by Universal Uclick
www.facebook.com/garfield
EVERYTHING'S FINE
© 2016 PAWS, INC. All Rights Reserved.
THE LESS SHE KNOWS, THE BETTER

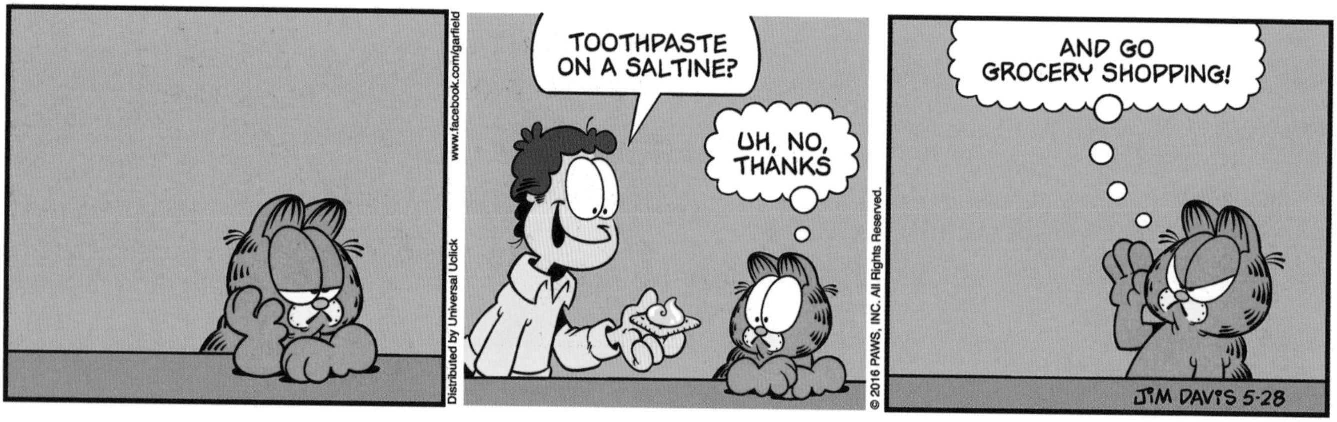
Distributed by Universal Uclick
www.facebook.com/garfield
TOOTHPASTE ON A SALTINE?
UH, NO, THANKS
© 2016 PAWS, INC. All Rights Reserved.
AND GO GROCERY SHOPPING!
JIM DAVIS 5-28

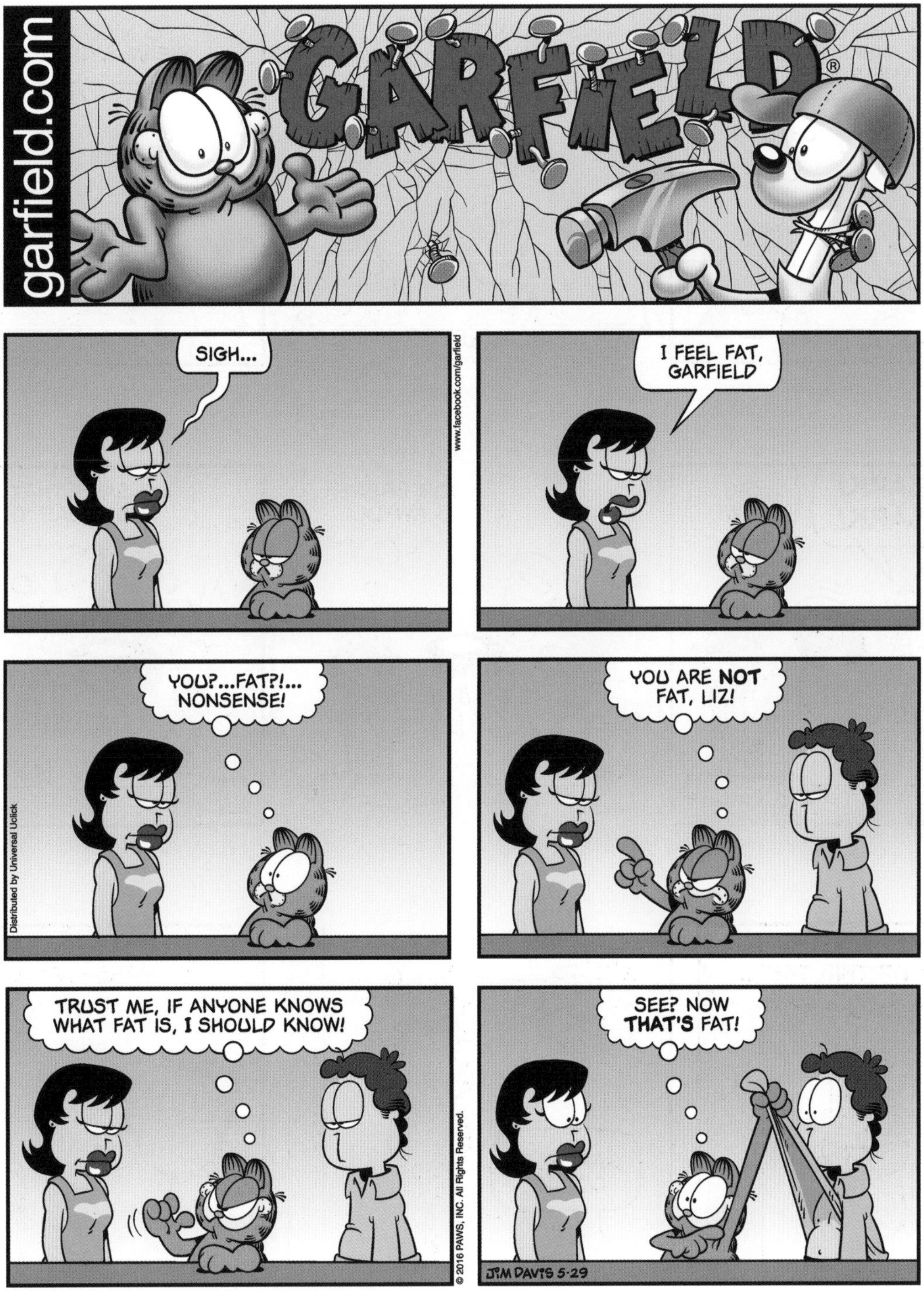
garfield.com
GARFIELD®
www.facebook.com/garfield
Distributed by Universal Uclick
© 2016 PAWS, INC. All Rights Reserved.
SIGH...
I FEEL FAT, GARFIELD
YOU?...FAT?!... NONSENSE!
YOU ARE NOT FAT, LIZ!
TRUST ME, IF ANYONE KNOWS WHAT FAT IS, I SHOULD KNOW!
SEE? NOW THAT'S FAT!
JIM DAVIS 5-29

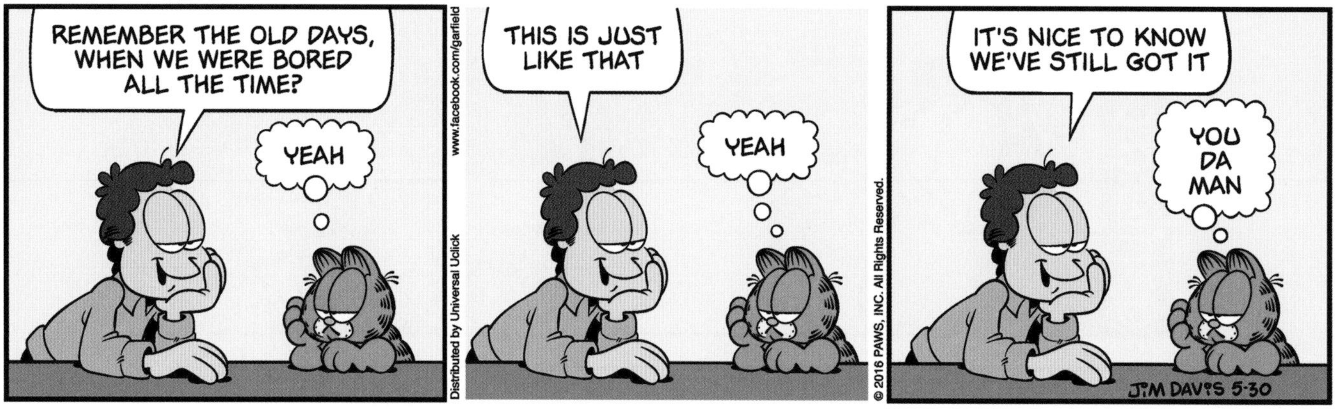
REMEMBER THE OLD DAYS, WHEN WE WERE BORED ALL THE TIME?
YEAH
THIS IS JUST LIKE THAT
YEAH
IT'S NICE TO KNOW WE'VE STILL GOT IT
YOU DA MAN
Distributed by Universal Uclick www.facebook.com/garfield
© 2016 PAWS, INC. All Rights Reserved.
JIM DAVIS 5-30

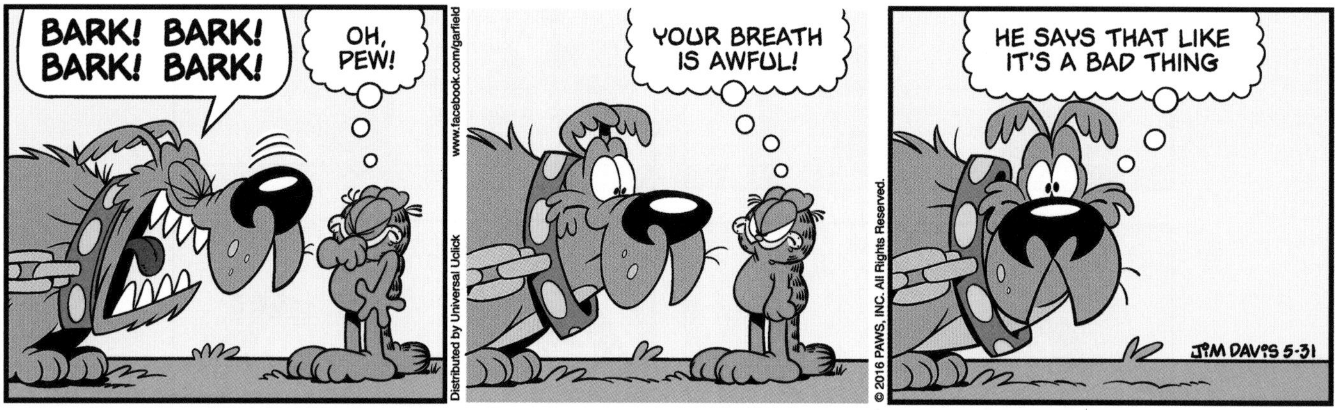
BARK! BARK! BARK! BARK!
OH, PEW!
YOUR BREATH IS AWFUL!
HE SAYS THAT LIKE IT'S A BAD THING
Distributed by Universal Uclick www.facebook.com/garfield
© 2016 PAWS, INC. All Rights Reserved.
JIM DAVIS 5-31

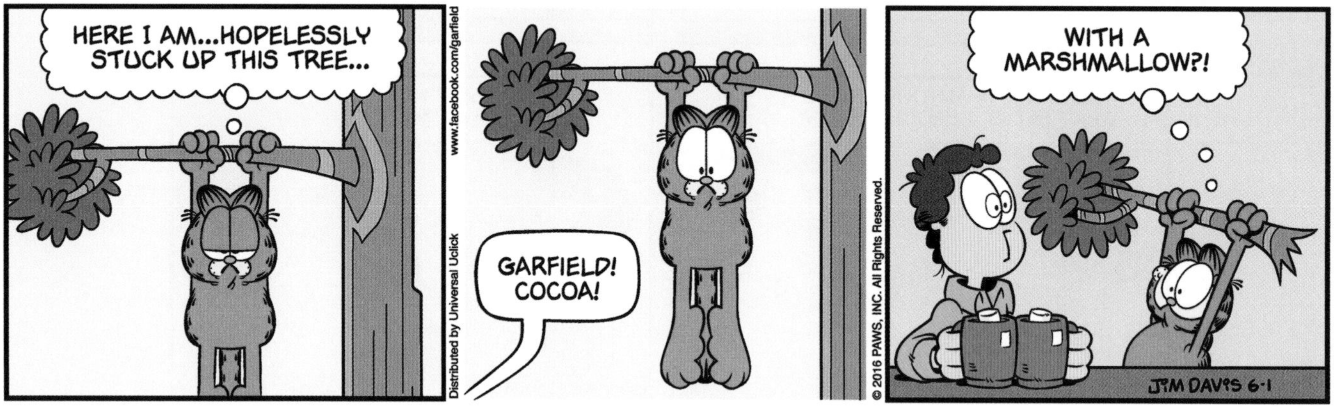
HERE I AM...HOPELESSLY STUCK UP THIS TREE...
GARFIELD! COCOA!
WITH A MARSHMALLOW?!
Distributed by Universal Uclick www.facebook.com/garfield
© 2016 PAWS, INC. All Rights Reserved.
JIM DAVIS 6-1

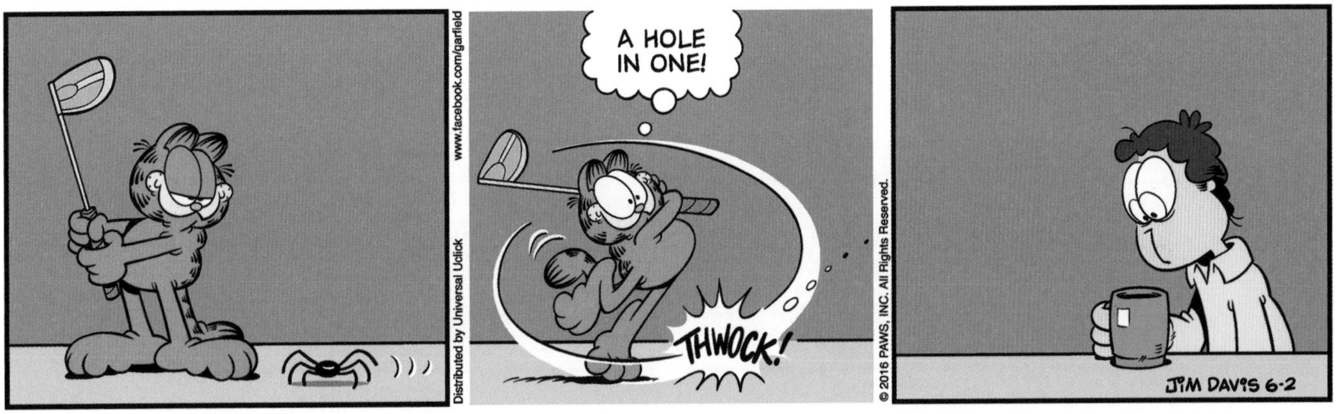
www.facebook.com/garfield
Distributed by Universal Uclick
A HOLE IN ONE!
THWOCK!
© 2016 PAWS, INC. All Rights Reserved.
JIM DAVIS 6-2

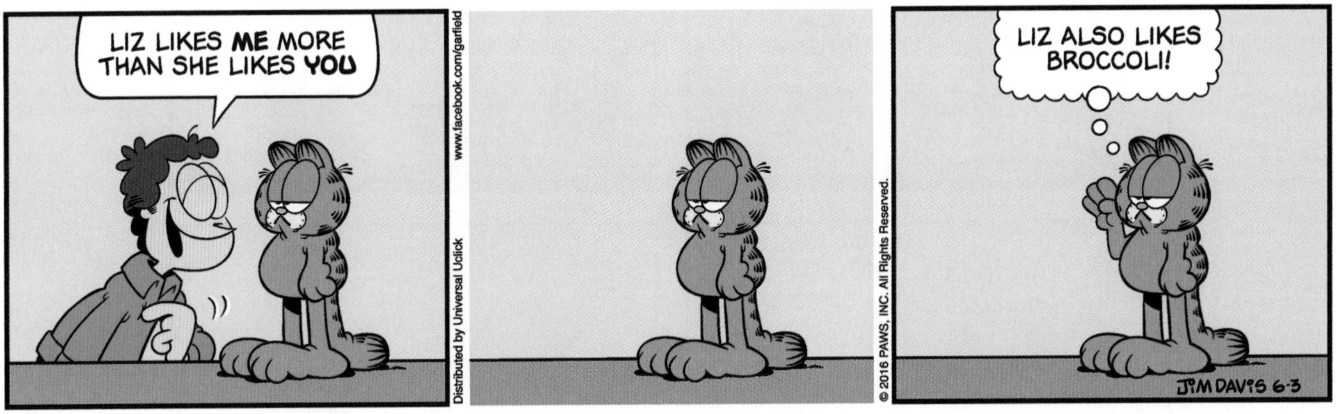
LIZ LIKES ME MORE THAN SHE LIKES YOU
www.facebook.com/garfield
Distributed by Universal Uclick
© 2016 PAWS, INC. All Rights Reserved.
LIZ ALSO LIKES BROCCOLI!
JIM DAVIS 6-3

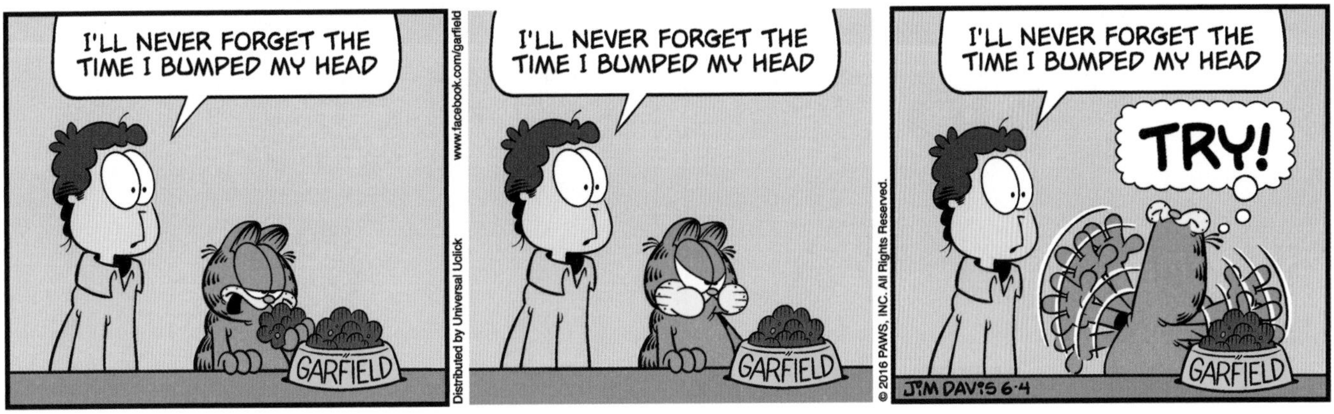
I'LL NEVER FORGET THE TIME I BUMPED MY HEAD
GARFIELD
www.facebook.com/garfield
Distributed by Universal Uclick
I'LL NEVER FORGET THE TIME I BUMPED MY HEAD
GARFIELD
© 2016 PAWS, INC. All Rights Reserved.
I'LL NEVER FORGET THE TIME I BUMPED MY HEAD
TRY!
GARFIELD
JIM DAVIS 6-4

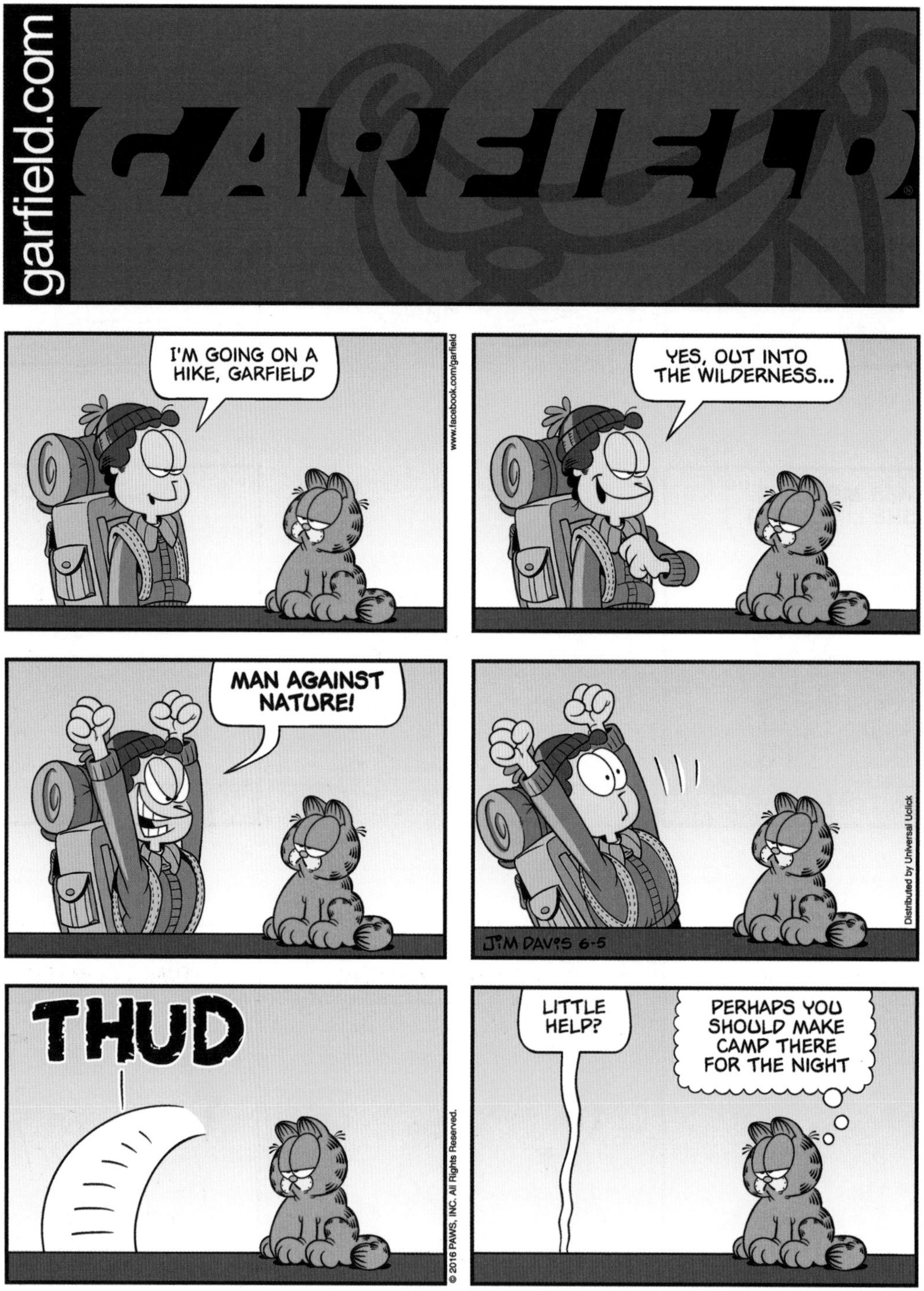
garfield.com
GARFIELD
I'M GOING ON A HIKE, GARFIELD
www.facebook.com/garfield
YES, OUT INTO THE WILDERNESS...
MAN AGAINST NATURE!
JIM DAVIS 6-5
Distributed by Universal Uclick
THUD
© 2016 PAWS, INC. All Rights Reserved.
LITTLE HELP?
PERHAPS YOU SHOULD MAKE CAMP THERE FOR THE NIGHT

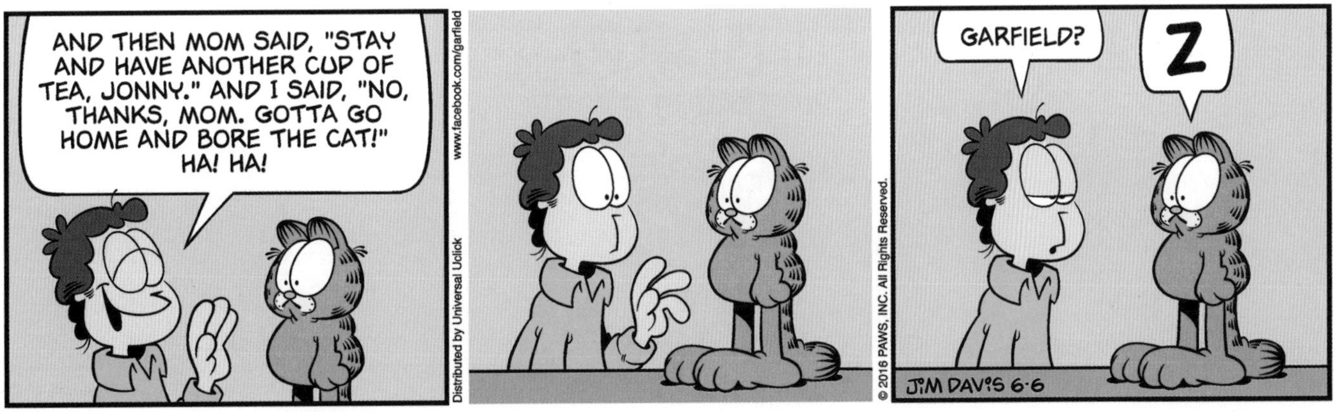
AND THEN MOM SAID, "STAY AND HAVE ANOTHER CUP OF TEA, JONNY." AND I SAID, "NO, THANKS, MOM. GOTTA GO HOME AND BORE THE CAT!" HA! HA!
GARFIELD?
Z
JIM DAVIS 6-6
www.facebook.com/garfield
Distributed by Universal Uclick
© 2016 PAWS, INC. All Rights Reserved.

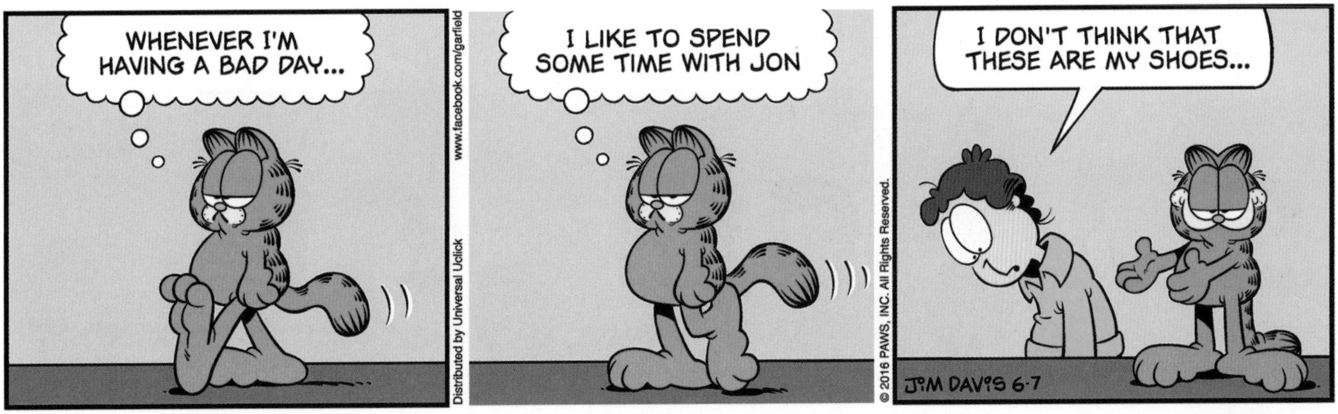
WHENEVER I'M HAVING A BAD DAY...
I LIKE TO SPEND SOME TIME WITH JON
I DON'T THINK THAT THESE ARE MY SHOES...
JIM DAVIS 6-7
www.facebook.com/garfield
Distributed by Universal Uclick
© 2016 PAWS, INC. All Rights Reserved.

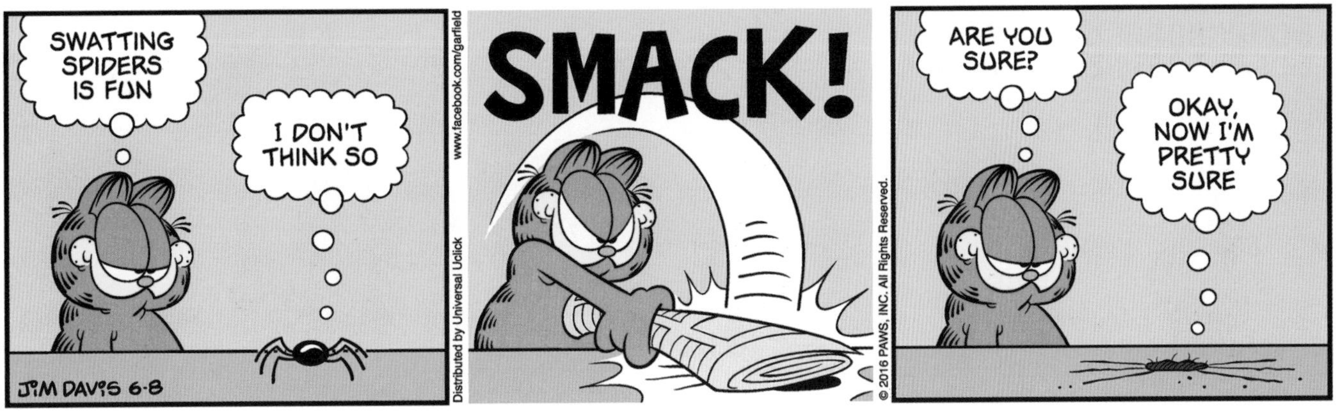
SWATTING SPIDERS IS FUN
I DON'T THINK SO
SMACK!
ARE YOU SURE?
OKAY, NOW I'M PRETTY SURE
JIM DAVIS 6-8
www.facebook.com/garfield
Distributed by Universal Uclick
© 2016 PAWS, INC. All Rights Reserved.

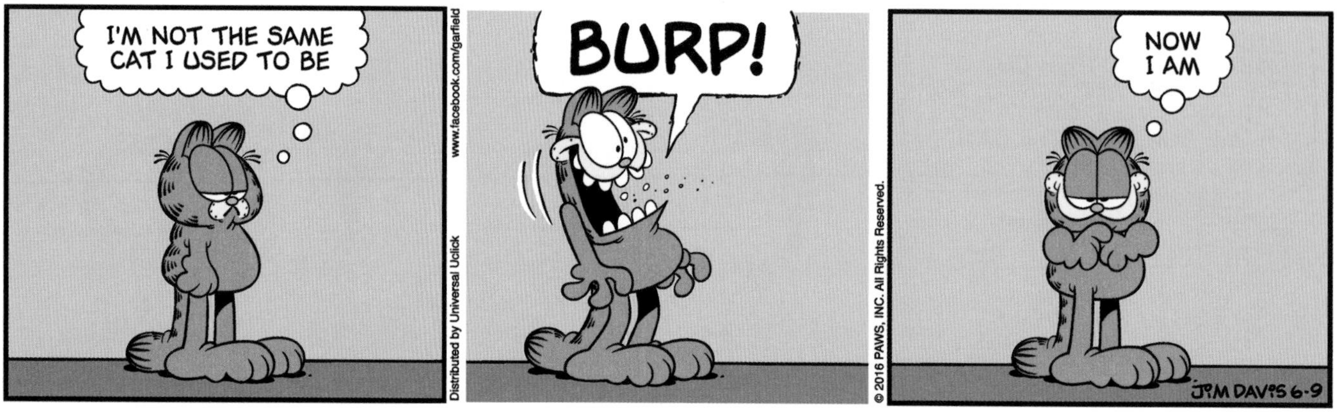
I'M NOT THE SAME CAT I USED TO BE
BURP!
NOW I AM
Distributed by Universal Uclick www.facebook.com/garfield
© 2016 PAWS, INC. All Rights Reserved.
JIM DAVIS 6-9

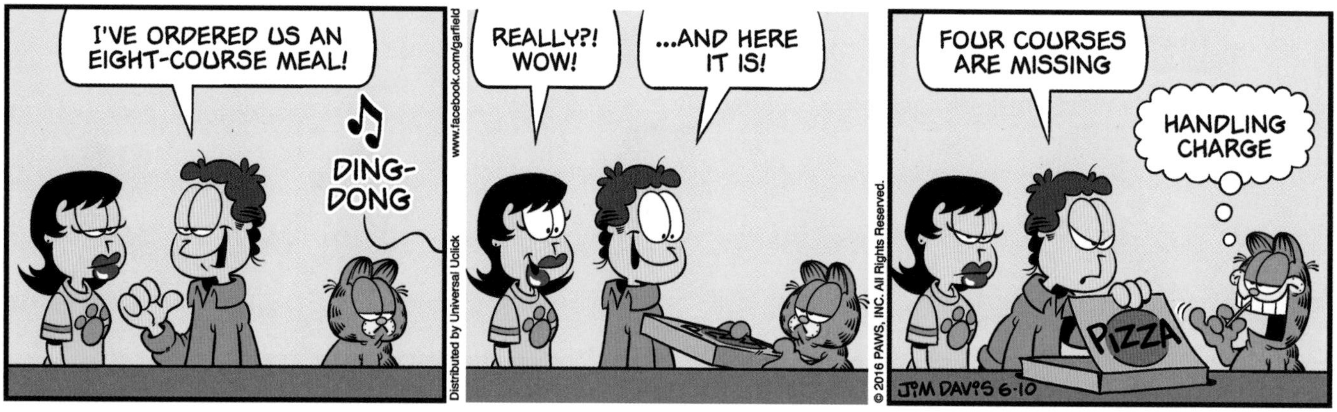
I'VE ORDERED US AN EIGHT-COURSE MEAL!
DING-DONG
REALLY?! WOW!
...AND HERE IT IS!
FOUR COURSES ARE MISSING
HANDLING CHARGE
PIZZA
Distributed by Universal Uclick www.facebook.com/garfield
© 2016 PAWS, INC. All Rights Reserved.
JIM DAVIS 6-10

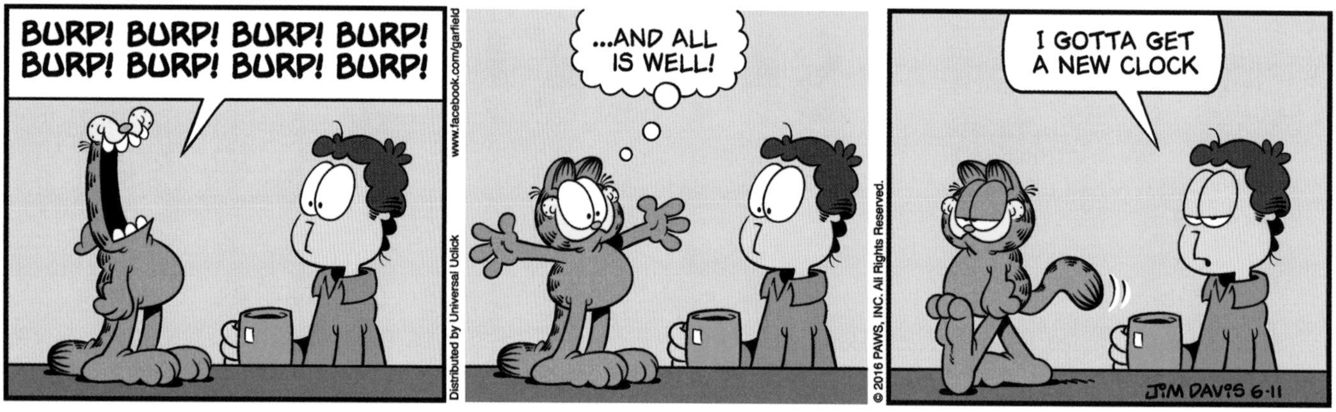
BURP! BURP! BURP! BURP! BURP! BURP! BURP! BURP!
...AND ALL IS WELL!
I GOTTA GET A NEW CLOCK
Distributed by Universal Uclick www.facebook.com/garfield
© 2016 PAWS, INC. All Rights Reserved.
JIM DAVIS 6-11

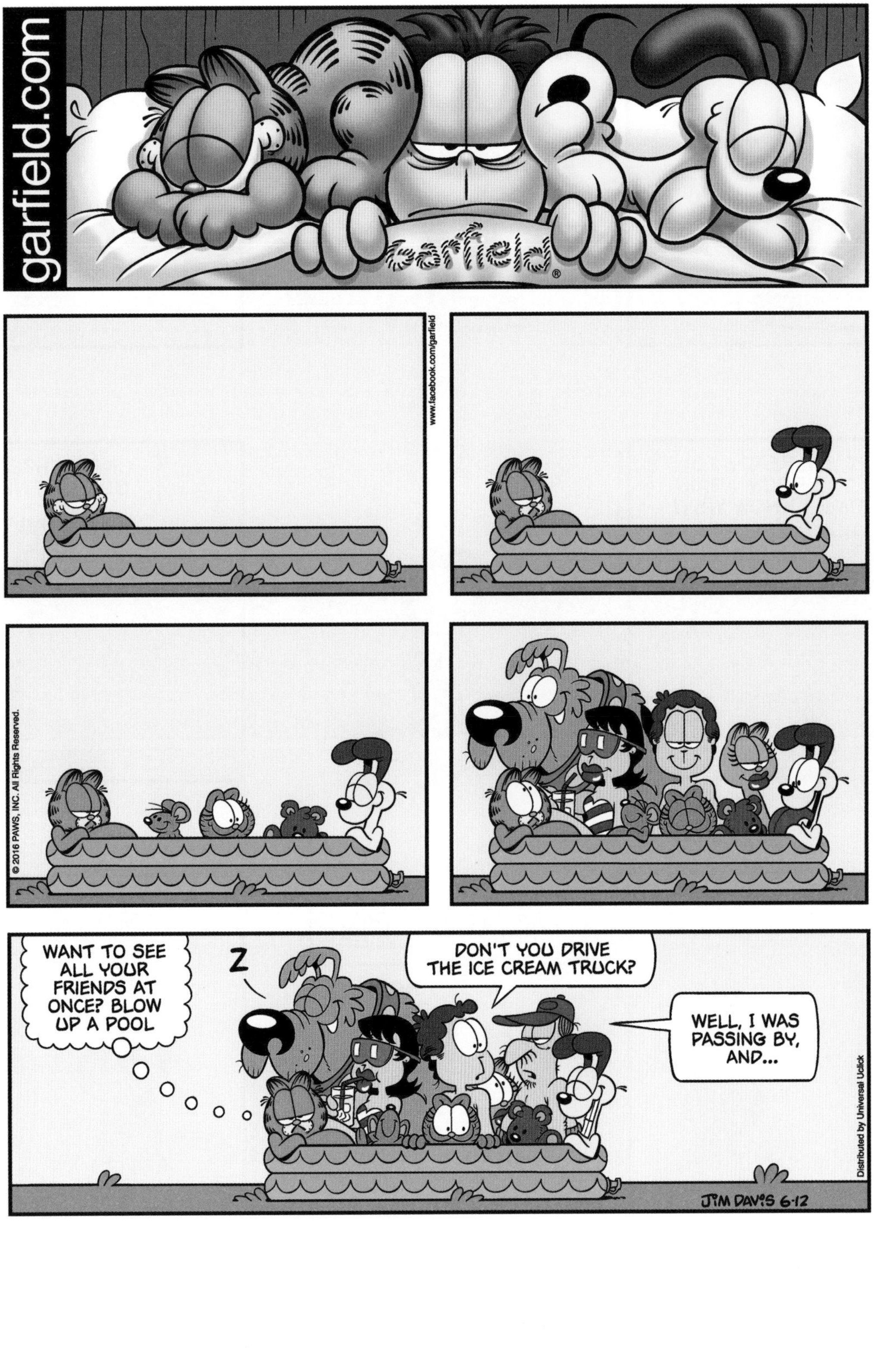
garfield.com
garfield®
www.facebook.com/garfield
© 2016 PAWS, INC. All Rights Reserved.
WANT TO SEE ALL YOUR FRIENDS AT ONCE? BLOW UP A POOL
Z
DON'T YOU DRIVE THE ICE CREAM TRUCK?
WELL, I WAS PASSING BY, AND...
Distributed by Universal Uclick
JIM DAVIS 6-12

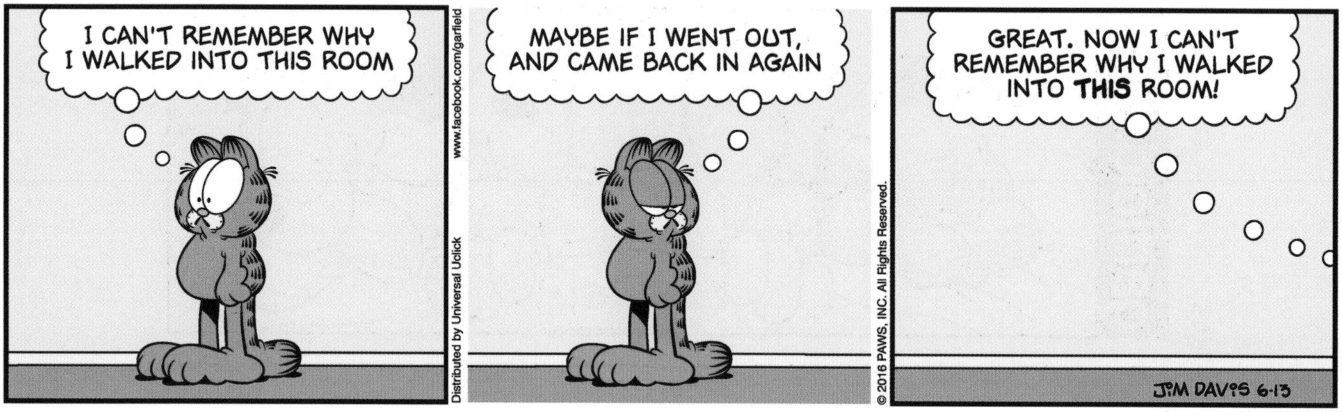
I CAN'T REMEMBER WHY I WALKED INTO THIS ROOM
Distributed by Universal Uclick www.facebook.com/garfield
MAYBE IF I WENT OUT, AND CAME BACK IN AGAIN
© 2016 PAWS, INC. All Rights Reserved.
GREAT. NOW I CAN'T REMEMBER WHY I WALKED INTO **THIS** ROOM!
JIM DAVIS 6-13

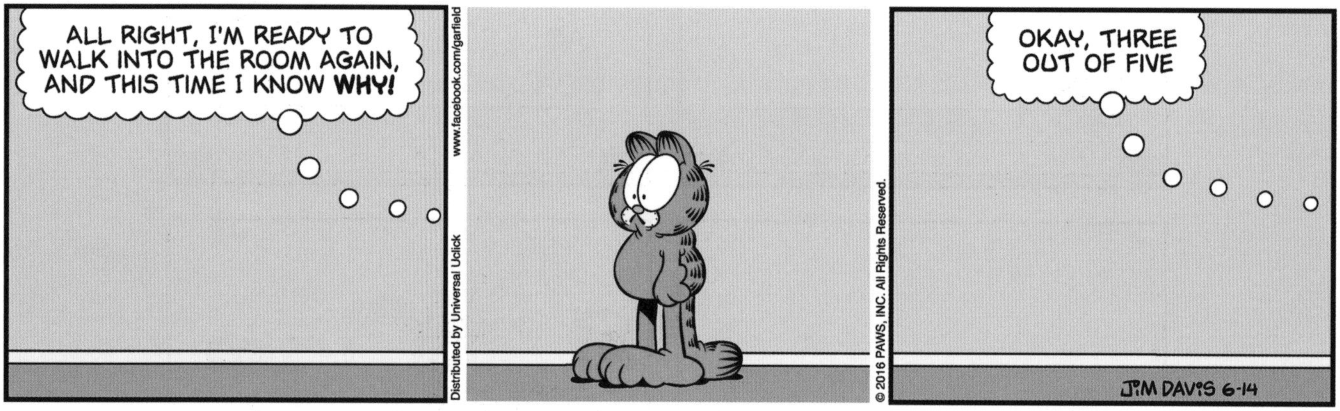
ALL RIGHT, I'M READY TO WALK INTO THE ROOM AGAIN, AND THIS TIME I KNOW **WHY!**
Distributed by Universal Uclick www.facebook.com/garfield
© 2016 PAWS, INC. All Rights Reserved.
OKAY, THREE OUT OF FIVE
JIM DAVIS 6-14

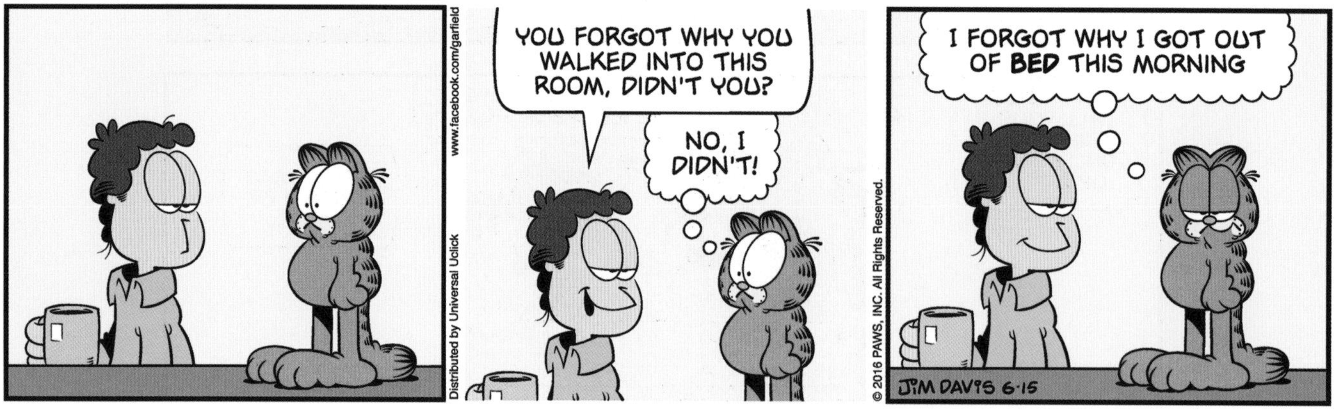
Distributed by Universal Uclick www.facebook.com/garfield
YOU FORGOT WHY YOU WALKED INTO THIS ROOM, DIDN'T YOU?
NO, I DIDN'T!
© 2016 PAWS, INC. All Rights Reserved.
I FORGOT WHY I GOT OUT OF **BED** THIS MORNING
JIM DAVIS 6-15

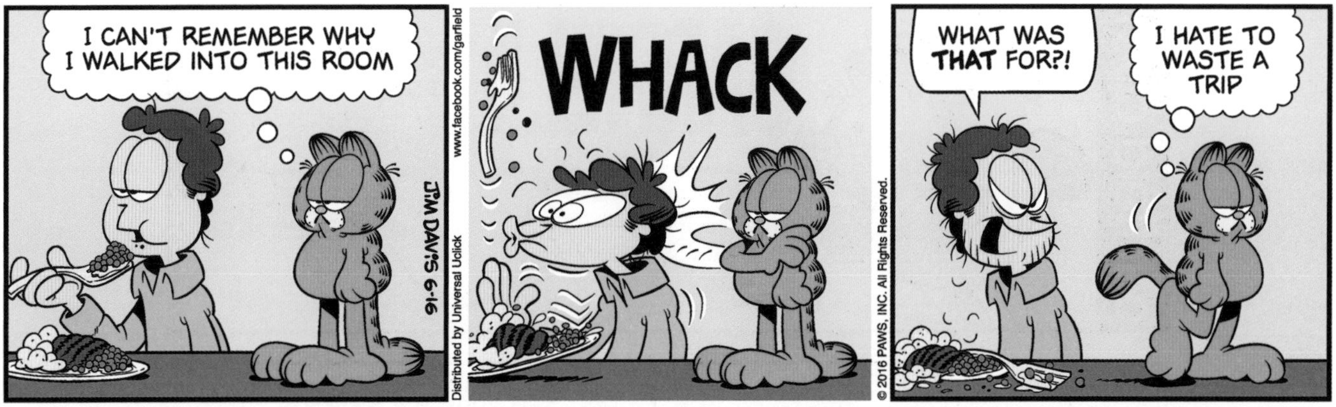
I CAN'T REMEMBER WHY I WALKED INTO THIS ROOM
JIM DAVIS 6-16
www.facebook.com/garfield
Distributed by Universal Uclick
WHACK
© 2016 PAWS, INC. All Rights Reserved.
WHAT WAS THAT FOR?!
I HATE TO WASTE A TRIP

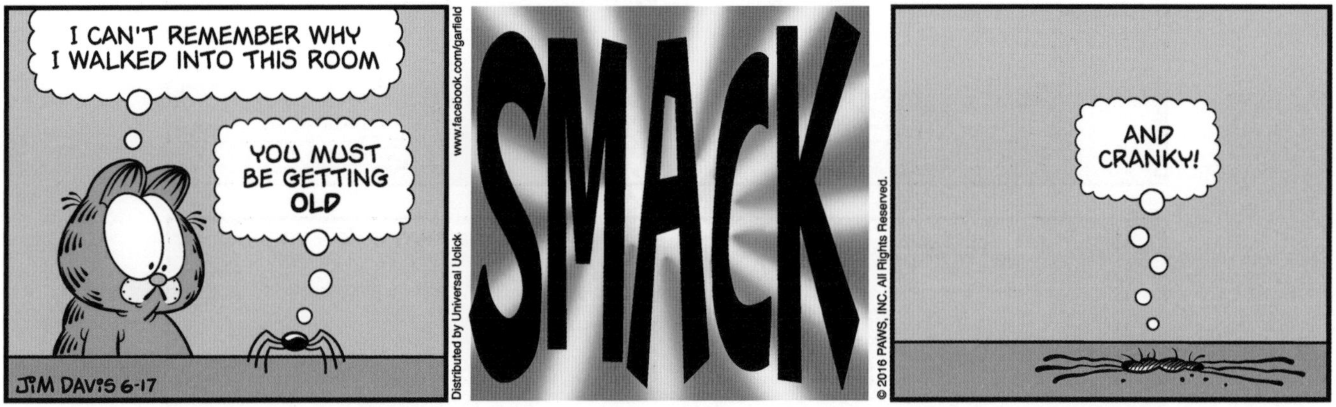
I CAN'T REMEMBER WHY I WALKED INTO THIS ROOM
YOU MUST BE GETTING OLD
JIM DAVIS 6-17
www.facebook.com/garfield
Distributed by Universal Uclick
SMACK
© 2016 PAWS, INC. All Rights Reserved.
AND CRANKY!

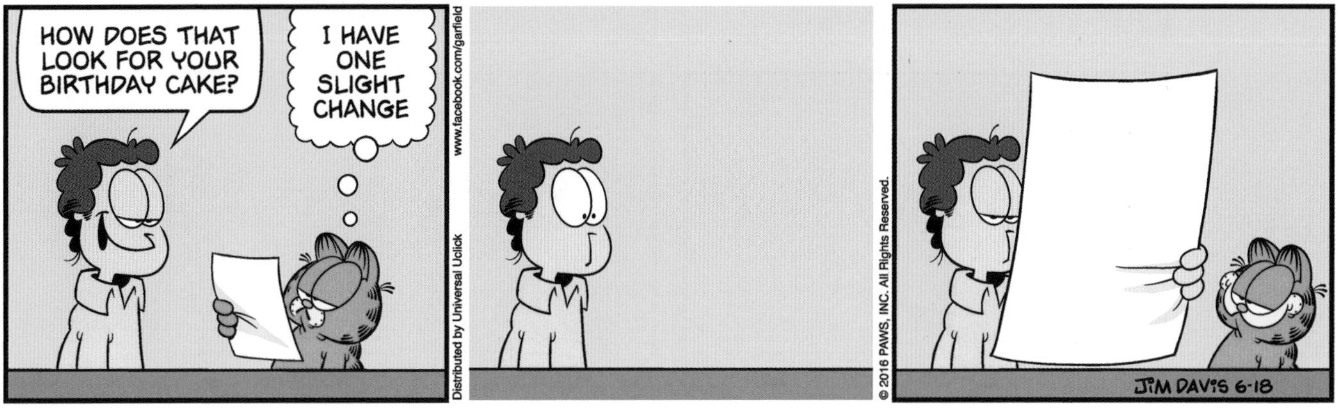
HOW DOES THAT LOOK FOR YOUR BIRTHDAY CAKE?
I HAVE ONE SLIGHT CHANGE
www.facebook.com/garfield
Distributed by Universal Uclick
© 2016 PAWS, INC. All Rights Reserved.
JIM DAVIS 6-18

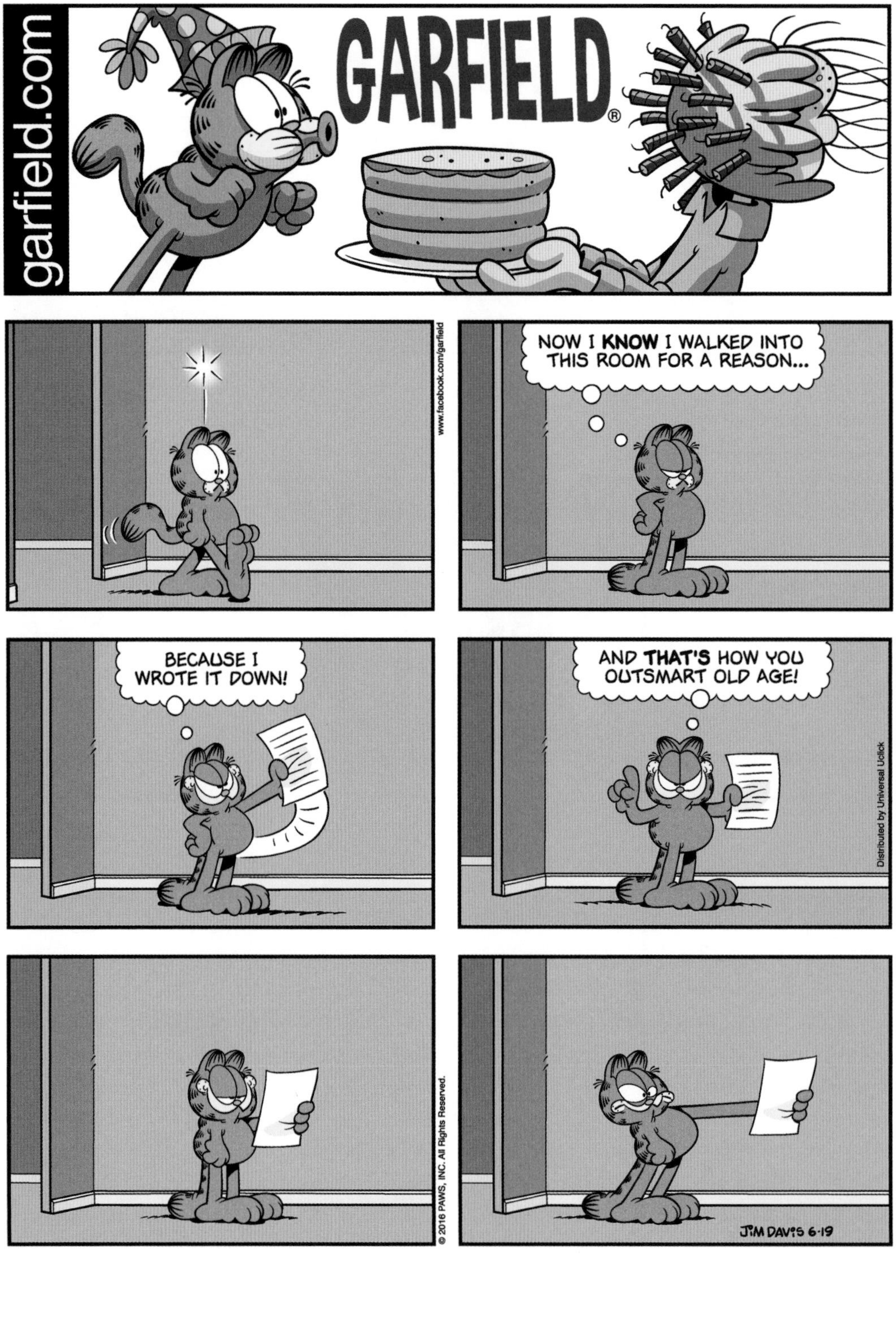
garfield.com
GARFIELD®
www.facebook.com/garfield
NOW I KNOW I WALKED INTO THIS ROOM FOR A REASON...
BECAUSE I WROTE IT DOWN!
AND THAT'S HOW YOU OUTSMART OLD AGE!
Distributed by Universal Uclick
© 2016 PAWS, INC. All Rights Reserved.
JIM DAVIS 6-19

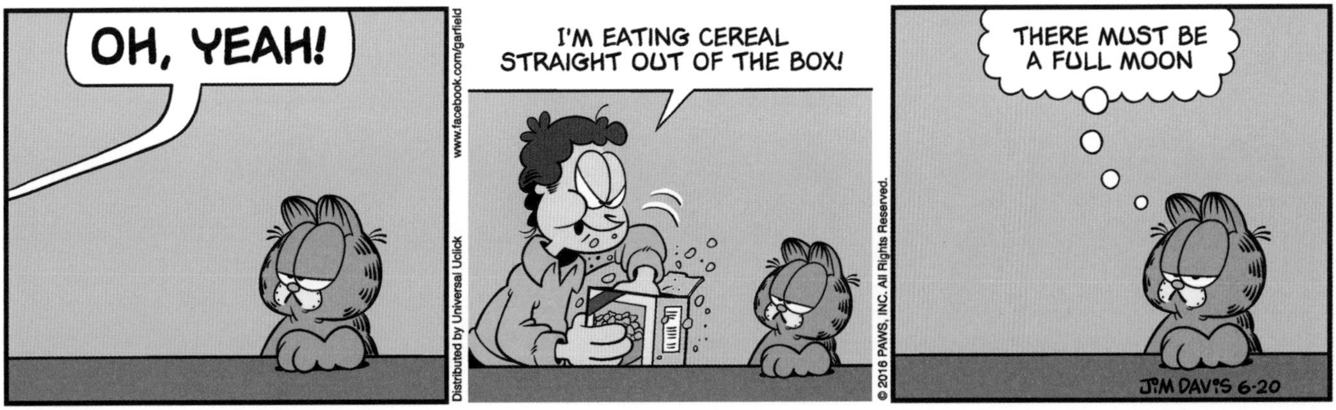
OH, YEAH!
Distributed by Universal Uclick
www.facebook.com/garfield
I'M EATING CEREAL STRAIGHT OUT OF THE BOX!
© 2016 PAWS, INC. All Rights Reserved.
THERE MUST BE A FULL MOON
JIM DAVIS 6-20

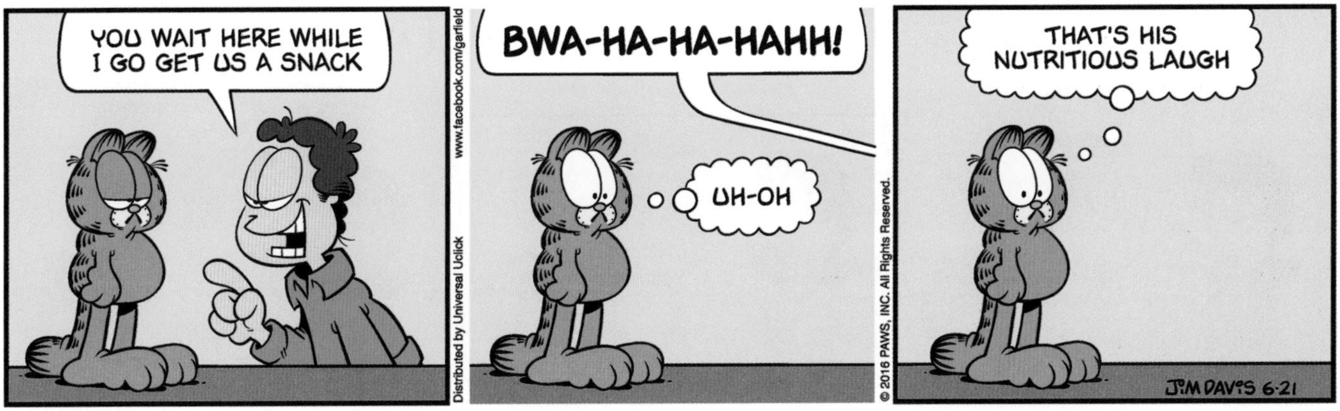
YOU WAIT HERE WHILE I GO GET US A SNACK
Distributed by Universal Uclick
www.facebook.com/garfield
BWA-HA-HA-HAHH!
UH-OH
© 2016 PAWS, INC. All Rights Reserved.
THAT'S HIS NUTRITIOUS LAUGH
JIM DAVIS 6-21

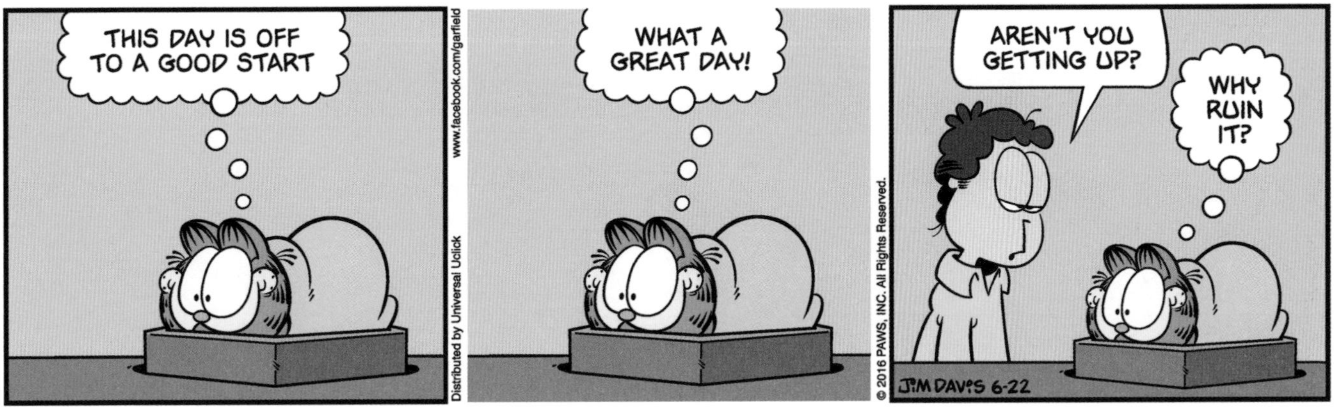
THIS DAY IS OFF TO A GOOD START
Distributed by Universal Uclick
www.facebook.com/garfield
WHAT A GREAT DAY!
© 2016 PAWS, INC. All Rights Reserved.
AREN'T YOU GETTING UP?
WHY RUIN IT?
JIM DAVIS 6-22

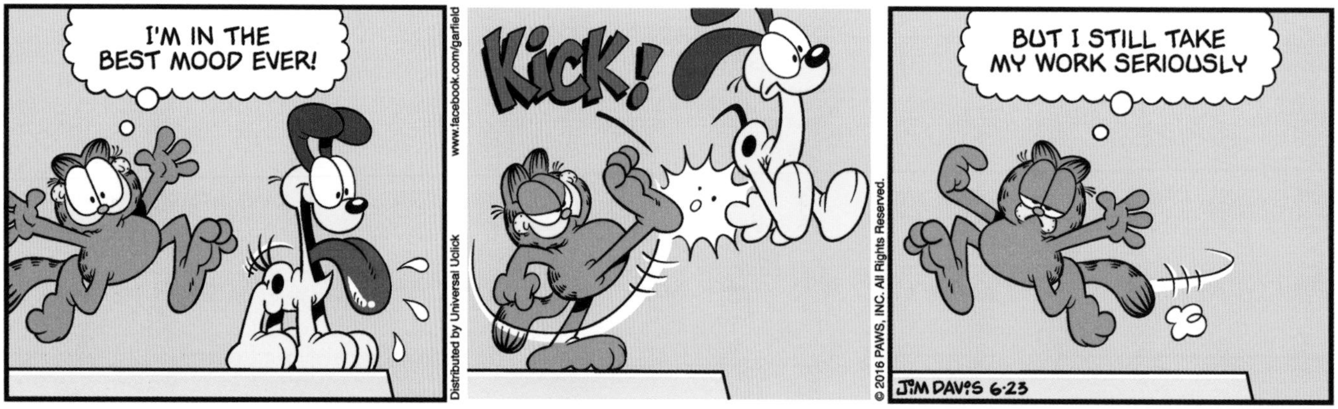
I'M IN THE BEST MOOD EVER!
KICK!
BUT I STILL TAKE MY WORK SERIOUSLY
JIM DAVIS 6-23
www.facebook.com/garfield
Distributed by Universal Uclick
© 2016 PAWS, INC. All Rights Reserved.

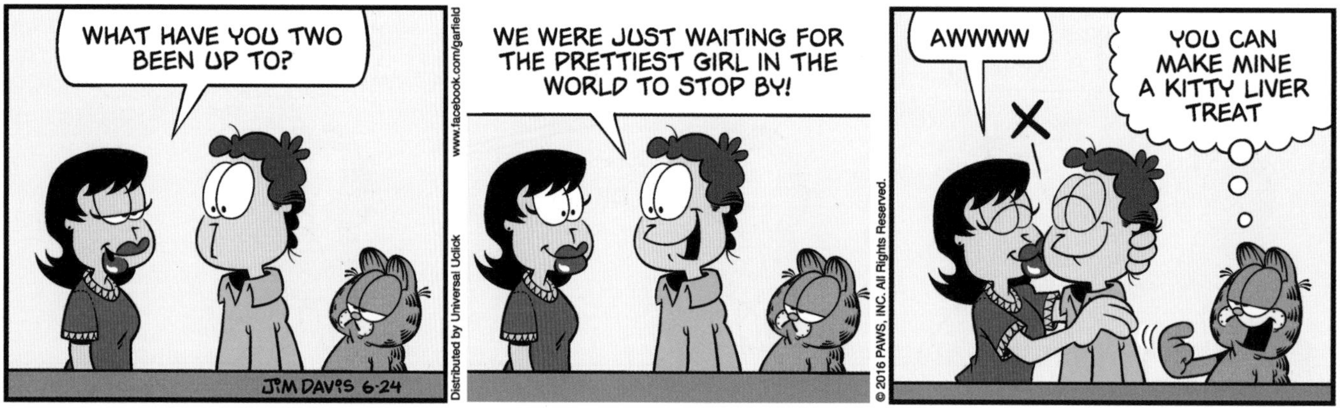
WHAT HAVE YOU TWO BEEN UP TO?
JIM DAVIS 6-24
WE WERE JUST WAITING FOR THE PRETTIEST GIRL IN THE WORLD TO STOP BY!
AWWWW
YOU CAN MAKE MINE A KITTY LIVER TREAT
www.facebook.com/garfield
Distributed by Universal Uclick
© 2016 PAWS, INC. All Rights Reserved.

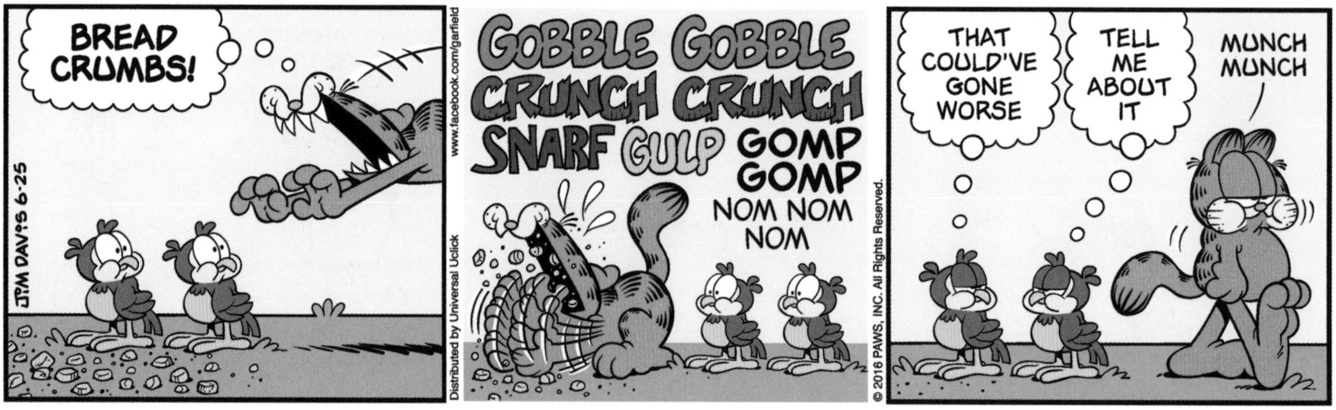
BREAD CRUMBS!
JIM DAVIS 6-25
GOBBLE GOBBLE
CRUNCH CRUNCH
SNARF GULP GOMP GOMP
NOM NOM NOM
THAT COULD'VE GONE WORSE
TELL ME ABOUT IT
MUNCH MUNCH
www.facebook.com/garfield
Distributed by Universal Uclick
© 2016 PAWS, INC. All Rights Reserved.

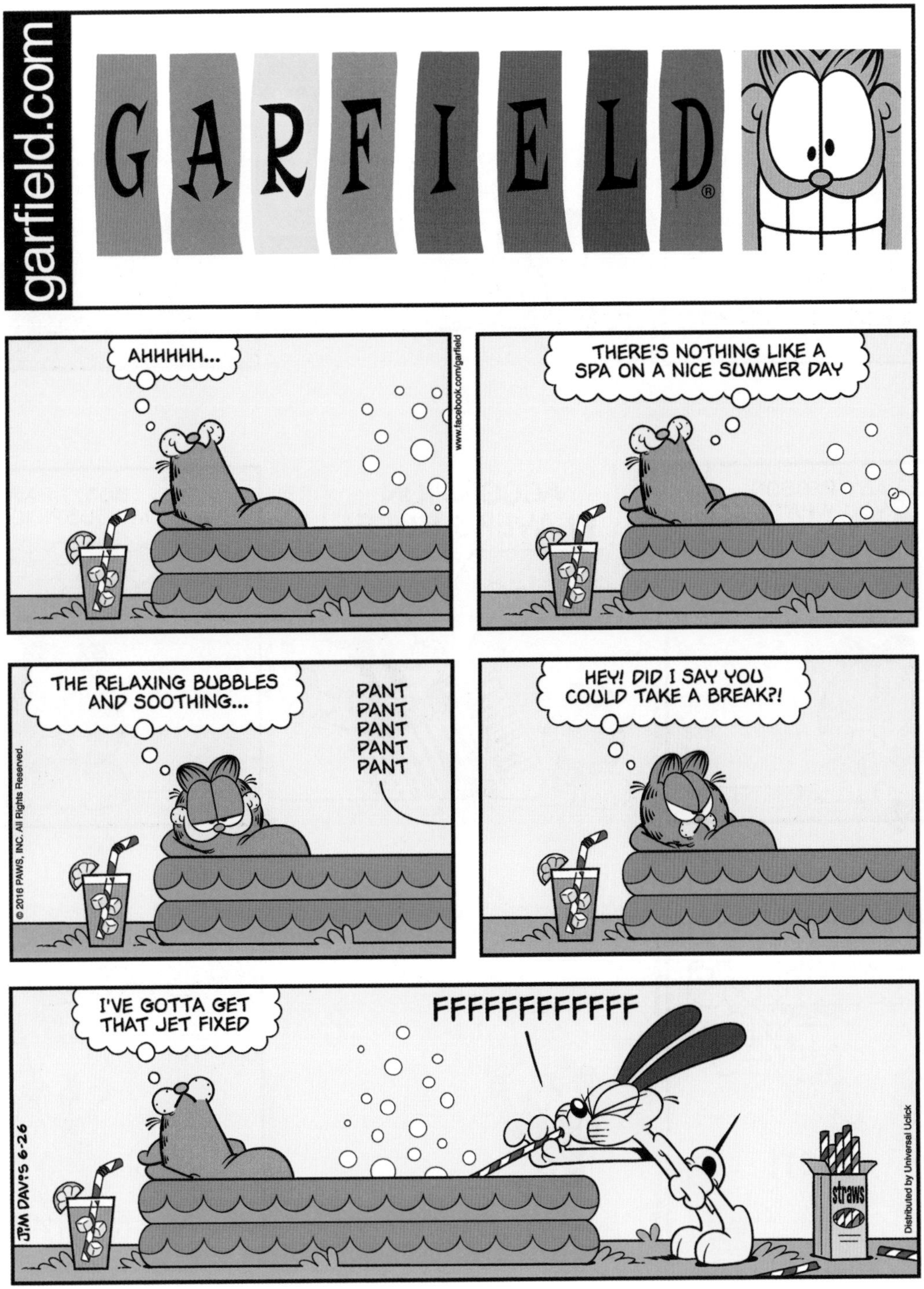
garfield.com
GARFIELD®
AHHHHH...
www.facebook.com/garfield
THERE'S NOTHING LIKE A SPA ON A NICE SUMMER DAY
© 2016 PAWS, INC. All Rights Reserved.
THE RELAXING BUBBLES AND SOOTHING...
PANT PANT PANT PANT PANT
HEY! DID I SAY YOU COULD TAKE A BREAK?!
JPM DAVIS 6-26
I'VE GOTTA GET THAT JET FIXED
FFFFFFFFFFFF
straws
Distributed by Universal Uclick

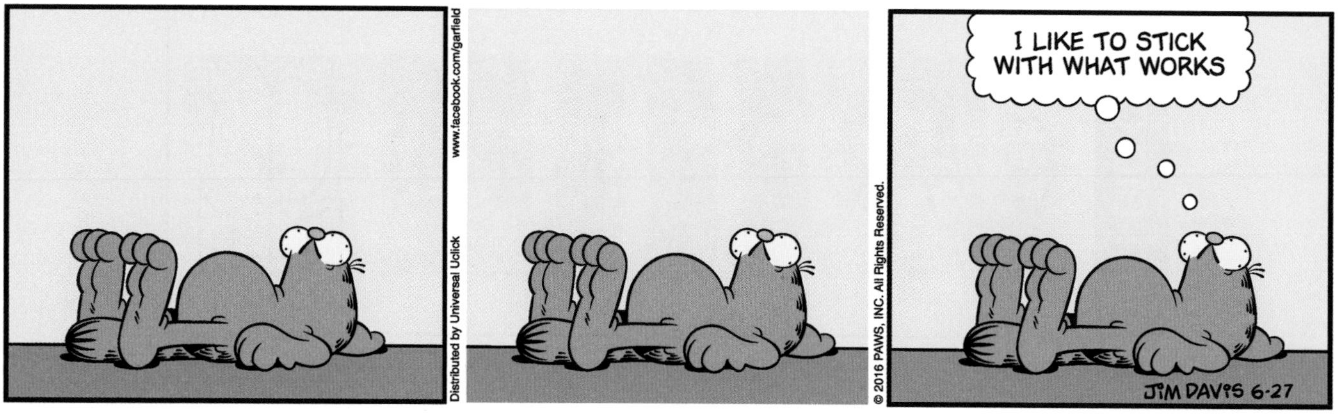
Distributed by Universal Uclick www.facebook.com/garfield
© 2016 PAWS, INC. All Rights Reserved.
I LIKE TO STICK WITH WHAT WORKS
JIM DAVIS 6-27

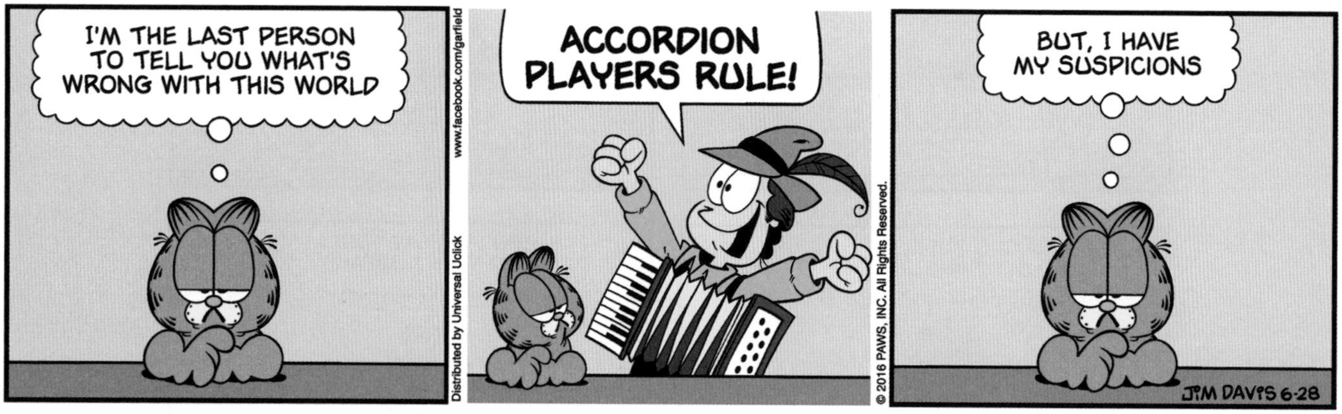
I'M THE LAST PERSON TO TELL YOU WHAT'S WRONG WITH THIS WORLD
Distributed by Universal Uclick www.facebook.com/garfield
ACCORDION PLAYERS RULE!
© 2016 PAWS, INC. All Rights Reserved.
BUT, I HAVE MY SUSPICIONS
JIM DAVIS 6-28

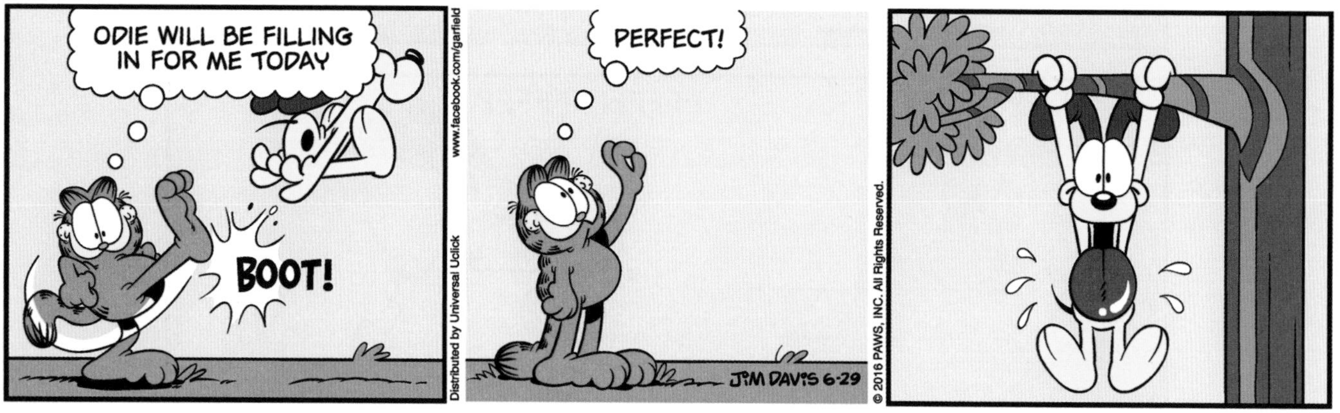
ODIE WILL BE FILLING IN FOR ME TODAY
BOOT!
Distributed by Universal Uclick www.facebook.com/garfield
PERFECT!
JIM DAVIS 6-29
© 2016 PAWS, INC. All Rights Reserved.

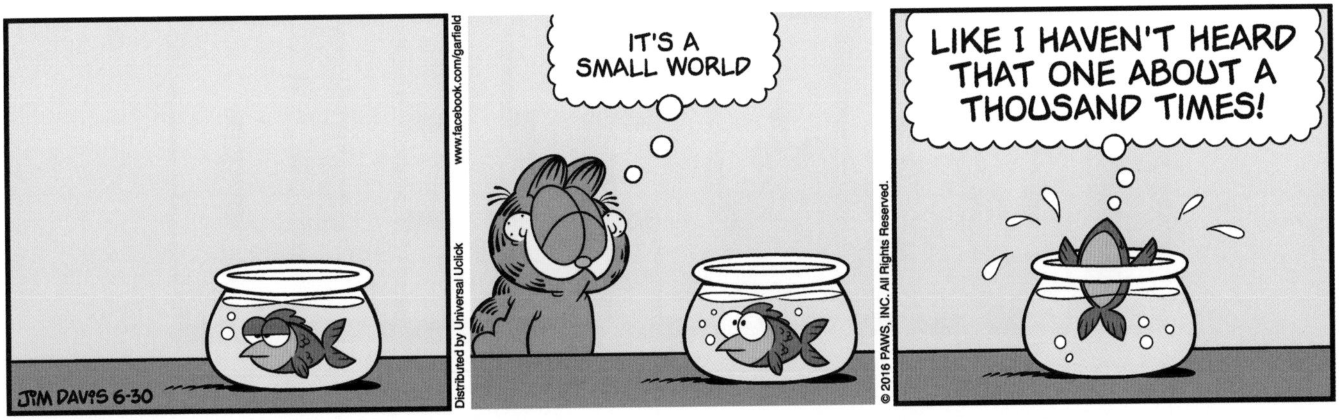
JIM DAVIS 6-30
www.facebook.com/garfield
Distributed by Universal Uclick
IT'S A SMALL WORLD
© 2016 PAWS, INC. All Rights Reserved.
LIKE I HAVEN'T HEARD THAT ONE ABOUT A THOUSAND TIMES!

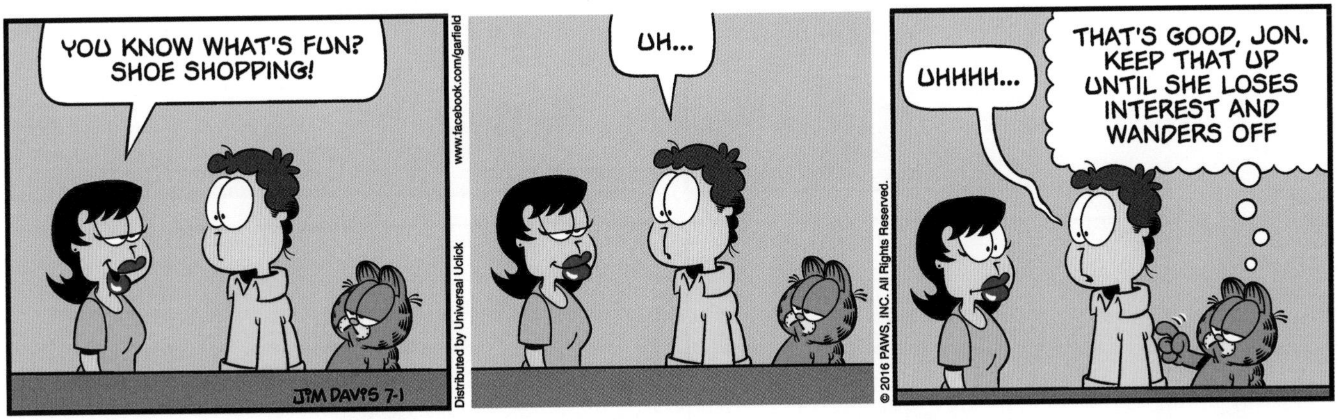
YOU KNOW WHAT'S FUN? SHOE SHOPPING!
JIM DAVIS 7-1
www.facebook.com/garfield
Distributed by Universal Uclick
UH...
© 2016 PAWS, INC. All Rights Reserved.
UHHHH...
THAT'S GOOD, JON. KEEP THAT UP UNTIL SHE LOSES INTEREST AND WANDERS OFF

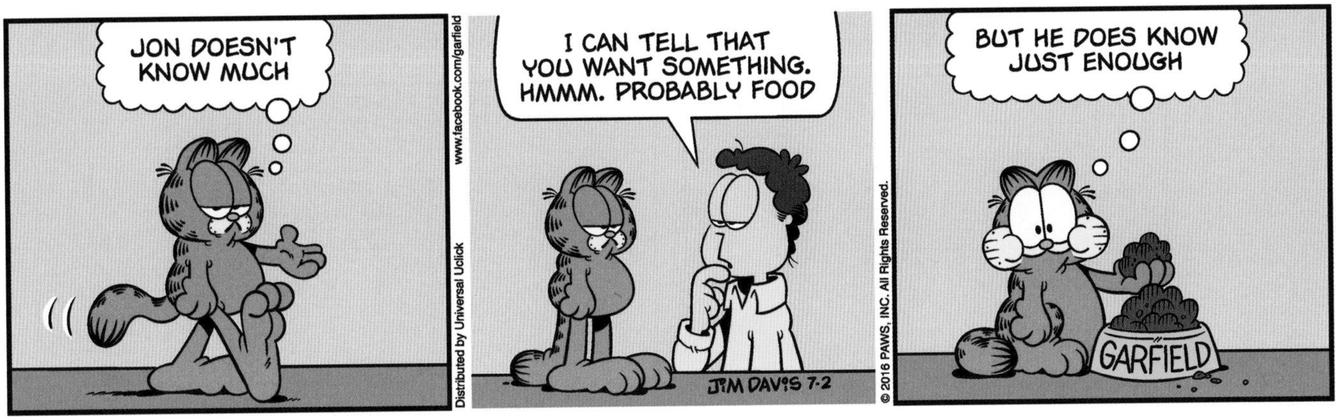
JON DOESN'T KNOW MUCH
www.facebook.com/garfield
Distributed by Universal Uclick
I CAN TELL THAT YOU WANT SOMETHING. HMMM. PROBABLY FOOD
JIM DAVIS 7-2
© 2016 PAWS, INC. All Rights Reserved.
BUT HE DOES KNOW JUST ENOUGH
GARFIELD

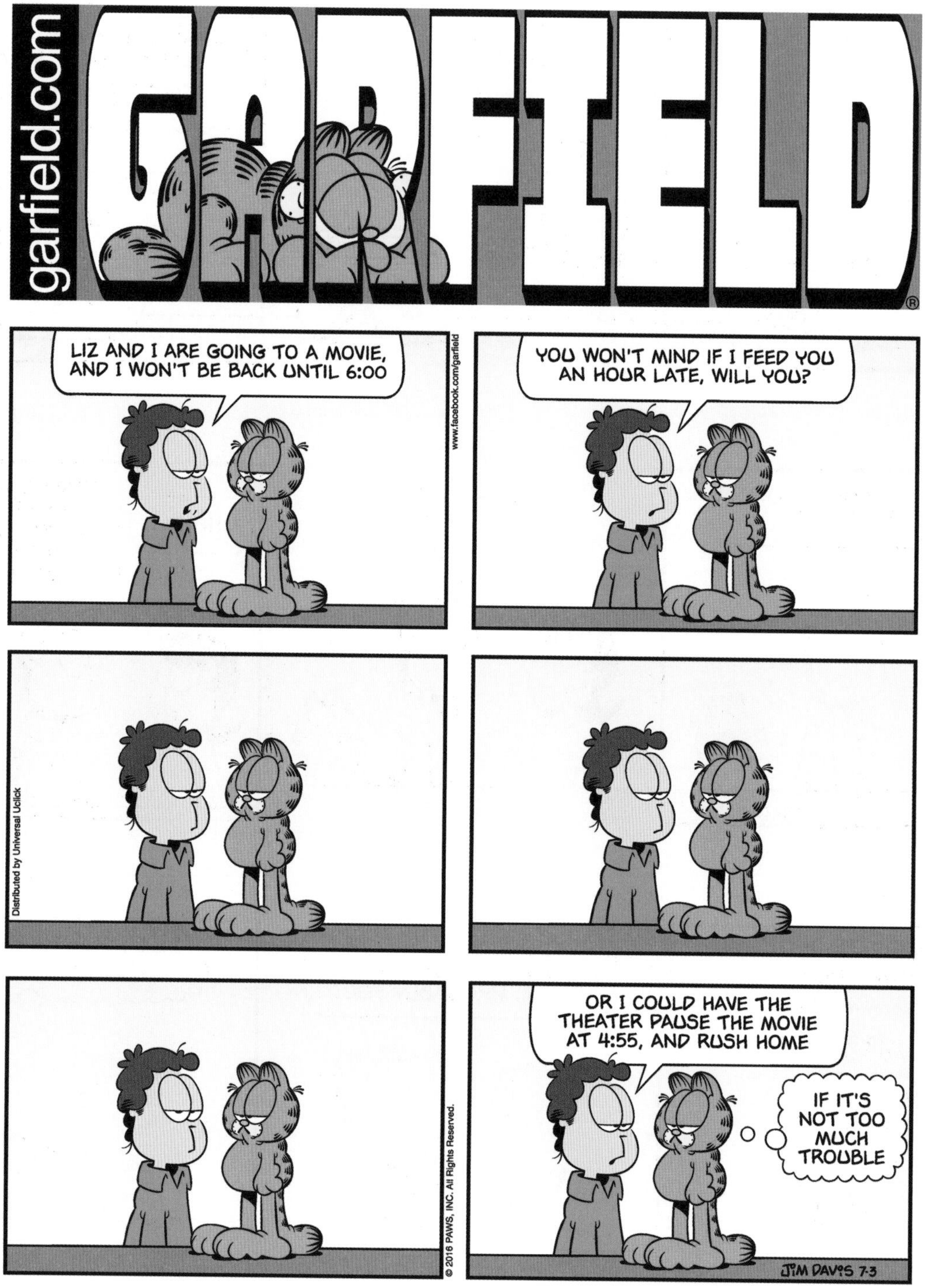
garfield.com
GARFIELD
LIZ AND I ARE GOING TO A MOVIE, AND I WON'T BE BACK UNTIL 6:00
www.facebook.com/garfield
YOU WON'T MIND IF I FEED YOU AN HOUR LATE, WILL YOU?
Distributed by Universal Uclick
© 2016 PAWS, INC. All Rights Reserved.
OR I COULD HAVE THE THEATER PAUSE THE MOVIE AT 4:55, AND RUSH HOME
IF IT'S NOT TOO MUCH TROUBLE
JIM DAVIS 7-3

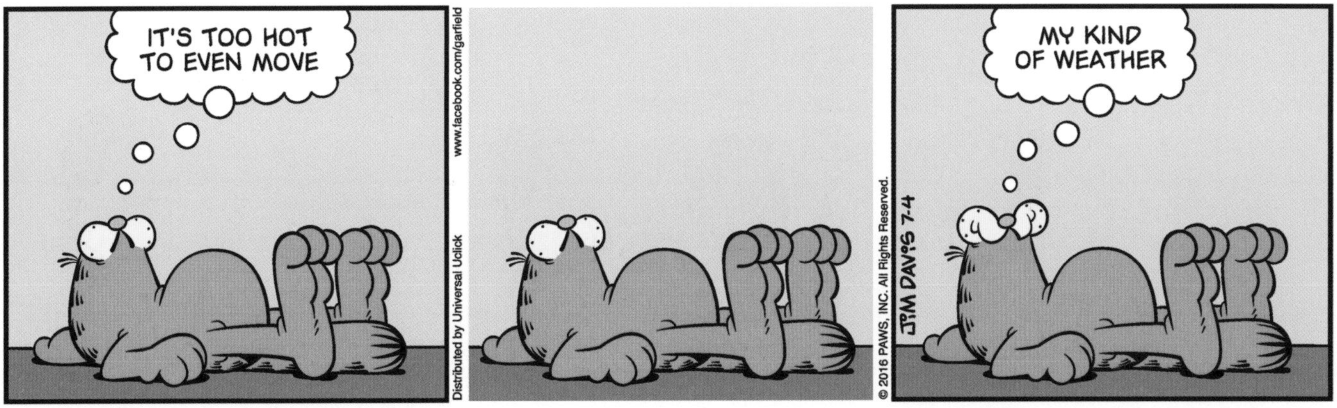
IT'S TOO HOT TO EVEN MOVE
Distributed by Universal Uclick
www.facebook.com/garfield
© 2016 PAWS, INC. All Rights Reserved.
JIM DAVIS 7-4
MY KIND OF WEATHER

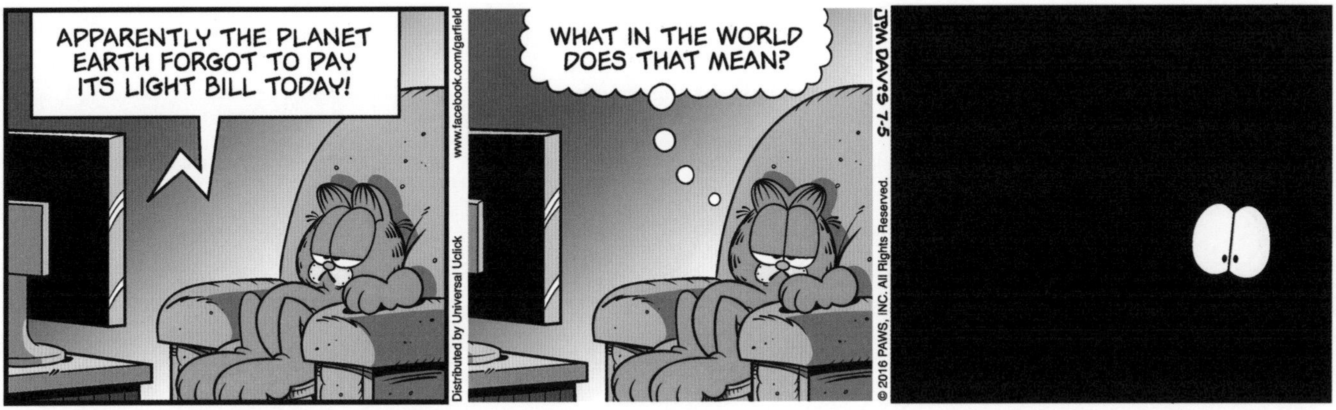
APPARENTLY THE PLANET EARTH FORGOT TO PAY ITS LIGHT BILL TODAY!
Distributed by Universal Uclick
www.facebook.com/garfield
WHAT IN THE WORLD DOES THAT MEAN?
© 2016 PAWS, INC. All Rights Reserved.
JIM DAVIS 7-5

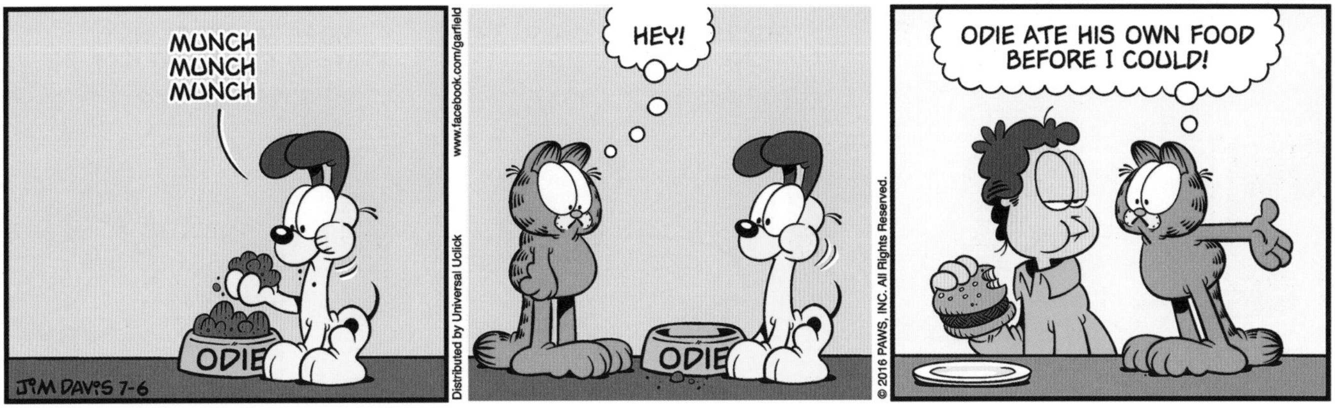
MUNCH MUNCH MUNCH
ODIE
JIM DAVIS 7-6
Distributed by Universal Uclick
www.facebook.com/garfield
HEY!
ODIE
© 2016 PAWS, INC. All Rights Reserved.
ODIE ATE HIS OWN FOOD BEFORE I COULD!

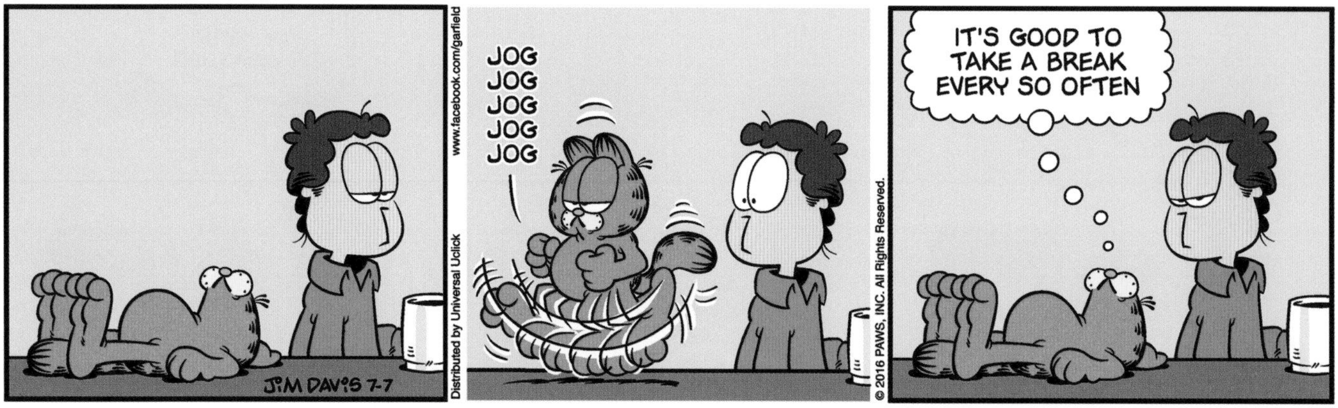
JIM DAVIS 7-7
Distributed by Universal Uclick
www.facebook.com/garfield
JOG
JOG
JOG
JOG
JOG
© 2016 PAWS, INC. All Rights Reserved.
IT'S GOOD TO TAKE A BREAK EVERY SO OFTEN

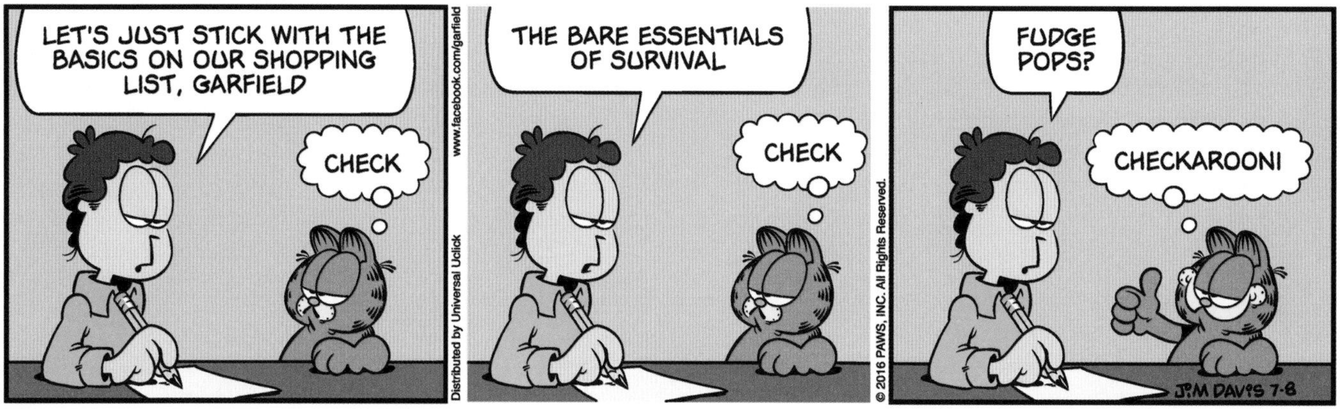
LET'S JUST STICK WITH THE BASICS ON OUR SHOPPING LIST, GARFIELD
CHECK
Distributed by Universal Uclick
www.facebook.com/garfield
THE BARE ESSENTIALS OF SURVIVAL
CHECK
© 2016 PAWS, INC. All Rights Reserved.
FUDGE POPS?
CHECKAROONI
JIM DAVIS 7-8

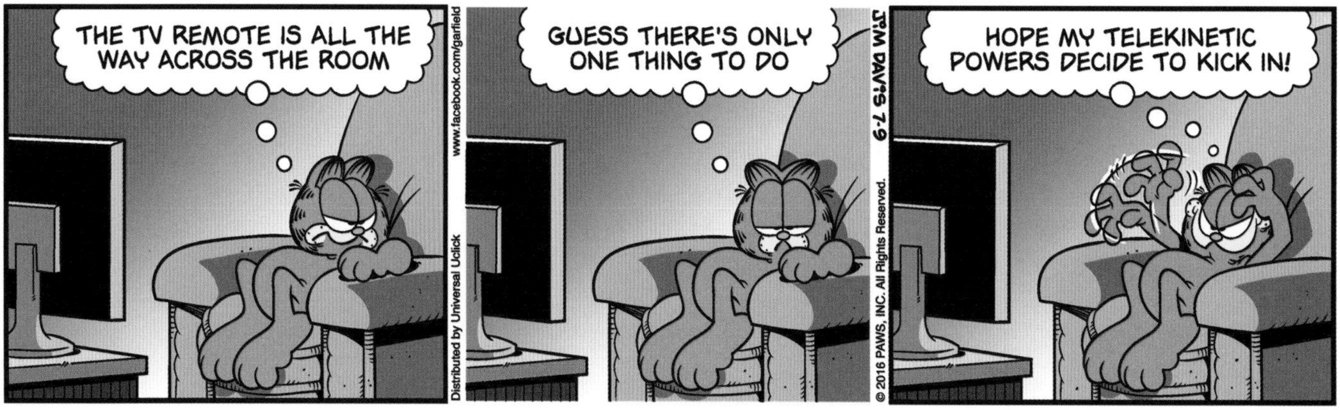
THE TV REMOTE IS ALL THE WAY ACROSS THE ROOM
Distributed by Universal Uclick
www.facebook.com/garfield
GUESS THERE'S ONLY ONE THING TO DO
JIM DAVIS 7-9
© 2016 PAWS, INC. All Rights Reserved.
HOPE MY TELEKINETIC POWERS DECIDE TO KICK IN!

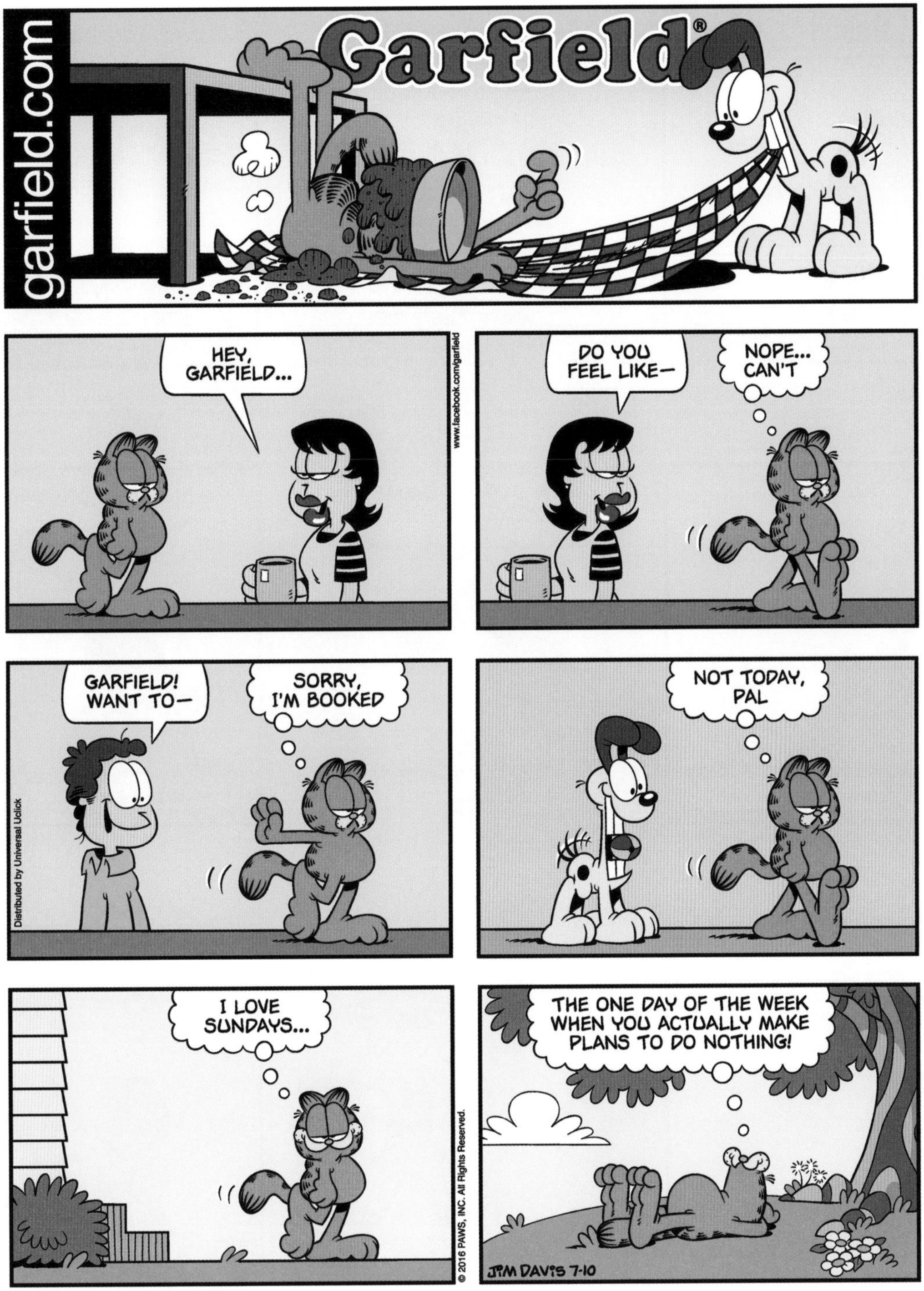
garfield.com
Garfield
HEY, GARFIELD...
www.facebook.com/garfield
DO YOU FEEL LIKE—
NOPE... CAN'T
GARFIELD! WANT TO—
SORRY, I'M BOOKED
Distributed by Universal Uclick
NOT TODAY, PAL
I LOVE SUNDAYS...
© 2016 PAWS, INC. All Rights Reserved.
THE ONE DAY OF THE WEEK WHEN YOU ACTUALLY MAKE PLANS TO DO NOTHING!
JIM DAVIS 7-10

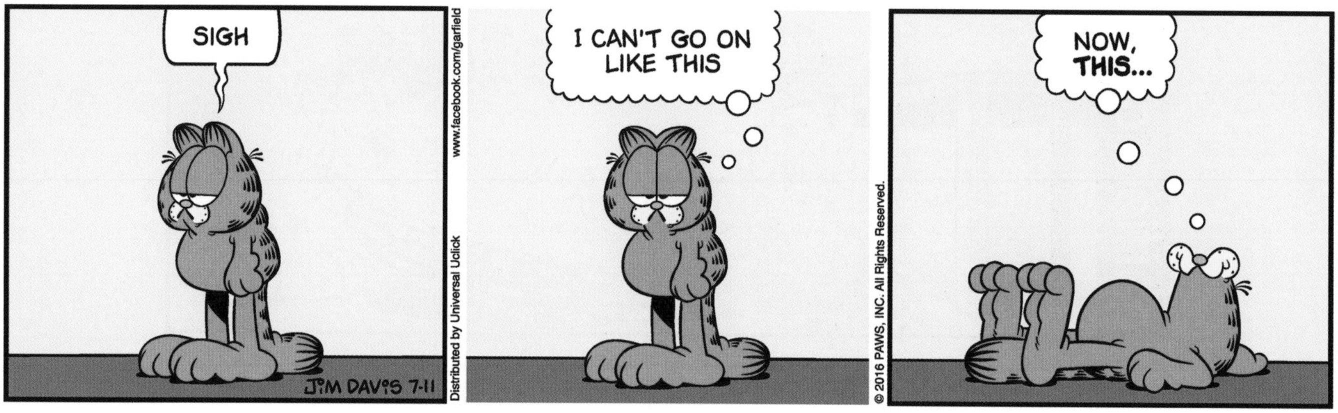
SIGH
JIM DAVIS 7-11
Distributed by Universal Uclick www.facebook.com/garfield
I CAN'T GO ON LIKE THIS
© 2016 PAWS, INC. All Rights Reserved.
NOW, THIS...

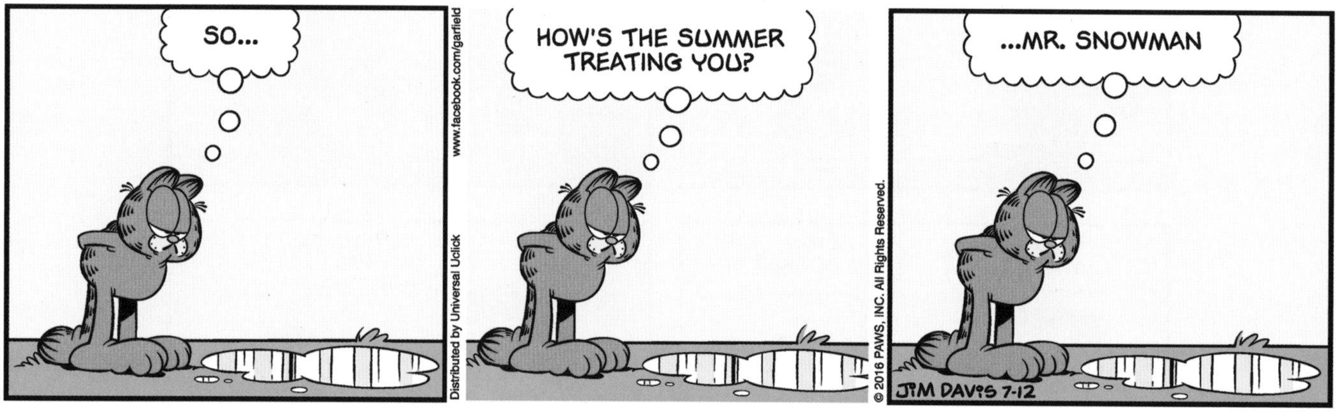
SO...
Distributed by Universal Uclick www.facebook.com/garfield
HOW'S THE SUMMER TREATING YOU?
© 2016 PAWS, INC. All Rights Reserved.
...MR. SNOWMAN
JIM DAVIS 7-12

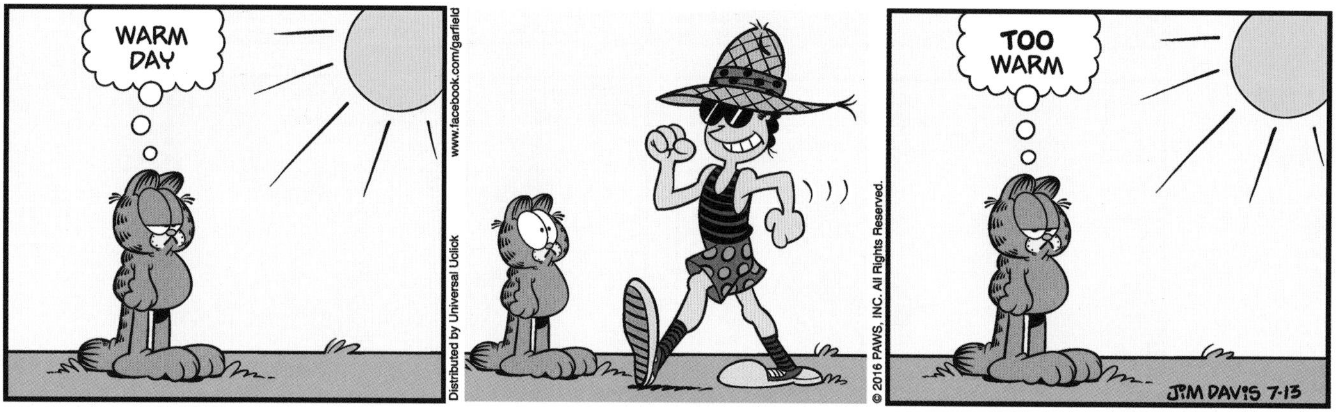
WARM DAY
Distributed by Universal Uclick www.facebook.com/garfield
© 2016 PAWS, INC. All Rights Reserved.
TOO WARM
JIM DAVIS 7-13

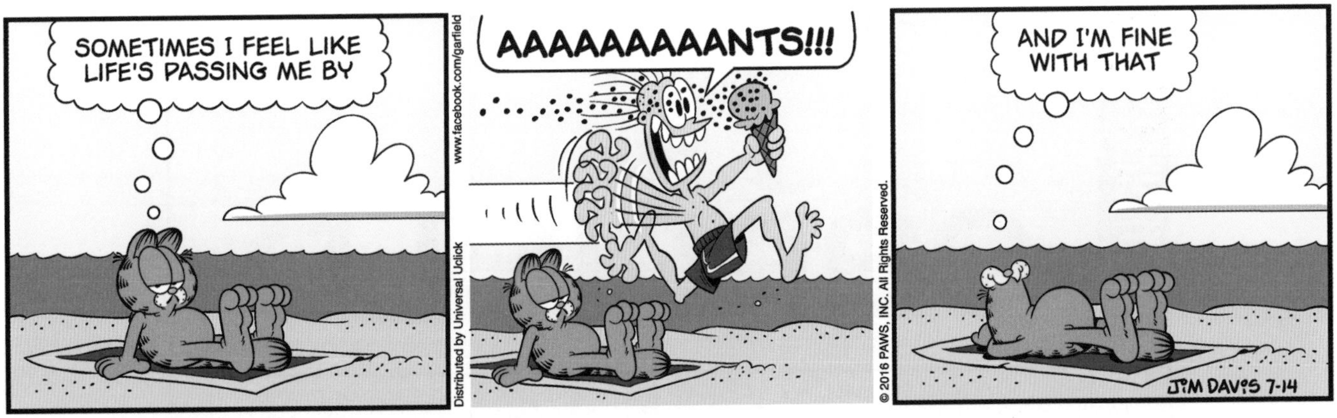
SOMETIMES I FEEL LIKE LIFE'S PASSING ME BY
www.facebook.com/garfield
Distributed by Universal Uclick
AAAAAAAAANTS!!!
© 2016 PAWS, INC. All Rights Reserved.
AND I'M FINE WITH THAT
JIM DAVIS 7-14

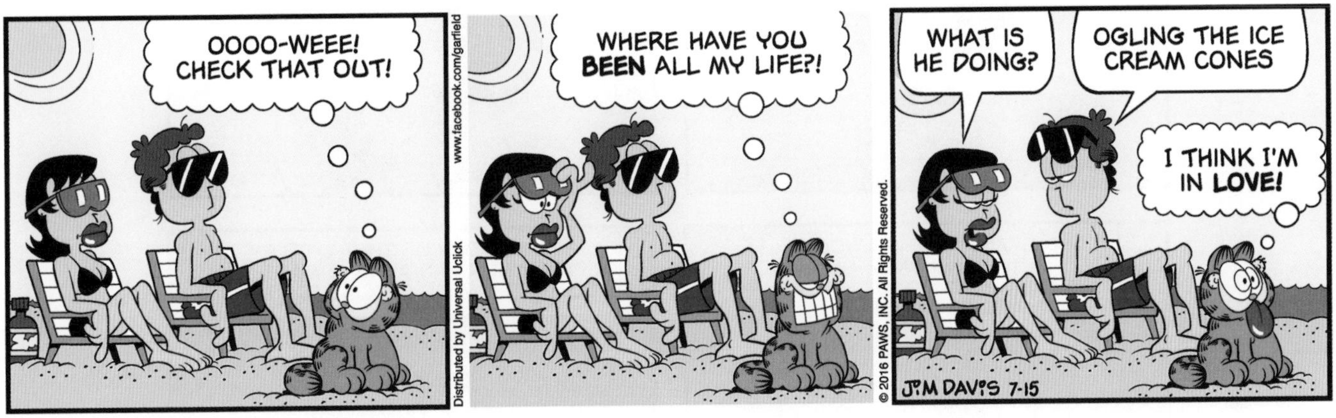
OOOO-WEEE! CHECK THAT OUT!
www.facebook.com/garfield
Distributed by Universal Uclick
WHERE HAVE YOU BEEN ALL MY LIFE?!
© 2016 PAWS, INC. All Rights Reserved.
WHAT IS HE DOING?
OGLING THE ICE CREAM CONES
I THINK I'M IN LOVE!
JIM DAVIS 7-15

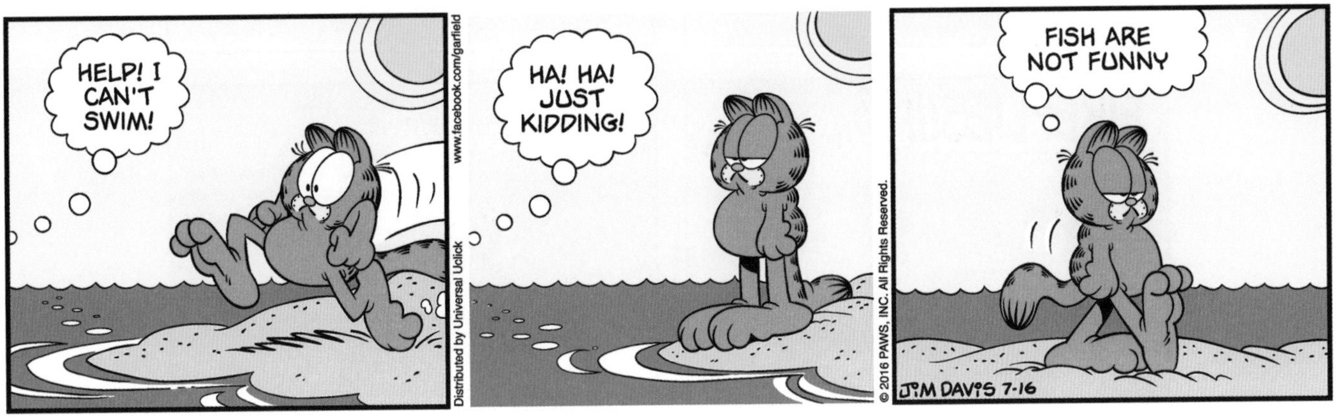
HELP! I CAN'T SWIM!
www.facebook.com/garfield
Distributed by Universal Uclick
HA! HA! JUST KIDDING!
© 2016 PAWS, INC. All Rights Reserved.
FISH ARE NOT FUNNY
JIM DAVIS 7-16

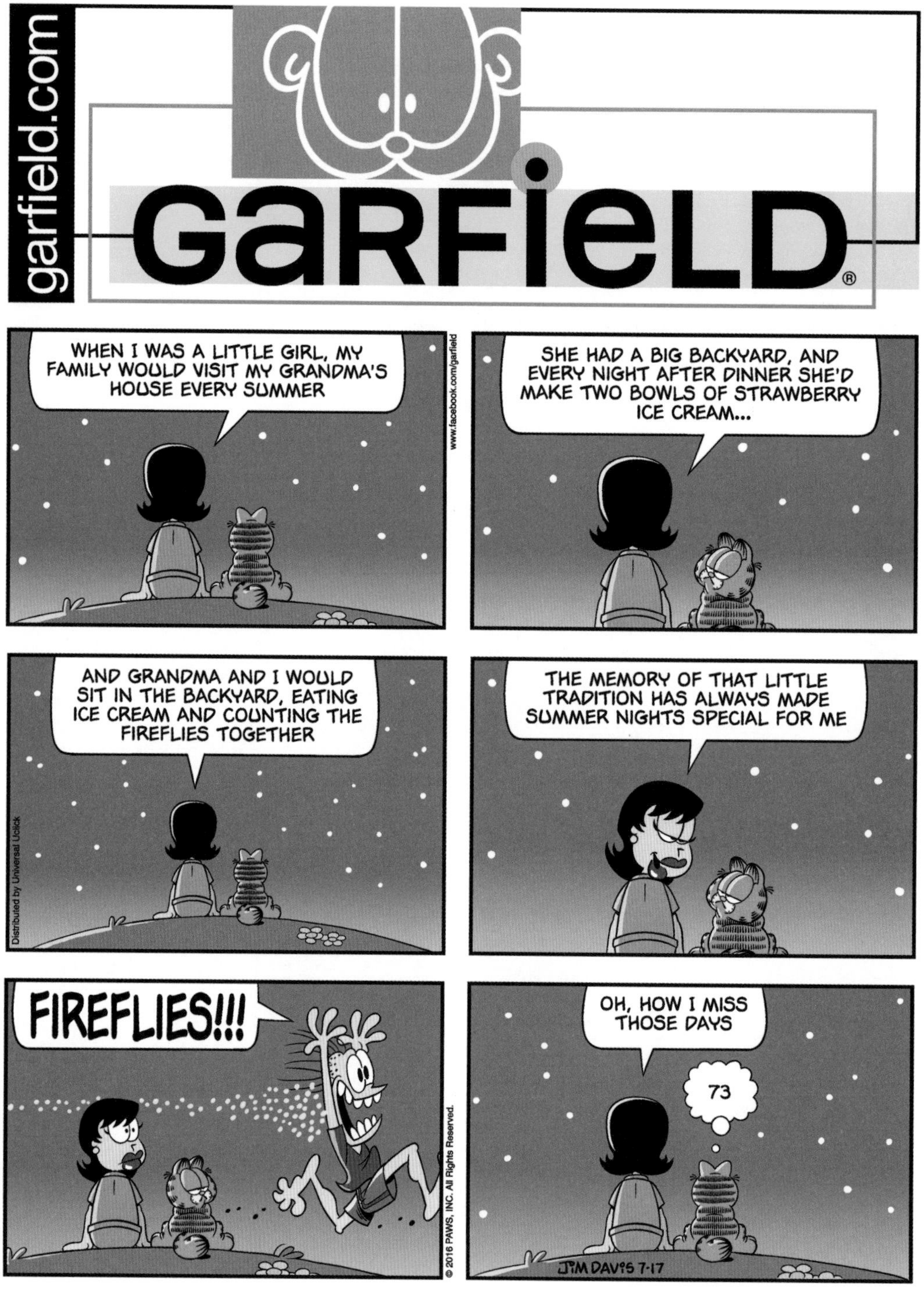
garfield.com
GARFIELD®
WHEN I WAS A LITTLE GIRL, MY FAMILY WOULD VISIT MY GRANDMA'S HOUSE EVERY SUMMER
www.facebook.com/garfield
SHE HAD A BIG BACKYARD, AND EVERY NIGHT AFTER DINNER SHE'D MAKE TWO BOWLS OF STRAWBERRY ICE CREAM...
AND GRANDMA AND I WOULD SIT IN THE BACKYARD, EATING ICE CREAM AND COUNTING THE FIREFLIES TOGETHER
Distributed by Universal Uclick
THE MEMORY OF THAT LITTLE TRADITION HAS ALWAYS MADE SUMMER NIGHTS SPECIAL FOR ME
FIREFLIES!!!
© 2016 PAWS, INC. All Rights Reserved.
OH, HOW I MISS THOSE DAYS
73
JIM DAVIS 7-17

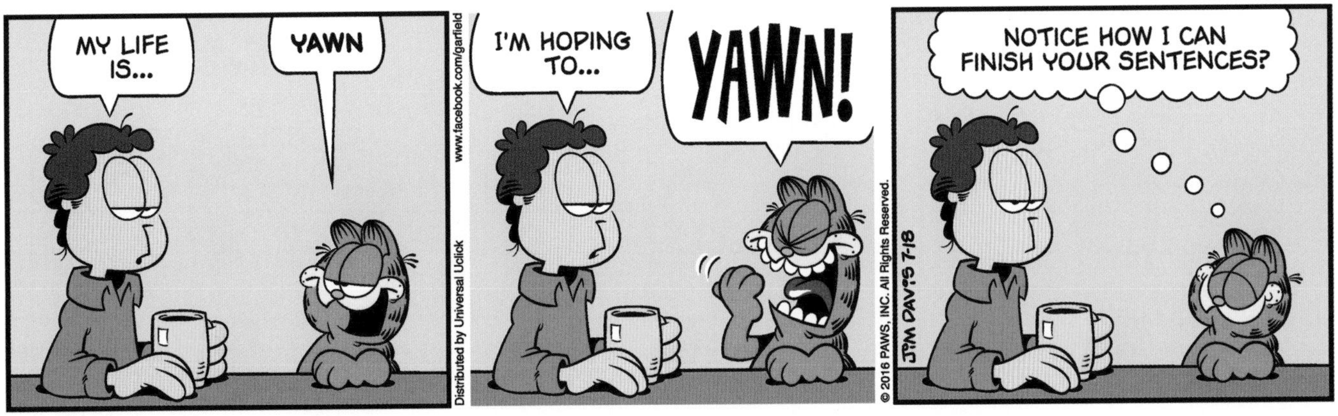
MY LIFE IS...
YAWN
www.facebook.com/garfield
Distributed by Universal Uclick
I'M HOPING TO...
YAWN!
© 2016 PAWS, INC. All Rights Reserved.
JIM DAVIS 7-18
NOTICE HOW I CAN FINISH YOUR SENTENCES?

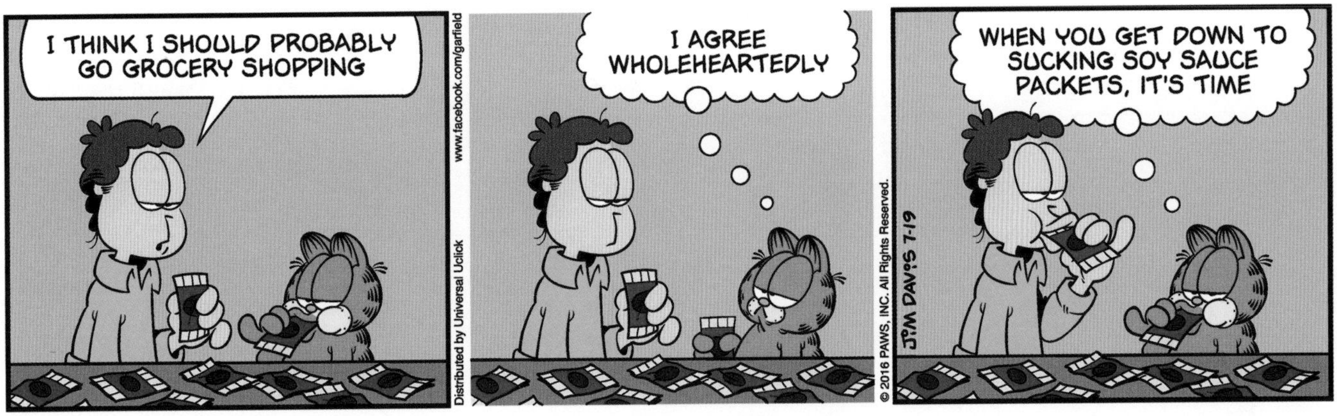
I THINK I SHOULD PROBABLY GO GROCERY SHOPPING
www.facebook.com/garfield
Distributed by Universal Uclick
I AGREE WHOLEHEARTEDLY
© 2016 PAWS, INC. All Rights Reserved.
JIM DAVIS 7-19
WHEN YOU GET DOWN TO SUCKING SOY SAUCE PACKETS, IT'S TIME

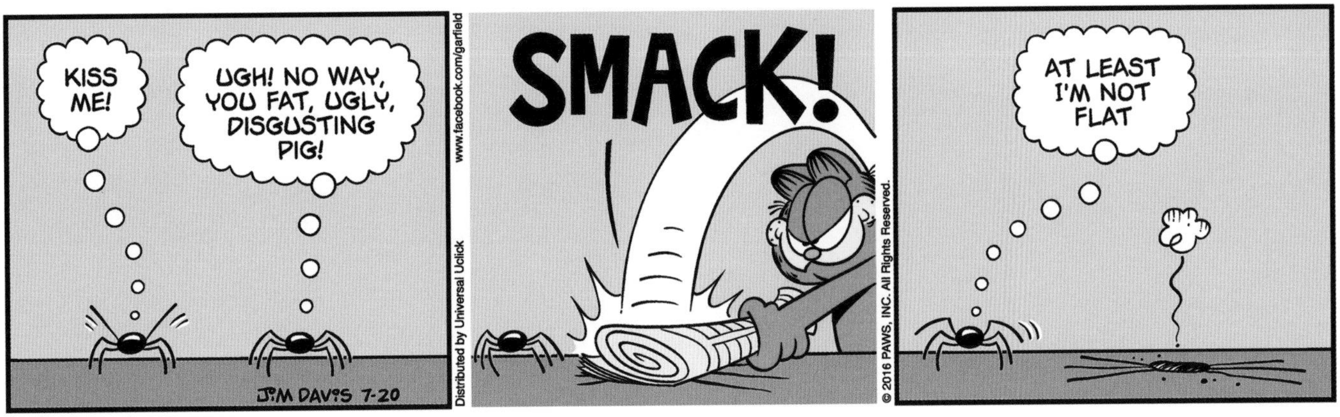
KISS ME!
UGH! NO WAY, YOU FAT, UGLY, DISGUSTING PIG!
JIM DAVIS 7-20
www.facebook.com/garfield
Distributed by Universal Uclick
SMACK!
© 2016 PAWS, INC. All Rights Reserved.
AT LEAST I'M NOT FLAT

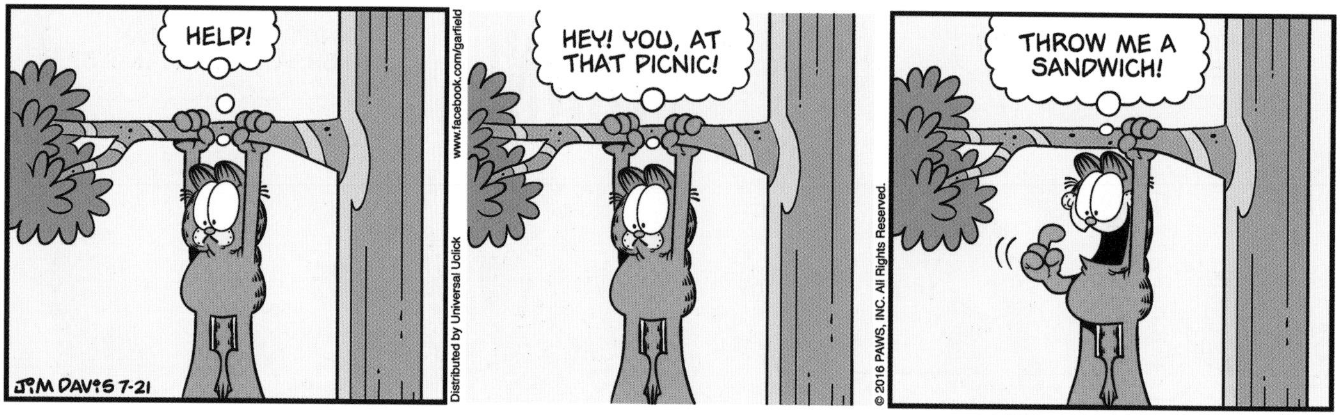
HELP!
HEY! YOU, AT THAT PICNIC!
THROW ME A SANDWICH!
JIM DAVIS 7-21
Distributed by Universal Uclick www.facebook.com/garfield
© 2016 PAWS, INC. All Rights Reserved.

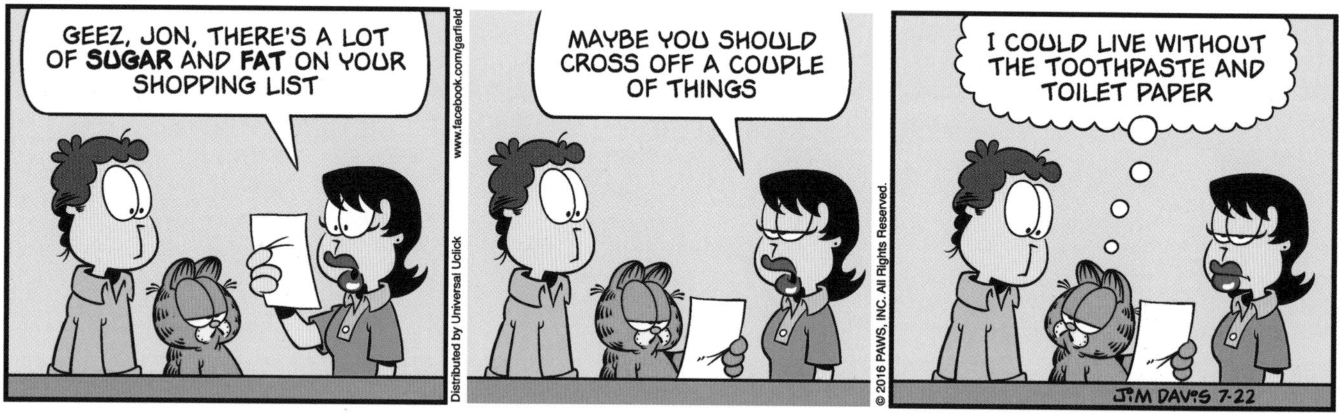
GEEZ, JON, THERE'S A LOT OF **SUGAR** AND **FAT** ON YOUR SHOPPING LIST
MAYBE YOU SHOULD CROSS OFF A COUPLE OF THINGS
I COULD LIVE WITHOUT THE TOOTHPASTE AND TOILET PAPER
JIM DAVIS 7-22
Distributed by Universal Uclick www.facebook.com/garfield
© 2016 PAWS, INC. All Rights Reserved.

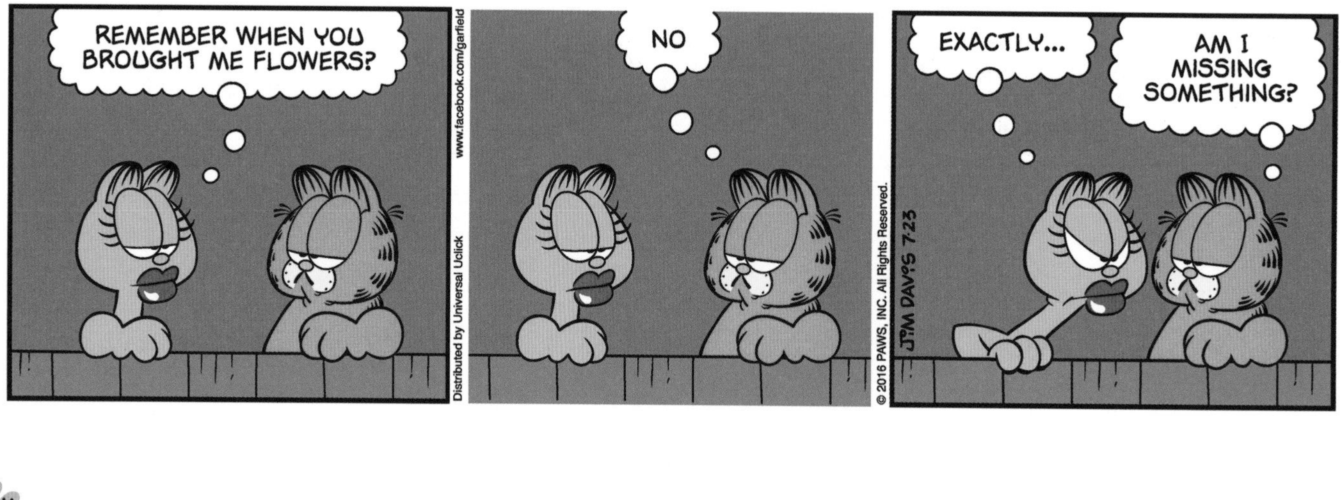
REMEMBER WHEN YOU BROUGHT ME FLOWERS?
NO
EXACTLY...
AM I MISSING SOMETHING?
JIM DAVIS 7-23
Distributed by Universal Uclick www.facebook.com/garfield
© 2016 PAWS, INC. All Rights Reserved.

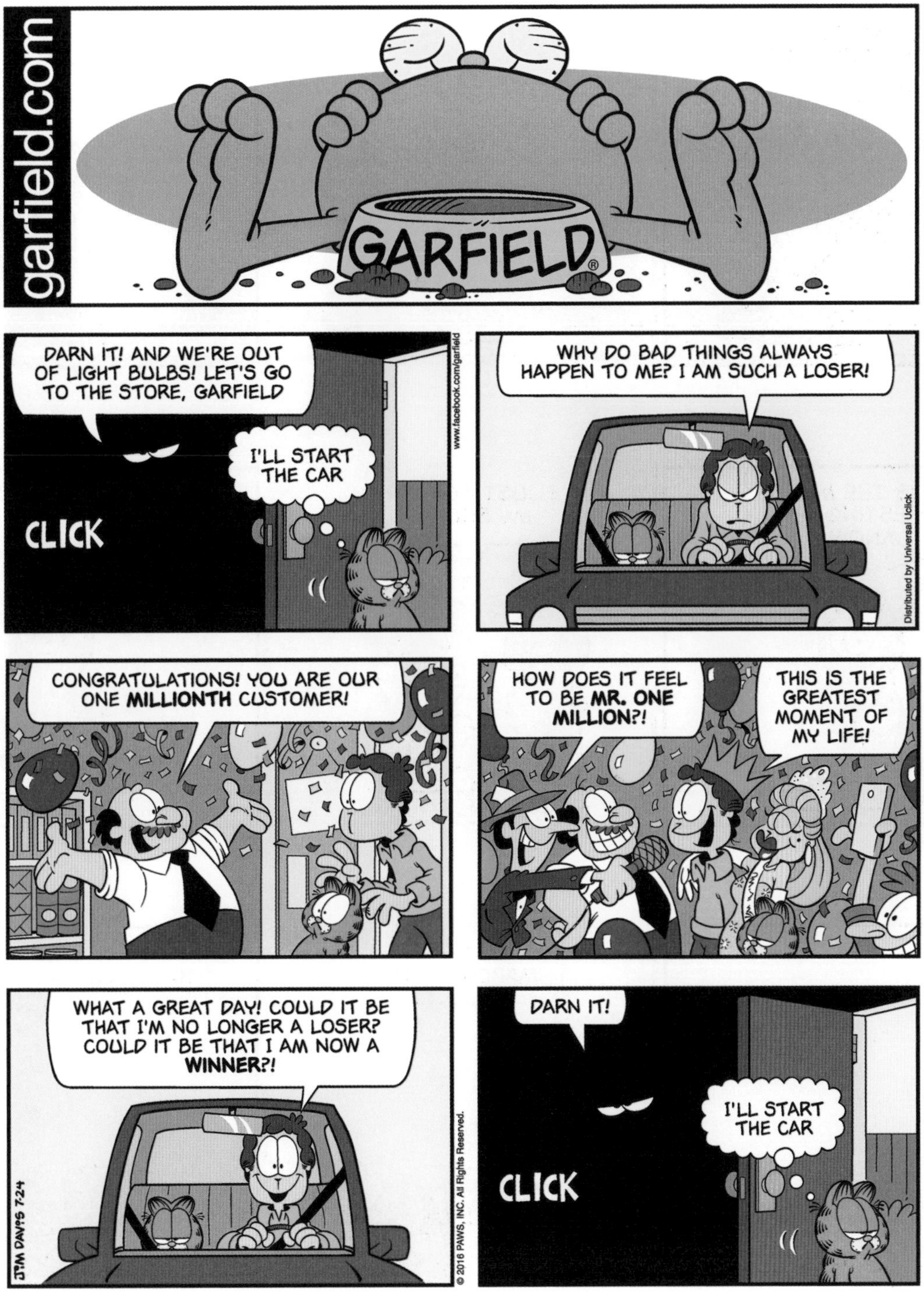
garfield.com
GARFIELD®
DARN IT! AND WE'RE OUT OF LIGHT BULBS! LET'S GO TO THE STORE, GARFIELD
I'LL START THE CAR
CLICK
www.facebook.com/garfield
WHY DO BAD THINGS ALWAYS HAPPEN TO ME? I AM SUCH A LOSER!
Distributed by Universal Uclick
CONGRATULATIONS! YOU ARE OUR ONE **MILLIONTH** CUSTOMER!
HOW DOES IT FEEL TO BE **MR. ONE MILLION?!**
THIS IS THE GREATEST MOMENT OF MY LIFE!
WHAT A GREAT DAY! COULD IT BE THAT I'M NO LONGER A LOSER? COULD IT BE THAT I AM NOW A **WINNER?!**
JIM DAVIS 7-24
© 2016 PAWS, INC. All Rights Reserved.
DARN IT!
I'LL START THE CAR
CLICK

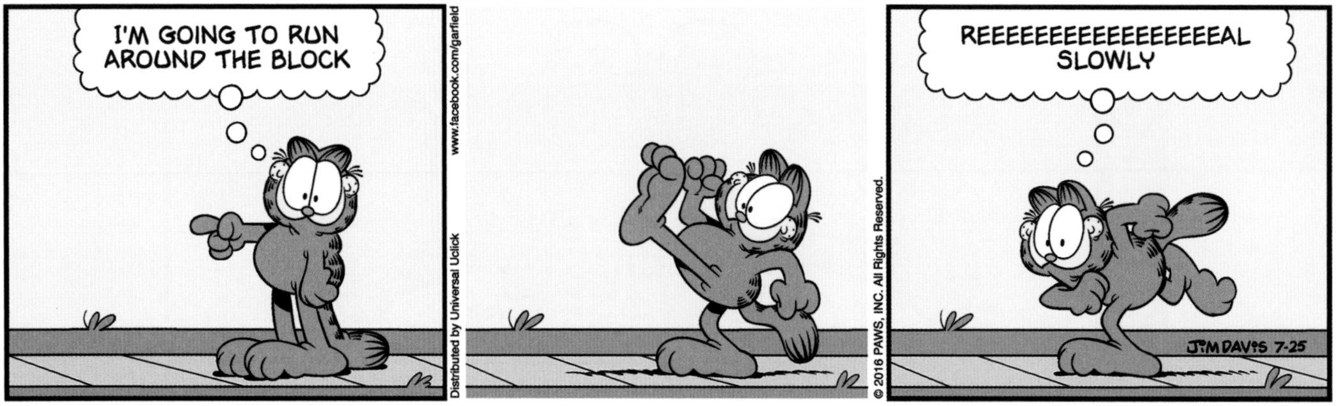
I'M GOING TO RUN AROUND THE BLOCK
REEEEEEEEEEEEEEEEEAL SLOWLY
JIM DAVIS 7-25
Distributed by Universal Uclick www.facebook.com/garfield
© 2016 PAWS, INC. All Rights Reserved.

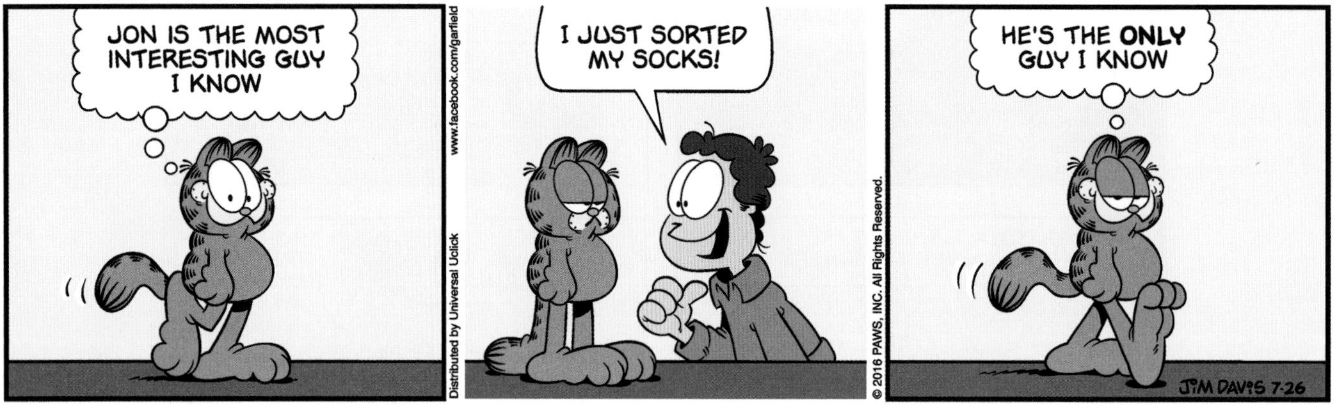
JON IS THE MOST INTERESTING GUY I KNOW
I JUST SORTED MY SOCKS!
HE'S THE **ONLY** GUY I KNOW
JIM DAVIS 7-26
Distributed by Universal Uclick www.facebook.com/garfield
© 2016 PAWS, INC. All Rights Reserved.

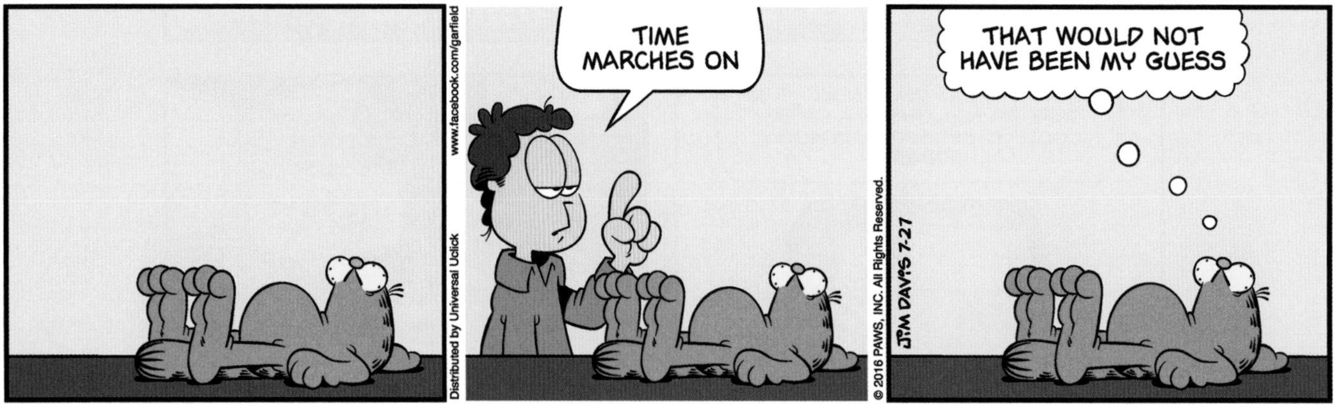
TIME MARCHES ON
THAT WOULD NOT HAVE BEEN MY GUESS
JIM DAVIS 7-27
Distributed by Universal Uclick www.facebook.com/garfield
© 2016 PAWS, INC. All Rights Reserved.

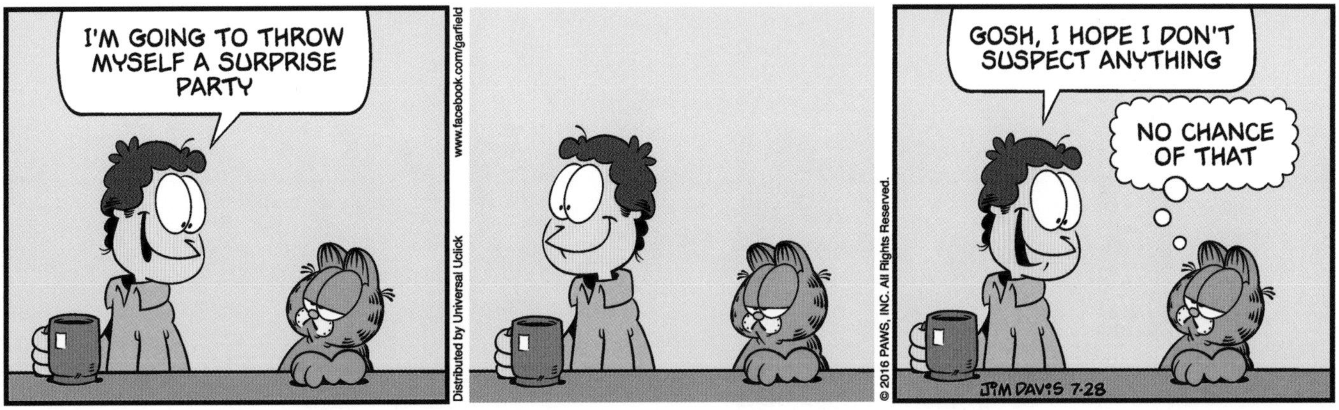
I'M GOING TO THROW MYSELF A SURPRISE PARTY
Distributed by Universal Uclick www.facebook.com/garfield
GOSH, I HOPE I DON'T SUSPECT ANYTHING
NO CHANCE OF THAT
© 2016 PAWS, INC. All Rights Reserved.
JIM DAVIS 7-28

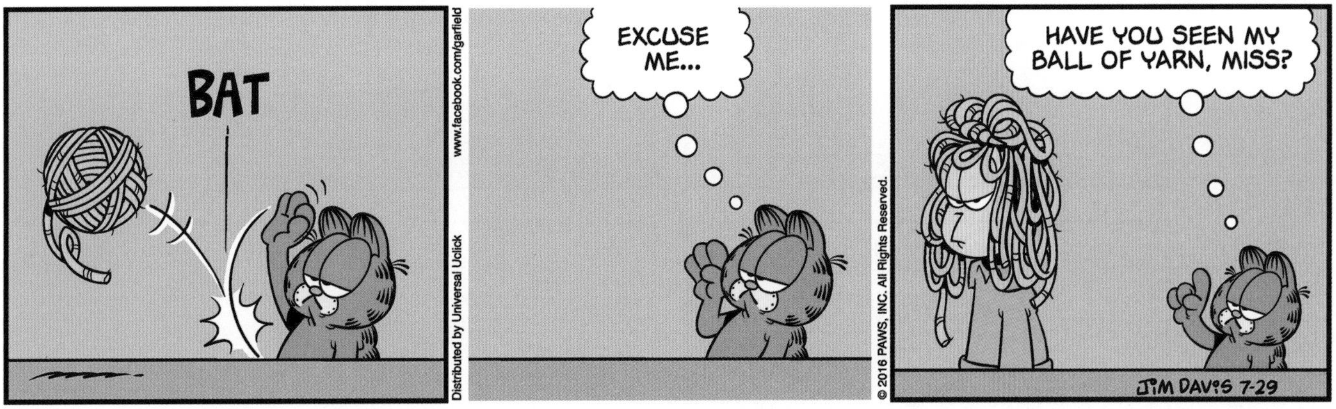
BAT
Distributed by Universal Uclick www.facebook.com/garfield
EXCUSE ME...
HAVE YOU SEEN MY BALL OF YARN, MISS?
© 2016 PAWS, INC. All Rights Reserved.
JIM DAVIS 7-29

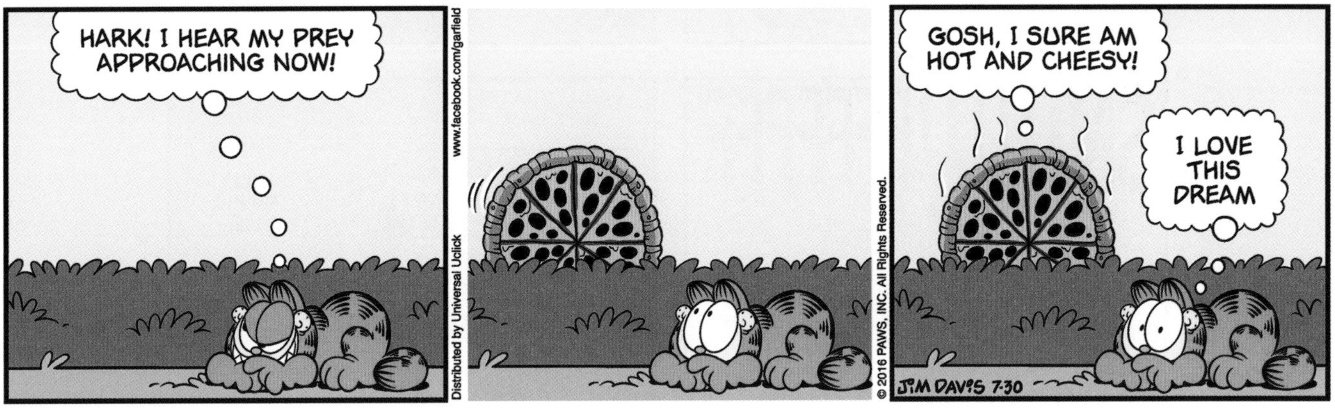
HARK! I HEAR MY PREY APPROACHING NOW!
Distributed by Universal Uclick www.facebook.com/garfield
GOSH, I SURE AM HOT AND CHEESY!
I LOVE THIS DREAM
© 2016 PAWS, INC. All Rights Reserved.
JIM DAVIS 7-30

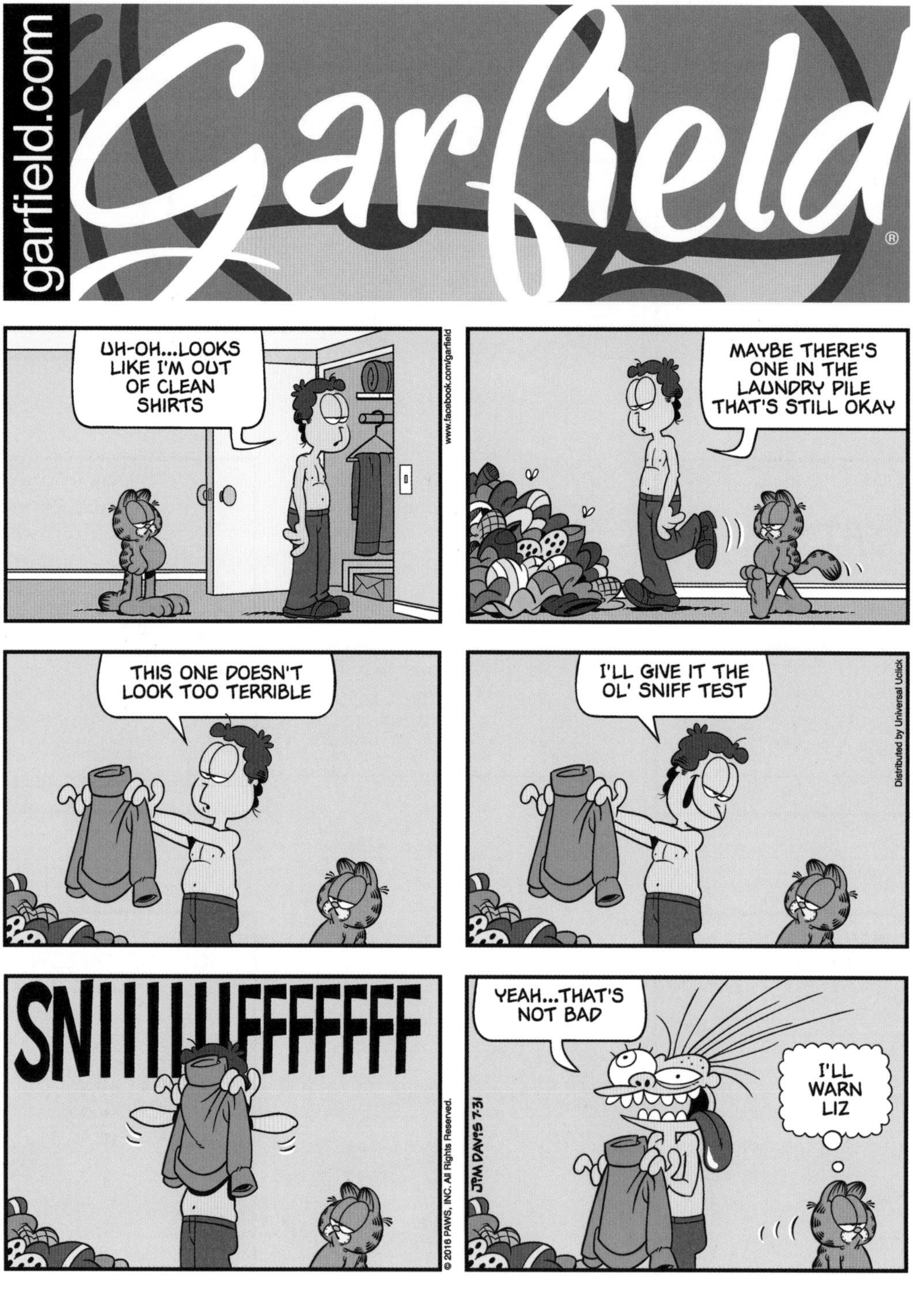
garfield.com
Garfield
UH-OH...LOOKS LIKE I'M OUT OF CLEAN SHIRTS
www.facebook.com/garfield
MAYBE THERE'S ONE IN THE LAUNDRY PILE THAT'S STILL OKAY
THIS ONE DOESN'T LOOK TOO TERRIBLE
I'LL GIVE IT THE OL' SNIFF TEST
Distributed by Universal Uclick
SNIIIIIFFFFFFF
© 2016 PAWS, INC. All Rights Reserved.
JIM DAVIS 7-31
YEAH...THAT'S NOT BAD
I'LL WARN LIZ

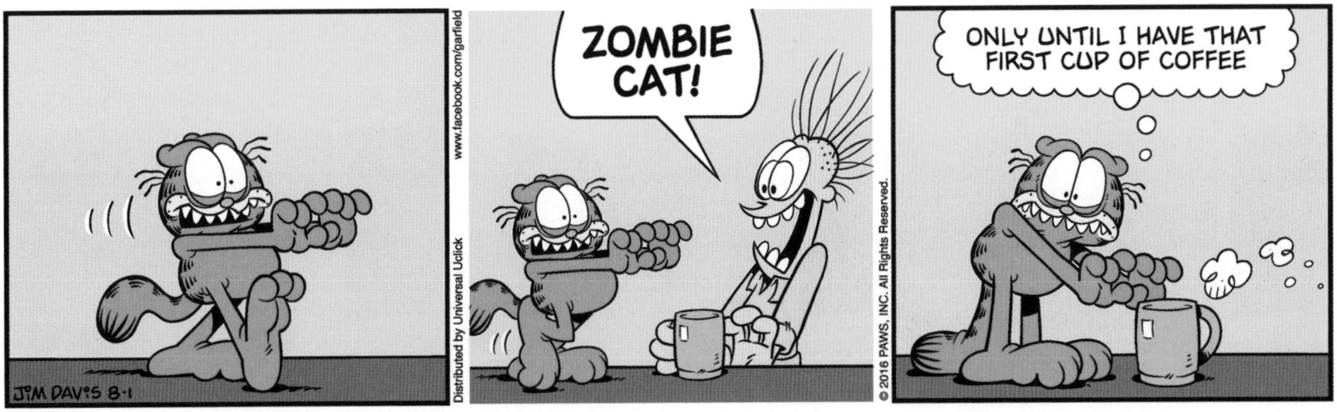
JIM DAVIS 8-1
Distributed by Universal Uclick
www.facebook.com/garfield
ZOMBIE CAT!
© 2016 PAWS, INC. All Rights Reserved.
ONLY UNTIL I HAVE THAT FIRST CUP OF COFFEE

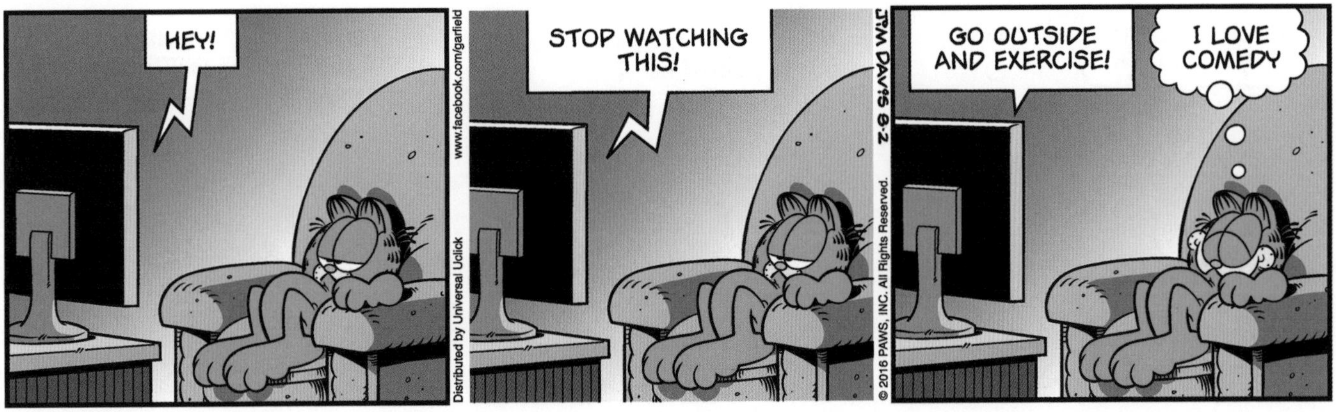
HEY!
Distributed by Universal Uclick
www.facebook.com/garfield
STOP WATCHING THIS!
JIM DAVIS 8-2
© 2016 PAWS, INC. All Rights Reserved.
GO OUTSIDE AND EXERCISE!
I LOVE COMEDY

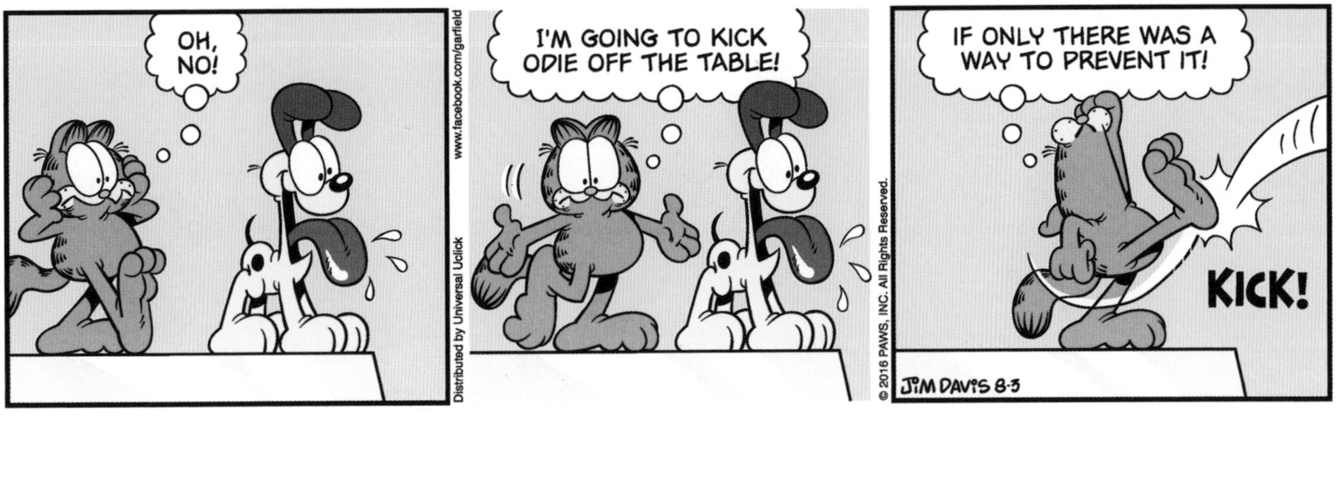
OH, NO!
Distributed by Universal Uclick
www.facebook.com/garfield
I'M GOING TO KICK ODIE OFF THE TABLE!
© 2016 PAWS, INC. All Rights Reserved.
IF ONLY THERE WAS A WAY TO PREVENT IT!
KICK!
JIM DAVIS 8-3

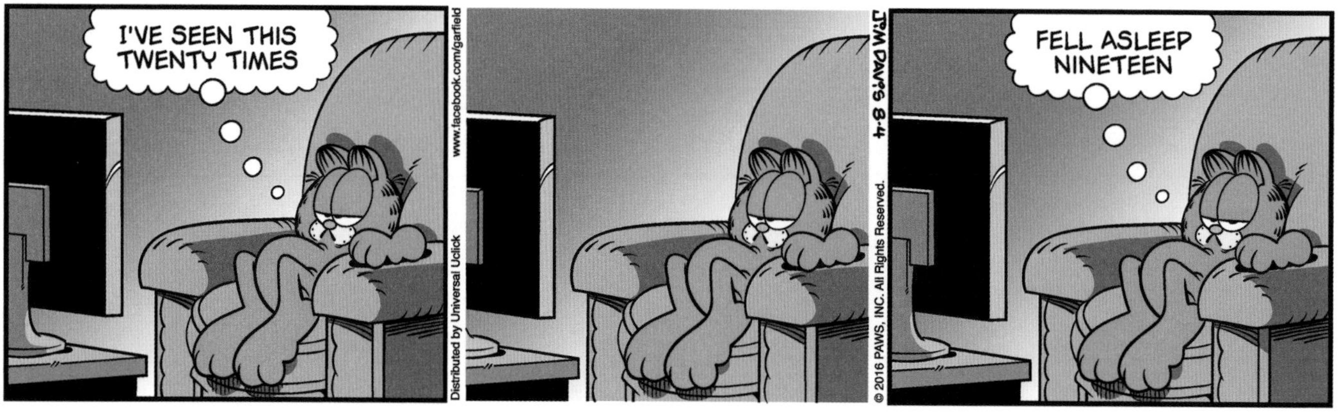
I'VE SEEN THIS TWENTY TIMES
FELL ASLEEP NINETEEN
JIM DAVIS 8-4

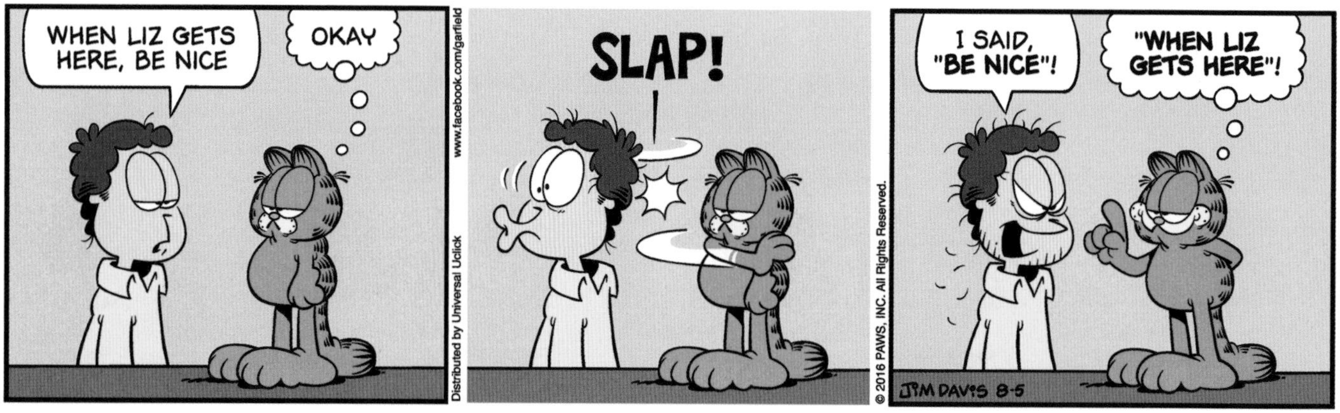
WHEN LIZ GETS HERE, BE NICE
OKAY
SLAP!
I SAID, "BE NICE"!
"WHEN LIZ GETS HERE"!
JIM DAVIS 8-5

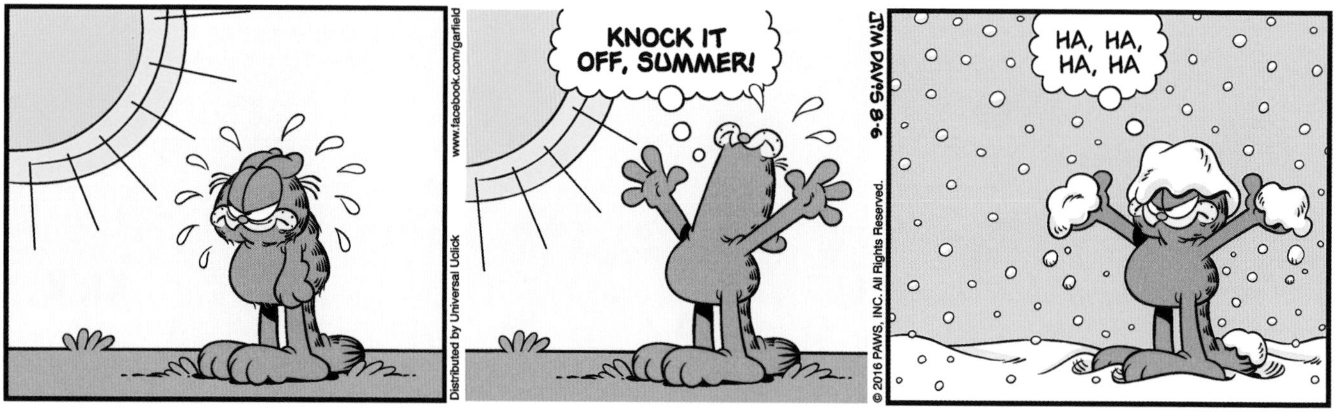
KNOCK IT OFF, SUMMER!
HA, HA, HA, HA
JIM DAVIS 8-6

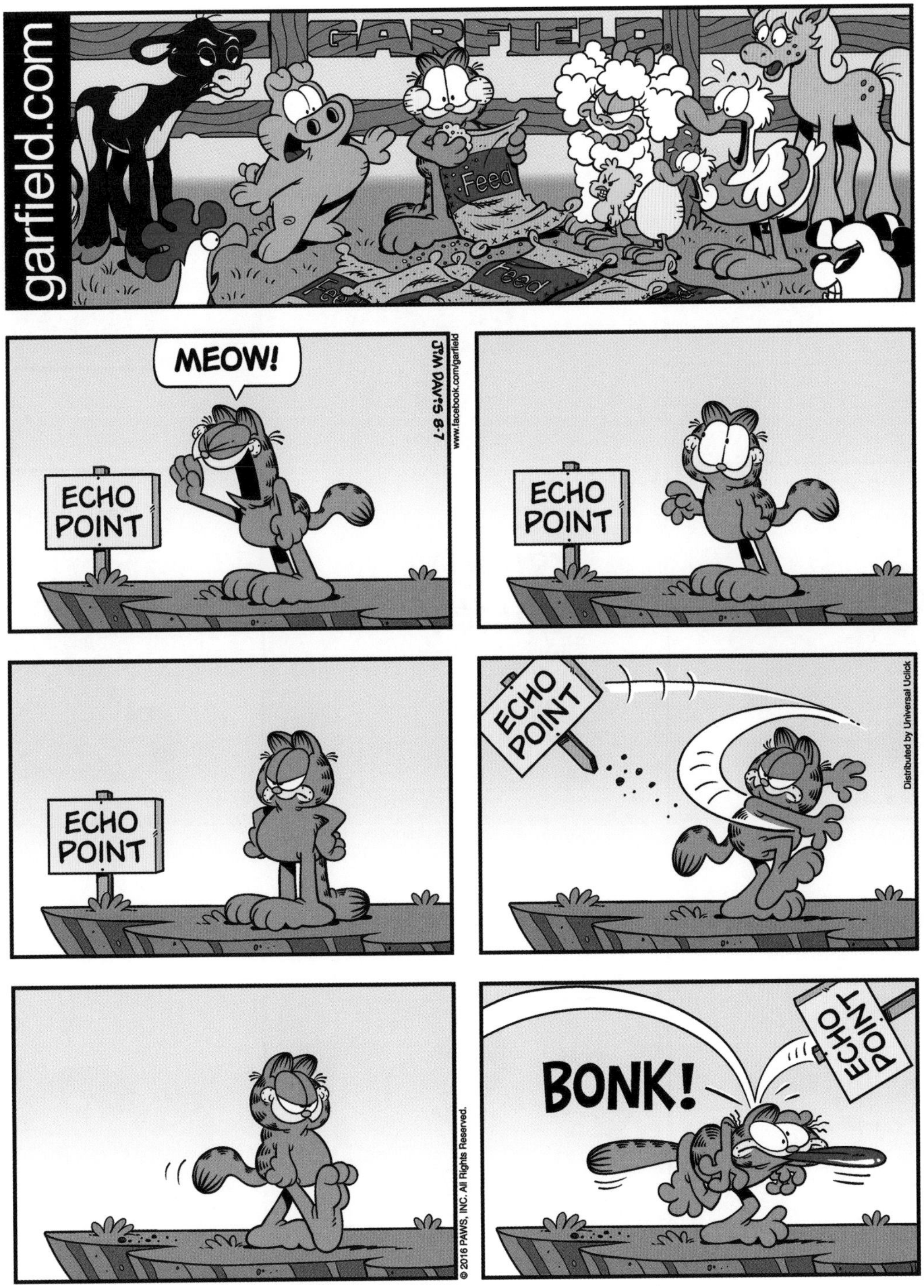
garfield.com
GARFIELD
Feed
Feed
Feed
JIM DAVIS 8-7
www.facebook.com/garfield
MEOW!
ECHO POINT
ECHO POINT
ECHO POINT
ECHO POINT
Distributed by Universal Uclick
© 2016 PAWS, INC. All Rights Reserved.
BONK!
ECHO POINT

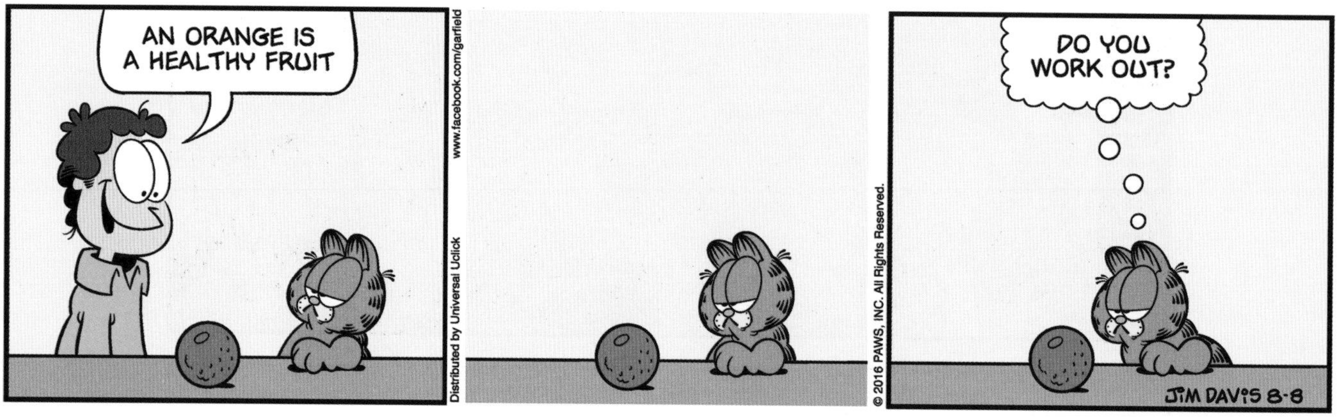
AN ORANGE IS A HEALTHY FRUIT
Distributed by Universal Uclick www.facebook.com/garfield
© 2016 PAWS, INC. All Rights Reserved.
DO YOU WORK OUT?
JIM DAVIS 8-8

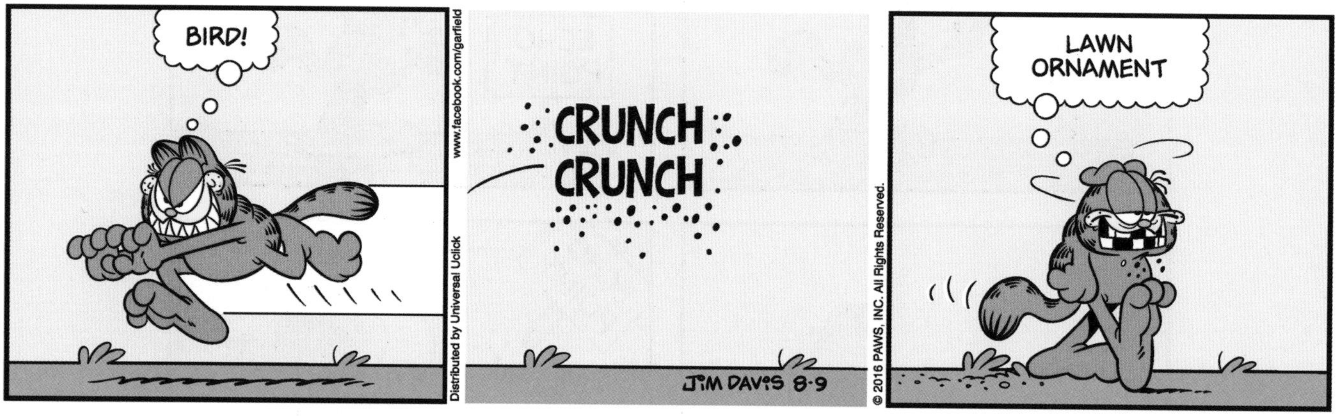
BIRD!
Distributed by Universal Uclick www.facebook.com/garfield
CRUNCH
CRUNCH
JIM DAVIS 8-9
© 2016 PAWS, INC. All Rights Reserved.
LAWN ORNAMENT

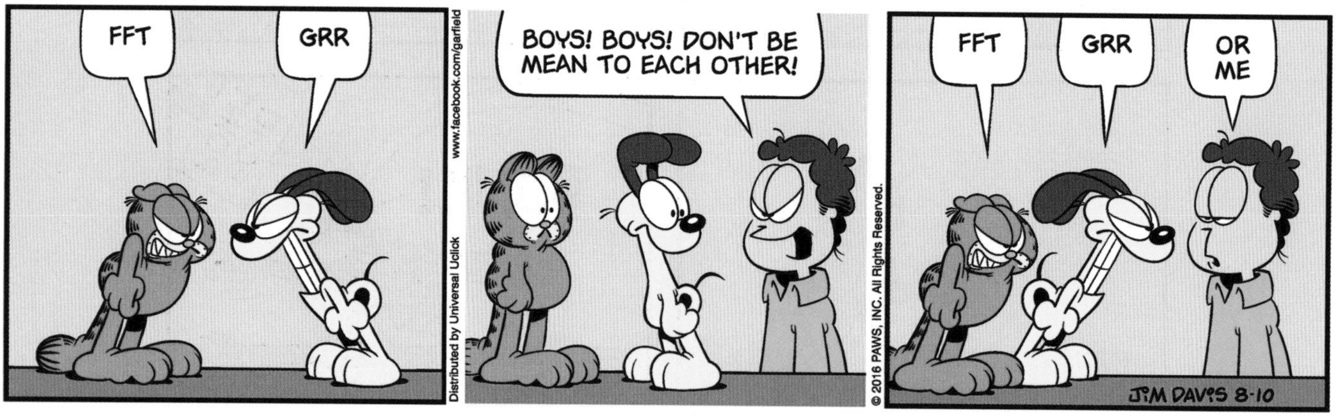
FFT
GRR
Distributed by Universal Uclick www.facebook.com/garfield
BOYS! BOYS! DON'T BE MEAN TO EACH OTHER!
© 2016 PAWS, INC. All Rights Reserved.
FFT
GRR
OR ME
JIM DAVIS 8-10

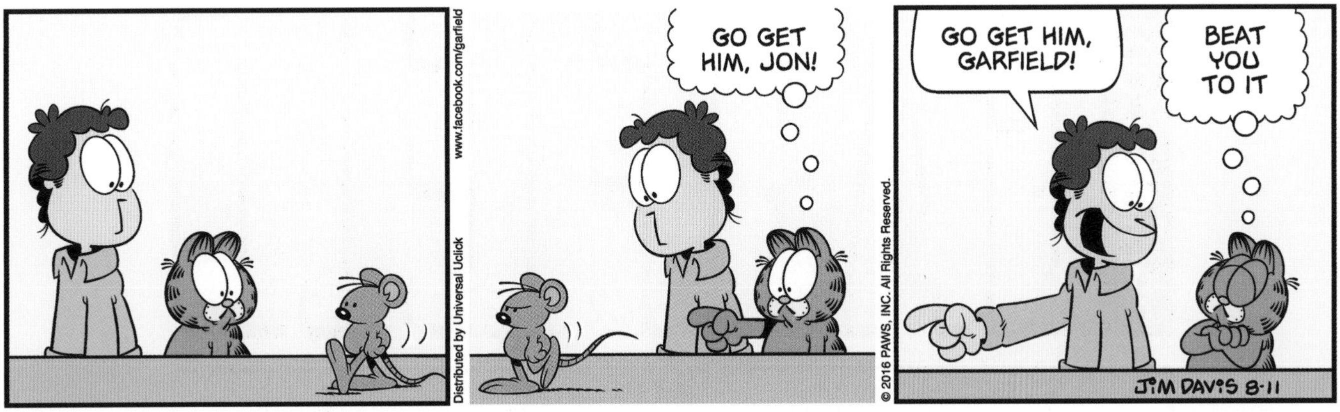
www.facebook.com/garfield
Distributed by Universal Uclick
GO GET HIM, JON!
© 2016 PAWS, INC. All Rights Reserved.
GO GET HIM, GARFIELD!
BEAT YOU TO IT
JIM DAVIS 8-11

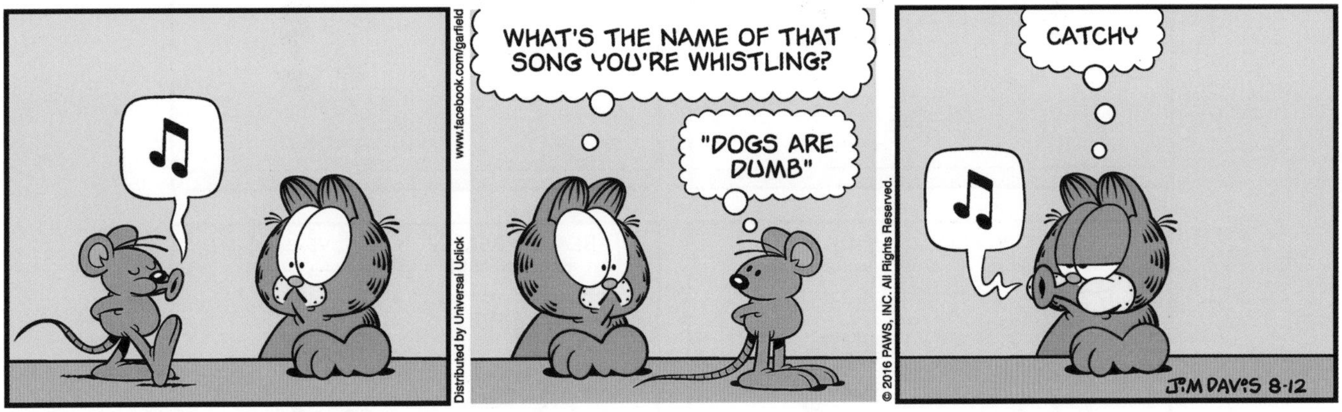
♫
www.facebook.com/garfield
Distributed by Universal Uclick
WHAT'S THE NAME OF THAT SONG YOU'RE WHISTLING?
"DOGS ARE DUMB"
© 2016 PAWS, INC. All Rights Reserved.
CATCHY
♫
JIM DAVIS 8-12

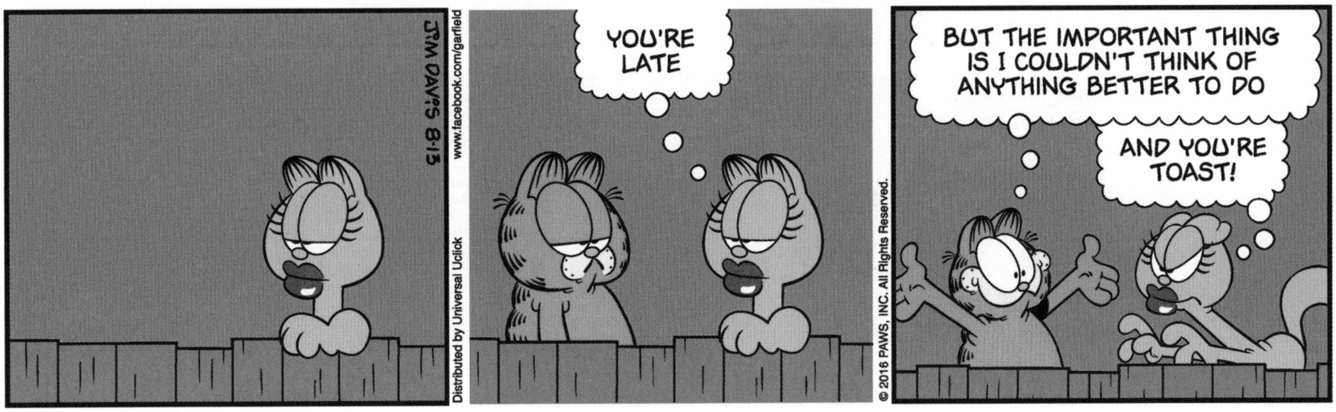
JIM DAVIS 8-13
www.facebook.com/garfield
Distributed by Universal Uclick
YOU'RE LATE
© 2016 PAWS, INC. All Rights Reserved.
BUT THE IMPORTANT THING IS I COULDN'T THINK OF ANYTHING BETTER TO DO
AND YOU'RE TOAST!

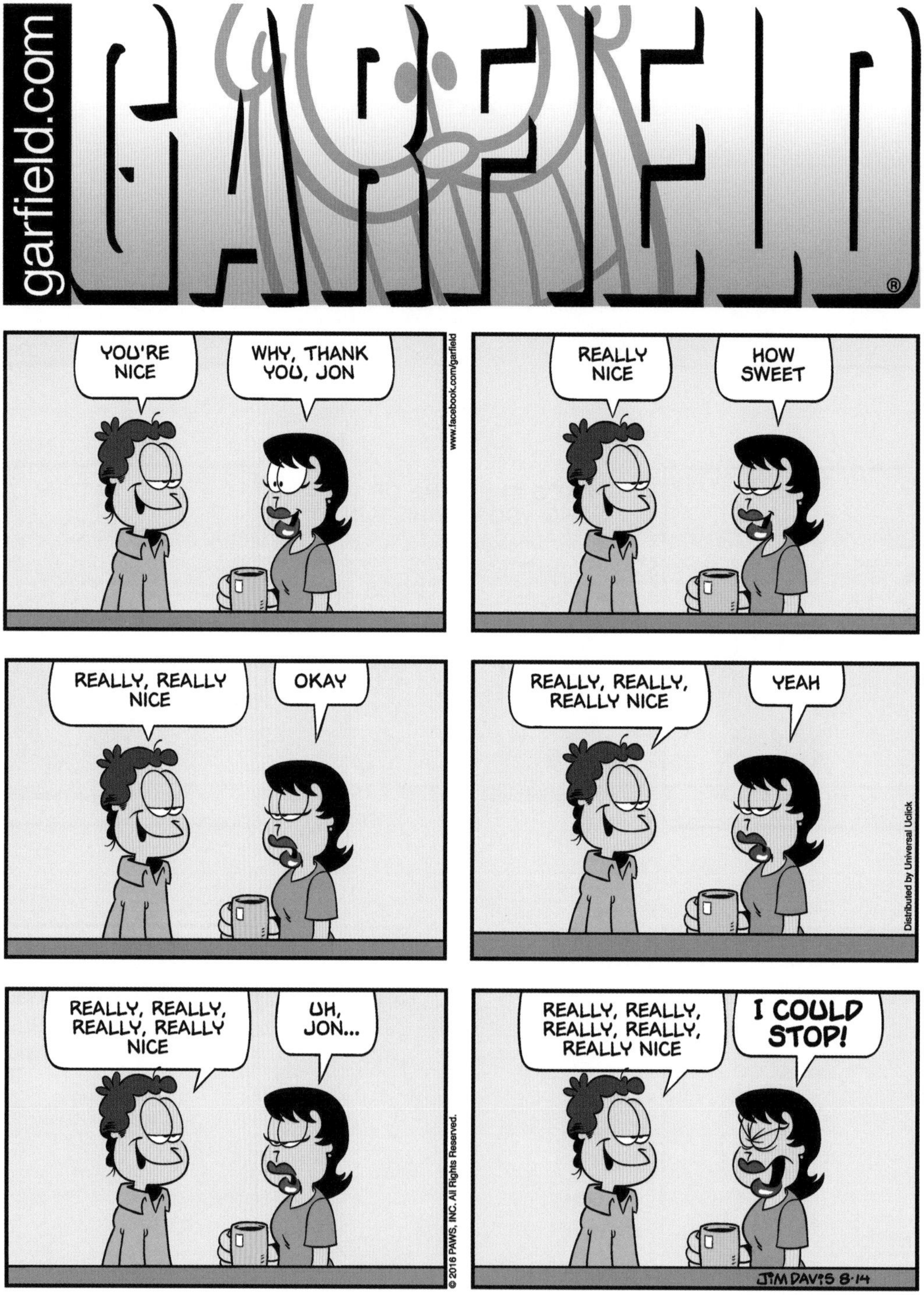
garfield.com
GARFIELD®
YOU'RE NICE
WHY, THANK YOU, JON
REALLY NICE
HOW SWEET
REALLY, REALLY NICE
OKAY
REALLY, REALLY, REALLY NICE
YEAH
REALLY, REALLY, REALLY, REALLY NICE
UH, JON...
REALLY, REALLY, REALLY, REALLY, REALLY NICE
I COULD STOP!
www.facebook.com/garfield
Distributed by Universal Uclick
© 2016 PAWS, INC. All Rights Reserved.
JIM DAVIS 8-14

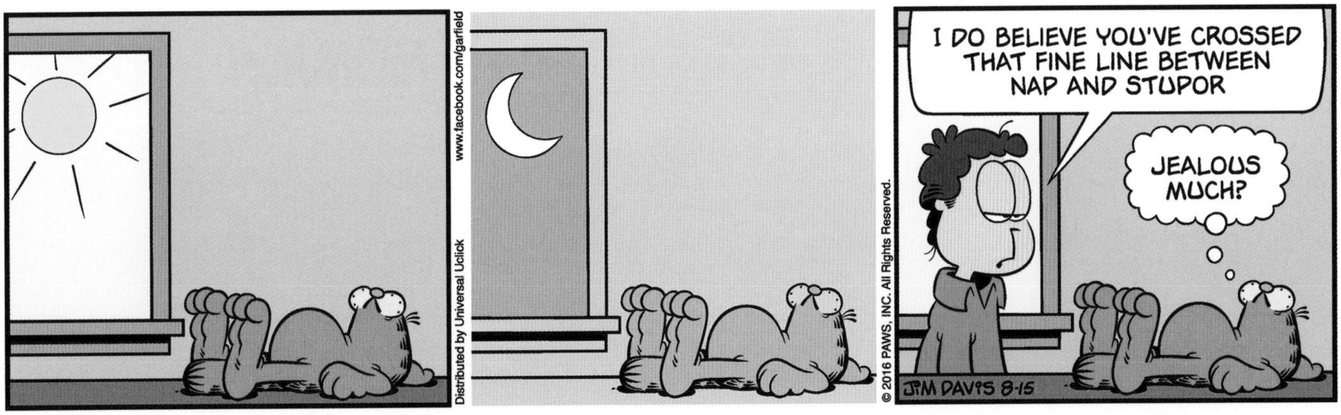
www.facebook.com/garfield
Distributed by Universal Uclick
I DO BELIEVE YOU'VE CROSSED THAT FINE LINE BETWEEN NAP AND STUPOR
JEALOUS MUCH?
© 2016 PAWS, INC. All Rights Reserved.
JIM DAVIS 8-15

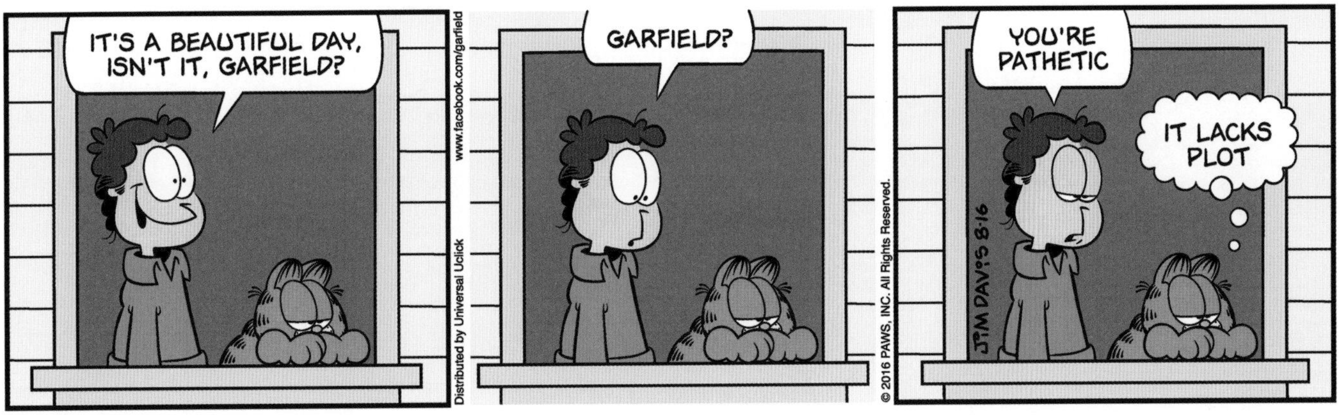
IT'S A BEAUTIFUL DAY, ISN'T IT, GARFIELD?
www.facebook.com/garfield
Distributed by Universal Uclick
GARFIELD?
© 2016 PAWS, INC. All Rights Reserved.
YOU'RE PATHETIC
IT LACKS PLOT
JIM DAVIS 8-16

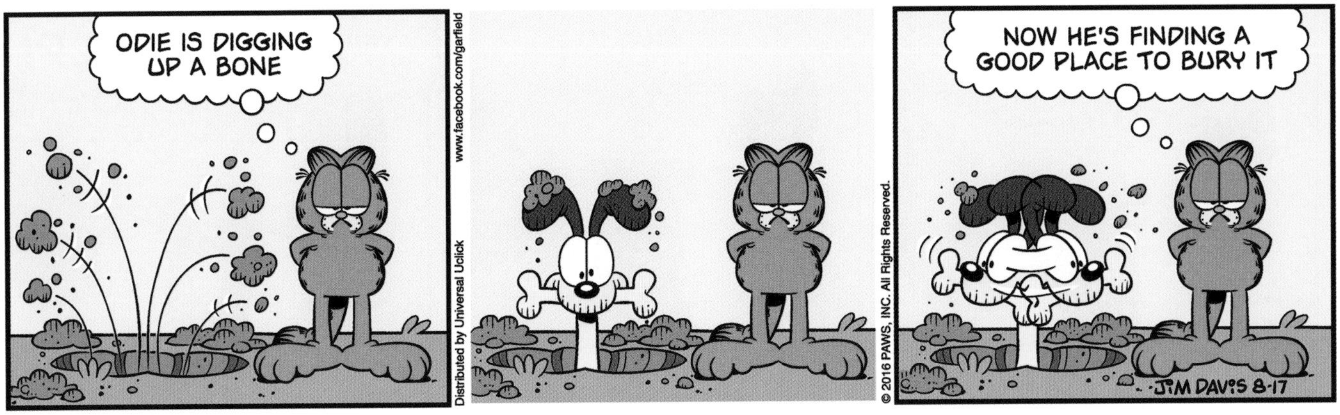
ODIE IS DIGGING UP A BONE
www.facebook.com/garfield
Distributed by Universal Uclick
© 2016 PAWS, INC. All Rights Reserved.
NOW HE'S FINDING A GOOD PLACE TO BURY IT
JIM DAVIS 8-17

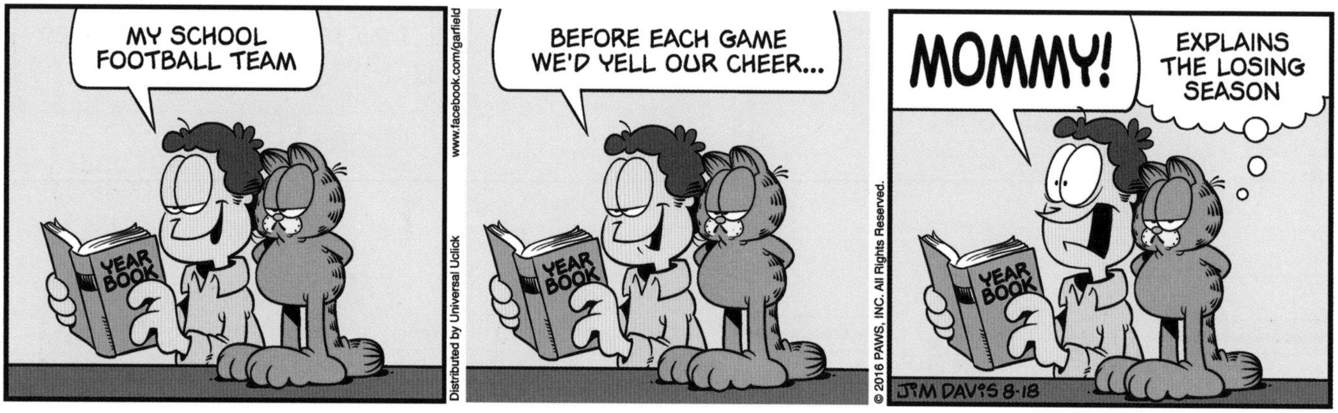
MY SCHOOL FOOTBALL TEAM
BEFORE EACH GAME WE'D YELL OUR CHEER...
MOMMY!
EXPLAINS THE LOSING SEASON
JIM DAVIS 8-18
www.facebook.com/garfield
Distributed by Universal Uclick
© 2016 PAWS, INC. All Rights Reserved.

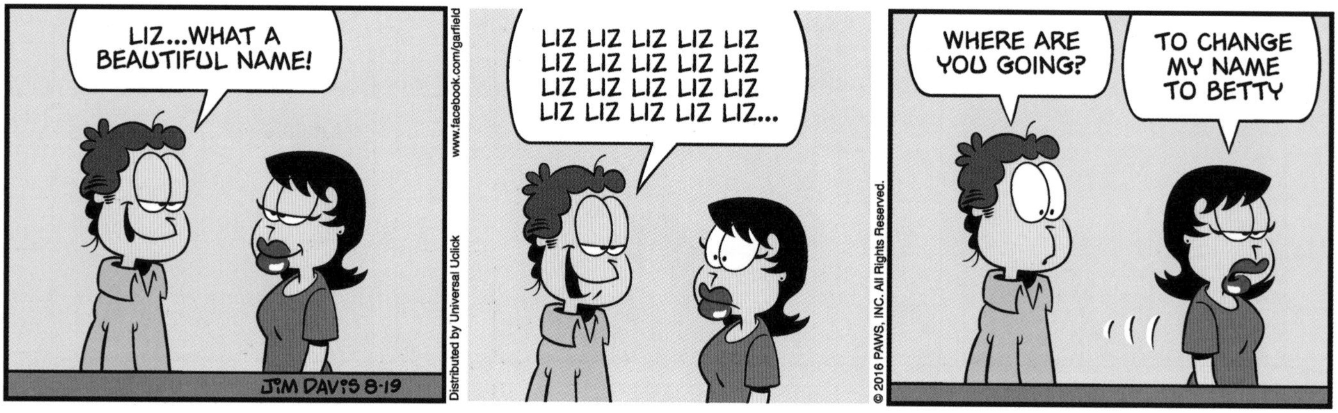
LIZ...WHAT A BEAUTIFUL NAME!
JIM DAVIS 8-19
LIZ LIZ LIZ LIZ LIZ
LIZ LIZ LIZ LIZ LIZ
LIZ LIZ LIZ LIZ LIZ
LIZ LIZ LIZ LIZ LIZ...
WHERE ARE YOU GOING?
TO CHANGE MY NAME TO BETTY
www.facebook.com/garfield
Distributed by Universal Uclick
© 2016 PAWS, INC. All Rights Reserved.

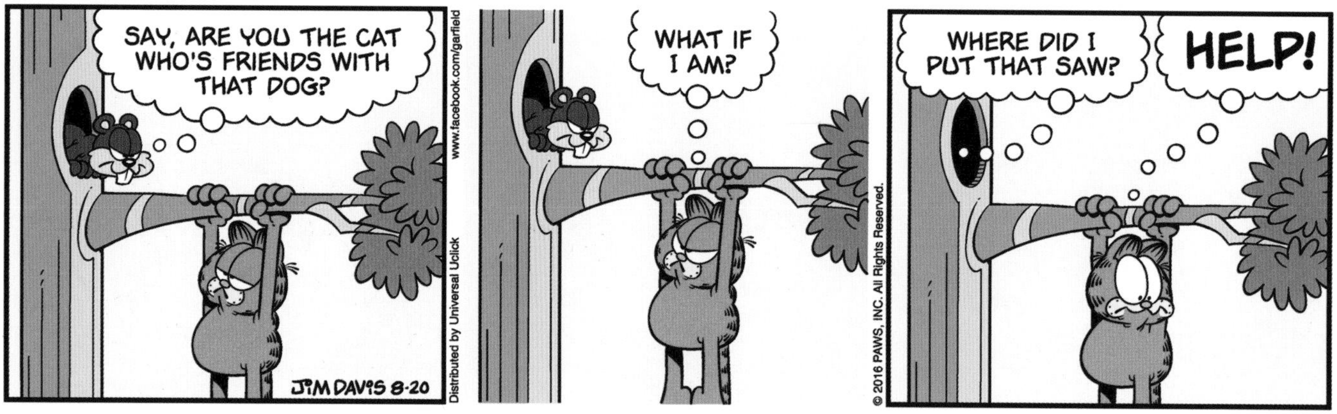
SAY, ARE YOU THE CAT WHO'S FRIENDS WITH THAT DOG?
JIM DAVIS 8-20
WHAT IF I AM?
WHERE DID I PUT THAT SAW?
HELP!
www.facebook.com/garfield
Distributed by Universal Uclick
© 2016 PAWS, INC. All Rights Reserved.

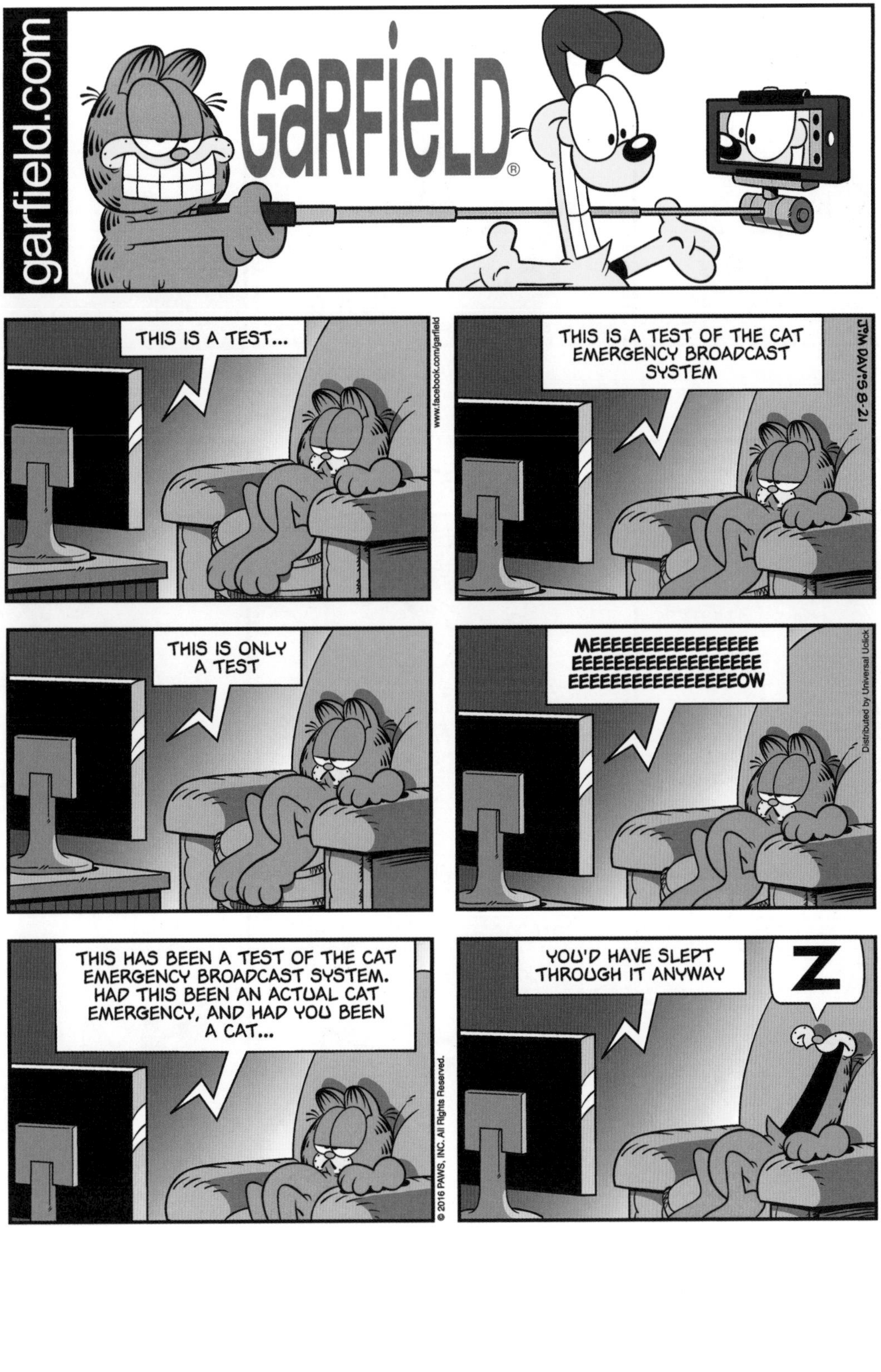
garfield.com
GARFIELD
THIS IS A TEST...
www.facebook.com/garfield
THIS IS A TEST OF THE CAT EMERGENCY BROADCAST SYSTEM
JIM DAVIS 8-21
THIS IS ONLY A TEST
MEEEEEEEEEEEEEEEE EEEEEEEEEEEEEEEEE EEEEEEEEEEEEEEEEOW
Distributed by Universal Uclick
THIS HAS BEEN A TEST OF THE CAT EMERGENCY BROADCAST SYSTEM. HAD THIS BEEN AN ACTUAL CAT EMERGENCY, AND HAD YOU BEEN A CAT...
© 2016 PAWS, INC. All Rights Reserved.
YOU'D HAVE SLEPT THROUGH IT ANYWAY
Z

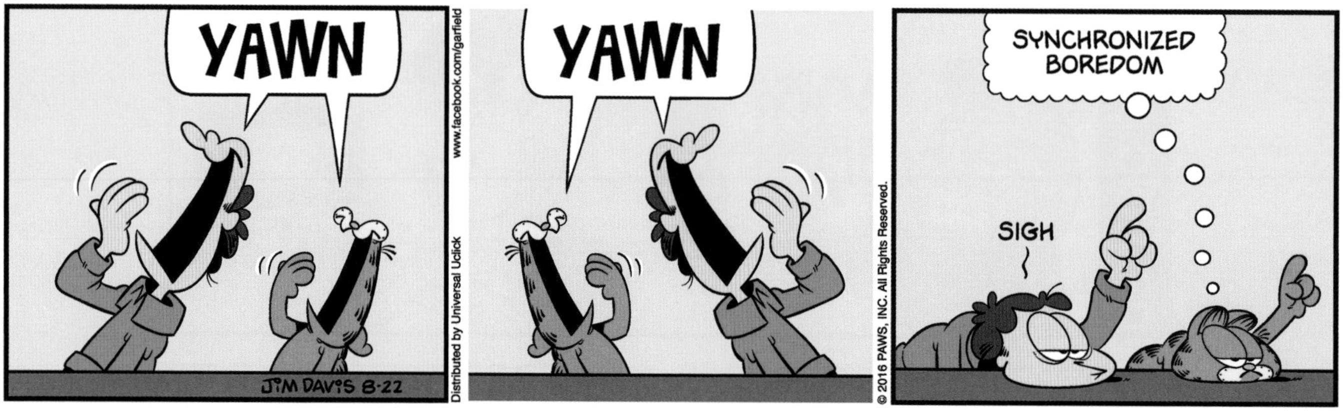
YAWN
JIM DAVIS 8-22
www.facebook.com/garfield
Distributed by Universal Uclick
YAWN
© 2016 PAWS, INC. All Rights Reserved.
SYNCHRONIZED BOREDOM
SIGH

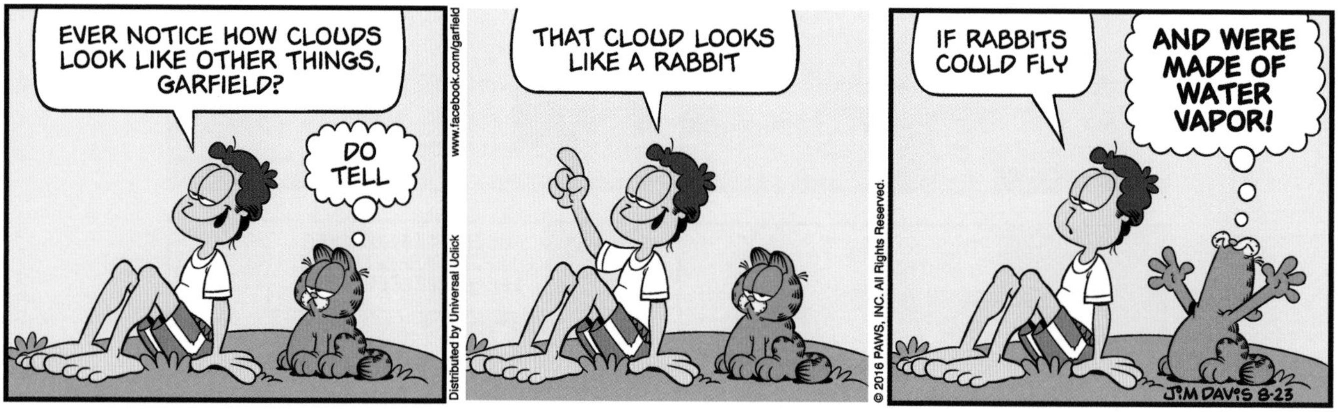
EVER NOTICE HOW CLOUDS LOOK LIKE OTHER THINGS, GARFIELD?
DO TELL
www.facebook.com/garfield
Distributed by Universal Uclick
THAT CLOUD LOOKS LIKE A RABBIT
© 2016 PAWS, INC. All Rights Reserved.
IF RABBITS COULD FLY
AND WERE MADE OF WATER VAPOR!
JIM DAVIS 8-23

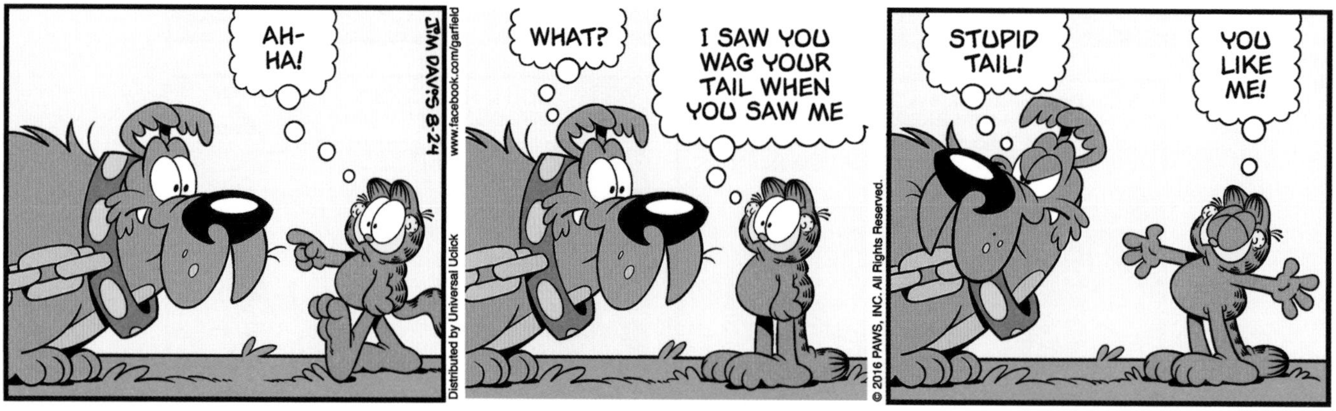
AH-HA!
JIM DAVIS 8-24
www.facebook.com/garfield
Distributed by Universal Uclick
WHAT?
I SAW YOU WAG YOUR TAIL WHEN YOU SAW ME
© 2016 PAWS, INC. All Rights Reserved.
STUPID TAIL!
YOU LIKE ME!

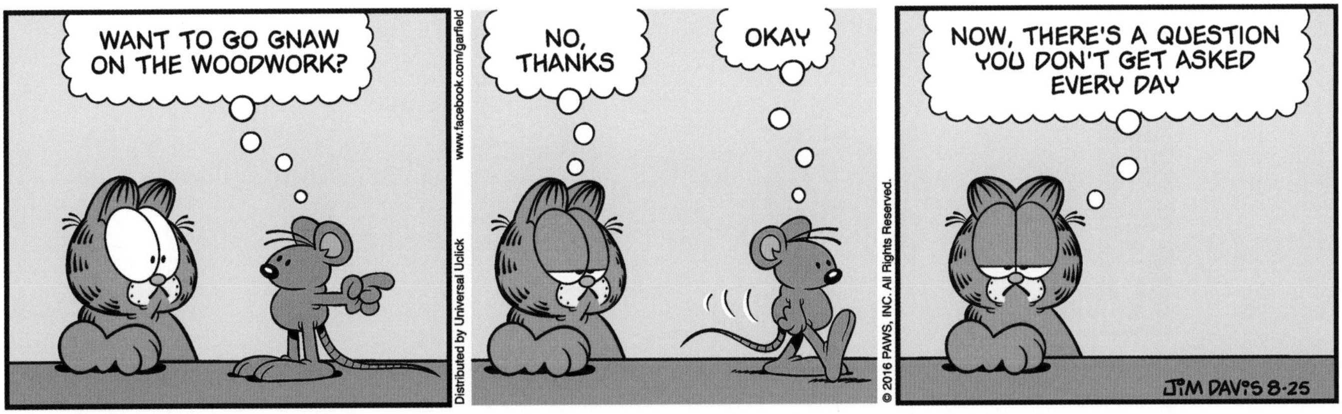
WANT TO GO GNAW ON THE WOODWORK?
www.facebook.com/garfield
Distributed by Universal Uclick
NO, THANKS
OKAY
© 2016 PAWS, INC. All Rights Reserved.
NOW, THERE'S A QUESTION YOU DON'T GET ASKED EVERY DAY
JIM DAVIS 8-25

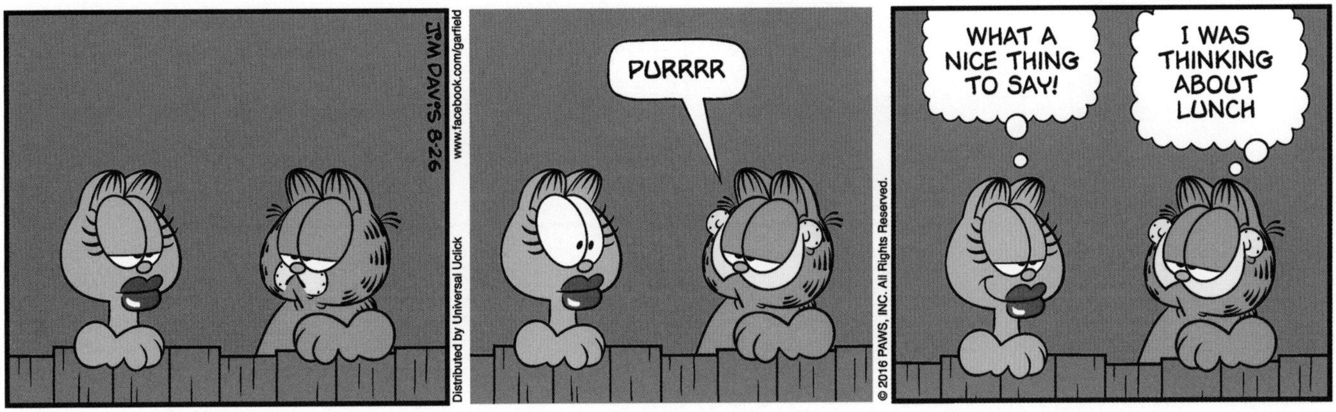
JIM DAVIS 8-26
www.facebook.com/garfield
Distributed by Universal Uclick
PURRRR
© 2016 PAWS, INC. All Rights Reserved.
WHAT A NICE THING TO SAY!
I WAS THINKING ABOUT LUNCH

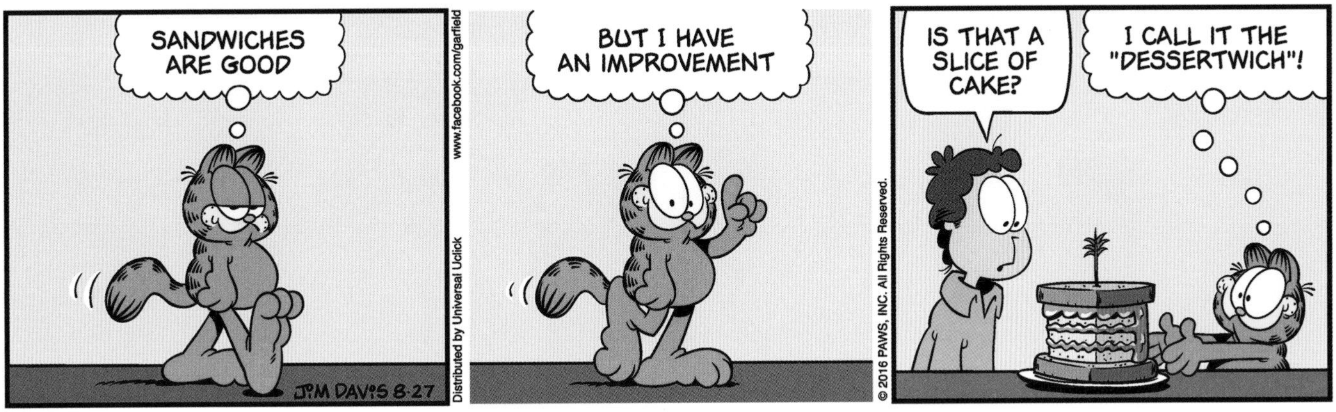
SANDWICHES ARE GOOD
JIM DAVIS 8-27
www.facebook.com/garfield
Distributed by Universal Uclick
BUT I HAVE AN IMPROVEMENT
© 2016 PAWS, INC. All Rights Reserved.
IS THAT A SLICE OF CAKE?
I CALL IT THE "DESSERTWICH"!

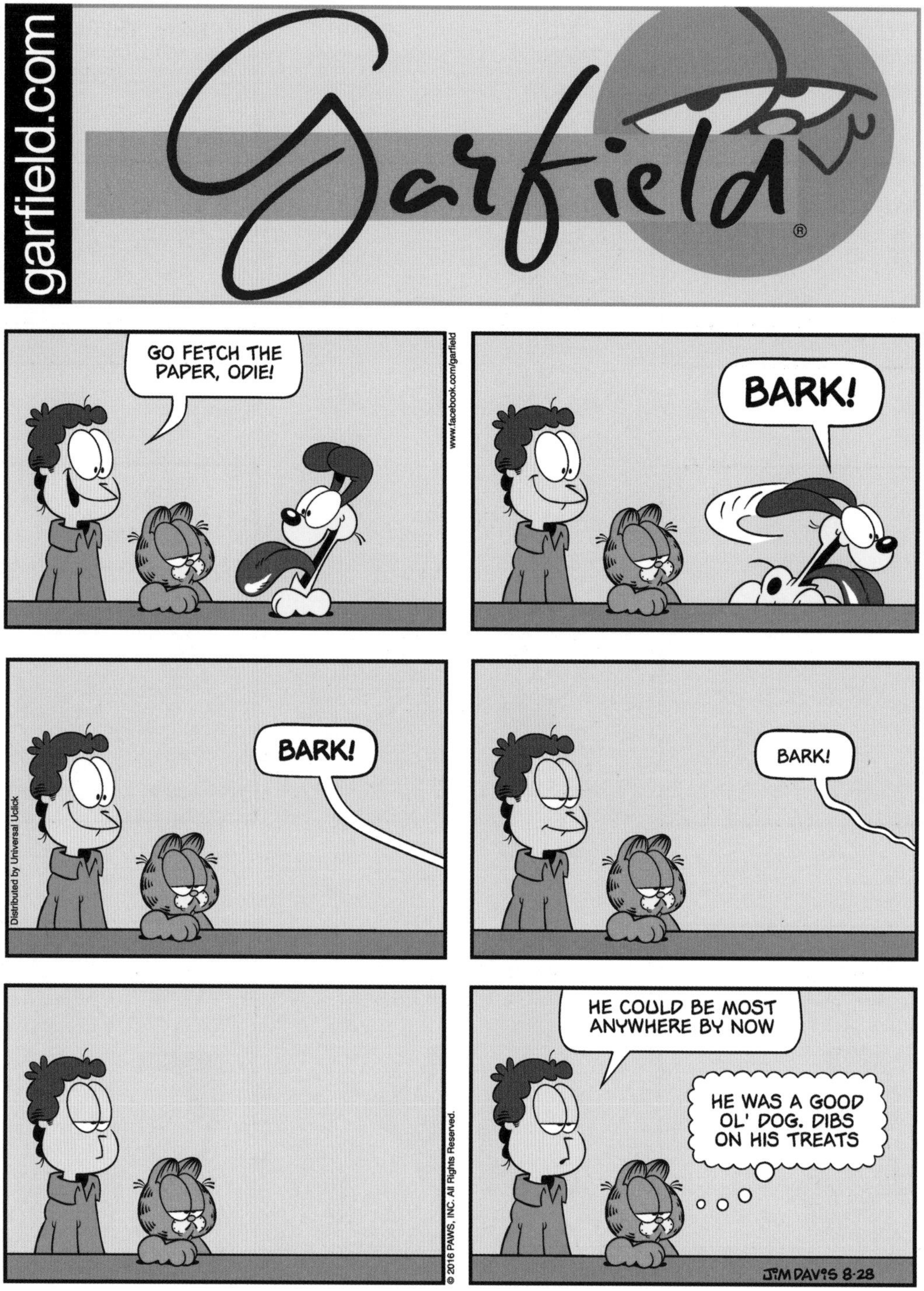
garfield.com
Garfield®
GO FETCH THE PAPER, ODIE!
www.facebook.com/garfield
BARK!
Distributed by Universal Uclick
BARK!
BARK!
© 2016 PAWS, INC. All Rights Reserved.
HE COULD BE MOST ANYWHERE BY NOW
HE WAS A GOOD OL' DOG. DIBS ON HIS TREATS
JIM DAVIS 8-28

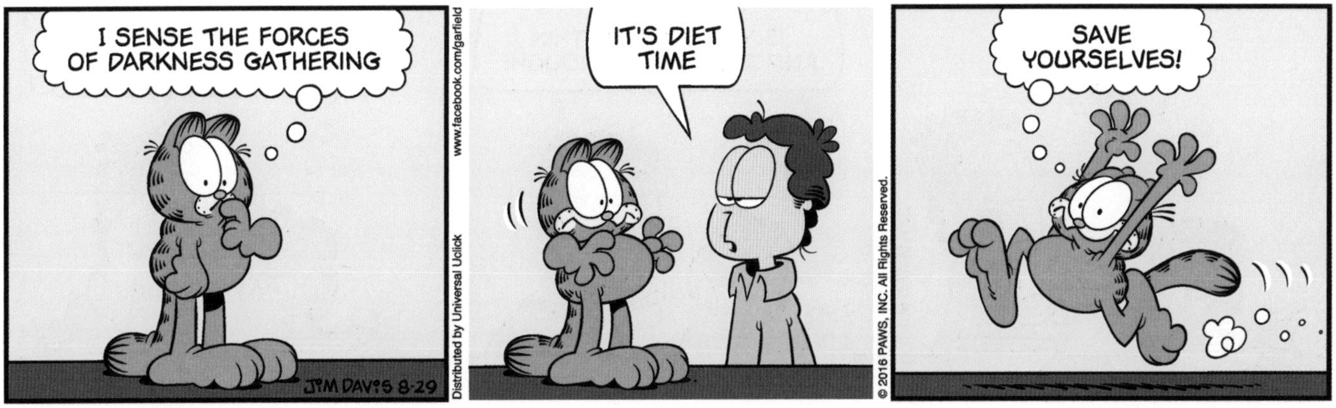
I SENSE THE FORCES OF DARKNESS GATHERING
JIM DAVIS 8-29
Distributed by Universal Uclick www.facebook.com/garfield
IT'S DIET TIME
© 2016 PAWS, INC. All Rights Reserved.
SAVE YOURSELVES!

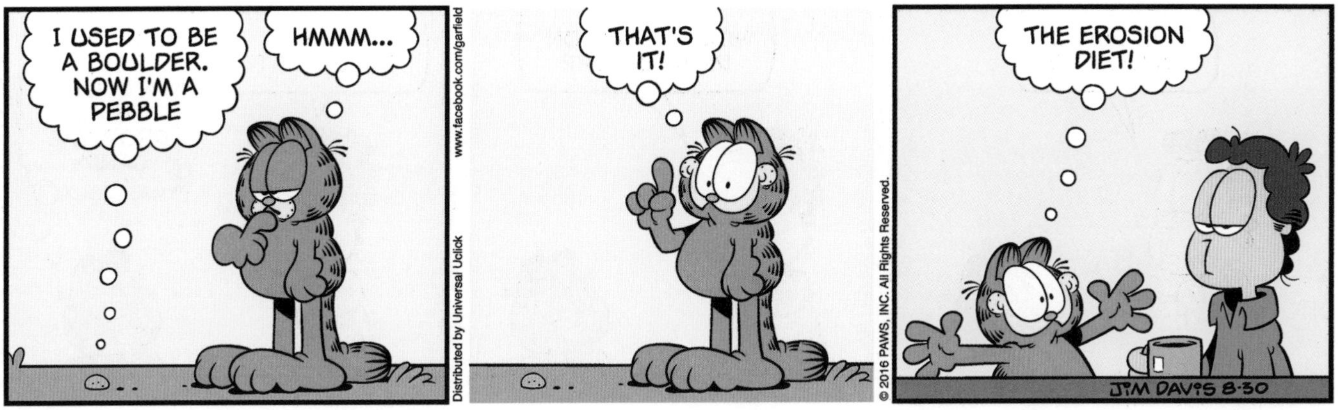
I USED TO BE A BOULDER. NOW I'M A PEBBLE
HMMM...
Distributed by Universal Uclick www.facebook.com/garfield
THAT'S IT!
© 2016 PAWS, INC. All Rights Reserved.
THE EROSION DIET!
JIM DAVIS 8-30

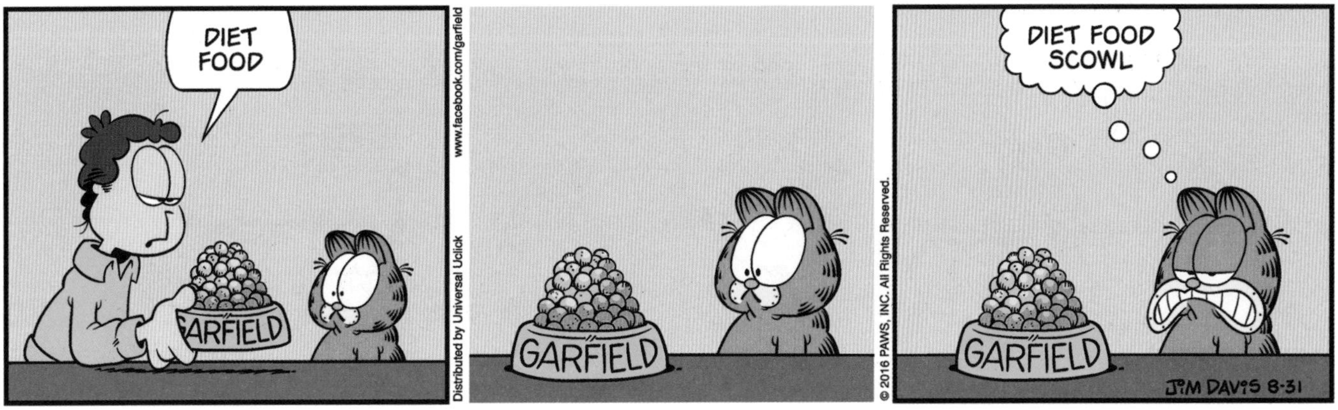
DIET FOOD
GARFIELD
Distributed by Universal Uclick www.facebook.com/garfield
GARFIELD
© 2016 PAWS, INC. All Rights Reserved.
DIET FOOD SCOWL
GARFIELD
JIM DAVIS 8-31

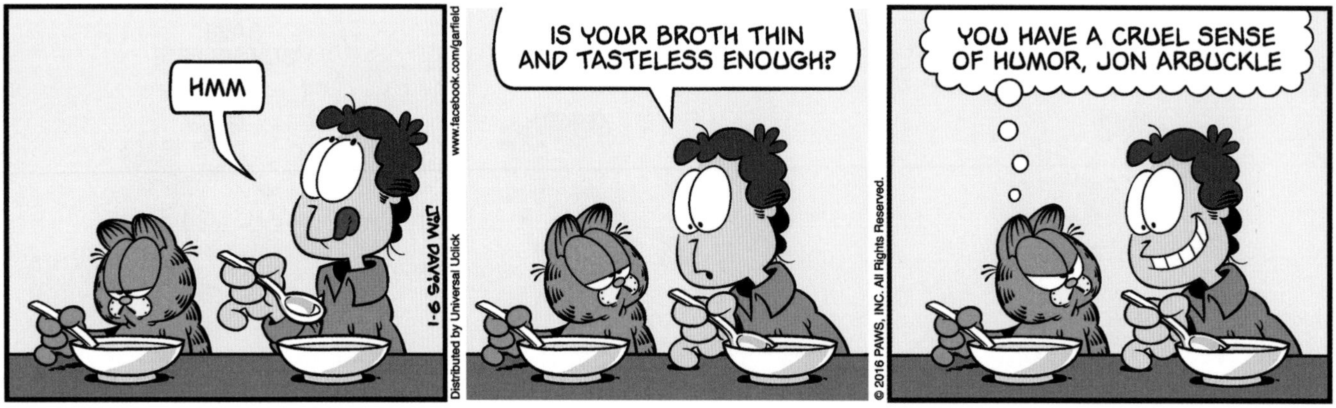
HMM
JIM DAVIS 9-1
Distributed by Universal Uclick www.facebook.com/garfield
IS YOUR BROTH THIN AND TASTELESS ENOUGH?
© 2016 PAWS, INC. All Rights Reserved.
YOU HAVE A CRUEL SENSE OF HUMOR, JON ARBUCKLE

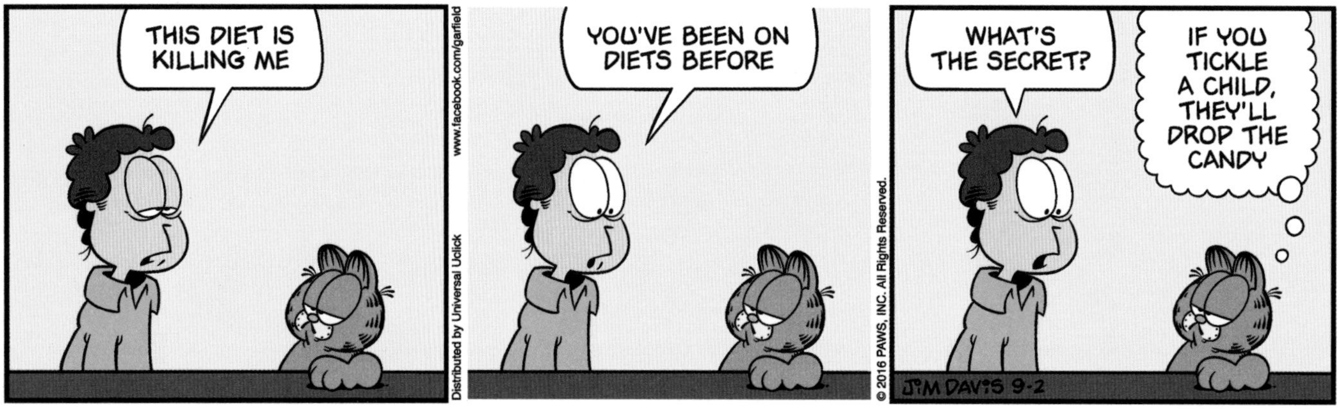
THIS DIET IS KILLING ME
Distributed by Universal Uclick www.facebook.com/garfield
YOU'VE BEEN ON DIETS BEFORE
© 2016 PAWS, INC. All Rights Reserved.
WHAT'S THE SECRET?
IF YOU TICKLE A CHILD, THEY'LL DROP THE CANDY
JIM DAVIS 9-2

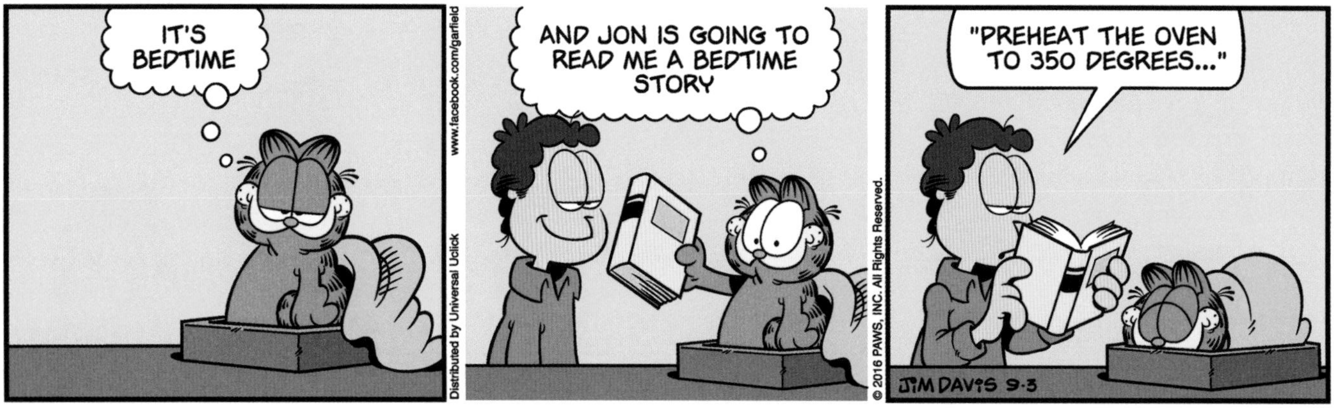
IT'S BEDTIME
Distributed by Universal Uclick www.facebook.com/garfield
AND JON IS GOING TO READ ME A BEDTIME STORY
© 2016 PAWS, INC. All Rights Reserved.
"PREHEAT THE OVEN TO 350 DEGREES..."
JIM DAVIS 9-3

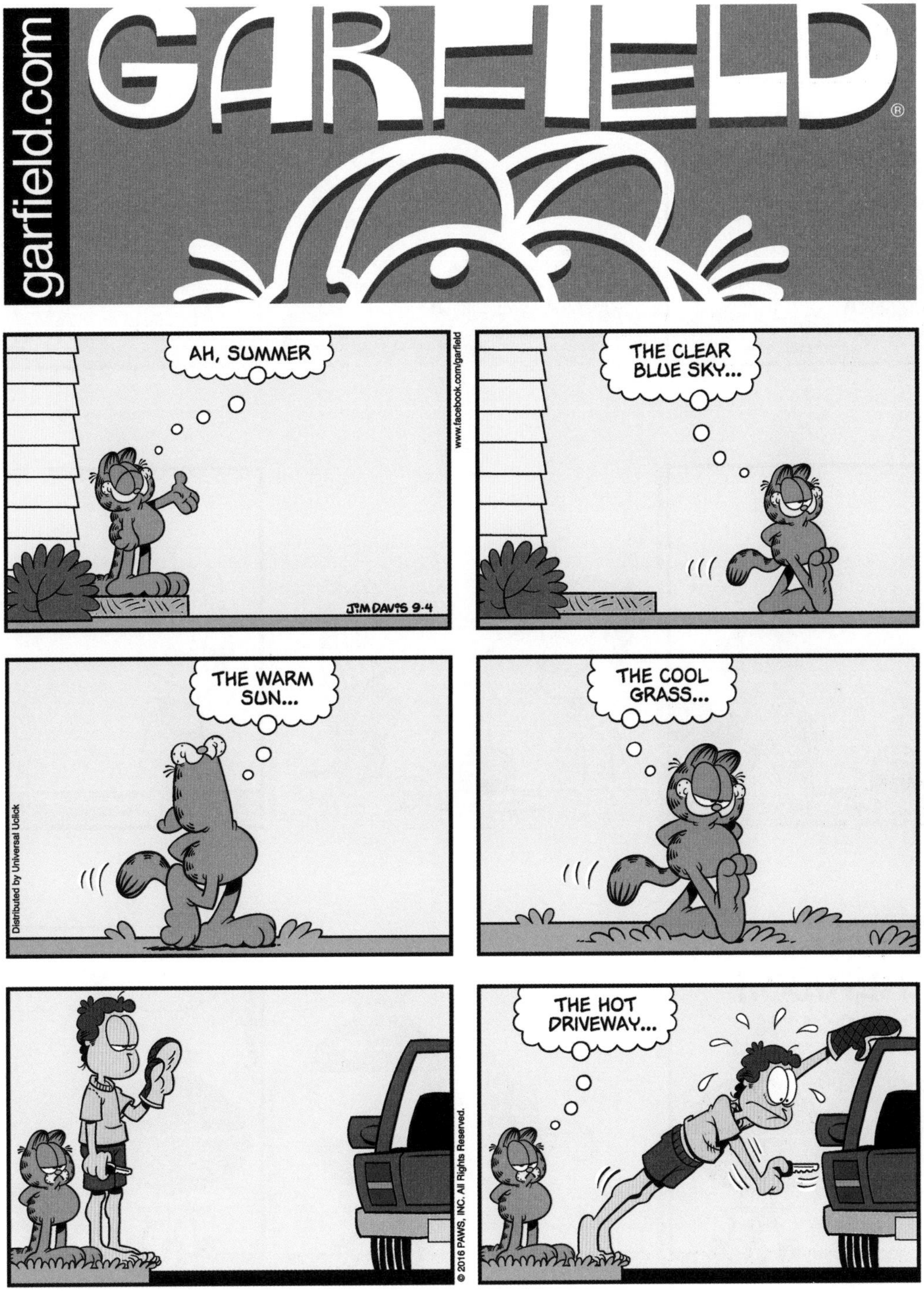
GARFIELD
garfield.com
AH, SUMMER
JIM DAVIS 9-4
www.facebook.com/garfield
THE CLEAR BLUE SKY...
THE WARM SUN...
Distributed by Universal Uclick
THE COOL GRASS...
© 2016 PAWS, INC. All Rights Reserved.
THE HOT DRIVEWAY...

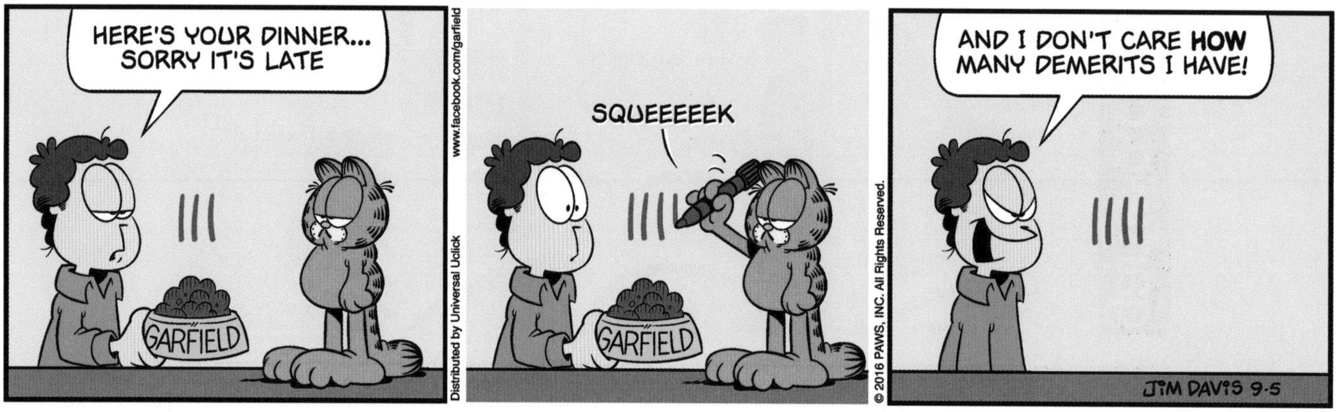
HERE'S YOUR DINNER... SORRY IT'S LATE
GARFIELD
www.facebook.com/garfield
Distributed by Universal Uclick
SQUEEEEEK
GARFIELD
© 2016 PAWS, INC. All Rights Reserved.
AND I DON'T CARE **HOW** MANY DEMERITS I HAVE!
JIM DAVIS 9-5

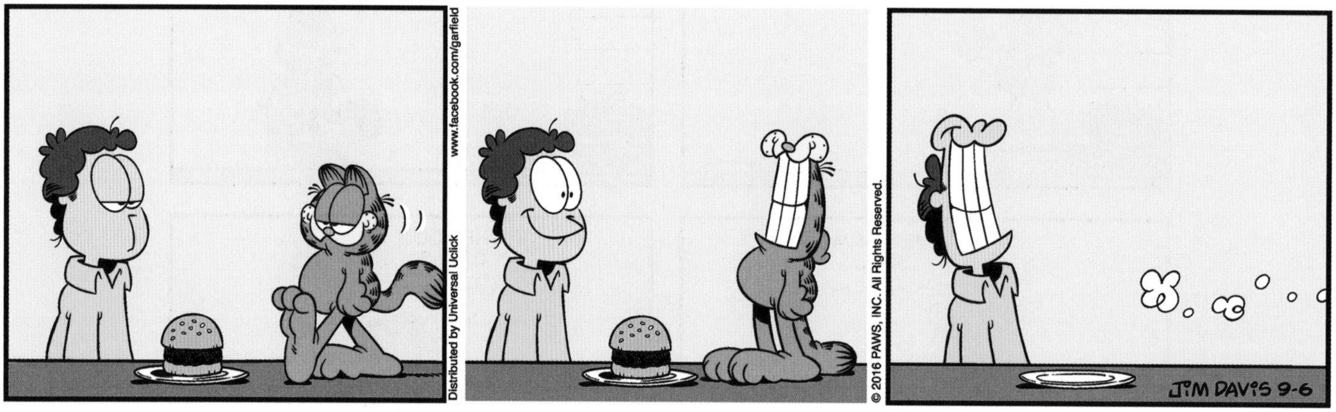
www.facebook.com/garfield
Distributed by Universal Uclick
© 2016 PAWS, INC. All Rights Reserved.
JIM DAVIS 9-6

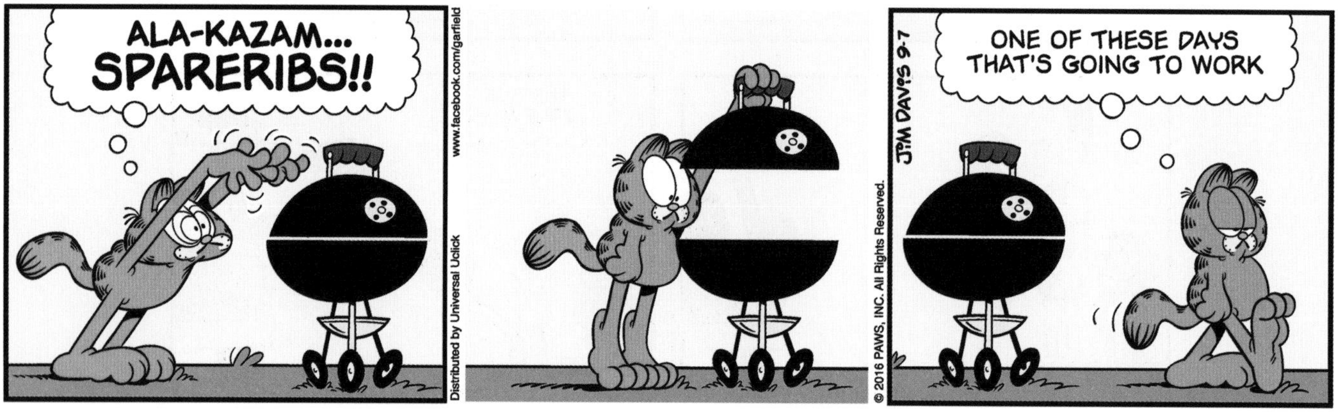
ALA-KAZAM... SPARERIBS!!
www.facebook.com/garfield
Distributed by Universal Uclick
JIM DAVIS 9-7
© 2016 PAWS, INC. All Rights Reserved.
ONE OF THESE DAYS THAT'S GOING TO WORK

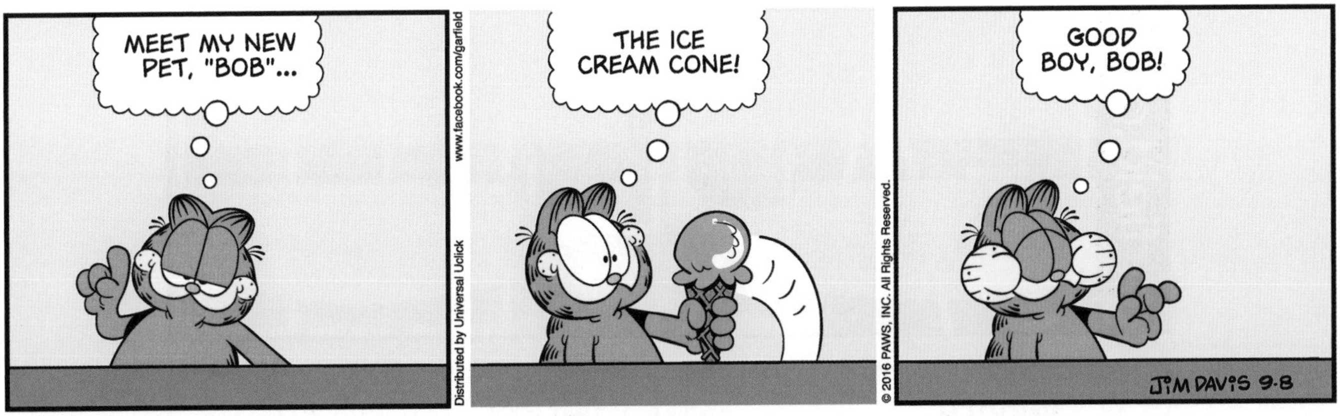
MEET MY NEW PET, "BOB"...
THE ICE CREAM CONE!
GOOD BOY, BOB!
JIM DAVIS 9-8
Distributed by Universal Uclick www.facebook.com/garfield
© 2016 PAWS, INC. All Rights Reserved.

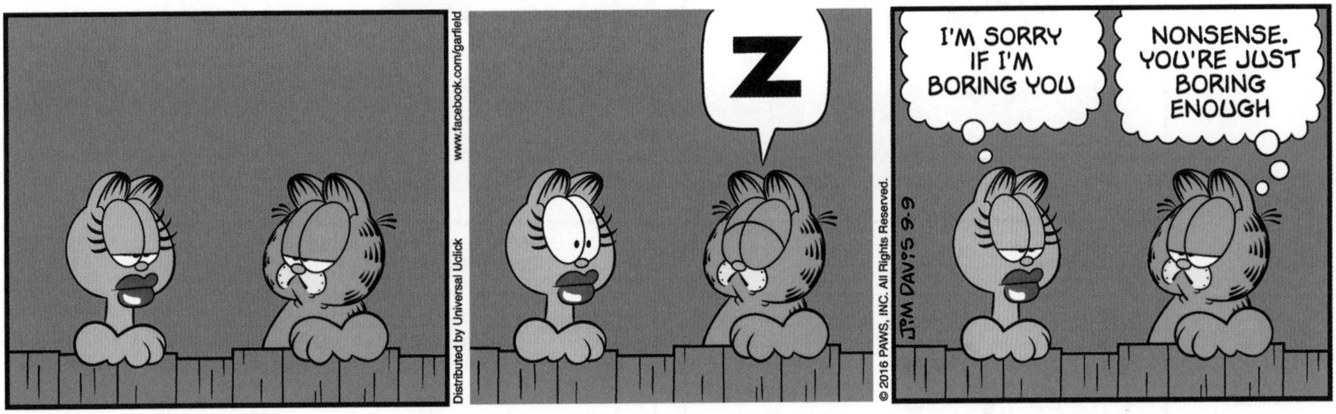
Z
I'M SORRY IF I'M BORING YOU
NONSENSE. YOU'RE JUST BORING ENOUGH
JIM DAVIS 9-9
Distributed by Universal Uclick www.facebook.com/garfield
© 2016 PAWS, INC. All Rights Reserved.

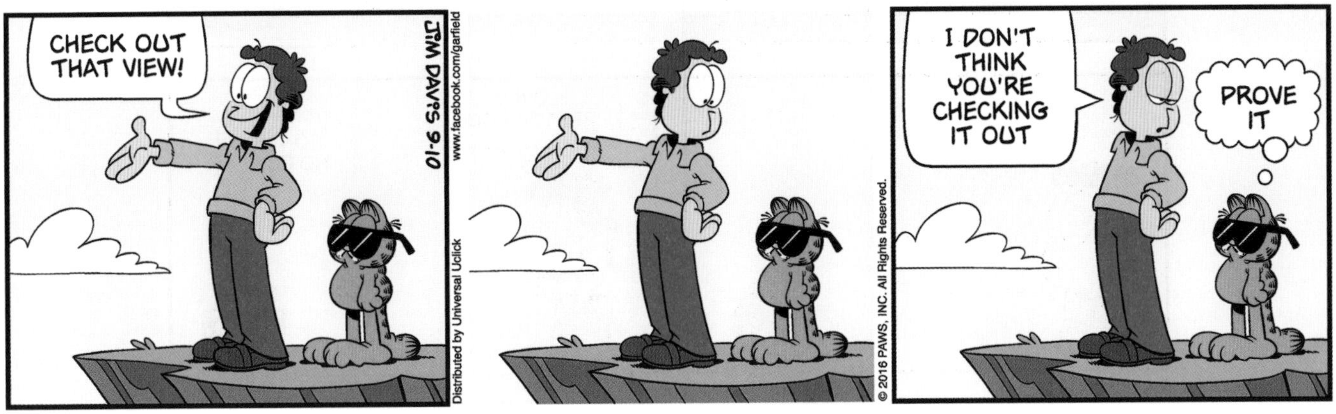
CHECK OUT THAT VIEW!
I DON'T THINK YOU'RE CHECKING IT OUT
PROVE IT
JIM DAVIS 9-10
Distributed by Universal Uclick www.facebook.com/garfield
© 2016 PAWS, INC. All Rights Reserved.

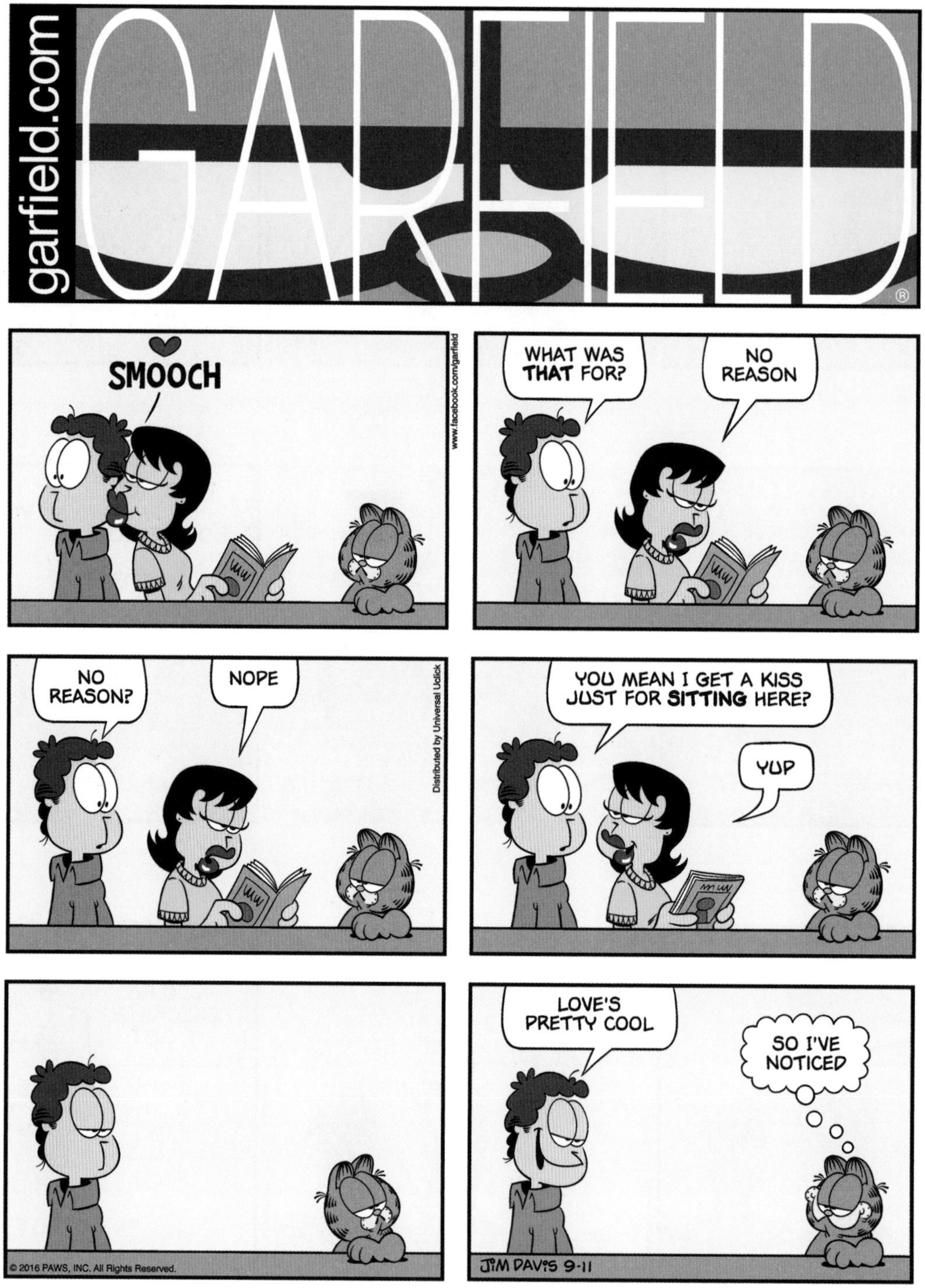
garfield.com
GARFIELD
SMOOCH
www.facebook.com/garfield
WHAT WAS THAT FOR?
NO REASON
NO REASON?
NOPE
Distributed by Universal Uclick
YOU MEAN I GET A KISS JUST FOR SITTING HERE?
YUP
© 2016 PAWS, INC. All Rights Reserved.
LOVE'S PRETTY COOL
SO I'VE NOTICED
JIM DAVIS 9-11

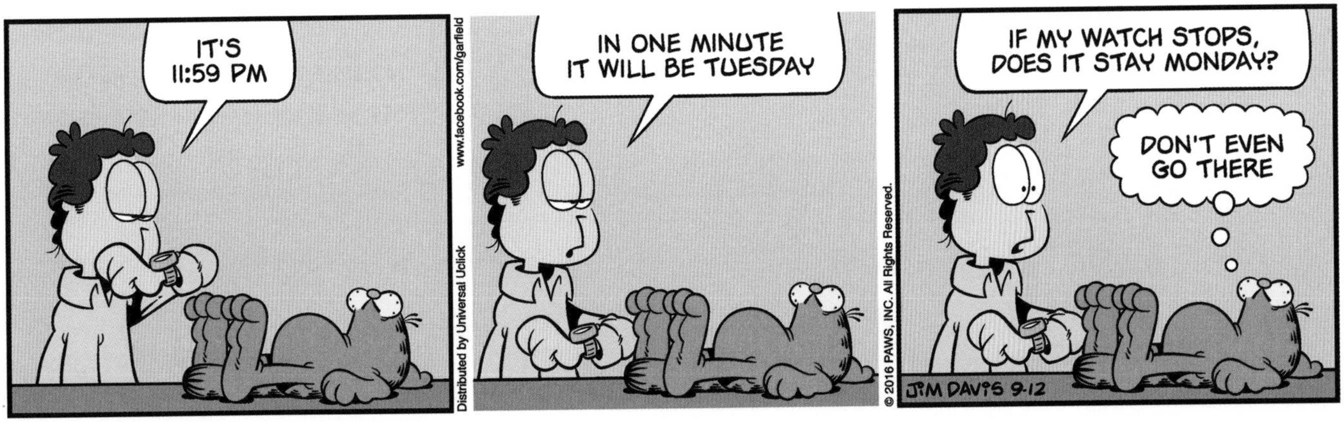
IT'S 11:59 PM
IN ONE MINUTE IT WILL BE TUESDAY
IF MY WATCH STOPS, DOES IT STAY MONDAY?
DON'T EVEN GO THERE
JIM DAVIS 9-12
www.facebook.com/garfield
Distributed by Universal Uclick
© 2016 PAWS, INC. All Rights Reserved.

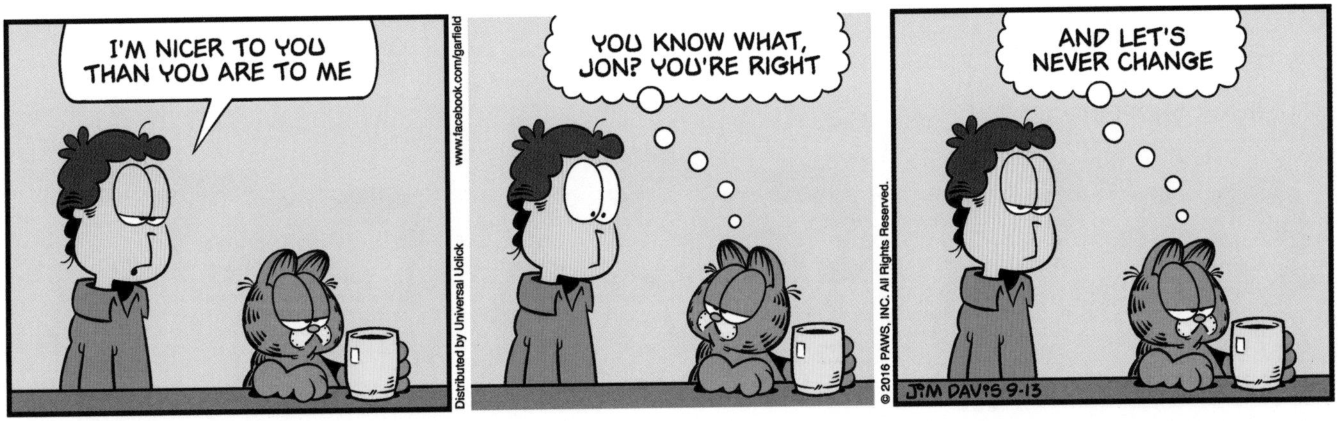
I'M NICER TO YOU THAN YOU ARE TO ME
YOU KNOW WHAT, JON? YOU'RE RIGHT
AND LET'S NEVER CHANGE
JIM DAVIS 9-13
www.facebook.com/garfield
Distributed by Universal Uclick
© 2016 PAWS, INC. All Rights Reserved.

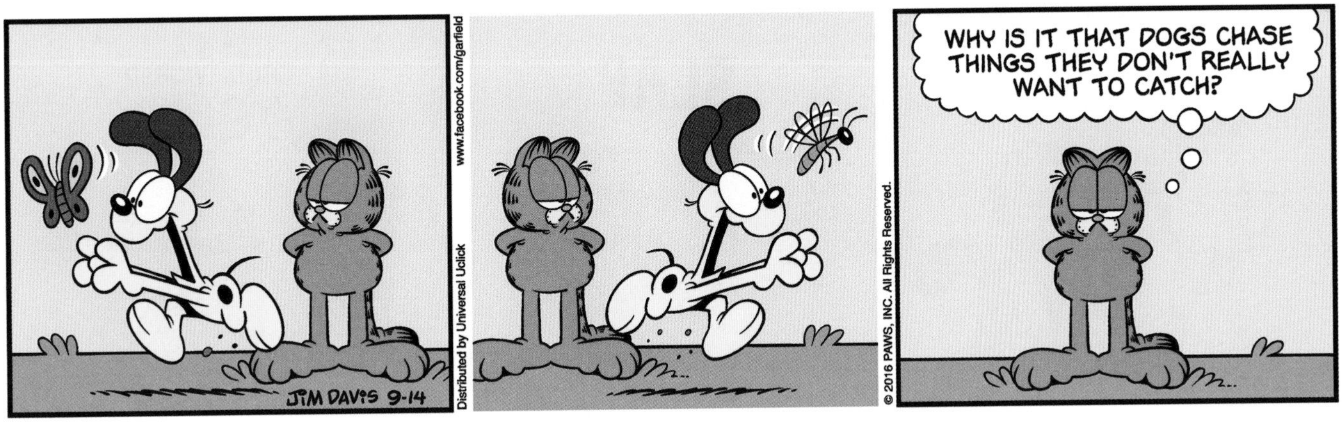
JIM DAVIS 9-14
WHY IS IT THAT DOGS CHASE THINGS THEY DON'T REALLY WANT TO CATCH?
www.facebook.com/garfield
Distributed by Universal Uclick
© 2016 PAWS, INC. All Rights Reserved.

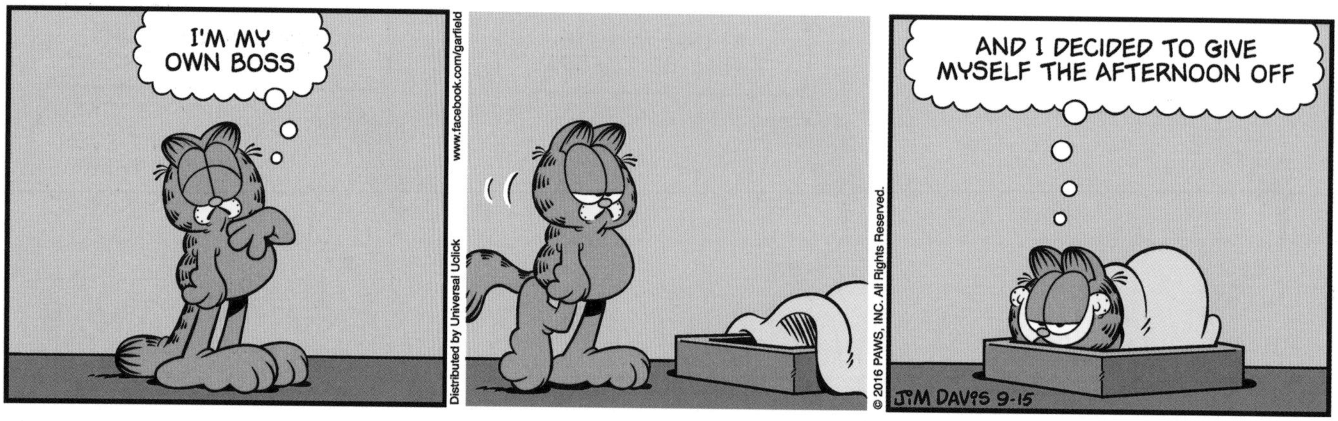
I'M MY OWN BOSS
AND I DECIDED TO GIVE MYSELF THE AFTERNOON OFF
Distributed by Universal Uclick
www.facebook.com/garfield
© 2016 PAWS, INC. All Rights Reserved.
JIM DAVIS 9-15

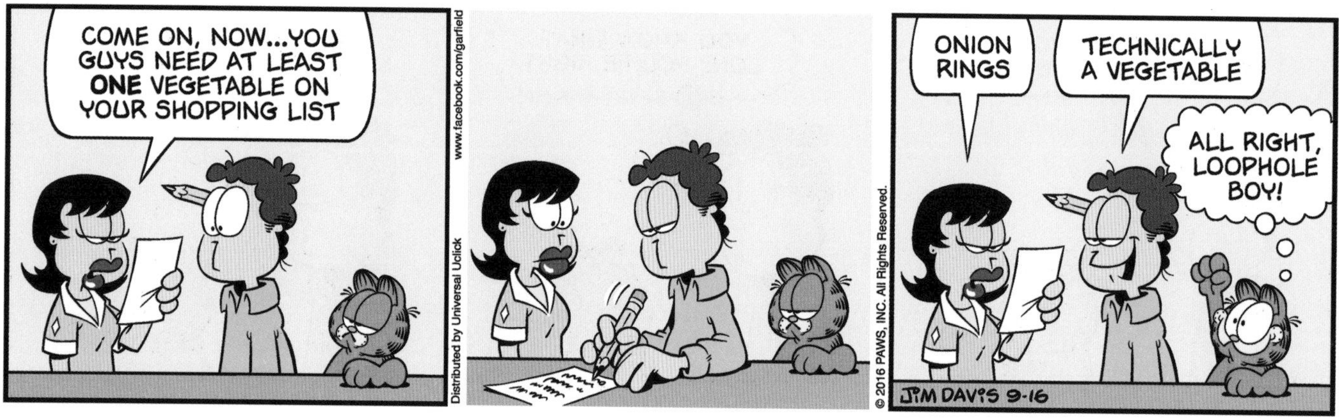
COME ON, NOW...YOU GUYS NEED AT LEAST **ONE** VEGETABLE ON YOUR SHOPPING LIST
ONION RINGS
TECHNICALLY A VEGETABLE
ALL RIGHT, LOOPHOLE BOY!
Distributed by Universal Uclick
www.facebook.com/garfield
© 2016 PAWS, INC. All Rights Reserved.
JIM DAVIS 9-16

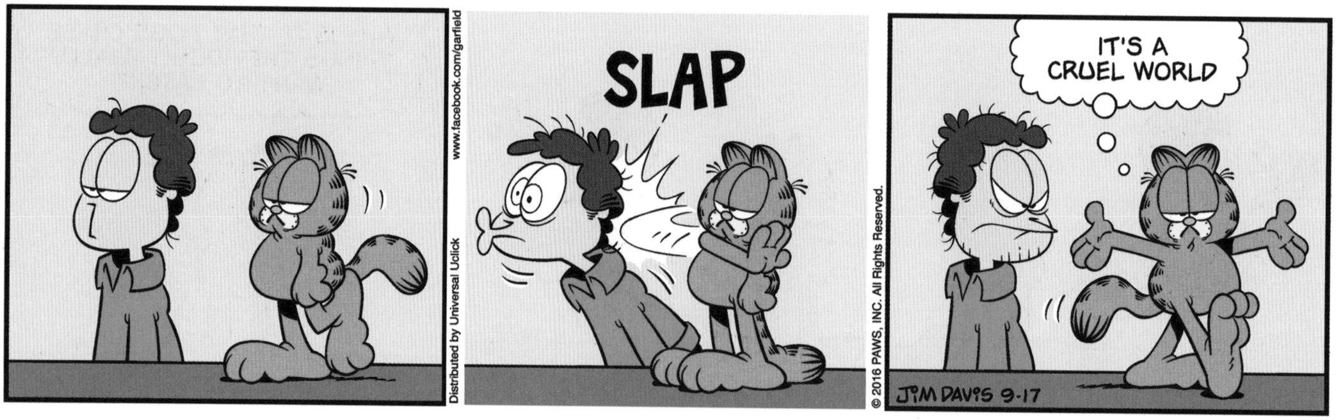
SLAP
IT'S A CRUEL WORLD
Distributed by Universal Uclick
www.facebook.com/garfield
© 2016 PAWS, INC. All Rights Reserved.
JIM DAVIS 9-17

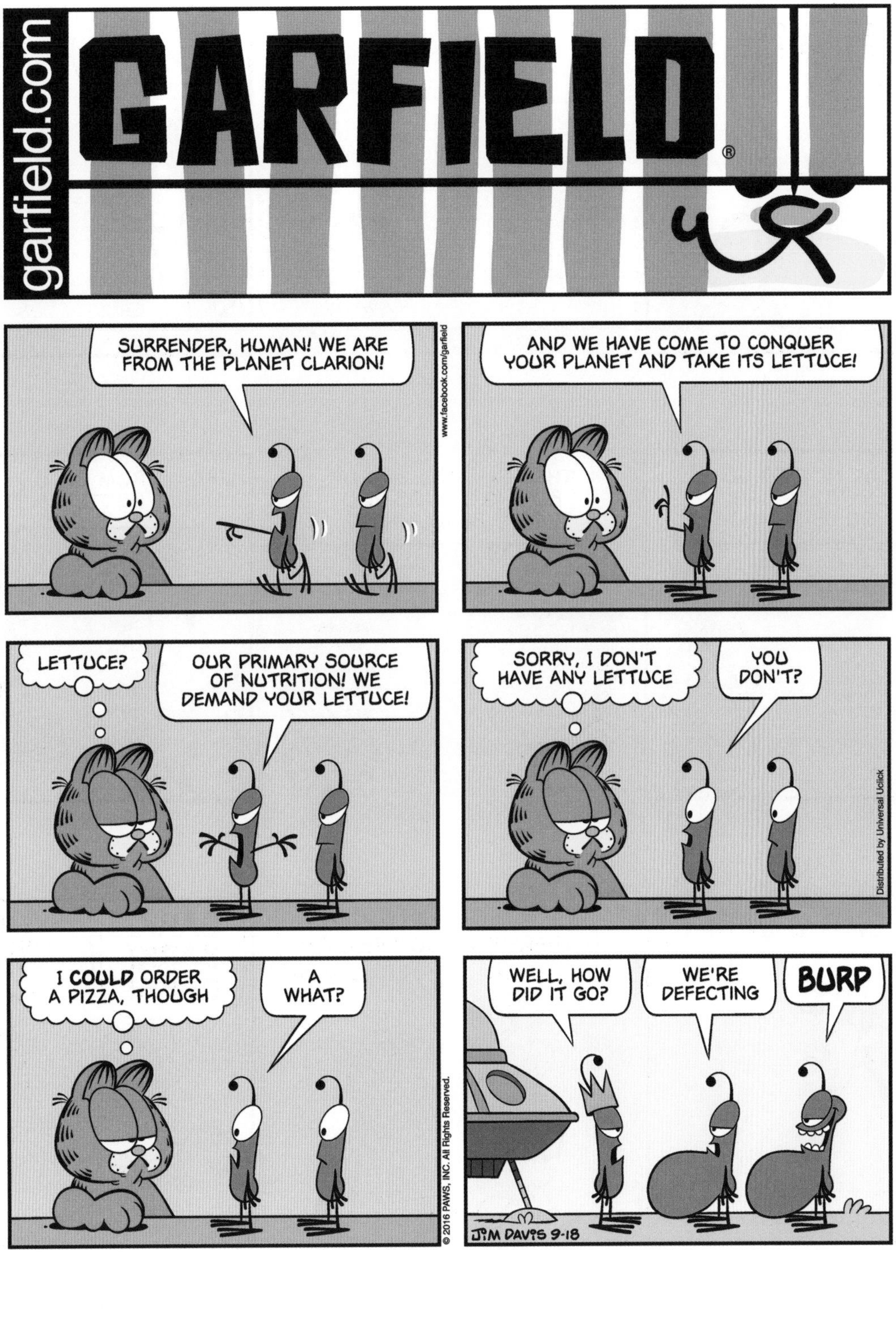
garfield.com
GARFIELD®
SURRENDER, HUMAN! WE ARE FROM THE PLANET CLARION!
www.facebook.com/garfield
AND WE HAVE COME TO CONQUER YOUR PLANET AND TAKE ITS LETTUCE!
LETTUCE?
OUR PRIMARY SOURCE OF NUTRITION! WE DEMAND YOUR LETTUCE!
SORRY, I DON'T HAVE ANY LETTUCE
YOU DON'T?
Distributed by Universal Uclick
I **COULD** ORDER A PIZZA, THOUGH
A WHAT?
© 2016 PAWS, INC. All Rights Reserved.
WELL, HOW DID IT GO?
WE'RE DEFECTING
BURP
JIM DAVIS 9-18

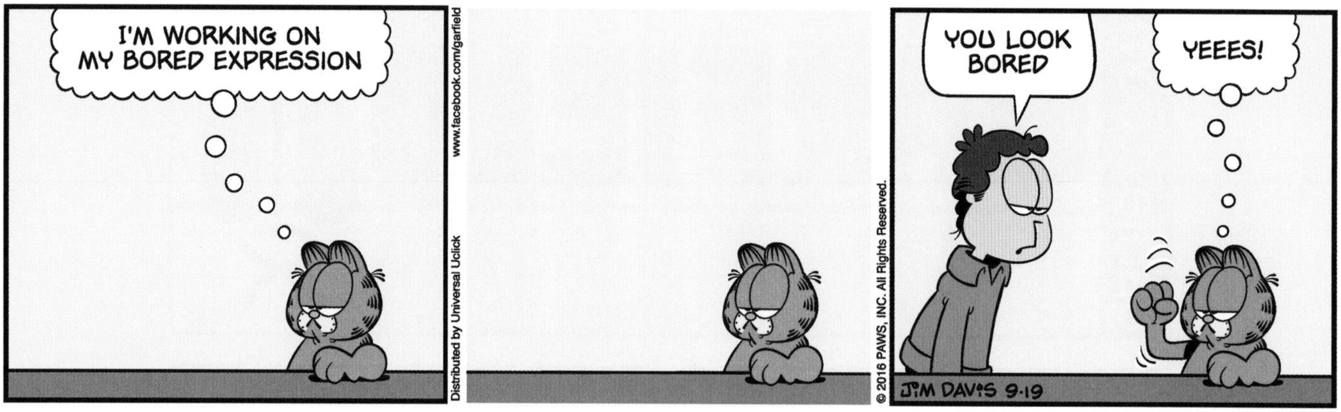
I'M WORKING ON MY BORED EXPRESSION
Distributed by Universal Uclick
www.facebook.com/garfield
YOU LOOK BORED
YEEES!
© 2016 PAWS, INC. All Rights Reserved.
JIM DAVIS 9·19

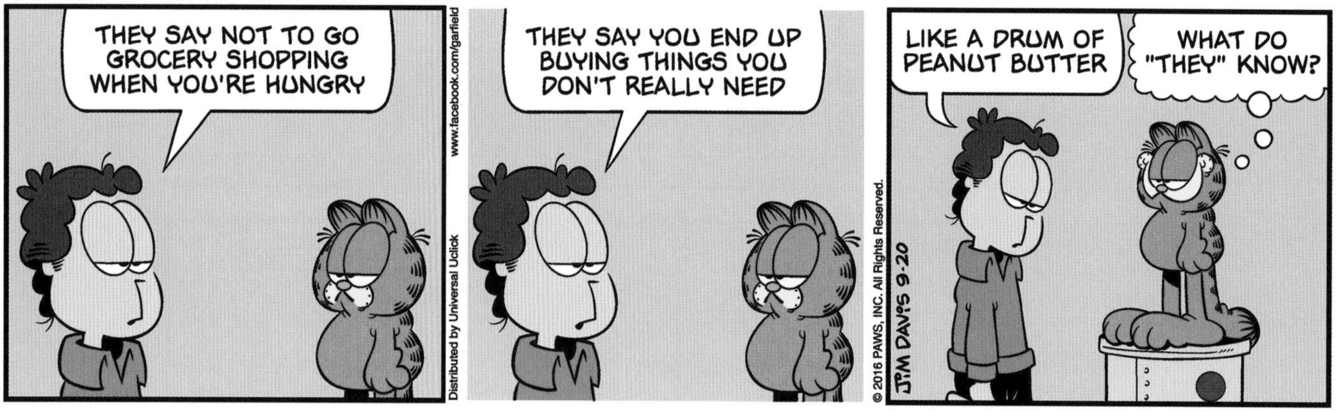
THEY SAY NOT TO GO GROCERY SHOPPING WHEN YOU'RE HUNGRY
Distributed by Universal Uclick
www.facebook.com/garfield
THEY SAY YOU END UP BUYING THINGS YOU DON'T REALLY NEED
LIKE A DRUM OF PEANUT BUTTER
WHAT DO "THEY" KNOW?
© 2016 PAWS, INC. All Rights Reserved.
JIM DAVIS 9·20

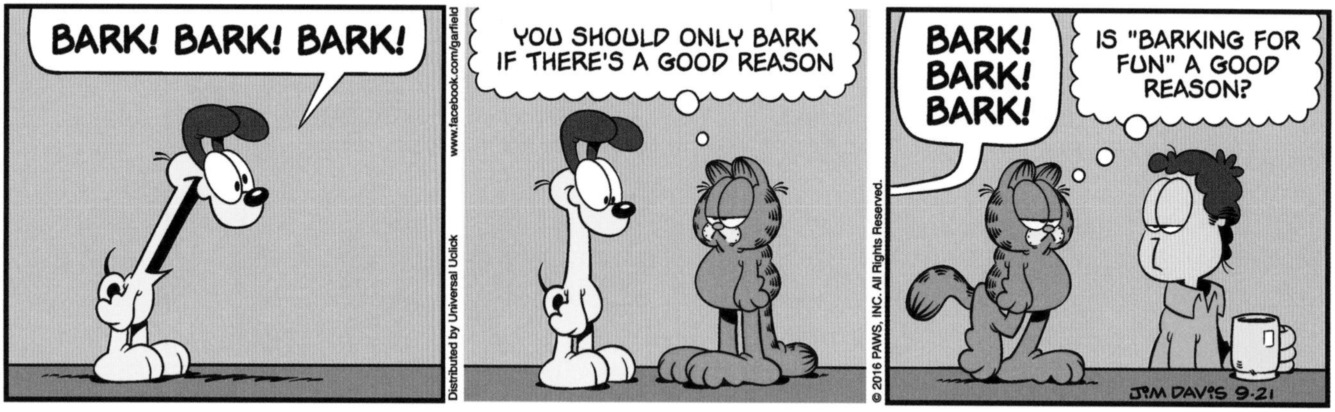
BARK! BARK! BARK!
Distributed by Universal Uclick
www.facebook.com/garfield
YOU SHOULD ONLY BARK IF THERE'S A GOOD REASON
BARK! BARK! BARK!
IS "BARKING FOR FUN" A GOOD REASON?
© 2016 PAWS, INC. All Rights Reserved.
JIM DAVIS 9·21

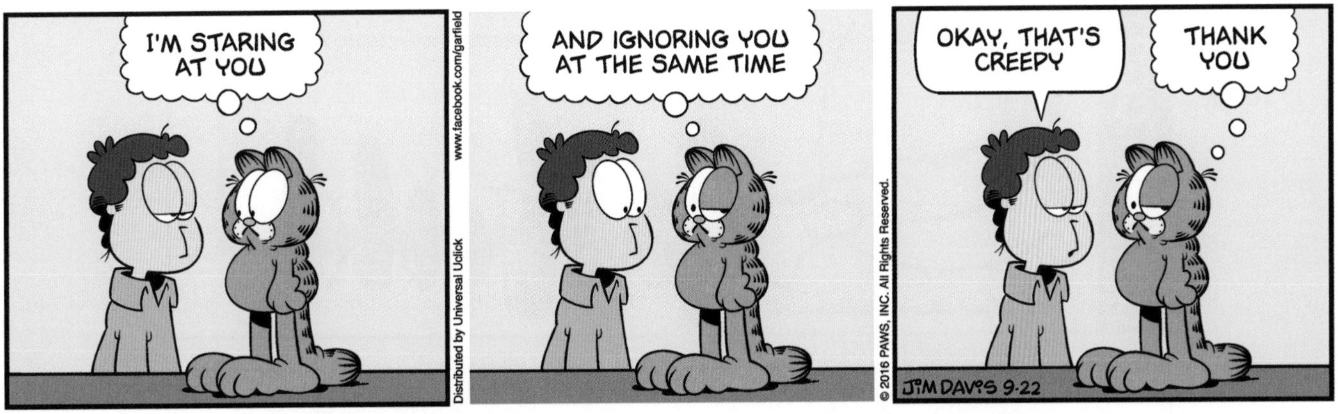
I'M STARING AT YOU
AND IGNORING YOU AT THE SAME TIME
OKAY, THAT'S CREEPY
THANK YOU
www.facebook.com/garfield
Distributed by Universal Uclick
© 2016 PAWS, INC. All Rights Reserved.
JIM DAVIS 9-22

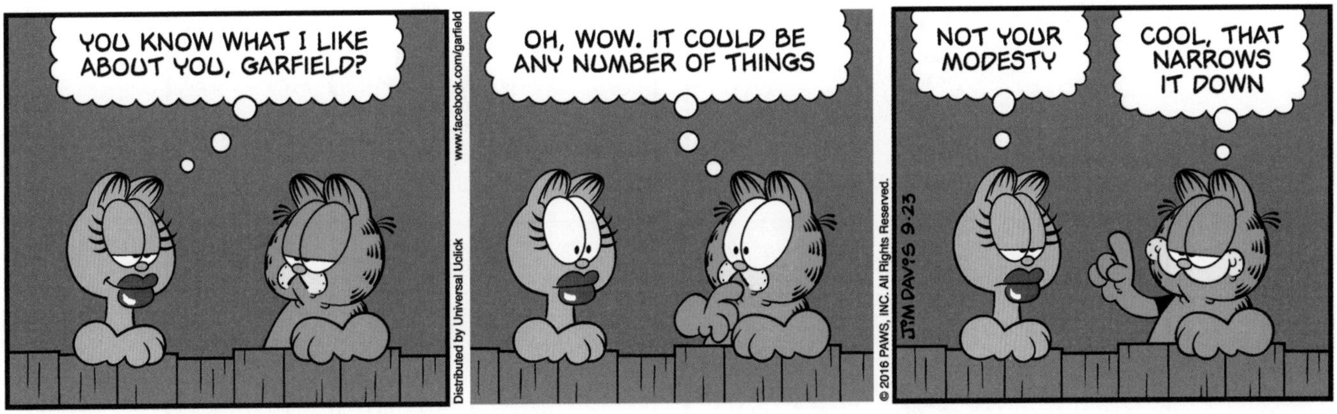
YOU KNOW WHAT I LIKE ABOUT YOU, GARFIELD?
OH, WOW. IT COULD BE ANY NUMBER OF THINGS
NOT YOUR MODESTY
COOL, THAT NARROWS IT DOWN
www.facebook.com/garfield
Distributed by Universal Uclick
© 2016 PAWS, INC. All Rights Reserved.
JIM DAVIS 9-23

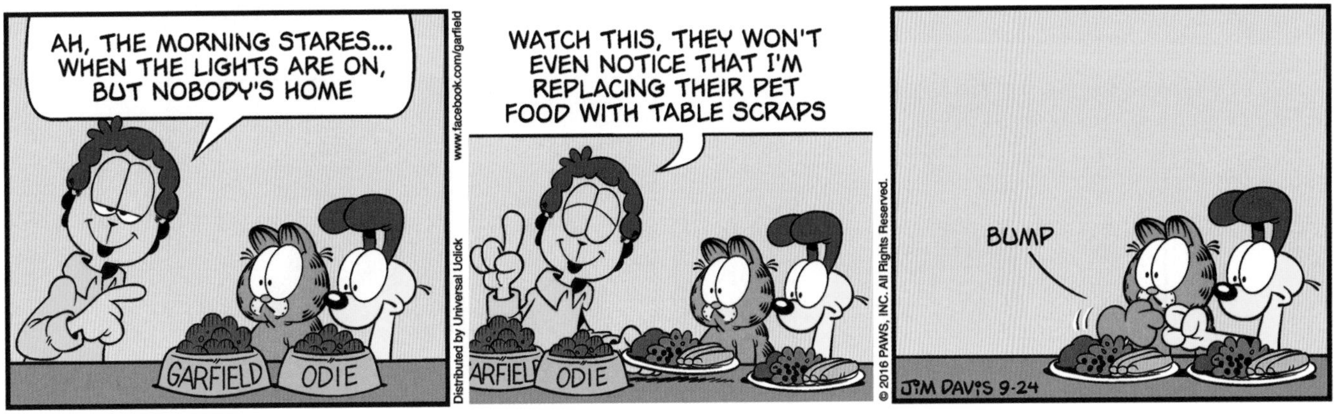
AH, THE MORNING STARES... WHEN THE LIGHTS ARE ON, BUT NOBODY'S HOME
GARFIELD
ODIE
WATCH THIS, THEY WON'T EVEN NOTICE THAT I'M REPLACING THEIR PET FOOD WITH TABLE SCRAPS
BUMP
www.facebook.com/garfield
Distributed by Universal Uclick
© 2016 PAWS, INC. All Rights Reserved.
JIM DAVIS 9-24

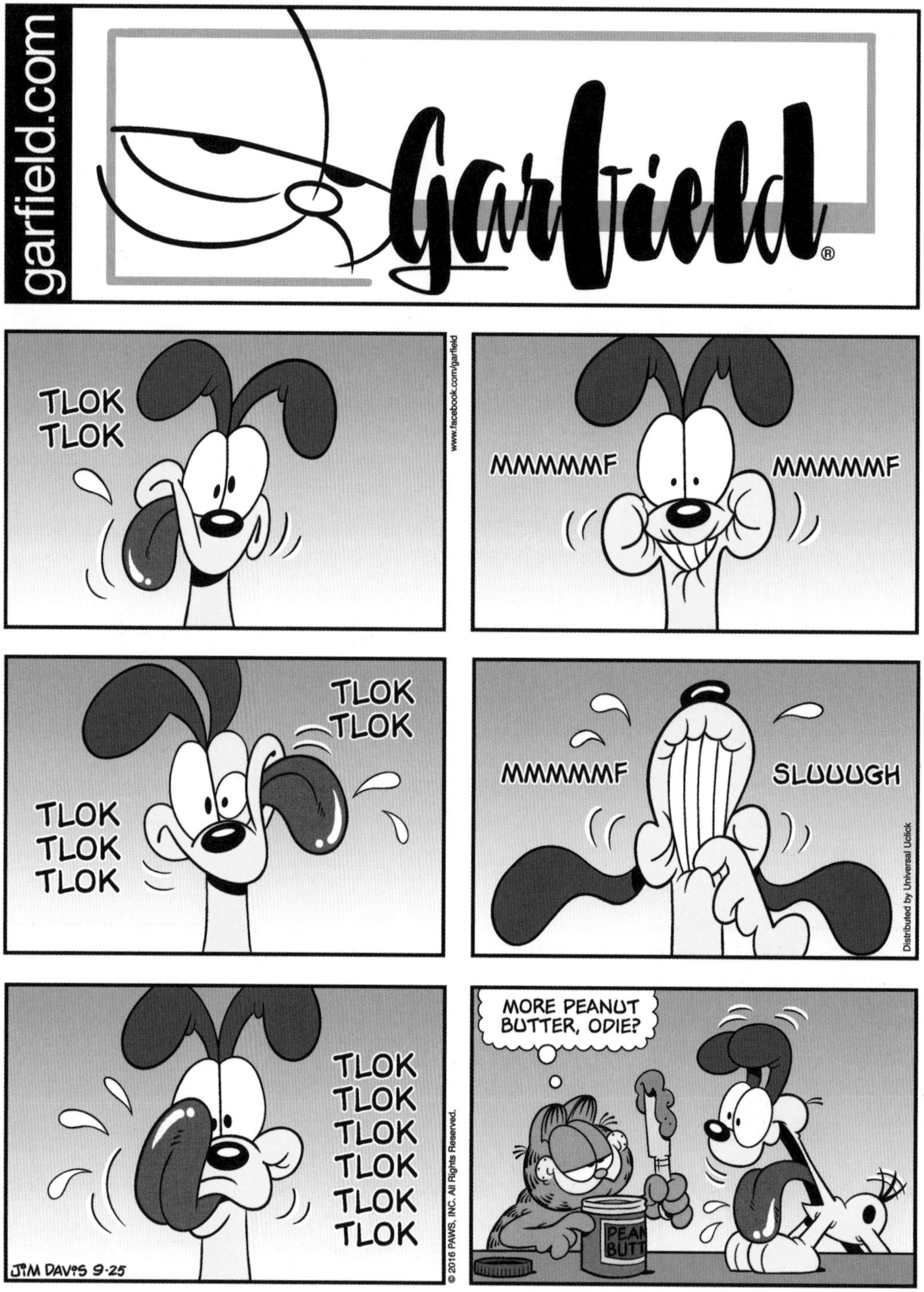
garfield.com
Garfield®
www.facebook.com/garfield
TLOK
TLOK
MMMMMF
MMMMMF
TLOK
TLOK
TLOK
TLOK
TLOK
MMMMMF
SLUUUGH
Distributed by Universal Uclick
TLOK
TLOK
TLOK
TLOK
TLOK
TLOK
JIM DAVIS 9-25
© 2016 PAWS, INC. All Rights Reserved.
MORE PEANUT BUTTER, ODIE?

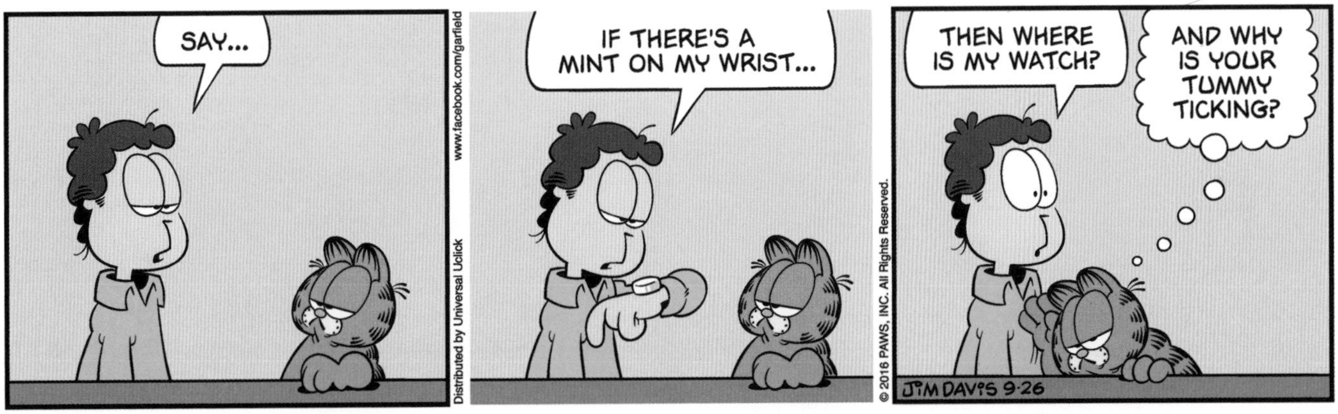
SAY...
IF THERE'S A MINT ON MY WRIST...
THEN WHERE IS MY WATCH?
AND WHY IS YOUR TUMMY TICKING?
JIM DAVIS 9-26
Distributed by Universal Uclick www.facebook.com/garfield
© 2016 PAWS, INC. All Rights Reserved.

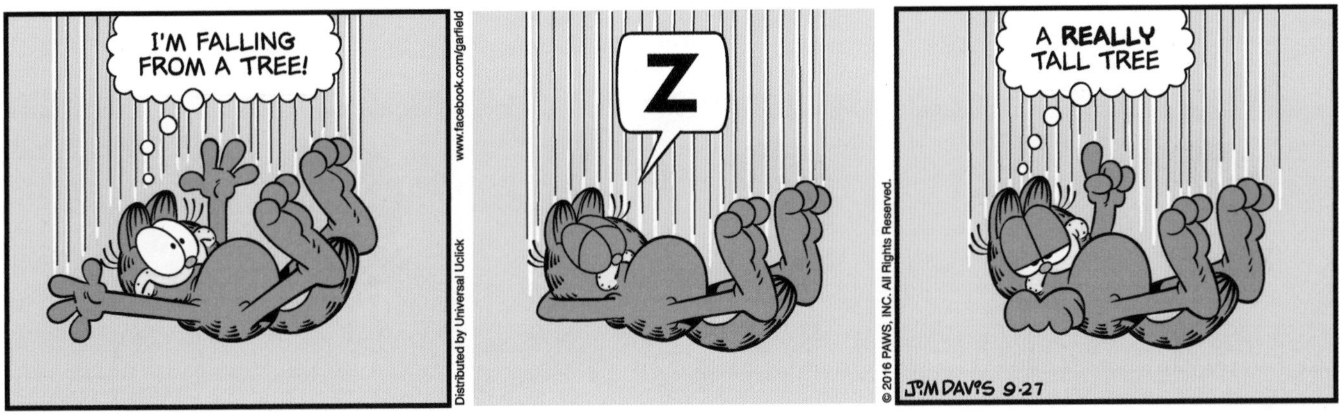
I'M FALLING FROM A TREE!
Z
A REALLY TALL TREE
JIM DAVIS 9-27
Distributed by Universal Uclick www.facebook.com/garfield
© 2016 PAWS, INC. All Rights Reserved.

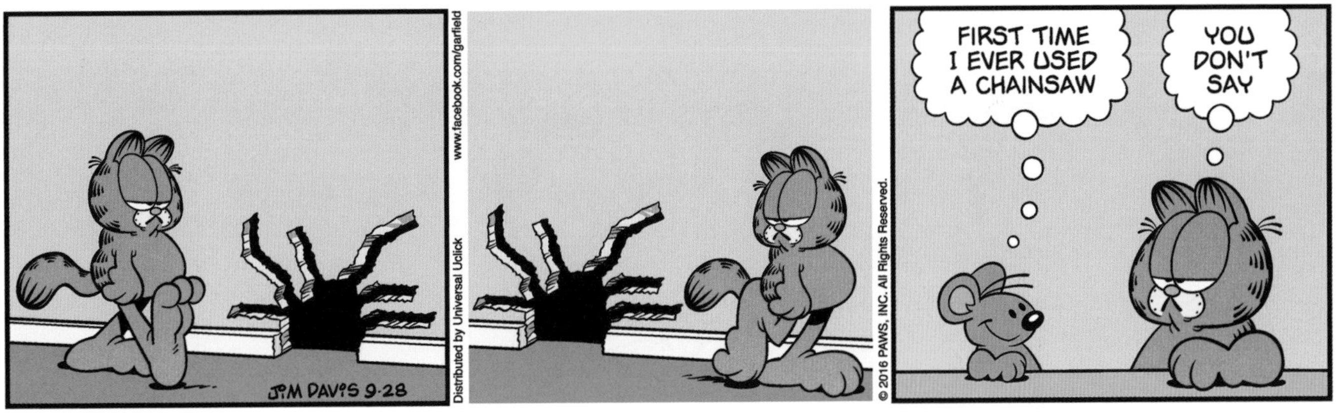
JIM DAVIS 9-28
FIRST TIME I EVER USED A CHAINSAW
YOU DON'T SAY
Distributed by Universal Uclick www.facebook.com/garfield
© 2016 PAWS, INC. All Rights Reserved.

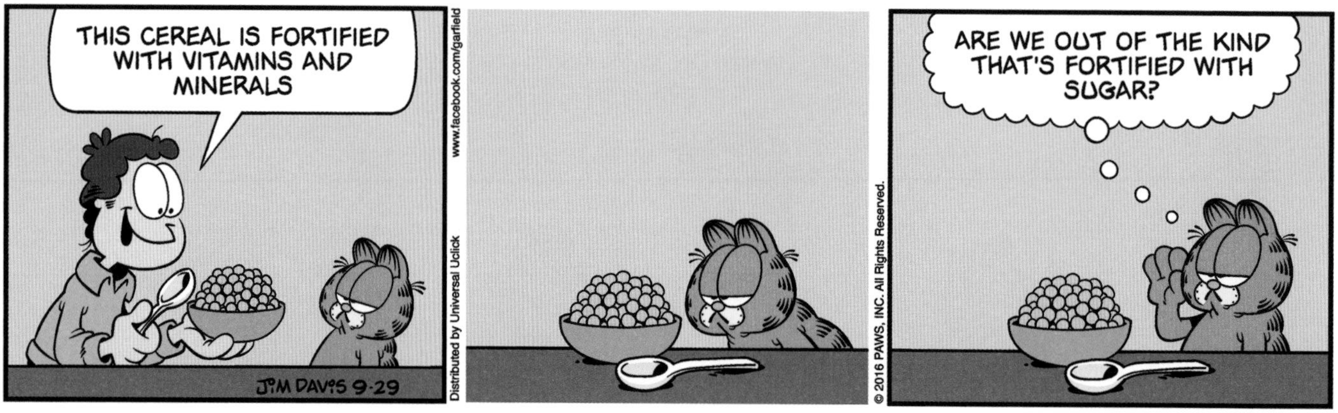
THIS CEREAL IS FORTIFIED WITH VITAMINS AND MINERALS
JIM DAVIS 9-29
Distributed by Universal Uclick www.facebook.com/garfield
© 2016 PAWS, INC. All Rights Reserved.
ARE WE OUT OF THE KIND THAT'S FORTIFIED WITH SUGAR?

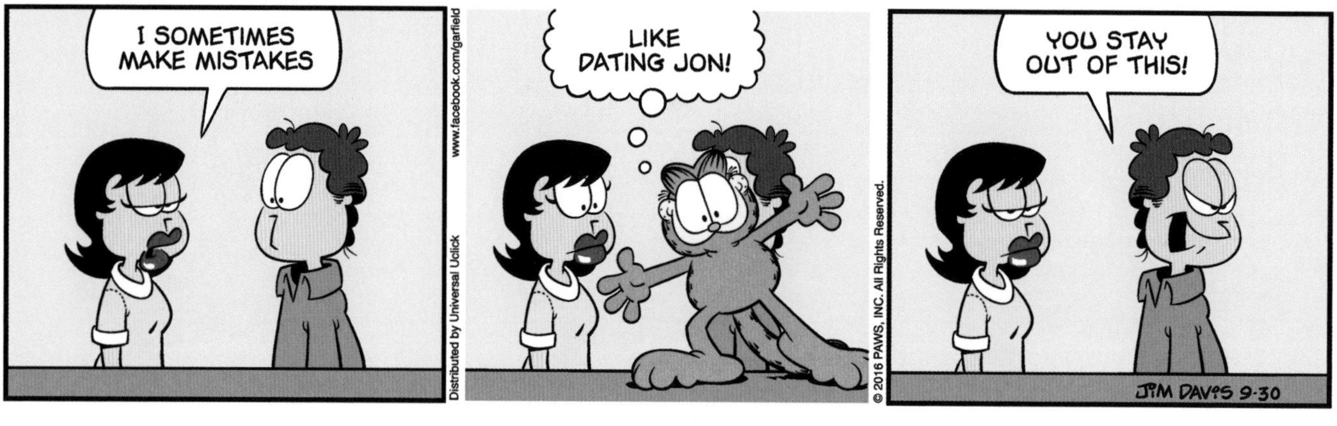
I SOMETIMES MAKE MISTAKES
Distributed by Universal Uclick www.facebook.com/garfield
LIKE DATING JON!
© 2016 PAWS, INC. All Rights Reserved.
YOU STAY OUT OF THIS!
JIM DAVIS 9-30

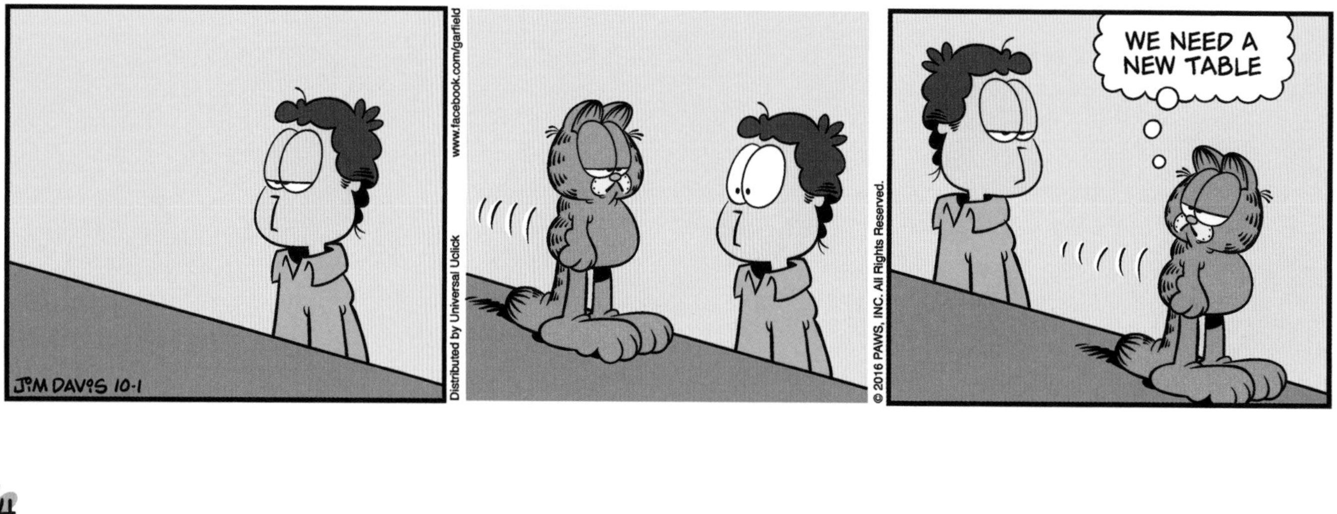
JIM DAVIS 10-1
Distributed by Universal Uclick www.facebook.com/garfield
© 2016 PAWS, INC. All Rights Reserved.
WE NEED A NEW TABLE

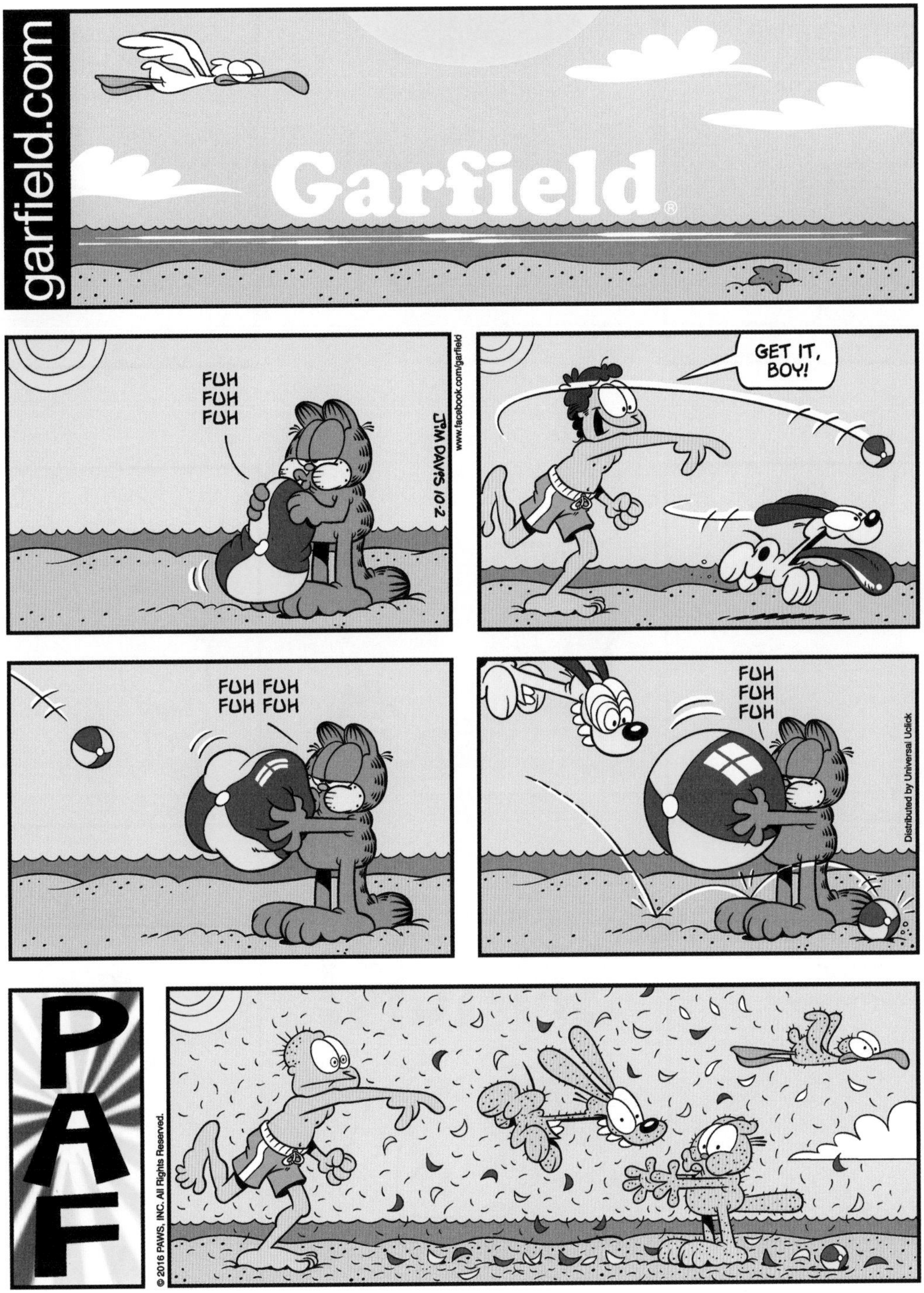
garfield.com
Garfield
FUH
FUH
FUH
JIM DAVIS 10-2
www.facebook.com/garfield
GET IT,
BOY!
FUH FUH
FUH FUH
FUH
FUH
FUH
Distributed by Universal Uclick
PAF
© 2016 PAWS, INC. All Rights Reserved.

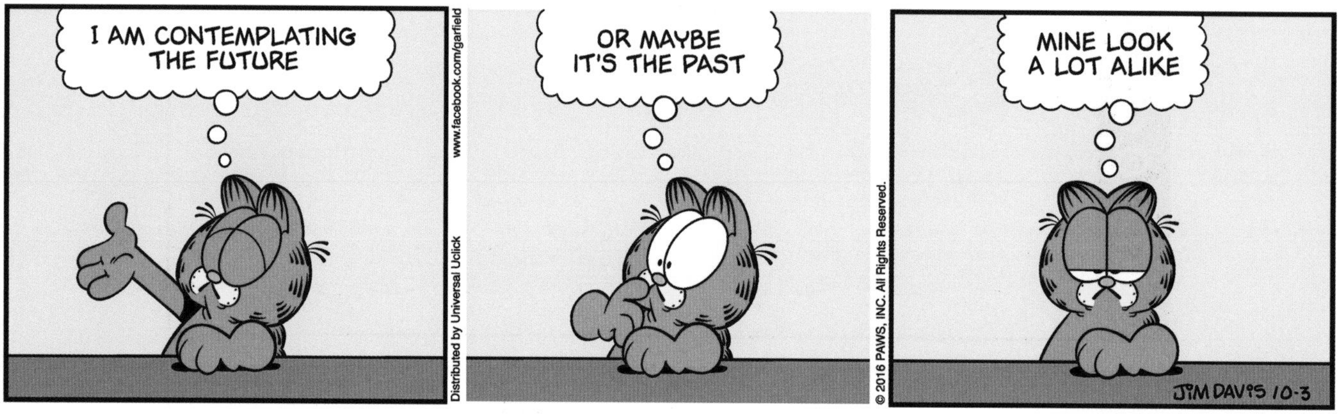
I AM CONTEMPLATING THE FUTURE
OR MAYBE IT'S THE PAST
MINE LOOK A LOT ALIKE
JIM DAVIS 10-3
Distributed by Universal Uclick www.facebook.com/garfield
© 2016 PAWS, INC. All Rights Reserved.

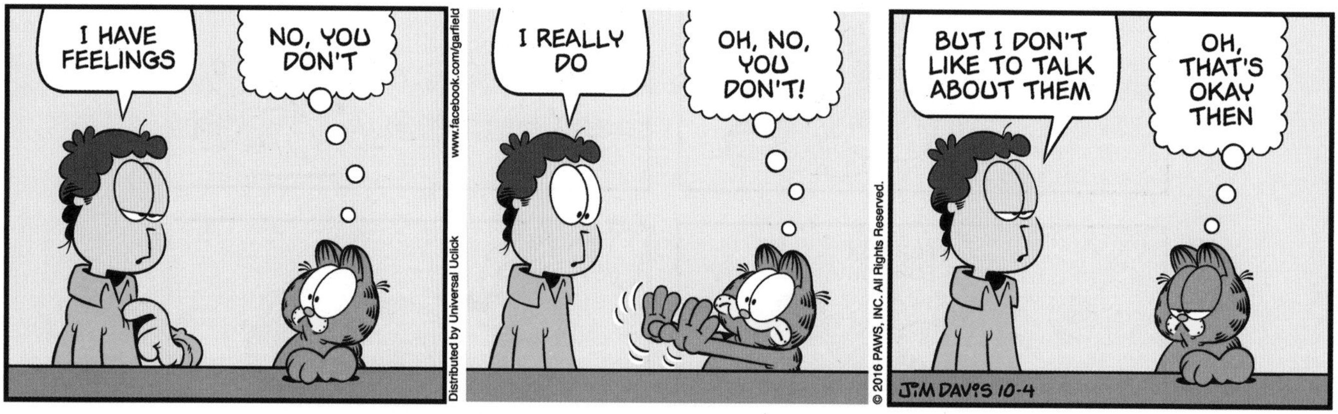
I HAVE FEELINGS
NO, YOU DON'T
I REALLY DO
OH, NO, YOU DON'T!
BUT I DON'T LIKE TO TALK ABOUT THEM
OH, THAT'S OKAY THEN
JIM DAVIS 10-4
Distributed by Universal Uclick www.facebook.com/garfield
© 2016 PAWS, INC. All Rights Reserved.

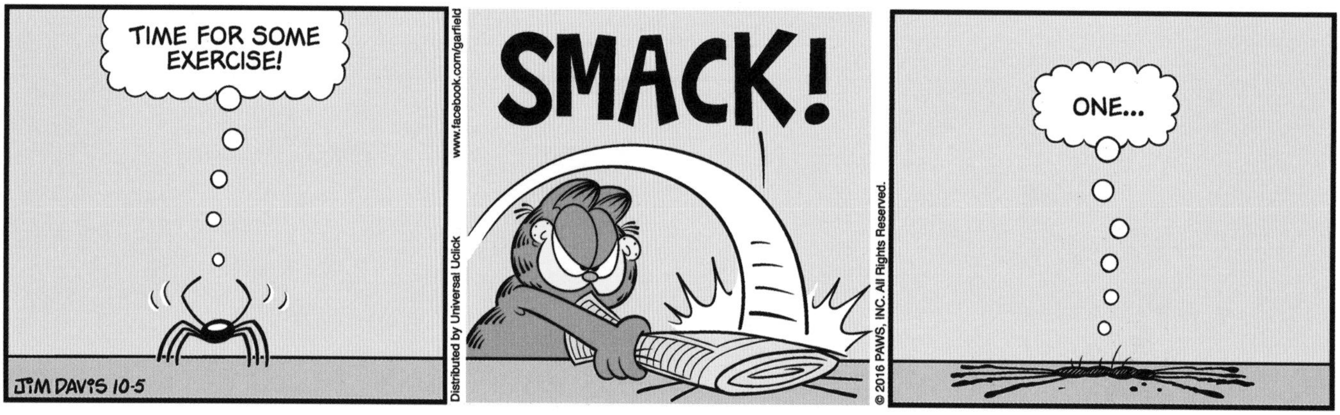
TIME FOR SOME EXERCISE!
JIM DAVIS 10-5
SMACK!
ONE...
Distributed by Universal Uclick www.facebook.com/garfield
© 2016 PAWS, INC. All Rights Reserved.

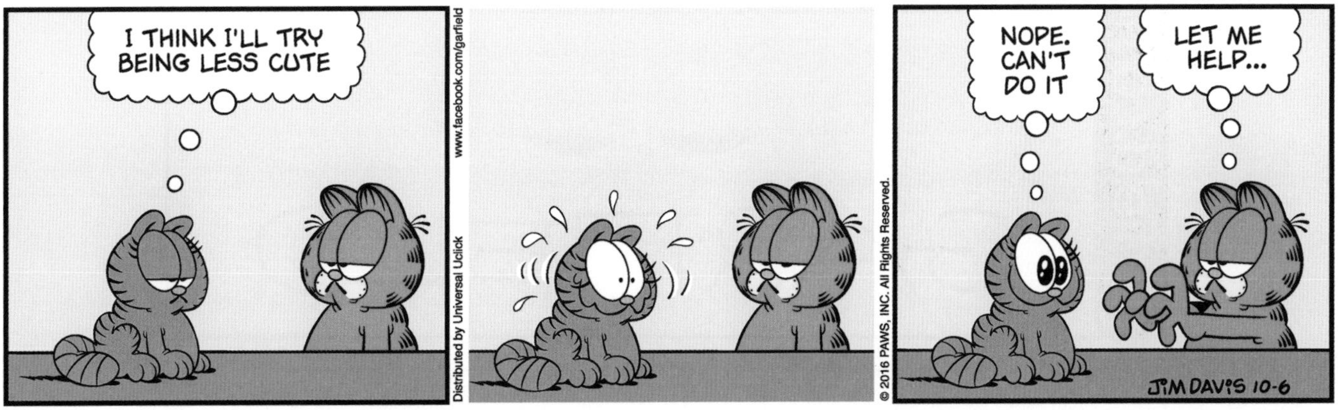
I THINK I'LL TRY BEING LESS CUTE
www.facebook.com/garfield
Distributed by Universal Uclick
© 2016 PAWS, INC. All Rights Reserved.
NOPE. CAN'T DO IT
LET ME HELP...
JIM DAVIS 10-6

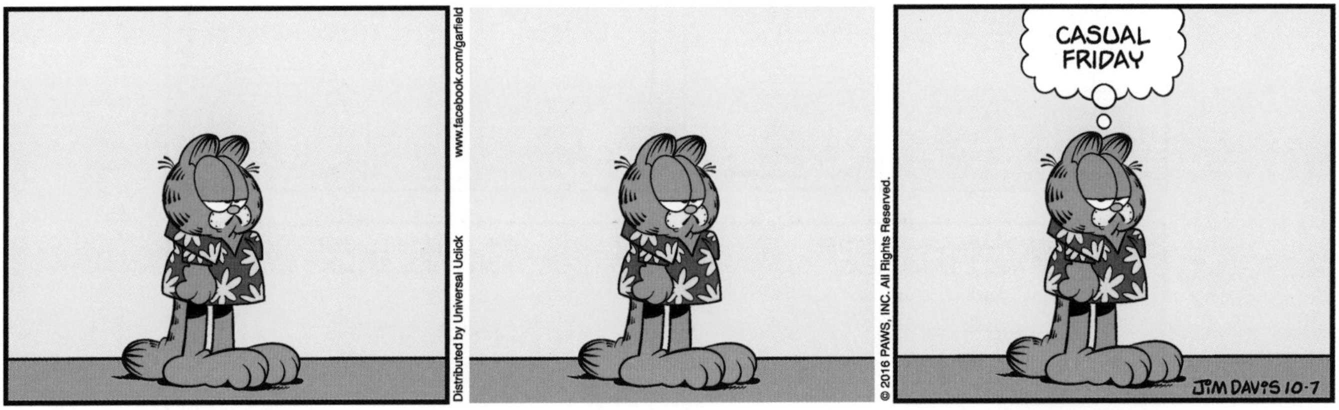
www.facebook.com/garfield
Distributed by Universal Uclick
© 2016 PAWS, INC. All Rights Reserved.
CASUAL FRIDAY
JIM DAVIS 10-7

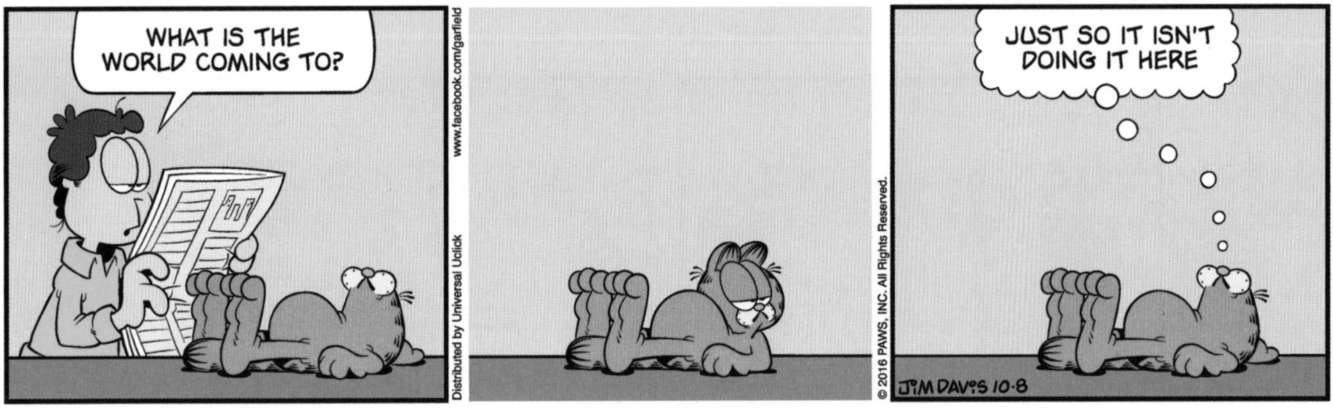
WHAT IS THE WORLD COMING TO?
www.facebook.com/garfield
Distributed by Universal Uclick
© 2016 PAWS, INC. All Rights Reserved.
JUST SO IT ISN'T DOING IT HERE
JIM DAVIS 10-8

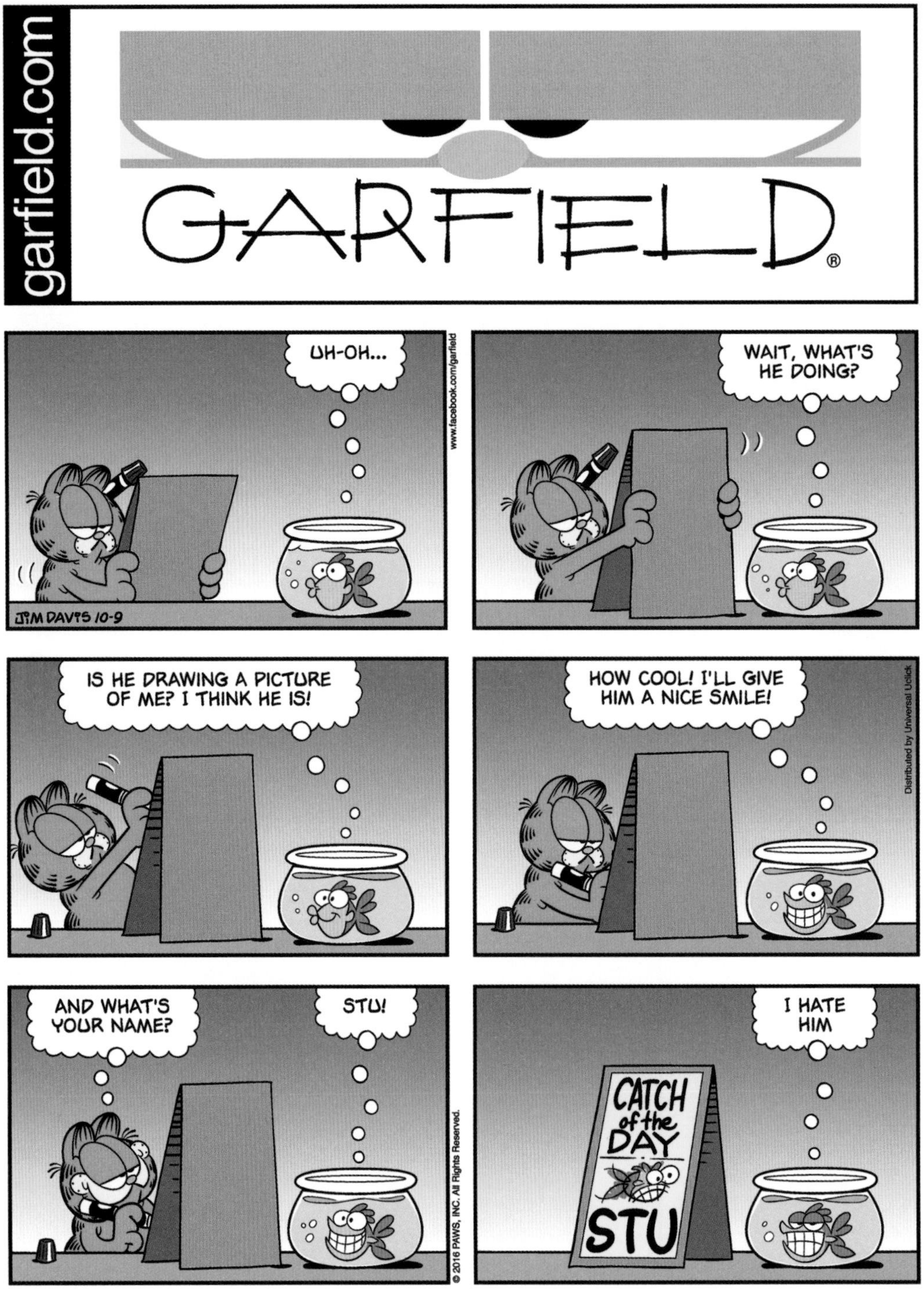
garfield.com
GARFIELD
UH-OH...
JIM DAVIS 10-9
www.facebook.com/garfield
WAIT, WHAT'S HE DOING?
IS HE DRAWING A PICTURE OF ME? I THINK HE IS!
HOW COOL! I'LL GIVE HIM A NICE SMILE!
Distributed by Universal Uclick
AND WHAT'S YOUR NAME?
STU!
© 2016 PAWS, INC. All Rights Reserved.
CATCH of the DAY
STU
I HATE HIM

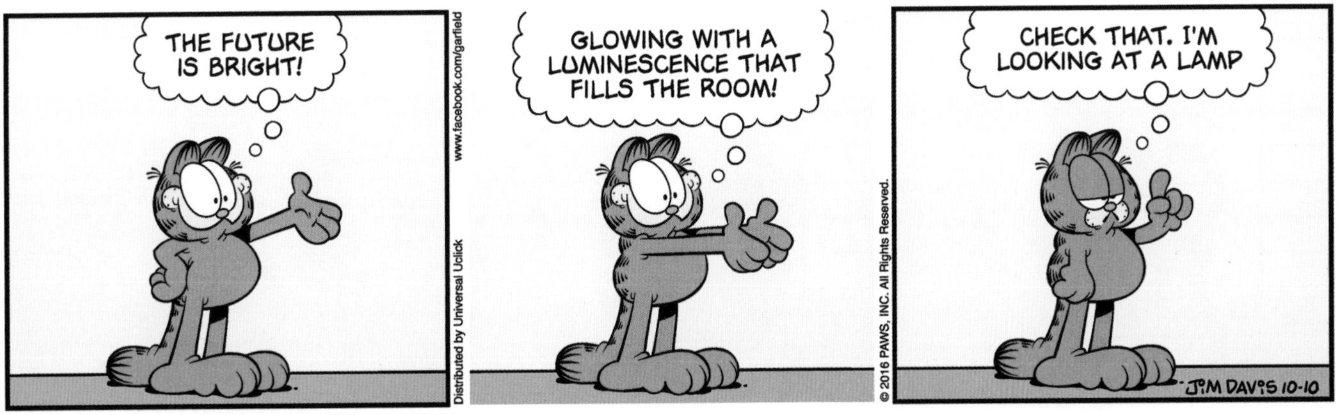
THE FUTURE IS BRIGHT!
www.facebook.com/garfield
Distributed by Universal Uclick
GLOWING WITH A LUMINESCENCE THAT FILLS THE ROOM!
© 2016 PAWS, INC. All Rights Reserved.
CHECK THAT. I'M LOOKING AT A LAMP
JIM DAVIS 10-10

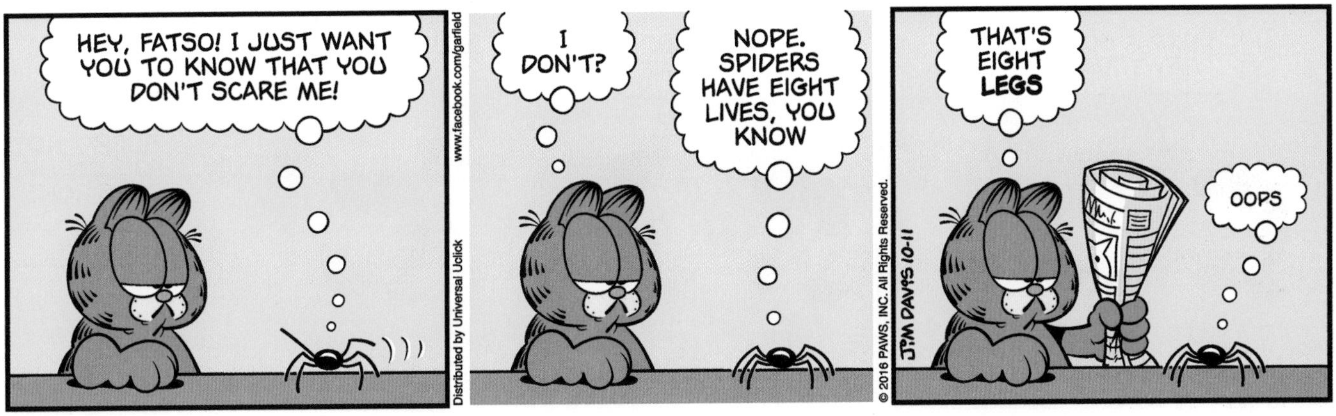
HEY, FATSO! I JUST WANT YOU TO KNOW THAT YOU DON'T SCARE ME!
Distributed by Universal Uclick
www.facebook.com/garfield
I DON'T?
NOPE. SPIDERS HAVE EIGHT LIVES, YOU KNOW
© 2016 PAWS, INC. All Rights Reserved.
JIM DAVIS 10-11
THAT'S EIGHT LEGS
OOPS

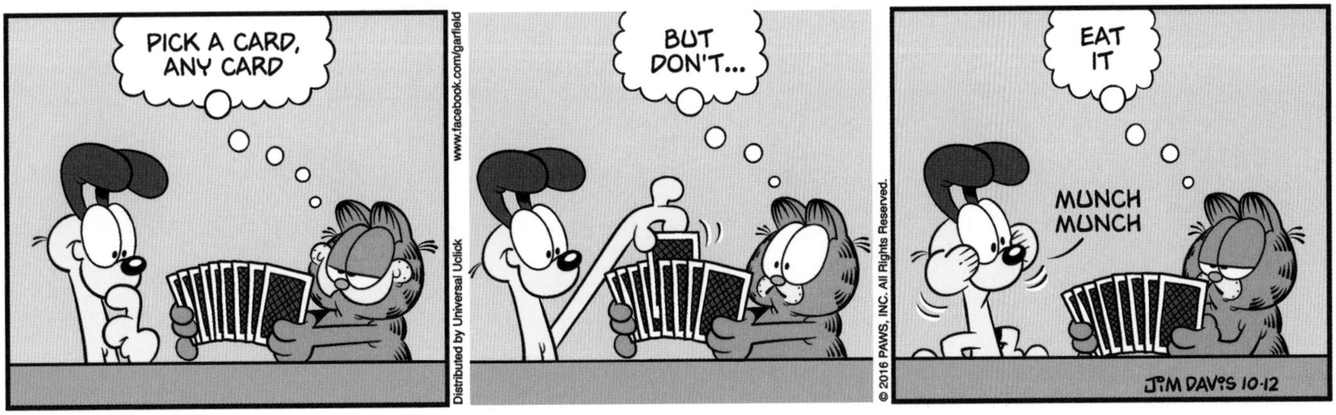
PICK A CARD, ANY CARD
www.facebook.com/garfield
Distributed by Universal Uclick
BUT DON'T...
© 2016 PAWS, INC. All Rights Reserved.
EAT IT
MUNCH MUNCH
JIM DAVIS 10-12

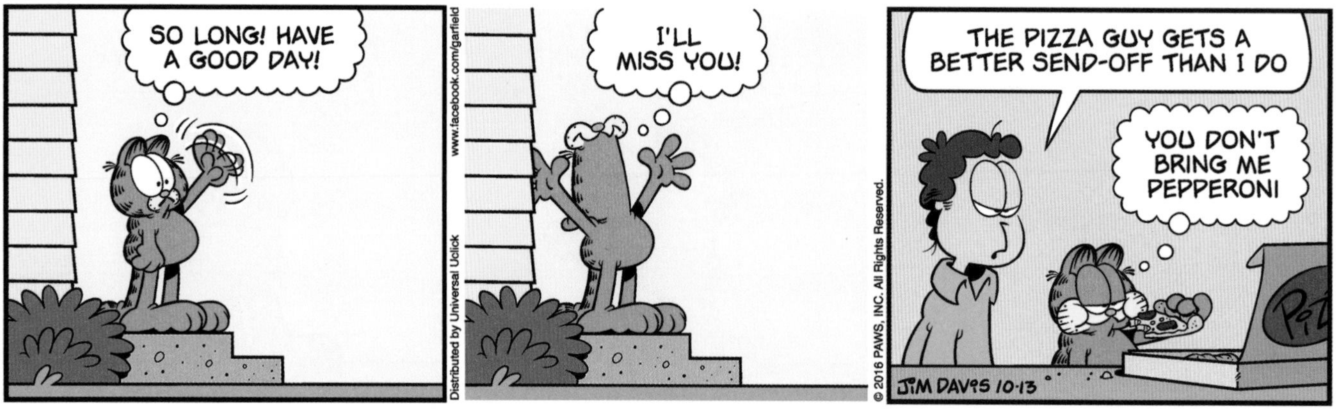
SO LONG! HAVE A GOOD DAY!
Distributed by Universal Uclick www.facebook.com/garfield
I'LL MISS YOU!
© 2016 PAWS, INC. All Rights Reserved.
THE PIZZA GUY GETS A BETTER SEND-OFF THAN I DO
YOU DON'T BRING ME PEPPERONI
JIM DAVIS 10-13

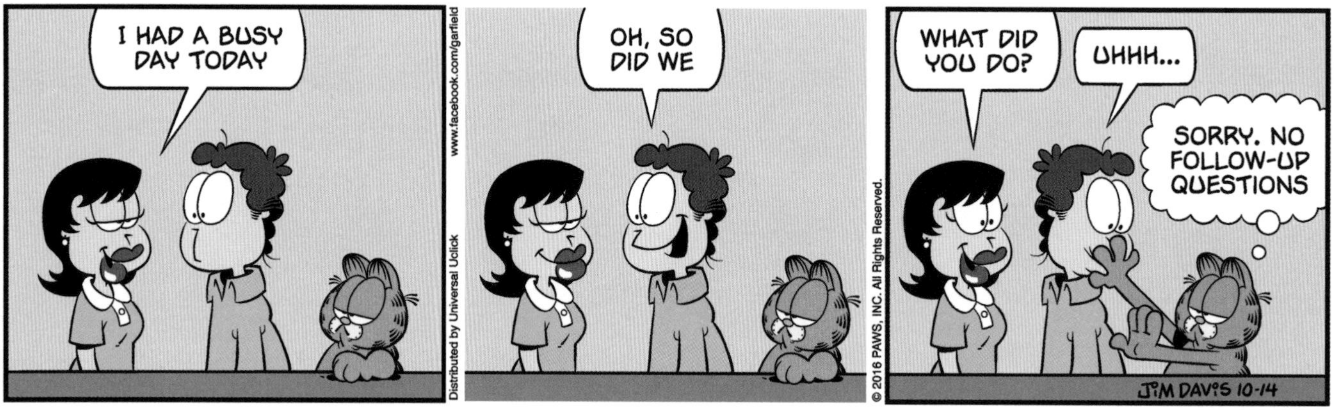
I HAD A BUSY DAY TODAY
Distributed by Universal Uclick www.facebook.com/garfield
OH, SO DID WE
© 2016 PAWS, INC. All Rights Reserved.
WHAT DID YOU DO?
UHHH...
SORRY. NO FOLLOW-UP QUESTIONS
JIM DAVIS 10-14

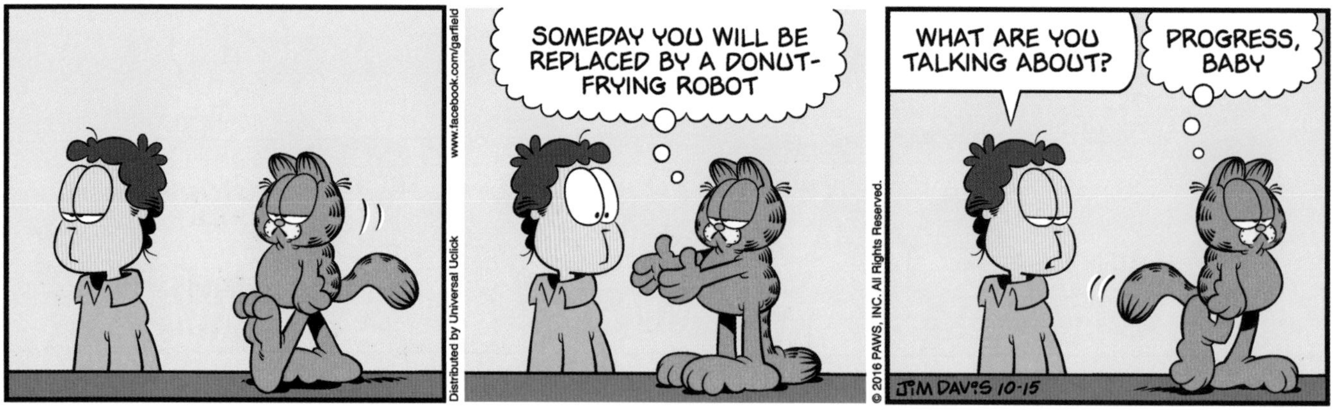
Distributed by Universal Uclick www.facebook.com/garfield
SOMEDAY YOU WILL BE REPLACED BY A DONUT-FRYING ROBOT
© 2016 PAWS, INC. All Rights Reserved.
WHAT ARE YOU TALKING ABOUT?
PROGRESS, BABY
JIM DAVIS 10-15

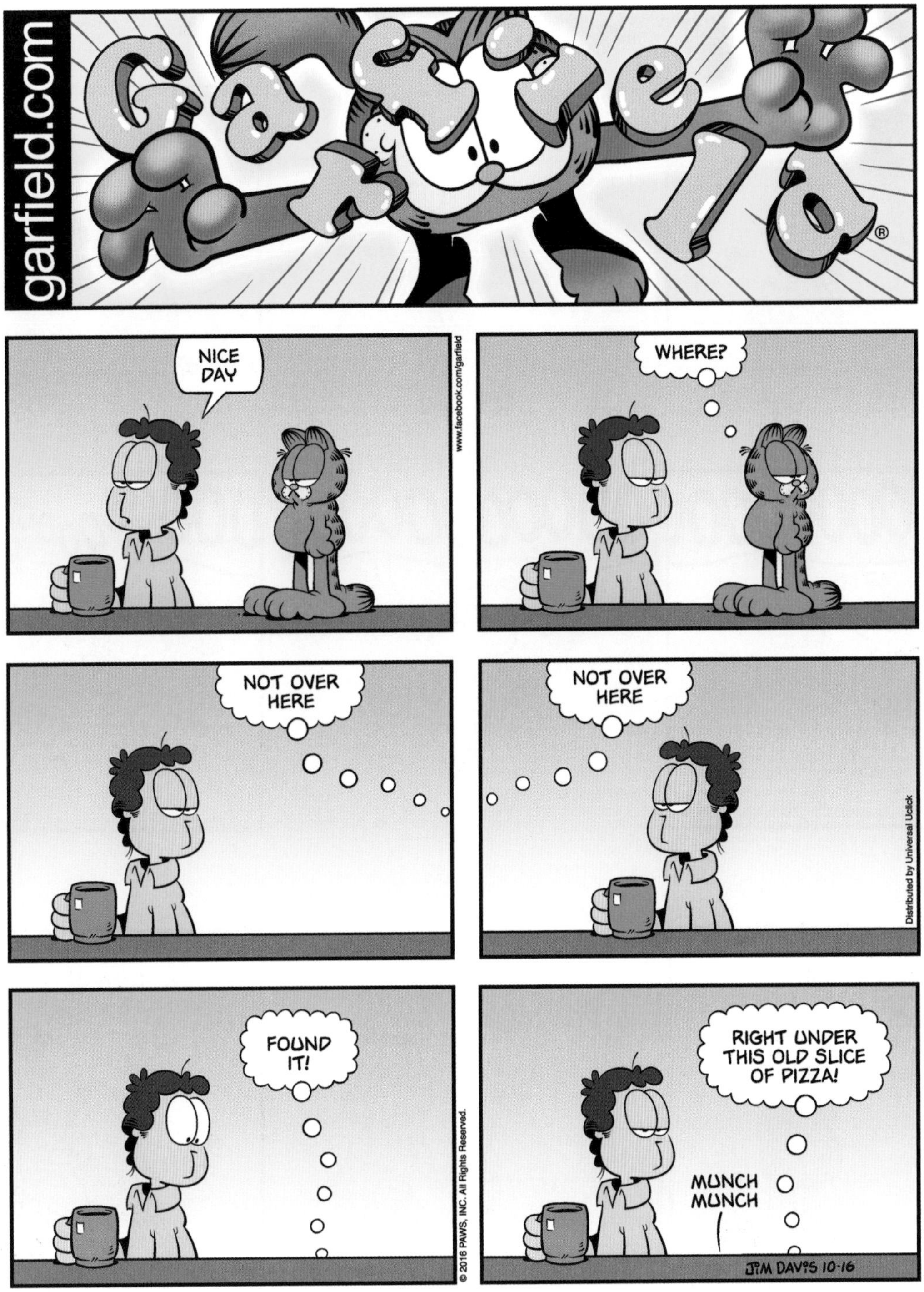
garfield.com
Garfield®
NICE DAY
www.facebook.com/garfield
WHERE?
NOT OVER HERE
NOT OVER HERE
Distributed by Universal Uclick
FOUND IT!
© 2016 PAWS, INC. All Rights Reserved.
RIGHT UNDER THIS OLD SLICE OF PIZZA!
MUNCH MUNCH
JIM DAVIS 10-16

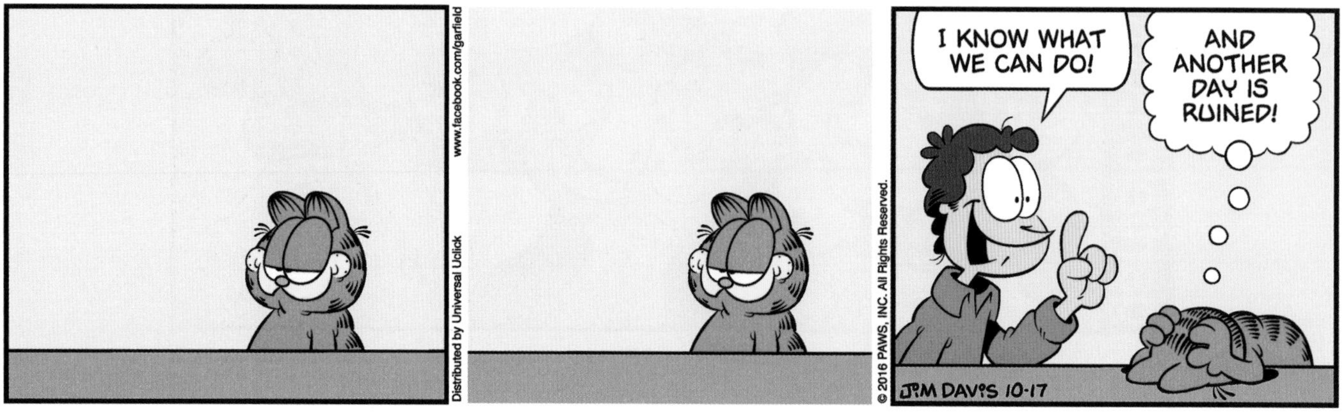
I KNOW WHAT WE CAN DO!
AND ANOTHER DAY IS RUINED!
JIM DAVIS 10-17
www.facebook.com/garfield
Distributed by Universal Uclick
© 2016 PAWS, INC. All Rights Reserved.

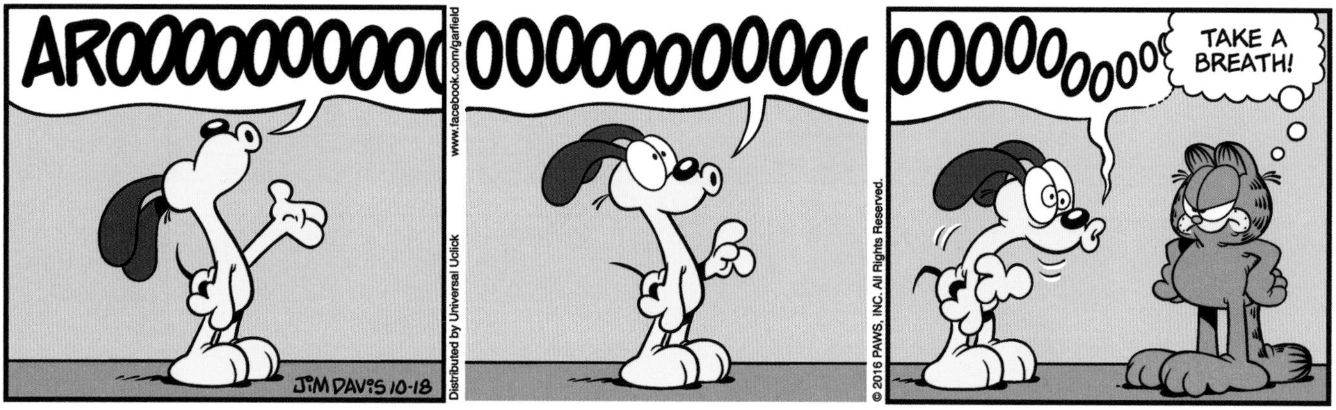
AROOOOOOOOOOOOOOOOOOOOOOOOOOOOOOOOO
TAKE A BREATH!
JIM DAVIS 10-18
www.facebook.com/garfield
Distributed by Universal Uclick
© 2016 PAWS, INC. All Rights Reserved.

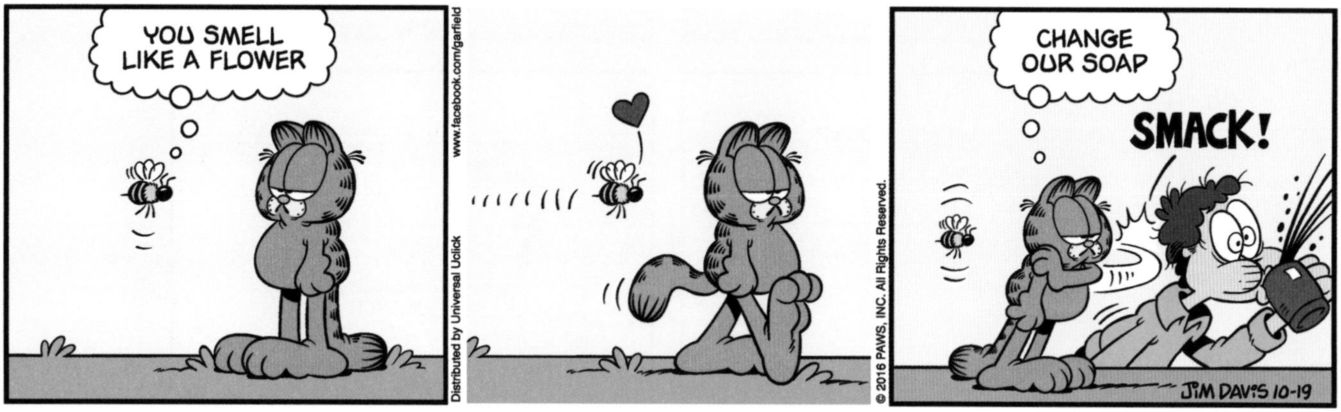
YOU SMELL LIKE A FLOWER
CHANGE OUR SOAP
SMACK!
JIM DAVIS 10-19
www.facebook.com/garfield
Distributed by Universal Uclick
© 2016 PAWS, INC. All Rights Reserved.

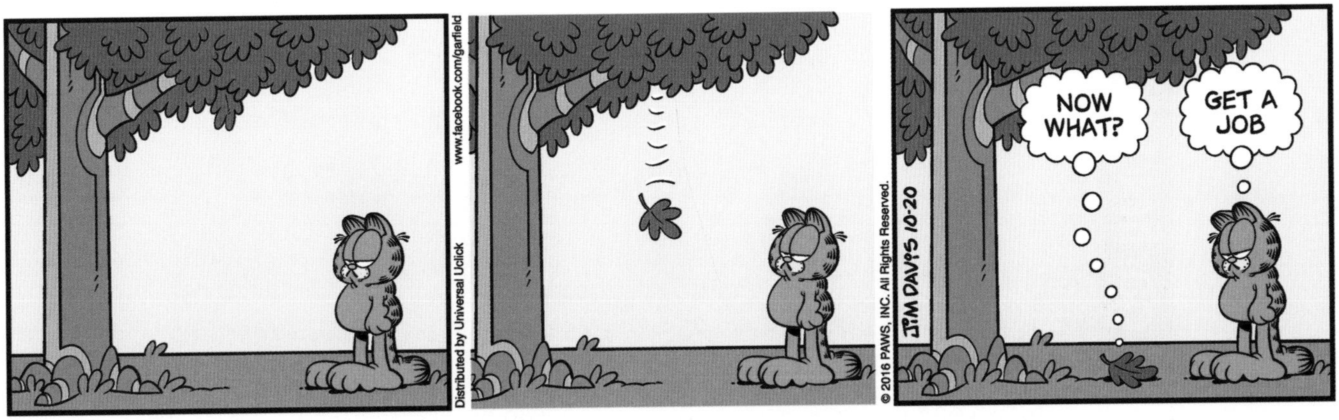
www.facebook.com/garfield
Distributed by Universal Uclick
© 2016 PAWS, INC. All Rights Reserved.
JIM DAVIS 10-20
NOW WHAT?
GET A JOB

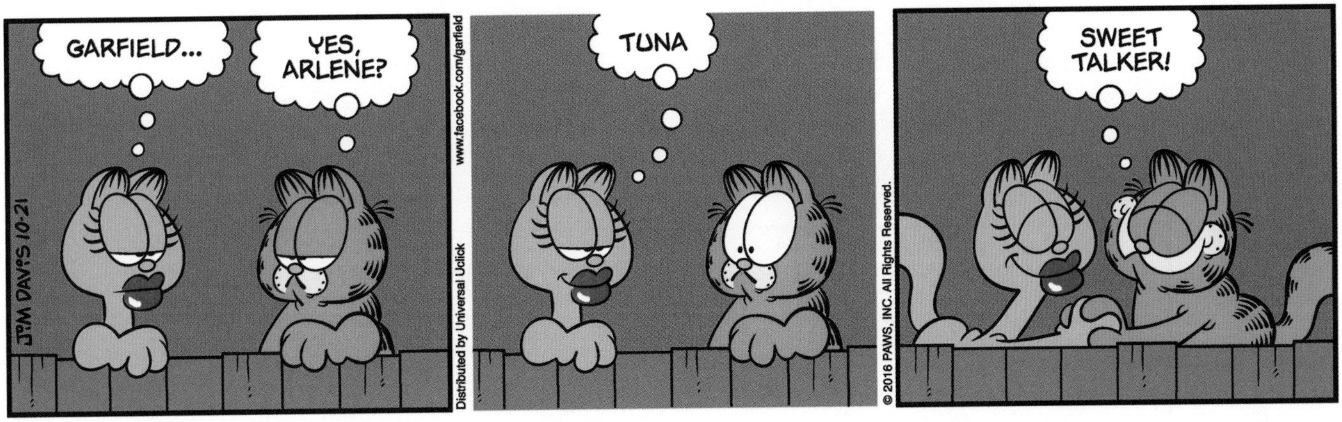
JIM DAVIS 10-21
GARFIELD...
YES, ARLENE?
www.facebook.com/garfield
Distributed by Universal Uclick
TUNA
© 2016 PAWS, INC. All Rights Reserved.
SWEET TALKER!

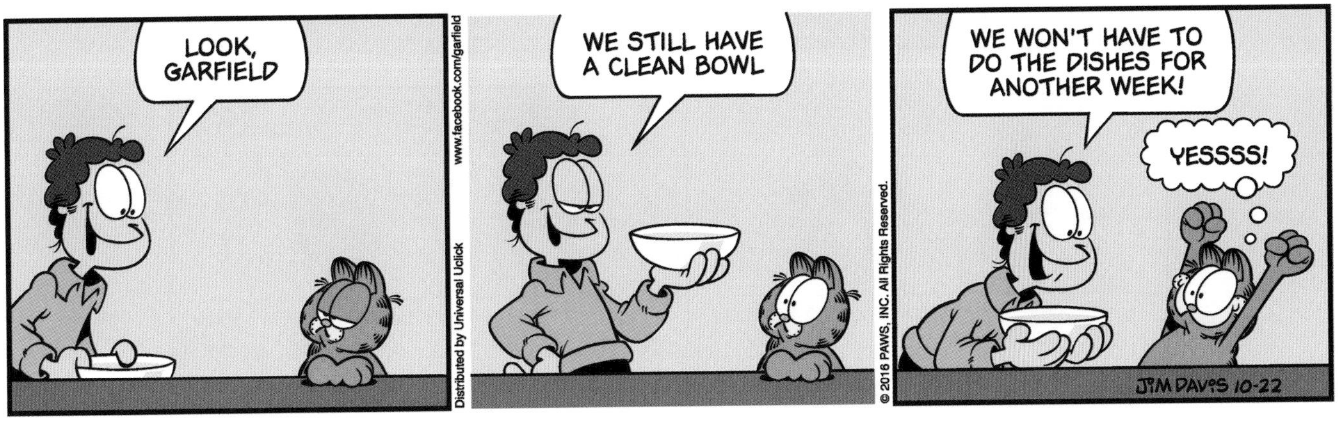
LOOK, GARFIELD
www.facebook.com/garfield
Distributed by Universal Uclick
WE STILL HAVE A CLEAN BOWL
© 2016 PAWS, INC. All Rights Reserved.
WE WON'T HAVE TO DO THE DISHES FOR ANOTHER WEEK!
YESSSS!
JIM DAVIS 10-22

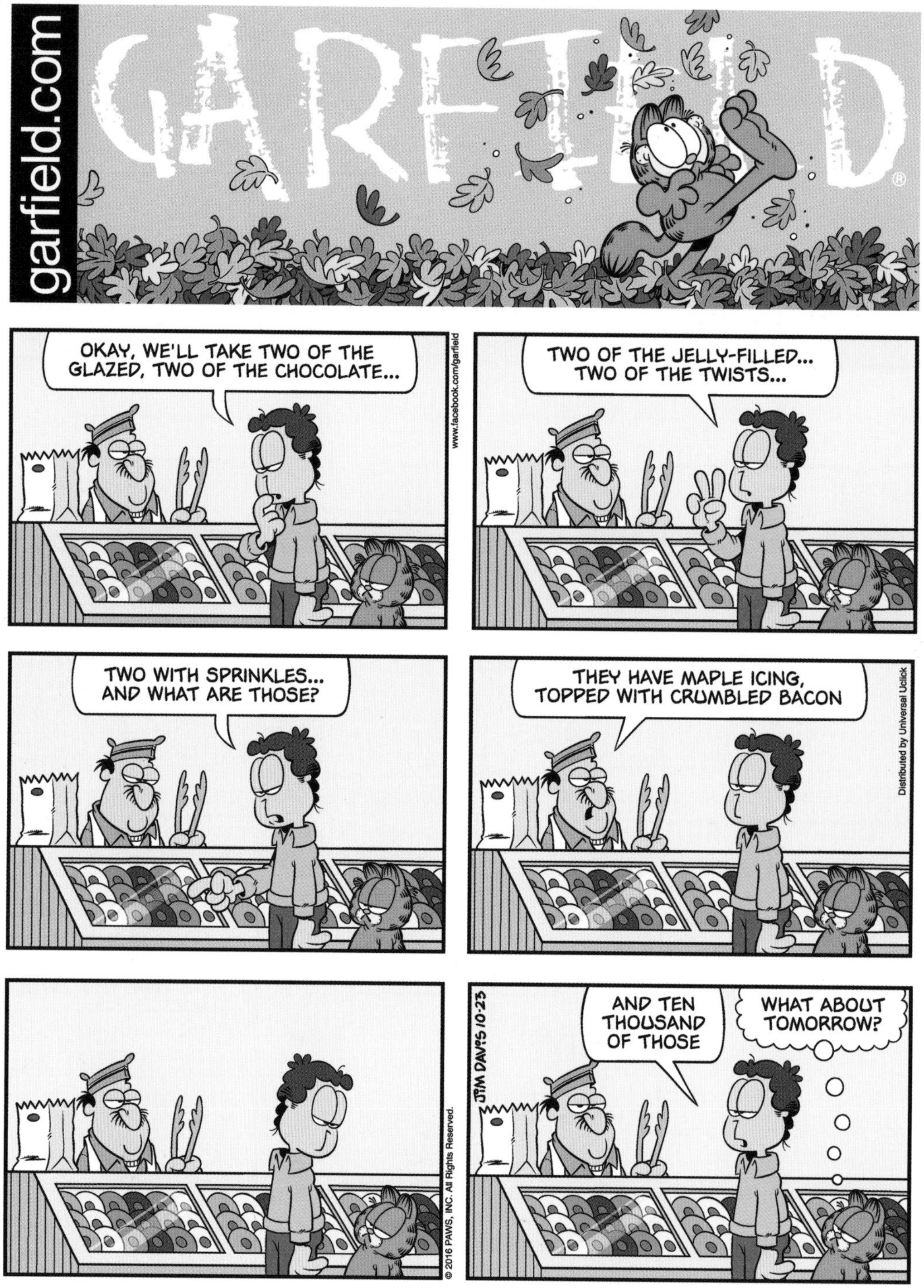
garfield.com
GARFIELD
OKAY, WE'LL TAKE TWO OF THE GLAZED, TWO OF THE CHOCOLATE...
www.facebook.com/garfield
TWO OF THE JELLY-FILLED... TWO OF THE TWISTS...
TWO WITH SPRINKLES... AND WHAT ARE THOSE?
THEY HAVE MAPLE ICING, TOPPED WITH CRUMBLED BACON
Distributed by Universal Uclick
© 2016 PAWS, INC. All Rights Reserved.
JIM DAVIS 10-23
AND TEN THOUSAND OF THOSE
WHAT ABOUT TOMORROW?

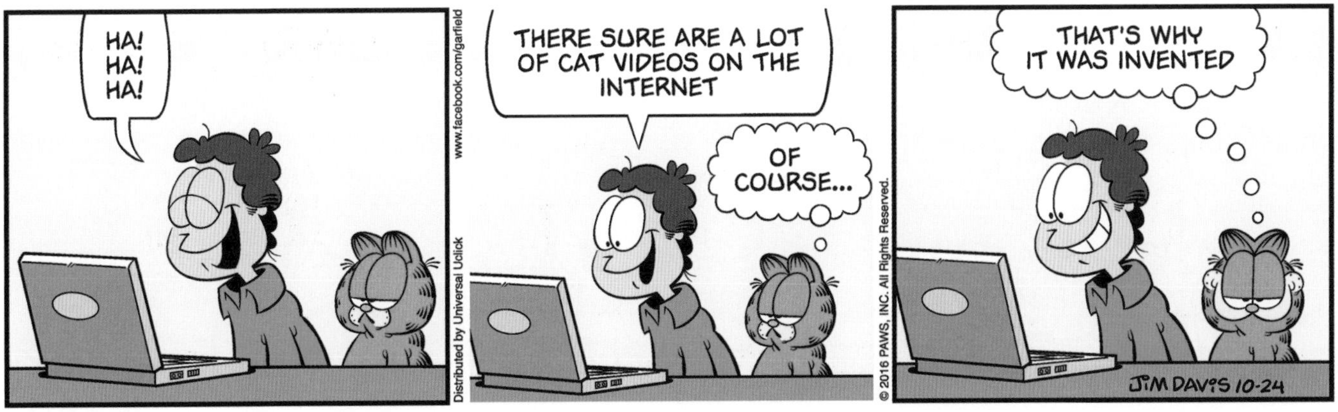
HA! HA! HA!
THERE SURE ARE A LOT OF CAT VIDEOS ON THE INTERNET
OF COURSE...
THAT'S WHY IT WAS INVENTED
JIM DAVIS 10-24
Distributed by Universal Uclick
www.facebook.com/garfield
© 2016 PAWS, INC. All Rights Reserved.

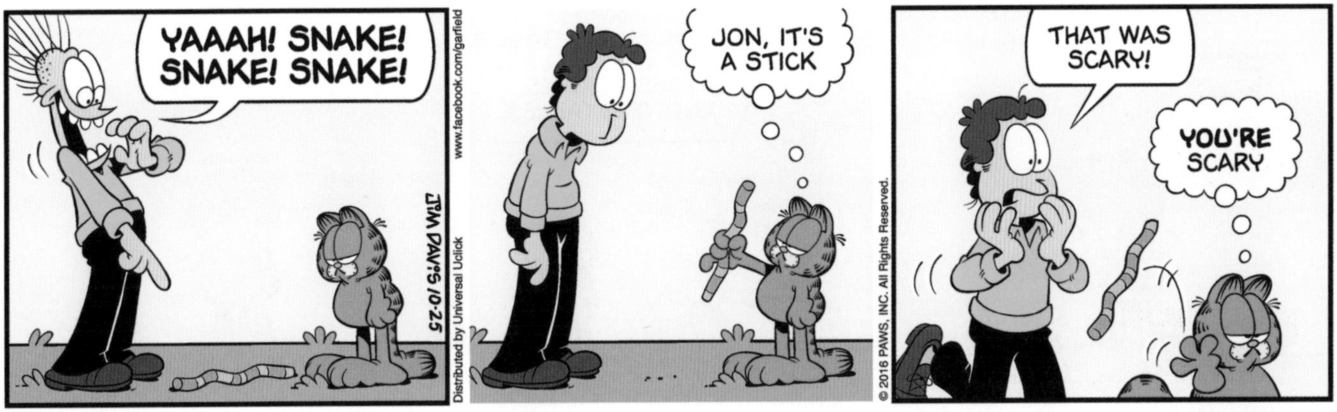
YAAAH! SNAKE! SNAKE! SNAKE!
JIM DAVIS 10-25
JON, IT'S A STICK
THAT WAS SCARY!
YOU'RE SCARY
Distributed by Universal Uclick
www.facebook.com/garfield
© 2016 PAWS, INC. All Rights Reserved.

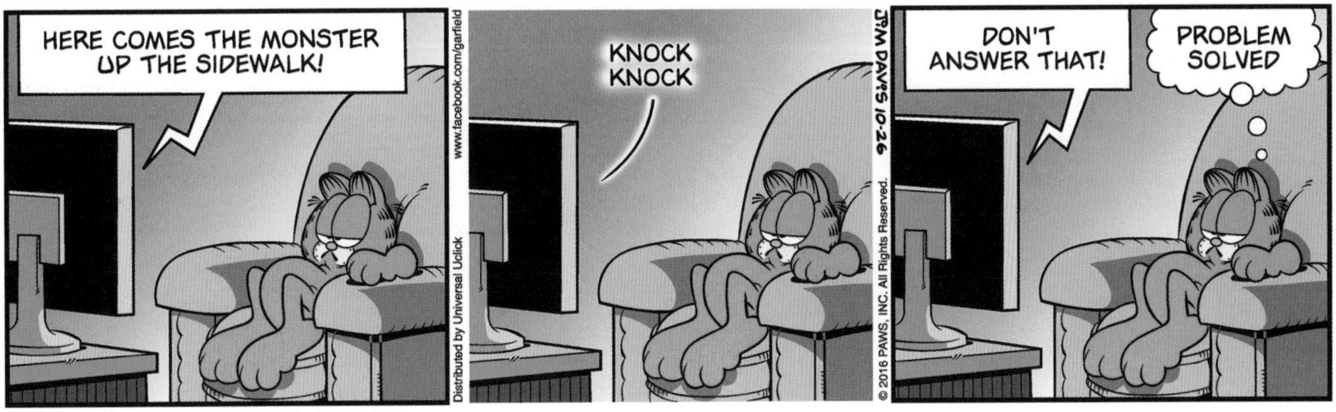
HERE COMES THE MONSTER UP THE SIDEWALK!
KNOCK KNOCK
DON'T ANSWER THAT!
PROBLEM SOLVED
JIM DAVIS 10-26
Distributed by Universal Uclick
www.facebook.com/garfield
© 2016 PAWS, INC. All Rights Reserved.

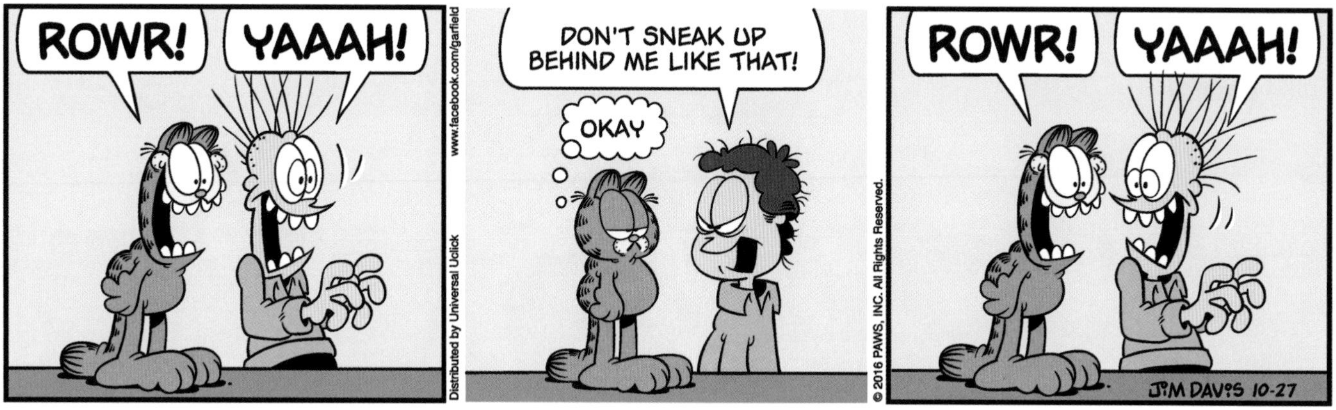
ROWR!
YAAAH!
Distributed by Universal Uclick
www.facebook.com/garfield
DON'T SNEAK UP BEHIND ME LIKE THAT!
OKAY
© 2016 PAWS, INC. All Rights Reserved.
ROWR!
YAAAH!
JIM DAVIS 10-27

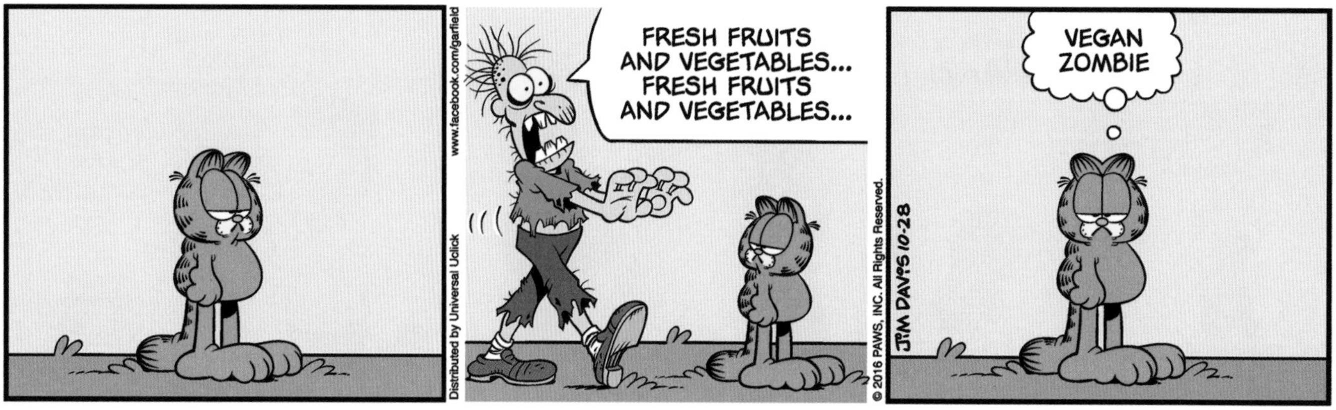
Distributed by Universal Uclick
www.facebook.com/garfield
FRESH FRUITS AND VEGETABLES... FRESH FRUITS AND VEGETABLES...
© 2016 PAWS, INC. All Rights Reserved.
JIM DAVIS 10-28
VEGAN ZOMBIE

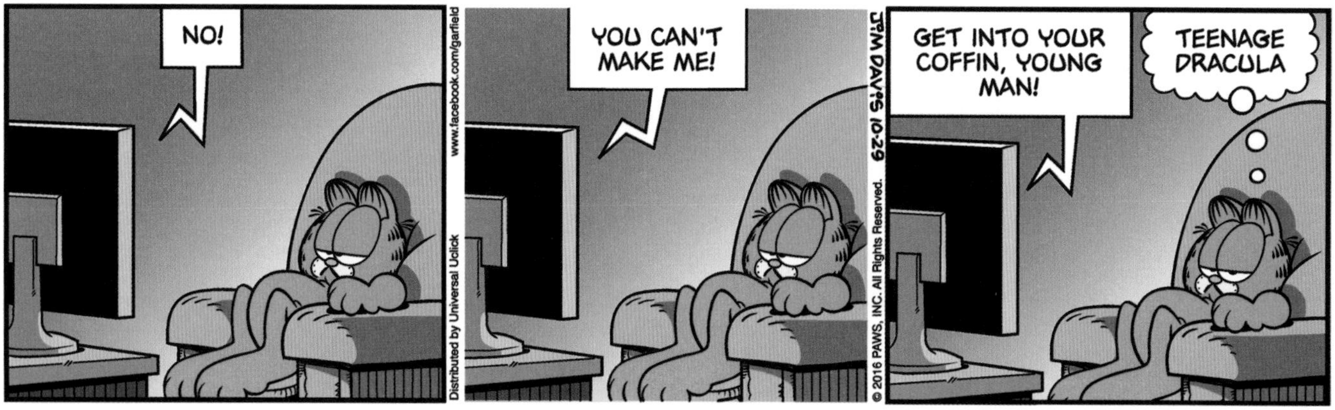
NO!
Distributed by Universal Uclick
www.facebook.com/garfield
YOU CAN'T MAKE ME!
© 2016 PAWS, INC. All Rights Reserved.
JIM DAVIS 10-29
GET INTO YOUR COFFIN, YOUNG MAN!
TEENAGE DRACULA

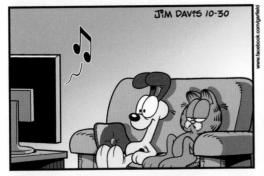

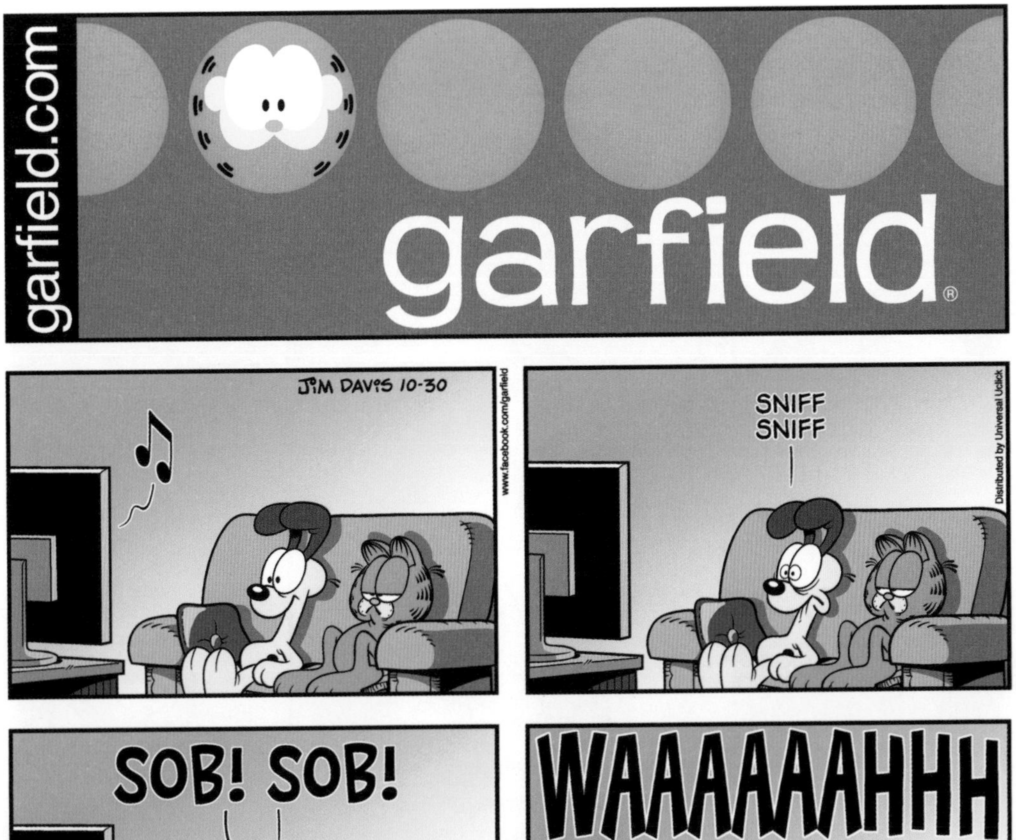

garfield.com
garfield
JIM DAVIS 10-30
www.facebook.com/garfield
SNIFF SNIFF
Distributed by Universal Uclick
SOB! SOB!
WAAAAAAHHH
AROOOOOOOOOO
© 2016 PAWS, INC. All Rights Reserved.
WE WILL RETURN TO "FIDO LOSES HIS SQUEAKY BONE"
WHY DO YOU WATCH THESE THINGS?!
HONK

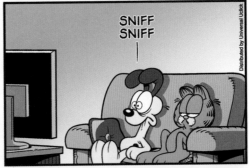

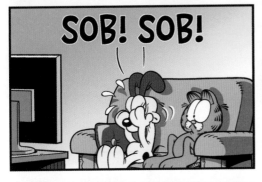

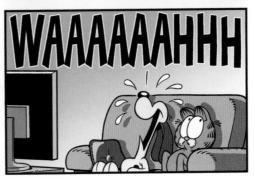

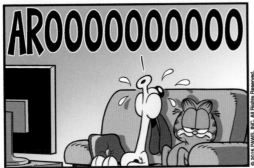

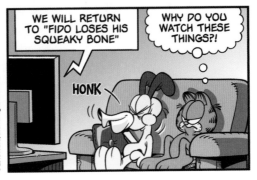

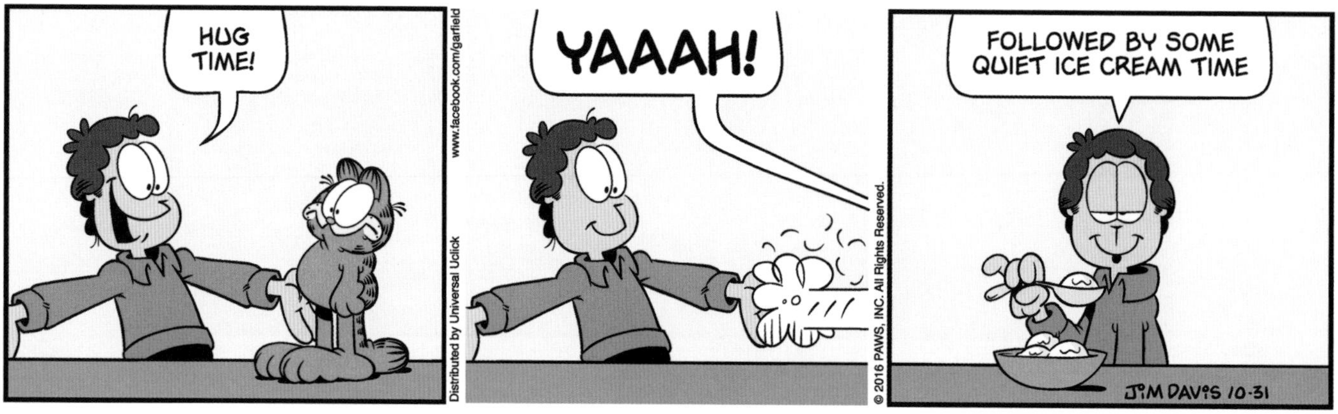
HUG TIME!
YAAAH!
FOLLOWED BY SOME QUIET ICE CREAM TIME
Distributed by Universal Uclick
www.facebook.com/garfield
© 2016 PAWS, INC. All Rights Reserved.
JIM DAVIS 10-31

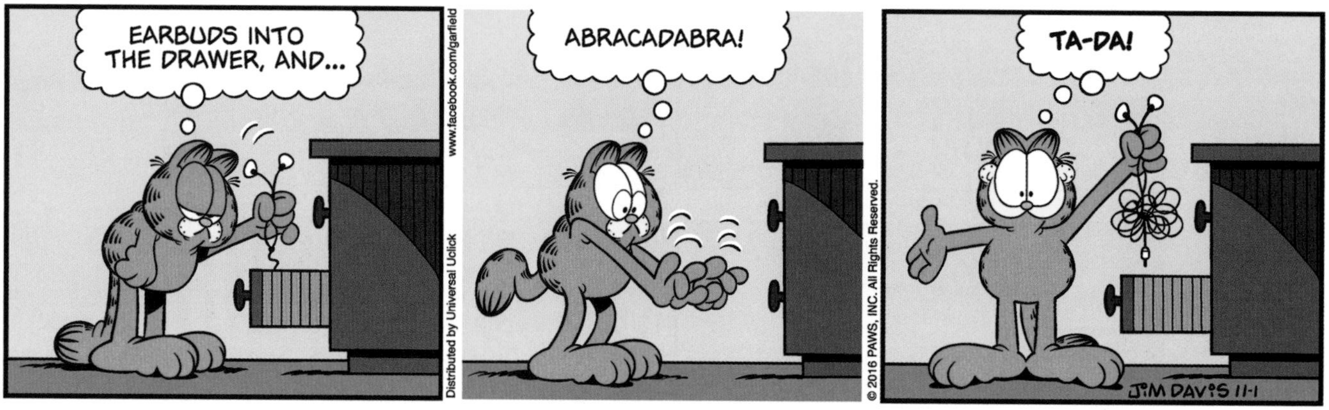
EARBUDS INTO THE DRAWER, AND...
ABRACADABRA!
TA-DA!
Distributed by Universal Uclick
www.facebook.com/garfield
© 2016 PAWS, INC. All Rights Reserved.
JIM DAVIS 11-1

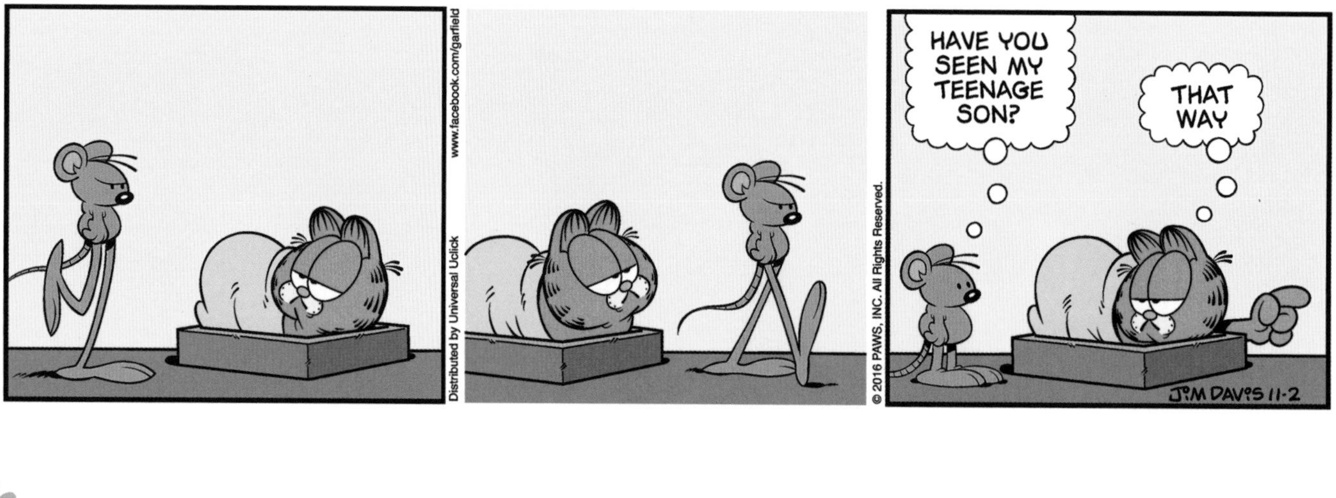
HAVE YOU SEEN MY TEENAGE SON?
THAT WAY
Distributed by Universal Uclick
www.facebook.com/garfield
© 2016 PAWS, INC. All Rights Reserved.
JIM DAVIS 11-2

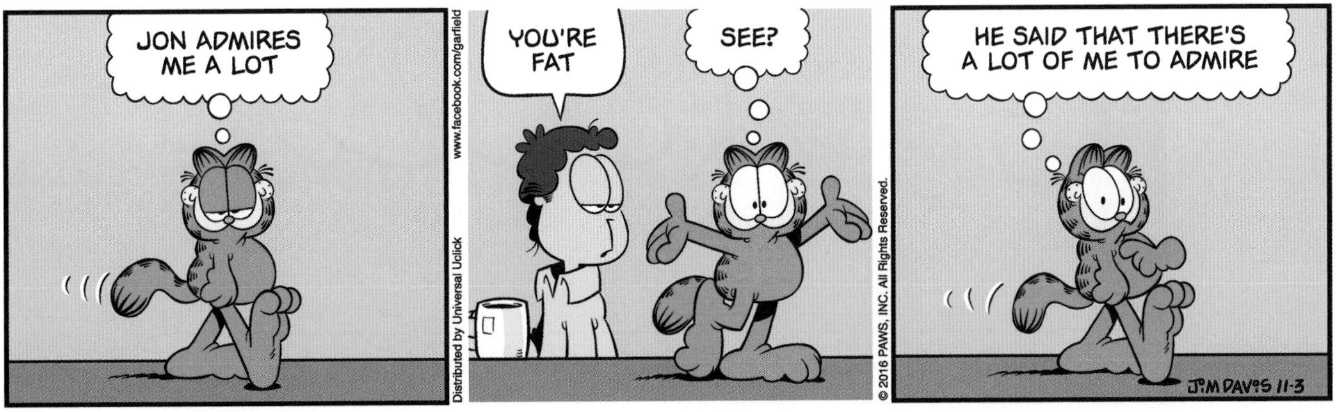
JON ADMIRES ME A LOT
YOU'RE FAT
SEE?
HE SAID THAT THERE'S A LOT OF ME TO ADMIRE
JIM DAVIS 11-3
Distributed by Universal Uclick www.facebook.com/garfield
© 2016 PAWS, INC. All Rights Reserved.

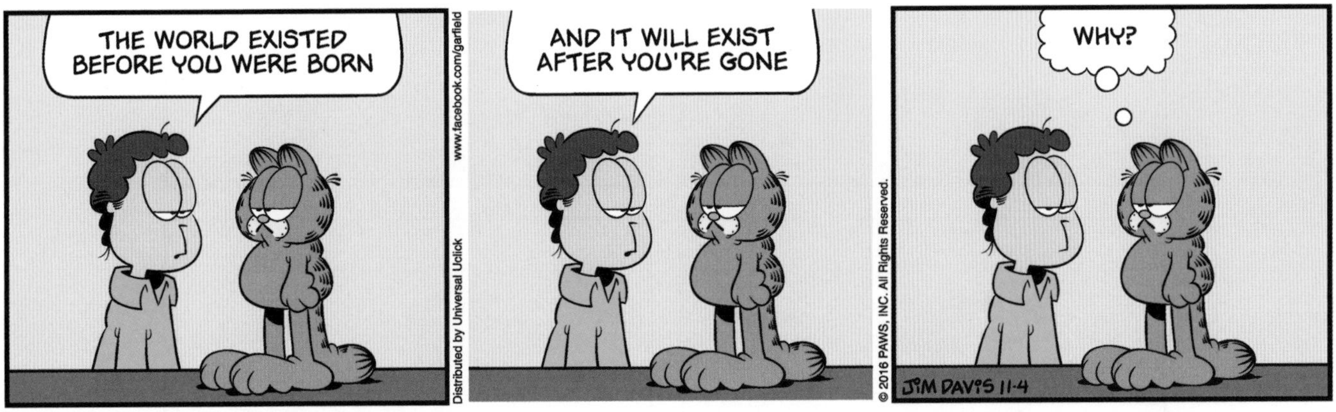
THE WORLD EXISTED BEFORE YOU WERE BORN
AND IT WILL EXIST AFTER YOU'RE GONE
WHY?
JIM DAVIS 11-4
Distributed by Universal Uclick www.facebook.com/garfield
© 2016 PAWS, INC. All Rights Reserved.

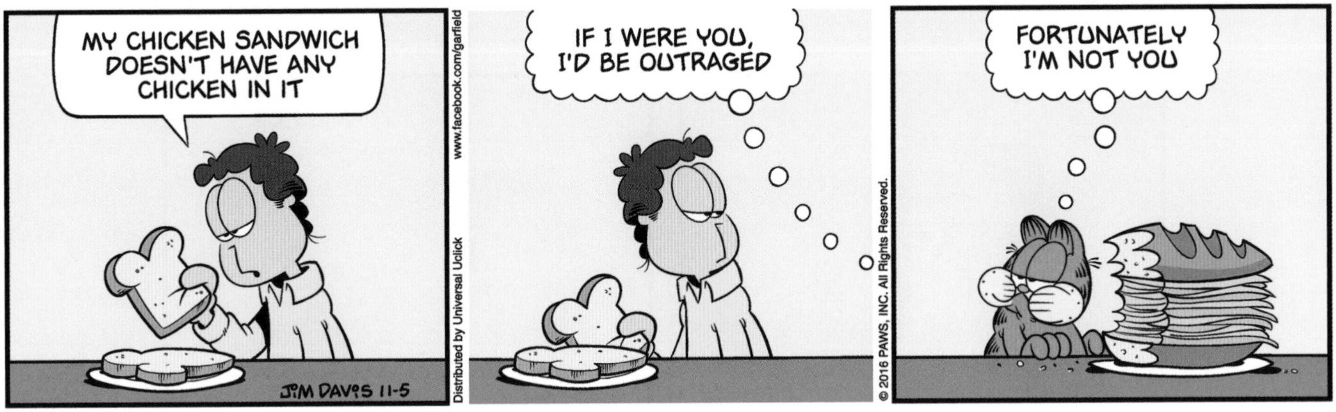
MY CHICKEN SANDWICH DOESN'T HAVE ANY CHICKEN IN IT
IF I WERE YOU, I'D BE OUTRAGED
FORTUNATELY I'M NOT YOU
JIM DAVIS 11-5
Distributed by Universal Uclick www.facebook.com/garfield
© 2016 PAWS, INC. All Rights Reserved.

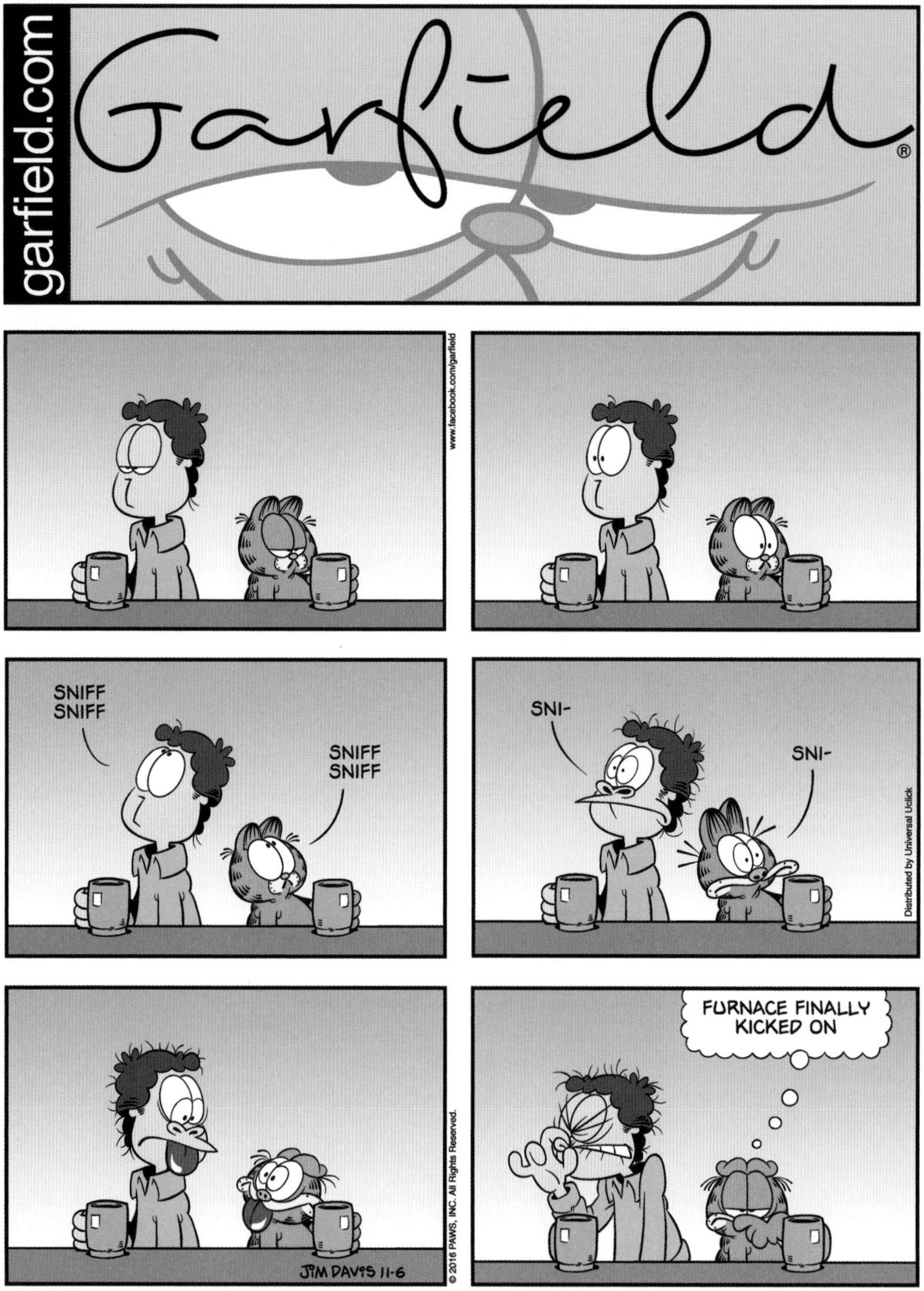
garfield.com
Garfield®
www.facebook.com/garfield
SNIFF SNIFF
SNIFF SNIFF
SNI-
SNI-
Distributed by Universal Uclick
JIM DAVIS 11-6
© 2016 PAWS, INC. All Rights Reserved.
FURNACE FINALLY KICKED ON

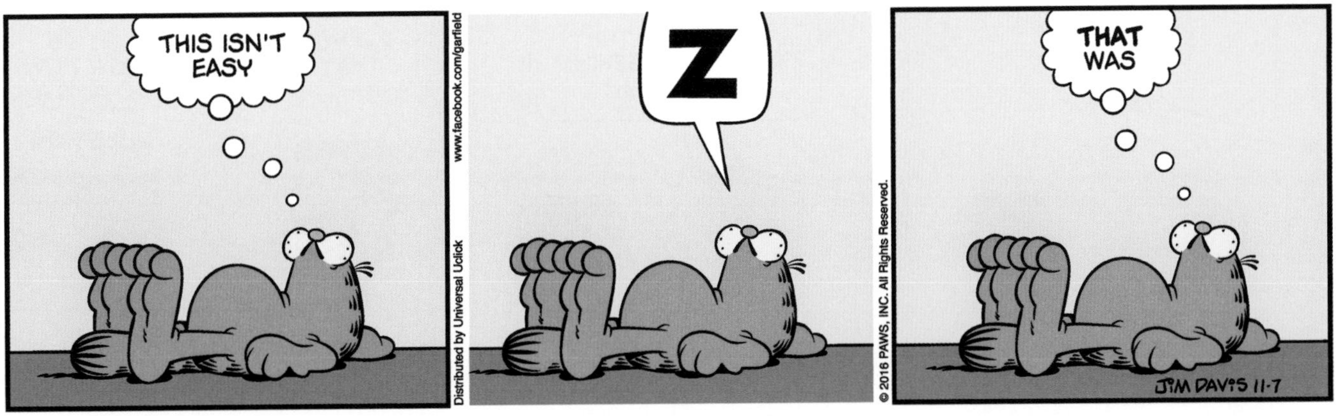
THIS ISN'T EASY
Distributed by Universal Uclick www.facebook.com/garfield
Z
© 2016 PAWS, INC. All Rights Reserved.
THAT WAS
JIM DAVIS 11-7

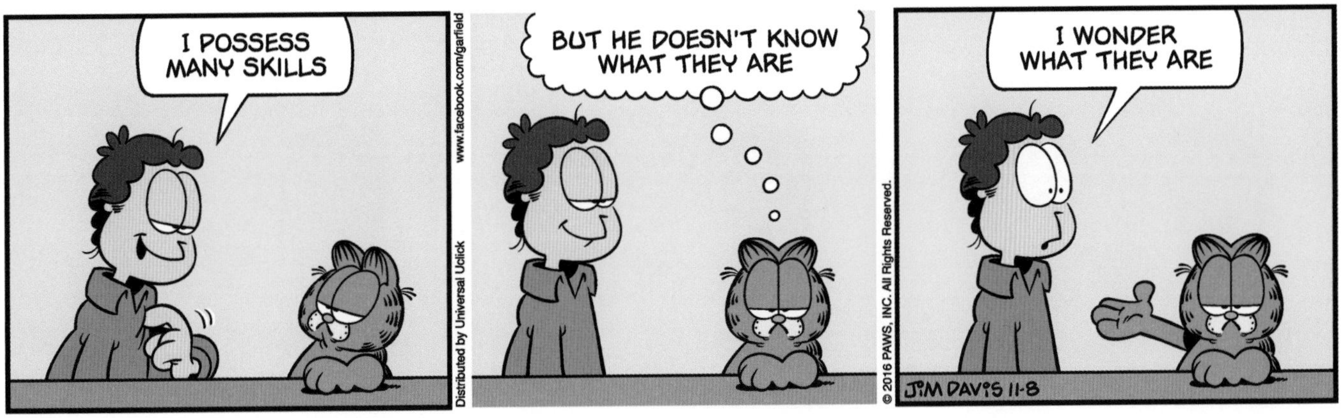
I POSSESS MANY SKILLS
Distributed by Universal Uclick www.facebook.com/garfield
BUT HE DOESN'T KNOW WHAT THEY ARE
© 2016 PAWS, INC. All Rights Reserved.
I WONDER WHAT THEY ARE
JIM DAVIS 11-8

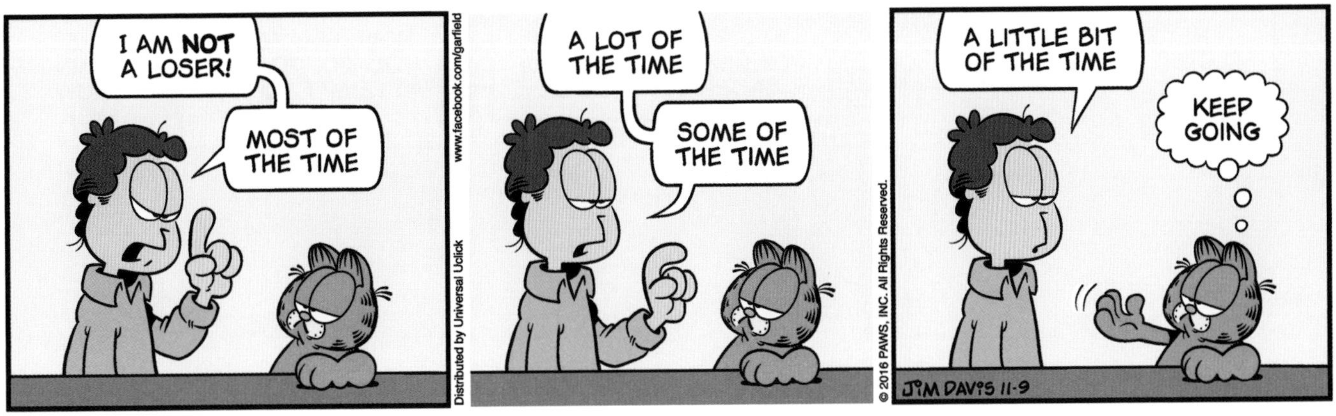
I AM **NOT** A LOSER!
MOST OF THE TIME
Distributed by Universal Uclick www.facebook.com/garfield
A LOT OF THE TIME
SOME OF THE TIME
© 2016 PAWS, INC. All Rights Reserved.
A LITTLE BIT OF THE TIME
KEEP GOING
JIM DAVIS 11-9

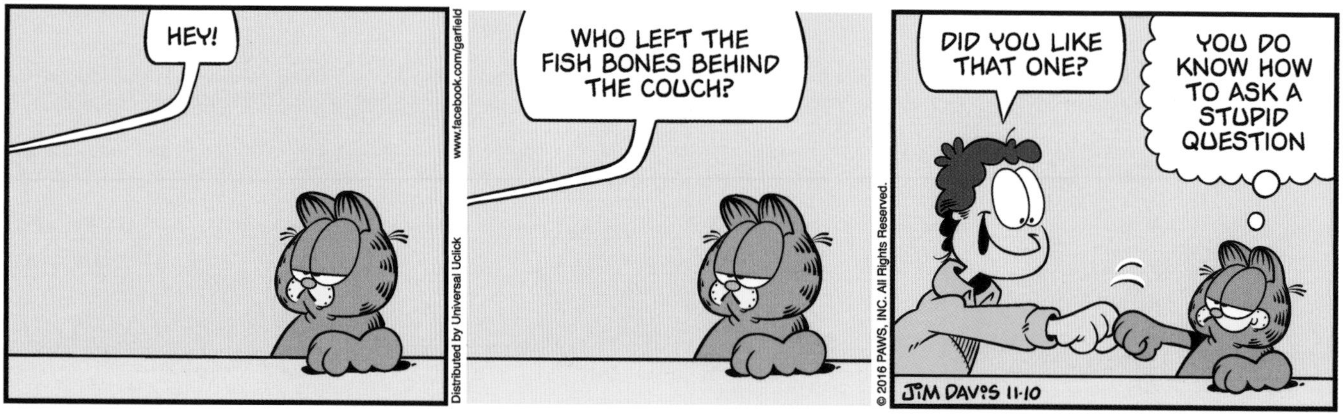
HEY!
WHO LEFT THE FISH BONES BEHIND THE COUCH?
DID YOU LIKE THAT ONE?
YOU DO KNOW HOW TO ASK A STUPID QUESTION
Distributed by Universal Uclick www.facebook.com/garfield
© 2016 PAWS, INC. All Rights Reserved.
JIM DAVIS 11-10

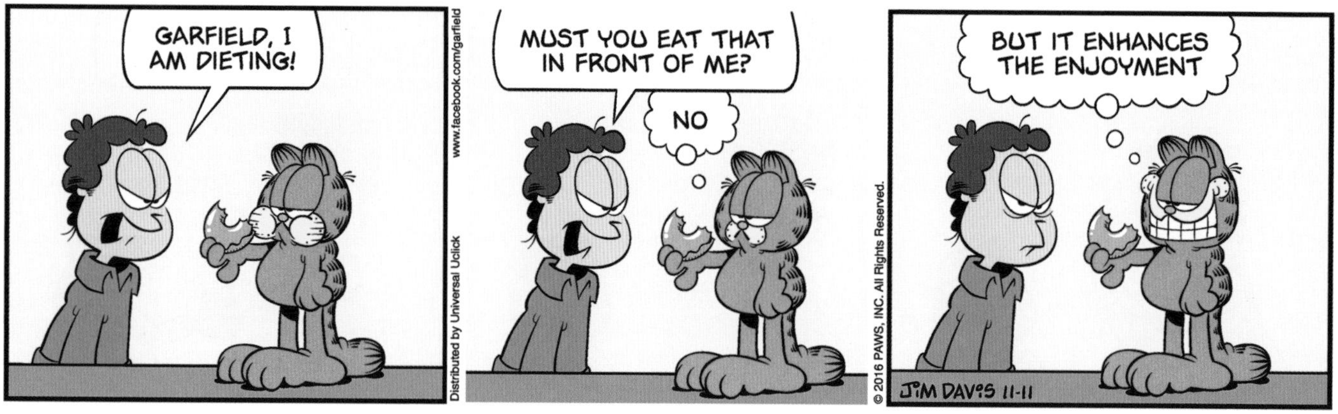
GARFIELD, I AM DIETING!
MUST YOU EAT THAT IN FRONT OF ME?
NO
BUT IT ENHANCES THE ENJOYMENT
Distributed by Universal Uclick www.facebook.com/garfield
© 2016 PAWS, INC. All Rights Reserved.
JIM DAVIS 11-11

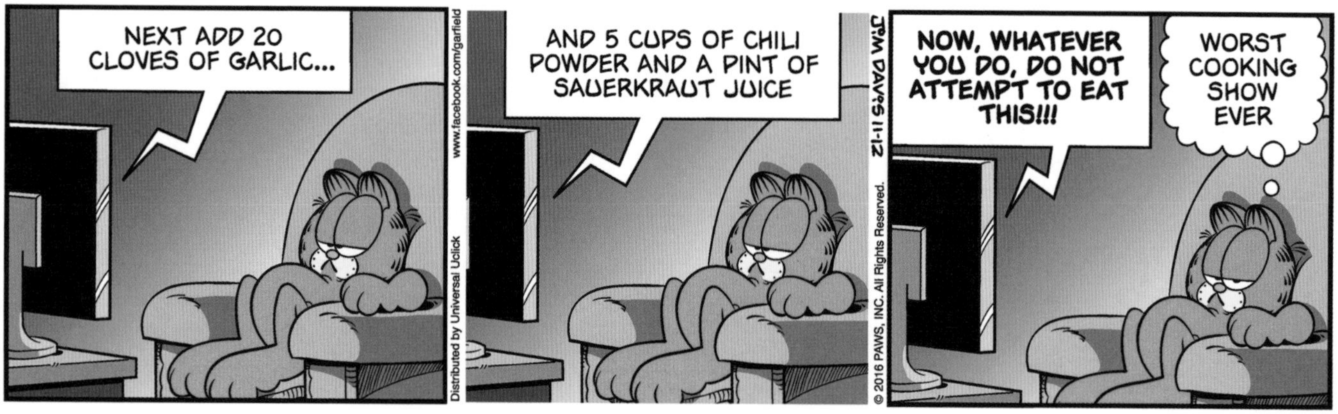
NEXT ADD 20 CLOVES OF GARLIC...
AND 5 CUPS OF CHILI POWDER AND A PINT OF SAUERKRAUT JUICE
NOW, WHATEVER YOU DO, DO NOT ATTEMPT TO EAT THIS!!!
WORST COOKING SHOW EVER
Distributed by Universal Uclick www.facebook.com/garfield
© 2016 PAWS, INC. All Rights Reserved.
JIM DAVIS 11-12

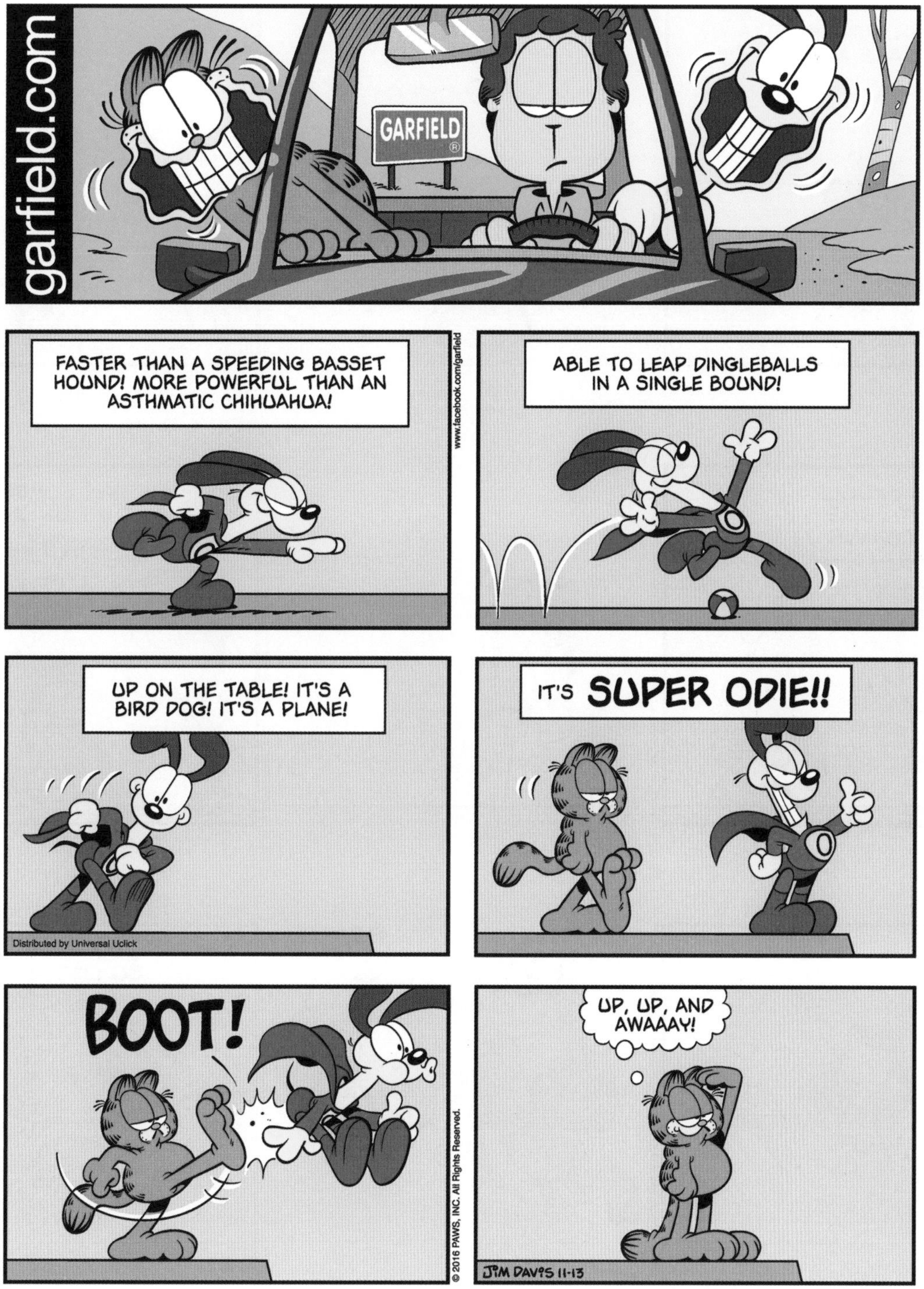
garfield.com
GARFIELD
FASTER THAN A SPEEDING BASSET HOUND! MORE POWERFUL THAN AN ASTHMATIC CHIHUAHUA!
www.facebook.com/garfield
ABLE TO LEAP DINGLEBALLS IN A SINGLE BOUND!
UP ON THE TABLE! IT'S A BIRD DOG! IT'S A PLANE!
Distributed by Universal Uclick
IT'S SUPER ODIE!!
BOOT!
© 2016 PAWS, INC. All Rights Reserved.
UP, UP, AND AWAAAY!
JIM DAVIS 11-13

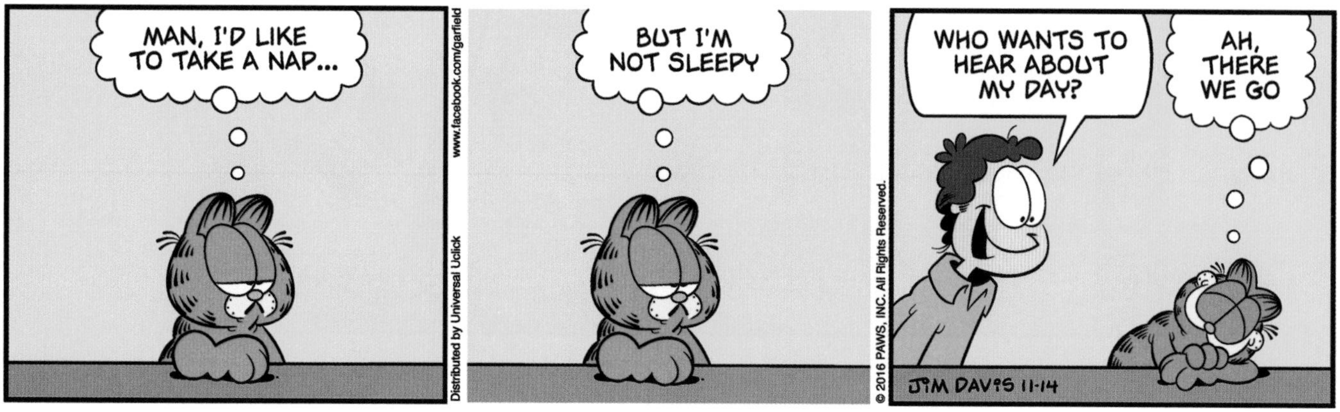
MAN, I'D LIKE TO TAKE A NAP...
Distributed by Universal Uclick
www.facebook.com/garfield
BUT I'M NOT SLEEPY
WHO WANTS TO HEAR ABOUT MY DAY?
AH, THERE WE GO
© 2016 PAWS, INC. All Rights Reserved.
JIM DAVIS 11-14

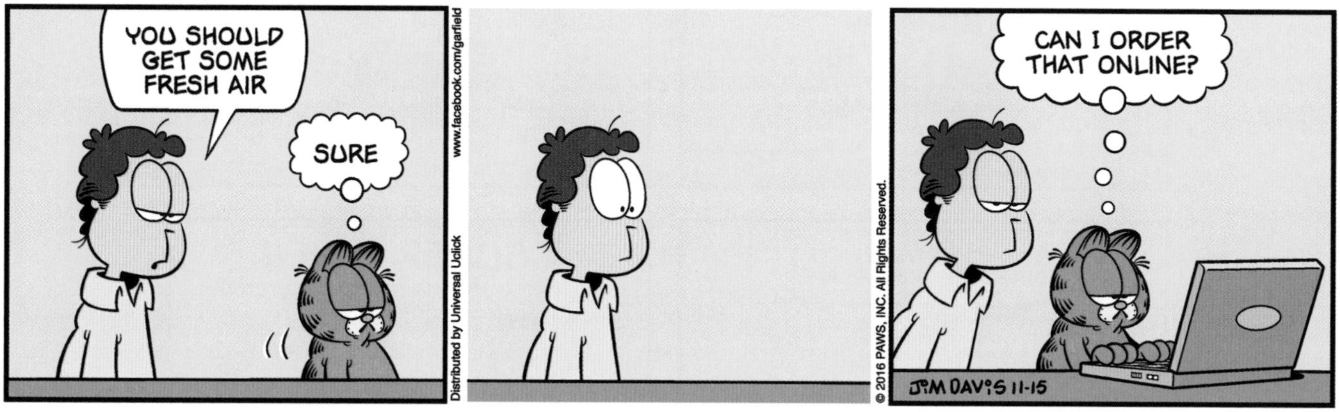
YOU SHOULD GET SOME FRESH AIR
SURE
Distributed by Universal Uclick
www.facebook.com/garfield
CAN I ORDER THAT ONLINE?
© 2016 PAWS, INC. All Rights Reserved.
JIM DAVIS 11-15

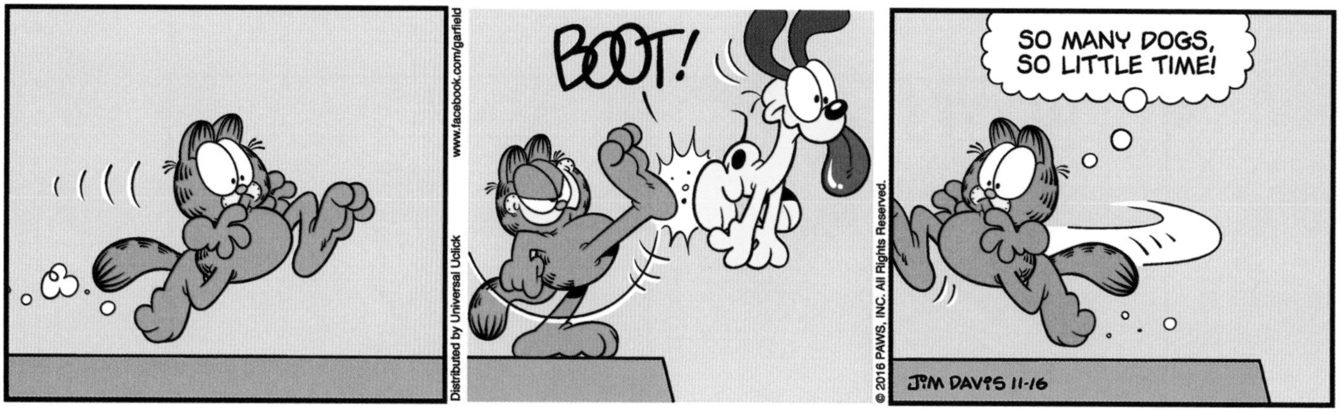
Distributed by Universal Uclick
www.facebook.com/garfield
BOOT!
SO MANY DOGS, SO LITTLE TIME!
© 2016 PAWS, INC. All Rights Reserved.
JIM DAVIS 11-16

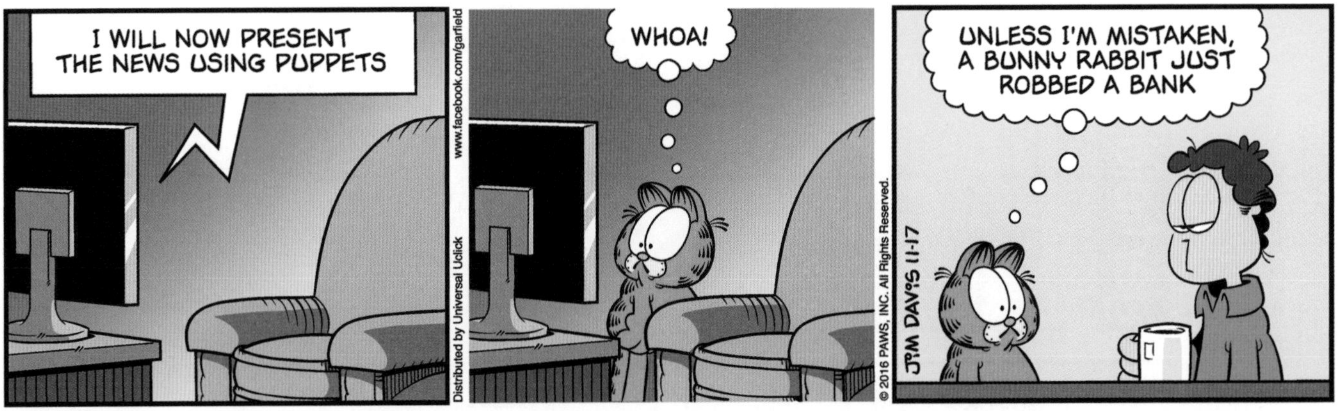
I WILL NOW PRESENT THE NEWS USING PUPPETS
WHOA!
UNLESS I'M MISTAKEN, A BUNNY RABBIT JUST ROBBED A BANK
Distributed by Universal Uclick www.facebook.com/garfield
© 2016 PAWS, INC. All Rights Reserved.
JIM DAVIS 11-17

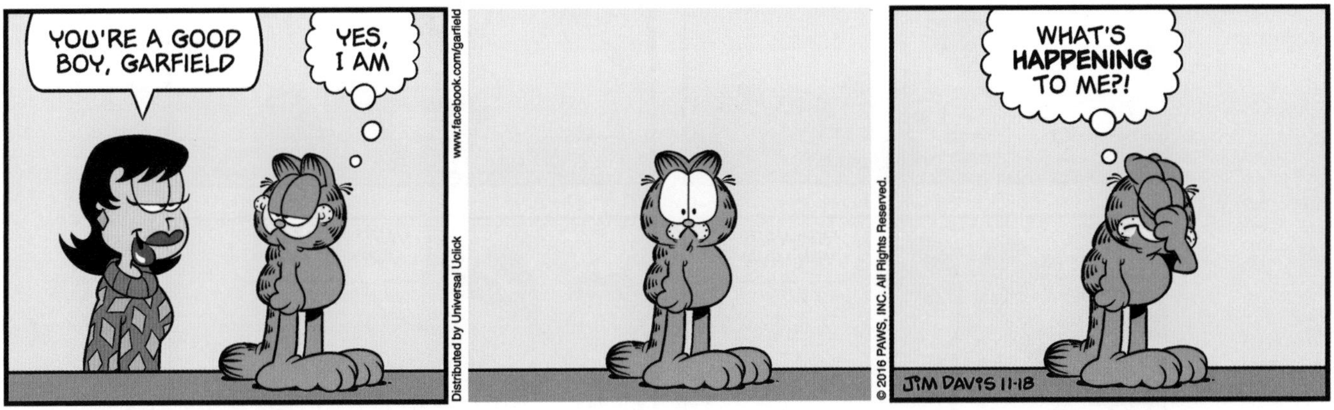
YOU'RE A GOOD BOY, GARFIELD
YES, I AM
WHAT'S **HAPPENING** TO ME?!
Distributed by Universal Uclick www.facebook.com/garfield
© 2016 PAWS, INC. All Rights Reserved.
JIM DAVIS 11-18

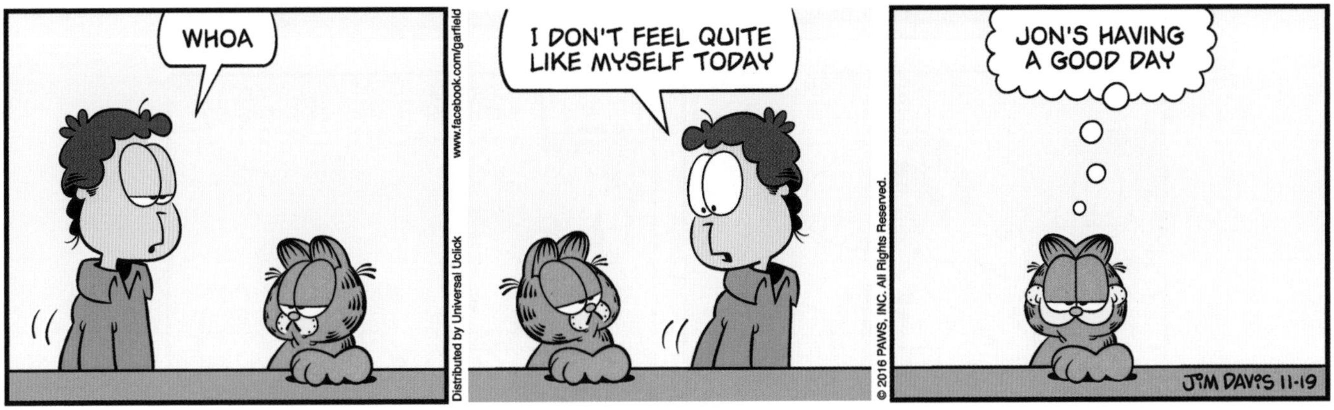
WHOA
I DON'T FEEL QUITE LIKE MYSELF TODAY
JON'S HAVING A GOOD DAY
Distributed by Universal Uclick www.facebook.com/garfield
© 2016 PAWS, INC. All Rights Reserved.
JIM DAVIS 11-19

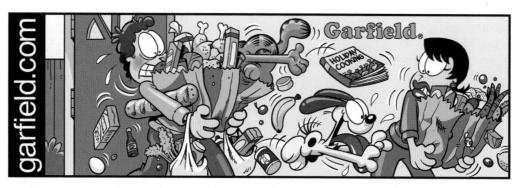

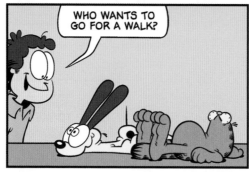

garfield.com
Garfield®
HOLIDAY COOKING
WHO WANTS TO GO FOR A WALK?
YIP! YIP! YIP!
YIP! YAP! YIP! YAP!
YAPPY! YAPPY! YIP! YIP! YAP!
COMING WITH US?
I'LL WAIT FOR THE LIMO
JIM DAVIS 11-20
www.facebook.com/garfield
© 2016 PAWS, INC. All Rights Reserved.
Distributed by Universal Uclick

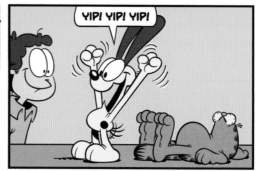

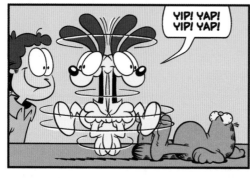

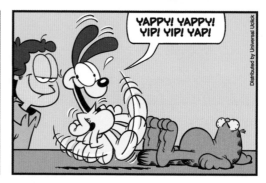

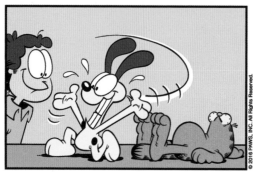

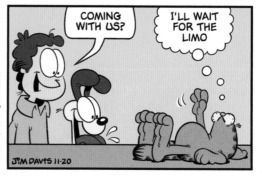

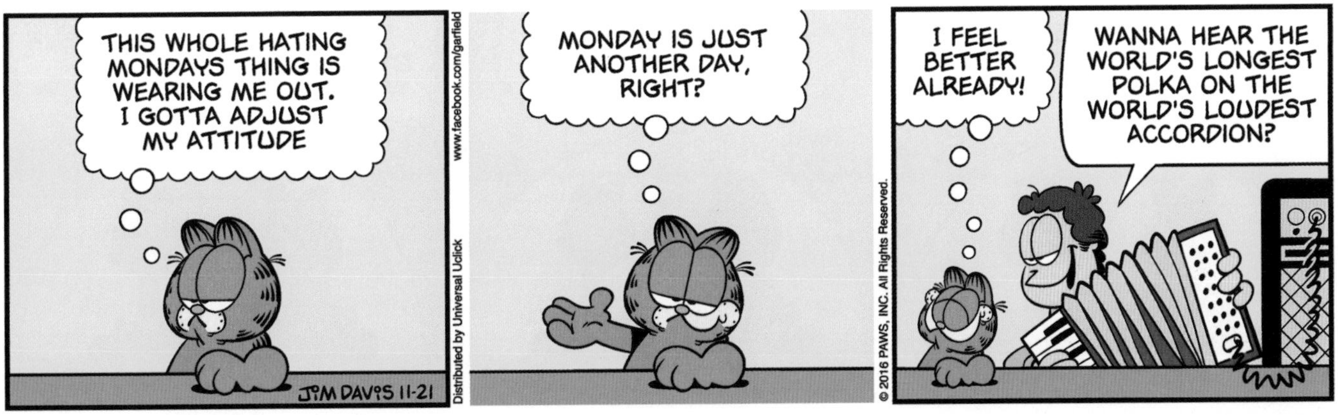
THIS WHOLE HATING MONDAYS THING IS WEARING ME OUT. I GOTTA ADJUST MY ATTITUDE
JIM DAVIS 11-21
www.facebook.com/garfield
Distributed by Universal Uclick
MONDAY IS JUST ANOTHER DAY, RIGHT?
© 2016 PAWS, INC. All Rights Reserved.
I FEEL BETTER ALREADY!
WANNA HEAR THE WORLD'S LONGEST POLKA ON THE WORLD'S LOUDEST ACCORDION?

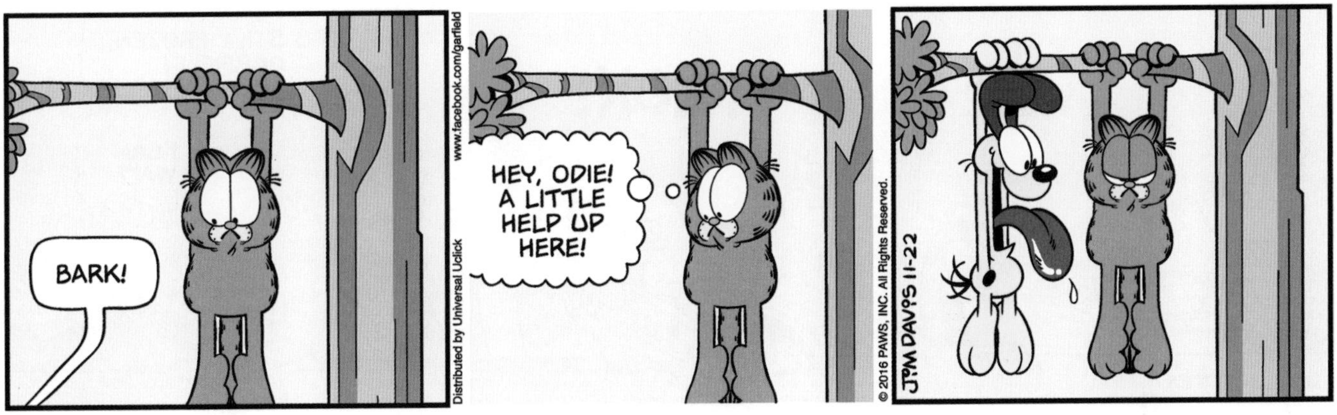
BARK!
www.facebook.com/garfield
Distributed by Universal Uclick
HEY, ODIE! A LITTLE HELP UP HERE!
© 2016 PAWS, INC. All Rights Reserved.
JIM DAVIS 11-22

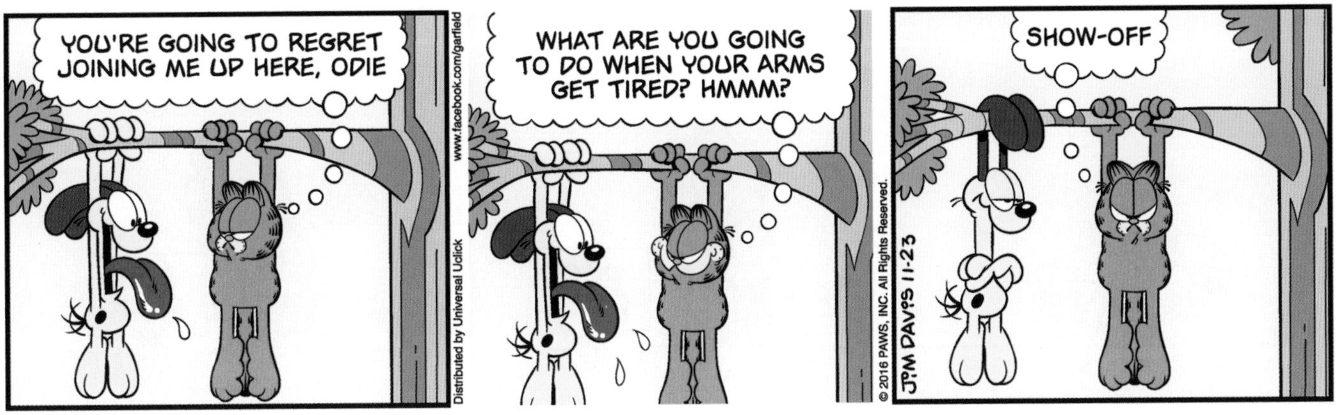
YOU'RE GOING TO REGRET JOINING ME UP HERE, ODIE
www.facebook.com/garfield
Distributed by Universal Uclick
WHAT ARE YOU GOING TO DO WHEN YOUR ARMS GET TIRED? HMMM?
© 2016 PAWS, INC. All Rights Reserved.
JIM DAVIS 11-23
SHOW-OFF

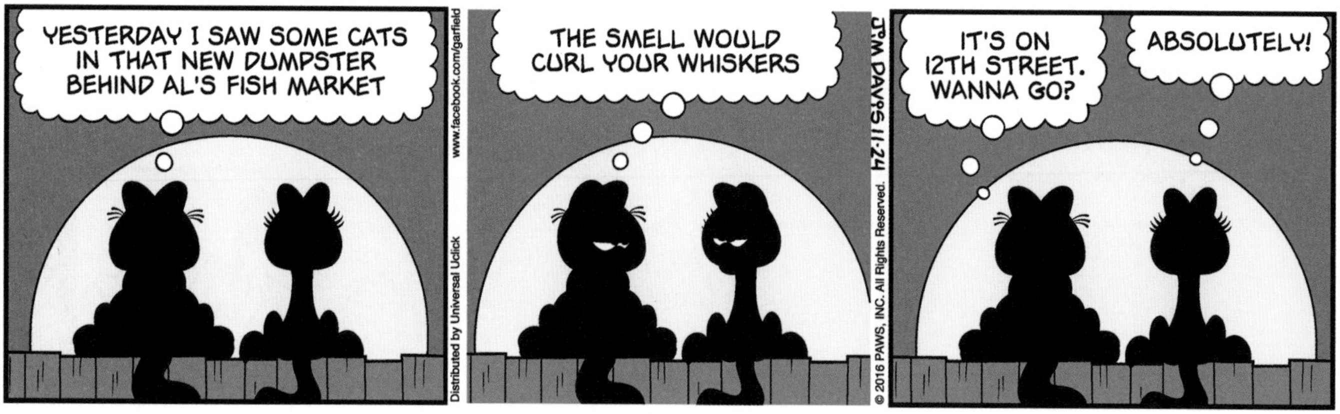
YESTERDAY I SAW SOME CATS IN THAT NEW DUMPSTER BEHIND AL'S FISH MARKET
THE SMELL WOULD CURL YOUR WHISKERS
IT'S ON 12TH STREET. WANNA GO?
ABSOLUTELY!
JIM DAVIS 11-24
Distributed by Universal Uclick www.facebook.com/garfield
© 2016 PAWS, INC. All Rights Reserved.

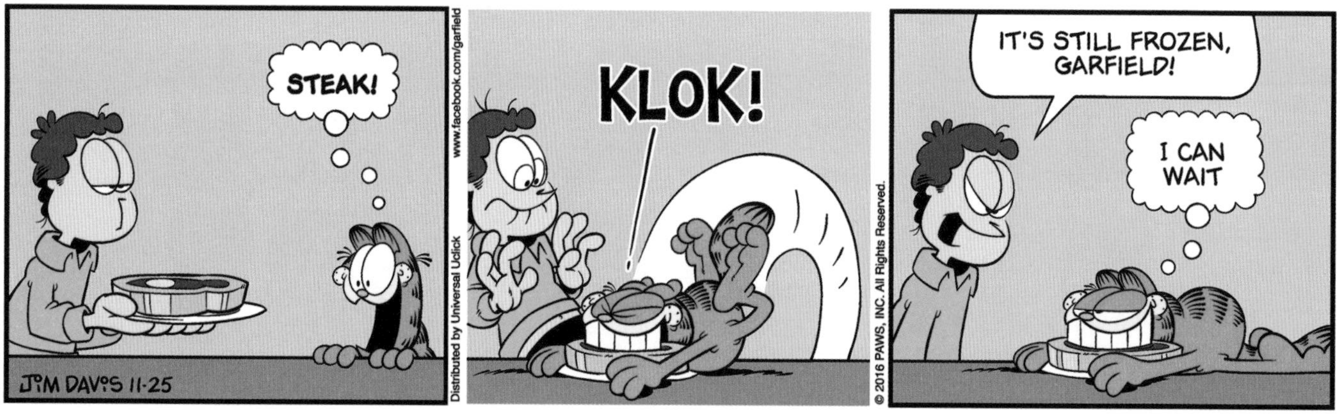
STEAK!
JIM DAVIS 11-25
Distributed by Universal Uclick www.facebook.com/garfield
KLOK!
© 2016 PAWS, INC. All Rights Reserved.
IT'S STILL FROZEN, GARFIELD!
I CAN WAIT

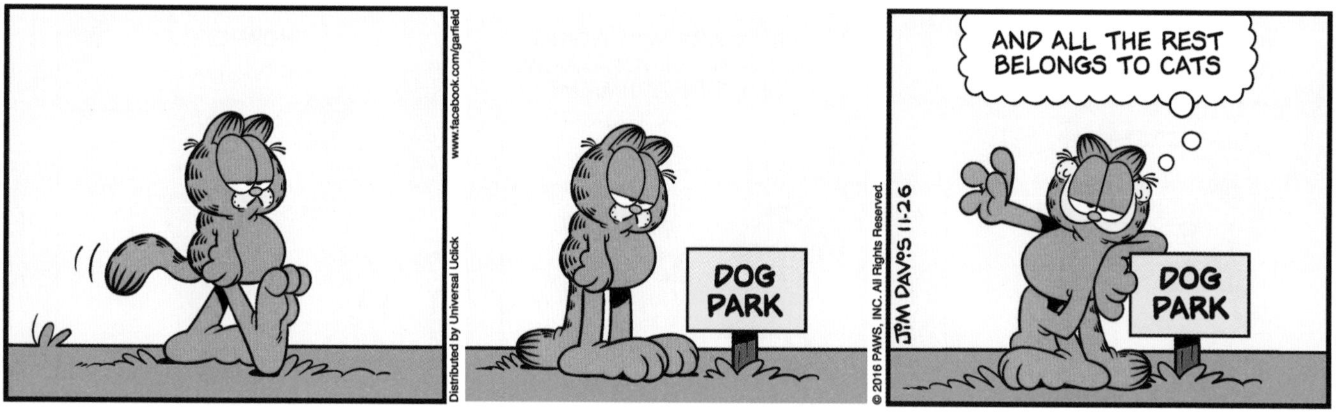
Distributed by Universal Uclick www.facebook.com/garfield
DOG PARK
© 2016 PAWS, INC. All Rights Reserved.
JIM DAVIS 11-26
AND ALL THE REST BELONGS TO CATS
DOG PARK

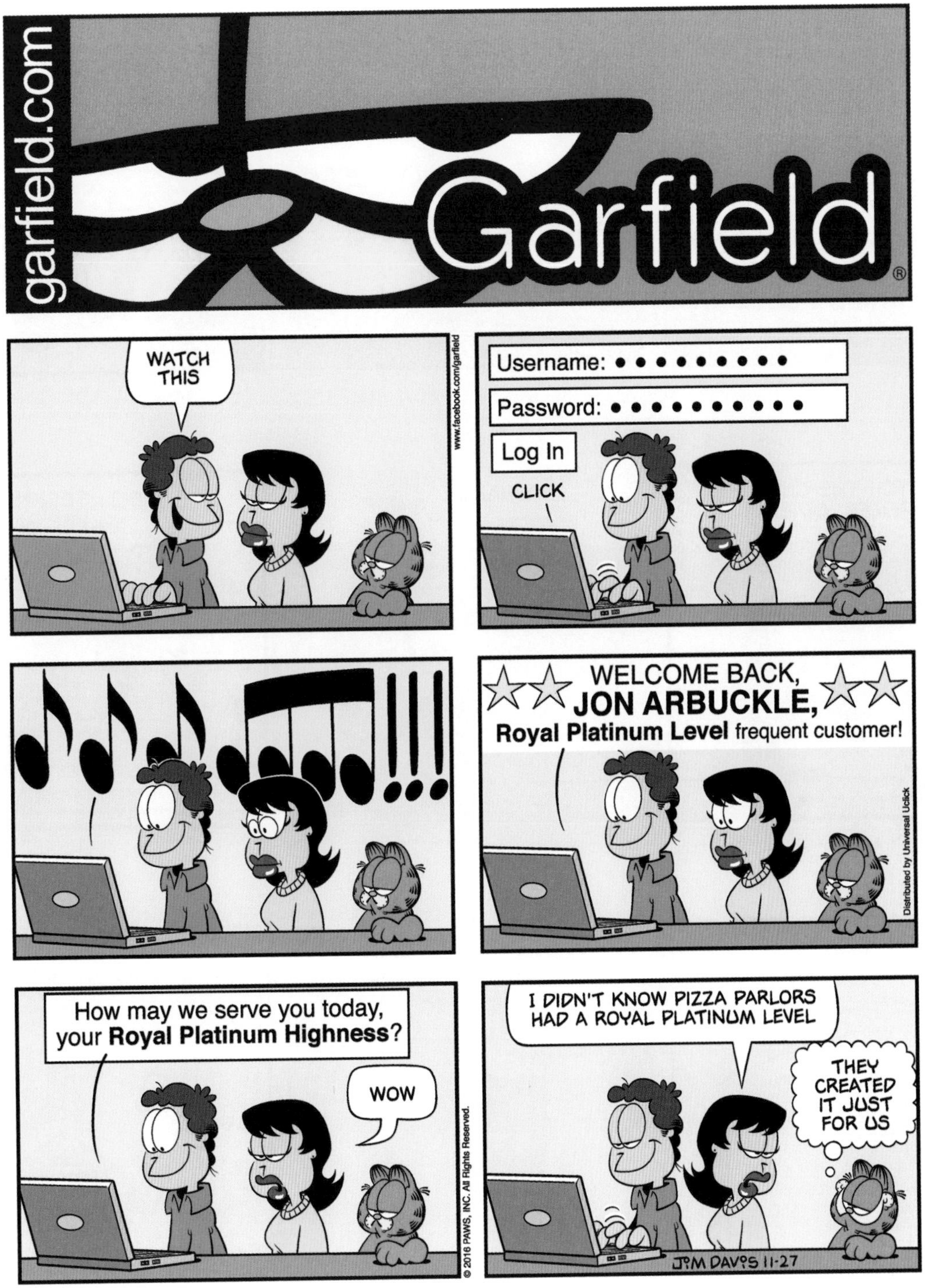
garfield.com
Garfield
www.facebook.com/garfield
WATCH THIS
Username: ●●●●●●●●●●
Password: ●●●●●●●●●●●
Log In
CLICK
WELCOME BACK, JON ARBUCKLE, Royal Platinum Level frequent customer!
Distributed by Universal Uclick
How may we serve you today, your Royal Platinum Highness?
WOW
© 2016 PAWS, INC. All Rights Reserved.
I DIDN'T KNOW PIZZA PARLORS HAD A ROYAL PLATINUM LEVEL
THEY CREATED IT JUST FOR US
JIM DAVIS 11-27

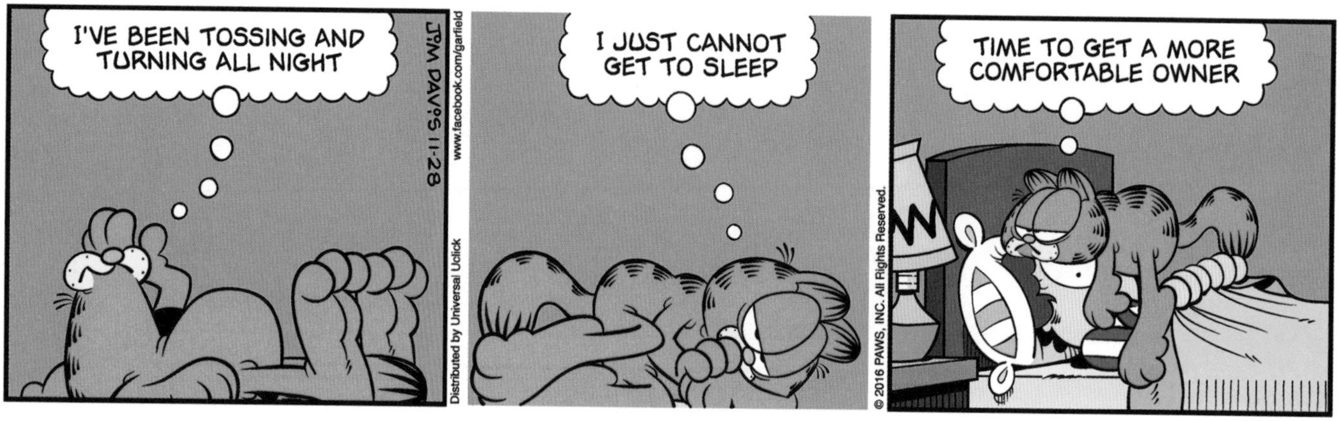
I'VE BEEN TOSSING AND TURNING ALL NIGHT
JIM DAVIS 11-28
www.facebook.com/garfield
Distributed by Universal Uclick
I JUST CANNOT GET TO SLEEP
TIME TO GET A MORE COMFORTABLE OWNER
© 2016 PAWS, INC. All Rights Reserved.

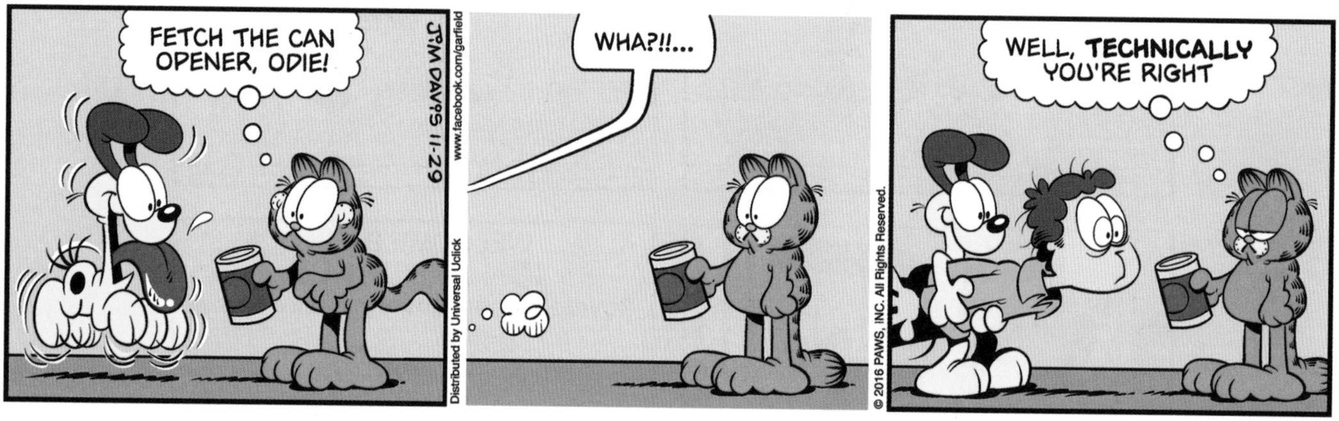
FETCH THE CAN OPENER, ODIE!
JIM DAVIS 11-29
www.facebook.com/garfield
Distributed by Universal Uclick
WHA?!!...
WELL, TECHNICALLY YOU'RE RIGHT
© 2016 PAWS, INC. All Rights Reserved.

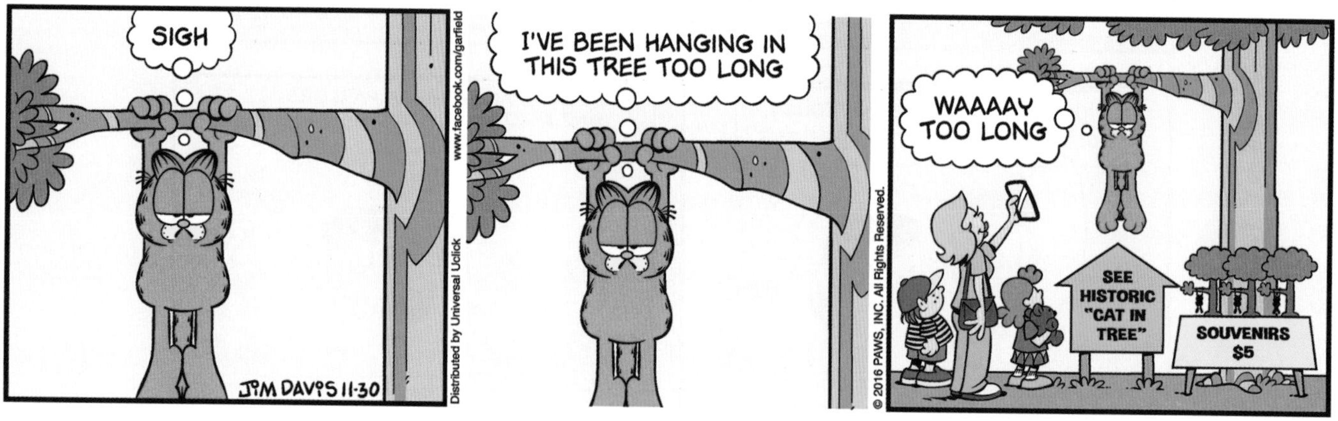
SIGH
JIM DAVIS 11-30
www.facebook.com/garfield
Distributed by Universal Uclick
I'VE BEEN HANGING IN THIS TREE TOO LONG
WAAAAY TOO LONG
SEE HISTORIC "CAT IN TREE"
SOUVENIRS $5
© 2016 PAWS, INC. All Rights Reserved.

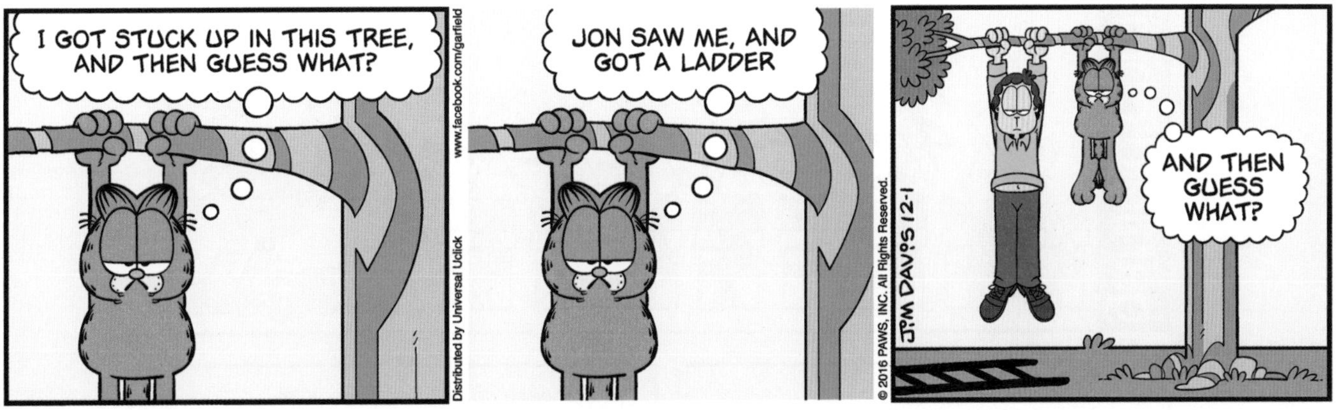
I GOT STUCK UP IN THIS TREE, AND THEN GUESS WHAT?
www.facebook.com/garfield
Distributed by Universal Uclick
JON SAW ME, AND GOT A LADDER
© 2016 PAWS, INC. All Rights Reserved.
JIM DAVIS 12-1
AND THEN GUESS WHAT?

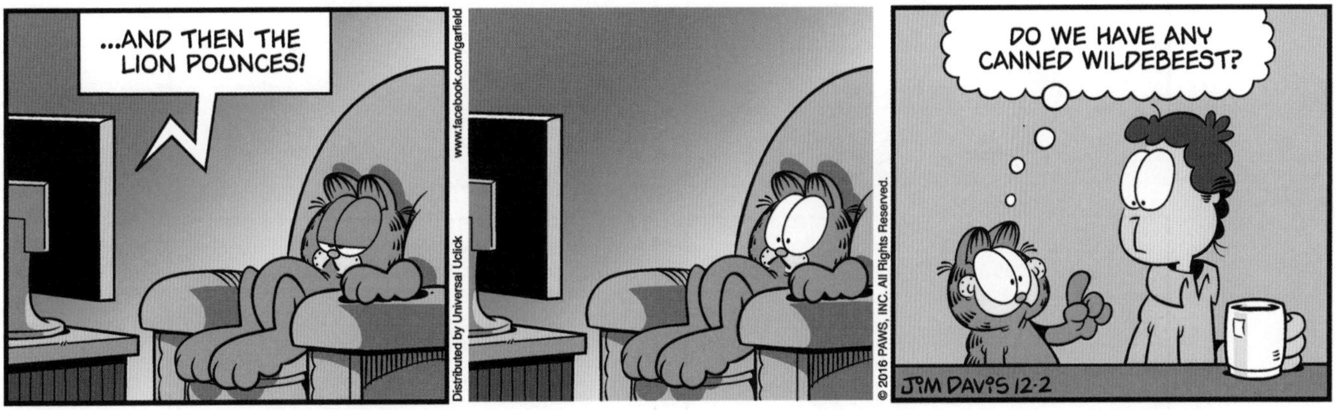
...AND THEN THE LION POUNCES!
www.facebook.com/garfield
Distributed by Universal Uclick
© 2016 PAWS, INC. All Rights Reserved.
DO WE HAVE ANY CANNED WILDEBEEST?
JIM DAVIS 12-2

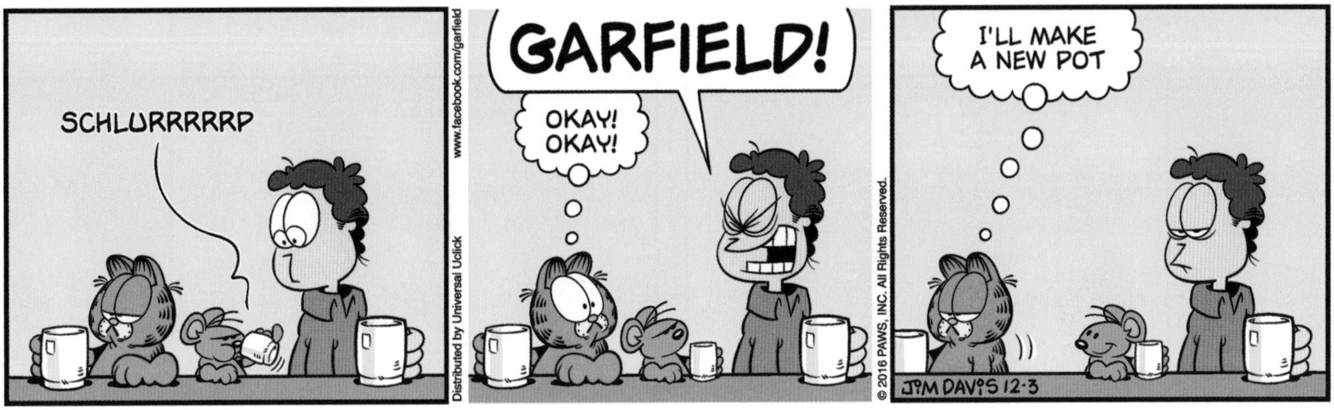
SCHLURRRRRP
www.facebook.com/garfield
Distributed by Universal Uclick
GARFIELD!
OKAY! OKAY!
© 2016 PAWS, INC. All Rights Reserved.
I'LL MAKE A NEW POT
JIM DAVIS 12-3

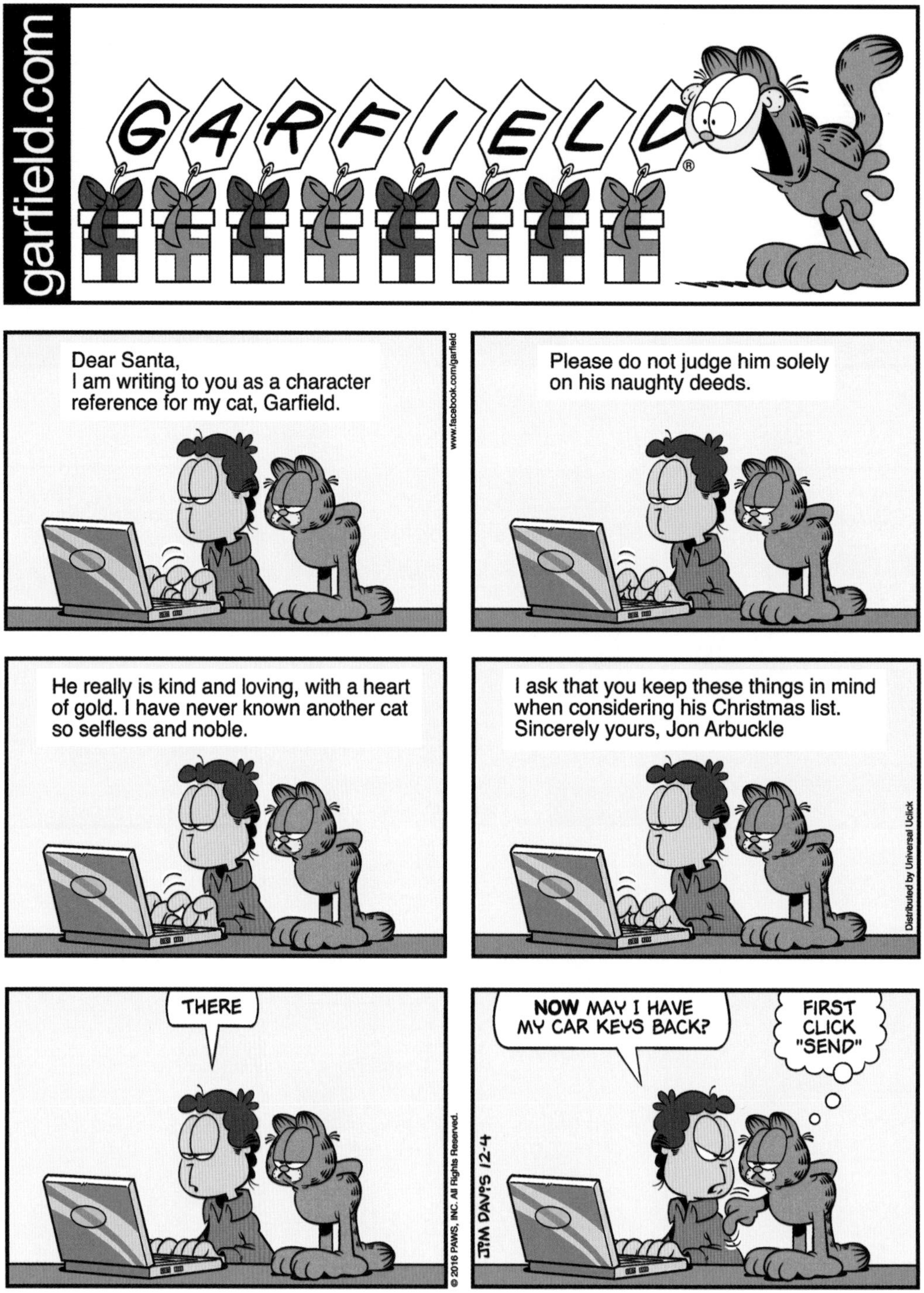
garfield.com
GARFIELD®
Dear Santa,
I am writing to you as a character reference for my cat, Garfield.
www.facebook.com/garfield
Please do not judge him solely on his naughty deeds.
He really is kind and loving, with a heart of gold. I have never known another cat so selfless and noble.
I ask that you keep these things in mind when considering his Christmas list.
Sincerely yours, Jon Arbuckle
Distributed by Universal Uclick
THERE
© 2016 PAWS, INC. All Rights Reserved.
JIM DAVIS 12-4
NOW MAY I HAVE MY CAR KEYS BACK?
FIRST CLICK "SEND"

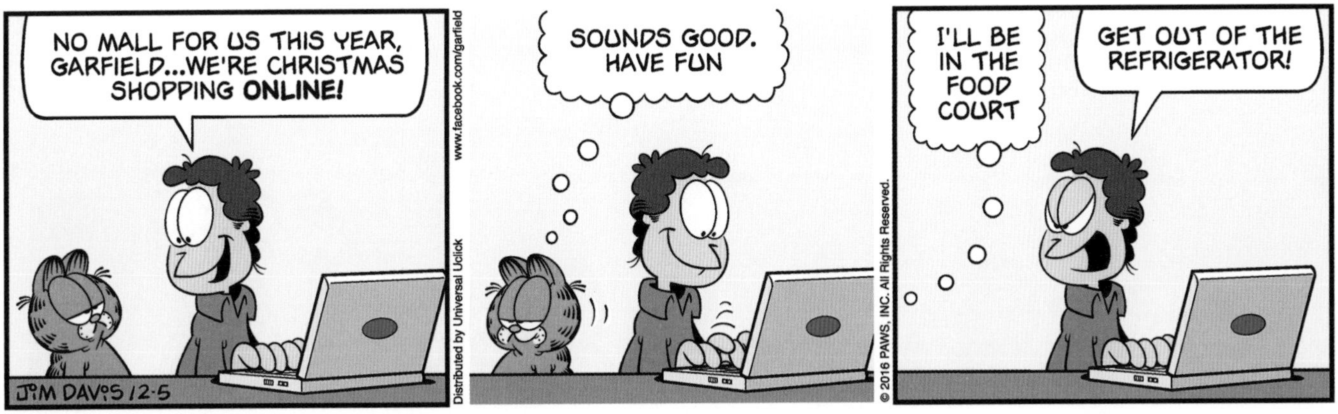
NO MALL FOR US THIS YEAR, GARFIELD...WE'RE CHRISTMAS SHOPPING **ONLINE!**
JIM DAVIS 12-5
Distributed by Universal Uclick www.facebook.com/garfield
SOUNDS GOOD. HAVE FUN
© 2016 PAWS, INC. All Rights Reserved.
I'LL BE IN THE FOOD COURT
GET OUT OF THE REFRIGERATOR!

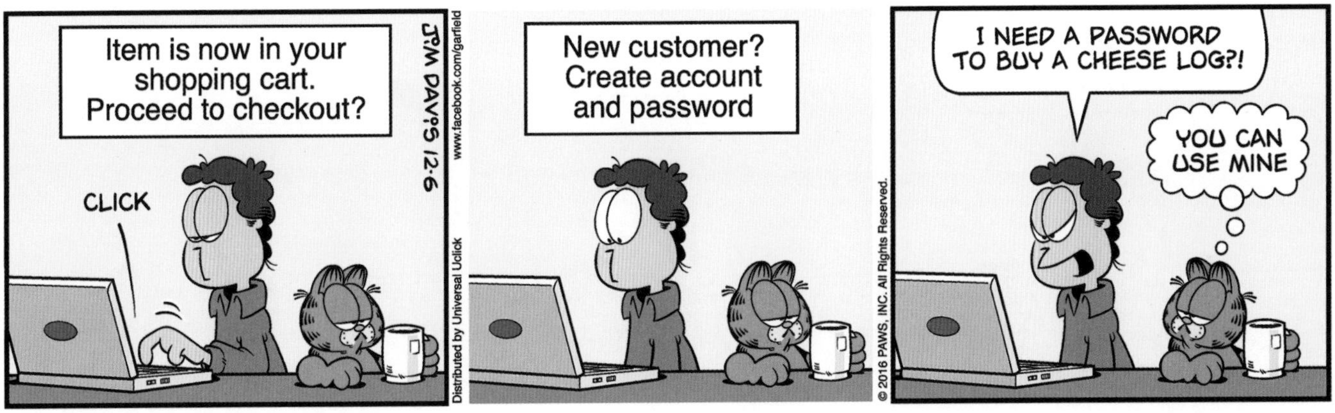
Item is now in your shopping cart. Proceed to checkout?
CLICK
JIM DAVIS 12-6
Distributed by Universal Uclick www.facebook.com/garfield
New customer? Create account and password
© 2016 PAWS, INC. All Rights Reserved.
I NEED A PASSWORD TO BUY A CHEESE LOG?!
YOU CAN USE MINE

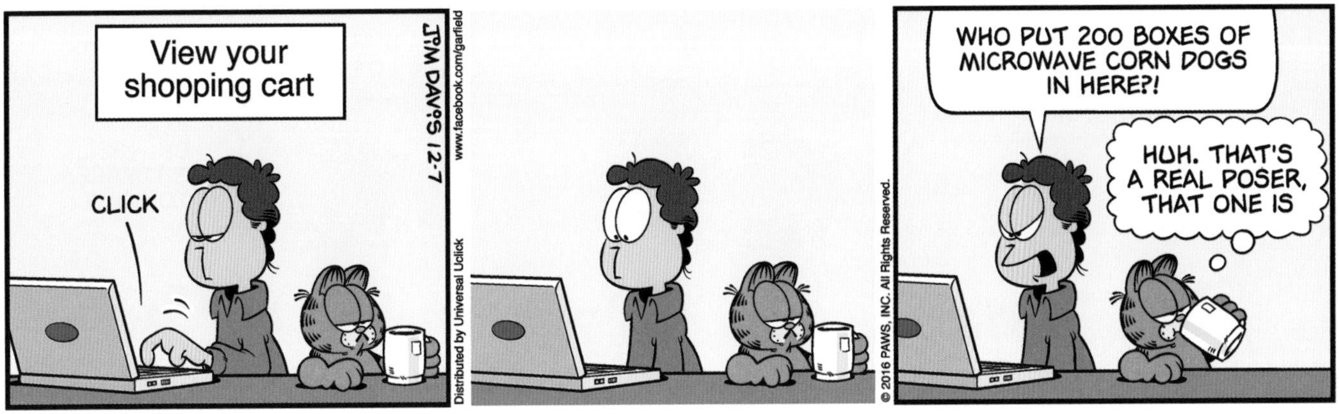
View your shopping cart
CLICK
JIM DAVIS 12-7
Distributed by Universal Uclick www.facebook.com/garfield
© 2016 PAWS, INC. All Rights Reserved.
WHO PUT 200 BOXES OF MICROWAVE CORN DOGS IN HERE?!
HUH. THAT'S A REAL POSER, THAT ONE IS

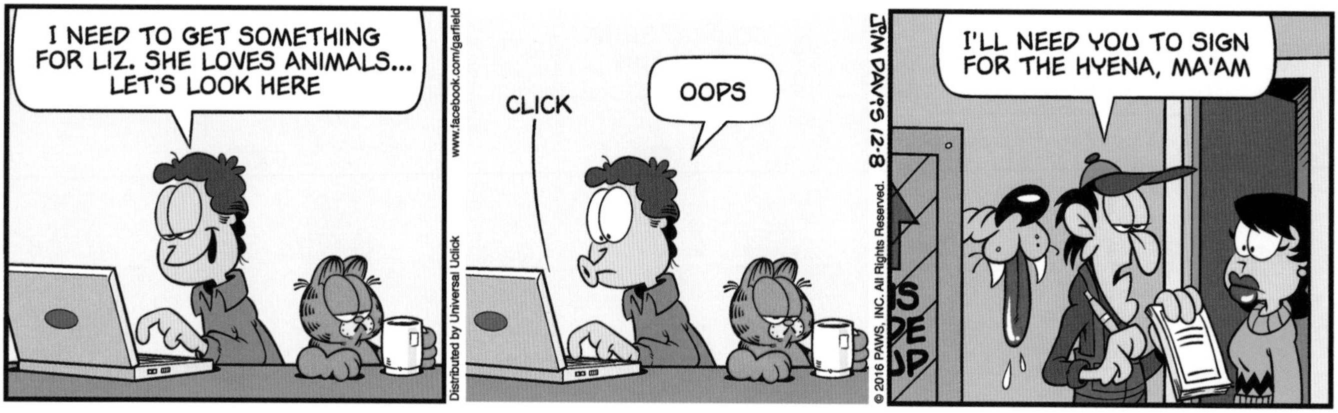
I NEED TO GET SOMETHING FOR LIZ. SHE LOVES ANIMALS... LET'S LOOK HERE
www.facebook.com/garfield
Distributed by Universal Uclick
CLICK
OOPS
JIM DAVIS 12-8
© 2016 PAWS, INC. All Rights Reserved.
I'LL NEED YOU TO SIGN FOR THE HYENA, MA'AM

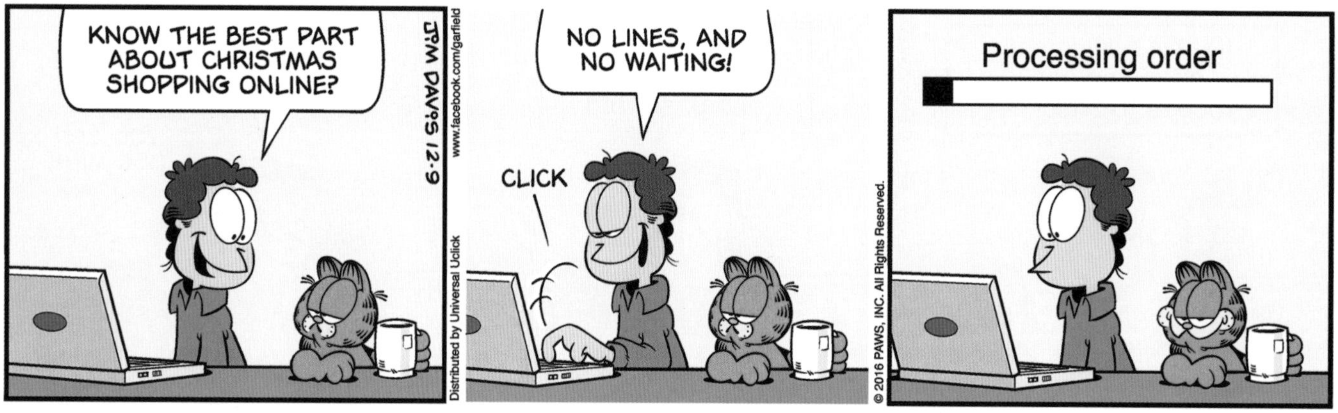
KNOW THE BEST PART ABOUT CHRISTMAS SHOPPING ONLINE?
JIM DAVIS 12-9
www.facebook.com/garfield
Distributed by Universal Uclick
NO LINES, AND NO WAITING!
CLICK
© 2016 PAWS, INC. All Rights Reserved.
Processing order

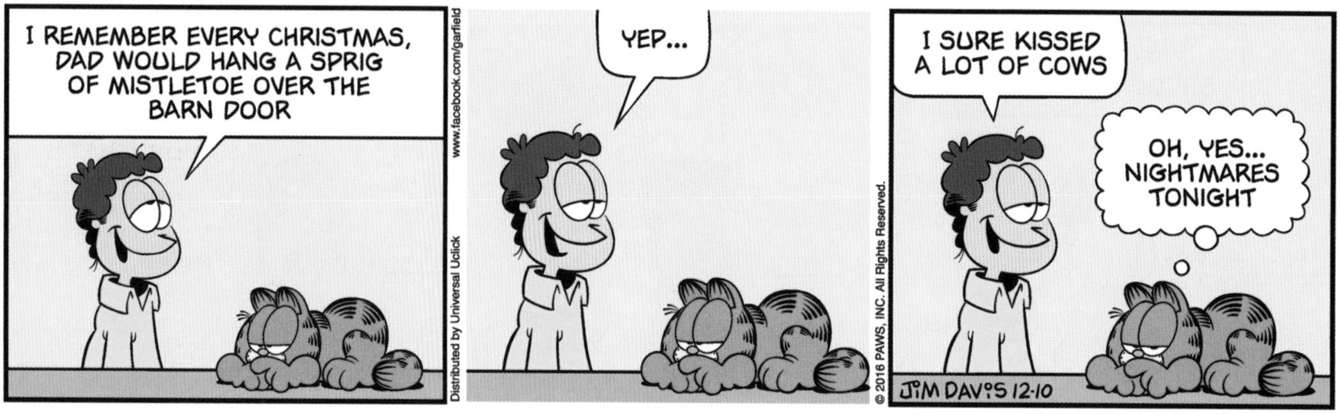
I REMEMBER EVERY CHRISTMAS, DAD WOULD HANG A SPRIG OF MISTLETOE OVER THE BARN DOOR
www.facebook.com/garfield
Distributed by Universal Uclick
YEP...
© 2016 PAWS, INC. All Rights Reserved.
I SURE KISSED A LOT OF COWS
OH, YES... NIGHTMARES TONIGHT
JIM DAVIS 12-10

Fat Cat Fan Art

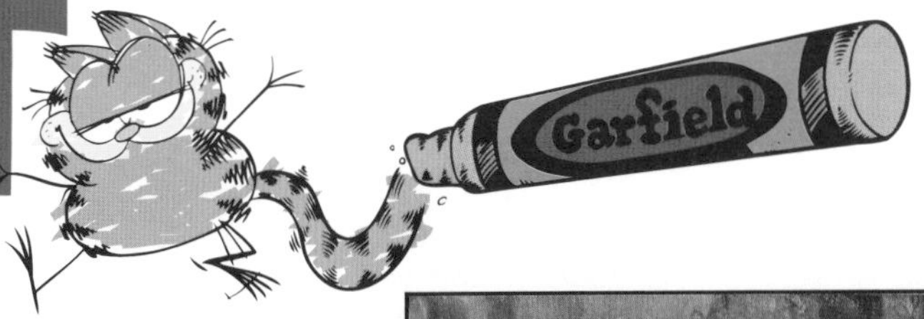
Garfield

Molly K.
Age 18
California

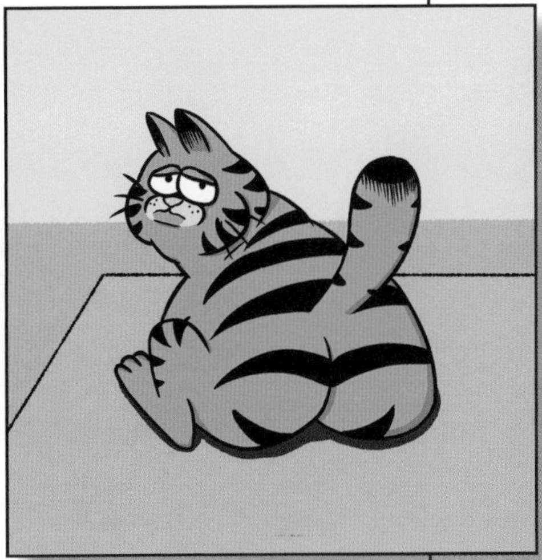

Cassy K.
Age 13
Canada

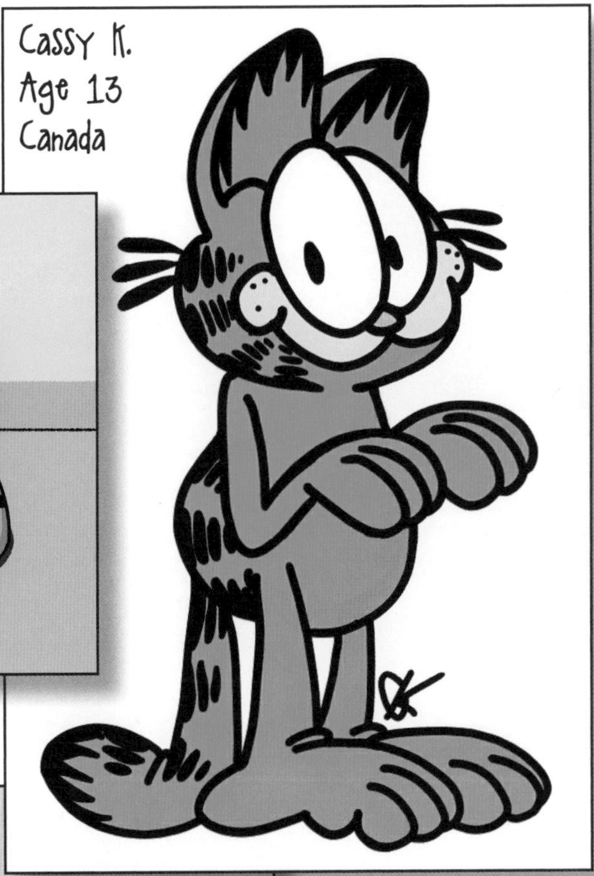

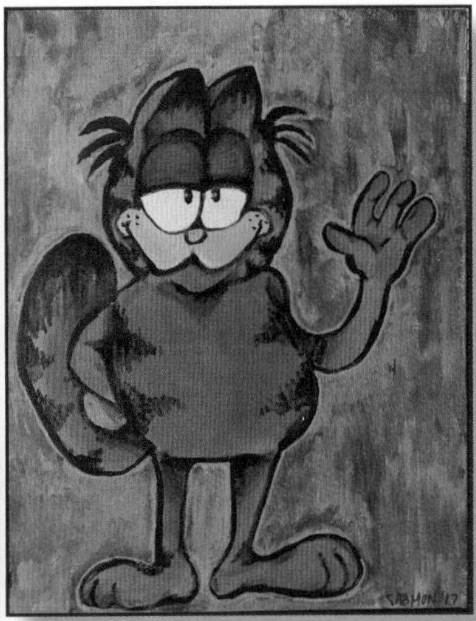

Sabrina M.
Age 16
California

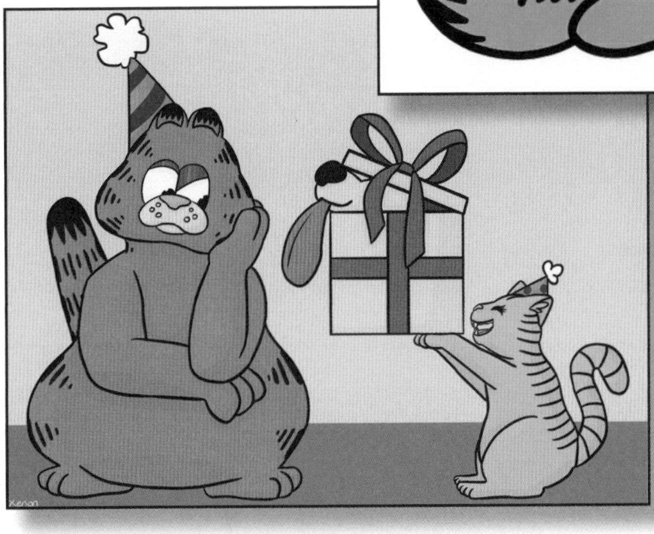

Xenon T.
Age 18
Canada

Julian H.
Age 23
Florida

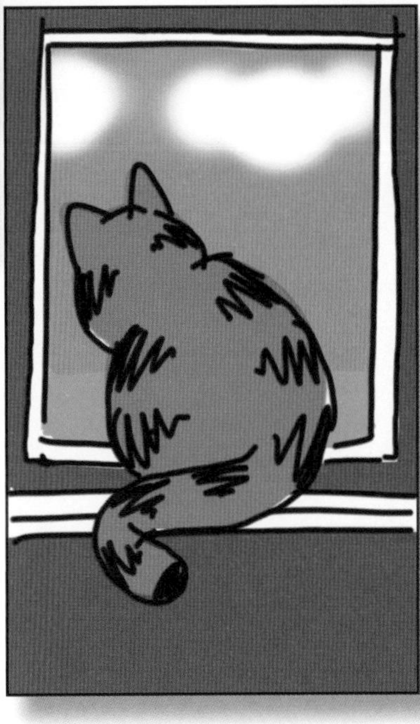

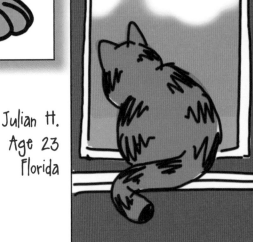

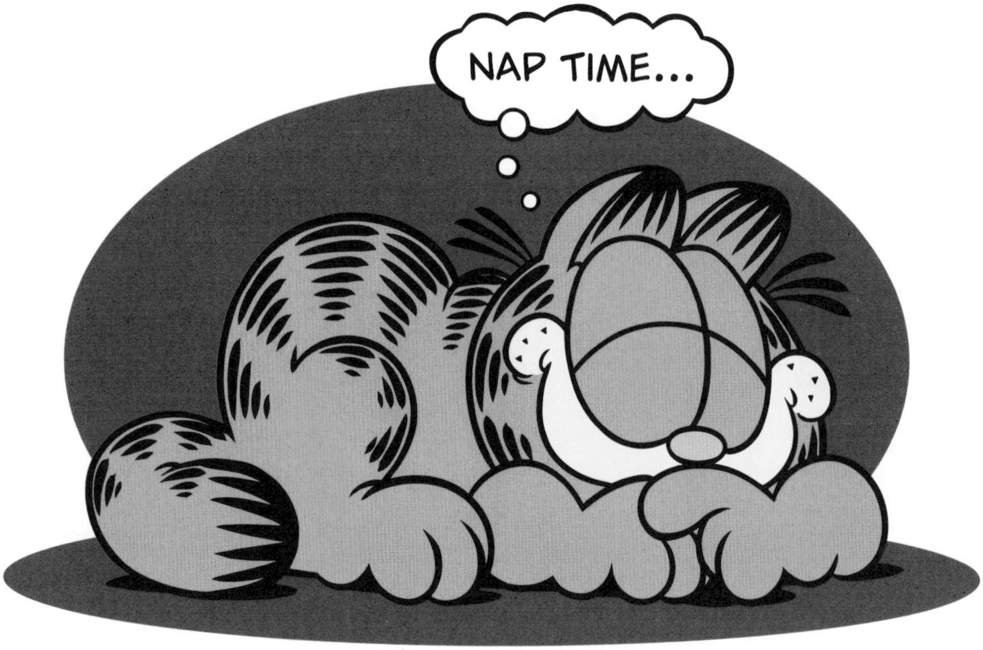
NAP TIME...

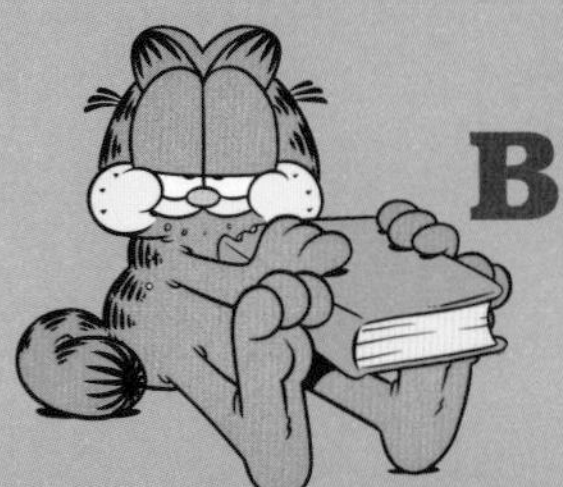

STRIPS, SPECIALS OR BESTSELLING BOOKS . . .

GARFIELD'S ON EVERYONE'S MENU.

Don't miss even one episode in the Tubby Tabby's hilarious series!

GARFIELD AT LARGE . . . (#1) 978-0-345-44382-3
GARFIELD GAINS WEIGHT . . . (#2) 978-0-345-44975-7
GARFIELD BIGGER THAN LIFE . . . (#3) 978-0-345-45027-2
GARFIELD WEIGHS IN . . . (#4) 978-0-345-45205-4
GARFIELD TAKES THE CAKE . . . (#5) 978-0-345-44978-8
GARFIELD EATS HIS HEART OUT . . . (#6) 978-0-345-46459-0
GARFIELD SITS AROUND THE HOUSE . . . (#7) 978-0-345-46463-7
GARFIELD TIPS THE SCALES . . . (#8) 978-0-345-46909-0
GARFIELD LOSES HIS FEET . . . (#9) 978-0-345-46467-5
GARFIELD MAKES IT BIG . . . (#10) 978-0-345-46468-2
GARFIELD ROLLS ON . . . (#11) 978-0-345-47561-9
GARFIELD OUT TO LUNCH . . . (#12) 978-0-345-47562-6
GARFIELD FOOD FOR THOUGHT . . . (#13) 978-0-345-47563-3
GARFIELD SWALLOWS HIS PRIDE . . . (#14) 978-0-345-91386-9
GARFIELD WORLDWIDE . . . (#15) 978-0-345-91754-6
GARFIELD ROUNDS OUT . . . (#16) 978-0-345-49169-5
GARFIELD CHEWS THE FAT . . . (#17) 978-0-345-49170-1
GARFIELD GOES TO WAIST . . . (#18) 978-0-345-49173-2
GARFIELD HANGS OUT . . . (#19) 978-0-345-49174-9
GARFIELD TAKES UP SPACE . . . (#20) 978-0-345-49178-7
GARFIELD SAYS A MOUTHFUL . . . (#21) 978-0-345-49179-4
GARFIELD BY THE POUND . . . (#22) 978-0-345-52558-1
GARFIELD KEEPS HIS CHINS UP . . . (#23) 978-0-345-52559-8
GARFIELD TAKES HIS LICKS . . . (#24) 978-0-345-52587-1
GARFIELD HITS THE BIG TIME . . . (#25) 978-0-345-52589-5
GARFIELD PULLS HIS WEIGHT . . . (#26) 978-0-345-52594-9
GARFIELD DISHES IT OUT . . . (#27) 978-0-345-52595-6
GARFIELD LIFE IN THE FAT LANE . . . (#28) 978-0-345-52600-7
GARFIELD TONS OF FUN . . . (#29) 978-0-345-52601-4
GARFIELD BIGGER AND BETTER . . . (#30) 978-0-345-52605-2
GARFIELD HAMS IT UP . . . (#31) 978-0-345-52606-9
GARFIELD THINKS BIG . . . (#32) 978-0-425-28516-9
GARFIELD THROWS HIS WEIGHT AROUND . . . (#33) 978-0-425-28559-6
GARFIELD LIFE TO THE FULLEST . . . (#34) 978-0-425-28564-0
GARFIELD FEEDS THE KITTY . . . (#35) 978-0-425-28569-5
GARFIELD HOGS THE SPOTLIGHT . . . (#36) 978-0-425-28574-9
GARFIELD BEEFS UP . . . (#37) 978-0-345-44109-6
GARFIELD GETS COOKIN' . . . (#38) 978-0-345-44582-7
GARFIELD EATS CROW . . . (#39) 978-0-345-45201-6
GARFIELD SURVIVAL OF THE FATTEST . . . (#40) 978-0-345-46458-3
GARFIELD OLDER AND WIDER . . . (#41) 978-0-345-46462-0
GARFIELD PIGS OUT . . . (#42) 978-0-345-46466-8
GARFIELD BLOTS OUT THE SUN . . . (#43) 978-0-345-46615-0
GARFIELD GOES BANANAS . . . (#44) 978-0-345-91346-3
GARFIELD LARGE & IN CHARGE . . . (#45) 978-0-345-49172-5
GARFIELD SPILLS THE BEANS . . . (#46) 978-0-345-49177-0
GARFIELD GETS HIS JUST DESSERTS . . . (#47) 978-0-345-91387-6
GARFIELD WILL EAT FOR FOOD . . . (#48) 978-0-345-49176-3
GARFIELD WEIGHS HIS OPTIONS . . . (#49) 978-0-345-49181-7
GARFIELD POTBELLY OF GOLD . . . (#50) 978-0-345-52244-3
GARFIELD SHOVELS IT IN . . . (#51) 978-0-345-52419-5
GARFIELD LARD OF THE JUNGLE . . . (#52) 978-0-345-52584-0
GARFIELD BRINGS HOME THE BACON . . . (#53) 978-0-345-52586-4
GARFIELD GETS IN A PICKLE . . . (#54) 978-0-345-52590-1
GARFIELD SINGS FOR HIS SUPPER . . . (#55) 978-0-345-52593-2
GARFIELD CAUTION: WIDE LOAD . . . (#56) 978-0-345-52596-3
GARFIELD SOUPED UP . . . (#57) 978-0-345-52598-7
GARFIELD GOES TO HIS HAPPY PLACE . . . (#58) 978-0-345-52602-1
GARFIELD THE BIG CHEESE . . . (#59) 978-0-345-52604-5
GARFIELD CLEANS HIS PLATE . . . (#60) 978-0-345-52608-3
GARFIELD CHICKENS OUT . . . (#61) 978-0-425-28515-2
GARFIELD LISTENS TO HIS GUT . . . (#62) 978-0-425-28557-2
GARFIELD COOKS UP TROUBLE . . . (#63) 978-0-425-28562-6
GARFIELD FEEDS HIS FACE . . . (#64) 978-0-425-28567-1
GARFIELD EATS AND RUNS . . . (#65) 978-0-425-28572-5
GARFIELD NUTTY AS A FRUITCAKE . . . (#66) 978-0-425-28576-3
GARFIELD SLURPS AND BURPS . . . (#67) 978-1-9848-1773-0
GARFIELD BELLY LAUGHS . . . (#68) 978-1-9848-1777-8

DVD TIE-INS

GARFIELD AS HIMSELF . . . 978-0-345-47805-4
GARFIELD HOLIDAY CELEBRATIONS . . . 978-0-345-47930-3
GARFIELD TRAVEL ADVENTURES . . . 978-0-345-48087-3

AND DON'T MISS . . .

GARFIELD AT 25: IN DOG YEARS I'D BE DEAD . . . 978-0-345-45204-7
GARFIELD'S JOKE ZONE/INSULTS . . . 978-0-345-46263-3
GARFIELD FAT CAT 3-PACK/ VOL. 1 . . . 978-0-345-46455-2
GARFIELD FAT CAT 3-PACK/ VOL. 2 . . . 978-0-345-46465-1
GARFIELD FAT CAT 3-PACK/ VOL. 3 . . . 978-0-345-48088-0
GARFIELD FAT CAT 3-PACK/ VOL. 4 . . . 978-0-345-49171-8
GARFIELD FAT CAT 3-PACK/ VOL. 5 . . . 978-0-345-49180-8
GARFIELD FAT CAT 3-PACK/ VOL. 6 . . . 978-0-345-52420-1
GARFIELD FAT CAT 3-PACK/ VOL. 7 . . . 978-0-345-52588-8
GARFIELD FAT CAT 3-PACK/ VOL. 8 . . . 978-0-345-52599-4
GARFIELD FAT CAT 3-PACK/ VOL. 9 . . . 978-0-345-52607-6
GARFIELD FAT CAT 3-PACK/ VOL. 10 . . . 978-0-425-28558-9
GARFIELD FAT CAT 3-PACK/ VOL. 11 . . . 978-0-425-28566-4
GARFIELD FAT CAT 3-PACK/ VOL. 12 . . . 978-0-425-28578-7
GARFIELD FAT CAT 3-PACK/ VOL. 13 . . . 978-0-345-46460-6
GARFIELD FAT CAT 3-PACK/ VOL. 14 . . . 978-0-345-49175-6
GARFIELD FAT CAT 3-PACK/ VOL. 15 . . . 978-0-345-52585-7
GARFIELD FAT CAT 3-PACK/ VOL. 16 . . . 978-0-345-52592-5
GARFIELD FAT CAT 3-PACK/ VOL. 17 . . . 978-0-345-52603-8
GARFIELD FAT CAT 3-PACK/ VOL. 18 . . . 978-0-399-59440-3
GARFIELD FAT CAT 3-PACK/ VOL. 19 . . . 978-0-425-28561-9
GARFIELD FAT CAT 3-PACK/ VOL. 20 . . . 978-0-425-28571-8
GARFIELD FAT CAT 3-PACK/ VOL. 21 . . . 978-1-984-81775-4
GARFIELD'S 20TH ANNIVERSARY COLLECTION . . . 978-0-345-42126-5
SEASON'S EATINGS: A VERY MERRY GARFIELD CHRISTMAS . . . 978-0-345-47560-2
GARFIELD'S GUIDE TO EVERYTHING . . . 978-0-345-46461-3
ODIE UNLEASHED! . . . 978-0-345-46464-4
GARFIELD'S BOOK OF CAT NAMES . . . 978-0-345-48516-8
THE GARFIELD JOURNAL . . . 978-0-345-46469-9
LIGHTS, CAMERA, HAIRBALLS!: GARFIELD AT THE MOVIES . . . 978-0-345-49134-3
30 YEARS OF LAUGHS AND LASAGNA . . . 978-0-345-50379-4
GARFIELD MINUS GARFIELD . . . 978-0-345-51387-8
GARFIELD FROM THE TRASH BIN . . . 978-0-345-51881-1
GARFIELD LEFT SPEECHLESS . . . 978-0-345-53058-5
MY LAUGHABLE LIFE WITH GARFIELD . . . 978-0-345-52591-8
GARFIELD'S SUNDAY FINEST . . . 978-0-345-52597-0
AGE HAPPENS: GARFIELD HITS THE BIG 4-0 . . . 978-0-345-52609-0
GARFIELD COMPLETE WORKS: VOLUME ONE: 1978 & 1979 . . . 978-0-425-28712-5
GARFIELD COMPLETE WORKS: VOLUME TWO: 1980 & 1981 . . . 978-0-425-28713-2

New larger, full-color format!